WIRELESS COMMUNICATIONS AND NETWORKS

A comprehensive, state-of-the art survey. Covers fundamental wireless communications topics, including antennas and propagation, signal encoding techniques, spread spectrum, and error correction techniques. Examines satellite, cellular, wireless local loop networks and wireless LANs, including Bluetooth and 802.11. Covers Mobile IP and WAP. ISBN 0-13-040864-6

CRYPTOGRAPHY AND NETWORK SECURITY, THIRD EDITION

A tutorial and survey on network security technology. Each of the basic building blocks of network security, including conventional and public-key cryptography, authentication, and digital signatures, are covered. The book covers important network security tools and applications, including S/MIME, IP Security, Kerberos, SSL/TLS, SET, and X509v3. In addition, methods for countering hackers and viruses are explored. **Second edition received the TAA award for the best Computer Science and Engineering Textbook of 1999.** ISBN 0-13-091429-0

NETWORK SECURITY ESSENTIALS, SECOND EDITION

A tutorial and survey on network security technology. The book covers important network security tools and applications, including S/MIME, IP Security, Kerberos, SSL/TLS, SET, and X509v3. In addition, methods for countering hackers and viruses are explored. ISBN 0-13-035128-8

LOCAL AND METROPOLITAN AREA NETWORKS, SIXTH EDITION

An in-depth presentation of the technology and architecture of local and metropolitan area networks. Covers topology, transmission media, medium access control, standards, internetworking, and network management. Provides an up-to-date coverage of LAN/MAN systems, including Fast Ethernet, Fibre Channel, and wireless LANs, plus LAN QoS. **Received the 2001 TAA award for long-term excellence in a Computer Science Textbook.** ISBN 0-13-012939-9

ISDN AND BROADBAND ISDN, WITH FRAME RELAY AND ATM: FOURTH EDITION

An in-depth presentation of the technology and architecture of integrated services digital networks (ISDN). Covers the integrated digital network (IDN), xDSL, ISDN services and architecture, signaling system no. 7 (SS7) and provides detailed coverage of the ITU-T protocol standards. Also provides detailed coverage of protocols and congestion control strategies for both frame relay and ATM. ISBN 0-13-973744-8

BUSINESS DATA COMMUNICATIONS

BUSINESS DATA COMMUNICATIONS

Fifth Edition

William Stallings

PEARSON
Prentice Hall

Upper Saddle River, NJ 07458

Library of Congress Cataloging-in-Publication Data

Stallings, William
  Business data communications/William Stallings.—5th ed.
     p. cm.
  Includes bibliographical references and index.
  ISBN 0-13-144257-0
   1. Business—Data processing. 2. Business—Communication systems—Data processing. 3.
  Local area networks (Computer networks) 4. Data transmission systems. 5. Business
  enterprises—Computer networks. 6. Electronic commerce. I. Title.

  HF5548.2S7728 2004
  004.6—dc22   2004044425

Vice President and Editorial Director, ECS:
  Marcia J. Horton
Publisher: *Alan Apt*
Associate Editor: *Toni D. Holm*
Editorial Assistant: *Patrick Lindner*
Vice President and Director of Production and
  Manufacturing, ESM: *David W. Riccardi*
Executive Managing Editor: *Vince O'Brien*
Managing Editor: *Camille Trentacoste*
Production Editor: *Rose Kernan*
Cover Photos: Tent Rocks in New Mexico, © Jess
  Alford/Getty Images, Photodisc Green. Field of
  Satellite Dishes, © Digital Vision Satellite Dish in

New Mexico, USA, © Edmond Van
  Hoorick/Getty Images, Photodisc Green
Director of Creative Services: *Paul Belfanti*
Creative Director: *Carole Anson*
Art Director: *Geoffrey Cussar*
Cover Designer: *Dina Curro*
Managing Editor, AV Management and Production:
  Patricia Burns
Art Editor: *Gregory Dulles*
Manufacturing Manager: *Trudy Pisciotti*
Manufacturing Buyer: *Lynda Castillo*
Marketing Manager: *Pamela Hersperger*
Marketing Assistant: *Barrie Reinhold*

©2005, 2001, 1998, 1995, 1992 Pearson Education, Inc.
Pearson Prentice Hall
Pearson Education, Inc.
Upper Saddle River, NJ 07458

Printed in the United States of America
10 9 8 7 6 5 4 3 2 1

ISBN: 0-13-144257-0

Pearson Education Ltd., *London*
Pearson Education Australia Pty. Ltd., *Sydney*
Pearson Education Singapore, Pte. Ltd.
Pearson Education North Asia Ltd., *Hong Kong*
Pearson Education Canada, Inc., *Toronto*
Pearson Educacíon de Mexico, S.A. de C.V.
Pearson Education—Japan, *Tokyo*
Pearson Education Malaysia, Pte. Ltd.
Pearson Education Inc., *Upper Saddle River, New Jersey*

For my loving wife, ATS
the best, the bravest, the kindest

Contents

PREFACE

Four trends have made a solid understanding of the fundamentals of **data communications** essential to business and information management students:

- **The increasing use of data processing equipment.** As the cost of computer hardware has dropped, data processing equipment has become an increasingly important and pervasive part of the office, factory, and engineering environments.
- **The increasing use of distributed systems.** Dropping hardware costs have resulted in the increasing use of small systems, including servers, workstations, and personal computers. These systems are distributed throughout a business and must be interconnected to exchange messages, share files, and share resources, such as printers.
- **The increasing diversity of networking options.** The emergence of a broad range of local area network (LAN) standards plus the evolution of LAN technology have led to a broad, overlapping range of products for local area communications. Similarly, the planning for the next generation of telephone equipment and networks and the evolution of new transmission and networking technologies have led to a broad, overlapping range of options for long-distance communications.
- **The emergence of the Internet and the World Wide Web.** In a very short time, the Internet and especially the World Wide Web have attracted millions of business and personal users. No business can ignore the potential of this enormous facility.

As a result of these factors, business data communications courses have become common in business and information management sequences, and this book intends to address the needs for such a course. However, a focus on data communications is no longer enough.

Over the past twenty years, as data processing capability has been introduced into the office, data communications products and services have gradually assumed increasing importance. Now, technological developments and the widespread acceptance of standards are transforming the ways in which information is used to support the business function. In addition to the traditional communications requirements for voice and data (meaning text and numerical data), there is now the need to deal with pictorial images and video information. These four types of information (voice, data, image, and video) are essential to the survival of any business in today's competitive international environment. What is needed is a treatment not just of data communications but also of **information communications** for the business environment.

Information communications and computer networking have become essential to the functioning of today's businesses, large and small. Furthermore, they have become a major and growing cost to organizations. Management and staff need a thorough understanding of information communications in order to assess needs; plan for the introduction of products, services, and systems; and manage the systems and technical personnel that operate them. This understanding must comprise the following:

- **Technology:** The underlying technology of information communications facilities, networking systems, and communications software
- **Architecture:** The way in which hardware, software, and services can be organized to provide computer and terminal interconnection
- **Applications:** How information communications and networking systems can meet the requirements of today's businesses

APPROACH

The purpose of this text is to present the concepts of information communications in a way that relates specifically to the business environment and to the concerns of business management and staff. To this end, the book takes an approach based on requirements, ingredients, and applications:

- **Requirements:** The need to provide services that enable businesses to utilize information is the driving force behind data and information communications technology. The text outlines the specific requirements that this technology is intended to address. This linkage between requirements and technology is essential to motivate a text of this nature.
- **Ingredients:** The technology of information communications includes the hardware, software, and communications services available to support distributed systems. An understanding of this technology is essential for a manager to make intelligent choices among the many alternatives.
- **Applications:** Management and staff must understand not only the technology but also the way in which that technology can be applied to satisfy business requirements.

These three concepts structure the presentation. They provide a way for the student to understand the context of what is being discussed at any point in the text, and they motivate the material. Thus, the student will gain a *practical* understanding of business information communications.

An important theme throughout the book is the essential role of standards. The proliferation of personal computers and other computer systems inevitably means that the manager will be faced with the need to integrate equipment from a variety of vendors. The only way to manage this requirement effectively is through standards. And, indeed, increasingly vendors are offering products and services that conform to international standards. This text addresses some of the key groupings of standards that are shaping the marketplace and that define the choices available to the decision maker.

INTENDED AUDIENCE

This book is addressed to students and professionals who now have or expect to have some information communications management responsibility. As a full-time job, some readers may have or plan to have responsibility for management of the company's telecommunications function. But virtually all managers and many staff personnel will need to have a basic understanding of business information communications to perform their tasks effectively.

For students, this text is intended as an introductory course in information communications for business and information management students. It does not assume any background in data communications but does assume a basic knowledge of data processing.

The book is also intended for self-study and is designed for use as both a tutorial and a reference book for those already involved in business information communications.

PLAN OF THE TEXT

This text is a survey of the broad and fast-changing field of information communications. It is organized in such a way that new material is seen to fit into the context of the material already presented. By emphasizing requirements and applications as well as technology, the student is provided with motivation and a means of assessing the importance of a particular topic with respect to the whole. The book is divided into six parts:

1. **Requirements:** Defines the needs for information communications in the business environment. It discusses the way in which various forms of information are used and the need for interconnection and networking facilities. An examination of the nature and role of distributed data processing is the highlight of this first part.

2. **The Internet and Distributed Applications:** Provides an overview of the Internet and the basic protocols that are the foundation of the Internet and also addresses the critical issue of quality of service. This part also deals with the specific business applications that require information communications facilities and networks. This part presents key applications, such as electronic mail and the World Wide Web, and includes a discussion of client/server computing and intranets.

3. **Local Area Networks:** Explores the technologies and architectures that have been developed for networking over shorter distances. The transmission media, topologies, and medium access control protocols that are the key ingredients of a LAN design are explored and specific standardized LAN systems examined.

4. **Wide Area Networks:** Examines the internal mechanisms and user-network interfaces that have been developed to support voice, data, and multimedia communications over long-distance networks. The traditional technologies of packet switching and circuit switching are examined, as well as the more recent ATM and wireless WANs.

5. **Data Communications:** Deals with the basic technology of the communication of information. The emphasis is on digital communications techniques, since these are rapidly displacing analog techniques for all products and services related to information communications. Key topics include transmission media, data link control protocols, and multiplexing.

6. **Management Issues:** Deals with two key areas: network security and network management.

In addition, the book includes an extensive glossary, a list of frequently used acronyms, and a bibliography. Each chapter includes review questions, problems and suggestions for further reading. Finally, a number of real-world cases studies are sprinkled throughout the book.

NOTE TO THE INSTRUCTOR

The major goal of this text is to make it as effective a teaching tool for this exciting and fast-moving subject as possible. This goal is reflected both in the structure of the book and in the supporting material.

The book contains a number of features that provide strong pedagogical support for the instructor. Each chapter begins with a list of chapter objectives, which provides, in effect, an outline of the chapter and alerts the student to look for certain key concepts as the chapter is read. Key terms are introduced in boldface in the chapter, and all of the new key terms for that chapter are listed at the end of the chapter. Acronyms are highlighted and listed on the back endpaper; this is important because the field of information communications is loaded with acronyms. A glossary at the end of the book provides a handy summary of key terms. The summary at the end of each chapter highlights the key concepts and places them in the context of the entire book. In addition, there are questions and homework problems to reinforce and extend what has been learned. The book is also liberally supplied with figures and tables to enhance points made in the text.

Throughout the book a number of case studies are presented. These are not "made-up" or "toy" cases but actual cases reported in the literature. Each case is chosen to reinforce or extend concepts introduced prior to the case study.

The text is also accompanied by supplementary material that will aid the instructor. A solutions manual provides answers to all of the problems and questions at the end of each chapter. A test bank of additional problems is also available. PDF figures and PowerPoint slides are available on line and on a CD-ROM version of the instructor's manual.

TOP-DOWN AND BOTTOM-UP APPROACHES

The book is laid out to present the material in a top-down fashion. This has the advantage of immediately focusing on the most visible part of the material, the applications, and then seeing, progressively, how each layer is supported by the next layer down. This approach makes the most sense for many instructors and students. The application layer is the most visible layer to the student and typically provides the most interest. An understanding of the applications motivates the mechanisms found at the transport layer. The treatment of the application and transport layers enables the student to understand the many design issues at the internet layer, including quality of service and routing issues. Finally, computer networks and data link mechanisms can be treated.

Some readers, and some instructors, are more comfortable with a bottom-up approach. With this approach, each part builds on the material in the previous part, so that it is always clear how a given layer of functionality is supported from below. Accordingly, the book is organized in a modular fashion. After reading Part One, the other parts can be read in a number of possible sequences.

INTERNET SERVICES FOR INSTRUCTORS AND STUDENTS

There is a Web page for this book that provides support for students and instructors. The page includes links to relevant sites, transparency masters of figures in the book in PDF

(Adobe Acrobat) format, PowerPoint slides, and sign-up information for the book's Internet mailing list. The Web page is at WilliamStallings.com/BDC/BDC5e.html. An Internet mailing list has been set up so that instructors using this book can exchange information, suggestions, and questions with each other and with the author. As soon as typos or other errors are discovered, an errata list for this book will be available at WilliamStallings.com.

NOTE TO THE READER

In a book on this topic, for this sort of audience, it is tempting to launch immediately into a description of communications and networking technology and to examine and compare the various approaches. Certainly, this is an essential element of a book that deals with business information communications. However, we believe that this approach is inappropriate. The business reader wants, and rightly so, to see the technical material in the context of the needs of the business and the ways in which communications and networking technology support desired business functions. Thus this book begins by defining the requirements for information communications in business. The types of information and their utility are examined first. This sets the stage for a discussion of the applications that can meet those requirements and the role of the Internet in supporting the applications. We are then in a position to examine the communications networks, both LANs and WANs, that form the infrastructure for distributed applications and the network. Continuing in this top-down fashion, the book then examines fundamental communications technologies. Finally, security and network management issues are discussed. It is hoped that this strategy will make the material more comprehensible and provide a structure that is more natural to a reader with a business orientation.

WHAT'S NEW IN THE FIFTH EDITION

In the four years since the fourth edition of this book was published, the field has seen continued innovations and improvements. In this new edition, we try to capture these changes while maintaining a broad and comprehensive coverage of the entire field. To begin the process of revision, the fourth edition of this book was extensively reviewed by a number of professors who teach the subject and by professionals working in the field. The result is that, in many places, the narrative has been clarified and tightened, and illustrations have been improved. Also, a number of new "field-tested" problems have been added.

Beyond these refinements to improve pedagogy and user friendliness, there have been major substantive changes throughout the book. Highlights include the following:

- **Top-down organization:** The organization of the book has been radically changed in response to professors' inputs and to provide a greater emphasis on the Internet and on applications.
- **The Internet:** Considerable new material has been added on the organization and operation of the Internet.
- **LANs and WANs:** The fourth edition provided five chapters in one part covering networking. The fifth edition splits this material into two parts, providing greater detail and with an increased emphasis on wireless networks.

In addition, throughout the book, virtually every topic has been updated to reflect the developments in standards and technology that have occurred since the publication of the fourth edition.

ACKNOWLEDGMENTS

This new edition has benefited from review by a number of people, who gave generously of their time and expertise. The following people reviewed all or a large part of the manuscript: Ron Fulle (Rochester Institute of Technology), Rangadhar Dash (University of Texas–Arlington), Hugo Moortgat (San Francisco State), Pramod Pandya (Cal. State–Fullerton), Bongsik Shin (San Diego State University), and Zhangxi Lin (Tennessee Tech).

Bruce Hartpence (Department of Information Technology, Rochester Institute of Technology) authored the application notes at the end of each chapter and contributed a number of review questions and homework problems. Ric Heishman (Assistant Dean–Computer Science & Information Technology, Northern Virginia Community College) also contributed homework problems. Fernando Ariel Gont contributed a number of homework problems; he also provided detailed reviews of all of the chapters of the fifth edition.

Steven Kilby contributed the case study on ING Life, plus he contributed part of Chapter 4. Professor Varadharajan Sridhar of the Indian Institute of Management contributed the case study on Staten Island University Hospital.

Richard Van Slyke of Brooklyn Polytechnic Institute has made substantial contributions to the second and third editions of this book and was listed as a coauthor. Much of his contribution has been retained and revised.

Finally, I would like to thank the many people responsible for the publication of the book, all of whom did their usual excellent job. This includes the staff at Prentice Hall, particularly my editors Alan Apt and Toni Holm, their assistant Patrick Lindner, production manager Rose Kernan, and supplements manager Sarah Parker. Also, Jake Warde of Warde Publishers managed the reviews; and Patricia M. Daly did the copy editing.

BUSINESS DATA COMMUNICATIONS

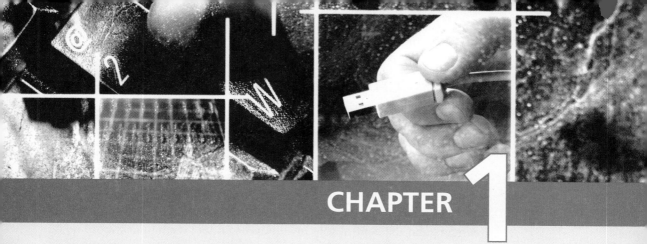

CHAPTER 1

INTRODUCTION

1

This introductory chapter begins with an overview of the role of data communications and networking in the enterprise. Then a brief discussion introduces each of the parts of this book.

1.1 INFORMATION AND COMMUNICATION

A confluence of computers, communication technologies, and demographics is transforming the way any enterprise conducts itself and carries out its organizational mandate. And it's happening fast. A business that ignores it will fall hopelessly to the rear in the global race for the competitive edge. At the heart of the transformation is information. No longer a byproduct—no longer, in many cases, even a cost center—the generation, storage, and movement of information have been made profitable by those companies that have taken up the technological challenge posed by the myriad machines that automate so much of our lives.

We are unquestionably dependent on computers and the communication devices and services that connect them. The number of computers and terminals at work in the world today is in the 100s of millions. It constitutes a critical mass: The overwhelming need of organizations and their workers now is for connectivity, for integration, for ease of access to information. So fundamental is information communication technology to business success that it is emerging as the foundation of a new strategy now taking shape in American businesses—using management structures to gain a competitive advantage.

As businesses are challenged by such forces as global competition, mergers, and acquisitions, time-tested management structures are putting a strain on corporate bottom lines. In response, companies are breaking down divisional walls and flattening top-heavy management pyramids to create new corporate structures that help them to compete more effectively. The technology that is making much of this possible is *networking*.

Communication technology helps companies overcome three kinds of basic organizational difficulties: Good networks make geographically dispersed companies more manageable; they help top-heavy companies trim down middle management; and they also help companies break down barriers between divisions. As we examine the technology and applications throughout this book, we will see the ways in which information communication technology solves these and other vital business problems.

1.2 DATA COMMUNICATIONS AND NETWORKING FOR TODAY'S ENTERPRISE

Effective and efficient data communication and networking facilities are vital to any enterprise. In this section, we first look at trends that are increasing the challenge for the business manager in planning and managing such facilities. Next we introduce the concept of business drivers that will guide the enterprise in developing an overall data communications and networking plan. Finally, we introduce the concept of convergence and show its importance in business data communications.

Trends

Three different forces have consistently driven the architecture and evolution of data communications and networking facilities: traffic growth, development of new services, and advances in technology.

Communication **traffic,** both local (within a building or building complex) and long distance, both voice and data, has been growing at a high and steady rate for decades. The increasing emphasis on office automation, remote access, online transactions, and other productivity measures means that this trend is likely to continue. Thus, managers are constantly struggling to maximize capacity and minimize transmission costs.

As businesses rely more and more on information technology, the range of **services** expands. This increases the demand for high-capacity networking and transmission facilities. In turn, the continuing growth in high-speed network offerings with the continuing drop in prices encourages the expansion of services. Thus, growth in services and growth in traffic capacity go hand in hand. Figure 1.1 gives some examples of information-based services and the data rates needed to support them [ELSA02].

Finally, trends in technology enable the provision of increasing traffic capacity and the support of a wide range of services. Four technology trends are particularly notable and need to be understood by the manager responsible for information technology:

1. The trend toward faster and cheaper, both in computing and communications, continues. In terms of computing, this means more powerful computers and

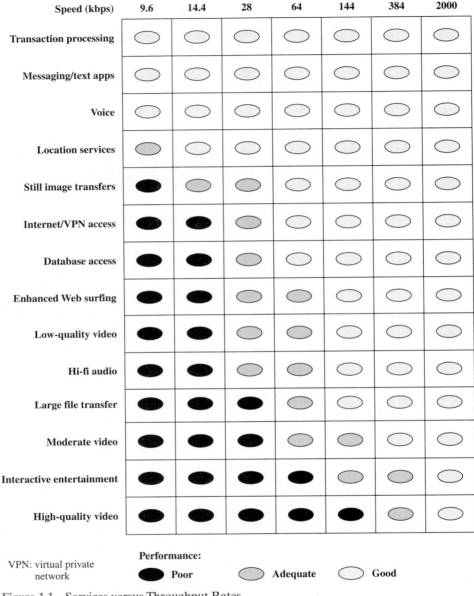

Figure 1.1   Services versus Throughput Rates

clusters of computers capable of supporting more demanding applications, such as multimedia applications. In terms of communications, the increasing use of optical fiber has brought transmission prices down and greatly increased capacity. For example, for long-distance telecommunication and data network links, recent offerings of dense wavelength division multiplexing (DWDM) enable capacities of many terabits per second. For local area networks (LANs) many enterprises now have Gigabit Ethernet backbone networks and some are beginning to deploy 10-Gbps Ethernet.[1]

2. Both voice-oriented telecommunications networks, such as the public switched telephone network (PSTN), and data networks, including the Internet, are more "intelligent" than ever. Two areas of intelligence are noteworthy. First, today's networks can offer differing levels of quality of service (QoS), which include specifications for maximum delay, minimum throughput, and so on. Second, today's networks provide a variety of customizable services in the areas of network management and security.

3. The Internet, the Web, and associated applications have emerged as dominant features of both the business and personal world, opening up many opportunities and challenges for managers. In addition to exploiting the Internet and the Web to reach customers, suppliers, and partners, enterprises have formed intranets and extranets[2] to isolate their proprietary information free from unwanted access.

4. There has been a trend toward ever-increasing mobility for decades, liberating workers from the confines of the physical enterprise. Innovations include voice mail, remote data access, pagers, fax, e-mail, cordless phones, cell phones and cellular networks, and Internet portals. The result is the ability of employees to take their business context with them as they move about. We are now seeing the growth of high-speed wireless access, which further enhances the ability to use enterprise information resources and services anywhere.

Business Drivers

The trends discussed in the preceding subsection are enabling the development of enterprise network and communications facilities that are increasingly better integrated with the information base, which the enterprise itself runs. Network management and operation depend on some key enterprise-specific information, such as names, network addresses, security capabilities, end-user groupings, priority designations, mailboxes, and application attributes. With the increasing capacity and functionality of enterprise networks, this information can be unified with the enterprise information base so that the information is correct, consistent, and available across all business applications.

The nature of the enterprise networking and communications facility depends on the business applications it must support. [MILO00] lists four main application areas that will serve as the drivers in determining the design and makeup of the enterprise network. Figure 1.2 lists these areas, along with their business motivators and the expected benefits.

---

[1]See Appendix 1A for an explanation of numerical prefixes, such as *tera* and *giga*.

[2]Briefly, an intranet uses Internet and Web technology in an isolated facility internal to an enterprise; an extranet extends a company's intranet out onto the Internet to allow selected customers, suppliers, and mobile workers to access the company's private data and applications. See Chapter 7 for a discussion.

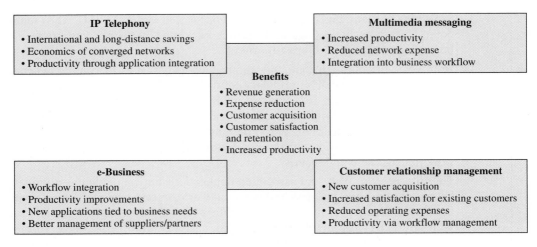

IP = Internet Protocol
e-Business = Enterprise activities based on mobile, global access to enterprise networks

Figure 1.2 Applications Driving Enterprise Networks

Convergence

A final concept we wish to introduce in this overview section is that of convergence [HETT03], which refers to the merger of previously distinct telephony and information technologies and markets. We can think of this convergence in terms of a four-layer model of enterprise communications:

- **Applications:** These are seen by the end users of a business. Convergence integrates communications applications, such as voice calling (telephone), voice mail, e-mail, and instant messaging, with business applications, such as workgroup collaboration, customer relationship management, and other back-office functions. With convergence, applications provide features that incorporate voice, data, and video in a seamless, organized, and value-added manner. One example is multimedia messaging, which enables a user to employ a single interface to access messages from a variety of sources (e.g., office voice mail, office e-mail, beeper, and fax).

- **Services:** At this level, the manager deals with the information network in terms of the services it supplies to support applications. The network manager needs design, maintenance, and support services related to the deployment of convergence-based facilities.

- **Management:** At this level, network managers deal with the enterprise network as a function-providing system. Such management services may include setting up authentication schemes; capacity management for various users, groups, and applications; and QoS provision.

- **Infrastructure:** The infrastructure consists of the communication links, LANs, WANs, and Internet connections available to the enterprise. The key aspect of

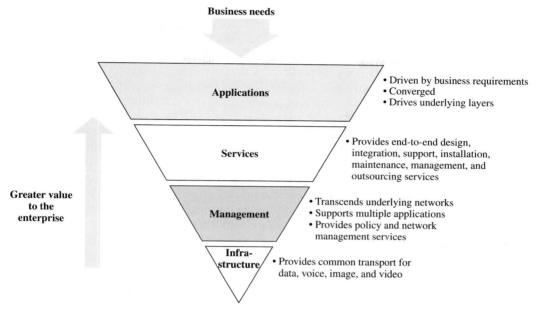

Figure 1.3   Business-Driven Convergence

convergence at this level is the ability to carry voice over data networks, such as the Internet.

Figure 1.3, based on [MILO00], illustrates the four layers and their associated convergence attributes.

1.3   THE NATURE OF BUSINESS INFORMATION REQUIREMENTS

A business survives and thrives on information: information within the organization and information exchanged with suppliers, customers, and regulators. Moreover, the information needs to be consistent, accessible, and at the right location. In Part One, Chapters 2 and 3, we consider information in four forms—voice, data, image, and video—and the implications of distributed data processing.

In this book, the term **voice communications** primarily refers to telephone-related communications. By far the most common form of communication in any organization and for most personnel is direct telephone conversation. The telephone has been a basic business tool for decades. Telephone communication has been enhanced by a variety of computer-based services, including voice mail and computerized telephone exchange systems. Voice mail provides the ability to send, forward, and reply to voice messages nonsimultaneously, and it has become a cost-efficient tool even for many small and midsize organizations. It provides savings on answering machines and services, as well as a more responsive service to customers and suppliers. Advances have also been made in computerized telephone exchange systems, including in-house digital private branch exchanges (PBX) and Centrex systems provided by the local telephone company. These new systems provide a host of features, including call forwarding, camp-on call waiting, least-cost routing of long-distance calls, and a variety of accounting and auditing features. More recently, the merger of voice and Internet technologies, based on the voice over IP (VoIP) protocol, has resulted in PBX offerings that provide full Internet support.

The term **data communications** is sometimes used to refer to virtually any form of information transfer other than voice. It is sometimes convenient to limit this term to information in the form of text (such as reports, memos, and other documents) and numerical data (such as accounting files). The rapid changes in technology have created fresh challenges for management in making effective use of data communications. Later in this chapter we briefly outline the changes in technology in transmission, networks, and communications software that present the manager with new and powerful business tools but also the necessity of making choices among complex alternatives.

Image communications is now an important component of the office environment. The best-known example of this technology is facsimile (fax). Like the tortoise who surpasses the hare, facsimile machines have caught up with higher-tech alternatives and have achieved status over the past few years as the preferred method of sending documents over a long distance. With fax, the document can have any content, including text, graphics, signatures, and even photographs. Newer machines can transmit these documents over telephone networks in seconds, and low-cost hardware, including personal computer attachments, is now available. In addition, image communications is coming to play an important role within the office. The arrival of the optical disc, based on the same technology as that of the familiar compact disc of the music industry, allows massive amounts of information to be stored inexpensively. Thus, all sorts of images, including engineering and design specifications, mixed documents (text, graphs, signatures, etc.), presentation material, and so on, can be moved quickly around the office and displayed on user workstations. This new technology for storing and transmitting images creates a demand for high-capacity networks and is one of the driving forces in the development of networking technology.

Video communications is also becoming important in the office environment. Traditionally, this technology has been used as a one-way delivery system of entertainment programs. Now, with the availability of high-capacity transmission links and networks, it has an increasing business application, most notably videoconferencing. Videoconferencing allows the linkup of two or more remotely located conference rooms to conduct such meetings as planning sessions, contract negotiations, and project reviews. The time and money saved on travel, food, and lodging make videoconferencing a powerful tool for increasing efficiency and productivity.

All these forms of information communications play a key role in today's businesses. The manager responsible for them must understand the technology sufficiently to be able to deal effectively with vendors of communications products and services and to make cost-effective choices among the growing array of options.

Chapter 2 examines the business uses of these four classes of information and the communications requirements that they generate.

1.4 DISTRIBUTED DATA PROCESSING

The steady drop over many years in the cost of data processing equipment, coupled with an increase in the capability of such equipment, has led to the introduction of many small- and medium-size computers into the business environment. Traditionally, the data processing function was centrally organized around a mainframe computer. Today, however, it is much more common to find a distributed data processing configuration, one that consists of a number of computers and terminals linked together by networks. Chapter 3 examines the motivation for distributed data processing and discusses the various forms that it takes.

1.5 THE INTERNET AND DISTRIBUTED APPLICATIONS

A business needs to be concerned with two dimensions of computer communications software: the application software that is provided for a community of terminals and computers, and the underlying interconnection software that allows these terminals and computers to work together cooperatively.

The mere existence of a large population of computers and terminals creates the demand that these devices work together. For example, when most employees in an organization have access to a terminal or a personal computer (PC), one of the most effective means of communication within the organization is electronic mail (e-mail). If one employee needs to communicate with another, a message sent by e-mail can be far more effective than hit-or-miss attempts to reach the person by telephone. A detailed e-mail message can be left in the recipient's "electronic mailbox," to be read and answered when the recipient returns to the office. Other applications, such as the exchange of documents, the use of a database that is distributed among a number of computers, and the ability to access many different computers from a single terminal, can be provided by applications software that is geared for the new networked environment.

The key to the success of these applications is that all the terminals and computers in the community "speak" the same language. This is the role of the underlying interconnection software. This software must ensure that all the devices transmit messages in such a way that they can be understood by the other computers and terminals in the community. With the introduction of the Systems Network Architecture (SNA) by IBM in the 1970s, this concept became a reality. However, SNA worked only with IBM equipment. Soon other vendors followed with their own proprietary communication architectures to tie together their equipment. Such an approach may be good business for the vendor, but it is bad business for the customer. Happily, that situation has changed radically with the adoption of standards for interconnection software. The manager needs to understand the scope and status of these standards to be able to exploit them in building a multiple-vendor, tailored installation.

Modern data communications and microelectronics are radically changing the architecture of modern information systems. Most applications have evolved away from large, general-purpose mainframe computers to *distributed computing*. Instead of dumb terminals enslaved to mainframes, powerful workstations and PCs provide, local to the user, powerful graphical interfaces and much of the application computing. The local workstations and PCs are supported by specialized servers specifically designed for a single function, such as printing, storing files, or supporting database activities. The workstations and PCs are often connected to the servers by high-speed LANs. This approach, called *client/server architecture*, requires sophisticated, reliable, and secure data communications, but its inherent flexibility and responsiveness make it an essential tool in the businessperson's information systems repertoire.

Part Two looks at a number of topics that deal with the infrastructure for supporting distributed applications.

The Internet

Virtually no business, and certainly no medium or large enterprise, can compete without exploiting the Internet and the Web. The Web provides a way to communicate with consumers and to publicize the company and can form the base for a number of e-commerce applications. Internet technology, in the form of intranets and extranets, enables secure communication both within an enterprise and with customers, suppliers, and partners. Chapter 4 provides important background on the Internet.

TCP/IP

One of the most difficult problems that has traditionally faced computer users is that different vendors have used different and incompatible architectures. Chapter 5 discusses the use of standardized communications protocols to integrate diverse equipment. The focus is on the TCP/IP (Transmission Control Protocol/Internet Protocol) protocol suite, which is now universally used for the communications software function across multiple vendor equipment and is the basis for the operation of the Internet.

Chapter 5 also briefly reviews the Open System Interconnection (OSI) architecture developed by the International Organization for Standardization (ISO).

Distributed Applications

Distributed information processing is essential in virtually all businesses. There is a growing use of applications that are designed to work among a distributed set of computers for both intracompany and intercompany information exchange. Chapter 6 examines some of the key applications that are likely to be the most important to a business.

Client/Server Architectures and Intranets

A remarkable transformation is taking place in the architecture of today's commercial computers. The large mainframe, although still important, has been replaced or supplemented in many applications by networked PCs and workstations, as is illustrated by the increased manufacture of computers of different types. The number of PCs and workstations is growing at a much greater rate than that of mainframes and midrange computers, with the result that computing is being more widely distributed. Increasingly, computation is provided by the *client/server* model. Separate computers (servers) support database functions, store files, perform printing services, and provide other specialized functions on a shared basis for many users (clients). These servers, which can offer enhanced performance and cost savings through specialization, are accessed over LANs and other communications networks.

Even more recently, a new approach has gained widespread support within organizations: the intranet. An intranet provides the same sorts of applications and interfaces as found on the Internet, especially the World Wide Web. The difference is that an intranet is confined to use within the organization, with no access to outsiders. The intranet is a flexible, easy-to-use, and easy-to-implement approach to many business applications.

Chapter 7 looks at client/server computing, intranets, and extranets.

1.6 NETWORKS

The number of computers in use worldwide is in the hundreds of millions. Moreover, the expanding memory and processing power of these computers means that users can put the machines to work on new kinds of applications and functions. Accordingly, the pressure from the users of these systems for ways to communicate among all these machines is irresistible. It is changing the way vendors think and the way all automation products and services are sold. This demand for connectivity is manifested in two specific requirements: the need for communications software, which is previewed in the next section, and the need for networks.

One type of network that has become increasingly common is the local area network (LAN). Indeed, the LAN is to be found in virtually all medium- and large-size office buildings. As the number and power of computing devices have grown, so have the number and capacity of LANs to be found in an office. Although standards have been developed that reduce somewhat the number of types of LANs, there are still half a dozen general types of local area networks to choose from. Furthermore, many offices need more than one such network, with the attendant problems of interconnecting and managing a diverse collection of networks, computers, and terminals.

Beyond the confines of a single office building, networks for voice, data, image, and video are equally important to business. Here, too, there are rapid changes. Advances in technology have led to greatly increased capacity and the concept of integration. *Integration* means that the customer equipment and networks can deal simultaneously with voice, data, image, and even video. Thus, a memo or report can be accompanied by voice commentary, presentation graphics, and perhaps even a short video introduction or summary. Image and video services impose large demands on wide area network transmission. Moreover, as LANs become ubiquitous and as their transmission rates increase, the demands on the wide area networks to support LAN interconnection have increased the demands on wide area network capacity and switching. On the other hand, fortunately, the enormous and ever-increasing capacity of fiber optic transmission provides ample resources to meet these demands. However, developing switching systems with the capacity and rapid response to support these increased requirements is a challenge not yet conquered.

The opportunities for using networks as an aggressive competitive tool and as a means of enhancing productivity and slashing costs are great. The manager who understands the technology and can deal effectively with vendors of service and equipment is able to enhance a company's competitive position.

In the remainder of this section, we provide a brief overview of various networks. Parts Three and Four cover these topics in depth.

Wide Area Networks

Wide area networks generally cover a large geographical area, require the crossing of public right-of-ways, and rely at least in part on circuits provided by a common carrier. Typically, a WAN consists of a number of interconnected switching nodes. A transmission from any attached device is routed through these internal nodes to the specified destination device. These nodes (including the boundary nodes) are not concerned with the content of the data; rather, their purpose is to provide a switching facility that will move the data from node to node until they reach their destination.

Traditionally, WANs have been implemented using one of two technologies: circuit switching and packet switching. More recently, frame relay and ATM networks have assumed major roles. Chapter 13 looks at frame relay and ATM.

Circuit Switching In a circuit-switching network, a dedicated communication path is established between two stations through the nodes of the network. That path is a connected sequence of physical links between nodes. On each link, a logical channel is dedicated to the connection. Data generated by the source station are transmitted along the dedicated path as rapidly as possible. At each node, incoming data are routed or switched to the appropriate outgoing channel without delay. The most common example of circuit switching is the telephone network.

Packet Switching A quite different approach is used in a packet-switching network. In this case, it is not necessary to dedicate transmission capacity along a path through the network. Rather, data are sent out in a sequence of small chunks, called packets. Each packet is passed through the network from node to node along some path leading from source to destination. At each node, the entire packet is received, stored briefly, and then transmitted to the next node. Packet-switching networks are commonly used for terminal-to-computer and computer-to-computer communications.

Frame Relay Packet switching was developed at a time when digital long-distance transmission facilities exhibited a relatively high error rate compared to today's facilities. As a result, there is a considerable amount of overhead built into packet-switching schemes to compensate for errors. The overhead includes additional bits added to each packet to introduce redundancy and additional processing at the end stations and the intermediate switching nodes to detect and recover from errors.

With modern high-speed telecommunications systems, this overhead is unnecessary and counterproductive. It is unnecessary because the rate of errors has been dramatically lowered and any remaining errors can easily be caught in the end systems by logic that operates above the level of the packet-switching logic. It is counterproductive because the overhead involved soaks up a significant fraction of the high capacity provided by the network.

Frame relay was developed to take advantage of these high data rates and low error rates. Whereas the original packet-switching networks were designed with a data rate to the end user of about 64 kbps, frame relay networks are designed to operate efficiently at user data rates of up to 2 Mbps. The key to achieving these high data rates is to strip out most of the overhead involved with error control.

ATM Asynchronous transfer mode (ATM), sometimes referred to as cell relay, is a culmination of developments in circuit switching and packet switching. ATM can be viewed as an evolution from frame relay. The most obvious difference between frame relay and ATM is that frame relay uses variable-length packets, called frames, and ATM uses fixed-length packets, called cells. As with frame relay, ATM provides little overhead for error control, depending on the inherent reliability of the transmission system and on higher layers of logic in the end systems to catch and correct errors. By using a fixed packet length, the processing overhead is reduced even further for ATM compared to frame relay. The result is that ATM is designed to work in the range of 10s and 100s of Mbps, and in the Gbps range.

ATM can also be viewed as an evolution from circuit switching. With circuit switching, only fixed-data-rate circuits are available to the end system. ATM allows the definition of multiple virtual channels with data rates that are dynamically defined at the time the virtual channel is created. By using small, fixed-size cells, ATM is so efficient that it can offer a constant-data-rate channel even though it is using a packet-switching technique. Thus, ATM extends circuit switching to allow multiple channels with the data rate on each channel dynamically set on demand.

Local Area Networks

As with WANs, a LAN is a communications network that interconnects a variety of devices and provides a means for information exchange among those devices. There are several key distinctions between LANs and WANs:

1. The scope of the LAN is small, typically a single building or a cluster of buildings. This difference in geographic scope leads to different technical solutions, as we shall see.

2. It is usually the case that the LAN is owned by the same organization that owns the attached devices. For WANs, this is less often the case, or at least a significant fraction of the network assets are not owned. This has two implications. First, care must be taken in the choice of LAN, because there may be a substantial capital

investment (compared to dial-up or leased charges for WANs) for both purchase and maintenance. Second, the network management responsibility for a LAN falls solely on the owner.

3. The internal data rates of LANs are typically much greater than those of WANs.

LANs come in a number of different configurations. The most common are switched LANs and wireless LANs. The most common switched LAN is a switched Ethernet LAN, which consists of a single switch with a number of attached devices, or a number of interconnected switches. Two other prominent examples are ATM LANs, which simply use an ATM network in a local area, and Fibre Channel. Wireless LANs use a variety of wireless transmission technologies and organizations.

Part Three covers LANs.

Wireless Networks

As was just mentioned, wireless LANs are common and are widely used in business environments. Wireless technology is also common for both wide area voice and data networks. Wireless networks provide advantages in the areas of mobility and ease of installation and configuration. Chapter 14 covers wireless WANs.

Metropolitan Area Networks

As the name suggests, a metropolitan area network (MAN) occupies a middle ground between LANs and WANs. Interest in MANs has come about as a result of a recognition that the traditional point-to-point and switched network techniques used in WANs may be inadequate for the growing needs of organizations. While frame relay and ATM promise to meet a wide range of high-speed needs, there is a requirement now for both private and public networks that provide high capacity at low costs over a large area. A number of approaches have been implemented, including wireless networks and metropolitan extensions to Ethernet.

The primary market for MANs is the customer that has high capacity needs in a metropolitan area. A MAN is intended to provide the required capacity at lower cost and greater efficiency than obtaining an equivalent service from the local telephone company.

An Example Configuration

To give some feel for the scope of concerns of Parts Two through Four, Figure 1.4 illustrates some of the typical communications and network elements in use today. In the upper left-hand portion of the figure, we see an individual residential user connected to an Internet service provider (ISP) through some sort of subscriber connection. Common examples of such a connection are the public switched telephone network, for which the user requires a dial-up modem (e.g., a 56-kbps modem); a digital subscriber line (DSL), which provides a high-speed link over telephone lines and requires a special DSL modem; and a cable TV facility, which requires a cable modem. In each case, there are separate issues concerning signal encoding, error control, and the internal structure of the subscriber network.

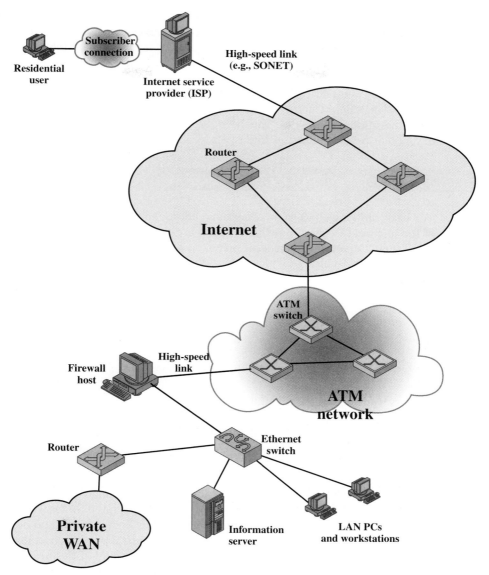

Figure 1.4 A Networking Configuration

Typically, an ISP will consist of a number of interconnected servers (only a single server is shown) connected to the Internet through a high-speed link. One example of such a link is a SONET (synchronous optical network) line, described in Chapter 17. The Internet consists of a number of interconnected routers that span the globe. These routers forward packets of data from source to destination through the Internet.

The lower portion of Figure 1.4 shows a LAN implemented using a single Ethernet switch. This is a common configuration at small businesses and other small organizations. The LAN is connected to the Internet through a firewall host that provides security services. In this example the firewall connects to the Internet through an ATM network. There is also a router off of the LAN hooked into a private WAN, which might be a private ATM or frame relay network.

A variety of design issues, such as signal encoding and error control, relate to the links between adjacent elements. Examples are links between routers on the Internet, between switches in the ATM network, and between a subscriber and an ISP. The internal structure of the various networks (telephone, ATM, Ethernet) raises additional issues. We will be occupied in Parts Two through Four with the design features suggested by Figure 1.4.

1.7 THE TRANSMISSION OF INFORMATION

The basic building block of any communications facility is the transmission line. Much of the technical detail of how information is encoded and transmitted across a line is of no real interest to the business manager. The manager is concerned with whether the particular facility provides the required capacity, with acceptable reliability, at minimum cost. However, there are certain aspects of transmission technology that a manager must understand to be able to ask the right questions and make informed decisions.

One of the basic choices facing a business user is the transmission medium. For use within the business premises, this choice is generally completely up to the business. For long-distance communications, the choice is generally but not always made by the long-distance carrier. In either case, changes in technology are rapidly changing the mix of media used. Of particular note are *fiber optic* transmission and *wireless* transmission (e.g., satellite and radio). These two media are now driving the evolution of data communications transmission.

The ever-increasing capacity of fiber optic channels is making channel capacity a virtually free resource. The growth of the market for optical fiber transmission systems since the beginning of the 1980s is without precedent. During the past 10 years, the cost of fiber optic transmission has dropped by more than an order of magnitude, and the capacity of such systems has grown at almost as rapid a rate. Long-distance telephone communications trunks within the United States will soon consist almost completely of fiber optic cable. Because of its high capacity and because of its security characteristics—fiber is almost impossible to tap—it is becoming increasingly used within office buildings to carry the growing load of business information. However, switching is now becoming the bottleneck. This problem is causing radical changes in communication architecture, including asynchronous transfer mode (ATM) switching, highly parallel processing in switches, and integrated network management schemes.

The second medium—wireless transmission—is a result of the trend toward universal personal telecommunications and universal access to communications. The first concept refers to the ability of a person to identify himself or herself easily and to use conveniently any communication system in a large area (e.g., globally, over a continent, or in an entire country) in terms of a single account. The second refers to the capability of using one's terminal in a wide variety of environments to connect to information services (e.g., to have a portable terminal that will work in the office, on the street, and on airplanes equally well). This revolution in personal computing obviously involves wireless communication in a fundamental way.

Despite the growth in the capacity and the drop in the cost of transmission facilities, transmission services remain the most costly component of a communications budget for most businesses. Thus, the manager needs to be aware of techniques that increase the efficiency of the use of these facilities. The two major approaches to greater efficiency are multiplexing and compression. *Multiplexing* refers to the ability of a number of devices to share a transmission facility. If each device needs the facility only a fraction of the time, then a sharing arrangement allows the cost of the facility to be spread over many users. *Compression*, as the name indicates, involves squeezing the data down so that a lower-capacity, cheaper transmission facility can be used to meet a given demand. These two techniques show up separately and in combination in a number of types of communications equipment. The manager needs to understand these technologies to be able to assess the appropriateness and cost-effectiveness of the various products on the market.

Chapters 15 and 16, in Part Five, examine the key issues and technologies in the area of information transmission.

Transmission and Transmission Media

Information can be communicated by converting it into an electromagnetic signal and transmitting that signal over some medium, such as a twisted-pair telephone line. The most commonly used transmission media are twisted-pair lines, coaxial cable, optical fiber cable, and terrestrial and satellite microwave. The data rates that can be achieved and the rate at which errors can occur depend on the nature of the signal and the type of medium. Chapter 15 examines the significant properties of electromagnetic signals Chapters 9, 11, and 14 discuss the various transmission media.

Communication Techniques

The transmission of information across a transmission medium involves more than simply inserting a signal on the medium. The technique used to encode the information into an electromagnetic signal must be determined. There are various ways in which the encoding can be done, and the choice affects performance and reliability. Furthermore, the successful transmission of information involves a high degree of cooperation. The interface between a device and the transmission medium must be agreed on. Some means of controlling the flow of information and recovering from its loss or corruption must be used. These latter functions may be performed by a data link control protocol. All these issues are examined in Chapters 16 and 17.

Transmission Efficiency

A major cost in any computer/communications facility is transmission cost. Because of this, it is important to maximize the amount of information that can be carried over a given resource or, alternatively, to minimize the transmission capacity needed to satisfy a given information communications requirement. The standard technique for achieving this objective is multiplexing. Chapter 17 examines the three most common multiplexing techniques—frequency division, synchronous time division, and statistical time division.

1.8 MANAGEMENT ISSUES

Part Six concludes the book by examining key management issues related to business data communications.

Network Security

As companies rely increasingly on networks and as access by outsiders via the Internet and other links grows, the vexing question of security becomes ever more important. Companies are at risk for the disclosure of confidential information and for the unauthorized altering of corporate data. Chapter 18 looks at the basic tools for achieving network security and discusses how they can be adapted to meet a company's needs.

Network Management

In the early years of data communications, in the 1970s, the key focus was the functionality and performance of the technology. The key questions were, What could the technology do? How fast? For how many transactions? As electronic information systems became part of the basic fabric of many businesses, managers discovered that the operation of their businesses had become dependent on their information systems and that the economic performance of their firms depended on the cost-effective use of the technology. That is, like any resource, information technology had to be managed. For example, managers of data communications are often most concerned today about network reliability. Many of the management functions required are common to other aspects of business management, but the following requirements are special to information technology:

- Networks have evolved from an easily controlled centralized (i.e., mainframe/dumb terminal) approach into peer-to-peer interconnections among highly distributed systems.
- Peer-to-peer networks have grown larger and larger—some have tens of thousands of attached devices—so that managing, monitoring, and maintaining them has become very complex.
- In many business sectors, such as banking, retailing, and other service industries, networks of computing devices constitute a critical strategic resource that cannot be allowed to fail.
- Communications costs, meanwhile, are climbing, and there is a shortage of skilled personnel to staff network command centers and to handle network management.

Network management must provide global visibility on corporate information flow. Techniques of centralized, remote monitoring and control provide rapid notification of failures and automatic invocation of recovery measures. On-the-fly analysis of network performance and dynamic adjustment of network parameters provide adaptation to varying cycles of business activity. Network management is a complex discipline, particularly in a multivendor environment. The manager must understand the requirements for network management and the tools and technologies available to be able to plan effectively for an automated network management strategy.

Chapter 19 focuses on network management.

1.9 STANDARDS

Standards have come to play a dominant role in the information communications marketplace. Virtually all vendors of products and services are committed to supporting international standards. A supporting document at this book's Web site explains the importance of standards and the current status of their use. It also provides an overview of the key organizations involved in developing these standards.

1.10 INTERNET RESOURCES

There are a number of resources available on the Internet and the Web to support this book and for keeping up with developments in this field.

Web Sites for This Book

There is a Web page for this book at WilliamStallings.com/BDC/BDC5e.html. The site includes the following:

- **Useful Web sites:** There are links to other relevant Web sites, including the sites listed throughout this book.
- **Errata sheet:** An errata list for this book will be maintained and updated as needed. Please e-mail any errors that you spot to me. Errata sheets for my other books are at **WilliamStallings.com.**
- **Figures:** All of the figures in this book in PDF (Adobe Acrobat) format.
- **Tables:** All of the tables in this book in PDF format.
- **Slides:** A set of PowerPoint slides, organized by chapter.
- **Internet mailing list:** The site includes sign-up information for the book's Internet mailing list.
- **BDC courses:** There are links to home pages for courses based on this book; these pages may be useful to other instructors in providing ideas about how to structure their course.

I also maintain the Computer Science Student Resource Site, at

WilliamStallings.com/StudentSupport.html

The purpose of this site is to provide documents, information, and links for computer science students and professionals. Links and documents are organized into four categories:

- **Math:** Includes a basic math refresher, a queuing analysis primer, a number system primer, and links to numerous math sites

- **How-to:** Advice and guidance for solving homework problems, writing technical reports, and preparing technical presentations
- **Research resources:** Links to important collections of papers, technical reports, and bibliographies
- **Miscellaneous:** A variety of other useful documents and links

Other Web Sites

There are numerous Web sites that provide information related to the topics of this book. In subsequent chapters, pointers to specific Web sites can be found in the "Recommended Reading" section. Because the addresses for Web sites tend to change frequently, I have not included these in the book. For all of the Web sites listed in the book, the appropriate link can be found at this book's Web site. Other links not mentioned in this book will be added to the Web site over time.

USENET Newsgroups

A number of USENET newsgroups are devoted to some aspect of data communications and networking. As with virtually all USENET groups, there is a high noise to signal ratio, but it is worth experimenting to see if any meet your needs. Here is a sample:

- **comp.dcom.lans, comp.dcom.lans.etherenet, and comp.dcom.lans.misc:** General discussions of LANs
- **comp.std.wireless:** General discussion of wireless networks including wireless LANs
- **comp.security.misc:** Computer security and encryption
- **comp.dcom.cell-relay:** Covers ATM and ATM LANs
- **comp.dcom.frame-relay:** Covers frame relay networks
- **comp.dcom.net-management:** Discussion of network management applications, protocols, and standards
- **comp.protocols.tcp-ip:** The TCP/IP protocol suite

1.11 USEFUL PUBLICATIONS

This book serves as a tutorial for learning about the field of business data communications and a reference that can be turned to for help on a specific topic. However, with the rapid changes taking place in this field, no book can hope to stand alone for very long. If you are truly interested in this field, you will need to invest some of your time keeping up with new developments, and the best way to do that is by reading a few relevant periodicals. The list of publications that could be recommended is huge. Included here is a small, select list of publications that will repay the time that you devote to them. All of these publications have Web sites (Table 1.1).

Business-Oriented Publications

Because of the growing importance of information communications to business, virtually all business periodicals now provide some coverage of this field. Two of the best for providing such coverage are *Forbes* and *Business Week*. *Forbes* includes a regular "Computer/Communications" section that includes two or three articles plus a regular column in each issue. The articles are timely, to the point, and cover a broad range. Periodically, the supplement *ASAP*

Table 1.1 Useful Periodicals

Name	Web Site
Business Communications Review	Links to Web pages of vendors that advertise in the magazine. Includes copies of some articles from past issues.
Telecommunications	Articles and new product information from past issues, plus an extensive international listing of industry trade shows. Product listings include a brief description plus the ability to request product information from the vendor. A useful search capability can be used to search articles and product listing by keyword.
Network World	The best Web site on this list. Contains a well-organized archive of the paper's contents. Also contains links to sites related to current news stories, sites related to various technical topics covered in the paper, and vendor information.
Network Computing	Articles from the magazine available plus pointers to advertisers. Site also includes a hypertext network design manual with useful practical tips for end-user network design.
Network Magazine	Links to Web pages of vendors that advertise in the magazine, plus a lot of useful online information.
IT Professional	Includes career resources and links related to information technology.
ACM Networker	Includes online copies of magazine articles.
Forbes/ASAP	Copies of some articles from past issues are provided.
Business Week	Copies of some articles from past issues are provided. Also has a considerable amount of supplemental information.

is included with *Forbes. ASAP* is a full-length magazine in its own right with broad coverage of business information systems and business data communications topics.

Business Week has a regular "Information Processing" section that includes two or three articles each week. The section is oriented more toward computers than communications but does provide coverage of the latter. In addition, the magazine from time to time has cover stories in this area that provide more in-depth discussion.

Trade/Technical Publications

The number of periodicals that cover some aspect of this field is vast and growing. A few of the most useful are discussed in this section.

Business Communications Review is a very useful monthly, oriented toward the business user, that integrates data and voice communications well. Besides clearly written features covering communications technology, management, and applications, it has a stable of well-qualified columnists writing on everything from the Washington regulatory scene and network management to the latest in broadband technologies.

Network Magazine is a monthly magazine that provides excellent coverage of the industry, including a regular column on communication tariffs, articles on particular companies, statistics on communications-related stocks, and coverage of industry trends and regulatory issues. The magazine also regularly features buyers' guide articles on particular products and services. In addition, every month there are one or two case-study articles that relate the experience of a particular company that has installed some sort of distributed system or network. Usually, these articles are written by someone with the company. *Telecommunications* is a monthly magazine that contains both industry-related and technical articles. The magazine concentrates heavily on long-distance networking topics, such as telephone, telecommunications, and regulatory issues.

Network World is a weekly tabloid-size newspaper that is an excellent source of information about the industry and market for information communications products and services. The coverage is quite thorough and includes buyers' guides on products and services. Each week there are one or more in-depth articles that touch upon a single area, such as network management. The treatment is from a management rather than a technical orientation. The newspaper also provides product comparisons. *Network Computing* focuses on networking products but also has some technical articles. That magazine, plus *Network Magazine*, provides an excellent means for tracking new product releases and for obtaining comparative analyses of product offerings.

IT Professional, put out by IEEE, is intended for developers and managers of enterprise information systems. The magazine is good at explaining technology to help you build and manage your information systems today, and provides advance notice of trends that may shape your business in the next few years. *Networker*, put out by ACM, is another good source of information for developers and managers of enterprise information systems, but with more emphasis on networking and data communications than *IT Professional*.

1.12 REVIEW QUESTIONS

1.1. What three kinds of basic organizational difficulties can communications technology help companies overcome?

1.2. Name four types of information that are found on networks.

1.3. How has the technology of the compact disc used in the music industry been used in image communications?

1.4. Why are the burdens on the manager greater today than in previous years when it comes to using new technology efficiently?

1.5. Why has optical fiber transmission become popular in the past few years?

1.6. What types of communications can be carried by satellite transmission?

1.7. Name two approaches that can be used for increasing the efficiency of transmission services.

1.8. Contrast the function of application software with that of interconnection software.

APPENDIX 1A PREFIXES FOR NUMERICAL UNITS

The **bit** (b) is the fundamental unit of discrete information. It represents the outcome of one choice: 1 or 0, yes or no, or on or off. One bit represents two potential outcomes. So, for example, one bit can represent the on/off state of a switch. Two bits can represent four outcomes: 00, 01, 10, 11, for example. Three bits represent eight outcomes: 000, 001, 010, 011, 100, 101, 110, 111, for example. Each time another bit is added, the numbers of outcomes double (Table 2.1). A **byte** (or **octet,** usually abbreviated as B) is the name given to 8 bits (e.g., 8 b = 1 B). The number of potential outcomes a byte represents is $2 \times 2 \times 2 \times 2 \times 2 \times 2 \times 2 \times 2 = 2^8 = 256$. Bytes are usually used in representing quantities of storage in computers. Bits are traditionally used in describing communication rates.

In the computer science literature, the prefixes kilo, mega, and so forth are often used on numerical units. These have two different interpretations (Table 1.2):

- **Data transmission:** For data transmission, the prefixes used are those defined for the International System of Units (SI), the international standard. In this scheme, prefixes

Table 1.2 Numerical Prefixes

Prefix Name	Prefix Symbol	Factor	
		SI	Computer Storage
tera	T	10^{12}	2^{40}
giga	G	10^{9}	$2^{30} = 1,073,741,824$
mega	M	10^{6}	$2^{20} = 1,048,576$
kilo	k	10^{3}	$2^{10} = 1024$
milli	m	10^{-3}	
micro	μ	10^{-6}	
nano	n	10^{-9}	

are used as a shorthand method of expressing powers of 10. For example, one kilobit per second (1 kbps) = 10^3 bps = 1000 bps.

- **Computer storage:** The amount of data in computer memory, in a file, or a message that is transmitted is typically measured in bytes. Because memory is indicated by binary addresses, the size of memory is expressed as powers of 2. The same prefixes are used in a way that approximates their use in the SI scheme. For example, one kilobyte (1 kB) = 2^{10} bytes = 1024 bytes.

PART ONE

Requirements

P art One defines the needs for information communications in the business environment. It discusses the ways in which various forms of information are used and the need for interconnection and networking facilities.

ROAD MAP FOR PART ONE

Chapter 2 Business Information

The requirements for data communications and networking facilities in an organization are driven by the nature and volume of information that is handled. Chapter 2 provides an overview of the four basic categories of information used in any organization: audio, data, image, and video. The chapter discusses some of the salient characteristics of each type and looks at their networking implications.

Chapter 3 Distributed Data Processing

Chapter 3 describes the nature and role of distrbuted data processing (DDP) in an organization. Virtually all business information systems organizations are distributed, and the networking and communications requirements are driven by the way in which data and applications are distributed.

CHAPTER 2

BUSINESS INFORMATION

It is important to understand how information communication relates to business requirements. A first step in this understanding is to examine the various forms of business information. There is a wide variety of applications, each with its own information characteristics. For the analysis and design of information networks, however, the kinds of information usually can be categorized as requiring one of a small number of services: **audio, data, image,** and **video.**

Our examination covers the following topics:

- How the impact of information sources on communications systems is measured
- The nature of the four major forms of business information: audio, data, image, and video
- The types of business services that relate to each of these forms of information
- An introductory look at the implications of these services from the point of view of the communications requirements that they generate

Information sources can produce information in **digital** or **analog** form. *Digital information* is represented as a sequence of discrete symbols from a finite "alphabet." Examples are text, numerical data, and binary data. For digital communication, the information rate and the capacity of a digital channel are measured in bits per second (bps).

Analog information is a continuous signal (for example, a voltage) that can take on a continuum of values. An example is the electrical signal coming out of a microphone when someone speaks into it. In this case, the analog electrical signal represents the continuous acoustic changes in air pressure that make up sound. For analog communication, information rate and channel capacity are measured in hertz (Hz) of bandwidth (1 Hz = 1 cycle per second). Virtually any communication signal can be expressed as a combination of pure oscillations of various frequencies. The bandwidth measures the limits of these frequencies. The higher the frequencies allowed, the more accurately a complex signal can be represented.

2.1 AUDIO

The audio service supports applications based on sound, usually of the human voice. The primary application using audio service is telephone communication. Other applications include telemarketing, voice mail, audio teleconferencing, and entertainment radio. The quality of sound is characterized mainly by the bandwidth used. Voice on a telephone is limited to about 3400 Hz of bandwidth, which is of moderate quality. Voice of teleconference quality requires about 7000 Hz of bandwidth. For high-fidelity sound of reasonable quality, about 15,000 Hz (approximately the range of the human ear) is needed. For compact discs, 20,000 Hz is supported for each of two channels for stereo.

Audio information can also be represented digitally. The details are given in Chapter 16. We give an abbreviated discussion here. To get a good representation of sound in digital format, we need to sample its amplitude at a rate (samples per second, or smp/s) equal to at least twice the maximum frequency (in Hz) of the analog signal. For voice of telephone quality, one usually samples at a rate of 8000 smp/s. For high-quality sound on compact discs, 44,100 smp/s is the rate used on each channel. After sampling, the signal amplitudes must be put in digital form, a process referred to as quantization. Eight bits per sample are usually used for telephone voice and 16 bits per sample for each channel for stereophonic compact disc. In the first case, 256 levels of amplitude can be distinguished, and in the second, 65,536 levels. Thus, without compression, digital voice requires 8 b/smp $\times$ 8,000 smp/s = 64,000 bps. In the case of CDs, a straightforward multiplication of the foregoing parameters leads to a data rate of about 1.41 Mbps for both channels. A CD is usually rated at a capacity of about 600 megabytes (MB). This leads to an audio capacity of about 1 hour of stereo sound.

Typical telephone conversations have an average length in the range of 1 to 5 min. For ordinary voice telephone communication, information in either direction is transmitted less than half the time; otherwise, the two parties would be talking at once. Speech typically takes place in bursts that average about 350 milliseconds (ms), separated by silent periods of about 650 ms [SPIR88].

Networking Implications

The requirements just discussed suggest the need for both a powerful and flexible intralocation facility plus access to a variety of outside telephone services. Outside services are provided by public telephone networks, including the local telephone company and long-distance carriers such as AT&T or a national PTT (postal, telegraph, and telephone) authority. In addition, various private networking facilities and leased line arrangements are possible. All of these are discussed in Chapter 12.

Intralocation services, plus access to outside services, is provided by means of either in-house equipment, often called customer premises equipment, such as a private branch exchange, or by Centrex.

The most effective way of managing voice requirements is to tie all of the phones at a given site into a single system. There are two main alternatives for this: the private branch exchange and Centrex. The **private branch exchange (PBX)** is an on-premise switching facility, owned or leased by an organization, that interconnects

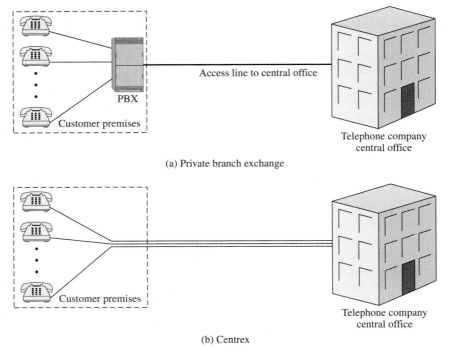

(a) Private branch exchange

(b) Centrex

Figure 2.1   Business Telephone Configurations

the telephones within the facility and provides access to the public telephone system (Figure 2.1a). Typically, a telephone user on the premises dials a three- or four-digit number to call another subscriber on the premises and dials one digit (usually 8 or 9) to get a dial tone for an outside line, which allows the caller to dial a number in the same fashion as a residential user.

Centrex is a telephone company offering that provides the same sort of service as a PBX but performs the switching function in equipment located in the telephone company's central office as opposed to the customer's premises (Figure 2.1b). All telephone lines are routed from the customer site to the central switch. The user can still make local calls with a short extension number, giving the appearance of an on-premise switch.

Either a PBX or Centrex facility can support a wide variety of voice-related services. Both voice mail and audio teleconferencing can be supported by either approach.

2.2   DATA

Data consist of information that can be represented by a finite alphabet of symbols, such as the digits 0 through 9 or the symbols represented on a terminal keyboard. Common examples of data include text and numerical information. Symbols are often represented in computers or for transmission by groups of 8 bits (octets or bytes).

A familiar example of digital data is **text** or character strings. While textual data are most convenient for human beings, they cannot, in character form, be easily stored or transmitted by data processing and communications systems. Such systems are designed for binary data. Thus a number of codes have been devised by which characters are represented by a sequence of bits. Perhaps the earliest common example of this is the Morse code. Today, the most commonly used text code is the International Reference Alphabet (IRA).[1] Each character in this code is represented by a unique 7-bit pattern; thus 128 different characters can be represented. This is a larger number than is necessary, and some of the patterns represent invisible *control characters*. IRA-encoded characters are almost always stored and transmitted using 8 bits per character. The eighth bit is a parity bit used for error detection. This bit is set such that the total number of binary 1s in each octet is always odd (**odd parity**) or always even (**even parity**). Thus a transmission error that changes a single bit, or any odd number of bits, can be detected.

Text, numerical data, and other types of data are typically organized into a database. This topic is explored in Chapter 3.

To get some practice in using the concepts introduced so far, let us estimate approximately how many bits are required to transmit a page of text. Commonly, a letter of the alphabet or a typographical symbol is represented by a byte, or 8 bits. Let us consider an 8.5-by-11-in. sheet, with a 1-in. margin on all sides. This leaves a 6.5-by-9 in. message space. A double-spaced page ordinarily has 3 lines to the inch, or 27 lines for the page. In a common typeface, there are 10 characters per inch, or 65 characters per line. This gives us a total $8 \times 27 \times 65 = 14{,}040$ bits. This overstates the situation because contiguous spaces at the ends of lines are not ordinarily included, and some pages are not full. As a round number, 10,000 bits per page is probably a fair estimate. For a PC or a terminal communicating with a computer over a telephone line using a modem, a typical channel capacity is 56,000 bps. Thus, it would take about 0.18 s to transmit a page.

To test our theory, we analyzed an 84-page report that was formatted with 1-in. margins and used a 10-point font except for headings. The formatted report consisted of 115,325 characters, which is equivalent to 1373 characters per page, or 10,983 bits, which is quite close to our rough estimate.

This is by no means the whole story. For example, English text is very redundant. That is, the same information can be sent by using many fewer bits. In the experiment just described, we used a standard compression routine to reduce the file to less than 40% of its size, or 4098 bits per page. Another feature that characterizes many data-oriented information sources is the response time required, discussed later in this chapter.

Networking Implications

The networking requirements for supporting data applications in an organization vary widely. We begin a consideration of these requirements in Chapter 3.

---

[1]IRA is defined in ITU-T Recommendation T.50 and was formerly known as International Alphabet Number 5 (IA5). The U.S. national version of IRA is referred to as the American Standard Code for Information Interchange (ASCII). A description and table of the IRA code is contained in a supporting document at this book's Web site.

2.3 IMAGE

The image service supports the communication of individual pictures, charts, or drawings. Image-based applications include facsimile, computer-aided design (CAD), publishing, and medical imaging.

As an example of the types of demands that can be placed by imaging systems, consider medical image transmission requirements. Table 2.1 summarizes the communication impact of various medical image types. As well as giving the bits per image and the number of images per exam, the table gives the transmission time per exam for three standard digital transmission rates: DS-0 = 56 kbps, DS-1 = 1.544 Mbps, and DS-3 = 44.736 Mbps.

Again, compression can be used. If we allow some barely perceivable loss of information, we can use "lossy" compression, which might reduce the data by factors of roughly 10 : 1 to 20 : 1. On the other hand, for medical imaging lossy compression usually is not acceptable, so that compression ratios for these applications run below 5 : 1.

Image Representation

There are a variety of techniques used to represent image information. These fall into two main categories:

- **Vector graphics:** An image is represented as a collection of straight and curved line segments. Simple objects, such as rectangles and ovals, and more complex objects are defined by the grouping of line segments.

Table 2.1 Transfer Time for Digital Radiology Images [DWYE92]

Image Type	Mbytes per image	Images per exam	DS-0 Time/exam (seconds)	DS-1 Time/exam (seconds)	DS-3 Time/exam (seconds)
Computerized tomography (CT)	0.52	30	2247	81	3
Magnetic resonance imagery (MRI)	0.13	50	928	34	1
Digital angiography	1	20	2857	104	4
Digital flourography	1	15	2142	78	3
Ultrasound	0.26	36	1337	48	2
Nuclear medicine	0.016	26	59	2	0.1
Computerized radiography	8	4	4571	166	6
Digitized film	8	4	4571	166	6

DS-0 = 56 kbps
DS-1 = 1.544 Mbps
DS-3 = 44.736 Mbps

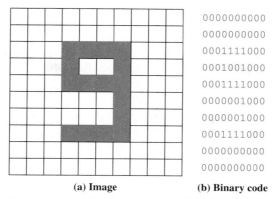

0000000000
0000000000
0001111000
0001001000
0001111000
0000001000
0000001000
0001111000
0000000000
0000000000

      (a) Image   **(b) Binary code**

Figure 2.2   A 100-Pixel Image and Its Binary Code

- **Raster graphics:** An image is represented as a two-dimensional array of spots, called pixels.[2] In the simplest form, each pixel is either black or white. This approach is used not only for computer image processing but also for facsimile.

All of the figures in this book were prepared with a graphics package that makes use of vector graphics. Vector graphics involves the use of binary codes to represent object type, size, and orientation. In all these cases, the image is represented and stored as a set of binary digits and can be transmitted using digital signals.

Figure 2.2 shows a simple 10×10 representation of an image using raster graphics. This could be a facsimile or raster-scan computer graphics image. The 10×10 representation is easily converted to a 100-bit code for the image. In this example, each pixel is represented by a single bit that indicates black or white. A **gray scale image** is produced if each pixel is defined by more than one bit, representing shades of gray. Figure 2.3 shows the use of a 3-bit gray scale to produce eight shades of gray, ranging from white to black. Gray scale can also be used in vector graphics to define the gray scale of line segments or the interior of closed objects such as rectangles.

Images can also be defined in color. There are a number of schemes in use for this purpose. One example is the RGB (red-green-blue) scheme, in which each pixel or image area is defined by three values, one for each of the three colors. The RGB scheme exploits the fact that a large percentage of the visible spectrum can be represented by mixing red, green, and blue in various proportions and intensities. The relative magnitude of each color value determines the actual color.

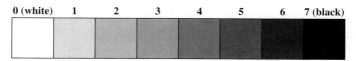

| 0 (white) | 1 | 2 | 3 | 4 | 5 | 6 | 7 (black) |

Figure 2.3   An Eight-Level Gray Scale

---

[2]A pixel, or picture element, is the smallest element of a digital image that can be assigned a gray level. Equivalently, a pixel is an individual dot in a dot-matrix representation of a picture.

Image and Document Formats

The most widely used format for raster-scan images is referred to as JPEG. The Joint Photographic Experts Group (JPEG) is a collaborative standards-making effort between ISO and ITU-T. JPEG has developed a set of standards for the compression of raster-scan images, both gray scale and color. The JPEG standard is designed to be general purpose, meeting a variety of needs in such areas as desktop publishing, graphic arts, newspaper wire photo transmission, and medical imaging. JPEG is appropriate for high-quality images, including photographs. Another format that is often seen on the Web is the Graphics Interchange Format (GIF). This is an 8-bit color format that can display up to 256 colors and is generally useful for nonphotographic images with a fairly narrow range of color, such as a company logo.

There are also two popular document formats that are suitable for documents that include text and images. The Portable Document Format (PDF) is widely used on the Web, and PDF readers are available for virtually all operating systems. Postscript is a page description language that is built into many desktop printers and virtually all high-end printing systems.

Networking Implications

The various configurations by which image information is used and communicated do not fundamentally differ from the configurations used for text and numerical data. The key difference is in the volume of data. A page of text may contain 300 words, which can be represented with about 13,000 bits (assuming 8 bits per character and an average of 5.5 characters per word). The bit image of a good-quality personal computer screen requires over 2 million bits (i.e., for the $640 \times 480 \times 256$ video mode). A facsimile page with a resolution of 200 dots per inch (which is an adequate but not unnecessarily high resolution) would generate about 4 million bits for a simple black-and-white image and considerably more bits for gray scale or color images. Thus, for image information, a tremendous number of bits is needed for representation in the computer.

The number of bits needed to represent an image can be reduced by the use of image compression techniques. In a typical document, whether it contains text or pictorial information, the black and white areas of the image tend to cluster. This property can be exploited to describe the patterns of black and white in a manner that is more concise than simply providing a listing of black and white values, one for each point in the image. Compression ratios (the ratio of the size of the uncompressed image, in bits, to the size of the compressed image) of from 8 to 16 are readily achievable.

Even with compression, the number of bits to be transmitted for image information is large. As usual, there are two concerns: response time and throughput. In some cases, such as a CAD/CAM application, the user is interactively manipulating an image. If the user's terminal is separated from the application by a communications facility, then the communications capacity must be substantial to give adequate response time. In other cases, such as facsimile, a delay of a few seconds or even a few minutes is usually of no consequence. However, the communications facility must still have a capacity great enough to keep up with the average rate of facsimile transmission. Otherwise, delays on the facility will grow over time as a backlog develops.

2.4   VIDEO

The video service carries sequences of pictures in time. In essence, video makes use of a sequence of raster-scan images. Here it is easier to characterize the data in terms of the viewer (destination) of the TV screen rather than the original scene (source) that is recorded by the TV camera. To produce a picture on the screen, an electron beam scans across the surface of the screen from left to right and top to bottom. For black-and-white television, the amount of illumination produced (on a scale from black to white) at any point is proportional to the intensity of the beam as it passes that point. Thus at any instant in time the beam takes on an analog value of intensity to produce the desired brightness at that point on the screen. Further, as the beam scans, the analog value changes. Thus the video image can be thought of as a time-varying analog signal.

Figure 2.4 depicts the scanning process. At the end of each scan line, the beam is swept rapidly back to the left (horizontal retrace). When the beam reaches the bottom, it is swept rapidly back to the top (vertical retrace). The beam is turned off (blanked out) during the retrace intervals.

To achieve adequate resolution, the beam produces a total of 483 horizontal lines at a rate of 30 complete scans of the screen per second. Tests have shown that this rate will produce a sensation of flicker rather than smooth motion. To provide a

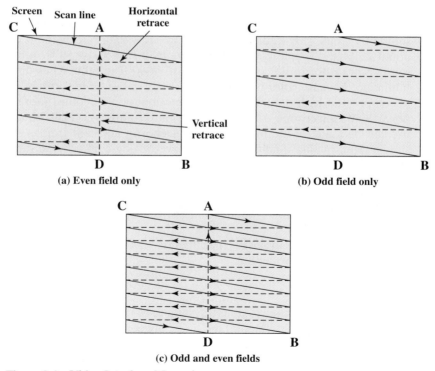

(a) Even field only

(b) Odd field only

(c) Odd and even fields

Figure 2.4   Video Interlaced Scanning

Table 2.2   Digital Television Formats

Format	Spatio-Temporal Resolution	Sampling Rate
CIF	$360 \times 288 \times 30$	3 MHz
CCIR	$720 \times 576 \times 30$	12 MHz
HDTV	$1280 \times 720 \times 60$	60 MHz

flicker-free image without increasing the bandwidth requirement, a technique known as **interlacing** is used. As Figure 2.4 shows, the odd numbered scan lines and the even numbered scan lines are scanned separately, with odd and even fields alternating on successive scans. The odd field is the scan from A to B and the even field is the scan from C to D. The beam reaches the middle of the screen's lowest line after 241.5 lines. At this point, the beam is quickly repositioned at the top of the screen and recommences in the middle of the screen's topmost visible line to produce an additional 241.5 lines interlaced with the original set. Thus the screen is refreshed 60 times per second rather than 30, and flicker is avoided.

Networking Implications

Applications based on video include instructional and entertainment television, teleconferencing, closed circuit TV, and multimedia. For example, a black-and-white TV signal for video conferencing might have a frame resolution of 360 by 280 pixels sent every 1/30 s with an intensity ranging from black through gray to white represented by 8 bits. This would correspond to a raw data rate, without compression, of about 25 Mbps. To add color, the bit rate might go up by 50%. Table 2.2 gives the sampling rate for three common types of video. The table gives only the rates for luminance because color is treated differently in the three formats. At the extreme, uncompressed high-definition color television would require more than a gigabit per second to transmit. As with images, lossy compression can be used. Moreover, use can be made of the fact that video scenes in adjacent frames are usually very similar. Reasonable quality can be achieved using compression ratios from about $20:1$ to $100:1$.

2.5   PERFORMANCE MEASURES

This section considers two key parameters related to performance requirements: response time and throughput.

Response Time

Response time is the time it takes a system to react to a given input. In an interactive transaction, it may be defined as the time between the last keystroke by the user and the beginning of the display of a result by the computer. For different types of applications, a slightly different definition is needed. In general, it is the time it takes for the system to respond to a request to perform a particular task.

Ideally, one would like the response time for any application to be short. However, it is almost invariably the case that shorter response time imposes greater cost. This cost comes from two sources:

- **Computer processing power:** The faster the computer, the shorter the response time. Of course, increased processing power means increased cost.

- **Competing requirements:** Providing rapid response time to some processes may penalize other processes.

Thus the value of a given level of response time must be assessed versus the cost of achieving that response time.

Table 2.3, based on [MART88], lists six general ranges of response times. Design difficulties are faced when a response time of less than 1 second is required.

That rapid response time is the key to productivity in interactive applications has been confirmed in a number of studies [SHNE84; THAD81; GUYN88; SEVC03]. These studies show that when a computer and a user interact at a pace that ensures that neither has to wait on the other, productivity increases significantly, the

Table 2.3 Response Time Ranges

Greater than 15 seconds
This rules out conversational interaction. For certain types of applications, certain types of users may be content to sit at a terminal for more than 15 seconds waiting for the answer to a single simple inquiry. However, for a busy person, captivity for more than 15 seconds seems intolerable. If such delays will occur, the system should be designed so that the user can turn to other activities and request the response at some later time.
Greater than 4 seconds
These are generally too long for a conversation requiring the operator to retain information in short-term memory (the operator's memory, not the computer's). Such delays would be very inhibiting in problem-solving activity and frustrating in data entry activity. However, after a major closure, delays from 4 to 15 seconds can be tolerated.
2 to 4 seconds
A delay longer than 2 seconds can be inhibiting to terminal operations demanding a high level of concentration. A wait of 2 to 4 seconds at a terminal can seem surprisingly long when the user is absorbed and emotionally committed to complete what he or she is doing. Again, a delay in this range may be acceptable after a minor closure has occurred.
Less than 2 seconds
When the terminal user has to remember information throughout several responses, the response time must be short. The more detailed the information remembered, the greater the need for responses of less than 2 seconds. For elaborate terminal activities, 2 seconds represents an important response-time limit.
Subsecond response time
Certain types of thought-intensive work, especially with graphics applications, require very short response times to maintain the user's interest and attention for long periods of time.
Decisecond response time
A response to pressing a key and seeing the character displayed on the screen or clicking a screen object with a mouse needs to be almost instantaneous—less than 0.1 second after the action. Interaction with a mouse requires extremely fast interaction if the designer is to avoid the use of alien syntax (one with commands, mnemonics, punctuation, etc.).

cost of the work done on the computer therefore drops, and quality tends to improve. It used to be widely accepted that a relatively slow response, up to 2 seconds, was acceptable for most interactive applications because the person was thinking about the next task. However, it now appears that productivity increases as rapid response times are achieved.

The results reported on response time are based on an analysis of online transactions. A transaction consists of a user command from a terminal and the system's reply. It is the fundamental unit of work for online system users. It can be divided into two time sequences:

- **User response time:** The time span between the moment a user receives a complete reply to one command and enters the next command. People often refer to this as *think time*.

- **System response time:** The time span between the moment the user enters a command and the moment a complete response is displayed on the terminal.

As an example of the effect of reduced system response time, Figure 2.5 shows the results of a study carried out on engineers using a computer-aided design graphics program for the design of integrated circuit chips and boards [SMIT88]. Each transaction consists of a command by the engineer that alters in some way the graphic image being displayed on the screen. The results show that the rate of transactions increases as system response time falls and rises dramatically once system response time falls below 1 second. What is happening is that as the system response time falls, so does the user response time. This has to do with the effects of short-term memory and human attention span.

In terms of the types of computer-based information systems that we have been discussing, rapid response time is most critical for transaction processing systems. The output of management information systems and decision support

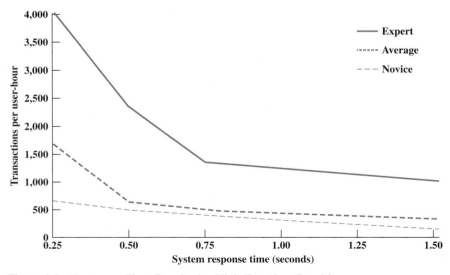

Figure 2.5   Response Time Results for High-Function Graphics

systems is generally a report or the results of some modeling exercise. In these cases, rapid turnaround is not essential. For office automation applications, the need for rapid response time occurs when documents are being prepared or modified, but there is less urgency for things such as electronic mail and computer teleconferencing. The implication in terms of communications is this: If there is a communications facility between an interactive user and the application and a rapid response time is required, then the communications system must be designed so that its contribution to delay is compatible with that requirement. Thus, if a transaction processing application requires a response time of 1 s and the average time it takes the computer application to generate a response is 0.75 s, then the delay due to the communications facility must be no more than 0.25 s.

Another area where response time has become critical is the use of the World Wide Web, either over the Internet or over a corporate intranet.[3] The time it takes for a typical Web page to come up on the user's screen varies greatly. Response times can be gauged based on the level of user involvement in the session; in particular, systems with very fast response times tend to command more user attention.

As Figure 2.6 indicates, Web systems with a 3-second or better response time maintain a high level of user attention. With a response time of between 3 and 10 seconds, some user concentration is lost, and response times above 10 seconds discourage the user, who may simply abort the session. For an organization that

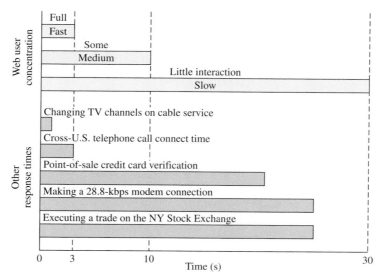

Figure 2.6   Response Time Requirements [SEVC96]

---

[3]*Intranet* is a term used to refer to the implementation of Internet technologies within a corporate organization, rather than for external connection to the global Internet; this topic is explored in Chapter 7.

maintains an Internet Web site, much of the response time is determined by forces beyond the organization's control, such as the Internet throughput, Internet congestion, and the end user's access speed. In such circumstances, the organization may consider keeping the image content of each page low and relying heavily on text, to promote rapid response time. For intranets, the organization has more control over delivery data rates and can afford more elaborate Web pages.

Throughput

The trend toward higher and higher transmission speed makes possible increased support for different services (e.g., Integrated Services Digital Network [ISDN]) and broadband-based multimedia services) that once seemed too demanding for digital communications. To make effective use of these new capabilities, it is essential to have a sense of the demands each service puts on the storage and communications of integrated information systems. Services can be grouped into data, audio, image, and video, whose demands on information systems vary widely. Figure 2.7 gives an indication of the data rates required for various information types.[4]

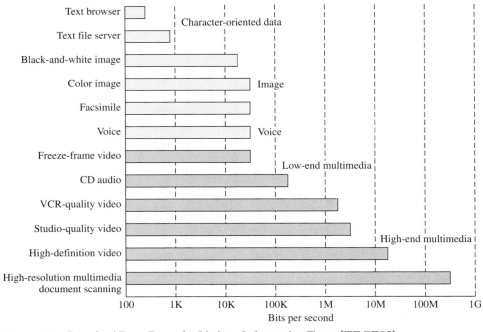

Figure 2.7   Required Data Rates for Various Information Types [TEGE95]

---

[4]Note the use of a log scale for the *x*-axis. A basic review of log scales is in the math refresher document at the Computer Science Student Resource Site at **WilliamStallings.com/StudentSupport.html.**

APPLICATION NOTE
Why Is the Type of Information Important?

This chapter provided an overview of the various forms (audio, video, image, data) information can take and some explanation of how this information is represented. When designing a network system and purchasing equipment, it is not always clear how these can directly effect the performance of the system and how slight changes in the information type can drastically affect the cost.

Generally speaking, it can be said that the amount of information increases as we move from simple data to audio to images to video. However, in order to truly understand the effect on your system, you must understand how the information gets from one place to another. For example, some organizations may build separate networks for running video conferencing between business sites in order to prevent the flood of video information from disabling the local network. Another organization may explore running video or audio the network using applications such as Microsoft's Net Meeting or Voice Over IP.

It is also important to understand that increasingly users include the various types of information in the same file. For example, a PowerPoint presentation may include graphics or pictures (image), a musical piece (audio) or a small video clip in addition to the standard text. Such a large presentation file affects the network while it is being transferred, but more significantly it affects the network storage that is required to house the presentation.

Many organizations prefer to have users save information or files "to the network" instead of using local storage such as hard drives or CDs. This is especially true of company financial or employee personal information. The result of policies like this is that the network storage required can dramatically increase depending on the type of information.

When a network system is designed, it is intended for a particular type of use. Older systems may have been designed to handle text messaging, for storage of these text messages and a small amount of off-site network communication. Once users of the system are provided with (or even introduced to) image, audio or video capability, the network system may no longer be able to support the user community. Response times will increase and individual throughput will be reduced. This is because of the larger files sizes and the bandwidth required by the information types introduced.

It is not unusual for capabilities to be introduced in advanced of network transmission capacity or storage improvements. Thus, system performance may degrade significantly with the introduction of different information types and can require costly upgrades to return to previous performance levels.

APPLICATION NOTE
File Sizes

Data or image file sizes are typically generated based on the amount of information on the page(s) and any color content. Audio files do not contain data or color but run over a period of time. The characteristics that change audio file sizes are sampling rate and bits per sample. The better the sound quality, the larger the file or the greater the bandwidth required to facilitate the transmission. Video includes all of the above and so the files can be quite large. In addition, video images are displayed (or sent) many times per second. This is called the frame rate and it can drastically change the file size or bandwidth required.

It is important to note that applications (e.g., FTP and word processors), operating systems (e.g., Windows or Linux) and the file systems (e.g., FAT32, NTFS) may all report the file sizes differently. The file system describes how data is organized for storage and how it is accessed. While these differences are not usually large, they can add some confusion.

So, what can you do to limit file size? Probably the principal thing that the end user can do is decide on the quality that is required. Following this, the user will select the appropriate file type. In reality, there is little to be done regarding data. Organizations typically standardize on a particular word processor and operating system so this is predetermined. All other forms of information (audio, image and video) are edited by the creator of the information and can be adjusted using the parameters discussed. Once the information and files have been created, there is little that the network or system administrator can do to change them. The administrator must simply supply sufficient network storage and bandwidth necessary to handle the information.

As an example, the following is a table of various image file sizes based on the type of information.

Information	Type	File type	Size
640 × 480 pixel picture	Image	24 bit bitmap	900 KB
640 × 480 pixel picture	Image	256 color (8 bit) bitmap	300 KB
640 × 480 pixel picture	Image	16 color (4 bit) bitmap	150 KB
640 × 480 pixel picture	Image	GIF	58 KB
640 × 480 pixel picture	Image	JPEG	45 KB

2.6 SUMMARY

Business communications systems and networks must deal with a variety of information types, which can be conveniently categorized as voice, data, image, and video. Each type presents its own requirements in terms of throughput, response time, and demands on the networking facility.

2.7 RECOMMENDED READING AND WEB SITES

Two books that provide expanded coverage of the topics explored in this chapter are [RAO02] and [STEI02].

RAO02   Rao, K.; Bojkovic, Z.; and Milovanovic, D. *Multimedia Communication Systems: Techniques, Standards, and Networks.* Upper Saddle River, NJ: Prentice Hall, 2002.

STEI02   Steinmetz, R., and Nahrstedt, K. *Multimedia Fundamentals, Volume 1: Media Coding and Content Processing.* Upper Saddle River, NJ: Prentice Hall, 2002.

Recommended Web Site:

- **Multimedia Communications Research Laboratory:** At Bell Labs. Good source of leading-edge research information.

2.8 KEY TERMS, REVIEW QUESTIONS, AND PROBLEMS

Key Terms

analog	GIF	Postscript
audio	gray scale image	Private branch exchange (PBX)
ASCII	interlacing	raster graphics
byte	JPEG	response time
Centrex	IRA	vector graphics
digital	PDF	video
data	pixel	voice

Review Questions

2.1. What are the two different interpretations of the prefixes *kilo*, *mega*, and *giga*? Define a context in which each interpretation is used.

2.2. What is the bandwidth of telephone voice?

2.3. The process that takes advantage of redundancy to reduce the number of bits sent for a given piece of data is called what?

2.4. What is the difference between Centrex and PBX?

2.5. What is the difference between a printable character and a control character?

2.6. Explain the basic principles of vector graphics and raster graphics.

2.7. List two common image formats.

2.8. List two common document formats.

2.9. Describe the process used to prevent flicker in a video screen.

2.10. Define response time.

2.11. What is considered an acceptable system response time for interactive applications and how does this response time relate to acceptable response times for Web sites?

Problems

2.1 How many CD-quality music channels can be transmitted simultaneously over a 10-Mbps Ethernet, assuming that no other traffic is carried on the same network and ignoring overhead?

2.2 The compact disc (CD) was originally designed to hold audio data. The information on the CD is arranged in a specific format that divides the data into segments. Hardware design considerations in effect at the time the CD was developed dictated that each second of audio would span exactly 75 sectors on the CD.
  a. Using stereo audio at a standard high-quality audio CD sample rate, what is the maximum number of bytes that can be stored in a single audio CD sector?
  b. How many minutes of CD quality audio can a 700-MB CD hold?
  c. How much storage is required to hold 5 minutes of CD-quality audio? What types of media are available to hold this amount of data?

2.3 A company's telephone exchange digitizes telephone channels at 8000 smp/s, using 8 bits for quantization. This telephone exchange must transmit simultaneously 24 of these telephone channels over a communications link.
  a. What's the required data rate?
  b. In order to provide answering-machine service, the telephone exchange can store 3-minute audio messages of the same quality as that of the telephone channels. How many megabytes of data storage space are needed to store each of these audio messages?

2.4 How many bits will it take to represent the following sets of outcomes?
  a. The uppercase alphabet A, B, ..., Z
  b. The digits 0, 1, ..., 9
  c. The seconds in a 24-hour day
  d. The people in the United States (about 300,000,000 of them)
  e. Population of the world (about 6 billion)

2.5 IRA is a 7-bit code that allows 128 characters to be defined. In the 1970s, many newspapers received stories from the wire services in a 6-bit code called TTS. This code carried upper and lowercase characters as well as many special characters and formatting commands. The typical TTS character set allowed over 100 characters to be defined. How do you think this could be accomplished?

2.6 Review the IRA code in the document at this book's Web site.
  a. Indicate the 7-bit code for the following letters: D, d, H, h.
  b. Repeat part (a), but this time show the 8-bit code that includes an odd parity bit.

2.7 In a document, what standard ASCII characters might fall into the category of invisible?

2.8 A primary primitive (due to its atomic nature) data type available to most programming languages is the character data type. This data type has traditionally been represented internally to the computer system using the ASCII (7-bit) or Extended Binary-Coded Decimal Interchange Code, EBCDIC (8-bit) encoding schemes. Programming languages such as Java use the Unicode (16-bit) encoding scheme to represent primitive character data elements (www.unicode.org). Discuss the implications, beneficial and detrimental, inherent in the decision process regarding the use of these various encoding schemes.

2.9 Base64 encoding allows arbitrary sequences of octets to be represented by printable characters. The encoding process represents 24-bit groups of input bits as strings of four encoded characters. The 24-bit groups are formed by concatenating three octets. These 24-bit groups are then treated as four concatenated 6-bit groups, each of which is translated to a character of the Base64 alphabet. The encoded output stream is represented by lines of no more than

76 printable characters, with line breaks being indicated by the "CR, LF" character sequence. How much will a file be expanded by encoding it with Base64?

2.10 The text of the *Encyclopaedia Britannica* is about 44 million words. For a sample of about 2000 words, the average word length was 5.1 characters per word.
   a. Approximately how many characters are there in the encyclopedia? (Be sure to allow for spaces and punctuation between words.)
   b. How long would it take to transmit the text over a T-1 line at 1.544 Mbps? On a fiber optic link at 2.488 Gbps?
   c. Could the text fit on a 600-MB CD?

2.11 A drawing in a 8.5-by-11-inch sheet is digitized by means of a 300 dpi (dots per inch) scanner.
   a. What is the visual resolution of the resulting image (number of dots in each dimension)?
   b. If 8 bits are used for the quantization of each pixel, how much data storage space is needed to store the image as raw data?

2.12 When examining X rays, radiologists often deal with four to six images at a time. For a faithful digital representation of an X ray photograph, a pixel array of 2048 by 2048 is typically used with a gray scale of intensity for each pixel of 12 bits. As you would hope, radiologists do not look kindly on compression that degrades quality.
   a. How many levels of gray scale are represented by 12 bits?
   b. How many bits does it take to represent an X ray based on these parameters?
   c. Suppose five X rays have to be sent to another site over a T-1 line (1.544 Mbps). How long would it take, at best—ignoring overhead?
   d. Suppose now that we wish to build a communications system that will provide the five X rays of part (c) upon demand; that is, that from the time the X rays are requested we want them available within 2 s. What is a lowest channel rate that can support this demand?
   e. The next generation of displays for X rays is planned for 4096 by 4096 pixels with a 12-bit gray scale. What does the answer to part d become when using this resolution?

2.13 A multimedia version of a multivolume reference book is being prepared for storage on compact disc (CD-ROM). Each disc can store about 700 MB (megabytes). The input to each volume consists of 1000 pages of text typed 10 characters to the inch, 6 lines to the inch, on 8-by-11-in. paper with 1-in. margins on each side. Each volume also has about 100 pictures, which will be displayed in color at Super VGA resolution (1024 × 768 pixel, 8 b/pixel). Moreover, each volume is enhanced for the CD version with 30 min of audio of teleconferencing quality (16,000 smp/s, 6 b/smp).
   a. How many bits are there on a 700-megabyte CD (1 megabyte = 2^{20} bytes)?
   b. Without compression and ignoring overhead, how many volumes can be put on one CD?
   c. Suppose the material is to be transmitted over a T-1 facility (1.544 Mbps). How long will it take, exclusive of overhead, to transmit a volume?
   d. Suppose the text can be compressed at a 3 : 1 rate, the pictures at 10 : 1, and the audio at 2 : 1. How many volumes, exclusive of overhead, will fit on a CD? How long will it take to transmit a compressed volume on a T-1 channel?

2.14 Commonly, medical digital radiology ultrasound studies consist of about 25 images extracted from a full-motion ultrasound examination. Each image consists of 512 by 512 pixels, each with 8 b of intensity information.
   a. How many bits are there in the 25 images?
   b. Ideally, however, doctors would like to use 512 × 512 × 8 bit frames at 30 fps. Ignoring possible compression and overhead factors, what is the minimum channel capacity required to sustain this full-motion ultrasound?
   c. Suppose each full-motion study consists of 25 s of frames. How many such studies could fit on a 600-MB CD-ROM?

2.15 An 800 × 600 image with 24-bit color depth needs to be stored on disc. Even though the image might contain 2^{24} different colors, only 256 colors are actually present. This image could be encoded by means of a table (palette) of 256 24-bit elements and, for each pixel, an index of its RGB value in the table. This type of encoding is usually called Color Look-Up Table (CLUT) encoding.

a. How many bytes are needed to store the image raw information?

b. How many bytes are needed to store the image using CLUT encoding?

c. What's the compression ratio achieved by using this simple encoding method?

2.16 A digital video camera provides an uncompressed output video stream with a resolution of 320×240 pixels, a frame rate of 30 fps, and 8 bits for quantization of each pixel.

a. What's the required bandwidth for the transmission of the uncompressed video stream?

b. How much data storage space is needed to record two minutes of the video stream?

2.17 An MPEG-encoded video stream with a resolution of 720×480 pixels and a frame rate of 30 fps is transmitted over a network. An old workstation is meant to receive and display the video stream. It takes 56 milliseconds for the workstation to decode each received frame and display it on the screen. Will this workstation display the video stream successfully? Why or why not?

2.18 Refer to Table 2.3 for a list and description of general system response time categories. Assume you are providing five computer systems for video game developer and the budget for hardware (e.g., CPU clock speed, RAM, bus data rate, disk I/O data rate, etc.) is limited by the consumer. The base price of a system is $1.5K (providing basic > 15 s response time for all application scenarios) and each increase in response time range adds $0.5K to the cost of the system hardware. Make a case for the classification of each of the systems running the application scenarios listed that will keep the customer's total cost for the five systems below $15K.

a. System 1 – word-processing application and basic Internet access

b. System 2 – skateboard equipment checkout terminal (for gamer recreation)

c. System 3 – graphic design and basic Internet access

d. System 4 – programming and basic Internet access

e. System 5 – video game testing

Note: There is no unique solution. In your answer, each lettered response should provide some rationalization as to why each category was selected, to show the student has given some thought to the impact on productivity that choices such as these can affect.

DISTRIBUTED DATA PROCESSING

CHAPTER OBJECTIVES

After reading this chapter, you should be able to

- Describe the difference between centralized and distributed data processing and discuss the pros and cons of each approach.

- Explain why a distributed data processing system needs to be interconnected with some sort of data communications or networking facility.

- Describe the different forms of distributed data processing for applications.

- Describe the different forms of distributed databases.

- Discuss the implications of distributed data processing in terms of the requirements for data communications and networking facilities.

- Understand the motivation behind the trend to client/server architectures.

In Chapter 2 we looked at the overall requirements for information in an organization and found that four types of information are vital to the competitive health of any business: data, voice, image, and video. In terms of data communications and networking facilities, it is the first of these types of information, data, that has shaped corporate strategy. Until recently, voice was treated as an entirely separate requirement, and indeed it still is treated that way in many organizations. As we shall see as the text progresses, the advent of digital transmission and networking facilities, plus the use of flexible transmission protocols such as ATM (asynchronous transfer mode), make it feasible for businesses to integrate voice, data, image, and in some cases video to provide cost-effective networking solutions.

Voice, image, and video have each produced separate communications technologies and what must be considered relatively straightforward solutions from the user's point of view. The situation with respect to data is much more complex, both because the variety of data processing facilities is wide and because the range of approaches to support the business data communications function is large. Therefore, so that the various approaches to business data communications and networking can be seen in context, we devote this chapter to looking at the types of data processing systems that are typical in organizations. We begin with a look at the two extremes in organization of the computing function: centralized and distributed data processing. The computing function in most organizations is implemented somewhere along a spectrum between these two extremes. By examining this spectrum, we can see the nature of the communications and networking requirements for business begin to emerge. We then focus on distributed data processing, examine various approaches, and look at the communications implications of these approaches. In particular, we examine the client/server architectures as one approach to achieving the best of centralized and decentralized architectures.

3.1 CENTRALIZED VERSUS DISTRIBUTED PROCESSING

Centralized and Distributed Organization

Traditionally, the data processing function was organized in a centralized fashion. In a **centralized data processing** architecture, data processing support is provided by one or a cluster of computers, generally large computers, located in a central data processing facility. Many of the tasks performed by such a facility are initiated at the center with the results produced at the center. An example is a payroll application. Other tasks may require interactive access by personnel who are not physically located in the data processing center. For example, a data entry function, such as inventory update, may be performed by personnel at sites throughout the organization. In a centralized architecture, each person is provided with a local terminal that is connected by a communications facility to the central data processing facility.

A fully centralized data processing facility is centralized in many senses of the word:

- **Centralized computers:** One or more computers are located in a central facility. In many cases, there are one or more large mainframe computers, which require special facilities such as air conditioning and a raised floor. In a smaller organization, the central computer or computers are high-performance servers or midrange systems. The iSeries from IBM is an example of a midrange system.

- **Centralized processing:** All applications are run on the central data processing facility. This includes applications that are clearly central or organization-wide in nature, such as payroll, as well as applications that support the needs of users in a particular organizational unit. As an example of the latter, a product design department may make use of a computer-aided design (CAD) graphics package that runs on the central facility.

- **Centralized data:** Most data are stored in files and databases at the central facility and are controlled by and accessible by the central computer or computers. This includes data that are of use to many units in the organization, such as inventory figures, as well as data that support the needs of, and should be used by, only one organizational unit. As an example of the latter, the marketing organization may maintain a database with information derived from customer surveys.

- **Centralized control:** A data processing or information systems manager has responsibility for the centralized data processing facility. Depending on the size and importance of the facility, control may be exercised at the middle-management level or may be very high in the organization. It is quite common to have control exercised at the vice-presidential level, and a number of organizations have the equivalent of a corporate information officer who has authority at the board level. In the case of very senior management, a subordinate generally has control of the centralized data processing facility, whereas the top data processing (DP) or information officer has broader authority in matters related to corporate acquisition, use, and protection of information.

- **Centralized support staff:** A centralized data processing facility must include a technical support staff to operate and maintain the data processing equipment. In addition, some (and in many cases all) programming is done by a central staff.

Such a centralized organization has a number of attractive aspects. There may be economies of scale in the purchase and operation of equipment and software. A large central DP shop can afford to have professional programmers on staff to meet the needs of the various departments. Management can maintain control over data processing procurement, enforce standards for programming and data file structure, and design and implement a security policy.

An example of a centralized data processing facility is that of Holiday Inn [LIEB95], shown in general terms in Figure 3.1. Holiday Inn's corporate offices in Atlanta are supported by a number of workstations and personal computers connected by internal local area networks (LANs) to a variety of server machines. The servers maintain many of the files used in day-to-day operation and in running the headquarters organization. The company's data center is located about 15 miles away; a leased 44-Mbps digital line connects the networked equipment in the two locations. The heart of the data center is a pair of IBM mainframe computers: one for running a transaction processing application that handles bookings by travel agents, hotels, and individuals; and the other for running core business applications such as financial and human resources. The data center is also linked via satellite to each of the approximately 1600 U.S. hotels, as well as having satellite links to Europe.

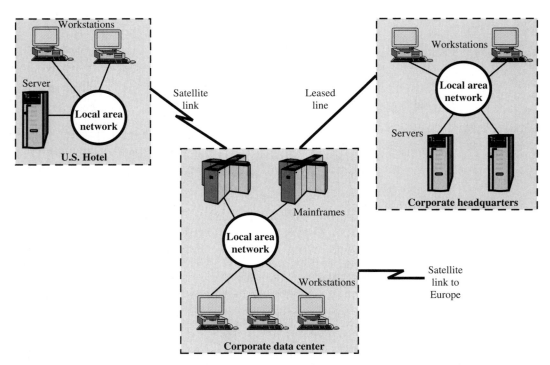

Figure 3.1   Holiday Inn Information Systems Architecture

This centralized configuration meets a number of business objectives for Holiday Inn. The mainframe reservation system is the largest of its kind in the world, handling around 25 million calls per year. The single, central reservation system means that there is one place with up-to-date information about availability in all the hotels; this timely information contributes to Holiday Inn's high occupancy rate. In addition, the central system collects and maintains detailed information on customer behavior and other details of individual hotel operation. This information can be analyzed in many different ways to provide top management with valuable guidance in meeting customer satisfaction objectives. Without a centralized system, it would be difficult to gather and use the many different types of data that go into the customer analysis applications.

A data processing facility may depart in varying degrees from the centralized data processing organization by implementing a **distributed data processing (DDP)** strategy. A distributed data processing facility is one in which computers, usually smaller computers, are dispersed throughout an organization. The objective of such dispersion is to process information in a way that is most effective based on operational, economic, and/or geographic considerations, or all three. A DDP facility may include a central facility plus satellite facilities, or it may more nearly resemble a community of peer computing facilities. In either case, some form of interconnection is usually needed; that is, the various computers in the system must be connected to one another. As may be expected, given the characterization of centralized data processing provided here, a DDP facility involves the distribution of computers, processing, and data.

An example of a distributed data processing facility is that of J. P. Morgan Securities' Fixed Income Market Department [HAIG92], shown in general terms in Figure 3.2. The main business of the department is trading mortgage-backed securities. These financial instruments provide their purchasers with interest payments for as long as the mortgages behind them are earning interest. Determining the value of such securities is a complex process that involves making estimates of how long the underlying mortgages will generate interest (interest stops if the property is sold, refinanced, or repossessed) and of future changes in interest rates. Traders compete by using a variety of algorithms to make these projections. Input to the algorithms includes a number of current factors as well as historical data from J. P. Morgan's huge database of previous transactions. For individual traders to have access to the required data, to be able to tailor the algorithms to their use, and to get immediate answers, each trader is equipped with his or her own fast computer to run the algorithms, with access to updated databases when needed.

As Figure 3.2 shows, individual traders have some leeway in choosing a computer. Depending on the trader's volume of work, personal preference, and chosen algorithms, a PC, Macintosh, or high-power Sun workstation is the most appropriate. Dozens of these machines are hooked together by means of local area networks (LANs). Machines are grouped on a single LAN based on the need of the traders to exchange data with each other. All of these LANs are in turn connected to a backbone LAN[1] that supports a set of high-performance, large-storage servers. The servers maintain a centralized database as well as supporting some specialized

---

[1]Multiple LANs are used to limit the amount of traffic on any given LAN. The LANs are connected by routers, which are devices that can route traffic between stations on different networks. Routers are described in Chapter 5.

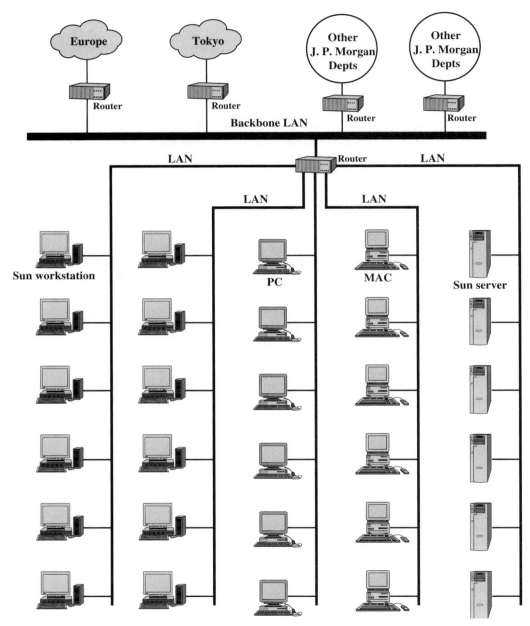

Figure 3.2   J. P. Morgan's Distributed Systems Architecture

applications, such as accounting and report preparation, that need not run on the individual traders' machines. Finally, links are maintained to other Morgan departments and to offices in Tokyo and Europe.

Technical Trends Leading to Distributed Data Processing

Until the early 1970s, the centralized data processing approach enjoyed near-universal use in businesses. Since that time, there has been a steady evolution to distributed processing. We can address this trend from two points of view: means and motive. First, let us look at the changes in the data processing industry that have given companies the means to choose distributed processing. We then turn to the question of why distributed data processing is coming to be preferred to centralized data processing.

The key factor that has made DDP possible is the dramatic and continuing decrease in cost of computer hardware, accompanied by an increase in its capabilities. Today's personal computers have speeds, instruction sets, and memory capacities comparable to those of minicomputers and even mainframes of just a few years ago. Equally important, today's personal computers boast graphical user interfaces (GUIs) that provide unprecedented ease of use and responsiveness.

Management and Organizational Considerations

The increasing availability of inexpensive yet powerful systems with a growing repertoire of applications software has made it possible for organizations to disperse computing capability throughout the organization rather than to continue to rely on a centralized facility with, at most, distributed terminals for access. However, the centralized option is still very much available to the organization. As with other types of computers, the powerful mainframes that are the heart of a centralized facility have also dropped in price and increased in power.

To begin, let us consider the requirements for the corporate computing function, that is, those needs that the computing facility must fulfill. Table 3.1 suggests nine specific requirements for the computing facility. A case can clearly be made that requirements 1, 3, 7, 8, and 9 can be satisfied with a distributed arrangement of

Table 3.1 Requirements for the Corporate Computing Function

1. Provide computing capability to all organizational units that legitimately require it.
2. Contain the capital and operations cost in provision of computing services within the organization.
3. Satisfy special computing needs of user departments
4. Maintain organizational integrity in operations that are dependent on computing (i.e., avoid mismatches in operation among departments).
5. Meet information requirements of management.
6. Provide computing services in a reliable, professional, and technically competent manner.
7. Allow organizational units sufficient autonomy in the conduct of their tasks to optimize creativity and performance at the unit level.
8. Preserve autonomy among organizational units and, if possible, increase their importance and influence within the larger organization.
9. Make the work of employees enjoyable as well as productive.

low-cost servers, workstations, and personal computers. Widespread use of small computers can provide highly individualistic service to all the departments needing computing, allow users to establish and maintain autonomy in their operations using their own equipment, and provide users with hands-on opportunity to enjoy computing use while improving departmental productivity.

Two aspects of the needs of users demonstrate the truth of the preceding statement: the need for new applications and the need for short response time. First, consider the need for new applications. For any organization to remain competitive, each department within the organization must continually strive to improve productivity and effectiveness. A major source of such improvement is increasing reliance on data processing and computers. The result is that in most well managed organizations, the demand for new applications is rising faster than the central data processing service can develop them. There are a variety of reasons for this, including the inadequacy of techniques for communicating requirements from users to professional programmers and the fact that much of the time of programmers in any mature data processing facility is taken up with software maintenance. For these reasons, the backlog of needed applications is growing. Indeed, a waiting time of from two to seven years for new user applications on central computer systems is not uncommon. A way around this dilemma is to make use of distributed servers, workstations, and personal computers. If end users have access to such machines, the application logjam can be broken in two ways:

- **Off-the-shelf applications:** There is a long list of applications software for common machines, such as UNIX-based servers and workstations, and for Windows-based and Macintosh personal computers.
- **End-user programming:** Many tools are available on small systems that allow users to construct modest applications without needing to use a traditional programming language. Examples are spreadsheet programs and project management tools.

The second need mentioned earlier is for short response time. As described in Chapter 2, in many applications it is critical to productivity that response time be short. On a mainframe computer with a complex operating system that is being time-shared by many users, it is often difficult to achieve reasonable response times, but a user on a dedicated personal computer or workstation or a user who is one of only a few sharing a powerful minicomputer can often experience extremely short response times.

We can see, then, that with distributed small systems that are both physically closer to the user and more dedicated to the user's particular applications, user productivity and computing effectiveness may be improved. However, the manager must exercise caution in adopting a distributed strategy. The lack of centralized computing may result in the loss of centralized control. Individual departments may adopt incompatible systems, making interdepartmental cooperation difficult. Procurement decisions may be made without systematic forecasts of requirements and cost and with no enforcement of standards for hardware, software, or departmental programming practices. These effects jeopardize objectives 4 and 6 of Table 3.1. Equally important, the devolvement of data processing activities to the departmental level can increase the difficulty of obtaining data for use by top management (objective 5).

The adoption of differing departmental standards and means of summarizing data makes uniform collection of data for upward reporting more difficult.

Tables 3.2 and 3.3 summarize some of the key potential benefits and potential drawbacks of distributed data processing.

Table 3.2 Potential Benefits of Distributed Data Processing

Responsiveness

Local computing facilities can be managed in such a way that they can more directly satisfy the needs of local organizational management than one located in a central facility and intended to satisfy the needs of the total organization.

Availability

With multiple interconnected systems, the loss of any one system should have minimal impact. Key systems and components (e.g., computers with critical applications, printers, mass storage devices) can be replicated so that a backup system can quickly take up the load after a failure.

Correspondence to Organizational Patterns

Many organizations employ a decentralized structure with corresponding policies and operational procedures. Requirements for data files and other automated resources tend to reflect these organizational patterns.

Resource Sharing

Expensive hardware, such as a laser printer, can be shared among users. Data files can be centrally managed and maintained, but with organization-wide access. Staff services, programs, and databases can be developed on an organization-wide basis and distributed to the dispersed facilities.

Incremental Growth

In a centralized facility, an increased workload or the need for a new set of applications usually involves a major equipment purchase or a major software upgrade. This involves significant expenditure. In addition, a major change may require conversion or reprogramming of existing applications, with the risk of error and degraded performance. With a distributed system, it is possible to gradually replace applications or systems, avoiding the "all-or-nothing" approach. In addition, old equipment can be left in the facility to run a single application if the cost of moving the application to a new machine is not justified.

Increased User Involvement and Control

With smaller, more manageable equipment physically located close to the user, the user has greater opportunity to affect system design and operation, either by direct interaction with technical personnel or through the user's immediate superior.

Decentralized Operation and Centralized Control

Decentralized applications and facilities can be tailored to the individual organizational unit's requirements and be enhanced by centralized services and databases with varying degrees of centralized control.

End-User Productivity

Distributed systems tend to give more rapid response time to the user, since each piece of equipment is attempting a smaller job. Also, the applications and interfaces of the facility can be optimized to the needs of the organizational unit. Unit managers are in a position to assess the effectiveness of the local portion of the facility and to make the appropriate changes.

Distance and Location Independence

Distributed systems introduce interfaces and access methods for utilizing computing services. These interfaces and access methods become independent of location or distance. Hence the user has access to organization-wide facilities with little or no additional training.

Privacy and Security

With a distributed system, it is easier to assign responsibility for security of data files and other resources to the owners and users of those resources. Physical and software means can be employed to prevent unauthorized access to data and resources.

Vendor Independence

Properly implemented, a distributed system will accommodate equipment and software from a variety of suppliers. This provides greater competition and enhanced bargaining power on the part of the buyer. The organization is less likely to become dependent on a single vendor with the risks that that position entails.

Flexibility

Users may be in a position to adapt their application software to changing circumstances if they have control over program maintenance and day-to-day running. Because their equipment is not used by other users, they are able to change the configuration if they need to with little trouble.

Table 3.3   Potential Drawbacks of Distributed Data Processing

More Difficult Test and Failure Diagnosis

Particularly when there is a high degree of interaction between elements of a distributed system, it is difficult to determine the cause of failure or performance degradation.

More Dependence on Communications Technology

To be effective, a distributed system must be interconnected by communication and networking facilities. These facilities become critical to the day-to-day operation of the organization.

Incompatibility among Equipment

Equipment from different vendors may not easily connect and communicate. To guarantee avoidance of this problem, the user must restrict applications and resources to those for which standards exist.

Incompatibility among Data

Similarly, data generated by one application may not be usable in the generated form by another application. Again, the user may need to restrict applications to those that are standardized.

Network Management and Control

Because equipment is physically dispersed, may involve multiple vendors, and may be controlled by various organizational units, it is difficult to provide overall management, to enforce standards for software and data, and to control the information available through the network. Thus, data processing facilities and services may evolve in an uncontrolled fashion.

Difficulty in Control of Corporate Information Resources

Data may be dispersed or, if not, at least access to data is dispersed. If distributed users can perform the update function (essential in many applications), it becomes difficult for a central authority to control the integrity and security of the data needed at the corporate level. In some cases, it may even be difficult to gather required management information from the dispersed and dissimilar detailed databases.

Suboptimization

With the dispersal of computer equipment and the ease of incrementally adding equipment and applications, it becomes easier for managers of suborganizations to justify procurement for their unit. Although each procurement may be individually justifiable, the totality of procurements throughout an organization may well exceed the total requirement.

Duplication of Effort

Technical personnel in various units may individually develop similar applications or data files, resulting in unnecessary and costly duplication of effort.

Client/Server Architecture

The widely used client/server architecture is intended to provide the best aspects of both distributed and centralized computing. Users work on powerful workstations or PCs, which supports the end-user programming, provides the ability to use off-the-shelf software, and gives the immediate response inherent in distributed architecture. These workstations, or "clients," are supported by specialized "servers." Examples of servers are specialized computers for providing database services, printing and fax services, file storage, and communications front ends, gateways, and bridges. This architecture has been made possible by the advent of high-speed local area networks (LANs) and LAN interconnections, along with more sophisticated systems software to provide intermachine processing.

Client/server architecture is attractive for several reasons. First, it is cost-effective and achieves economies of scale by centralizing support for specialized functions. File servers and database servers also make it easier to provide universal access to information by authorized users and to maintain consistency and security of files and data. The physical architecture of the computers used can be designed especially to support their service function. Finally, this architecture is very flexible. One reason is that functional services are not necessarily in a one-to-one relation with physical computers. That is, file service and database services can be on the same computer, or for an example at the other extreme, database services can be provided by several geographically dispersed machines. Services can share processors for smaller information systems, and they can be split among processors in larger systems to increase availability, capacity, and responsiveness. This popular approach is examined in more detail in Chapter 7.

An example of a client/server architecture is that used by MasterCard International, described in the Case Study following this chapter.

Intranets

One of the latest developments in the ongoing evolution of distributed data processing is the intranet. In essence, an intranet provides users the features and applications of the Internet but isolated within the organization. Key features of an intranet are as follows:

- Uses Internet-based standards, such as the HyperText Markup Language (HTML) and the Simple Mail Transfer Protocol (SMTP)
- Uses the TCP/IP protocol suite for local and wide area networking
- Comprises wholly owned content not accessible to the public Internet even though the corporation has Internet connections and runs a Web server on the Internet
- Can be managed, unlike the Internet

In general terms, an intranet can be considered as a form of client/server architecture. The advantages of the intranet approach include ease of implementation and ease of use. Intranets are examined in detail in Chapter 7.

Extranets

Another recent development is that of the extranet. Like the intranet, the extranet makes use of TCP/IP protocols and applications, especially the Web. The distinguishing feature of the extranet is that it provides access to corporate resources by outside clients, typically suppliers and customers of the organization. This outside access can be through the Internet or through other data communications networks. An extranet provides more than the simple Web access for the public that virtually all companies now provide. Instead, the extranet provides more extensive access to corporate resources, usually in a fashion that enforces a security policy. As with the intranet, the typical model of operation for the extranet is client/server.

Extranets are examined in detail in Chapter 7.

3.2 FORMS OF DISTRIBUTED DATA PROCESSING

We have defined a DDP system as a computing facility in which computers are dispersed within an organization with some means of interconnection among them. This general definition conceals the wide variety of forms that DDP can take. One way to gain an appreciation of this variety is to consider in more detail the following functions or objects that are supported by distributed processors:

- Applications
- Device controllers
- Control
- Data

It is often the case that more than one of these functions or objects is distributed in a DDP system. For our purposes, it is sufficient to examine them one at a time to gain insight into the configurations that are implemented in DDP. We examine the first three topics in this section and the last topic in the next section.

Distributed Applications

Two dimensions characterize the distribution of applications. First, there is the allocation of application functions:

- One application split up into components that are dispersed among a number of machines
- One application replicated on a number of machines
- A number of different applications distributed among a number of machines

Distributed application processing can also be characterized by whether the distribution is vertical or horizontal. In general, vertical partitioning involves one application split up into components that are dispersed among a number of machines, whereas horizontal partitioning involves either one application replicated on a number of machines or a number of different applications distributed among a number of machines.

With **vertical partitioning,** data processing is distributed in a hierarchical fashion. This distribution may reflect organizational structure, or it may simply be the most appropriate for the application. Examples include the following:

- **Insurance:** Data processing distribution is often a two-level hierarchy. Each branch has a computer system that it uses for preparing new contracts and for processing claims. In most cases, these transactions can be handled directly by the local office. Summary information is sent to a head office. The head office uses contract and claim information to perform risk analysis and actuarial calculations. On the basis of the company's financial position and current exposure, the head office can adjust rates and communicate the changes to the branches.

- **Retail chain:** Each retail store includes point-of-sale terminals and terminals for use by sales and office personnel. A convenient arrangement is a single powerful workstation or server that houses all the information used at the store. An interconnected set of personal computers is also possible, but the nature of the application lends itself more readily to a single site for storing all branch information. Point-of-sale terminals make use of pricing information from the computer system. Sales transactions record sales and changes in inventory and accounts receivable. Sales and office personnel can use terminals to display summary sales information, inventory, accounts receivable, and customer statements. Store management can display information on sales performance, goods aging, and other analyses. Periodically, perhaps once a day, sales and inventory information is transmitted to the head office system.

- **Process control:** The process-control function in a factory adapts readily to a vertical DDP system. Each major operational area is controlled by a workstation, which is fed information from individual process-control microprocessors. These microprocessors are responsible for the automated control of sensors and effector devices on the shop floor. The operations workstation scans sensor readings, looking for exceptions or analyzing trends. It may also control part of the operation to vary the rate or mix of production. These distributed workstations ensure rapid response to conditions at the process level. All the workstations are linked to a higher-level computer concerned with operations planning, optimization, provision of management information, and general corporate data processing.

As these examples illustrate, a vertically partitioned DDP system generally consists of a central computer system with one or more levels of satellite systems. The nature of the partition reflects organizational structure or the structure of the task to be performed, or both. The objective is to assign processing load to the level of the hierarchy at which it is most cost-effective. Such an arrangement combines some of the best features of both centralized and distributed data processing.

With **horizontal partitioning,** data processing is distributed among a number of computers that have a peer relationship. That is, there is no concept of client/server. Computers in a horizontal configuration normally operate autonomously, although in some cases this configuration is used for load balancing. In many cases, horizontal partitioning reflects organizational decentralization. Two examples follow:

- **Office automation support system:** Typically, secretarial staff and other personnel are equipped with personal computers linked together by a network. Each user's personal computer contains software packages useful to that user (e.g., word processing, spreadsheet). The systems are linked together so that users may exchange messages, files, and other information.

- **Air traffic control system:** Each regional center for air traffic control operates autonomously of the other centers, performing the same set of applications. Within the center, several computers are used to process radar and radio data and to provide a visual status to the air traffic controllers.

It is more often the case that an organization's computing function will include both horizontal and vertical partitioning. Corporate headquarters may maintain a mainframe computer facility with a corporate management information system and a decision support system. Central staff functions, such as public relations, strategic planning, and corporate finance and accounting, may be supported here. A vertical partition is created by providing subordinate computing facilities at branch offices. Within each branch office, a horizontal partition will provide office automation support.

Other Forms of DDP

In addition to, or instead of, the distribution of applications or data, a DDP system may involve the distribution of device controllers, or network management. Let us briefly examine each of these possibilities.

Distributed Devices One natural use of DDP is to support a distributed set of devices that can be controlled by processors, such as automatic teller machines or laboratory interface equipment. One common application of this approach is in factory automation. A factory may contain a number of sensors, programmable controllers, microprocessors, and even robots that are involved in the automation of the manufacturing process. Such a system involves the distribution of processing technology to the various locations of the manufacturing process.

Network Management Any distributed system requires some form of management and control, including control of access to some of the facilities in the distributed system, monitoring of the status of various components of the distributed system, and management of the communications facility to ensure availability and responsiveness. In most cases, some sort of central network management system is required. However, such a system needs to obtain status information from the various computers in the distributed system and to issue commands to those computers. Thus, each computer in the distributed system must include some management and control logic to be able to interact with the central network management system. A more detailed look at these issues can be found in Chapter 19.

3.3 DISTRIBUTED DATA

Before beginning our discussion of distributed data, it is necessary to say something about the nature of the organization of data in a computer system. In some cases, an organization can function with a relatively simple collection of files of data. Each file may contain text (e.g., copies of memos and reports) or numerical data (e.g., spreadsheets). A more complex file consists of a set of records. However, for an organization of any appreciable size, a more complex organization known as a database is required. A **database** is a structured collection of data stored for use in one or more applications. In addition to data, a database contains the relationships between data items and groups of data items. As an example of the distinction between data files and a database, consider the following. A simple personnel file might consist of a set of records, one for each employee. Each record gives the employee's name, address, date of birth, position, salary, and other details needed by the personnel department. A personnel database includes a personnel file, as just described. It may also include a time and attendance file, showing for each week the hours worked by each employee. With a database organization, these two files are tied together so that a payroll program can extract the information about time worked and salary for each employee to generate paychecks.

A **distributed database** is one in which portions of the data are dispersed among a number of computer systems. A distributed database must include a directory that identifies the physical location of each data element in the database. In general terms, we can distinguish three ways of organizing data for use by an organization: centralized, replicated, and partitioned.

Centralized Database

A centralized database is housed in a central computer facility. If the computing function is distributed, then users and application programs at remote locations may have access to the centralized database. A centralized database is often used with a vertical DDP organization. It is desirable when the security and integrity of the data are paramount, because the central facility is more easily controlled than is a dispersed collection of data. On the other hand, there are a number of reasons why a distributed data organization might be attractive, including the following:

1. A distributed design can reflect an organization's structure or function. This makes the design of the data organization and the use of the data more understandable and easier to implement and maintain.

2. Data can be stored locally, under local control. Local storage decreases response times and communications costs and increases data availability.

3. Distributing data across multiple autonomous sites confines the effects of a computer breakdown to its point of occurrence; the data on the surviving computers can still be processed.

4. The size of the total collection of data and the number of users of those data need not be limited by a computer's size and processing power.

Replicated Database

When data are distributed, one of two overall strategies may be adopted: replicated or partitioned. In a **replicated database,** all or part of the database is copied at two or more computers. Before looking at the general principles of this important strategy, we briefly describe two examples from [CONN99].

The first example is Golden Gate Financial Group, which makes about $1 billion in trades per month. The trades are recorded at their system in San Francisco and, as each trade is made, it is also recorded in a remote office in San Jose. Golden Gate makes use of a leased line to transfer about 6.6 Gbytes of data each month to achieve replication. The company recouped its investment in replication software and line charges for the year when San Francisco was hit by a daylong power outage. Employees traveled to San Jose, set up shop, and used current replicated data to do their work. As a result, trading was down only for half an hour.

A different strategy is used by Merrill Lynch, which must distribute 2 Gbytes of critical financial information to three remote offices daily for use by staff. Previously, Information systems (IS) staff copied the entire database to remote offices once per week by manual command. Now, data are updated twice per day to servers in each remote location. Only changed data, amounting to about 200 Mbytes, is sent, thus saving bandwidth and time. Now users have access to the latest data, and the data are local, avoiding the need to use long-distance hookups.

Data replication has become increasingly popular. Numerous vendors offer data replication technology for Windows and UNIX platforms for backing up mainframe-based data. Its use is virtually mandated in the banking industry. The key advantage of data replication is that it provides backup and recovery from both network and server failure.

Three variants of data replication are in common use: real time, near real time, and deferred, as shown in Table 3.4 (based on [GOLI99]). **Real-time replication** is often used in transactional systems, such as order entry, where all copies of data must be synchronized immediately. Updates involve the use of an algorithm called the two-phase commit, which attempts to avoid inconsistencies in the two databases (primary and backup) by adding a confirmation step to each update. This operation doubles the response time and may not always succeed, however.

Table 3.4   Replication Strategy Variants [GOLI99]

	Real Time	**Near Real Time**	**Deferred**
Design Architecture	Two-phase commit	Cascade or broadcast distribution	Messaging and queuing
Benefits	Tight data synchronization Distributed transactions Data currency	Data consolidation Data distribution Improved response time Less WAN loading	Heterogeneous database updates Guaranteed delivery across any network Multiple network protocol support
Drawbacks	Longer response time Difficult to implement Two-phase commit does not always work	Lack of data currency Single-vendor solution	Time delay in updates More programming work required

Near-real-time replication is more commonly used. In this case backups occur in batches, with a small amount of lag time (e.g., 30 minutes). This is adequate for most applications.

Deferred replication involves bulk transfer of a large number of changes at infrequent intervals, such as once or twice a day. The transfer is in the nature of a message or bulk file transfer, which may involve a large amount of data. This approach minimizes network resource requirements but does not provide current data.

Partitioned Database

In a partitioned database, the database exists as distinct and nonoverlapping segments that are dispersed among multiple computer systems. In general, there is no duplication of data among the segments of a partitioned database. This strategy can be used with either a horizontal or vertical DDP organization.

The main advantage of this approach is that it disperses the load and it eliminates a single point of failure. This approach can be counterproductive if the typical database request will involve data from multiple partitions.

Table 3.5 provides a simplified comparison of these three approaches to database organization. In practice, a mixture of strategies will be used. A more detailed look at strategies for database organization is provided in Table 3.6 (based on [[HOFF02]). For replicated databases, two strategies are possible. First, a central database is maintained, and copies of portions of the database may be extracted for local use. Typically, such systems lock the affected portion of the central database if the satellite computer has the authority to update. If this is the case, then the remote computer transmits the updates back to the central database upon completion of

Table 3.5 Advantages and Disadvantages of Database Distribution Methods

Type of Distribution	Advantages	Disadvantages
Common database accessed by all processors. (**Centralized**)	No duplication of data, little reorganization required.	Contention among multiple processors attempting to access data simultaneously. Database is large, so response time is slow. During disc failures, all processors lose access to data.
Copy of the common central database stored at each processor. (**Replicated**)	Each processor has access to database without contention. Short response time. During failure, new copy can be obtained.	High storage cost due to extensive duplication of data. Updates of one copy must subsequently be made on all other copies. High database reorganization costs.
Individual database for each processor. (**Partitioned**)	No duplication of data minimizes storage cost. Size of database determined by application of node, not total corporate requirement. Short response time.	Ad hoc or management reports must be obtained from different databases.

Table 3.6 Strategies for Database Organization

Strategy	Reliability	Expandability	Communications Overhead	Manageability	Data Consistency or Integrity
Centralized					
Centralized database Database resides in one location on host; data values may be distributed to geographically dispersed users for local processing	**Poor** Highly dependent on central server	**Poor** Limitations are barriers to performance	**Very high** High traffic to one site	**Very good** One monolithic site requires little coordination	Excellent All users always have same data
Replicated					
Distributed snapshot databases Copy of portion of the central database created by extraction and replication for use at remote sites	**Good** Redundancy and tolerated delays	**Very good** Cost of additional copies may be less than linear	**Low to medium** Periodic snapshots can cause bursts of network traffic	**Very good** All copies are identical	**Medium** Fine as long as delays are tolerated by business needs
Replicated, distributed database Data are replicated and synchronized at multiple sites	**Excellent** Redundancy and minimal delays	**Very good** Cost of additional copies may be low	**Medium** Messages are constant, but some delays are tolerated	**Medium** Collisions add some complexity to manageability	**Medium to very good** Close to precise consistency
Partitioned					
Distributed, nonintegrated databases Independent databases that can be accessed by applications on remote computers	**Good** Depends on local database availability	**Good** New sites independent of existing ones	**Low** Little if any need to pass data or queries across a network	**Very good** Easy for each site, until there is a need to share data across sites	**Low** No guarantees of consistency
Distributed, integrated database Data span multiple computers and software	**Very good** Effective use of partitioning	**Very good** New nodes get only data they need without changes in overall database design	**Low to medium** Most queries are local but queries that require data from multiple sites can cause a temporary load	**Difficult** Especially difficult for queries that need data from distributed tables, and updates must be tightly coordinated	**Very poor** Considerable effort and inconsistencies not tolerated

the task. Alternatively, a more elaborate synchronization technique can be employed so that updates to one copy of a replicated database are automatically propagated throughout the DDP system to update all copies. This strategy requires considerably more software and communications load but provides the user with a more flexible system.

The simplest partitioned strategy is one in which there are a number of independently operated databases with remote access allowed. In effect, we have a collection of centralized databases, with more than one center. A more complex system is one in which the databases are integrated so that a single query by the user may require access to any of the databases. In a sophisticated system, this access is invisible to the user, who need not specify where the data are located and who need not use a different command style for different portions of the distributed database.

Thus, we can see that a variety of strategies is possible. In designing a distributed database, two sets of objectives are paramount: database objectives and communications objectives. *Database objectives* include accessibility of the data, security and privacy, and completeness and integrity of the data. *Communications objectives* are to minimize the communications load and the delays imposed by the use of communications facilities.

3.4 NETWORKING IMPLICATIONS OF DDP

We can characterize the requirements for communications and networking generated by the use of distributed data processing as falling into three key areas: connectivity, availability, and performance.

The **connectivity** of a distributed system refers to the ability of components in the system to exchange data. In a vertically partitioned DDP system, components of the system generally need links only to components above and below them in the hierarchical structure. Such a requirement can often be met with simple direct links between systems. In a horizontally partitioned system, it may be necessary to allow data exchange between any two systems. For example, in an office automation system, any user should be able to exchange electronic mail and files with any other user, subject to any security policy. In a system requiring high connectivity, some sort of network may be preferable to a large number of direct links. To see this, consider Figure 3.3. If we have a distributed system requiring full connectivity and use a direct link between each pair of systems, the number of links and the communication interfaces needed grows rapidly with the number of systems. With four computers, six links are required; with five computers, ten links are required. Instead, suppose we create a network by providing a central switch and connecting each computer system to that switch. The results are shown in Figure 3.4. In this case, with four computers, four links are required, and with five computers, five links are required.

If the components of a distributed system are geographically dispersed, the requirement for connectivity dictates that some method of transmitting data over long distances is needed. This involves the use of public telecommunications facilities or some private installation.

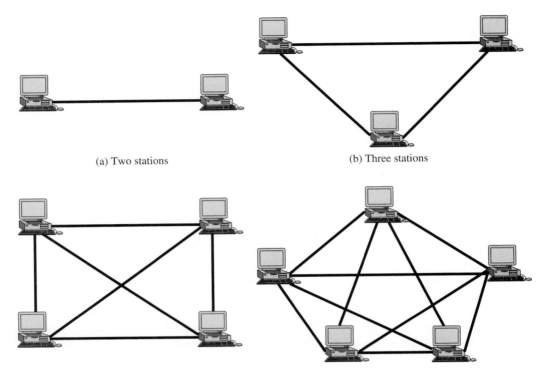

(a) Two stations   (b) Three stations

Figure 3.3   Full Connectivity Using Direct Links

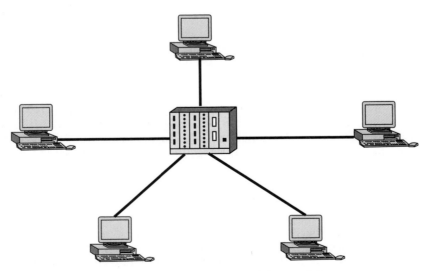

Figure 3.4   The Use of a Central Switch for Full Connectivity

Availability refers to the percentage of time that a particular function or application is available for users. Depending on the application, availability may be merely desirable or it may be essential. For example, in an air traffic control system, the availability of the computer system that supports the air traffic controllers is critical. High availability requirements mean that the distributed system must be designed in such a way that the failure of a single computer or other device will not deny access to the application. For example, backup processors can be employed. High availability requirements also mean that the communications facility must be highly available. Thus, some form of redundancy and backup in the communications facility is needed.

Finally, the **performance** of the communications facility can be assessed, given the nature of the DDP system and the applications that it supports. In a highly interactive system, such as a data entry system or a graphics design application, we have seen that response time is critically important. Thus, not only must the processors that execute the applications respond rapidly but also, if the interaction involves transmission across a network, the network must have sufficient capacity and flexibility to provide the required response time. If the system is used instead to move a lot of data around but without the time being critical, the concern may be more one of throughput. That is, the communications facility must be designed to handle large volumes of data.

Once we have examined the details of the available data communications techniques and facilities, we will return to this topic and examine strategies for communications and network planning.

3.5 SUMMARY

With the increasing availability of inexpensive yet powerful personal computers and workstations, there has been an increasing trend toward distributed data processing (DDP). With DDP, processors, data, and other aspects of a data processing system may be dispersed within an organization. This provides a system that is more responsive to user needs, is able to provide better response times, and may minimize communications costs compared to a centralized approach. A DDP system involves either the horizontal or vertical partitioning of the computing function and may also involve a distributed organization of databases, device control, and interaction (network) control. This trend has been facilitated by the advent of client/server architectures.

At this stage, we are not yet ready to translate our description of DDP characteristics into an analysis of the needed data communications and networking facilities. In general terms, we can say that a DDP system involves requirements in the areas of connectivity, availability, and performance. These requirements, in turn, dictate the type of data communications or networking approach that is appropriate for a given DDP system.

3.6 RECOMMENDED READING

One of the best treatments of distributed data processing is [COUL02]. This book is a broad survey of the issues involved, including networking, file and database design, protocols, transaction issues, and security. A worthwhile and thorough discussion of distributed databases is found in [OZSU99].

COUL02   Coulouris, G.; Dollimore, J.; and Kindberg, T. *Distributed Systems: Concepts and Design.* Reading, MA: Addison-Wesley, 2002.

OZSU99   Ozsu, M., and Valduriez, P. *Principles of Distributed Database Systems.* Upper Saddle River, NJ: Prentice Hall, 1999.

APPLICATION NOTE
Working with a Decentralized System

Processing power, large disk storage, and low cost of workstations or personal computers serves to increase the number of these machines that an organization will purchase. After understanding the pros and cons of such an investment, we sometimes see that there are several issues that go unnoticed until they start to create problems. It is important to realize that many problems can be resolved easily if the IT staff is skilled and has a solid support structure. IT departments have labored under the belief that they are not part of the core business and so receive only sporadic attention or a "fix it when it is broken approach."

Because personal computers are inexpensive and are less complex than mainframes, organizations may staff themselves with personnel having a corresponding level of training and skill. While this may be a cost effective means of providing support to the organization, it may not be appropriate long-range planning. The IT staff must not only be capable of installing, troubleshooting and maintaining the network infrastructure and all of the computers, they must also be professional. Working with a variety of people across the organization, they must be able to communicate in verbal and written form, be courteous and prompt. As a service component, customer satisfaction is paramount. Other departments must be viewed as customers. In any business, the ability to convey verbal and written information, solve problems in a timely fashion while being polite can mean the difference between success and failure.

Another component often underestimated is the helpdesk or trouble call center. Staffing and reliability are important aspects of this particular area. For large organizations, the number of trouble calls can be staggering. An ineffective or understaffed group answering the telephones or going out on the calls can slow the primary business functions down and have a significant effect on the bottom line in terms of man-hours and downtime. The software used to support such a system should be simple but also have functions such as trend analysis, searching, categorizing and various reporting capabilities. Organizations should commit to the appropriate level of support for the helpdesk.

Many departments retain their own "local" computer expert. This is someone who, in addition to their regular duties, also takes on the responsibility of keeping the department machines up to date and doing repairs. In most cases, this is a significant problem for the regular IT staff because the local expert will typically not document maintenance of the machines or inform the IT staff of any changes made. Equipment is purchased from two or more different budgets and often the "local" expert is an expert in name only. It is important to leave repairs and installations to a single organizational entity.

Perhaps the single most important approach that a business can take in order to save money, time and energy when dealing with computers and data networks is to standardize on a set of applications, computing platforms and networking hardware. While there are always a few exceptions, where possible the choices should be minimal. By selecting a single set of applications for desktop and laptop use, licensing and software fees can be reduced by buying in bulk. Licenses in particular can be very expensive on a per seat basis but site licensing can be much more cost effective. In addition, the maintenance of the software becomes easier as technicians have fewer variables to contend with in their troubleshooting and updates.

The same is true of hardware. With a single manufacturer to deal with, fewer spares need to be kept on hand, technicians become very familiar with the equipment and the vendors are known and have a vested interest in keeping their customer happy. It is a troubleshooting nightmare moving from one machine equipped with Windows to the next machine equipped with Mac OS.

To conclude this section we will examine decentralized systems and viruses. When a virus is downloaded, it is often shared between users. This is particularly true if it is in the guise of a cute program, picture or false offer of some sort. In the case of a fully distributed environment, the best cure for this eventuality is prevention. Most viruses come through email downloads and so a good virus package on individual machines and on the server are important.

Once the virus has been contracted by the network and by the machines, a virus removal process must be initiated immediately. Some thought should go into a procedure for handling this because often, scans are not enough to remove the virus. In some cases, scanning from a bootable floppy disk or an inoculation procedure must be followed to remove the virus. Worse yet, the infected machine(s) may be backed up to the network resulting in infected servers and potential large-scale loss of organization data. If this occurs, it is possible that the data cannot be recovered. Any removable media that was in use at the time of the infection must also be considered infected.

Decentralized or distributed systems can pose a unique problems not experienced by fully centralized systems. With the increasing use of autonomous nodes an understanding of these problems can minimize the financial impact, staffing problems and reduce downtime of the communications system.

3.7 KEY TERMS, REVIEW QUESTIONS, AND PROBLEMS

Key Terms

availability centralized database centralized data processing client/server architecture connectivity database	distributed database distributed data processing (DDP) extranet horizontal partitioning intranet	partitioned database performance replicated database vertical partitioning

Review Questions

3.1. What are some functions that are centralized in a fully centralized data processing facility?

3.2. What are some advantages of a centralized data processing facility?

3.3. Based on your reading of the chapter, name five components that might be part of a fully centralized system.

3.4. What is a distributed data processing (DDP) strategy?

3.5. Applications for the distributed environment are available much sooner than those in the centralized environment. What are the main sources of these applications?

3.6. Describe three ways that an application can be allocated in a distributed environment.

3.7. What major problems for the data processing manager result from distributed small systems?

3.8. What are some reasons for wanting to interconnect distributed data processing systems?

3.9. Distinguish between horizontal and vertical partitioning of applications.

3.10. Why would a company want a distributed database?

3.11. In designing a distributed database, database objectives and communications objectives are not always the same. Distinguish between these two sets of objectives.

3.12. How does a factory often reflect the use of distributed devices?

3.13. Name three types of communications and networking requirements generated by the use of distributed data processing.

3.14. Why do we still need mainframe computers even though personal computers and workstations have become so much more powerful?

Problems

3.1 The new corporate CIO (Chief Information Officer) has devised a nine-point mission statement for the company's Information Technology division (refer to Table 3.1). As one of the operations managers in the department, you have received a memo on the new policy and an associated task. The CIO wants to address the new strategy in a three-phase rollout plan and wants your feedback on which three of the nine points are of highest importance and therefore should be the focus for the initial rollout phase. Select the three you feel meet this criteria and prepare a case for each of your selections.

3.2 You have just accepted the position as CIO for Holiday Inn. As your first official act, the CEO has asked you to assess the corporation's computer operations (refer to Figure 3.1) and report back to her with your recommendation on whether to remain with the status quo (i.e., a centralized IS architecture), migrate to a distributed architecture, or create a hybrid solution using aspects from both general architectures. Choose your position and prepare a case for presentation at the next staff meeting.

3.3 The Internet, if viewed from a global client/server perspective, generally consists of web servers and their associated databases and other data repositories on the server side and various web browser applications and associated plug-ins on the client side. Is a system of this sort best described as vertically distributed application processing, horizontally distributed application processing, or some hybrid of these two characterizations?

3.4 How many direct connections does it take to connect *n* computers together? (*Hint:* Count the number of "ends" of connections and divide by 2.) Suppose you have a computer in each of the 50 states in the United States; how many direct connections would you need?

3.5 While many systems are considered centralized such as a company mainframe performing financial functions, there are fewer and fewer "dumb terminals" accessing the mainframe. Instead, terminal emulation programs that simulate the terminal environment are used. The Windows operating system family has a program like this built in. What is it called?

3.6 This chapter describes several components and advantages of a fully centralized system. What do might be some of the major drawbacks of a system like this?

3.7 This chapter describes both "off the shelf" and "end user programming" as types of applications. Discuss what is meant by these terms and provide some examples of each.

3.8 In the client/server architecture, what in meant by the term "server"?

3.9 Two data centers used for retail credit authorization are located in two different major population centers, which are separated from each other by a large zone of very little population. Each data center is intended to cover a particular geographical area and thus contains data that reflect the account status of the card holders in that area (only). Terminals for each area are connected to the corresponding data center. Communication between both data centers occurs only in case a card holder from one geographical area shops in a retail credit establishment of the geographical area covered by the other data center.
   a. Classify the relationship between each terminal and the corresponding data center as either client/server or peer-to-peer.
   b. Classify the relationship between both data centers as either client/server or peer-to-peer.
   c. Classify the database of the retail credit system as either partitioned or replicated.
   d. Is this approach to distributed data processing suitable for the scenario described? Why or why not?
   e. Would this approach be suitable if the two major population centers were close to each other? Why or why not?

3.10 An online terminal system implemented on one computer is being used to service four cities. Discuss how the overall system availability could be increased by
   a. reducing the scope of failures
   b. reducing the impact of failures

3.11 Retail is one of the first areas in adopting distributed data processing. Instead of centralizing the POS (Point-Of-Sale) systems, retailers deploy distributed databases, so all of their POS systems are local, but linked to a central system. Prices for all merchandise are determined and maintained at the central system. Each day, before trading starts, relevant prices are downloaded to the POS system at each store, replicating the data of the central system. Analyze the economic advantages of the adoption of distributed data processing in the retail area.

3.12 Napster was a famous music exchange system that additionally offered many add-on services. It was sentenced to go out of business due to copyright infringement. The system worked as follows. The Napster server held a database of all music files offered by the participating users. Users had to login to the Napster server, and send the list of files they offered. Each user could then send search requests to the Napster server, in order to receive a list of the users that offered files that matched the query. The requester could then choose a user from that list, establish a direct connection with him, and request a download of the file.

 a. Categorize the relationship between the Napster server and the users of the system as either client/server or peer-to-peer.

 b. Categorize the relationship between the users of the system as either client/server or peer-to-peer.

 c. Categorize the database of music files as centralized, decentralized, or distributed, and analyze the economic implications on the system.

 d. Categorize the database containing the list available music files as either centralized or distributed, and analyze its technical implications.

 e. Analyze the relationship between the Napster system architecture and the vulnerability of Napster against legal actions.

3.13 A company will deploy a credit sales system which will provide service to ten large population centers. A database will be used to store user information and record credit transactions. The IT department is considering two choices:

 a. A centralized database, where a single copy of the data is stored in one datacenter and used from all population centers.

 b. A replicated database, where one copy of the data is stored at multiple datacenters (one in each each population center) and all copies of the data are synchronized.

Give some criteria for deciding which type of database should be used for this project.

Case Study I: MasterCard International

An example of a client/server architecture is that used by MasterCard International [HIGG03, STEI02b]. The company's computer facility authorizes, clears, and settles each credit card transaction in real time as a cardholder's credit card is swiped. The client/server system ties together 25,000 member banks with MasterCard's massive data warehouse, which helps the credit card giant and its bank clients make more effective business decisions. MasterCard has converted the 50 terabytes (TB)[1] of transactional and financial data into a business-intelligence engine for use by banks and MasterCard employees.

Planning for the data warehouse began in the mid-1990s. Interestingly, the IT (information technology) staff did not feel the need to present a detailed business case to upper management for this major project. Rather, the data warehouse was presented as a strategic move to give MasterCard a competitive edge. Specifically, MasterCard wanted to improve market share. At the time, MasterCard accounted for only about 25% of charges for goods sold worldwide using credit cards, with Visa accounting for 50%. Today, that market share is closer to one-third, and growing.

Financial institutions that use MasterCard rely on the history of credit card transactions to provide information for targeted marketing and business planning. For example, a bank that issues credit cards might notice a large volume of charges to flights from a specific airline. The bank can use this information to negotiate a deal with the airline to provide special offers and incentives to cardholders.

The company runs a combination of homegrown and off-the-shelf analytic tools to identify buying trends, credit card fraud, and other useful information. The company can correlate and analyze transactions to determine a consumer's interest or detect anomalies that suggest a card has been stolen. MasterCard offers bank clients access to these tools, as well as custom reports.

Among the signature applications provided by MasterCard is the Business Performance Intelligence suite of operational reporting tools. This suite includes about 70 standard reports that let members analyze transactions every day, week, or month and compare the results to different parts of the country, other parts of the world, or predefined groups of similar banks. For example, one member bank found that it had a disproportionally high rate of turning down transactions. It was not because of any analysis of the cardholder's creditworthiness; instead, the bank's systems simply timed out.

Another popular tool is MarketScope, which helps banks monitor, analyze, and develop campaigns to increase use of their cards. For example, a card issuer in New York might use the data to see how many cardholders spent $25 or more in January and February on sporting goods at Wal-Mart

---

[1]See Appendix 1A for an explanation of numerical prefixes, such as *tera* and *giga*.

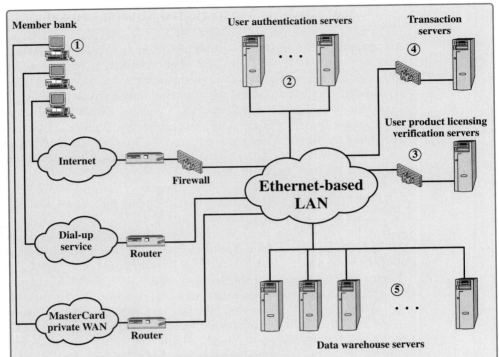

Figure I.1 MasterCard Client/Server Architecture

stores. Then, it might propose to Wal-Mart a mail marketing campaign before the opening of baseball season, tied to heavy spenders with an affinity to the New York Mets or Yankees.

The configuration is shown in general terms in Figure I.1. A client/server transaction proceeds in the following way:

1. Member bank connects to MasterCard facility, known as MasterCard Online. This could be by Internet, by means of a private dial-up access service, or by means of a private wide area network, such as a frame relay network. In the case of Internet access, all traffic must go through a firewall, which assures that unwanted traffic is blocked.

2. User authenticates to MasterCard Online. A dedicated group of servers is assigned the task of authenticating all incoming transaction request to assure that the user has permission to use the facility and to specify the user's level of privilege.

3. MasterCard Online verifies user product licensing. This has to do with which business enterprise software tools the bank client is able to use.

4. User request is forwarded to a transaction server, which invokes the appropriate application software for this transaction. The application translates the request into the corresponding database requests and updates.

5. The transaction server forwards a transaction request to the data warehouse, which processes the request and returns a response to the member user.

MasterCard continues to expand the size of the database and the tool set. The goal is to include every transaction handled by members over a three-year period, capturing the dollar amount, the card number, the location, and the merchant in each instant. But it is the set of applications provided to members that is crucial in gaining competitive edge. Master-Card aims to gain favor with the portfolio managers and member banks, who decide whether to push Visa or MasterCard. If the online tools help those managers analyze the profitability of the cards in their portfolio better or gain more customers and transaction volume faster, then Master-Card benefits. To keep ahead of Visa, the MasterCard IT shop has 35 full-time developers, tasked to come up with new tools to put in the hands of the banks. The developers also work with banks to create repeatable custom reports that can focus on any aspect of authorizing a card or transaction, including charge backs for disputed amounts and fraud.

Discussion Points

1. The IT managers responsible for selling the data warehouse concept to upper management say that it would be much harder to make the case in today's climate of shrinking IT budgets, because most organizations are trying to cut costs rather than launch new initiatives. Discuss the approach that the IT shop would need to take in presenting a business case for a data warehouse with application tools such as that of MasterCard International.

2. MasterCard makes its tools available to all of its member banks. [STEI02b] states that these tools are more likely to be attractive to state and regional banks. Big national and international banks are likely to have developed and use their own analytical tools. Discuss the implications of this in terms of the marketing of MasterCard's IT services. Include in your discussion a consideration of what MasterCard can offer the big banks.

3. Suggest applications or tools that MasterCard could provide that would be attractive to member banks.

PART TWO

The Internet and Distributed Applications

Part Two provides an overview of the Internet and the basic protocols that are the foundation of the Internet. This part then looks at the services perceived by end users, including Internet-based distributed applications and client/server support. Finally, Part Two looks at some of the details of Internet operation.

Chapter 7 Client/Server and Intranet Computing

A more general treatment of distributed applications is in Chapter 7, which deals with client/server computing and with intranets. The client/server approach provides an architecture to support distributed applications that is an ideal match for today's PC-dominated business environment. An intranet is an Internet-style facility that makes use of Internet technologies to provide a client/server base. An extranet extends these Internet-based facilities to business partners, such as customers and suppliers.

Chapter 8 Internet Operation

Chapter 8 continues the discussion of TCP/IP technology begun in Chapters 4 and 5 by looking at the critical issue of addressing on the Internet and the related issues of routing. The remainder of the chapter looks at recent efforts to provide a given level of Quality of Service (QoS) to various applications, with emphasis on the area of differentiated services.

THE INTERNET

CHAPTER OBJECTIVES

After reading this chapter, you should be able to

- Discuss the history of the Internet and explain its explosive growth.
- Describe the overall Internet architecture and its key components, including ISPs, POPs, and NAPs.
- Explain Internet domains and domain names.
- Discuss the operation of the Domain Name System.

4.1   INTERNET HISTORY

Beginnings

The Internet evolved from the ARPANET, which was developed in 1969 by the Advanced Research Projects Agency (ARPA) of the U.S. Department of Defense. It was the first operational packet-switching network. ARPANET began operations in four locations. Today the number of hosts is in the hundreds of millions, the number of users in the billions, and the number of countries participating nearing 200. The number of connections to the Internet continues to grow exponentially (Figure 4.1).

ARPANET made use of the new technology of packet switching, which offered advantages over circuit switching, both of which were briefly introduced in Section 1.6.

Traditionally, the two primary paradigms for electronic communications were circuit switching (essentially, voice communication; see Chapter 12), and message switching (telegraph and Telex). In **circuit switching** (Figure 4.2), when source S communicates with destination T through a network, a dedicated path of transmission facilities is established (e.g., S, A, C, E, T) connecting S to T. All of these facilities are held for the duration of the "call." In particular, if there were lulls in the conversation, the path of facilities would remain unused during these periods. On

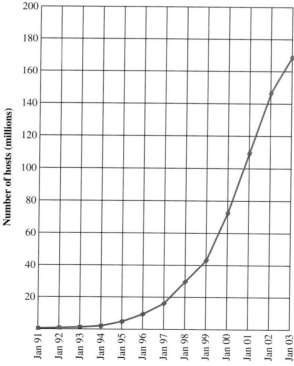

Figure 4.1   Number of Internet Hosts
Source: Internet Software Consortium (http://www.isc.org)

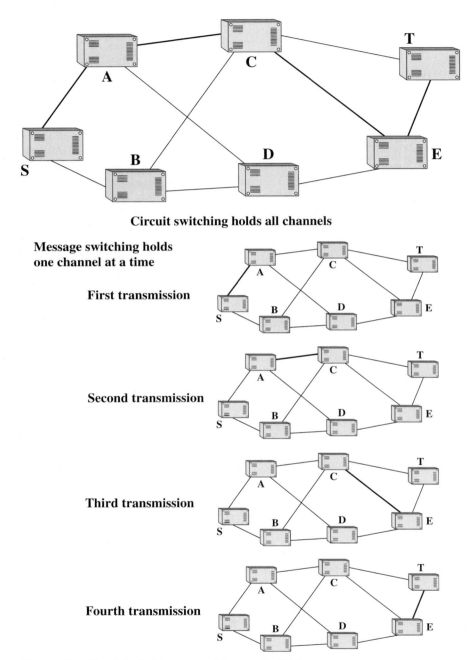

Figure 4.2   Circuit Switching versus Message Switching

the other hand, after the connection is established there is minimal delay through the network. Moreover, once the "call" was set up, the network could basically be passive. Because switching was often electromechanical, this was a big plus.

In **message switching** (Figure 4.2), a message is sent from S to T in stages. First the transmission facility from S to A might be seized and the message is transmitted from S to A, where it is temporarily stored. At this point the S to A channel is released. Then a channel from A to C is accessed and the message is sent to C, and so on. In this case the transmission channels are only used when they are needed, and not wasted when they are not needed. In exchange for this more efficient transmission, the delay can be substantial and quite variable. The messages were frequently stored at each intermediate location on slow peripheral processors such as discs, magnetic drums, or, in the early days, on punched paper tapes. These peripherals are slow. Moreover, each time the message is transmitted, a transmission time equal to the length of the message divided by the channel's data rate was incurred. Very long messages would incur very long delays on each hop. There would be one such delay for each hop on the path connecting the source to the destination. So the delay due to transmissions would vary widely depending on the length of the message and the number of hops on the path connecting source to destination.

Packet switching is a special case of message switching with special properties. First the transmitted data unit, the packet, is limited in length. If a message is bigger than the maximum packet size, it is broken up into a number of packets. Second, when packets are passed from switch to switch they are stored in high-speed random access memory (RAM) rather than in the slower peripherals ordinarily used in message switching systems. Packet switching has several obvious advantages compared to message switching. The delay is much shorter. The delay of the first packet to arrive is only the transmission time of the first packet times the number of hops on the path used. Subsequent packets follow in sequence immediately behind. If high-speed channels are used, the delay, even across the United States, is a few hundred milliseconds. The ARPANET used 50-kbps links. Thus for a path with 5 or less hops and a packet length of less than 1000 bytes, the transmission time is less than $1000 \times 8/50,000 = 0.16$ seconds. At the same time, the channels are used as efficiently as for message switching.

The ARPANET technology offered other new advantages, as discussed in the following paragraphs.

When circuit switching is used for data transmission, the data rates of the transmitting device and the receiving device must be the same. With packet switching, this is not necessary. A packet can be sent at the data rate of the transmitting device into the network, travel through the network at a variety of different data rates, usually higher than the transmitter's rate, and then be metered out at the data rate that the receiver was expecting. The packet-switching network and its interfaces can buffer backed-up data to make speed conversion from a higher rate to a lower one possible. It was not just differing data rates that made interconnections difficult at the time of ARPANET's invention; the complete lack of open communication standards made it very difficult for a computer made by one manufacturer to communicate electronically with a computer made by another. Therefore, a key part of the ARPANET effort was the development of standardized communication and application protocols, as discussed subsequently. Of particular interest to its military sponsors, ARPANET also offered adaptive routing. Each packet, individually, was routed to its destination by whatever route seemed fastest at the time of its transmission. Thus, if parts of the network got congested or failed, packets would automatically be routed around the obstacles.

Some of the early applications developed for the ARPANET also offered new functionality. The first two important applications were Telnet and FTP. Telnet provided a universal language for remote computer terminals. When the ARPANET was introduced, each different computer system supported a different terminal. The Telnet application provided a common denominator terminal. If software was written for each type of computer to support the "Telnet terminal," then one terminal could interact with all computer types. The File Transfer Protocol (FTP) offered a similar open functionality. FTP allowed the transparent transfer of files from one computer to another over the network. This is not as trivial as it may sound because various computers had different word sizes, stored their bits in different orders, and used different word formats. However, the first "killer app" for the ARPANET was electronic mail. Before ARPANET there were electronic mail systems, but they were all single computer systems. In 1972, Ray Tomlinson of Bolt Beranek and Newman (BBN) wrote the first system to provide distributed mail service across a computer network using multiple computers. By 1973, an ARPA study had found that three quarters of all ARPANET traffic was e-mail [HAFN96].

The network was so successful that ARPA applied the same packet-switching technology to tactical radio communication (packet radio) and to satellite communication (SATNET). Because the three networks operated in very different communication environments, the appropriate values for certain parameters, such as maximum packet size, were different in each case. Faced with the dilemma of integrating these networks, Vint Cerf and Bob Kahn of ARPA started to develop methods and protocols for *internetworking;* that is, communicating across arbitrary, multiple, packet-switched networks. They published a very influential paper in May of 1974 [CERF74] outlining their approach to a Transmission Control Protocol. The proposal was refined and details filled in by the ARPANET community, with major contributions from participants from European networks, such as Cyclades (France), and EIN, eventually leading to the TCP (Transmission Control Protocol) and IP (Internet Protocol) protocols, which, in turn, formed the basis for what eventually became the TCP/IP protocol suite. This provided the foundation for the Internet. In 1982–1983, ARPANET converted from the original NCP protocol to TCP/IP. Many networks then were connected using this technology throughout the world. Nevertheless, use of the ARPANET was generally restricted to ARPA contractors.

The 1980s saw the widespread deployment of local area networks (LAN), personal computers (PC), and workstations. Many of these were connected to the Internet, resulting in large-scale expansion. As the scale of the Internet increased, new innovations were required to meet new challenges. Originally, hosts were given numeric addresses, but these quickly became cumbersome. The Domain Name System (DNS) was invented so hosts could be assigned names that were easier to remember, with DNS providing a translation from the domain names to numeric addresses. New routing algorithms were also invented to handle the ever-increasing complexity of the many connected networks.

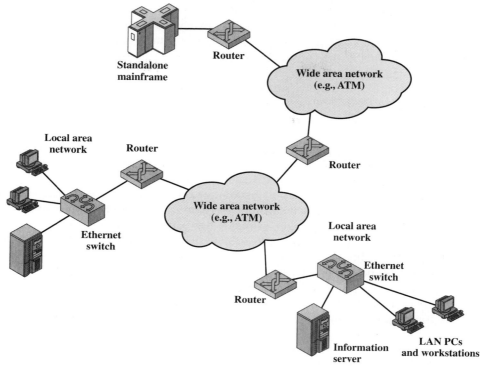

Figure 4.3   Key Elements of the Internet

Figure 4.3 illustrates the key elements that comprise the Internet. The purpose of the Internet, of course, is to interconnect end systems, called **hosts;** these include PCs, workstations, servers, mainframes, and so on. Most hosts that use the Internet are connected to a **network,** such as a local area network (LAN) or a wide area network (WAN). These networks are in turn connected by **routers.** Each router attaches to two or more networks. Some hosts, such as mainframes or servers, connect directly to a router rather than through a network.

In essence, the Internet operates as follows. A host may send data to another host anywhere on the Internet. The source host breaks the data to be sent into a sequence of packets, called **IP datagrams** or **IP packets.** Each packet includes a unique numeric, address of the destination host. This address is referred to as an **IP address,** because the address is carried in an IP packet. Based on this destination address, each packet travels through a series of routers and networks from source to destination. Each router, as it receives a packet, makes a routing decision and forwards the packet along its way to the destination. We have more to say about this process in Chapter 5.

National Science Foundation Takes on a Role

In 1985 the U.S. National Science Foundation (NSF) announced plans to establish NSFNET to serve U.S. universities. The NSF also agreed to provide the backbone for the U.S. Internet service. Within three years the NSFNET backbone was implemented and servicing traffic at T-1 speed (1.544 Mbps). This version of the Internet, however, excluded "purposes not in support of research and education"; this purpose was codified in an *acceptable use policy,* which limited commercial exploitation of the Internet. Eventually, NSF offered interconnection through its backbone to regional packet-switching networks across the country.

The NSF extended support to other computer science research groups with CSNET in 1980–1981; in 1986, NSF extended Internet support to all the disciplines of the general research community with the NSFNET backbone. In 1990 the ARPANET was shut down.

The NSF was responsible for many of the policy decisions that led to the modern Internet. One of the primary goals of the foundation was to establish a wide area networking infrastructure that was not directly funded by the federal government. To this end, the foundation encouraged regional networks that were part of NSFNET to expand their facilities to commercial customers. The NSF also helped standardize the use of many technologies we are familiar with today, such as TCP/IP. The foundation also standardized the requirements for Internet gateways to ensure interoperability between the pieces of the Internet.

NSF policies deliberately fostered competition, and in 1995 the Internet went "private" as the role of the NSFNET backbone was taken over by private long-haul networks. From this point onward the Internet became open to virtually unlimited commercial activity.

Internet Interconnection Points

In 1991, General Atomics, which operated CERFnet (a California regional network); Performance Systems International operating PSINet (a commercial spin-off from New York's regional network, NYSERnet); and UUNET Technologies, a commercial Internet service provider that owned Alternet provided nearly all the commercial TCP/IP services in the United States. On their own networks, because they did not use the NSF backbone, they were not subject to NSF's Acceptable Use Policy. However, to communicate between their networks they had been using the NSF backbone, which brought them under the policy. To get around this problem they formed the Commercial Information Interchange (CIX). Originally, it was a mechanism for the networks of the three founders to interchange traffic carried on their networks at a West Coast router so that each network's customers would have access to customers on others' networks at no extra charge. As other providers entered the market, they too found the concept useful and joined the exchange. By 1996, CIX had 147 member networks. One feature of the CIX is that there are no *settlements*, that is, no traffic-based fees for use of the interchange. A similar interconnection point was formed in 1994 in England, the London Internet Exchange (LINX); in 1996, it had 24 member networks. Also in 1991, the U.S. government announced that it would no longer subsidize the Internet after 1995. As part of the privatization plan, the government mandated interconnection points called network access points. There are also metropolitan area exchanges, MAE East and MAE West. After the U.S. government privatized the national backbone in 1995, commercial activity began to dominate.

The World Wide Web

In the spring of 1989, at CERN (the European Laboratory for Particle Physics), Tim Berners-Lee proposed the idea of a distributed hypermedia technology to facilitate the international exchange of research findings using the Internet. Two years later, a prototype World Wide Web (WWW or the Web for short) was developed at CERN using the NeXT computer as a platform. By the end of 1991, CERN released a line-oriented *browser* or reader to a limited population. The explosive growth of the technology came with the development of the first graphically oriented browser, *Mosaic,* developed at the NCSA Center at the University of Illinois by Mark Andreasson and others in 1993. Two million copies of Mosaic were delivered over the Internet. Today, the characteristic Web addresses, the URLs (uniform resource locators), are ubiquitous. One cannot read a newspaper or watch TV without seeing the addresses everywhere.

The Web is a system consisting of an internationally distributed collection of *multimedia files* supported by clients (users) and servers (information providers). Each file is addressed in a consistent manner using its URL. The files from the providers are viewed by the clients using *browsers* such as Netscape Navigator or Microsoft's Internet Explorer. Most browsers have graphical display and support multimedia—text, audio, image, video. The user can move from file to file by clicking with a mouse or other pointing device on specially highlighted text or image elements on the browser display; the transfer from one file to the next is called a *hyperlink.* The layout of the browser display is controlled by the *HyperText Markup Language* (HTML) standard, which defines embedded commands in text files that specify features of the browser display, such as the fonts, colors, images and their placement on the display, and the location of the locations where the user can invoke the hyperlinks and their targets. Another important feature of the Web is the Hypertext Transfer Protocol (HTTP), which is a communications protocol for use in TCP/IP networks for fetching the files from the appropriate servers as specified by the hyperlinks.

4.2 INTERNET ARCHITECTURE

What the Internet Looks Like Today

The Internet today is made up of thousands of overlapping hierarchical networks. Because of this, it is not practical to attempt a detailed description of the exact architecture or topology of the Internet. However, an overview of the common, general characteristics can be made. Figure 4.4 illustrates the discussion and Table 4.1 summarizes the terminology.

A key element of the Internet is the set of hosts attached to it. Simply put, a host is a computer. Today, computers come in many forms, including mobile phones and even cars. All of these forms can be hosts on the Internet. Hosts are sometimes grouped together in a LAN. This is the typical configuration in a corporate environment. Individual hosts and LANs are connected to an **Internet service provider (ISP)** through a **point of presence (POP).** The connection is made in a series of steps starting with the **customer premises equipment (CPE).** The CPE is the communications equipment located onsite with the host.

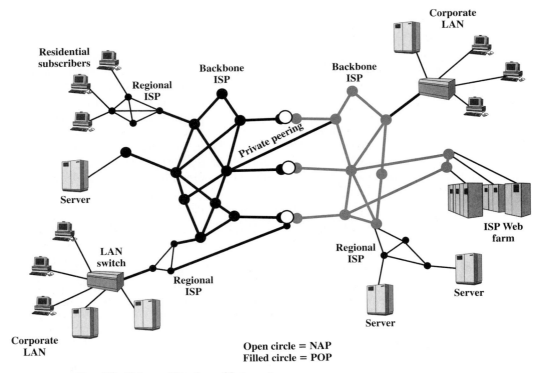

Figure 4.4   Simplified View of Portion of Internet

For the typical home user, the CPE is a 56K modem. This is perfectly adequate for e-mail and related services but marginal for graphics-intensive Web surfing. Newer CPE offerings provide greater capacity and guaranteed service in some cases. A sample of these new access technologies includes DSL, cable modem, and satellite. Users who connect to the Internet through their work often use workstations or PCs connected to their employer-owned LANs, which in turn connect through shared organizational trunks to an ISP. In these cases the shared circuit is often a T-1 connection (1.544 Mbps), while for very large organizations T-3 connections (44.736 Mbps) are sometimes found. Alternatively, an organization's LAN may be hooked to a wide area network (WAN), such as a frame relay network, which in turn connects to an ISP.

The CPE is physically attached to the "local loop" or "last mile." This is the infrastructure between a provider's installation and the site where the host is located. For example, a home user with a 56K modem attaches the modem to the telephone line. The telephone line is typically a pair of copper wires that runs from the house to a **central office (CO)** owned and operated by the telephone company. In this instance the local loop is the pair of copper wires running between the home and the CO. If the home user has a cable modem, the local loop is the coaxial cable that runs from the home to the cable company facilities. The preceding examples are a bit of an oversimplification, but they suffice for this discussion. In many cases the wires that leave a home are aggregated with wires from other homes and then

Table 4.1   Internet Terminology

Central Office (CO)

The place where telephone companies terminate customer lines and locate switching equipment to interconnect those lines with other networks.

Customer Premises Equipment (CPE)

Telecommunications equipment that is located on the customer's premises (physical location) rather than on the provider's premises or in between. Telephone handsets, modems, cable TV set-top boxes, and digital subscriber line routers are examples. Historically, this term referred to equipment placed at the customer's end of the telephone line and usually owned by the telephone company. Today, almost any end-user equipment can be called customer premises equipment and it can be owned by the customer or by the provider.

Internet Service Provider (ISP)

A company that provides other companies or individuals with access to, or presence on, the Internet. An ISP has the equipment and the telecommunication line access required to have a POP on the Internet for the geographic area served. The larger ISPs have their own high-speed leased lines so that they are less dependent on the telecommunication providers and can provide better service to their customers.

Network Access Point (NAP)

In the United States, a network access point (NAP) is one of several major Internet interconnection points that serve to tie all the ISPs together. Originally, four NAPs—in New York, Washington, D.C., Chicago, and San Francisco—were created and supported by the National Science Foundation as part of the transition from the original U.S. government-financed Internet to a commercially operated Internet. Since that time, several new NAPs have arrived, including WorldCom's "MAE West" site in San Jose, California and ICS Network Systems' "Big East."

The NAPs provide major switching facilities that serve the public in general. Companies apply to use the NAP facilities. Much Internet traffic is handled without involving NAPs, using peering arrangements and interconnections within geographic regions.

Network Service Provider (NSP)

A company that provides backbone services to an Internet service provider (ISP). Typically, an ISP connects at a point called an Internet exchange (IX) to a regional ISP that in turn connects to an NSP backbone.

Point of Presence (POP)

A site that has a collection of telecommunications equipment, usually refers to ISP or telephone company sites. An ISP POP is the edge of the ISP's network; connections from users are accepted and authenticated here. An Internet access provider may operate several POPs distributed throughout its area of operation to increase the chance that their subscribers will be able to reach one with a local telephone call. The largest national ISPs have POPs all over the country.

converted to a different media such as fiber. In these cases the term *local loop* still refers to the path from the home to the CO or cable facility. The local loop provider is not necessarily the ISP. In many cases the local loop provider is the telephone company and the ISP is a large, national service organization. Often times, however, the local loop provider is also the ISP.

The ISP provides access to its larger network through a POP. A POP is simply a facility where customers can connect to the ISP network. The facility is sometimes owned by the ISP, but often the ISP leases space from the local loop carrier. A POP can be as simple as a bank of modems and an access server installed in a rack at the CO. The POPs are usually spread out over the geographic area where the provider offers service. The ISP acts as a gateway to the Internet, providing many important services. For most home users, the ISP provides the unique numeric IP address needed to communicate with other Internet hosts. Most ISPs also provide name resolution and other essential network services. The most important service an ISP provides, though, is access to other ISP networks. Access is facilitated by formal peering agreements between providers. Physical access can be implemented by connecting POPs from different ISPs. This can be done directly with a local connection if the POPs are collocated or with leased lines when the POPs are not collocated. A more commonly used mechanism is the **network access point (NAP).**

A NAP is a physical facility that provides the infrastructure to move data between connected networks. In the United States, the NSF privatization plan called for the creation of four NAPs. The NAPs were built and are operated by the private sector. The number of NAPs has grown significantly over the years, and the technology employed has shifted from Fiber Distributed Data Interface (FDDI) and Ethernet to ATM and Gigabit Ethernet. Most NAPs today have an ATM core. The networks connected at a NAP are owned and operated by **network service providers (NSPs).** A NSP can also be an ISP, but this is not always the case. Peering agreements are between NSPs and do not include the NAP operator. The NSPs install routers at the NAP and connect them to the NAP infrastructure. The NSP equipment is responsible for routing, and the NAP infrastructure provides the physical access paths between routers.

A small hypothetical example can help make the picture clearer. In this example there are two companies, one named A, Inc. and the other B, Inc. and they are both NSPs. A, Inc. and B, Inc. have a peering agreement and they both install routers in two NAPs, one located on the east coast of the United States and the other on the west coast. There are also two other companies known as Y, Inc. and Z, Inc. and they are both ISPs. Finally, there is a home user named Bob and a small company named Small, Inc.

Small, Inc. has four hosts connected together into a LAN. Each of the four hosts can communicate and share resources with the other three. Small, Inc. would like access to a broader set of services so they contract with ISP Y, Inc. for a connection. Small, Inc. installs a CPE to drive a leased T-1 line into a Y, Inc. POP. Once the CPE is connected, software automatically assigns a numeric address to each Small, Inc. host. The Small, Inc. hosts can now communicate and share resources with any other host connected to the larger ISP network. On the other side of the country, Bob decides to contract with ISP Z, Inc. He installs a modem on his phone line to dial into a Z, Inc. POP. Once the modem connects, a numeric address is automatically assigned to his home computer. His computer can now communicate and share resources with any other computer connected to the larger ISP network.

Bob's home machine and the hosts owned by Small, Inc. cannot yet communicate. This becomes possible when their respective ISPs contract with NSPs that have a peering agreement. In this example, the ISP Y, Inc. decides to expand its service coverage to the opposite coast and contracts with the NSP A, Inc. A, Inc. sells bandwidth on its high speed coast-to-coast network. The ISP Z, Inc. also wishes to expand its service coverage and contracts with the NSP B, Inc. Like A, Inc., B, Inc. also sells bandwidth on a high speed coast-to-coast network. Because A, Inc. and B, Inc. have a peering agreement and have implemented the agreement at two NAPs, Bob's home machine and the hosts of Small, Inc. can now communicate and share resources. Although this example is contrived, in principle this is what the Internet is. The differences are that the Internet has millions of hosts and many thousands of networks using dozens of access technologies, including satellite, radio, leased T-1, and DSL.

Commercial Use of the Internet

The commercial uses of the Internet came in stages. In the early days, limited by the access rules of the ARPANET and, later, by the Acceptable Use Policy, commercial use was limited to research and development (R&D) or other technical units using the Net for research and educational uses, although some informational activities that could be considered marketing were carried on under the name of research and education. When the Internet was privatized in 1995, the first new applications were mainly informational ones for sales and marketing information and public relations. Electronic data interchange (EDI) transactions for intercompany invoices, billing, and the like, which were originally designed for use on dedicated wide area networks and commercial public networks, began to be carried on the Internet. Commercial networks, especially America Online, have long played a customer service role by providing bulletin board type services dealing with technical and usage problems. These activities were gradually extended to the Internet as well. However, the most significant activity is direct sales to the tens of millions of Internet users throughout the world. The initial infrastructure of the Internet did not support online transactions well. There were three limitations: lack of an easy to use graphical user interface, lack of security, and lack of effective payment systems. The most popular and easy to use interface, the World Wide Web and its browsers, did not become commonly available until the early 1990s. In its early incarnations there was very little support to allow the client browser to submit information (forms) to the server. Moreover, there were not many options for payment for online ordering, and all the options were insecure. One obvious payment method is to use credit card accounts. However, many people are uncomfortable about sending credit card numbers over the Internet, with good reason, because of the lack of security. For example, if the credit card information is not encrypted it is very easy to "listen in" on Internet communications. Moreover, several files of customer's credit card numbers on merchant's computers have been compromised. The ease of collecting and integrating information on customer transactions when they are in electronic form also raises privacy concerns for customers. One of the hottest application areas in financial information systems is "data mining," which often involves collecting large amounts of customer transaction information to improve the targeting of marketing efforts. These limitations have been addressed. Today's browsers support secure communication with the server for the filling out of forms and providing credit card information.

4.3   INTERNET DOMAINS

Internet Names and Addresses

Recall from Section 4.1 that data traverse the Internet in the form of packets, with each packet including a numeric destination address. These addresses are 32-bit binary numbers. The 32-bit IP address provides a way of uniquely identifying devices attached to the Internet. This address is interpreted as having two components: a network number, which identifies a network on the Internet, and a host address, which identifies a unique host on that network. The use of IP addresses presents two problems:

1. Routers devise a path through the Internet on the basis of the network number. If each router needed to keep a master table that listed every network and the preferred path to that network, the management of the tables would be cumbersome and time consuming. It would be better to group the networks in such a way as to simplify the routing function.

2. The 32-bit address is usually written as four decimal numbers, corresponding to the four octets of the address. This number scheme is effective for computer processing but is not convenient for users, who can more easily remember names than numeric addresses.

These problems are addressed by the concept of **domain** and the use of **domain names.** In general terms, a domain refers to a group of hosts that are under the administrative control of a single entity, such as a company or government agency. Domains are organized hierarchically, so that a given domain may consist of a number of subordinate domains. Names are assigned to domains and reflect this hierarchical organization.

Figure 4.5 shows a portion of the domain naming tree. At the very top level are a small number of domains that encompass the entire Internet. Table 4.2 lists the currently defined top-level domains. Each subordinate level is named by prefixing a subordinate name to the name at the next highest level. For example,

- edu is the domain of college-level educational institutions.
- mit.edu is the domain for the Massachusetts Institute of Technology (MIT).
- lcs.mit.edu is the domain for the Laboratory for Computer Science at MIT.

As you move down the naming tree, you eventually get to leaf nodes that identify specific hosts on the Internet. These hosts are assigned Internet addresses. Domain names are assigned hierarchically in such a way that every domain name is unique. At a top level, the creation of new top-level names and the assignment of

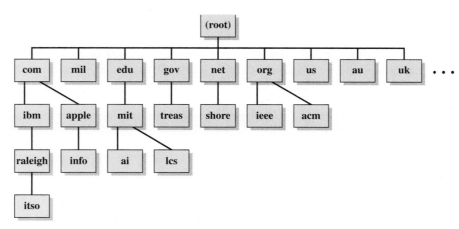

Figure 4.5   Portion of Internet Domain Tree

Table 4.2 Top-Level Internet Domains

Domain	Contents
com	Commercial organizations
edu	Educational institutions
gov	U.S. federal government agencies
mil	U.S. military
net	Network support centers, Internet service providers, and other network-related organizations
org	Nonprofit organizations
us	U.S. state and local government agencies, schools, libraries, and museums
country code	ISO standard 2-letter identifier for country-specific domains (e.g., au, ca, uk)
biz	Dedicated exclusively for private businesses
info	Unrestricted use
name	Individuals, for e-mail addresses and personalized domain names
museum	Restricted to museums, museum organizations, and individual members of the museum profession
coop	Member-owned cooperative organizations, such as credit unions
aero	Aviation community
pro	Medical, legal, and accounting professions
arpa	Temporary ARPA domain (still used)
int	International organizations

names and addresses is administered by the Internet Corporation for Assigned Names and Numbers (ICANN). The actual assignment of addresses is delegated down the hierarchy. Thus, the mil domain is assigned a large group of addresses. The U.S. Department of Defense (DoD) then allocates portions of this address space to various DoD organizations for eventual assignment to hosts.

For example, the main host at MIT, with a domain name of mit.edu, has four IP addresses: 18.7.21.77, 18.7.21.69, 18.7.21.70, and 18.7.21.110. The subordinate domain lcs.mit.edu has the IP address 18.26.0.36.

Domain Name System

The Domain Name System (DNS) is a directory lookup service that provides a mapping between the name of a host on the Internet and its numeric address. DNS is essential to the functioning of the Internet.

Four elements comprise the DNS:

- **Domain name space:** DNS uses a tree-structured name space to identify resources on the Internet.
- **DNS database:** Conceptually, each node and leaf in the name space tree structure names a set of information (e.g., IP address, name server for this domain name, etc.) that is contained in resource record (RRs). The collection of all RRs is organized into a distributed database.

- **Name servers:** These are server programs that hold information about a portion of the domain name tree structure and the associated RRs.
- **Resolvers:** These are programs that extract information from name servers in response to client requests. A typical client request is for an IP address corresponding to a given domain name.

We have already looked at domain names. The remaining DNS elements are discussed in the remainder of this subsection.

The DNS Database   DNS is based on a hierarchical database containing **resource records (RRs)** that include the name, IP address, and other information about hosts. The key features of the database are as follows:

- **Variable-depth hierarchy for names:** DNS allows essentially unlimited levels and uses the period (.) as the level delimiter in printed names, as described earlier.
- **Distributed database:** The database resides in DNS servers scattered throughout the Internet.
- **Distribution controlled by the database:** The DNS database is divided into thousands of separately managed zones, which are managed by separate administrators. Distribution and update of records is controlled by the database software.

Using this database, DNS servers provide a name-to-address directory service for network applications that need to locate specific servers. For example, every time an e-mail message is sent or a Web page is accessed, there must be a DNS name lookup to determine the IP address of the e-mail server or Web server.

DNS Operation   DNS operation typically includes the following steps (Figure 4.6):

1. A user program requests an IP address for a domain name.
2. A resolver module in the local host or local ISP queries a local name server in the same domain as the resolver.
3. The local name server checks to see if the name is in its local database or cache, and, if so, returns the IP address to the requestor. Otherwise, the name server queries other available name servers, if necessary going to the root server, as explained subsequently.
4. When a response is received at the local name server, it stores the name/address mapping in its local cache and may maintain this entry for the amount of time specified in the time to live field of the retrieved RR.
5. The user program is given the IP address or an error message.

The distributed DNS database that supports the DNS functionality must be updated frequently because of the rapid and continued growth of the Internet. Further, the DNS must cope with dynamic assignment of IP addresses, such as is done for home DSL users by their ISP. Accordingly, dynamic updating functions for DNS have been defined. In essence, DNS name servers automatically send out updates to other relevant name servers as conditions warrant.

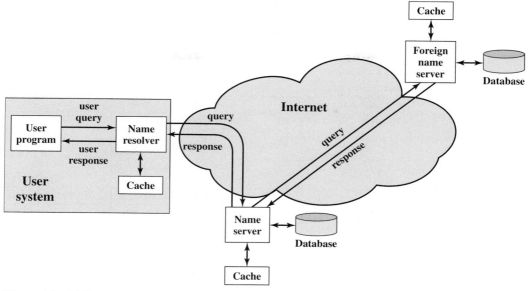

Figure 4.6 DNS Name Resolution

The Server Hierarchy The DNS database is distributed hierarchically, residing in DNS name servers scattered throughout the Internet. Name servers can be operated by any organization that owns a domain; that is, any organization that has responsibility for a subtree of the hierarchical domain name space. Each name server is configured with a subset of the domain name space, known as a **zone,** which is a collection of one or more (or all) subdomains within a domain, along with the associated RRs. This set of data is called authoritative, because this name server is responsible for maintaining an accurate set of RRs for this portion of the domain name space. The hierarchical structure can extend to virtually any depth. Thus, a portion of the name space assigned to an authoritative name server can be delegated to a subordinate name server in a way that corresponds to the structure of the domain name tree. For example, a name server is authoritative for the domain ibm.com. A portion of that domain is defined by the name watson.ibm.com, which corresponds to the node watson.ibm.com and all of the branches and leaf nodes underneath the node watson.ibm.com.

At the top of the server hierarchy are 13 **root name servers** that share responsibility for the top-level zones (Table 4.3). This replication is to prevent the root server from becoming a bottleneck, and for reliability. Even so, each individual root server is quite busy. For example, the Internet Software Consortium reports that its server (F) answers almost 300 million DNS requests daily (www.isc.org/services/public/F-root-server.html).

Consider a query by a program on a user host for watson.ibm.com. This query is sent to the local name server, and the following steps occur:

1. If the local server already has the IP address for watson.ibm.com in its local cache, it returns the IP address.

Table 4.3   Internet Root Servers

Server	Operator	Cities	IP Addr
A	VeriSign Global Registry Services	Herndon VA, US	198.41.0.4
B	Information Sciences Institute	Marina Del Rey CA, US	128.9.0.107
C	Cogent Communications	Herndon VA, US	192.33.4.12
D	University of Maryland	College Park MD, US	128.8.10.90
E	NASA Ames Research Center	Mountain View CA, US	192.203.230.10
F	Internet Software Consortium	Palo Alto CA, US; San Francisco CA, US	IPv4: 192.5.5.241 IPv6: 2001:500::1035
G	U.S. DOD Network Information Center	Vienna VA, US	192.112.36.4
H	U.S. Army Research Lab	Aberdeen MD, US	128.63.2.53
I	Autonomica	Stockholm, SE	192.36.148.17
J	VeriSign Global Registry Services	Herndon VA, US	192.58.128.30
K	Reseaux IP Europeens—Network Coordination Centre	London, UK	193.0.14.129
L	Internet Corporation for Assigned Names and Numbers	Los Angeles CA, US	198.32.64.12
M	WIDE Project	Tokyo, JP	202.12.27.33

2. If the name is not in the local name server's cache, it sends the query to a root server. The root server returns the names and addresses of the domain name servers that contain information for ibm.com.

3. The local name server sends a request to the appropriate name server. If this server has the information for watson.ibm.com, it returns the IP address.

4. If there is a delegated name server just for watson.ibm.com, then the ibm.com name server forwards the request to the watson.ibm.com name server, which returns the IP address.

Name Resolution   As Figure 4.6 indicates, each query begins at a name resolver located in the user host system (e.g., gethostbyname in UNIX). Each resolver is configured to know the IP address of a local DNS name server. If the resolver does not have the requested name in its cache, it sends a DNS query to the local DNS server, which either returns an address immediately or does so after querying one or more other servers.

There are two methods by which queries are forwarded and results returned. Suppose a resolves issues a request to local name server (A). If A has the name/address in its local cache or local database, it can return the IP address to the resolver. If not, then A can do either of the following:

1. Query another name server for the desired result and then send the result back to the resolver. This is known as a **recursive** technique.

2. Return to the resolver the address of the next server (B) to whom the request should be sent. The resolver then sends out a new DNS request to B. This is known as the **iterative** technique.

4.4 SUMMARY

The most important networking facility available to organizations is the Internet. The Internet can be used to link to customers and suppliers and can function as a portion of the wide area networking strategy for linking corporate facilities. The Internet is an unusual corporate tool in that it is not owned or managed by a single entity. Instead, each organization that uses the Internet must understand and deploy the standardized protocols necessary for communication across the Internet.

The Internet, and any private intranet, consists of multiple separate networks that are interconnected by routers. Data are transmitted in packets from a source system to a destination across a path involving multiple networks and routers. A router accepts packets and relays them on toward their destination and is responsible for determining the route, much the same way as packet-switching nodes operate.

An essential element of the Internet is its addressing scheme. It is necessary that each attached host have a unique address to make routing and delivery possible. Internet standards define a 32-bit addressing scheme for this purpose. The Domain Name System provides a means of translating host names to Internet addresses, making it easier for users to identify Internet resources.

4.5 RECOMMENDED READING AND WEB SITES

[COME00] is an excellent in-depth discussion of the topics covered in this chapter.

COME00	Comer, D. *The Internet Book.* Upper Saddle River, NJ: Prentice Hall, 2000.

Recommended Web Site:

- **The Living Internet:** Provides comprehensive and in-depth information about the history of the Internet, plus links to numerous other relevant sites

4.6 KEY TERMS, REVIEW QUESTIONS, AND PROBLEMS

Key Terms

ARPANET	Internet service provider (ISP)	point of presence (POP)
central office	IP address	root name server
customer premises equipment (CPE)	IP datagram	router
	IP packet	Transmission Control Protocol (TCP)
domain	message switching	World Wide Web (WWW)
domain name system (DNS)	network	
host	network access point (NAP)	
Internet Protocol (IP)	network service provider (NSP)	

APPLICATION NOTE
Fitting DNS into Your Organizational Structure

The Domain Name System or DNS is an integral part of communicating over your local network and the Internet. Every time a name or Uniform Resource Locator (URL) is entered into a program that runs over a network, the name must be converted to the Internet Protocol (IP) address. The best example is a Web browser. The DNS allows us to dispense with difficult to remember IP addresses like 207.42.16.185, in favor of easier "human readable" names like www.yahoo.com. The Yahoo website is actually comprised of servers accessed by their IP addresses after the name has been converted from what was entered into the browser.

DNS is also used for services other than Web sites. Telnet and FTP are but two programs we use to access information over our networks. Typically, servers on organization networks are also contacted by name rather than by IP address. We might issue a command or open a terminal emulation program that connects to one of these servers. The command ftp www.georgia.com uses a name that must be resolved to a numerical address for the server. E-mail is another service that resolves names to IP addresses.

At some point, nearly every single computer must contact the DNS in order to complete a transmission or transaction. So, where are the machines providing this service? The answer is that you can either have this service provided to you or handle part of it yourself. The size of your organization network usually determines your choice. Small networks usually have no need or desire to maintain their own DNS server. It is only when you have large number of servers and services running internally that you might opt to run your own service.

When the service is provided to you, it is usually by your Internet service provider, or ISP. The ISP may also automatically provide other services like the IP addresses for the organizations computers and e-mail. If you receive an IP address automatically, the address of the DNS server can be provided at the same time. This is not required. Another option is to manually configure the DNS server address on the individual computers. An institution may decide to do this if the network is configured with private IP addresses that do not come from the ISP.

Should the institution decide that it is time to run their own DNS server, there are several configurations possible. However, is should be understood that the DNS is actually a huge collection of servers working together in a hierarchy. These servers will be both on site (your local DNS) and off site (those servers used by everyone connected to the Internet). This means that unless the server is designed to be isolated, it will have to communicate with DNS servers external to and upstream of the local network.

Just about any computer can be configured as a DNS server. While the technical details are beyond the scope of this text, it should be understood that like all computing elements, it adds an additional layer of complexity and management. The DNS server must be kept up to date and have a backup system. Should the local DNS server be off line, all the machines depending on it may have difficulty connecting.

Modern operating systems such as Windows XP have DNS services interoperating with what is called active directory. Active Directory is a repository or database of organization objects. These objects can describe people, groups, services and many others. Previously, Windows networks were supported by domain controllers, NetBIOS and by DNS. NetBIOS is a protocol used by Windows. Active Directory changes all that by replacing the NetBIOS portion with DNS. Thus, the Windows system is even more dependent on the proper operation of DNS. In this case, it would be best to run your own DNS server. This is because of all of the organization specific information that must be stored there. If run by the ISP, all of the updates would have to be sent to the ISP for changes and the off-site network connection would have increased levels of traffic as the DNS must be queried by the Windows system.

DNS is an integral part of any data communications network. The decision to implement your own or rely on services provided from an external organization must be given a good deal of thought as it requires a significant amount of time for configuration and ongoing management. The decision to make use of advanced directory services from operating systems must also be carefully planned as it can have a dramatic effect on current and future DNS implementations.

Review Questions

4.1. What is the difference between ARPANET and the Internet?

4.2. What two protocols form the foundation of and govern the way we communicate on the Internet?

4.3. What are the roles of host, network, and routers in the Internet?

4.4. What were two of the first applications developed for use over a network?

4.5. What is an IP address?

4.6. What is Mosaic?

4.7. What are two applications programs that have taken the place of Mosaic?

4.8. What is the programming language used to display Web pages?

4.9. What is the difference between an ISP and a POP?

4.10. What is the difference between an NAP and an NSP?

4.11. What is an Internet domain?

4.12. What is DNS?

4.13. Name the four major components of the domain name system.

4.14. What is the difference between a name server and a resolver in DNS?

4.15. What is a DNS resource record?

4.16. Give a brief description of DNS operation.

4.17. What is a root name server?

4.18. Explain the difference between the recursive technique and the iterative technique in DNS.

Problems

4.1 Compare and contrast circuit switching and packet switching. Describe the tradeoffs between the two technologies. Why is packet switching the more appropriate mechanism for the operation of the Internet?

4.2 Two seemingly unrelated events took place in late 1992 and early 1993 that together seeded the explosive growth of the Internet that is rooted in the early 1990s. One was a piece of legislation authored by Congressman Rick Boucher and the other was a piece of software authored by Marc Andreessen. Explain how and why these two events were major contributors to the state of the Internet as we know it today.
References: http://www.house.gov/boucher/docs/boucherinfotech.htm
http://www.webhistory.org/www.lists/www-talk.1993q1/0262.html

4.3 The dig tool provides easy interactive access to the DNS. The dig tool is available for UNIX and Windows operating systems. It can also be used from the Web. Here are three sites that, at the time of this writing, provided free access to dig:
http://www.gont.com.ar/tools/dig
http://www.webmaster-toolkit.com/dig.shtml
http://www.webhostselect.com/whs/dig-tool.jsp

Use the dig tool to get the list of root servers.

4.4 Choose a root server, and use the dig tool to send it a query for the IP address of www.example.com, with the RD (Recursion Desired) bit set. Does it support recursive lookups? Why or why not?

4.5 A user on the host 170.210.17.145 is using a Web browser to visit www.example.com. In order to resolve the www.example.com domain to an IP address, a query is sent to an authoritative name server for the 'example.com' domain. In response, the name server returns a list of four IP addresses, in the following order: {192.168.0.1, 128.0.0.1, 200.47.57.1, 170.210.10.130}. Even though it is the last IP address in the list returned by the name server, the Web browser creates a connection to 170.210.17.130. Why?

4.6 Before the deployment of the Domain Name System, a simple text file ('HOSTS.TXT') centrally maintained at the SRI Network Information Center was used to enable mapping between host names and addresses. Each host connected to the Internet had to have an updated local copy of it to be able to use host names instead of having to cope directly with their IP addresses. Discuss the main advantages of the DNS over the old centralized HOSTS.TXT system.

4.7 Every machine connected to a network should have an IP address. This is true whether the address comes from a server or is manually configured. Use the following tools to determine your IP address. To use each one, you must first open up either a DOS shell (for Windows) or a Bourne shell (most often used Linux shell). These shells are sometimes called command windows. In Windows operating systems, the shell can be accessed typing "command" in the Start/Run box. For Linux, the shell may be the default or can be accessed by the shell icon on the task bar.

Windows 98/2000/XP–type "ipconfig" in the shell window then press "Enter"
Linux–type "ifconfig eth0" in the shell window then press "Enter"

4.8 What is the name of the protocol used to provide your IP address automatically?

4.9 In this same window, you can interact with the server providing the IP address for your computer. For Linux you can use the command ifdown eth0 followed by the command ifup eth0. This will send a series of requests to the server. On the Windows 98/2000/XP machine, type the command ipconfig /?, which will display a series of options. Release and renew your IP address using these options. Did you get the same IP address?

4.10 Windows 2000/XP and Linux have a program built in that will allow you to interact with the DNS server. This program is called "nslookup". Type this name into the command windows and press "Enter". What is the automatic feedback you receive and what does it mean? Typing "exit" will close the program.

4.11 From the previous exercise you learned your IP address. Type the command nslookup and use your IP as an argument. For example, nslookup 10.20.30.40. This will look up your IP address with the DNS system. What does the server return?

4.12 What kind of lookup did your perform in the last problem?

CHAPTER 5

TCP/IP AND OSI

CHAPTER OBJECTIVES

After reading this chapter, you should be able to

- Define the term *protocol architecture* and explain the need for and benefits of a communications architecture.

- Describe the TCP/IP protocol architecture and explain the functioning of each layer.

- Explain the motivation for the development of a standardized architecture and the reasons why a customer should use products based on a protocol architecture standard in preference to products based on a proprietary architecture.

- Explain the need for internetworking.

- Describe the operation of a router within the context of TCP/IP to provide internetworking.

- Give a brief description of the OSI architecture and each of its constituent layers.

This chapter examines the underlying communications software required to support distributed applications. We will see that the required software is substantial. To make the task of implementing this communications software manageable, a modular structure known as a protocol architecture is used.

We begin this chapter by introducing a simple protocol architecture consisting of just three modules, or layers. This will allow us to present the key characteristics and design features of a protocol architecture without getting bogged down in details. With this background, we are then ready to examine the most important such architecture: TCP/IP (Transmission Control Protocol/Internet Protocol). TCP/IP is an Internet-based standard and is the framework for developing a complete range of computer communications standards. Virtually all computer vendors now provide support for this architecture. Open Systems Interconnection (OSI) is another standardized architecture that is often used to describe communications functions but that is now rarely implemented. For the interested reader, OSI is covered at the end of this chapter.

Following a discussion of TCP/IP, the important concept of internetworking is examined. Inevitably, a business will require the use of more than one communications network. Some means of interconnecting these networks is required, and this raises issues that relate to the protocol architecture.

5.1 A SIMPLE PROTOCOL ARCHITECTURE

The Need for a Protocol Architecture

When computers, terminals, and/or other data processing devices exchange data, the procedures involved can be quite complex. Consider, for example, the transfer of a file between two computers. There must be a data path between the two computers, either directly or via a communication network. But more is needed. Typical tasks to be performed include the following:

1. The source system must either activate the direct data communication path or inform the communication network of the identity of the desired destination system.

2. The source system must ascertain that the destination system is prepared to receive data.

3. The file transfer application on the source system must ascertain that the file management program on the destination system is prepared to accept and store the file for this particular user.

4. If the file formats or data representation used on the two systems are incompatible, one or the other system must perform a format translation function.

The exchange of information between computers for the purpose of cooperative action is generally referred to as *computer communications*. Similarly, when two or more computers are interconnected via a communication network, the set of computer stations is referred to as a *computer network*. Because a similar level of cooperation is required between a terminal and a computer, these terms are often used when some of the communicating entities are terminals.

In discussing computer communications and computer networks, two concepts are paramount:

- Protocols
- Computer communications architecture, or protocol architecture

A **protocol** is used for communication between entities in different systems. The terms *entity* and *system* are used in a very general sense. Examples of entities are user application programs, file transfer packages, database management systems, electronic mail facilities, and terminals. Examples of systems are computers, terminals, and remote sensors. Note that in some cases the entity and the system in which it resides are coextensive (e.g., terminals). In general, an entity is anything capable of sending or receiving information, and a system is a physically distinct object that contains one or more entities. For two entities to communicate successfully, they must "speak the same language." What is communicated, how it is communicated, and when it is communicated must conform to mutually agreed conventions between the entities involved. The conventions are referred to as a protocol, which may be defined as a set of rules governing the exchange of data between two entities. The key elements of a protocol are as follows:

- **Syntax:** Includes such things as data format and signal levels
- **Semantics:** Includes control information for coordination and error handling
- **Timing:** Includes speed matching and sequencing

Appendix 5A provides a specific example of a protocol, the Internet standard Trivial File Transfer Protocol (TFTP).

Having introduced the concept of a protocol, we can now introduce the concept of a **protocol architecture.** It is clear that there must be a high degree of cooperation between the two computer systems. Instead of implementing the logic for this as a single module, the task is broken up into subtasks, each of which is implemented separately. As an example, Figure 5.1 suggests the way in which a file transfer facility could be implemented. Three modules are used. Tasks 3 and 4 in the preceding list could be performed by a file transfer module. The two modules on the two systems exchange files and commands. However, rather than requiring the file transfer module to deal with the details of actually transferring data and commands, the file transfer modules each rely on a communications service module. This module is responsible for making sure that the file transfer commands and data are reliably exchanged between systems. The manner in which a communications service module functions is explored subsequently. Among other things, this module would perform task 2. Finally, the nature of the exchange between the two communications service modules is independent of the nature of the network that interconnects them. Therefore, rather than building details of the network interface into the communications service module, it makes sense to have a third module, a network access module, that performs task 1 by interacting with the network.

To summarize, the file transfer module contains all the logic that is unique to the file transfer application, such as transmitting passwords, file commands, and file records. These files and commands must be transmitted reliably. However, the same sorts of reliability requirements are relevant to a variety of applications (e.g., electronic mail, document transfer). Therefore, these requirements are met by a separate communications service module that can be used by a variety of applications. The communications service module is concerned with assuring that the two computer systems are active and ready for data transfer and for keeping track of the data that are being exchanged to assure delivery. However, these tasks are independent of the

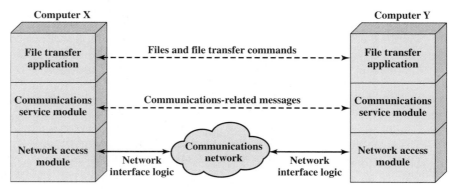

Figure 5.1 A Simplified Architecture for File Transfer

type of network that is being used. Therefore, the logic for actually dealing with the network is put into a separate network access module. If the network to be used is changed, only the network access module is affected.

Thus, instead of a single module for performing communications, there is a structured set of modules that implements the communications function. That structure is referred to as a protocol architecture. An analogy might be useful at this point. Suppose an executive in office X wishes to send a document to an executive in office Y. The executive in X prepares the document and perhaps attaches a note. This corresponds to the actions of the file transfer application in Figure 5.1. Then the executive in X hands the document to a secretary or administrative assistant (AA). The AA in X puts the document in an envelope and puts Y's address and X's return address on the outside. Perhaps the envelope is also marked "confidential." The AA's actions correspond to the communications service module in Figure 5.1. The AA in X then gives the package to the shipping department. Someone in the shipping department decides how to send the package: mail, UPS, or express courier. The shipping department attaches the appropriate postage or shipping documents to the package and ships it out. The shipping department corresponds to the network access module of Figure 5.1. When the package arrives at Y, a similar layered set of actions occurs. The shipping department at Y receives the package and delivers it to the appropriate AA or secretary based on the name on the package. The AA opens the package and hands the enclosed document to the executive to whom it is addressed.

In the remainder of this section, we generalize the example of Figure 5.1 to present a simplified protocol architecture. Following that, we look at the real-world example of TCP/IP.

A Three-Layer Model

In very general terms, distributed data communications can be said to involve three agents: applications, computers, and networks. In Chapter 6, we look at several applications; examples include file transfer and electronic mail. These applications execute on computers that typically support multiple simultaneous applications. Computers are connected to networks, and the data to be exchanged are transferred by the network from one computer to another. Thus, the transfer of data from one application to another involves first getting the data to the computer in which the application resides and then getting it to the intended application within the computer.

With these concepts in mind, it appears natural to organize the communication task into three relatively independent layers: network access layer, transport layer, and application layer

The **network access layer** is concerned with the exchange of data between a computer and the network to which it is attached. The sending computer must provide the network with the address of the destination computer, so that the network may route the data to the appropriate destination. The sending computer may wish to invoke certain services, such as priority, that might be provided by the network. The specific software used at this layer depends on the type of network to be used; different standards have been developed for circuit switching, packet switching, local area networks (LANs), and others. For example, IEEE 802 is a standard that specifies the access to a LAN; this standard is described in Part Three. It makes sense to put those functions having to do with network access into a separate layer. By doing this, the remainder of the communications software, above the network access layer, need not be concerned about the specifics of the network to be used. The same higher-layer software should function properly regardless of the particular network to which the computer is attached.

Regardless of the nature of the applications that are exchanging data, there is usually a requirement that data be exchanged reliably. That is, we would like to be assured that all of the data arrive at the destination application and that the data arrive in the same order in which they were sent. As we shall see, the mechanisms for providing reliability are essentially independent of the nature of the applications. Thus, it makes sense to collect those mechanisms in a common layer shared by all applications; this is referred to as the **transport layer.**

Finally, the **application layer** contains the logic needed to support the various user applications. For each different type of application, such as file transfer, a separate module is needed that is peculiar to that application.

Figures 5.2 and 5.3 illustrate this simple architecture. Figure 5.2 shows three computers connected to a network. Each computer contains software at the network access and transport layers and software at the application layer for one or more applications. For successful communication, every entity in the overall system must have a unique address. Actually, two levels of addressing are needed. Each computer on the network must have a unique network address; this allows the network to deliver data to the proper computer. Each application on a computer must have an address that is unique within that computer; this allows the transport layer to support multiple applications at each computer. These latter addresses are known

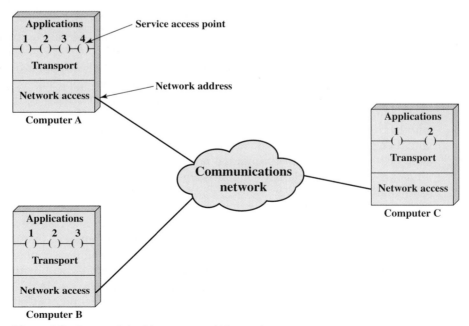

Figure 5.2   Protocol Architectures and Networks

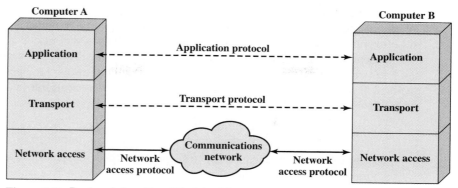

Figure 5.3   Protocols in a Simplified Architecture

as **service access points** (SAPs), or **ports,** connoting the fact that each application is individually accessing the services of the transport layer.

Figure 5.3 indicates the way in which modules at the same layer on different computers communicate with each other: by means of a protocol. Let us trace a simple operation. Suppose that an application, associated with port 1 at computer A, wishes to send a message to another application, associated with port 2 at computer B. The application at A hands the message over to its transport layer with instructions to send it to port 2 on computer B. The transport layer hands the message over to the network access layer, which instructs the network to send the message to computer B. Note that the network need not be told the identity of the destination port. All that it needs to know is that the data are intended for computer B.

To control this operation, control information, as well as user data, must be transmitted, as suggested in Figure 5.4. Let us say that the sending application generates a block of data and passes this to the transport layer. The transport layer may break this block into two smaller pieces for convenience, as discussed subsequently. To

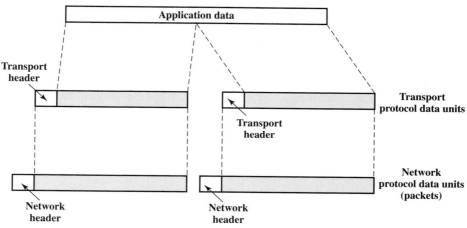

Figure 5.4   Protocol Data Units

each of these pieces the transport layer appends a transport **header,** containing protocol control information. The combination of data from the next higher layer and control information is known as a **protocol data unit** (PDU); in this case, it is referred to as a transport PDU. Transport PDUs are typically called transport **segments.** The header in each segment contains control information to be used by the peer transport protocol at computer B. Examples of items that may be stored in this header include the following:

- **Destination port:** When the destination transport layer receives the segment, it must know to which application the data are to be delivered.
- **Sequence number:** Because the transport protocol is sending a sequence of segments, it numbers them sequentially so that if they arrive out of order, the destination transport entity may reorder them.
- **Error-detection code:** The sending transport entity may include a code that is a function of the contents of the segment. The receiving transport protocol performs the same calculation and compares the result with the incoming code. A discrepancy results if there has been some error in transmission. In that case, the receiver can discard the segment and take corrective action. This code is also referred to as a **checksum** or **frame check sequence.**

The next step is for the transport layer to hand each segment over to the network layer, with instructions to transmit it to the destination computer. To satisfy this request, the network access protocol must present the data to the network with a request for transmission. As before, this operation requires the use of control information. In this case, the network access protocol appends a network access header to the data it receives from the transport layer, creating a network access PDU, typically called a **packet** or a **frame.** Examples of the items that may be stored in the header include the following:

- **Destination computer address:** The network must know to which computer on the network the data are to be delivered.
- **Facilities requests:** The network access protocol might want the network to make use of certain facilities, such as priority.

Figure 5.5 puts all of these concepts together, showing the interaction between modules to transfer one block of data. Let us say that the file transfer module in computer A is transferring a file one record at a time to computer B. Each record is handed over to the transport layer module. We can picture this action as being in the form of a command or procedure call. The arguments of this procedure call include the destination computer address, the destination service access point, and the record. The transport layer appends the destination service access point and other control information to the record to create a transport segment. This is then handed down to the network access layer by another procedure call. In this case, the arguments for the command are the destination computer address and the transport segment. The network access layer uses this information to construct a network PDU, generally called a **packet.** The transport segment is the data field of the packet, and the packet header includes the addressing information to enable delivery to B. Note that the transport header is not "visible" at the network access layer; the network access layer is not concerned with the contents of the transport segment.

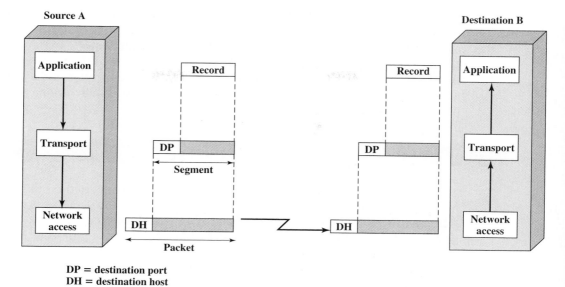

DP = destination port
DH = destination host

Figure 5.5   Operation of a Protocol Architecture

The network accepts the network packet from A and delivers it to B. The network access module in B receives the packet, strips off the packet header, and transfers the enclosed transport segment to B's transport layer module. The transport layer examines the segment header and, on the basis of the port field in the header, delivers the enclosed record to the appropriate application, in this case the file transfer module in B.

Standardized Protocol Architectures

When communication is desired among computers from different vendors, the software development effort can be a nightmare. Different vendors use different data formats and data exchange protocols. Even within one vendor's product line, different model computers may communicate in unique ways.

Now that computer communications and computer networking are ubiquitous, a one-at-a-time special-purpose approach to communications software development is too costly to be acceptable. The only alternative is for computer vendors to adopt and implement a common set of conventions. For this to happen, standards are needed. Such standards would have two benefits:

- Vendors feel encouraged to implement the standards because of an expectation that, because of wide usage of the standards, their products would be less marketable without them.

- Customers are in a position to require that the standards be implemented by any vendor wishing to propose equipment to them.

Two protocol architectures have served as the basis for the development of interoperable protocol standards: the TCP/IP protocol suite and the OSI reference model. TCP/IP is by far the most widely used interoperable architecture. OSI, though well known, has never lived up to its early promise. There is also a widely used proprietary scheme: IBM's Systems Network Architecture (SNA). Although IBM provides support for TCP/IP, it continues to use SNA, and this latter architecture will remain important for some years to come. The remainder of the chapter looks in some detail at TCP/IP and OSI. SNA is summarized in a document at this book's Web site.

5.2 THE TCP/IP PROTOCOL ARCHITECTURE

TCP/IP is a result of protocol research and development conducted on the experimental packet-switched network, ARPANET, funded by the Defense Advanced Research Projects Agency (DARPA), and is generally referred to as the TCP/IP protocol suite. This protocol suite consists of a large collection of protocols that have been issued as Internet standards by the Internet Activities Board (IAB). A document at this book's Web site provides a discussion of Internet standards.

TCP/IP Layers

There is no official TCP/IP protocol model as there is in the case of OSI. However, based on the protocol standards that have been developed, we can organize the communication task for TCP/IP into five relatively independent layers:

- Application layer
- Host-to-host, or transport layer
- Internet layer
- Network access layer
- Physical layer

The **physical layer** covers the physical interface between a data transmission device (e.g., workstation, computer) and a transmission medium or network. This layer is concerned with specifying the characteristics of the transmission medium, the nature of the signals, the data rate, and related matters.

The **network access layer** is concerned with the exchange of data between an end system (server, workstation, etc.) and the network to which it is attached. The sending computer must provide the network with the address of the destination computer, so that the network may route the data to the appropriate destination. The sending computer may wish to invoke certain services, such as priority, that might be provided by the network. The specific software used at this layer depends on the type of network to be used; different standards have been developed for circuit switching, packet switching (e.g., frame relay), LANs (e.g., Ethernet), and others. Thus it makes sense to separate those functions having to do with network access into a separate layer. By doing this, the remainder of the communications software, above the network access layer, need not be concerned about the specifics of the network to be used. The same higher-layer software should function properly regardless of the particular network to which the computer is attached.

The network access layer is concerned with access to and routing data across a network for two end systems attached to the same network. In those cases where two devices are attached to different networks, procedures are needed to allow data to traverse multiple interconnected networks. This is the function of the internet layer. The **Internet Protocol (IP)** is used at this layer to provide the routing function across multiple networks. This protocol is implemented not only in the end systems but also in routers. A **router** is a processor that connects two networks and whose primary function is to relay data from one network to the other on a route from the source to the destination end system.

Regardless of the nature of the applications that are exchanging data, there is usually a requirement that data be exchanged reliably. That is, we would like to be assured that all the data arrive at the destination application and that the data arrive in the same order in which they were sent. As we shall see, the mechanisms for providing reliability are essentially independent of the nature of the applications. Thus, it makes sense to collect those mechanisms in a common layer shared by all applications; this is referred to as the host-to-host layer, or **transport layer.** The Transmission Control Protocol (TCP) is the most commonly used protocol to provide this functionality.

Finally, the **application layer** contains the logic needed to support the various user applications. For each different type of application, such as file transfer, a separate module is needed that is peculiar to that application.

TCP and UDP

For most applications running as part of the TCP/IP protocol architecture, the transport layer protocol is TCP. TCP provides a reliable connection for the transfer of data between applications. A connection is simply a temporary logical association between two entities in different systems. For the duration of the connection each entity keeps track of segments coming and going to the other entity, in order to regulate the flow of segments and to recover from lost or damaged segments.

Figure 5.6a shows the header format for TCP, which is a minimum of 20 octets, or 160 bits. The Source Port and Destination Port fields identify the applications at the source and destination systems that are using this connection. The Sequence Number, Acknowledgment Number, and Window fields provide flow control and error control. The checksum is a 16-bit frame check sequence used to detect errors in the TCP segment. For the interested reader, Section 5.4 provides more detail.

In addition to TCP, there is one other transport-level protocol that is in common use as part of the TCP/IP protocol suite: the User Datagram Protocol (UDP). UDP does not guarantee delivery, preservation of sequence, or protection against duplication. UDP enables a process to send messages to other processes with a minimum of protocol mechanism. Some transaction-oriented applications make use of UDP; one example is SNMP (Simple Network Management Protocol), the standard network management protocol for TCP/IP networks. Because it is connectionless, UDP has very little to do. Essentially, it adds a port addressing capability to IP. This is best seen by examining the UDP header, shown in Figure 5.6b.

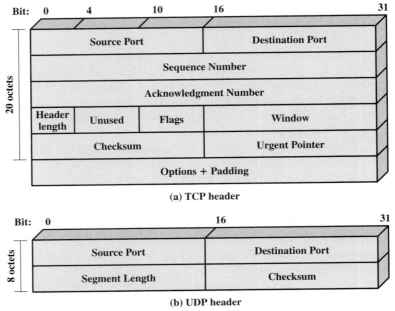

Figure 5.6 TCP and UDP Headers

IP and IPv6

For decades, the keystone of the TCP/IP protocol architecture has been IP. Figure 5.7a shows the IP header format, which is a minimum of 20 octets, or 160 bits. The header, together with the segment from the transport layer form an IP-level PDU referred to as an IP datagram or an IP packet. The header includes 32-bit source and destination addresses. The Header Checksum field is used to detect errors in the header to avoid misdelivery. The Protocol field indicates which higher-layer protocol is using IP. The ID, Flags, and Fragment Offset fields are used in the fragmentation and reassembly process. For the interested reader, Section 5.4 provides more detail.

In 1995, the Internet Engineering Task Force (IETF), which develops protocol standards for the Internet, issued a specification for a next-generation IP, known then as IPng. This specification was turned into a standard in 1996 known as IPv6. IPv6 provides a number of functional enhancements over the existing IP, designed to accommodate the higher speeds of today's networks and the mix of data streams, including graphic and video, that are becoming more prevalent. But the driving force behind the development of the new protocol was the need for more addresses. The current IP uses a 32-bit address to specify a source or destination. With the explosive growth of the Internet and of private networks attached to the Internet, this address length became insufficient to accommodate all systems needing addresses. As Figure 5.7b shows, IPv6 includes 128-bit source and destination address fields.

Ultimately, all installations using TCP/IP are expected to migrate from the current IP to IPv6, but this process will take many years, if not decades.

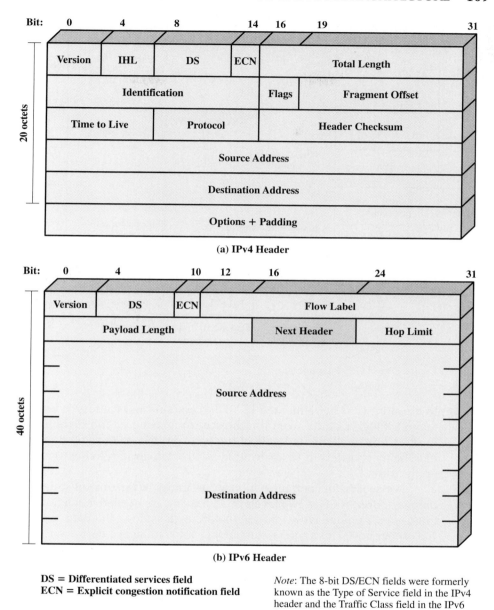

Figure 5.7   IP Headers

DS = Differentiated services field
ECN = Explicit congestion notification field

Note: The 8-bit DS/ECN fields were formerly known as the Type of Service field in the IPv4 header and the Traffic Class field in the IPv6 header.

Operation of TCP/IP

Figure 5.8 indicates how these protocols are configured for communications. Some sort of network access protocol, such as the Ethernet logic, is used to connect a computer to a network. This protocol enables the host to send data across the network to another host or, in the case of a host on another network,

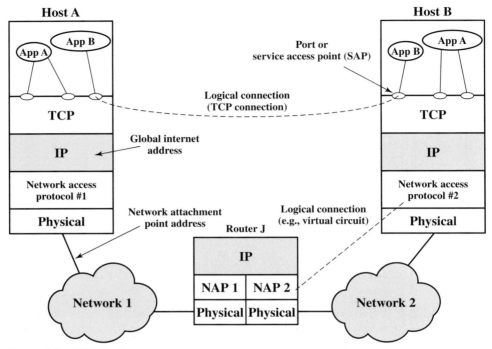

Figure 5.8 TCP/IP Concepts

to a router. IP is implemented in all end systems and routers. It acts as a relay to move a block of data from one host, through one or more routers, to another host. TCP is implemented only in the end systems; it keeps track of the blocks of data being transferred to assure that all are delivered reliably to the appropriate application.

For successful communication, every entity in the overall system must have a unique address. In fact, two levels of addressing are needed. Each host on a network must have a unique global internet address; this allows the data to be delivered to the proper host. This address is used by IP for routing and delivery. Each application within a host must have an address that is unique within the host; this allows the host-to-host protocol (TCP) to deliver data to the proper process. These latter addresses are known as ports.

Let us trace a simple operation. Suppose that a process, associated with port 3 at host A, wishes to send a message to another process, associated with port 2 at host B. The process at A hands the message down to TCP with instructions to send it to host B, port 2. TCP hands the message down to IP with instructions to send it to host B. Note that IP need not be told the identity of the destination port. All it needs to know is that the data are intended for host B. Next, IP hands the message down to the network access layer (e.g., Ethernet logic) with instructions to send it to router J (the first hop on the way to B).

To control this operation, control information as well as user data must be transmitted, as suggested in Figure 5.9. Let us say that the sending process generates

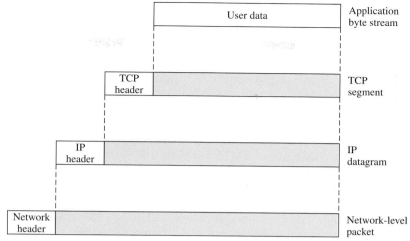

Figure 5.9   Protocol Data Units (PDUs) in the TCP/IP Architecture

a block of data and passes this to TCP. TCP appends control information known as the TCP header (Figure 5.6a), forming a TCP segment. The control information is to be used by the peer TCP protocol entity at host B.

Next, TCP hands each segment over to IP, with instructions to transmit it to B. These segments must be transmitted across one or more networks and relayed through one or more intermediate routers. This operation, too, requires the use of control information. Thus IP appends a header of control information (Figure 5.7) to each segment to form an **IP datagram.** An example of an item stored in the IP header is the destination host address (in this example, B).

Finally, each IP datagram is presented to the network access layer for transmission across the first network in its journey to the destination. The network access layer appends its own header, creating a packet, or frame. The packet is transmitted across the network to router J. The packet header contains the information that the network needs in order to transfer the data across the network. Examples of items that may be contained in this header include the following:

- **Destination network address:** The network must know to which attached device the packet is to be delivered, in this case router J.

- **Facilities requests:** The network access protocol might request the use of certain network facilities, such as priority.

At router J, the packet header is stripped off and the IP header examined. On the basis of the destination address information in the IP header, the IP module in the router directs the datagram out across network 2 to B. To do this, the datagram is again augmented with a network access header.

When the data are received at B, the reverse process occurs. At each layer, the corresponding header is removed, and the remainder is passed on to the next higher layer, until the original user data are delivered to the destination process.

TCP/IP Applications

A number of applications have been standardized to operate on top of TCP. We mention three of the most common here.

The **Simple Mail Transfer Protocol** (SMTP) provides a basic electronic mail facility. It provides a mechanism for transferring messages among separate hosts. Features of SMTP include mailing lists, return receipts, and forwarding. The SMTP protocol does not specify the way in which messages are to be created; some local editing or native electronic mail facility is required. Once a message is created, SMTP accepts the message, and makes use of TCP to send it to an SMTP module on another host. The target SMTP module will make use of a local electronic mail package to store the incoming message in a user's mailbox. SMTP is examined in more detail in Chapter 6

The **File Transfer Protocol** (FTP) is used to send files from one system to another under user command. Both text and binary files are accommodated, and the protocol provides features for controlling user access. When a user wishes to engage in file transfer, FTP sets up a TCP connection to the target system for the exchange of control messages. This connection allows user ID and password to be transmitted and allows the user to specify the file and file actions desired. Once a file transfer is approved, a second TCP connection is set up for the data transfer. The file is transferred over the data connection, without the overhead of any headers or control information at the application level. When the transfer is complete, the control connection is used to signal the completion and to accept new file transfer commands.

TELNET provides a remote logon capability, which enables a user at a terminal or personal computer to logon to a remote computer and function as if directly connected to that computer. The protocol was designed to work with simple scroll-mode terminals. TELNET is actually implemented in two modules: User TELNET interacts with the terminal I/O module to communicate with a local terminal. It converts the characteristics of real terminals to the network standard and vice versa. Server TELNET interacts with an application, acting as a surrogate terminal handler so that remote terminals appear as local to the application. Terminal traffic between User and Server TELNET is carried on a TCP connection.

Protocol Interfaces

Each layer in the TCP/IP protocol suite interacts with its immediate adjacent layers. At the source, the application layer makes use of the services of the transport layer and provides data down to that layer. A similar relationship exists at the interface between the transport and internet layers and at the interface of the internet and network access layers. At the destination, each layer delivers data up to the next higher layer.

This use of each individual layer is not required by the architecture. As Figure 5.10 suggests, it is possible to develop applications that directly invoke the services of any one of the layers. Most applications require a reliable transport protocol and thus make use of TCP. Some special-purpose applications do not need the services of TCP. Some of these applications, such as the Simple Network Management Protocol (SNMP), use another transport protocol known as the User Datagram Protocol (UDP); others may make use of IP directly. Applications that do not involve internetworking and that do not need TCP have been developed to invoke the network access layer directly.

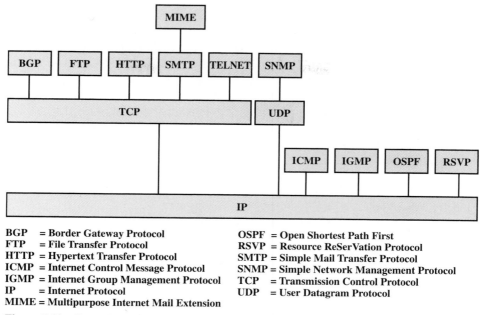

BGP   = Border Gateway Protocol
FTP   = File Transfer Protocol
HTTP   = Hypertext Transfer Protocol
ICMP   = Internet Control Message Protocol
IGMP   = Internet Group Management Protocol
IP   = Internet Protocol
MIME   = Multipurpose Internet Mail Extension

OSPF   = Open Shortest Path First
RSVP   = Resource ReSerVation Protocol
SMTP   = Simple Mail Transfer Protocol
SNMP   = Simple Network Management Protocol
TCP   = Transmission Control Protocol
UDP   = User Datagram Protocol

Figure 5.10   Some Protocols in the TCP/IP Protocol Suite

5.3 INTERNETWORKING

In most cases, a LAN or wide area network (WAN) is not an isolated entity. An organization may have more than one type of LAN at a given site to satisfy a spectrum of needs. An organization may have multiple LANs of the same type at a given site to accommodate performance or security requirements. And an organization may have LANs at various sites and need them to be interconnected via WANs for central control of distributed information exchange.

Table 5.1 lists some commonly used terms relating to the interconnection of networks, or internetworking. An interconnected set of networks, from a user's point of view, may appear simply as a larger network. However, if each of the constituent networks retains its identity, and special mechanisms are needed for communicating across multiple networks, then the entire configuration is often referred to as an **internet,** and each of the constituent networks as a **subnetwork.** The most important example of an internet is referred to simply as the Internet. As the Internet has evolved from its modest beginnings as a research-oriented packet-switching network, it has served as the basis for the development of internetworking technology and as the model for private internets within organizations. These latter are also referred to as **intranets.** If an organization extends access to its intranet, over the Internet, to selected customers and suppliers, then the resulting configuration is often referred to as an **extranet.**

Table 5.1   Internetworking Terms

Communication Network

A facility that provides a data transfer service among devices attached to the network.

Internet

A collection of communication networks interconnected by bridges and/or routers.

Intranet

An internet used by a single organization that provides the key Internet applications, especially the World Wide Web. An intranet operates within the organization for internal purposes and can exist as an isolated, self-contained internet, or may have links to the Internet.

Extranet

The extension of a company's intranet out onto the Internet to allow selected customers, suppliers, and mobile workers to access the company's private data and applications via the World Wide Web.

Subnetwork

Refers to a constituent network of an internet. This avoids ambiguity because the entire internet, from a user's point of view, is a single network.

End System (ES)

A device attached to one of the networks of an internet that is used to support end-user applications or services.

Intermediate System (IS)

A device used to connect two networks and permit communication between end systems attached to different networks.

Bridge

An IS used to connect two LANs that use similar LAN protocols. The bridge acts as an address filter, picking up packets from one LAN that are intended for a destination on another LAN and passing those packets on. The bridge does not modify the contents of the packets and does not add anything to the packet. The bridge operates at layer 2 of the OSI model.

Router

An IS used to connect two networks that may or may not be similar. The router employs an internet protocol present in each router and each end system of the network. The router operates at layer 3 of the OSI model.

Each constituent subnetwork in an internet supports communication among the devices attached to that subnetwork; these devices are referred to as **end systems** (ESs). In addition, subnetworks are connected by devices referred to in the ISO documents as **intermediate systems** (ISs). ISs provide a communications path and perform the necessary relaying and routing functions so that data can be exchanged between devices attached to different subnetworks in the internet.

Two types of ISs of particular interest are **bridges** and **routers.** The differences between them have to do with the types of protocols used for the internetworking logic. We look at the role and functions of bridges in Chapter 10. The role and functions of routers were introduced in the context of IP earlier in this chapter. However, because of the importance of routers in the overall networking scheme, it is worth providing additional comment in this section.

Routers

Internetworking is achieved by using intermediate systems, or routers, to interconnect a number of independent networks. Essential functions that the router must perform include the following:

1. Provide a link between networks.
2. Provide for the routing and delivery of data between end systems attached to different networks.
3. Provide these functions in such a way as to not require modifications of the networking architecture of any of the attached networks.

Point 3 means that the router must accommodate a number of differences among networks, such as the following:

- **Addressing schemes:** The networks may use different schemes for assigning addresses to devices. For example, an IEEE 802 LAN uses 48-bit binary addresses for each attached device; an ATM network typically uses 15-digit decimal addresses (encoded as 4 bits per digit for a 60-bit address). Some form of global network addressing must be provided, as well as a directory service.
- **Maximum packet sizes:** Packets from one network may have to be broken into smaller pieces to be transmitted on another network, a process known as **fragmentation.** For example, Ethernet imposes a maximum packet size of 1500 bytes; a maximum packet size of 1600 bytes is common on frame relay networks. A packet that is transmitted on an frame relay network and picked up by a router for forwarding on an Ethernet LAN may have to be fragmented into two smaller ones.
- **Interfaces:** The hardware and software interfaces to various networks differ. The concept of a router must be independent of these differences.
- **Reliability:** Various network services may provide anything from a reliable end-to-end virtual circuit to an unreliable service. The operation of the routers should not depend on an assumption of network reliability.

The preceding requirements are best satisfied by an internetworking protocol, such as IP, that is implemented in all end systems and routers.

Internetworking Example

Figure 5.11 depicts a configuration that we will use to illustrate the interactions among protocols for internetworking. In this case, we focus on a server attached to a frame relay WAN and a workstation attached to an IEEE 802 LAN such as Ethernet, with a router connecting the two networks. The router provides a link between the server and the workstation that enables these end systems to ignore the details of the intervening networks. For the frame relay network, what we have referred to as the network access layer consists of a single frame relay protocol. In the case of the IEEE 802 LAN, the network access layer consists of two sublayers: the logical link control (LLC) layer and the medium access control (MAC) layer. For purposes of this discussion, we need not describe these layers in any detail, but they are explored in subsequent chapters.

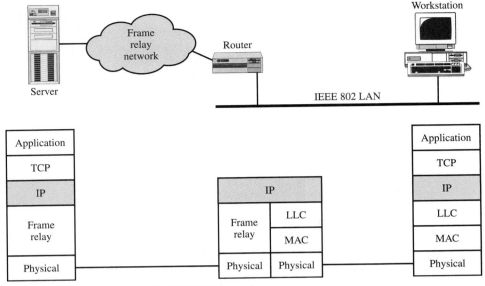

Figure 5.11   Configuration for TCP/IP Example

Figures 5.12 through 5.14 outline typical steps in the transfer of a block of data, such as a file or a Web page, from the server, through an internet, and ultimately to an application in the workstation. In this example, the message passes through just one router. Before data can be transmitted, the application and transport layers in the server establish, with the corresponding layers in the workstation, the applicable ground rules for a communication session. These include character code to be used, error-checking method, and the like. The protocol at each layer is used for this purpose and then is used in the transmission of the message.

5.4 TCP AND IP DETAILS

Having looked at the TCP/IP architecture and the basic functionality of internetworking, we can now return to TCP and IP and look at a few details.

TCP

TCP uses only a single type of segment. The header is shown in Figure 5.6a. Because one header must serve to perform all protocol mechanisms, it is rather large, with a minimum length of 20 octets. The fields are as follows:

- **Source Port (16 bits):** Source TCP user.
- **Destination Port (16 bits):** Destination TCP user.
- **Sequence Number (32 bits):** Sequence number of the first data octet in this segment except when the SYN flag is set. If SYN is set, this field contains the initial sequence number (ISN) and the first data octet in this segment has sequence number ISN +1.

1. Preparing the data. The application protocol prepares a block of data for transmission: for example, an e-mail message (SMTP), a file (FTP), or a block of user input (TELNET).

2. Using a common syntax. If necessary, the data are converted to a form expected by the destination. This may include a different character code, the use of encryption, and/or compression.

3. Segmenting the data. TCP may break the data block into a number of segments, keeping track of their sequence. Each TCP segment includes a header containing a sequence number and a frame check sequence to detect errors.

4. Duplicating segments. A copy is made of each TCP segment, in case the loss or damage of a segment necessitates retransmission. When an acknowledgment is received from the other TCP entity, a segment is erased.

5. Fragmenting the segments. IP may break a TCP segment into a number of datagrams to meet size requirements of the intervening networks. Each datagram includes a header containing a destination address, a frame check sequence, and other control information.

6. Framing. A frame relay header and trailer is added to each IP datagram. The header contains a connection identifier and the trailer contains a frame check sequence.

Peer-to-peer dialogue
Before data are sent, the sending and receiving applications agree on format and encoding and agree to exchange data.

Peer-to-peer dialogue
The two TCP entities agree to open a connection.

Peer-to-peer dialogue
Each IP datagram is forwarded through networks and routers to the destination system.

Peer-to-peer dialogue
Each frame is forwarded through the frame relay network.

7. Transmission. Each frame is transmitted over the medium as a sequence of bits.

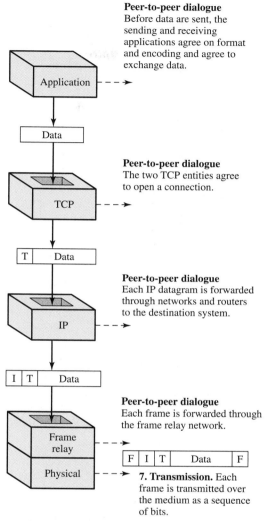

Figure 5.12 Operation of TCP/IP: Action at Sender

- **Acknowledgment Number (32 bits):** Contains the sequence number of the next data octet that the TCP entity expects to receive from the other TCP entity.
- **Header Length (4 bits):** Number of 32-bit words in the header.
- **Reserved (4 bits):** Reserved for future use.
- **Flags (6 bits):** For each flag, if set to 1, the meaning is as follows:

  CWR: congestion window reduced.

  ECE: ECN-Echo; the CWR and ECE bits, defined in RFC 3168, are used for the explicit congestion notification function, which is described in Chapter 8.

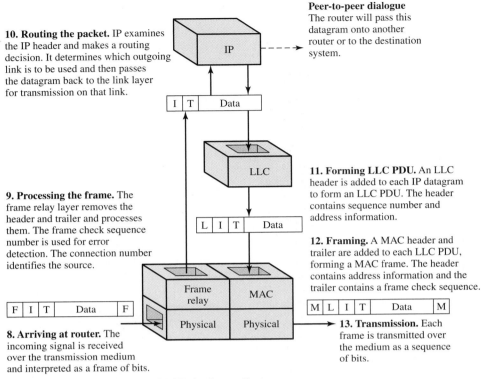

10. Routing the packet. IP examines the IP header and makes a routing decision. It determines which outgoing link is to be used and then passes the datagram back to the link layer for transmission on that link.

Peer-to-peer dialogue
The router will pass this datagram onto another router or to the destination system.

11. Forming LLC PDU. An LLC header is added to each IP datagram to form an LLC PDU. The header contains sequence number and address information.

9. Processing the frame. The frame relay layer removes the header and trailer and processes them. The frame check sequence number is used for error detection. The connection number identifies the source.

12. Framing. A MAC header and trailer are added to each LLC PDU, forming a MAC frame. The header contains address information and the trailer contains a frame check sequence.

8. Arriving at router. The incoming signal is received over the transmission medium and interpreted as a frame of bits.

13. Transmission. Each frame is transmitted over the medium as a sequence of bits.

Figure 5.13 Operation of TCP/IP: Action at Router

URG: urgent pointer field significant.

ACK: acknowledgment field significant.

PSH: push function.

RST: reset the connection.

SYN: synchronize the sequence numbers.

FIN: no more data from sender.

- **Window (16 bits):** Flow control credit allocation, in octets. Contains the number of data octets, beginning with the sequence number indicated in the acknowledgment field that the sender is willing to accept.

- **Checksum (16 bits):** The ones complement of the ones complement sum modulo of all the 16-bit words in the segment plus a pseudoheader, described subsequently.[1]

- **Urgent Pointer (16 bits):** This value, when added to the segment sequence number, contains the sequence number of the last octet in a sequence of urgent data. This allows the receiver to know how much urgent data are coming.

- **Options (Variable):** Zero or more options may be included.

---

[1]A discussion of this checksum is contained in a supporting document at this book's Web site.

20. Delivering the data. The application performs any needed transformations, including decompression and decryption, and directs the data to the appropriate file or other destination.

19. Reassembling user data. If TCP has broken the user data into multiple segments, these are reassembled and the block is passed up to the application.

18. Processing the TCP segment. TCP removes the header. It checks the frame check sequence and acknowledges if there is a match and discards for mismatch. Flow control is also performed.

17. Processing the IP datagram. IP removes the header. The frame check sequence and other control information are processed.

16. Processing the LLC PDU. The LLC layer removes the header and processes it. The sequence number is used for flow and error control.

15. Processing the frame. The MAC layer removes the header and trailer and processes them. The frame check sequence number is used for error detection.

14. Arriving at destination. The incoming signal is received over the transmission medium and interpreted as a frame of bits.

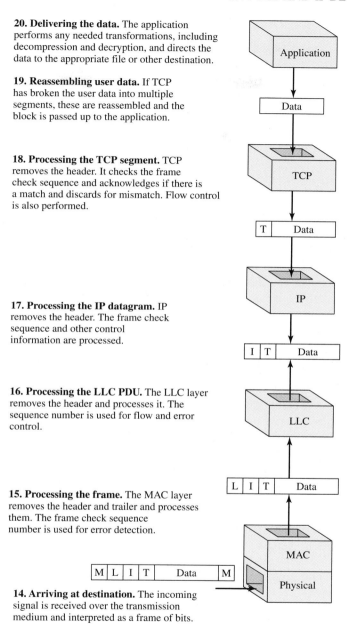

Figure 5.14   Operation of TCP/IP: Action at Receiver

The Source Port and Destination Port specify the sending and receiving users of TCP. There are a number of common users of TCP that have been assigned fixed numbers; some examples are shown in Table 5.2. These numbers should be reserved for that purpose in any implementation. Other port numbers must be arranged by agreement between the two communicating parties.

Table 5.2   Some Assigned Port Numbers

5	Remote Job Entry		79	Finger
7	Echo		80	World Wide Web (HTTP)
20	FTP (Default Data)		88	Kerberos
21	FTP (Control)		119	Network News Transfer Protocol
23	TELNET		161	SNMP Agent Port
25	SMTP		162	SNMP Manager Port
43	WhoIs		179	Border Gateway Protocol
53	Domain Name Server		194	Internet Relay Chat Protocol
69	TFTP		389	Lightweight Directory Access Protocol

The Sequence Number and Acknowledgment Number are bound to octets rather than to entire segments. For example, if a segment contains Sequence Number 1001 and includes 600 octets of data, the Sequence Number refers to the first octet in the data field; the next segment in logical order will have Sequence Number 1601. Thus, TCP is logically stream oriented: It accepts a stream of octets from the user, groups them into segments as it sees fit, and numbers each octet in the stream. These numbers are used for flow control, together with the window field. The scheme works as follows, for a TCP segment traveling from X to Y. The Acknowledgement Number is the number of the next octet expected by X; that is, X has already received data octets up to this number. The Window indicates how many additional octets X is prepared to receive from Y. By limiting the value of Window, X can limit the rate at which data arrive from Y.

The Checksum field is used to detect errors. This field is calculated based on the bits in the entire segment plus a pseudoheader prefixed to the header at the time of calculation (at both transmission and reception). The sender calculates this Checksum and adds it to the segment. The receiver performs the same calculation on the incoming segment and compares that calculation to the Checksum field in that incoming segment. If the two values don't match, then one or more bits have been accidentally altered in transit. The pseudoheader includes the following fields from the IP header: Source and Destination Address and Protocol, plus a segment length field. By including the pseudoheader, TCP protects itself from misdelivery by IP. That is, if IP delivers a segment to the wrong host, even if the segment contains no bit errors, the receiving TCP entity will detect the delivery error.

IPv4

Figure 5.7a shows the IP header format, which is a minimum of 20 octets, or 160 bits. The fields are as follows:

- **Version (4 bits):** Indicates version number, to allow evolution of the protocol; the value is 4.
- **Internet Header Length (IHL) (4 bits):** Length of header in 32-bit words. The minimum value is five, for a minimum header length of 20 octets.

- **DS/ECN (8 bits):** Prior to the introduction of differentiated services, this field was referred to as the **Type of Service** field and specified reliability, precedence, delay, and throughput parameters. This interpretation has now been superseded. The first 6 bits of the TOS field are now referred to as the DS (differentiated services) field, discussed in Chapter 8. The remaining 2 bits are reserved for an ECN (explicit congestion notification) field, discussed in Chapter 8.

- **Total Length (16 bits):** Total datagram length, including header plus data, in octets.

- **Identification (16 bits):** A sequence number that, together with the source address, destination address, and user protocol, is intended to identify a datagram uniquely. Thus, this number should be unique for the datagram's source address, destination address, and user protocol for the time during which the datagram will remain in the internet.

- **Flags (3 bits):** Only two of the bits are currently defined. The More bit is used for fragmentation and reassembly, as previously explained. The Don't Fragment bit prohibits fragmentation when set. This bit may be useful if it is known that the destination does not have the capability to reassemble fragments. However, if this bit is set, the datagram will be discarded if it exceeds the maximum size of an en route network. Therefore, if the bit is set, it may be advisable to use source routing to avoid networks with small maximum packet size.

- **Fragment Offset (13 bits):** Indicates where in the original datagram this fragment belongs, measured in 64-bit units. This implies that fragments other than the last fragment must contain a data field that is a multiple of 64 bits in length.

- **Time to Live (8 bits):** Specifies how long, in seconds, a datagram is allowed to remain in the internet. Every router that processes a datagram must decrease the TTL by at least one, so the TTL is somewhat similar to a hop count.

- **Protocol (8 bits):** Indicates the next-higher-level protocol that is to receive the data field at the destination; thus, this field identifies the type of the next header in the packet after the IP header.

- **Header Checksum (16 bits):** An error-detecting code applied to the header only. Because some header fields may change during transit (e.g., time to live, fragmentation-related fields), this is reverified and recomputed at each router. The checksum is formed by taking the ones complement of the 16-bit ones complement addition of all 16-bit words in the header. For purposes of computation, the checksum field is itself initialized to a value of zero.[2]

- **Source Address (32 bits):** Coded to allow a variable allocation of bits to specify the network and the end system attached to the specified network, as discussed subsequently.

- **Destination Address (32 bits):** Same characteristics as source address.

- **Options (variable):** Encodes the options requested by the sending user.

- **Padding (variable):** Used to ensure that the datagram header is a multiple of 32 bits in length.

---

[2]A discussion of this checksum is contained in a supporting document at this book's Web site.

Table 5.3   Some Assigned Protocol Numbers

1	Internet Control Message Protocol	17	User Datagram Protocol
2	Internet Group Management Protocol	46	Reservation Protocol (RSVP)
6	Transmission Control Protocol	89	Open Shortest Path First (OSPF)
8	Exterior Gateway Protocol		

- **Data (variable):** The data field must be an integer multiple of 8 bits in length. The maximum length of the datagram (data field plus header) is 65,535 octets.

The protocol field indicates to which IP user the data in this IP datagram are to be delivered. Although TCP is the most common user of IP, other protocols can access IP. For common protocols that use IP, specific protocol numbers have been assigned and should be used. Table 5.3 lists some of these assignments.

5.5   THE OSI PROTOCOL ARCHITECTURE

The **Open Systems Interconnection (OSI) reference model** was developed by the International Organization for Standardization (ISO) as a model for a computer protocol architecture and as a framework for developing protocol standards. As with TCP, the OSI model uses the structuring technique known as layering. The communications functions are partitioned into a hierarchical set of layers. Each layer performs a related subset of the functions required to communicate with another system. It relies on the next lower layer to perform more primitive functions and to conceal the details of those functions. It provides services to the next higher layer. Ideally, the layers should be defined so that changes in one layer do not require changes in the other layers. Thus, we have decomposed one problem into a number of more manageable subproblems.

The task of ISO was to define a set of layers and the services performed by each layer. The partitioning should group functions logically and should have enough layers to make each layer manageably small but should not have so many layers that the processing overhead imposed by the collection of layers is burdensome. The resulting reference model has seven layers, which are listed with a brief definition in Figure 5.15. The intent of the OSI model is that protocols be developed to perform the functions of each layer.

The designers of OSI assumed that this model and the protocols developed within this model would come to dominate computer communications, eventually replacing proprietary protocol implementations and rival multivendor models such as TCP/IP. This did not happen. Although many useful protocols have been developed in the context of OSI, the overall seven-layer model has not flourished. Instead, the TCP/IP architecture has come to dominate. There are a number of reasons for this outcome. Perhaps the most important is that the key TCP/IP protocols were mature and well tested at a time when similar OSI protocols were in the development stage. When businesses began to recognize the need for interoperability across networks, only TCP/IP was available and ready to go. Another reason is that

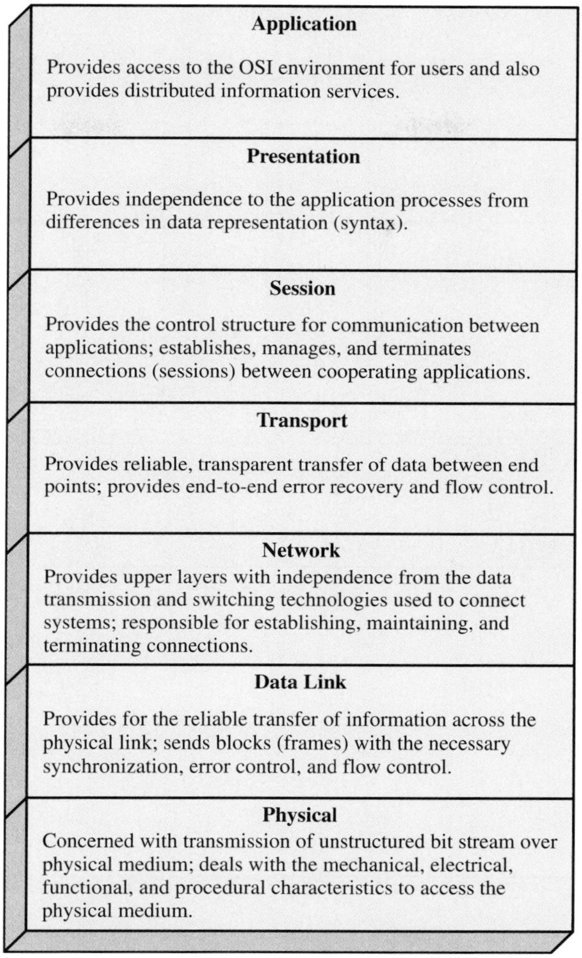

| **Application** |
| Provides access to the OSI environment for users and also provides distributed information services. |

| **Presentation** |
| Provides independence to the application processes from differences in data representation (syntax). |

| **Session** |
| Provides the control structure for communication between applications; establishes, manages, and terminates connections (sessions) between cooperating applications. |

| **Transport** |
| Provides reliable, transparent transfer of data between end points; provides end-to-end error recovery and flow control. |

| **Network** |
| Provides upper layers with independence from the data transmission and switching technologies used to connect systems; responsible for establishing, maintaining, and terminating connections. |

| **Data Link** |
| Provides for the reliable transfer of information across the physical link; sends blocks (frames) with the necessary synchronization, error control, and flow control. |

| **Physical** |
| Concerned with transmission of unstructured bit stream over physical medium; deals with the mechanical, electrical, functional, and procedural characteristics to access the physical medium. |

Figure 5.15   The OSI Layers

the OSI model is unnecessarily complex, with seven layers to accomplish what TCP/IP does with fewer layers.

Figure 5.16 illustrates the OSI architecture. Each system contains the seven layers. Communication is between applications in the two computers, labeled application X and application Y in the figure. If application X wishes to send a message to application Y, it invokes the application layer (layer 7). Layer 7 establishes a peer relationship with layer 7 of the target computer, using a layer 7 protocol (application protocol). This protocol requires services from layer 6, so the two layer 6 entities use a protocol of their own, and so on down to the physical layer, which actually transmits bits over a transmission medium.

Note that there is no direct communication between peer layers except at the physical layer. That is, above the physical layer, each protocol entity sends data down

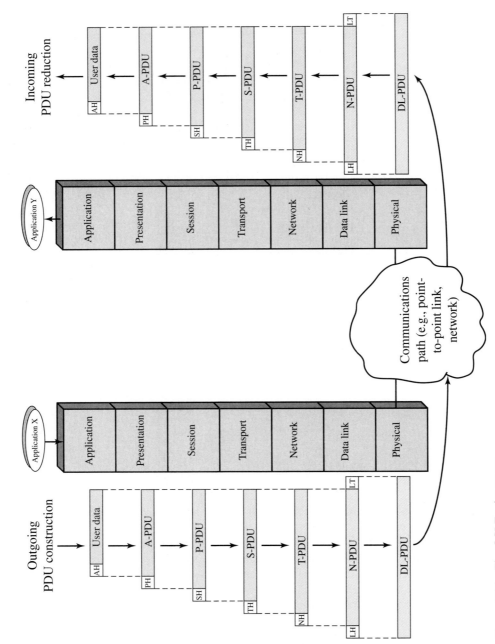

Figure 5.16   The OSI Environment

to the next lower layer to get the data across to its peer entity. Even at the physical layer, the OSI model does not stipulate that two systems be directly connected. For example, a packet-switched or circuit-switched network may be used to provide the communication link.

Figure 5.16 also highlights the use of PDUs within the OSI architecture. First, consider the most common way in which protocols are realized. When application X has a message to send to application Y, it transfers those data to an application entity in the application layer. A header is appended to the data that contains the required information for the peer layer 7 protocol (encapsulation). The original data, plus the header, are now passed as a unit to layer 6. The presentation entity treats the whole unit as data and appends its own header (a second encapsulation). This process continues down through layer 2, which generally adds both a header and a trailer (e.g., HDLC). This layer 2 unit, called a frame, is then passed by the physical layer onto the transmission medium. When the frame is received by the target system, the reverse process occurs. As the data ascend, each layer strips off the outermost header, acts on the protocol information contained therein, and passes the remainder up to the next layer.

At each stage of the process, a layer may fragment the data unit it receives from the next higher layer into several parts, to accommodate its own requirements. These data units must then be reassembled by the corresponding peer layer before being passed up.

Figure 5.17 shows roughly the correspondence in functionality of the layers of the TCP/IP and OSI architectures.

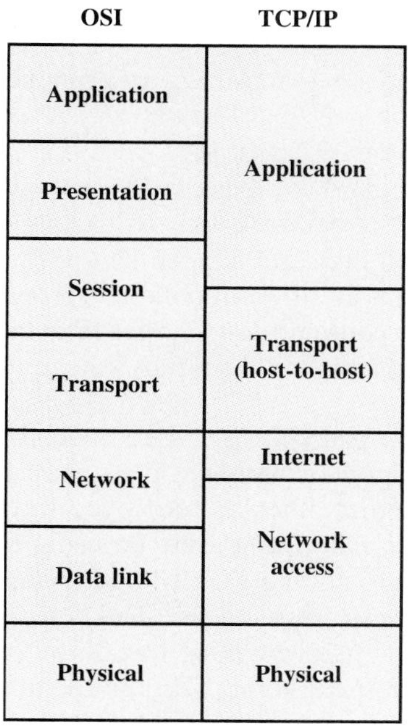

OSI	TCP/IP
Application	Application
Presentation	
Session	
Transport	Transport (host-to-host)
Network	Internet
Data link	Network access
Physical	Physical

Figure 5.17 A Comparison of the OSI and TCP/IP Protocol Architectures

APPLICATION NOTE
Practical Guide to Networking

There are a large number of protocols and models to select from when building a communication system. Trying to understand them all can be challenging to say the least. It may be helpful to know that this is actually not necessary. It turns out that a majority of networking decisions can be made for you if you understand what everyone else is doing and what works well.

For example, you may decide that the best local area network protocol is Token Ring. In certain scenarios, Token Ring outperforms many other local area network protocols. Alas, the rest of the world has decided upon Ethernet. This means that vendor support, product availability, cost and variety all favor an Ethernet infrastructure.

This is true in many other areas. Another example can be found in the Apple Computers. For many years, Apple had its own protocol stack (AppleTalk) that was deployed with its computers, and applications such as file sharing worked very well with these protocols. However, the TCP/IP protocol suite has had such tremendous success that system administrators often spent a good deal of their time trying to get the Apple computers to talk to machines running TCP/IP. This resulted in major changes to recent versions of the MacOS to not only include support for TCP/IP but also remove many of the AppleTalk protocols. Thus, when in doubt, go with TCP/IP. This isn't to say that an organization should only use TCP/IP over Ethernet. However, it should be understood that when other protocols are used or when protocols are mixed, additional levels of complexity and management are introduced.

Local area networks are usually defined by the type of layer 2 protocol that is used. Thus we usually have Ethernet, Token Ring, 802.11, or FDDI networks. Most networking equipment is built to handle a particular layer 2 protocol. The bridges that were mentioned in this chapter might be specific to Ethernet. In order to ensure that they can handle additional types of traffic, extra modules or cards would have to be purchased and installed.

Routers are independent of the layer 2 protocols with the exception that the router interface connected to a particular layer 2 network must be of the same type. So, all of the traffic leaving a Token Ring network will go through the router's Token Ring interface on it's way out. Though they are independent of the layer 2 protocol, they must be able to handle such things as different data field sizes. This can result in additional processing. Default router configurations target IP at layer 3. Basic setup can be very simple but is made more complex if there is a need to handle an additional layer 3 protocol such as IPX.

Finally, when multiple upper-layer protocols are used, specialized equipment or software may have to be installed. A good example of this can be seen where mainframes are positioned. Often IBM mainframes are deployed to handle large-scale applications for finance or sales. The mainframe may be using the SNA protocol suite for communication. A computer running TCP/IP and trying to communicate with the mainframe would not be able to do so unless it had help. This help comes in the form of a protocol translator or gateway. This translator either converts or encapsulates one transmission so that the other end can understand the data.

While there are many communication choices available, standardizing on one particular set of popular protocols can make administration easier and reduce costs and complexity. Reduced complexity can also translate into increased up time and reduced configuration time. It is very common to see companies deploying TCP/IP-based applications supported by equipment optimized for TCP/IP. The network is very typically Ethernet, especially with gigabit speeds to the desktop available. Particular vendors are chosen based on their expertise in this area. Most notable are companies like Cisco, Nortel and Extreme. As we move from one technical generation to another, many of the decisions are made for us as in the case of the AppleTalk protocols. However, these kinds of decisions will have to be made as newer protocols are developed and where equipment of the previous generation is still in use.

5.6 SUMMARY

The communication functionality required for distributed applications is quite complex. This functionality is generally implemented as a structured set of modules. The modules are arranged in a vertical, layered fashion, with each layer providing a particular portion of the needed functionality and relying on the next lower layer for more primitive functions. Such a structure is referred to as a protocol architecture.

One motivation for the use of this type of structure is that it eases the task of design and implementation. It is standard practice for any large software package to break the functions up into modules that can be designed and implemented separately. After each module is designed and implemented, it can be tested. Then the modules can be combined and tested together. This motivation has led computer vendors to develop proprietary layered protocol architectures. An example of this is the Systems Network Architecture (SNA) of IBM.

A layered architecture can also be used to construct a standardized set of communication protocols. In this case, the advantages of modular design remain. But, in addition, a layered architecture is particularly well suited to the development of standards. Standards can be developed simultaneously for protocols at each layer of the architecture. This breaks down the work to make it more manageable and speeds up the standards-development process. The TCP/IP protocol architecture is the standard architecture used for this purpose. This architecture contains five layers. Each layer provides a portion of the total communications function required for distributed applications. Standards have been developed for each layer. Development work still continues, particularly at the top (application) layer, where new distributed applications are still being defined.

Another standardized architecture is the Open Systems Interconnection (OSI) model. This seven-layer model was intended to be the international standard that would govern all protocol design. However, OSI never achieved market acceptance and has yielded to TCP/IP.

5.7 RECOMMENDED READING AND WEB SITES

[STAL04] provides a detailed description of the TCP/IP model and of the standards at each layer of the model. A very useful reference work on TCP/IP is [RODR02], which covers the spectrum of TCP/IP-related protocols in a technically concise but thorough fashion.

RODR02 Rodriguez, A., et al. *TCP/IP Tutorial and Technical Overview.* Upper Saddle River: NJ: Prentice Hall, 2002.

STAL04 Stallings, W. *Data and Computer Communications,* 7th edition. Upper Saddle River, NJ: Prentice Hall, 2004.

Recommended Web sites:

- **Networking Links:** Excellent collection of links related to TCP/IP
- **IPng:** Information about IPv6 and related topics.

5.8 KEY TERMS, REVIEW QUESTIONS, AND PROBLEMS

Key Terms

application layer	IP datagram	protocol data unit (PDU)
checksum	IPv4	router
end system	IPv6	service access point (SAP)
extranet	network layer	subnetwork
frame check sequence (FCS)	Open Systems Interconnec-	Transmission Control Protocol
header	tion (OSI)	(TCP)
intermediate system	packet	TCP segment
Internet	physical layer	transport layer
Internet Protocol (IP)	port	User Datagram Protocol
Internetworking	protocol	(UDP)
Intranet	protocol architecture	

Review Questions

5.1. What is the major function of the network access layer?

5.2. What tasks are performed by the transport layer?

5.3. What is a protocol?

5.4. What is a protocol data unit (PDU)?

5.5. What is a protocol architecture?

5.6. What is TCP/IP?

5.7. There are several protocol models that have been developed. Examples of these include SNA, Appletalk, OSI and TCP/IP as well as more general models such as three-layer models. What model is actually used for communications that travel over the Internet?

5.8. What are some advantages of layering as seen in the TCP/IP architecture?

5.9. Which version of IP is the most prevalent today?

5.10. Does all traffic running on the Internet use TCP?

5.11. Compare the address space between IPv4 and IPv6. How many bits are used in each?

5.12. Large files sent over the network must be broken up into smaller packets. How does the IP layer keep the packets from getting misplaced or collected out of order?

5.13. What is a router?

5.14. Does a router require that all attached layer 2 protocols are the same?

Problems

5.1 Using the layer models in Figure 5.18, describe the ordering and delivery of a pizza, indicating the interactions at each level.

5.2 a. The French and Chinese prime ministers need to come to an agreement by telephone, but neither speaks the other's language. Further, neither has on hand a translator that can translate to the language of the other. However, both prime ministers have English translators on their staffs. Draw a diagram similar to Figure 5.18 to depict the situation, and describe the interaction at each layer.

b. Now suppose that the Chinese prime minister's translator can translate only into Japanese and that the French prime minister has a German translator available. A translator between German and Japanese is available in Germany. Draw a new diagram that reflects this arrangement and describe the hypothetical phone conversation.

5.3 List the major disadvantages of the layered approach to protocols.

5.4 Assume you have two machines on separate networks that are communicating via e-mail. Machine A is attached to a frame relay network and Machine B is attached to an Ethernet network. For a given set of network conditions (i.e., congestion, path selection, etc.), will an email message transmitted from A to B take the same amount of time and effort as an identical message transmitted from B to A?

5.5 A TCP segment consisting of 1500 bits of data and 160 bits of header is sent to the IP layer, which appends another 160 bits of header. This is then transmitted through two networks, each of which uses a 24-bit packet header. The destination network has a maximum packet size of 800 bits. How many bits, including headers, are delivered to the network layer protocol at the destination?

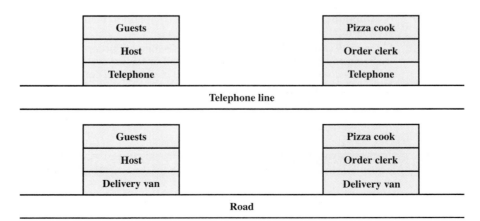

Figure 5.18 Architecture for Problem 5.1

5.6 Why is UDP needed? Why can't a user program directly access IP?

5.7 IP, TCP, and UDP all discard a packet that arrives with a checksum error and do not attempt to notify the source. Why?

5.8 Why does the TCP header have a header length field while the UDP header does not?

5.9 OSI has seven layers. Design an architecture with eight layers and make a case for it. Design one with six layers and make a case for that.

5.10 The previous version of the TFTP specification, RFC 783, included the following statement:

All packets other than those used for termination are acknowledged individually unless a timeout occurs.

The new specification revises this to say:

All packets other than duplicate ACKs and those used for termination are acknowledged unless a timeout occurs.

The change was made to fix a problem referred to as the "Sorcerer's Apprentice." Deduce and explain the problem.

5.11 What is the limiting factor in the time required to transfer a file using TFTP?

5.12 This chapter mentions the use of Frame Relay as a specific protocol or system used to connect to a wide area network. Each organization will have a certain collection of services available (like Frame Relay), but this is dependent upon provider provisioning, cost, and customer premises equipment. What are some of the services available to you in your area?

5.13 Ethereal is a free packet sniffer that allows you to capture traffic on a local area network. It can be used on a variety of operating systems and is available at www.ethereal.com. You must also install the WinPcap packet capture driver, which can be obtained from http://winpcap.mirror.ethereal.com/.

After starting a capture from Ethereal, start a TCP-based application like telnet, FTP, or http (Web browser). Can you determine the following from your capture?
a. Source and destination layer 2 addresses (MAC)
b. Source and destination layer 3 addresses (IP)
c. Source and destination layer 4 addresses (port numbers)

5.14 Packet capture software or sniffers can be powerful management and security tools. By using the filtering capability that is built in, you can trace traffic based on several different criteria and eliminate everything else. Use the filtering capability built into Ethereal to do the following:
a. Capture only traffic coming from your computer's MAC address.
b. Capture only traffic coming from your computer's IP address.
c. Capture only UDP based transmissions.

5.15 Figure 5.10 shows the protocols built into IP. Ping is a program used to test connectivity between machines and is available on all operating systems. Which of the built in protocols does Ping use and what does the payload data consist of? *Hint:* You can use Ethereal to help you determine the answers.

5.16 What other programs are built into your operating system to help you troubleshoot or provide feedback about your connectivity.

APPENDIX 5A THE TRIVIAL FILE TRANSFER PROTOCOL

This appendix provides an overview of the Internet standard Trivial File Transfer Protocol (TFTP). Our purpose is to give the reader some flavor for the elements of a protocol.

Introduction to TFTP

TFTP is far simpler than the Internet standard File Transfer Protocol (FTP). There are no provisions for access control or user identification, so TFTP is only suitable for public access file directories. Because of its simplicity, TFTP is easily and compactly implemented. For example, some diskless devices use TFTP to download their firmware at boot time.

TFTP runs on top of UDP. The TFTP entity that initiates the transfer does so by sending a read or write request in a UDP segment with a destination port of 69 to the target system. This port is recognized by the target UDP module as the identifier of the TFTP module. For the duration of the transfer, each side uses a transfer identifier (TID) as its port number.

TFTP Packets

TFTP entities exchange commands, responses, and file data in the form of packets, each of which is carried in the body of a UDP segment. TFTP supports five types of packets (Figure 5.19); the first two bytes contain an opcode that identifies the packet type:

- **RRQ:** The read request packet requests permission to transfer a file from the other system. The packet includes a file name, which is a sequence of ASCII[3] bytes terminated by a zero byte. The zero byte is the means by which the receiving TFTP entity knows when the file name is terminated. The packet also includes a mode field, which indicates whether the data file is to be interpreted as a string of ASCII bytes or as raw 8-bit bytes of data.

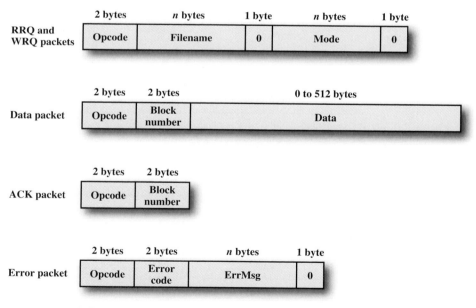

Figure 5.19   TFTP Packet Formats

---

[3]ASCII is the American Standard Code for Information Interchange, a standard of the American National Standards Institute. It designates a unique 7-bit pattern for each letter, with an eighth bit used for parity. ASCII is equivalent to the International Reference Alphabet (IRA), defined in ITU-T Recommendation T.50. A description and table of the IRA code is contained in a supporting document at this book's Web site.

- **WRQ:** The write request packet requests permission to transfer a file to the other system.
- **Data:** The block numbers on data packets begin with one and increase by one for each new block of data. This convention enables the program to use a single number to discriminate between new packets and duplicates. The data field is from zero to 512 bytes long. If it is 512 bytes long, the block is not the last block of data; if it is from zero to 511 bytes long, it signals the end of the transfer.
- **ACK:** This packet is used to acknowledge receipt of a data packet or a WRQ packet. An ACK of a data packet contains the block number of the data packet being acknowledged. An ACK of a WRQ contains a block number of zero.
- **Error:** An error packet can be the acknowledgment of any other type of packet. The error code is an integer indicating the nature of the error. The error message is intended for human consumption, and should be in ASCII. Like all other strings, it is terminated with a zero byte.

All packets other than duplicate ACKs (explained subsequently) and those used for termination are to be acknowledged. Any packet can be acknowledged by an error packet. If there are no errors, then the following conventions apply. A WRQ or a data packet is acknowledged by an ACK packet. When a RRQ is sent, the other side responds (in the absence of error) by beginning to transfer the file; thus, the first data block serves as an acknowledgment of the RRQ packet. Unless a file transfer is complete, each ACK packet from one side is followed by a data packet from the other, so that the data packet functions as an acknowledgment. An error packet can be acknowledged by any other kind of packet, depending on the circumstance.

Figure 5.20 shows a TFTP data packet in context. When such a packet is handed down to UDP, UDP adds a header to form a UDP segment. This is then passed to IP, which adds an IP header to form an IP datagram.

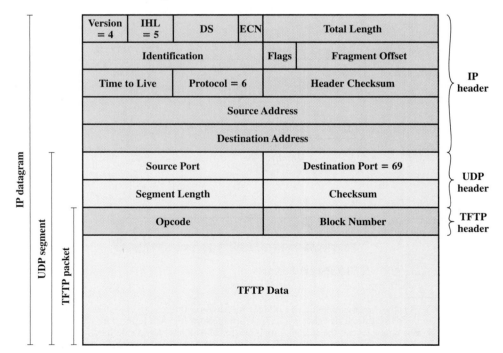

Figure 5.20 A TFTP Packet in Context

Overview of a Transfer

The example illustrated in Figure 5.21 is of a simple file transfer operation from A to B. No errors occur and the details of the option specification are not explored.

The operation begins when the TFTP module in system A sends a write request (WRQ) to the TFTP module in system B. The WRQ packet is carried as the body of a UDP segment. The write request includes the name of the file (in this case, XXX) and a mode of octet, or raw data. In the UDP header, the destination port number is 69, which alerts the receiving UDP entity that this message is intended for the TFTP application. The source port number is a TID selected by A, in this case 1511. System B is prepared to accept the file and so responds with an ACK with a block number of 0. In the UDP header, the destination port is 1511, which enables the UDP entity at A to route the incoming packet to the TFTP module, which can match this TID with the TID in the WRQ. The source port is a TID selected by B for this file transfer, in this case 1660.

Following this initial exchange, the file transfer proceeds. The transfer consists of one or more data packets from A, each of which is acknowledged by B. The final data packet contains less than 512 bytes of data, which signals the end of the transfer.

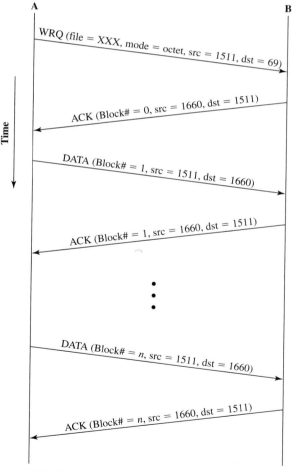

Figure 5.21   Example TFTP Operation

Errors and Delays

If TFTP operates over a network or internet (as opposed to a direct data link), it is possible for packets to be lost. Because TFTP operates over UDP, which does not provide a reliable delivery service, there needs to be some mechanism in TFTP to deal with lost packets. TFTP uses the common technique of a timeout mechanism. Suppose that A sends a packet to B that requires an acknowledgment (i.e., any packet other than duplicate ACKs and those used for termination). When A has transmitted the packet, it starts a timer. If the timer expires before the acknowledgment is received from B, A retransmits the same packet. If in fact the original packet was lost, then the retransmission will be the first copy of this packet received by B. If the original packet was not lost but the acknowledgment from B was lost, then B will receive two copies of the same packet from A and simply acknowledges both copies. Because of the use of block numbers, this causes no confusion. The only exception to this rule is for duplicate ACK packets. The second ACK is ignored.

Syntax, Semantics, and Timing

In Section 5.1, it was mentioned that the key features of a protocol can be classified as syntax, semantics, and timing. These categories are easily seen in TFTP. The formats of the various TFTP packets form the **syntax** of the protocol. The **semantics** of the protocol are shown in the definitions of each of the packet types and the error codes. Finally, the sequence in which packets are exchanged, the use of block numbers, and the use of timers are all aspects of the **timing** of TFTP.

Case Study II: Florida Department of Management Services

By the early 1990s the Florida Department of Management Service (DMS) had built up a large information systems network that served state government agencies in 10 regional sites and connected these to the data center in Tallahassee. The network was based on the use of the proprietary Systems Network Architecture (SNA) from IBM and a mainframe at the data center that housed most of the applications.

Although relatively happy with the SNA operation, DMS saw a need to expand applications and services by providing TCP/IP capability and Internet access. The goal was met in a remarkably short time. Over the course of 30 months, DMS built a statewide TCP/IP network, began offering Internet services to local and state agencies, and created a suite of Internet applications that will ultimately move personnel, accounting, and billing systems online [JOHN96]. To complete the success story, DMS managed to accomplish all that while saving the state of Florida more than $4 million. The breakdown is shown in Table II.1.

The aim of this upgrade was to exploit the Internet. Internet connectivity, together with key Internet applications such as the Web, could make it easier for agencies across the state to communicate with each other, with suppliers, and with users, thereby improving employee productivity.

The IP Infrastructure

The first step was to build an IP infrastructure. The then-current configuration, based on SNA, made heavy use of telephone-company (telco) supplied equipment and services. DMS considered the possibility of outsourcing the IP capability but rejected this for the following reasons:

1. None of the telcos had a router-based service at that time, which meant DMS would have to wait for the carrier to build its own network.

Table II.1   DMS Cost Breakdown

What Was Spent		What Was Not Spent	
Personnel	$450,000	Terminal upgrades	$150,000
Application development	$300,000	Mainframe application development	$1,000,000
Software (including Web software, databases, and development tools)	$850,000	Mainframe hardware upgrades	$6,000,000
Hardware (servers, routers, telco services)	$1,525,000	Mainframe software upgrades	$600,000
Maintenance	$450,000		
TOTAL	$3,575,000	**TOTAL**	$7,750,000

2. DMS wanted to select the routers. The telcos wouldn't purchase the products picked by DMS because they did not fit in with their plans. Finally, a regulatory prohibition against colocation meant that user-owned equipment couldn't be installed at telco central offices.

3. The existing SNA network could easily be adapted to TCP/IP.

The existing configuration had been put in place to allow some 6000 users throughout the state to access mainframe application in Tallahassee. SNA network control processors (NCP) in 10 cities were linked via T-1 (1.544 Mbps) and T-3 (45 Mbps) lines to a communications controller on a token ring LAN in the DMS data center. The communications controller handled SNA traffic into and out of the mainframe. The token ring also supported SNA terminals, personal computers, and other equipment.

To transform the SNA backbone into a router network, all DMS had to do, in essence, was deploy routers at each site, connect the boxes, and link them to a central-site router at the data center (Figure II.1). Put that

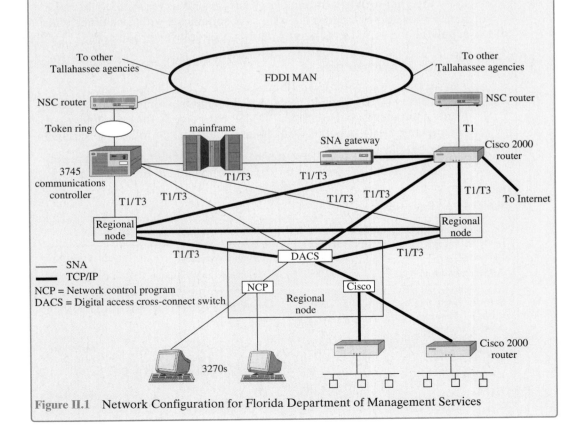

Figure II.1   Network Configuration for Florida Department of Management Services

way, it sounds easy, and in fact the installation and startup went remarkably smoothly.

DMS chose the Cisco 7000 as its backbone router, with one deployed at each of the 10 regional sites. The Cisco gear came with strong network management and could be booted and configured centrally. At each site the Cisco router and the NCP are hooked to a digital access cross-connect switch (DACS). This switch segregates SNA from TCP/IP traffic and directs it accordingly. The DACS now provides the T-1/T-3 link to the SNA communications controller at the data center. In addition, each DACS is connected to the DACS at each of the nine other regional centers to create a mesh for IP traffic. Finally, there is a link from each DACS to a router at the data center.

At the regional center, SNA traffic is handled as before from IBM 3270 terminals. This traffic only goes from the regional center to the mainframe at the data center. For connection to the IP backbone and the Internet applications, each regional center is equipped with Cisco 2000 routers to connect workstations, personal computers, and servers via LANs.

At the data center, there is a high-capacity Cisco 2000 router that has a direct leased link to each of the 10 regional centers. This router is also connected to the Internet and provides the entry point for the entire far-flung DMS network into the Internet. Finally, there are several Network Systems Corp. routers that connect the data center to the Tallahassee MAN, which is an FDDI ring owned and operated by Sprint Corporation. The MAN gives agencies located throughout Tallahassee access to the data center and to each other.

The Applications

Once the IP infrastructure was in place, DMS began to add applications. The first, and still the most popular, application was a client/server employment system. The original system stored information about some 125,000 state employees on the mainframe. About 1200 users throughout the state accessed it over the SNA network. Although the system was secure and reliable, services were slow and the interface clumsy. The applications around the database had been developed and installed in the early 1980s and were batch-mode with fixed-transaction access. Users couldn't configure their own request and searches on the fly. If they wanted anything out of the ordinary, they had to contact mainframe programmers, who might take days or weeks to develop what was needed. The new application makes use of a UNIX server at the data center that is hooked to the mainframe and downloads the employee database at least weekly to store in its own server database. Users at workstations at the various agencies and centers access the server over the IP network running an application called Copesview.

Another client/server application that generates a lot of traffic over the IP network is Spursview, a purchasing application. Like Copesview, it was adapted from a mainframe application—SPURS (Statewide Purchasing

System). SPURS, which was used by roughly 4000 employees, stored information on the mainframe about products purchased by the site, including vendor, model number, and price. Here again, users were limited as to the type of searches they could perform. With Spursview, users gained a variety of new capabilities, such as wild-card searches on any parameters (data of purchase, vendor, type of product, etc.). They also can create graphs and bar charts and import data directly into PC-based spreadsheets.

Intranet and Internet Applications

The data center maintains a link to the Internet through which all traffic between the data center's IP network and the Internet pass. This link is equipped with a firewall that prevents unauthorized access.

With the Internet link and the IP network up, DMS was in a position to offer Internet access to state employees as well as to set up Web services for both intranet and Internet access. Like the servers in the client/server configuration, the Web server has a link to the mainframe and is able to construct databases accessible from Web browsers.

One of the most popular Web-based applications is a job-posting service that lets users search for vacancies within the state system by location, salary ranges, and type of work. The state has about 8000 job vacancies on any given day. Applicants can fill out an online job application and store it for multiple submissions. This application averages about 100,000 hits per week.

Another well-used site eliminates the need for state employees to process information regarding government contracts and suppliers. Previously, when a vendor won a bid, it submitted pricing and product data on floppy discs. The DMS employed several people full time just to review that information, format it, and enter it onto the mainframe. That information is now available on the Web. Users can access this information on the DMS Web server and on Web servers at vendor sites. For example, users can search for contracted suppliers that offer computers priced below $2000. The search generates a list of names, each of which is a Web link. Because the data resides on the vendors' Web servers, it is up to the suppliers, not the DMS, to make sure all data are accurate and up to date.

DMS is also working on an online purchasing system running over the Web. Users not only would be able to view vendor information but also could order products online. This application will take a lot of coordination, because it involves the purchasing department, comptroller's office, and accounting. It also involves authenticating users to ensure they are authorized to make purchases.

DMS has not neglected those who pay state employees' salaries: the citizens of Florida. The Web service available to the public is called the Florida Community Network (FCN), and it has been a success story and a model for other states [REGE96]. The FCN is currently averaging a million hits per month. Online access to information can in many cases eliminate two or three layers of bureaucracy and provide a self-service connection to the government. For example, one of the projects under development is automatic fishing and gaming licensing. Mrs. X in Palm Beach wants to go fishing but knows she needs a license. She logs on to the FCN site, chooses the search option, and types "fishing." Within seconds, a form appears that lets Mrs. X apply and pay for a license from the comfort of her home. She fills out the form, submits it, and moments later a license is e-mailed to her. No clerks, no lines, no trips to the Office of the Tax Collector or a sporting goods store.

Yet another popular Web service is the Statewide Telephone Directory, which includes listings for state and local government, universities, community colleges, and school boards.

Most recently, DMS has worked with the state Board of Regents to set up a distance learning service, which make use of the DMS networking facilities [MADA98].

The DMS Web site is undergoing constant evolution and refinement. It is located at http://fcn.state.fl.us/dms.

Discussion Points

1. What security mechanisms are needed to protect the DMS systems from both state employees and users accessing over the Internet?

2. Visit the DMS Web site and list the major services found there. Discuss the relative merits of each.

3. Suggest improvements to existing services and suggest new services that should be added.

CHAPTER 6

INTERNET-BASED APPLICATIONS

CHAPTER OBJECTIVES

After reading this chapter, you should be able to

- Discuss the applications for electronic mail.
- Explain that basic functionality of SMTP.
- Explain the need for MIME as an enhancement to ordinary e-mail.
- Describe the key elements of MIME.
- Explain the role of HTTP in the operation of the Web.
- Describe the functions of proxies, gateways, and tunnels in HTTP.
- Explain Web caching.
- Discuss the role of SIP.
- Explain the relationship between SIP and SDP.

As we discussed in Chapters 2 and 3, distributed information processing is essential in virtually all businesses. Much of the distributed processing is tailored to specific types of data and is supported by proprietary vendor software. However, there is a growing use of distributed applications for both intracompany and intercompany exchange that are general purpose in nature and that are defined by international standards or by industry de facto standards. These applications can have a direct impact on the efficiency and competitiveness of a business. In this chapter, we look at three of the most important and widespread of these distributed applications: electronic mail, Web access, and multimedia support including voice over IP. In each case, international standards have been developed. As these standards become more widely implemented by computer vendors and software houses, these applications become increasingly important and useful in the business environment.

6.1 ELECTRONIC MAIL AND SMTP

Electronic mail is a facility that allows users at workstations and terminals to compose and exchange messages. The messages need never exist on paper unless the user (sender or recipient) desires a paper copy of the message. Some electronic mail systems only serve users on a single computer; others provide service across a network of computers. Table 6.1 lists some of the common features provided by an electronic mail facility.

In this section, we look at the basic functioning of electronic mail, its use in a distributed environment, and finally the international standards for electronic mail.

Public versus Private Electronic Mail

A public electronic mail service is one provided by a third-party electronic mail vendor. The service is usually available over one or more public networks, especially the dial-up public telephone network. Users gain access to the facility from a terminal or personal computer by connecting to the facility across the public network. Messages can be sent to any other registered subscriber. Thus, a corporation could use a public mail system for internal electronic mail communication and could also exchange messages with customers and suppliers who are also registered with this facility. Examples of public mail systems are MCI Mail, available over the MCI public telecommunications network, and the mail systems provided by online services, such as AOL.

A private electronic mail facility is one that is integrated with the user's computer equipment. This may be in the form of software from an independent software house that runs on the equipment of one or more computer vendors. More commonly, the electronic mail facility is provided by the computer vendor, often as part of an integrated office system such as IBM's PROFS. As their name implies, private electronic mail facilities are owned and operated by a company for its own internal messaging requirements; for external messaging, a connection to other systems is required.

In general, the services offered on private and public electronic mail systems are quite similar. One factor in deciding between the two is cost. For private systems, there is the initial cost of the software and hardware. If the facility is implemented on computers already used for other purposes, the only hardware costs will be additional terminals and their connections for users who need the terminal only for electronic mail. For public systems, the cost is number and length of messages transmitted and stored in mailboxes on the system. Other factors to consider: Private mail systems are able to offer better integration with customer-owned computer systems, whereas public mail systems are able to offer a wider range of delivery options (e.g., links to telex and courier services) and a broader community of users.

Internet electronic mail does not fit into either of the categories just discussed. Strictly speaking, Internet mail is not a complete electronic mail facility but merely the transfer mechanism for exchanging mail among subscribing systems. This distinction is explained in the next subsection.

Single–Computer versus Multiple–Computer Electronic Mail

The simplest form of electronic mail is the single-system facility (Figure 6.1a). This facility allows all the users of a shared computer system to exchange messages.

Table 6.1   Typical Electronic Mail Facilities

Message Preparation

Word Processing

Facilities for the creation and editing of messages. Usually these need not be as powerful as a full word processor, since electronic mail documents tend to be simple. However, most electronic mail packages allow "offline" access to word processors: The user creates a message using the computer's word processor, stores the message as a file, and then uses the file as input to the message preparation function of the word processor.

Annotation

Messages often require some sort of short reply. A simple technique is to allow the recipient to attach annotation to an incoming message and send it back to the originator or on to a third party.

Message Sending

User Directory

Used by the system. May also be accessible to users to be able to look up addresses.

Timed Delivery

Allows the sender to specify that a message be delivered before, at, or after a specified date/time. A message is considered delivered when it is placed in the recipient's mailbox.

Multiple Addressing

Copies of a message are sent to multiple addressees. The recipients are designated by listing each in the header of the message or by the use of a distribution list. The latter is a file containing a list of users. Distribution lists can be created by the user and by central administrative functions.

Message Priority

A message may be labeled at a given priority level. Higher-priority messages will be delivered more rapidly, if that is possible. Also, the recipient will be notified or receive some indication of the arrival of high-priority messages.

Status Information

A user may request notification of delivery or of actual retrieval by the recipient. A user may also be able to query the current status of a message (e.g., queued for transmission, transmitted but receipt confirmation not yet received).

Interface to Other Facilities

These would include other electronic systems, such as telex, and physical distribution facilities, such as couriers and the public mail service (e.g., U.S. postal service).

Message Receiving

Mailbox Scanning

Allows the user to scan the current contents of mailbox. Each message may be indicated by subject, author, date, priority, and so on.

Message Selection

The user may select individual messages from the mailbox for display, printing, storing in a separate file, or deletion.

Message Notification

Many systems notify an online user of the arrival of a new message and indicate to a user during log on that there are messages in his or her mailbox.

Message Reply

A user may reply immediately to a selected message, avoiding the necessity of keying in the recipient's name and address.

Message Rerouting

A user who has moved, either temporarily or permanently, may reroute incoming messages. An enhancement is to allow the user to specify different forwarding addresses for different categories of messages.

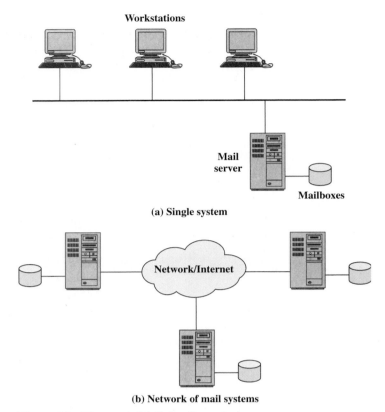

Figure 6.1 Electronic Mail Configurations

Each user is registered on the system and has a unique identifier, usually the person's last name. Associated with each user is a mailbox. The electronic mail facility is an application program available to any user logged onto the system. A user may invoke the electronic mail facility, prepare a message, and "send" it to any other user on the system. The act of sending simply involves putting the message in the recipient's mailbox. The mailbox is actually an entity maintained by the file-management system and is in the nature of a file directory. One mailbox is associated with each user. Any "incoming" mail is simply stored as a file under that user's mailbox directory. The user may later go and fetch that file to read the message. The user reads messages by invoking the mail facility and "reading" rather than "sending." In most systems, when the user logs on, he or she is informed if there is any new mail in that user's mailbox.

Many public mail systems are single-computer systems, with a single host system maintaining all the mailboxes of all users. In the private context, a single central host may support single-computer mail. More typically, in a LAN configuration, the central mail system is a dedicated mail server or a mail facility on a multipurpose server. In this latter case, the software for preparing and processing mail may be on each individual's workstation, while the mailboxes themselves are on the server.

With a single-system electronic mail facility, messages can only be exchanged among users of that particular system. Clearly, this is too limited. In a distributed environment, we would like to be able to exchange messages with users attached to other systems. Thus, we would like to treat electronic mail as a distributed application.

For a distributed mail system, a number of mail handlers (e.g., mail servers) connect over a network facility (e.g., public or private WAN or the Internet) and exchange mail (Figure 6.1b). With this configuration, it is useful to group electronic mail functions into two distinct categories: user agent and message transfer agent.

The **user agent** functions are visible to the electronic mail user. These include facilities for preparing and submitting messages for routing to the destination(s), as well as utility functions to assist the user in filing, retrieving, replying, and forwarding. The **message transfer agent** accepts messages from the user agent for transmission across a network or internetwork. The message transfer agent is concerned with the protocol operation needed to transmit and deliver messages.

The user does not directly interact with the message transfer agent. If the user designates a local recipient for a message, the user agent stores the message in the local recipient's mailbox. If a remote recipient is designated, the user agent passes the message to the message transfer agent for transmission to a remote message transfer agent and ultimately to a remote mailbox.

Many vendors offer a network version of their basic electronic mail facility. However, this will only allow the user to send mail to users on systems of the same vendor. Several forms of interconnection are needed. It is most desirable to provide an interconnection between a private electronic mail network and a public electronic mail service. Also desirable is the ability to interconnect private systems based on computers from different vendors. To provide these interconnections, a set of standards is needed, a topic to which we now turn.

Simple Mail Transfer Protocol

SMTP is the standard protocol for transferring mail between hosts in the TCP/IP protocol suite; it is defined in RFC 821.

Although messages transferred by SMTP usually follow the format defined in RFC 822, described later, SMTP is not concerned with the format or content of messages themselves, with two exceptions. This concept is often expressed by saying that SMTP uses information written on the envelope of the mail (message header), but does not look at the contents (message body) of the envelope. The two exceptions are as follows:

1. SMTP standardizes the message character set as 7-bit ASCII.
2. SMTP adds log information to the start of the delivered message that indicates the path the message took.

Basic Electronic Mail Operation Figure 6.2 illustrates the overall flow of mail in a typical distributed system. Although much of this activity is outside the scope of SMTP, the figure illustrates the context within which SMTP typically operates.

To begin, mail is created by a user agent program in response to user input. Each created message consists of a header that includes the recipient's e-mail address and other information, and a body containing the message to be sent. These messages are then queued in some fashion and provided as input to an SMTP Sender program, which is typically an always-present server program on the host.

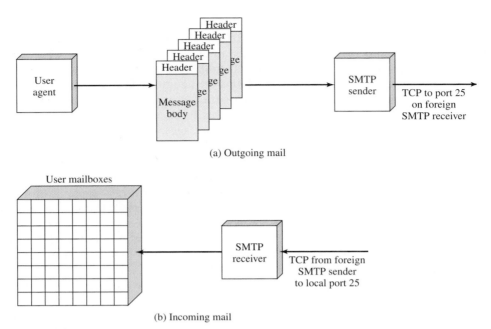

(a) Outgoing mail

(b) Incoming mail

Figure 6.2   SMTP Mail Flow

Although the structure of the outgoing mail queue will differ depending on the host's operating system, each queued message conceptually has two parts:

1. The message text, consisting of
   - The RFC 822 header: This constitutes the message envelope and includes an indication of the intended recipient or recipients.
   - The body of the message, composed by the user.
2. A list of mail destinations.

The list of mail destinations for the message is derived by the user agent from the 822 message header. In some cases, the destination or destinations are literally specified in the message header. In other cases, the user agent may need to expand mailing list names, remove duplicates, and replace mnemonic names with actual mailbox names. If any blind carbon copies (BCCs) are indicated, the user agent needs to prepare messages that conform to this requirement. The basic idea is that the multiple formats and styles preferred by humans in the user interface are replaced by a standardized list suitable for the SMTP send program.

The **SMTP sender** takes messages from the outgoing mail queue and transmits them to the proper destination host via SMTP transactions over one or more TCP connections to port 25 on the target hosts. A host may have multiple SMTP senders active simultaneously if it has a large volume of outgoing mail and should also have the capability of creating SMTP receivers on demand so that mail from one host cannot delay mail from another.

Whenever the SMTP sender completes delivery of a particular message to one or more users on a specific host, it deletes the corresponding destinations from that message's destination list. When all destinations for a particular message are processed, the message is deleted from the queue. In processing a queue, the SMTP sender can perform a variety of optimizations. If a particular message is be sent to multiple users on a single host, the message text needs to be sent only once. If multiple messages are ready to send to the same host, the SMTP sender can open a TCP connection, transfer the multiple messages, and then close the connection, rather than opening and closing a connection for each message.

The SMTP sender must deal with a variety of errors. The destination host may be unreachable, out of operation, or the TCP connection may fail while mail is being transferred. The sender can requeue the mail for later delivery but give up after some period rather then keep the message in the queue indefinitely. A common error is a faulty destination address, which can occur due to user input error or because the intended destination user has a new address on a different host. The SMTP sender must either redirect the message if possible or return an error notification to the message's originator.

The **SMTP protocol** is used to transfer a message from the SMTP sender to the SMTP receiver over a TCP connection. SMTP attempts to provide reliable operation but does not guarantee to recover from lost messages. SMTP does not return an end-to-end acknowledgment to a message's originator to indicate that a message is successfully delivered to the message's recipient. Error indications are not guaranteed to be returned either. However, the SMTP-based mail system is generally considered reliable.

The **SMTP receiver** accepts each arriving message and either places it in the appropriate user mailbox or copies it to the local outgoing mail queue if forwarding is required. The SMTP receiver must be able to verify local mail destinations and deal with errors, including transmission errors and lack of disc file capacity.

The SMTP sender is responsible for a message up to the point where the SMTP receiver indicates that the transfer is complete; however, this simply means that the message has arrived at the SMTP receiver, not that the message has been delivered to and retrieved by the intended final recipient. The SMTP receiver's error handling responsibilities are generally limited to giving up on TCP connections that fail or are inactive for very long periods. Thus, the sender has most of the error recovery responsibility. Errors during completion indication may cause duplicate, but not lost, messages.

In most cases, messages go directly from the mail originator's machine to the destination machine over a single TCP connection. However, mail will occasionally go through intermediate machines via an SMTP forwarding capability, in which case the message must traverse a series of TCP connections between source and destination. One way for this to happen is for the sender to specify a route to the destination in the form of a sequence of servers. A more common event is forwarding required because a user has moved.

It is important to note that the SMTP protocol is limited to the conversation that takes place between the SMTP send and the SMTP receiver. SMTP's main function is the transfer of messages, although there are some ancillary functions dealing with mail destination verification and handling. The rest of the mail-handling apparatus depicted in Figure 6.2 is beyond the scope of SMTP and may differ from one system to another.

We now turn to a discussion of the main elements of SMTP.

SMTP Overview The operation of SMTP consists of a series of commands and responses exchanged between the SMTP sender and receiver. The initiative is with the SMTP sender, which establishes the TCP connection. Once the connection is established, the SMTP sender sends commands over the connection to the receiver. Each command generates exactly one reply from the SMTP receiver.

Basic SMTP operation occurs in three phases: connection setup, exchange of one or more command-response pairs, and connection termination. We examine each phase in turn.

Connection Setup An SMTP sender will attempt to set up a TCP connection with a target host when it has one or more mail messages to deliver to that host. The sequence is quite simple:

1. The sender opens a TCP connection with the receiver.
2. Once the connection is established, the receiver identifies itself with "220 Service Ready".
3. The sender identifies itself with the HELO command.
4. The receiver accepts the sender's identification with "250 OK".

If the mail service on the destination is unavailable, the destination host returns a "421 Service Not Available" reply in step 2 and the process is terminated.

Mail Transfer Once a connection has been established, the SMTP sender may send one or more messages to the SMTP receiver. There are three logical phases to the transfer of a message:

1. A MAIL command identifies the originator of the message.
2. One or more RCPT commands identify the recipients for this message.
3. A DATA command transfers the message text.

The **MAIL command** gives the reverse path, which can be used to report errors. If the receiver is prepared to accept messages from this originator, it returns a "250 OK" reply. Otherwise the receiver returns a reply indicating failure to execute the command or an error in the command.

The **RCPT command** identifies an individual recipient of the mail data; multiple recipients are specified by multiple use of this command. A separate reply is returned for each RCPT command, with one of the following possibilities:

1. The receiver accepts the destination with a 250 reply; this indicates that the designated mailbox is on the receiver's system.
2. The destination will require forwarding and the receiver will forward.
3. The destination requires forwarding but the receiver will not forward; the sender must resend to the forwarding address.
4. A mailbox does not exist for this recipient at this host.
5. The destination is rejected due to some other failure to execute or an error in the command.

The advantage of using a separate RCPT phase is that the sender will not send the message until it is assured that the receiver is prepared to receive the message for at least one recipient, thereby avoiding the overhead of sending an entire message only to learn that the destination is unknown. Once the SMTP receiver has agreed to receive the mail message for at least one recipient, the SMTP sender uses the DATA command to initiate the transfer of the message. If the SMTP receiver is still prepared to receive the message, it returns a Start message; otherwise the receiver returns a reply indicating failure to execute the command or an error in the command. If the Start reply is returned, the SMTP sender proceeds to send the message over the TCP connection as a sequence of ASCII lines. The end of the message is indicated by a line containing only a period. The SMTP receiver responds with an OK reply if the message is accepted or with the appropriate error code.

An example, taken from RFC 821, illustrates the process:

```
S: MAIL FROM:<Smith@Alpha.ARPA>
R: 250 OK

S: RCPT TO:<Jones@Beta.ARPA>
R: 250 OK

S: RCPT TO:<Green@Beta.ARPA>
R: 550 No such user here

S: RCPT TO:<Brown@Beta.ARPA>
R: 250 OK

S: DATA
R: 354 Start mail input; end with <CRLF>.<CRLF>
S: Blah blah blah...
S: ...etc. etc. etc.
S: <CRLF>.<CRLF>
R: 250 OK
```

The SMTP sender is transmitting mail that originates with the user Smith@Alpha.ARPA. The message is addressed to three users on machine Beta.ARPA, namely, Jones, Green, and Brown. The SMTP receiver indicates that it has mailboxes for Jones and Brown but does not have information on Green. Because at least one of the intended recipients has been verified, the sender proceeds to send the text message.

Connection Closing The SMTP sender closes the connection in two steps. First, the sender sends a QUIT command and waits for a reply. The second step is to initiate a TCP close operation for the TCP connection. The receiver initiates its TCP close after sending its reply to the QUIT command.

RFC 822 RFC 822 defines a format for text messages that are sent using electronic mail. The SMTP standard adopts RFC 822 as the format for use in constructing messages for transmission via SMTP. In the RFC 822 context, messages are viewed as having an envelope and contents. The envelope contains whatever information is needed to accomplish transmission and delivery. The contents compose the object to be delivered to the recipient. The RFC 822 standard applies only to the contents. However, the content standard includes a set of header fields that may be used by the mail system to create the envelope, and the standard is intended to facilitate the acquisition of such information by programs.

An RFC 822 message consists of a sequence of lines of text and uses a general "memo" framework. That is, a message consists of some number of header lines, which follow a rigid format, followed by a body portion consisting of arbitrary text.

A header line usually consists of a keyword, followed by a colon, followed by the keyword's arguments; the format allows a long line to be broken up into several lines. The most frequently used keywords are From, To, Subject, and Date. Here is an example message:

Date: Thur, 16 Jan 1997 10:37:17 (EST)
From: "William Stallings" <ws@host.com>
Subject: The Syntax in RFC 822
To: Smith@Other-host.com
Cc: Jones@Yet-Another-Host.com

Hello. This section begins the actual message body, which is delimited from the message heading by a blank line.

Another field that is commonly found in RFC 822 headers is Message-ID. This field contains a unique identifier associated with this message.

Multipurpose Internet Mail Extensions (MIME)

MIME is an extension to the RFC 822 framework that is intended to address some of the problems and limitations of the use of SMTP and RFC 822 for electronic mail. [RODR02] lists the following limitations of the SMTP/822 scheme:

1. SMTP cannot transmit executable files or other binary objects. A number of schemes are in use for converting binary files into a text form that can be used by SMTP mail systems, including the popular UNIX uuencode/uudecode scheme. However, none of these is a standard or even a de facto standard.

2. SMTP cannot transmit text data that include national language characters because these are represented by 8-bit codes with values of 128 decimal or higher, and SMTP is limited to 7-bit ASCII.

3. SMTP servers may reject mail message over a certain size.

4. SMTP gateways that translate between ASCII and the character code EBCDIC do not use a consistent set of mappings, resulting in translation problems.

5. SMTP gateways to X.400 electronic mail networks cannot handle nontextual data included in X.400 messages.

6. Some SMTP implementations do not adhere completely to the SMTP standards defined in RFC 821. Common problems include the following:
   - Deletion, addition, or reordering of carriage return and linefeed
   - Truncating or wrapping lines longer than 76 characters
   - Removal of trailing white space (tab and space characters)
   - Padding of lines in a message to the same length
   - Conversion of tab characters into multiple space characters

These limitations make it difficult to use encryption with electron mail and to use SMTP to carry multimedia objects and electronic data interchange (EDI) messages. MIME is intended to resolve these problems in a manner that is compatible with existing RFC 822 implementations.

Overview The MIME specification includes the following elements:

1. Five new message header fields are defined, which may be included in an RFC 822 header. These fields provide information about the body of the message.
2. A number of content formats are defined, thus standardizing representations that support multimedia electronic mail.
3. Transfer encodings are defined that enable the conversion of any content format into a form that is protected from alteration by the mail system.

In this subsection, we introduce the five message header fields. The next two subsections deal with content formats and transfer encodings.

The five header fields defined in MIME are as follows:

- **MIME-Version:** Must have the parameter value 1.0. This field indicates that the message conforms to the RFCs.
- **Content-Type:** Describes the data contained in the body with sufficient detail that the receiving user agent can pick an appropriate agent or mechanism to represent the data to the user or otherwise deal with the data in an appropriate manner.
- **Content-Transfer-Encoding:** Indicates the type of transformation that has been used to represent the body of the message in a way that is acceptable for mail transport.
- **Content-ID:** Used to uniquely identify MIME entities in multiple contexts.
- **Content-Description:** A plain text description of the object with the body; this is useful when the object is not readable (e.g., audio data).

Any or all of these fields may appear in a normal RFC 822 header. A compliant implementation must support the MIME-Version, Content-Type, and Content-Transfer-Encoding fields; the Content-ID and Content-Description fields are optional and may be ignored by the recipient implementation.

MIME Content Types The bulk of the MIME specification is concerned with the definition of a variety of content types. This reflects the need to provide standardized ways of dealing with a wide variety of information representations in a multimedia environment.

Table 6.2   MIME Content Types

Type	Subtype	Description
Text	Plain	Unformatted text; may be ASCII or ISO 8859.
Multipart	Mixed	The different parts are independent but are to be transmitted together. They should be presented to the receiver in the order that they appear in the mail message.
	Parallel	Differs from Mixed only in that no order is defined for delivering the parts to the receiver.
	Alternative	The different parts are alternative versions of the same information. They are ordered in increasing faithfulness to the original and the recipient's mail system should display the "best" version to the user.
	Digest	Similar to Mixed, but the default type/subtype of each part is message/rfc822.
Message	rfc822	The body is itself an encapsulated message that conforms to RFC 822.
	Partial	Used to allow fragmentation of large mail items, in a way that is transparent to the recipient.
	External-body	Contains a pointer to an object that exists elsewhere.
Image	jpeg	The image is in JPEG format, JFIF encoding.
	gif	The image is in GIF format.
Video	mpeg	MPEG format.
Audio	Basic	Single-channel 8-bit ISDN mu-law encoding at a sample rate of 8 kHz.
Application	PostScript	Adobe Postscript.
	octet-stream	General binary data consisting of 8-bit bytes.

Table 6.2 lists the MIME content types. There are seven different major types of content and a total of 14 subtypes. In general, a content type declares the general type of data, and the subtype specifies a particular format for that type of data.

For the **text type** of body, no special software is required to get the full meaning of the text, aside from support of the indicated character set. The only defined subtype is plain text, which is simply a string of ASCII characters.

The **multipart type** indicates that the body contains multiple, independent parts. The Content-Type header field includes a parameter, called boundary, that defines the delimiter between body parts. This boundary should not appear in any parts of the message. Each boundary starts on a new line and consists of two hyphens followed by the boundary value. The final boundary, which indicates the end of the last part, also has a suffix of two hyphens. Within each part, there may be an optional ordinary MIME header.

Here is a simple example of a multipart message, containing two parts both consisting of simple text:

```
From: John Smith <js@company.com>
To: Ned Jones <ned@soft.com>
Subject: Sample message
MIME-Version: 1.0
Content-type: multipart/mixed; boundary="simple boundary"

This is the preamble.  It is to be ignored, though it is a handy place
for mail composers to include an explanatory note to non-MIME
conformant readers.
—simple boundary
This is implicitly typed plain ASCII text. It does NOT end with a
linebreak.

—simple boundary
Content-type: text/plain; charset=us-ascii
This is explicitly typed plain ASCII text. It DOES end with a line-
break.

—simple boundary—
This is the epilogue. It is also to be ignored.
```

There are four subtypes of the multipart type, all of which have the same overall syntax. The **multipart/mixed subtype** is used when there are multiple independent body parts that need to be bundled in a particular order. For the **multipart/parallel subtype,** the order of the parts is not significant. If the recipient's system is appropriate, the multiple parts can be presented in parallel. For example, a picture or text part could be accompanied by a voice commentary that is played while the picture or text is displayed.

For the **multipart/alternative subtype,** the various parts are different representations of the same information. The following is an example:

```
From: John Smith <js@company.com>
To: Ned Jones <ned@soft.com>
Subject: Formatted text mail
MIME-Version: 1.0
Content-Type: multipart/alternative; boundary=boundary42

—boundary42

Content-Type: text/plain; charset=us-ascii

 ...plain text version of message goes here....
—boundary42
Content-Type: text/richtext

 .... RFC 1341 richtext version of same message goes here ...
—boundary42—
```

In this subtype, the body parts are ordered in terms of increasing preference. For this example, if the recipient system is capable of displaying the message in the richtext format, this is done; otherwise, the plain text format is used.

The **multipart/digest subtype** is used when each of the body parts is interpreted as an RFC 822 message with headers. This subtype enables the construction of a message whose parts are individual messages. For example, the moderator of a group might collect e-mail messages from participants, bundle these messages, and send them out in one encapsulating MIME message.

The **message type** provides a number of important capabilities in MIME. The **message/rfc822 subtype** indicates that the body is an entire message, including header and body. Despite the name of this subtype, the encapsulated message may be not only a simple RFC 822 message, but also any MIME message.

The **message/partial subtype** enables fragmentation of a large message into a number of parts, which must be reassembled at the destination. For this subtype, three parameters are specified in the Content-Type: Message/Partial field:

- **id:** A value that is common to each fragment of the same message, so that the fragments can be identified at the recipient for reassembly, but unique across different messages.

- **number:** A sequence number that indicates the position of this fragment in the original message. The first fragment is numbered 1, the second 2, and so on.

- **total:** The total number of parts. The last fragment is identified by having the same value for the *number* and *total* parameters.

The **message/external-body subtype** indicates that the actual data to be conveyed in this message are not contained in the body. Instead, the body contains the information needed to access the data. As with the other message types, the message/external-body subtype has an outer header and an encapsulated message with its own header. The only necessary field in the outer header is the Content-type field, which identifies this as a message/external-body subtype. The inner header is the message header for the encapsulated message.

The Content-type field in the outer header must include an access-type parameter, which has one of the following values:

- **FTP:** The message body is accessible as a file using the File Transfer Protocol (FTP). For this access type, the following additional parameters are mandatory: name, the name of the file; and site, the domain name of the host where the file resides. Optional parameters are as follows: directory, the directory in which the file is located; and mode, which indicates how FTP should retrieve the file (e.g., ASCII, image). Before the file transfer can take place, the user will need to provide a used id and password. These are not transmitted with the message for security reasons.

- **TFTP:** The message body is accessible as a file using the Trivial File Transfer Protocol (TFTP). The same parameters as for FTP are used, and the user id and password must also be supplied.

- **Anon-FTP:** Identical to FTP, except that the user is not asked to supply a user id and password. The parameter name supplies the name of the file.

- **local-file:** The message body is accessible as a file on the recipient's machine.
- **AFS:** The message body is accessible as a file via the global AFS (Andrew File System). The parameter name supplies the name of the file.
- **mail-server:** The message body is accessible by sending an e-mail message to a mail server. A *server* parameter must be included that gives the e-mail address of the server. The body of the original message, known as the phantom body, should contain the exact command to be sent to the mail server.

The **image type** indicates that the body contains a displayable image. The subtype, jpeg or gif, specifies the image format. In the future, more subtypes will be added to this list.

The **video type** indicates that the body contains a time-varying picture image, possibly with color and coordinated sound. The only subtype so far specified is mpeg.

The **audio type** indicates that the body contains audio data. The only subtype, basic, conforms to an ISDN service known as "64-kbps, 8-kHz Structured, Usable for Speech Information," with a digitized speech algorithm referred to as μ-*law* PCM (pulse code modulation). This general type is the typical way of transmitting speech signals over a digital network. The term μ-*law* refers to the specific encoding technique; it is the standard technique used in North America and Japan. A competing system, known as A-law, is standard in Europe.

The **application type** refers to other kinds of data, typically either uninterpreted binary data or information to be processed by a mail-based application. The **application/octet-stream subtype** indicates general binary data in a sequence of octets. RFC 1521 recommends that the receiving implementation should offer to put the data in a file or use the data as input to a program.

The **application/Postscript subtype** indicates the use of Adobe Postscript.

6.2 WEB ACCESS AND HTTP

The Hypertext Transfer Protocol (HTTP) is the foundation protocol of the World Wide Web (WWW) and can be used in any client/server application involving hypertext. The name is somewhat misleading in that HTTP is not a protocol for transferring hypertext; rather it is a protocol for transmitting information with the efficiency necessary for making hypertext jumps. The data transferred by the protocol can be plaintext, hypertext, audio, images, or any Internet-accessible information.

We begin with an overview of HTTP concepts and operation and then look at some of the details, basing our discussion on the most recent version to be put on the Internet standards track, HTTP 1.1. A number of important terms defined in the HTTP specification are summarized in Table 6.3; these will be introduced as the discussion proceeds.

HTTP Overview

HTTP is a transaction-oriented client/server protocol. The most typical use of HTTP is between a Web browser and a Web server. To provide reliability, HTTP makes use of TCP. Nevertheless, HTTP is a **stateless protocol:** Each transaction

Table 6.3   Key Terms Related to HTTP

Cache

A program's local store of response messages and the subsystem that controls its message storage, retrieval, and deletion. A cache stores cacheable responses in order to reduce the response time and network bandwidth consumption on future, equivalent requests. Any client or server may include a cache, though a cache cannot be used by a server while it is acting as a tunnel.

Client

An application program that establishes connections for the purpose of sending requests.

Connection

A transport layer virtual circuit established between two application programs for the purposes of communication.

Entity

A particular representation or rendition of a data resource, or reply from a service resource, that may be enclosed within a request or response message. An entity consists of entity headers and an entity body.

Gateway

A server that acts as an intermediary for some other server. Unlike a proxy, a gateway receives requests as if it were the original server for the requested resource; the requesting client may not be aware that it is communicating with a gateway. Gateways are often used as server-side portals through network firewalls and as protocol translators for access to resources stored on non-HTTP systems.

Message

The basic unit of HTTP communication, consisting of a structured sequence of octets transmitted via the connection.

Origin Server

The server on which a given resource resides or is to be created.

Proxy

An intermediary program that acts as both a server and a client for the purpose of making requests on behalf of other clients. Requests are serviced internally or by passing them, with possible translation, on to other servers. A proxy must interpret and, if necessary, rewrite a request message before forwarding it. Proxies are often used as client-side portals through network firewalls and as helper applications for handling requests via protocols not implemented by the user agent.

Resource

A network data object or service that can be identified by a URI.

Server

An application program that accepts connections in order to service requests by sending back responses.

Tunnel

An intermediary program that is acting as a blind relay between two connections. Once active, a tunnel is not considered a party to the HTTP communication, though the tunnel may have been initiated by an HTTP request. A tunnel ceases to exist when both ends of the relayed connections are closed. Tunnels are used when a portal is necessary and the intermediary cannot, or should not, interpret the relayed communication.

User Agent

The client that initiates a request. These are often browsers, editors, spiders, or other end-user tools.

is treated independently. Accordingly, a typical implementation will create a new TCP connection between client and server for each transaction and then terminate the connection as soon as the transaction completes, although the specification does not dictate this one-to-one relationship between transaction and connection lifetimes.

The stateless nature of HTTP is well suited to its typical application. A normal session of a user with a Web browser involves retrieving a sequence of Web pages and documents. The sequence is, ideally, performed rapidly, and the locations of the various pages and documents may be a number of widely distributed servers.

Another important feature of HTTP is that it is flexible in the formats that it can handle. When a client issues a request to a server, it may include a prioritized list of formats that it can handle, and the server replies with the appropriate format. For example, a lynx browser cannot handle images, so a Web server need not transmit any images on Web pages. This arrangement prevents the transmission of unnecessary information and provides the basis for extending the set of formats with new standardized and proprietary specifications.

Figure 6.3 illustrates three examples of HTTP operation. The simplest case is one in which a user agent establishes a direct connection with an origin server. The **user agent** is the client that initiates the request, such as a Web browser being run on behalf of an end user. The **origin server** is the server on which a resource of interest resides; an example is a Web server at which a desired Web home page resides. For this case, the client opens a TCP connection that is end-to-end between the client and the server. The client then issues an HTTP request. The request consists of a specific command, referred to as a method, an address [referred to as a Uniform Resource Locator[1] (URL)], and a MIME-like message containing request parameters, information about the client, and perhaps some additional content information.

When the server receives the request, it attempts to perform the requested action and then returns an HTTP response. The response includes status information, a success/error code, and a MIME-like message containing information about the server, information about the response itself, and possible body content. The TCP connection is then closed.

The middle part of Figure 6.3 shows a case in which there is not an end-to-end TCP connection between the user agent and the origin server. Instead, there are one or more intermediate systems with TCP connections between logically adjacent systems. Each intermediate system acts as a relay, so that a request initiated by the client is relayed through the intermediate systems to the server, and the response from the server is relayed back to the client.

Three forms of intermediate system are defined in the HTTP specification: proxy, gateway, and tunnel, all of which are illustrated in Figure 6.4.

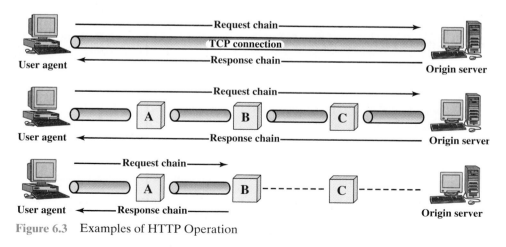

Figure 6.3   Examples of HTTP Operation

---

[1]A discussion of URLs is contained in a supporting document at this book's Web site.

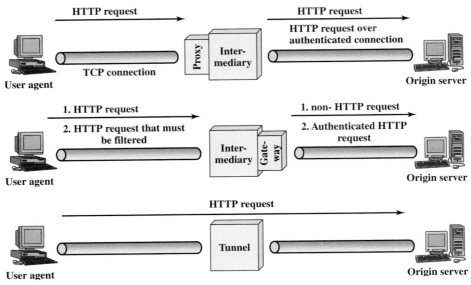

Figure 6.4 Intermediate HTTP Systems

Proxy A proxy acts on behalf of other clients and presents requests from other clients to a server. The proxy acts as a server in interacting with a client and as a client in interacting with a server. There are two scenarios that call for the use of a proxy:

- **Security intermediary:** The client and server may be separated by a security intermediary such as a firewall, with the proxy on the client side of the firewall. Typically, the client is part of a network secured by a firewall and the server is external to the secured network. In this case, the server must authenticate itself to the firewall to set up a connection with the proxy. The proxy accepts responses after they have passed through the firewall.

- **Different versions of HTTP:** If the client and server are running different versions of HTTP, then the proxy can implement both versions and perform the required mapping.

In summary, a proxy is a forwarding agent, receiving a request for a URL object, modifying the request, and forwarding the request toward the server identified in the URL.

Gateway A gateway is a server that appears to the client as if it were an origin server. It acts on behalf of other servers that may not be able to communicate directly with a client. There are two scenarios in which gateways can be used.

- **Security intermediary:** The client and server may be separated by a security intermediary such as a firewall, with the gateway on the server side of the firewall. Typically, the server is connected to a network protected by a firewall, with the client external to the network. In this case the client must authenticate itself to the gateway, which can then pass the request on to the server.

- **Non-HTTP server:** Web browsers have built into them the capability to contact servers for protocols other than HTTP, such as FTP and Gopher servers. This capability can also be provided by a gateway. The client makes an HTTP request to a gateway server. The gateway server then contacts the relevant FTP or Gopher server to obtain the desired result. This result is then converted into a form suitable for HTTP and transmitted back to the client.

Tunnel Unlike the proxy and the gateway, the tunnel performs no operations on HTTP requests and responses. Instead, a tunnel is simply a relay point between two TCP connections, and the HTTP messages are passed unchanged as if there were a single HTTP connection between user agent and origin server. Tunnels are used when there must be an intermediary system between client and server but it is not necessary for that system to understand the contents of messages. An example is a firewall in which a client or server external to a protected network can establish an authenticated connection and then maintain that connection for purposes of HTTP transactions.

Cache Returning to Figure 6.3, the lowest portion of the figure shows an example of a cache. A cache is a facility that may store previous requests and responses for handling new requests. If a new request arrives that is the same as a stored request, then the cache can supply the stored response rather than accessing the resource indicated in the URL. The cache can operate on a client or server or on an intermediate system other than a tunnel. In the figure, intermediary B has cached a request/response transaction, so that a corresponding new request from the client need not travel the entire chain to the origin server, but is handled by B.

Not all transactions can be cached, and a client or server can dictate that a certain transaction may be cached only for a given time limit.

Messages

The best way to describe the functionality of HTTP is to describe the individual elements of the HTTP message. HTTP consists of two types of messages: requests from clients to servers, and responses from servers to clients. The general structure of such messages is shown in Figure 6.5.

The Simple-Request and Simple-Response messages were defined in HTTP/0.9. The request is a simple GET command with the requested URL; the response is simply a block containing the information identified in the URL. In HTTP/1.1, the use of these simple forms is discouraged because it prevents the client from using content negotiation and the server from identifying the media type of the returned entity.

With full requests and responses, the following fields are used:

- **Request-Line:** Identifies the message type and the requested resource
- **Response-Line:** Provides status information about this response
- **General-Header:** Contains fields that are applicable to both request and response messages but that do not apply to the entity being transferred
- **Request-Header:** Contains information about the request and the client

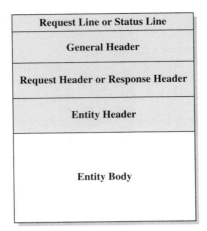

Figure 6.5 General Structure of HTTP Messages

- **Response-Header:** Contains information about the response
- **Entity-Header:** Contains information about the resource identified by the request and information about the entity body
- **Entity-Body:** The body of the message

All of the HTTP headers consist of a sequence of fields, following the same generic format as RFC 822 (described in Section 6.1). Each field begins on a new line and consists of the field name followed by a colon and the field value.

6.3 INTERNET TELEPHONY AND SIP

The Session Initiation Protocol (SIP), defined in RFC 3261, is an application-level control protocol for setting up, modifying, and terminating real-time sessions between participants over an IP data network. The key driving force behind SIP is to enable Internet telephony, also referred to as voice over IP (VoIP). SIP can support any type of single media or multimedia session, including teleconferencing.

SIP is just one component in the set of protocols and services needed to support multimedia exchanges over the Internet. SIP is the signaling protocol that enables one party to place a call to another party and to negotiate the parameters of a multimedia session. The actual audio, video, or other multimedia content is exchanged between session participants using an appropriate transport protocol. In many cases, the transport protocol to use is the Real-Time Transport Protocol (RTP). Directory access and lookup protocols are also needed.

The key driving force behind SIP is to enable Internet telephony, also referred to as voice over IP (VoIP). There is wide industry acceptance that SIP will be the standard IP signaling mechanism for voice and multimedia calling services. Further, as older PBXs and network switches are phased out, industry is moving toward a voice networking model that is SIP signaled, IP based, and packet switched, not only in the wide area but also on the customer premises [BORT02, BORT03].

SIP supports five facets of establishing and terminating multimedia communications:

- **User location:** Users can move to other locations and access their telephony or other application features from remote locations.
- **User availability:** Determination of the willingness of the called party to engage in communications.
- **User capabilities:** Determination of the media and media parameters to be used.
- **Session setup:** Setup up point-to-point and multiparty calls, with agreed session parameters.
- **Session management:** Including transfer and termination of sessions, modifying session parameters, and invoking services.

SIP employs design elements developed for earlier protocols. SIP is based on an HTTP-like request/response transaction model. Each transaction consists of a client request that invokes a particular method, or function, on the server and at least one response. SIP uses most of the header fields, encoding rules, and status codes of HTTP. This provides a readable text-based format for displaying information. SIP incorporates the use of a Session Description Protocol (SDP), which defines session content using a set of types similar to those used in MIME.

SIP Components and Protocols

An SIP network can be viewed of consisting of components defined on two dimensions: client/server and individual network elements. RFC 3261 defines **client** and **server** as follows:

- **Client:** A client is any network element that sends SIP requests and receives SIP responses. Clients may or may not interact directly with a human user. User agent clients and proxies are clients.
- **Server:** A server is a network element that receives requests in order to service them and sends back responses to those requests. Examples of servers are proxies, user agent servers, redirect servers, and registrars.

The individual elements of a standard SIP network are as follows:

- **User Agent:** Resides in every SIP end station. It acts in two roles:
  - **—User Agent Client (UAC):** Issues SIP requests.
  - **—User Agent Server (UAS):** Receives SIP requests and generates a response that accepts, rejects, or redirects the request.
- **Redirect Server:** Used during session initiation to determine the address of the called device. The redirect server returns this information to the calling device, directing the UAC to contact an alternate URI.
- **Proxy Server:** An intermediary entity that acts as both a server and a client for the purpose of making requests on behalf of other clients. A proxy server primarily plays the role of routing, which means its job is to ensure that a request is sent to another entity closer to the targeted user. Proxies are also useful for

enforcing policy (for example, making sure a user is allowed to make a call). A proxy interprets, and, if necessary, rewrites specific parts of a request message before forwarding it.

- **Registrar:** A server that accepts REGISTER requests and places the information it receives (the SIP address and associated IP address of the registering device) in those requests into the location service for the domain it handles.
- **Location Service:** A location service is used by a SIP redirect or proxy server to obtain information about a callee's possible location(s). For this purpose, the location service maintains a database of SIP-address/IP-address mappings.

The various servers are defined in RFC 3261 as logical devices. They may be implemented as separate servers configured on the Internet or they may be combined into a single application that resides in a physical server.

Figure 6.6 shows how some of the SIP components relate to one another and the protocols that are employed. A user agent acting as a client (in this case UAC alice) uses SIP to set up a session with a user agent that will act as a server (in this case UAS bob). The session initiation dialogue uses SIP and involves one or more proxy servers to forward requests and responses between the two user agents. The user agents also make use of the Session Description Protocol (SDP), which is used to describe the media session.

The proxy servers may also act as redirect servers as needed. If redirection is done, a proxy server will need to consult the location service database, which may be

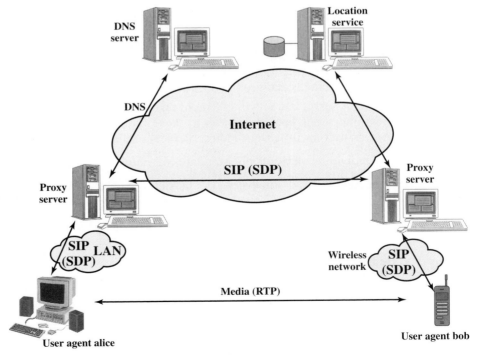

Figure 6.6 SIP Components and Protocols

colocated with a proxy server or not. The communication between the proxy server and the location service is beyond the scope of the SIP standard. The Domain Name Service (DNS), described in Chapter 7, is also an important part of SIP operation. Typically, a UAC will make a request using the domain name of the UAS, rather than an IP address. A proxy server will need to consult a DNS server to find a proxy server for the target domain.

SIP typically runs on top of UDP for performance reasons and provides its own reliability mechanisms but may also use TCP. If a secure, encrypted transport mechanism is desired, SIP messages may alternatively be carried over the Transport Layer Security (TLS) protocol, described in Chapter 17.

Associated with SIP is the Session Description Protocol (SDP), defined in RFC 2327. SIP is used to invite one or more participants to a session, while the SDP-encoded body of the SIP message contains information about what media encodings (e.g., voice, video) the parties can and will use. Once this information is exchanged and acknowledged, all participants are aware of the participants' IP addresses, available transmission capacity, and media type. Then data transmission begins, using an appropriate transport protocol. Typically, the Real-Time Transport Protocol (RTP) is used. RTP is a transport protocol that provides direct support for real-time traffic, unlike TCP. Throughout the session, participants can make changes to session parameters, such as new media types or new parties to the session, using SIP messages.

SIP Uniform Resource Identifier

A resource within a SIP network is identified by a Uniform Resource Identifier (URI).[2] Examples of communications resources include the following:

- A user of an online service
- An appearance on a multiline phone
- A mailbox on a messaging system
- A telephone number at a gateway service
- A group (such as "sales" or "helpdesk") in an organization

SIP URIs have a format based on e-mail address formats, namely user@domain. There are two common schemes. An ordinary SIP URI is of the form

sip:bob@biloxi.com

The URI may also include a password, port number, and related parameters. If secure transmission is required, "sip:" is replaced by "sips:". In the latter case, SIP messages are transported over TLS.

Examples of Operation

The SIP specification is quite complex; the main document, RFC 3261, is 269 pages long. To give some feel for its operation, we present a few examples.

---

[2]A URI is a generic identifier used to name any resource on the Internet. The URL, used for Web addresses is a type of URI. See RFC 2396 or the supporting document at this book's Web site for more detail.

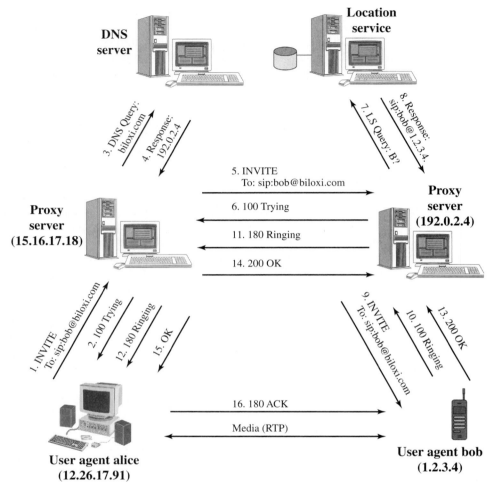

Figure 6.7 SIP Successful Call Setup

Figure 6.7 shows a successful attempt by user Alice to establish a session with user Bob, whose URI is bob@biloxi.com.[3] Alice's UAC is configured to communicate with a proxy server (the outbound server) in its domain and begins by sending an INVITE message to the proxy server that indicates its desire to invite Bob's UAS into a session (1); the server acknowledges the request (2). Although Bob's UAS is identified by its URI, the outbound proxy server needs to take into account the possibility that Bob is not currently available or that Bob has moved. Accordingly, the outbound proxy server should forward the INVITE request to the proxy server that is responsible for the domain biloxi.com. The outbound proxy thus consults a local DNS server to obtain the IP address of the biloxi.com proxy

---

[3]Figures 6.7 through 6.9 are adapted from ones developed by Professor H. Charles Baker of Southern Methodist University.

server (3), by asking for the resource record that contains information on the proxy server for biloxi.com.

The DNS server responds (4) with the IP address of the biloxi.com proxy server (the inbound server). Alices's proxy server can now forward the INVITE message to the inbound proxy server (5), which acknowledges the message (6). The inbound proxy server now consults a location server to determine the location of Bob (7), and the location server responds with Bob's location, indicating that Bob is signed in, and therefore available for SIP messages (8). The proxy server can now send the INVITE message on to Bob (9). A ringing response is sent from Bob back to A (10, 11, 12) while the UAS at Bob is alerting the local media application (e.g., telephony). When the media application accepts the call, Bob's UAS sends back an OK response to Alice (13, 14, 15).

Finally, Alice's UAC sends an acknowledgement message to Bob's UAS to confirm the reception of the final response (16). In this example, the ACK is sent directly from Alice to Bob, bypassing the two proxies. This occurs because the endpoints have learned each other's address from the INVITE/200 (OK) exchange, which was not known when the initial INVITE was sent. The media session has now begun, and Alice and Bob can exchange data over one or more RTP connections.

The next example (Figure 6.8) makes use of two message types that are not yet part of the SIP standard but that are documented in RFC 2848 and are likely to be incorporated in a later revision of SIP. These message types support telephony applications. Suppose that in the preceding example, Alice was informed that Bob was not available. Alice's UAC can then issue a SUBSCRIBE message (1), indicating that it wants to be informed when Bob is available. This request is forwarded through the two proxies in our example to a PINT (PSTN-Internet Networking) server (2, 3). A PINT server acts as a gateway between an IP network from which comes a request to place a telephone call and a telephone network that executes the call by connecting to the destination telephone. In this example, we assume that the PINT server logic is colocated with the location service. It could also be the case that Bob is attached to the Internet rather than a PSTN, in which case, the equivalent of PINT logic is needed to handle SUBSCRIBE requests. In this example, we assume that latter and assume that the PINT functionality is implemented in the location service. In any case, the location service authorizes subscription by returning an OK message (4), which is passed back to Alice (5, 6). The location service then immediately sends a NOTIFY message with Bob's current status of not signed in (7, 8, 9), which Alice's UAC acknowledges (10, 11, 12).

Figure 6.9 continues the example of Figure 6.8. Bob signs on by sending a REGISTER message to the proxy in its domain (1). The proxy updates the database at the location service to reflect registration (2). The update is confirmed to the proxy (3), which confirms the registration to Bob (4). The PINT functionality learns of Bob's new status from the location server (here we assume that they are colocated) and sends a NOTIFY message containing the new status of Bob (5), which is forwarded to Alice (6, 7). Alice's UAC acknowledges receipt of the notification (8, 9, 10).

SIP Messages

As was mentioned, SIP is a text-based protocol with a syntax similar to that of HTTP. There are two different types of SIP messages, requests and responses. The format difference between the two types of messages is seen in the first line. The first line of a

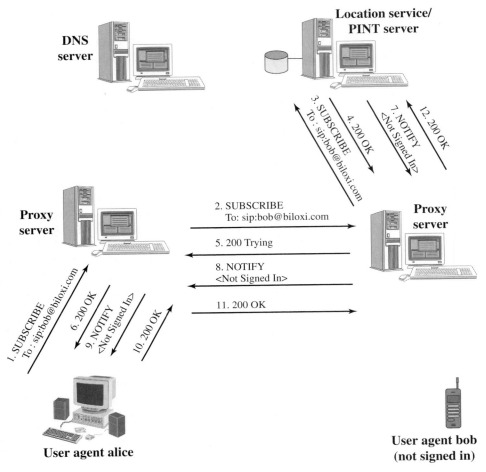

Figure 6.8   SIP Presence Example

request has a **method,** defining the nature of the request, and a Request-URI, indicating where the request should be sent. The first line of a response has a **response code.** All messages include a header, consisting of a number of lines, each line beginning with a header label. A message can also contain a body such as an SDP media description.

For **SIP requests**, RFC 3261 defines the following methods:

- **Register:** Used by a user agent to notify a SIP configuration of its current IP address and the URLs for which it would like to receive calls
- **Invite:** Used to establish a media session between user agents
- **Ack:** Confirms reliable message exchanges
- **Cancel:** Terminates a pending request but does not undo a completed call
- **Bye:** Terminates a session between two users in a conference
- **Options:** Solicits information about the capabilities of the callee but does not set up a call.

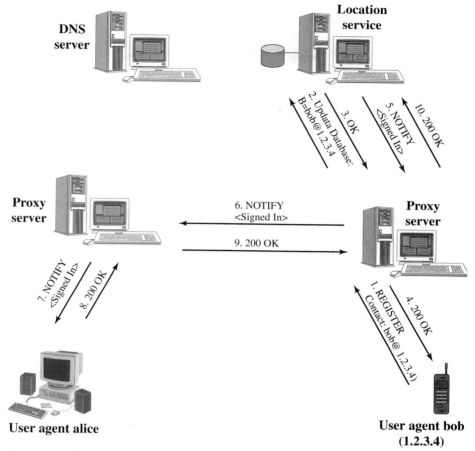

Figure 6.9 SIP Registration and Notification Example

For example, the header of message (1) in Figure 6.7 might look like this:

> **INVITE** sip:bob@biloxi.com SIP/2.0
> **Via:** SIP/2.0/UDP 12.26.17.91:5060
> **Max-Forwards:** 70
> **To:** Bob <sip:bob@biloxi.com>
> **From:** Alice <sip:alice@atlanta.com>;tag=1928301774
> **Call-ID:** a84b4c76e66710@12.26.17.91
> **CSeq:** 314159 INVITE
> **Contact:** <sip:alice@atlanta.com>
> **Content-Type:** application/sdp
> **Content-Length:** 142

The boldface type used for header labels is not typical but is used here for clarity. The first line contains the method name (**INVITE**), a SIP URI, and the version number of SIP that is used. The lines that follow are a list of header fields. This example contains the minimum required set.

The **Via** headers show the path the request has taken in the SIP configuration (source and intervening proxies) and are used to route responses back along the same path. As the INVITE message leaves, there is only the header inserted by Alice. The line contains the IP address (12.26.17.91), port number (5060), and transport protocol (UDP) that Alice wants Bob to use in his response.

Max-Forwards serves to limit the number of hops a request can make on the way to its destination. It consists of an integer that is decremented by one by each proxy that forwards the request. If the Max-Forwards value reaches 0 before the request reaches its destination, it will be rejected with a 483 (Too Many Hops) error response.

To contains a display name (Bob) and a SIP or SIPS URI (sip:bob@biloxi.com) toward which the request was originally directed. **From** also contains a display name (Alice) and a SIP or SIPS URI (sip:alice@atlanta.com) that indicate the originator of the request. This header field also has a tag parameter containing a random string (1928301774) that was added to the URI by the UAC. It is used to identify the session.

Call-ID contains a globally unique identifier for this call, generated by the combination of a random string and the host name or IP address. The combination of the To tag, From tag, and Call-ID completely defines a peer-to-peer SIP relationship between Alice and Bob and is referred to as a dialog.

CSeq or Command Sequence contains an integer and a method name. The CSeq number is initialized at the start of a call (314159 in this example), incremented for each new request within a dialog, and is a traditional sequence number. The CSeq is used to distinguish a retransmission from a new request.

The **Contact** header contains a SIP URI for direct communication between UAs. While the Via header field tells other elements where to send the response, the Contact header field tells other elements where to send future requests for this dialog.

The **Content-Type** indicates the type of the message body. **Content-Length** gives the length in octets of the message body.

The **SIP response** types defined in RFC 3261 are in the following categories:

- **Provisional (1xx):** Request received and being processed.
- **Success (2xx):** The action was successfully received, understood, and accepted.
- **Redirection (3xx):** Further action needs to be taken in order to complete the request.
- **Client Error (4xx):** The request contains bad syntax or cannot be fulfilled at this server.
- **Server Error (5xx):** The server failed to fulfill an apparently valid request.
- **Global Failure (6xx):** The request cannot be fulfilled at any server.

For example, the header of message (13) in Figure 6.7 might look like this:

```
SIP/2.0 200 OK
Via: SIP/2.0/UDP server10.biloxi.com
Via: SIP/2.0/UDP bigbox3.site3.atlanta.com
Via: SIP/2.0/UDP 12.26.17.91:5060
To: Bob <sip:bob@biloxi.com>;tag=a6c85cf
From: Alice <sip:alice@atlanta.com>;tag=1928301774
Call-ID: a84b4c76e66710@12.26.17.91
CSeq: 314159 INVITE
Contact: <sip:bob@biloxi.com>
Content-Type: application/sdp
Content-Length: 131
```

The first line contains the version number of SIP that is used and the response code and name. The lines that follow are a list of header fields. The Via, To, From, Call-ID, and CSeq header fields are copied from the INVITE request. (There are three Via header field values—one added by Alice's SIP UAC, one added by the atlanta.com proxy, and one added by the biloxi.com proxy.) Bob's SIP phone has added a tag parameter to the To header field. This tag will be incorporated by both endpoints into the dialog and will be included in all future requests and responses in this call.

Session Description Protocol

The Session Description Protocol (SDP), defined in RFC 2327, describes the content of sessions, including telephony, Internet radio, and multimedia applications. SDP includes information about the following: [SCHU99]:

- **Media streams:** A session can include multiple streams of differing content. SDP currently defines audio, video, data, control, and application as stream types, similar to the MIME types used for Internet mail (Table 6.2).
- **Addresses:** Indicates the destination addresses, which may be a multicast address, for a media stream.
- **Ports:** For each stream, the UDP port numbers for sending and receiving are specified.
- **Payload types:** For each media stream type in use (e.g., telephony), the payload type indicates the media formats that can be used during the session.
- **Start and stop times:** These apply to broadcast sessions, like a television or radio program. The start, stop, and repeat times of the session are indicated.
- **Originator:** For broadcast sessions, the originator is specified, with contact information. This may be useful if a receiver encounters technical difficulties.

APPLICATION NOTE
To Serve or Not to Serve?

Web servers and mail servers are possibly the most difficult kinds of systems to manage. They are constantly barraged with requests from valid users and assailed by attacks from not so valid users. Before deciding to deploy either of these, there are some questions that an organization should ask itself. Very often, there is no need to manage these types of services internally.

Perhaps the best place to start is determining what the system will be required to do. In other words, what do we need and want? For mail servers, questions such as the numbers of accounts needed, security required, and internal versus external mail should be answered. Small companies or individuals running their own companies may be able to take advantage free mail services such as hotmail.com. This does not provide a real identity for the organization but does facilitate communication.

Groups falling into the small category often have their Web pages hosted by their Internet service provider (ISP) or a specialized hosting firm. This allows them to have a Web presence without the need to run a Web server. In addition, Web hosting services or ISPs will often register a domain name with the DNS for you. At a small cost (typically less than $100) this provides an identity to the group and often includes several e-mail accounts, some security/logging tools, and management services.

Using Web hosting and mail services from an ISP or hosting company can serve companies with several employees. For a few extra dollars the number of accounts can be increased and the space or scripting required by the Web site can be enlarged. There is a point at which the outside services become less attractive. For large organizations with dozens or hundreds of people, complex human resources, or internal communication demands and a fully staffed IT department, it may be much more attractive to run your own services.

Setting up e-mail or Web servers internally can be a daunting task for the unprepared. Like most installations, it is not difficult to put the software on a machine or set up a few accounts. It is the maintenance and security of the systems that becomes the struggle. In addition, installing services internally can affect other systems. It is important to understand the operation and requirements of such a system before it is installed.

For example, when running a Web or mail server that is to be accessed from outside the company network, any firewalls that have been configured need to be updated to allow this sort of traffic. This is directly related to the ports used by these applications. The firewall rules may also be written based on other criterion such as IP address. In addition, the type of client software must be considered, as not all external systems will have the necessary software. If the users will be carrying their own laptops around with them, then they are likely to have the proper software. However, stopping at Starbuck's without the laptop will not allow them to check their mail unless the client software is installed there or the mail server allows browser access.

Allowing access from outside can be tricky if the organization regularly handles sensitive data. If this is the case, security will be a top priority and the firewalls a main focus. A security policy should be established and careful consideration given to the personnel allowed external access to internal systems. Often companies will have two or more sets of servers running. These will be for internal or external use exclusively. For example, employee information and benefits may be run on an internal server while the company Web site and contact information may be on the external one.

For the staff running the servers the never-ending tasks of security patching and virus protection take up a good deal of time. Exploits for security installations pop up as fast as older holes can be closed and new viruses arrive as we are filtering out the existing ones. Viruses are a particularly tricky problem that has led many administrators to do a good amount of mail filtering on the server itself. This means that many messages will arrive to the end user with a note describing how a potentially dangerous file was automatically removed from the original message. This is particularly true of executable files. End users should also be running virus protection software that examines incoming mail and the local computer. In the end, the real problem with viruses is that the end user will download them to a computer either by going around the installed security or because the security measures didn't catch the virus.

There are advantages and disadvantages to running your own services. On one hand local configuration permits tailored security changes, rapid account creation, and content modification. On the other hand, server management headaches, costs, and labor hours can make external provisioning attractive.

6.4 SUMMARY

Standardized distributed applications are becoming increasingly important to businesses, for three main reasons:

- Standardized applications are more readily acquired and used than special-purpose software, which may have inadequate support and is accompanied by inadequate training.
- Standardized software allows the user to procure computers from a variety of vendors and yet have those computers work together.
- Standards promote the ability for different companies to exchange data.

This chapter examines three important distributed applications. Standards have been developed for these applications, and their use continues to grow.

A general-purpose electronic mail facility provides a means of exchanging unstructured messages, usually text messages. Electronic mail is a rapid and convenient method for communication, supplementing, and, in many instances, replacing telephone and paper communications. Because electronic mail is so general purpose in nature, it is perhaps the most popular distributed application and can have the most widespread benefits.

The most widely used protocol for the transmission of electronic mail is SMTP. SMTP assumes that the content of the message is a simple text block. The recent MIME standard expands SMTP to support transmission of multimedia information.

The rapid growth in the use of the Web is due to the standardization of all the elements that support Web applications. A key element is HTTP, which is the protocol for the exchange of Web-based information between Web browsers and Web servers. Three types of intermediate devices can be used in an HTTP networks: proxies, gateways, and tunnels. HTTP uses a request/response style of communication.

The Session Initiation Protocol (SIP) is an application-level control protocol for setting up, modifying, and terminating real-time sessions between participants over an IP data network. One important use for SIP is to support telephony over the Internet, known as voice over IP. SIP uses the Session Description Protocol (SDP) to describe the media content to be used during a session.

6.5 RECOMMENDED READING AND WEB SITES

[KHAR98] provides a concise overview of SMTP. [HOFF00] is a good overview of SMTP and related e-mail standards. [KANE98] is a comprehensive look at SMTP and related mail standards, plus a comparison with proprietary schemes. [ROSE98] provides a book-length treatment of electronic mail, including some coverage of SMTP and MIME.

[GOUR02] provides comprehensive coverage of HTTP. Another good treatment is [KRIS01]. [SCHU98] is a good overview of SIP. [GOOD02] and [SCHU99] discuss SIP in the context of VoIP. [DIAN02] looks at SIP in the context of the support of multimedia services over the Internet.

DIAN02   Dianda, J.; Gurbani, V.; and Jones, M. "Session Initiation Protocol Services Architecture." *Bell Labs Technical Journal*, Volume 7, Number 1, 2002.

GOOD02   Goode, B. "Voice Over Internet Protocol (VoIP)." *Proceedings of the IEEE*, September 2002.

GOUR02   Gourley, D., et al. *HTTP: The Definitive Guide.* Sebastopol, CA: O'Reilly, 2002.

HOFF00   Hoffman, P. "Overview of Internet Mail Standards." *The Internet Protocol Journal*, June 2000 (www.cisco.com/warp/public/759)

KANE98   Kanel, J.; Givler, J.; Leiba, B.; and Segmuller, W. "Internet Messaging Frameworks." *IBM Systems Journal*, No. 1, 1998.

KHAR98   Khare, R. "The Spec's in the Mail." *IEEE Internet Computing*, September/ October 1998.

KRIS01   Krishnamurthy, B., and Rexford, J. *Web Protocols and Practice: HTTP/1.1, Networking Protocols, Caching, and Traffic Measurement.* Upper Saddle River, NJ: Prentice Hall, 2001.

ROSE98   Rose, M., and Strom, D. *Internet Messaging: From the Desktop to the Enterprise.* Upper Saddle River, NJ: Prentice Hall, 1998.

SCHU98   Schulzrinne, H. and Rosenberg, J. "The Session Initiation Protocol: Providing Advanced Telephony Access Across the Internet." *Bell Labs Technical Journal*, October-December 1998.

SCHU99   Schulzrinne, H., and Rosenberg, J. "The IETF Internet Telephony Architecture and Protocols." *IEEE Network*, May/June 1999.

Recommended Web Sites:

- **WWW consortium:** Contains up-to-date information on HTTP and related topics.
- **SIP Forum:** Nonprofit organization to promote SIP. Site contains product information, white papers, and other useful information and links.
- **SIP working group:** Chartered by IETF to develop standards related to SIP. The Web site includes all relevant RFCs and Internet drafts.

6.6 KEY TERMS, REVIEW QUESTIONS, AND PROBLEMS

Key Terms

electronic mail	RFC 822	SIP proxy server
HTTP gateway	Session Description Protocol	SIP redirect server
HTTP method	(SDP)	SIP registrar
HTTP proxy	Session Initiation Protocol	Uniform Resource Identifier
HTTP tunnel	(SIP)	(URI)
Hypertext Transfer Protocol	Simple Mail Transfer Protocol	Uniform Resource Locator
(HTTP)	(SMTP)	(URL)
Multipurpose Internet Mail	SIP location service	voice over IP (VoIP)
Extensions (MIME)	SIP method	

Review Questions

6.1. With a single-system mail facility or native mail facility, what major elements are needed?

6.2. By installing a mail client on your computer, are you storing your unread e-mail on your system?

6.3. In extending a single-system mail system to a distributed mail system, what key additions must be included?

6.4. What is the port used by SMTP?

6.5. What is the difference between the RFC 821 and RFC 822?

6.6. What are the SMTP and MIME standards?

6.7. What are some of the limitations of SMTP that MIME was intended to address?

6.8. What is meant by saying that HTTP is a stateless protocol?

6.9. Explain the differences among HTTP proxy, gateway, and tunnel.

6.10. What is the function of the cache in HTTP?

6.11. What port is used by HTTP?

6.12. What are the five key services provided by SIP?

6.13. List and briefly define the major components in an SIP network.

6.14. Provide an example of a transport protocol used to convey audio or video content during a SIP based transmission.

6.15. What is the Session Description Protocol?

Problems

6.1 Electronic mail systems differ in the manner in which multiple recipients are handled. In some systems, the originating user agent or mail sender makes all the necessary copies and these are sent out independently. An alternative approach is to determine the route for each destination first. Then a single message is sent out on a common portion of the route and copies are only made when the routes diverge; this process is referred to as mail bagging. Discuss the relative advantages and disadvantages of the two methods.

6.2 Excluding the connection establishment and termination, what is the minimum number of network round trips to send a small e-mail message using SMTP?

6.3 HTTP caching is an operation that can be controlled at the originating server, an intermediate node, or at the client browser application. What are the potential benefits and detriments associated with this mechanism (from the perspective of both the originator and client) as it is implemented?

6.4 RFC 3298 describes the Spirits protocol requirements. What is Sprits and how might it be relative to a discussion of SIP and PINT?

6.5 Many mail clients allow you to view the mail header that will display the path that the message traveled. Does your mail client or program have this option? If so, can you trace the message from source to destination?

6.6 What TCP port does your mail system use?

6.7 In discovering the port your mail system uses, what port is your machine using?

6.8 Why is it important for the local systems administrator to understand what ports are being used by applications?

6.9 What are POP3 and IMAP?

6.10 What is HTTPS?

6.11 Netmeeting is a video conferencing program built into the Windows family of operating systems. It allows video, audio or video/audio combined communications. Using Netmeeting and some basic communications gear (microphone, speakers, camera), establish communication between two stations. What protocols and codecs are being used?

CHAPTER 7

CLIENT/SERVER AND INTRANET COMPUTING

A number of distributed applications, such as those discussed in the preceding chapter, involve what might be referred to as a peer interaction between systems. There is also a fundamentally different style of distributed computing, one that is having a profound impact on the way in which businesses use computers: client/server computing.

We begin this chapter with a general description of the client/server philosophy and the implications for businesses. Next, we examine the nature of the application support provided by the client/server architecture. Then we look at the rather fuzzy but very important concept of middleware.

Following this survey of client/server computing, we examine a more recent approach referred to as an intranet. An intranet uses Internet technology and applications (especially Web-based applications) to provide in-house support for distributed applications. Finally, this chapter covers the concept of the extranet.

7.1 THE GROWTH OF CLIENT/SERVER COMPUTING

Perhaps the most significant trend in information systems in recent years is the rise of client/server computing. This mode of computing is rapidly replacing both mainframe-dominated, centralized computing approaches and alternative forms of distributed data processing.

What Is Client/Server?

As with other new waves in the computer field, client/server computing comes with its own set of jargon words. Table 7.1 lists some of the terms that are commonly found in descriptions of client/server products and applications.

Table 7.1   Client/Server Terminology

Application Programming Interface (API)

A set of function and call programs that allow clients and servers to intercommunicate.

Client

A networked information requester, usually a PC or workstation, that can query database and/or other information from a server.

Middleware

A set of drivers, APIs, or other software that improves connectivity between a client application and a server.

Relational Database

A database in which information access is limited to the selection of rows that satisfy all search criteria.

Server

A computer, usually a high-powered workstation or a mainframe, that houses information for manipulation by networked clients.

Structured Query Language (SQL)

A language developed by IBM and standardized by ANSI for addressing, creating, updating, or querying relational databases.

Figure 7.1 attempts to capture the essence of these themes. As the term suggests, a client/server environment is populated by clients and servers. The **client** machines are generally single-user PCs or workstations that provide a highly user-friendly interface to the end user. The client-based station generally presents the type of graphical interface that is most comfortable to users, including the use of windows and a mouse. Common examples of such interfaces are provided by Microsoft Windows and Macintosh OS X. Client-based applications are tailored for ease of use and include such familiar tools as the spreadsheet.

Each **server** in the client/server environment provides a set of shared user services to the clients. The most common type of server currently is the database server, usually controlling a relational database. The server enables many clients to share access to the same database and enables the use of a high-performance computer system to manage the database.

In addition to clients and servers, the third essential ingredient of the client/server environment is the **network.** Client/server computing is distributed computing. Users, applications, and resources are distributed in response to business requirements and linked by a single LAN or WAN or by an internet.

How does a client/server configuration differ from any other distributed processing solution? There are a number of characteristics that stand out and that together make client/server distinct from ordinary distributed processing:

- There is a heavy reliance on bringing user-friendly applications to the user on his or her system. This gives the user a great deal of control over the timing and style of computer usage and gives department-level managers the ability to be responsive to their local needs.

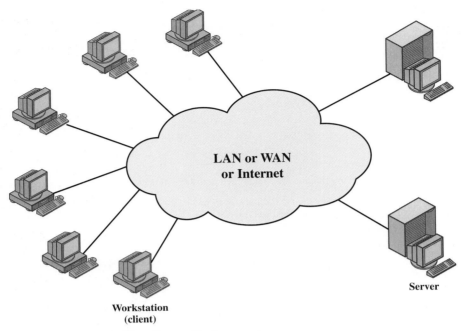

LAN or WAN or Internet

Server

Workstation (client)

Figure 7.1 Generic Client/Server Environment

- Although the applications are dispersed, there is an emphasis on centralizing corporate databases and many network management and utility functions. This enables corporate management to maintain overall control of the total capital investment in computing and information systems and enables corporate management to provide interoperability so that systems are tied together. At the same time, it relieves individual departments and divisions of much of the overhead of maintaining sophisticated computer-based facilities but enables them to choose just about any type of machine and interface they need to access data and information.

- There is a commitment, both by user organizations and vendors, to open and modular systems. This means that the user has greater choice in selecting products and in mixing equipment from a number of vendors.

- Networking is fundamental to the operation. Thus, network management and network security have a high priority in organizing and operating information systems.

Client/server computing is, on the one hand, a natural solution from the product point of view, because it exploits the growing availability and affordability of microcomputers and networks. On the other hand, client/server computing may be the ideal choice to support the direction that business is taking in the organization of work.

This latter point deserves elaboration. The success of client/server computing in the marketplace is not just a matter of new jargon on top of old solutions.

Client/server computing is indeed a new technical approach to distributed comput-ing. But beyond that, client/server computing is responsive to, and indeed creates the conditions for, new ways of organizing business. Let us consider two significant trends in industry that illustrate the point.

The first of these is the permanent shedding of jobs by companies in an effort to downsize and streamline for success in a fiercely competitive market. Why have companies needed to shed jobs to remain competitive and how have they managed to increase productivity so fast as to have sales growth without pay-roll growth? The cost per employee is rising rapidly, with wage increases coupled to mandated benefits increases. At the same time, business equipment, especially computer and network equipment and services, has suffered only modest cost increases. This has led, as one might expect, to substantial increases in investment in computers and other information technology in an effort to compensate for a smaller employee base.

This trend occurs in small as well as large businesses and is affecting middle managers as well as clerical staff. What client/server computing provides is a way of automating tasks and eliminating barriers to information, which allows companies to eliminate layers of management and to add work without adding workers.

Another trend that illustrates the effectiveness of client/server computing is the so-called internal market. This is a business strategy that affects primarily large businesses, which seek to combine entrepreneurial zeal with corporate might to have the best of both worlds: the economies of scale of a large business with the agility of a small business. In an era of rapid technological and market changes, many large companies are tearing down traditional functional hierarchies and replacing them with collections of relatively independent business units. These units must then compete with external companies for business from other units. In an internal market, every business unit operates as an independent company. Each one decides to buy its inputs from internal sources (other units of the corporation) or from outside suppliers. Even traditional "overhead" departments, such as informa-tion systems, accounting, and legal, must sell their services to other units and com-pete with outside providers.

This dose of internal competition is designed to correct the flaws of the tradi-tional way of doing business. As Jay Forrester of MIT observes [ROTH93], "American corporations are some of the largest socialist bureaucracies in the world. They have central planning, central ownership of capital, central allocation of resources, subjective evaluation of people, lack of internal competition, and decisions made at the top in response to political pressures."

Internal markets have already transformed some companies and promise to have a major impact on others. But, until recently, there has been a formidable obstacle to implementing such a scheme. In a large company, the use of an internal market can result in thousands of teams making agreements among themselves and with outsiders. Somehow, the ledgers for all the resulting transactions have to be reconciled. Analyses of this situation have suggested that the cost and complexity of bookkeeping would overwhelm the benefits of an internal market. The evolution of computing technology has overcome this obstacle. Today, a number of multination-als are using the latest database software running on client/server networks to set up internal markets.

The Evolution of Client/Server Computing

The way in which client/server computing has evolved is worth noting. This style of organizing computer resources began at the workgroup and departmental level. Departmental managers found that relying on central, mainframe-based applications hindered their ability to rapidly respond to business demands. Application development time within the central IS shop was too slow, and the results were not tailored to the specific needs of the department. The deployment of PCs enabled workers to have computing power and data at their command and enabled department-level managers to select needed applications quickly.

However, in a pure PC environment, cooperation among users was difficult. Even within the department, there needed to be a departmental-level database and departmental formatting and data usage standards. The solution to these requirements is a departmental-level client/server architecture. Typically, such an architecture involves a single LAN, a number of PCs, and one or two servers.

The success of departmental-level client/server systems paved the way for the introduction of enterprise-wide client/server computing. Ideally, such an architecture will enable the integration of departmental and IS organization resources, allowing for applications that give individual users ready but controlled access to corporate databases. The dominant theme of such architectures is the reestablishment of control over data by the central IS organization but in the context of a distributed computing system.

7.2 CLIENT/SERVER APPLICATIONS

The central feature of a client/server architecture is the allocation of application-level tasks between clients and servers. Figure 7.2 illustrates the general case. In both client and server, of course, the basic software is an operating system running

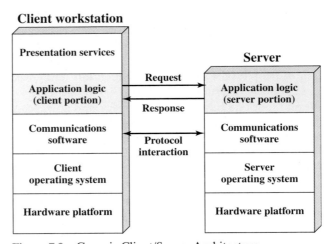

Figure 7.2 Generic Client/Server Architecture

on the hardware platform. The platforms and the operating systems of client and server may differ. Indeed, there may be a number of different types of client platforms and operating systems and a number of different types of server platforms and operating systems in a single environment. As long as a particular client and server share the same communications protocols and support the same applications, these lower-level differences are irrelevant.

It is the communications software that enables client and server to interoperate. The principal example of such software is TCP/IP. Of course, the point of all this support software (communications and operating system) is to provide a base for distributed applications. Ideally, the actual functions performed by the application can be split up between client and server in a way that optimizes platform and network resources and that optimizes the ability of users to perform various tasks and to cooperate with one another in using shared resources. In some cases, these requirements dictate that the bulk of the applications software executes at the server, while in other cases, most of the application logic is located at the client.

An essential factor in the success of a client/server environment is the way in which the user interacts with the system as a whole. Thus, the design of the user interface to the client machine is critical. In most client/server systems, there is heavy emphasis on providing a **graphical user interface (GUI)** that is easy to use, easy to learn, yet powerful and flexible. Thus, we can think of a presentation services module[1] in the client workstation responsible for providing a user-friendly interface to the distributed applications available in the environment.

Database Applications

As an example that illustrates the concept of splitting application logic between client and server, let us consider the most common family of client/server applications: those that make use of relational databases. In this environment, the server is essentially a database server. Interaction between client and server is in the form of transactions in which the client makes a database request and receives a database response.

Figure 7.3 illustrates, in general terms, the architecture of such a system. The server is responsible for maintaining the database, for which purpose a complex database management system software module is required. A variety of applications that make use of the database can be housed on client machines. The "glue" that ties client and server together is software that enables the client to make requests for access to the server's database. A popular example of such logic is the Structured Query Language (SQL).

Figure 7.3 suggests that all of the application logic—the software for "number crunching" or other types of data analysis—is on the client side, while the server is only concerned with managing the database. Whether such a configuration is appropriate depends on the style and intent of the application. For example, suppose that the primary purpose is to provide online access for record lookup. Figure 7.4a suggests how

---

[1]Not to be confused with the presentation layer of the OSI model. The presentation layer is concerned with the formatting of data so that they can be properly interpreted by the two communicating machines. A presentation services module is concerned with the way in which the user interacts with an application and with the layout and functionality of what is presented to the user on the screen.

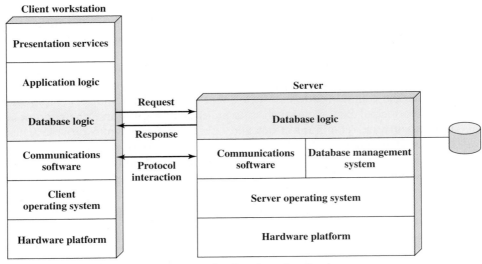

Figure 7.3 Client/Server Architecture for Database Applications

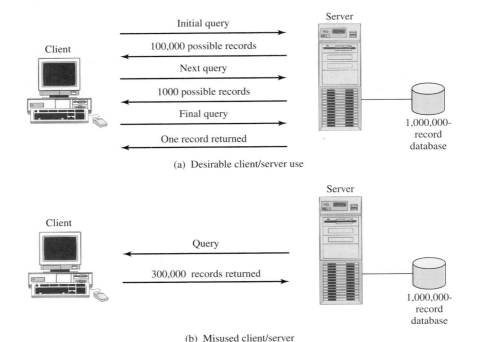

Figure 7.4 Client/Server Database Usage

this might work. Suppose that the server is maintaining a database of one million records (called rows in relational database jargon), and the user wants to perform a lookup that should result in zero, one, or at most a few records. The user could search for these records using a number of search criteria (e.g., records older than 1992; records referring to individuals in Ohio; records referring to a specific event or characteristic, etc.). An initial client query may yield a server response that there are 100,000 records that satisfy the search criteria. The user then adds additional qualifiers and issues a new query. This time, a response indicating that there are 1000 possible records is returned. Finally, the client issues a third request with additional qualifiers. The resulting search criteria yield a single match, and the record is returned to the client.

The preceding application is well suited to a client/server architecture for two reasons:

1. There is a massive job of sorting and searching the database. This requires a large disc or bank of discs, a high-speed CPU, and a high-speed I/O architecture. Such capacity and power is not needed and is too expensive for a single-user workstation or PC.

2. It would place too great a traffic burden on the network to move the entire one-million-record file to the client for searching. Therefore, it is not enough for the server to just be able to retrieve records on behalf of a client; the server needs to have database logic that enables it to perform searches on behalf of a client.

Now consider the scenario of Figure 7.4b, which has the same one-million-record database. In this case, a single query results in the transmission of 300,000 records over the network. This might happen if, for example, the user wishes to find the grand total or mean value of some field across many records or even the entire database.

Clearly, this latter scenario is unacceptable. One solution to this problem, which maintains the client/server architecture with all its benefits, is to move part of the application logic over to the server. That is, the server can be equipped with application logic for performing data analysis as well as data retrieval and data searching.

Classes of Client/Server Applications

Within the general framework of client/server, there is a spectrum of implementations that divide the work between client and server differently. The exact distribution of data and application processing depends on the nature of the database information, the types of applications supported, the availability of interoperable vendor equipment, and the usage patterns within an organization.

Figure 7.5 illustrates some of the major options for database applications. Other splits are possible, and the options may have a different characterization for other types of applications. In any case, it is useful to examine this figure to get a feel for the kind of trade-offs possible.

The figure depicts four classes:

*   **Host-based processing:** Host-based processing is not true client/server computing as the term is generally used. Rather, host-based processing refers to the traditional mainframe environment in which all or virtually all of the processing is

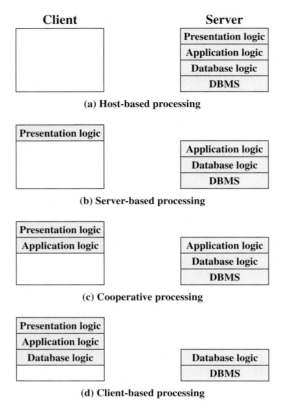

Figure 7.5   Classes of Client/Server Applications

done on a central host. Often the user interface is via a dumb terminal. Even if the user is employing a microcomputer, the user's station is generally limited to the role of a terminal emulator.

- **Server-based processing:** The simplest class of client/server configuration is one in which the client is principally responsible for providing a graphical user interface, while virtually all of the processing is done on the server.

- **Client-based processing:** At the other extreme, virtually all application processing may be done at the client, with the exception of data validation routines and other database logic functions that are best performed at the server. Generally, some of the more sophisticated database logic functions are housed on the client side. This architecture is perhaps the most common client/server approach in current use. It enables the user to employ applications tailored to local needs.

- **Cooperative processing:** In a cooperative processing configuration, the application processing is performed in an optimized fashion, taking advantage of the strengths of both client and server machines and of the distribution of data. Such a configuration is more complex to set up and maintain but, in the long run, this type of configuration may offer greater user productivity gains and greater network efficiency than other client/server approaches.

Figures 7.5c and d correspond to configurations in which a considerable fraction of the load is on the client. This so-called fat client model has been popularized by application development tools such as Powersoft Corp.'s PowerBuilder and Gupta Corp.'s SQL Windows. Applications developed with these tools are typically departmental in scope, supporting between 25 and 150 users [ECKE95]. The main benefit of the fat client model is that it takes advantage of desktop power, off-loading application processing from servers and making them more efficient and less likely to be bottlenecks.

There are, however, several disadvantages to the fat client strategy. The addition of more functions rapidly overloads the capacity of desktop machines, forcing companies to upgrade. If the model extends beyond the department to incorporate many users, the company must install high-capacity LANs to support the large volumes of transmission between the thin servers and the fat clients. Finally, it is difficult to maintain, upgrade, or replace applications distributed across tens or hundreds of desktops.

Figure 7.5b is representative of a fat server approach. This approach more nearly mimics the traditional host-centered approach and is often the migration path for evolving corporate-wide applications from the mainframe to a distributed environment.

Three–Tier Client/Server Architecture

The traditional client/server architecture involves two levels, or tiers: a client tier and a server tier. In recent years, a three-tier architecture has become increasingly common (Figure 7.6). In this architecture, the application software is distributed among three types of machines: a user machine, a middle-tier server, and a backend server. The user machine is the client machine we have been discussing and, in the three-tier model, is typically a thin client. The middle-tier machines are essentially gateways between the

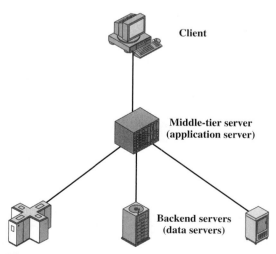

Figure 7.6   Three-Tier Client/Server Architecture

thin user clients and a variety of backend database servers. The middle-tier machines can convert protocols and map from one type of database query to another. In addition, the middle-tier machine can merge/integrate results from different data sources. Finally, the middle-tier machine can serve as a gateway between the desktop applications and the backend legacy applications by mediating between the two worlds.

The interaction between the middle-tier server and the backend server also follows the client/server model. Thus, the middle tier system acts as both a client and a server.

7.3 MIDDLEWARE

The development and deployment of client/server products has far outstripped efforts to standardize all aspects of distributed computing, from the physical layer up to the application layer. This lack of standards makes it difficult to implement an integrated, multivendor, enterprise-wide client/server configuration. Because much of the benefit of the client/server approach is tied up with its modularity and the ability to mix and match platforms and applications to provide a business solution, this interoperability problem must be solved.

To achieve the true benefits of the client/server approach, developers must have a set of tools that provide a uniform means and style of access to system resources across all platforms. This will enable programmers to build applications that not only look and feel the same on various PCs and workstations but that use the same method to access data regardless of the location of that data.

The most common way to meet this requirement is by the use of standard programming interfaces and protocols that sit between the application above and communications software and operating system below. Such standardized interfaces and protocols have come to be referred to as **middleware**. With standard programming interfaces, it is easy to implement the same application on a variety of server types and workstation types. This obviously has benefit to the customer, but vendors are also motivated to provide such interfaces. The reason is that customers buy applications, not servers; customers will only choose among those server products that run the applications they want. The standardized protocols are needed to link these various server interfaces back to the clients that need access to them.

There is a variety of middleware packages ranging from the very simple to the very complex. What they all have in common is the capability to hide the complexities and disparities of different network protocols and operating systems. Client and server vendors generally provide a number of the more popular middleware packages as options. Thus, a user can settle on a particular middleware strategy and then assemble equipment from various vendors that support that strategy.

Middleware Architecture

Figure 7.7 suggests the role of middleware in a client/server architecture. The exact role of the middleware component will depend on the style of client/server computing being used. Referring back to Figure 7.5, recall that there are a number of different client/server approaches, depending on the way in which application

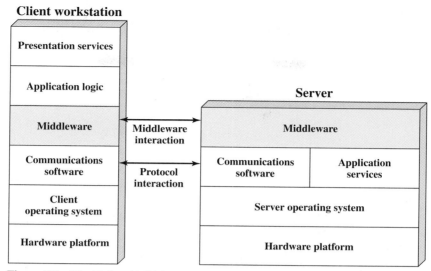

Figure 7.7   The Role of Middleware in Client/Server Architecture

functions are split up. In any case, Figure 7.7 gives a good general idea of the architecture involved.

Note that there is both a client and server component of middleware. The basic purpose of middleware is to enable an application or user at a client to access a variety of services on servers without being concerned about differences among servers. To look at one specific application area, the Structured Query Language (SQL) is supposed to provide a standardized means for access to a relational database by either a local or remote user or application. However, many relational database vendors, although they support SQL, have added their own proprietary extensions to SQL. This enables vendors to differentiate their products but also creates potential incompatibilities.

As an example, consider a distributed system used to support, among other things, the personnel department. The basic employee data, such as employee name and address, might be stored on a Gupta database, whereas salary information might be contained on an Oracle database. When a user in the personnel department requires access to particular records, that user does not want to be concerned with which vendor's database contains the records needed. Middleware provides a layer of software that enables uniform access to these differing systems.

It is instructive to look at the role of middleware from a logical, rather than an implementation, point of view. This viewpoint is illustrated in Figure 7.8 [BERN96b]. Middleware enables the realization of the promise of distributed client/server computing. The entire distributed system can be viewed as a set of applications and resources available to users. Users need not be concerned with the location of data or indeed the location of applications. All applications operate over a uniform **application programming interface (API)**. The middleware, which cuts across all client and server platforms, is responsible for routing client requests to the appropriate server.

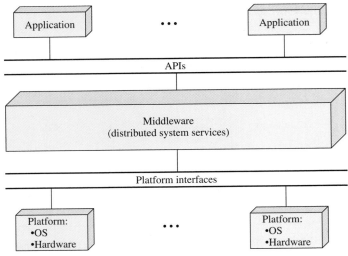

Figure 7.8 Logical View of Middleware

Although there is a wide variety of middleware products, these products are typically based on one of three underlying mechanisms: message passing, remote procedure calls, and object-oriented mechanisms. The remainder of this section provides an overview of these mechanisms.

Message Passing

Figure 7.9a shows the use of distributed message passing to implement client/server functionality. A client process requires some service (e.g., read a file, print) and sends a message containing a request for service to a server process. The server process honors the request and sends a message containing a reply. In its simplest form, only two functions are needed: Send and Receive. The Send function specifies a destination and includes the message content. The Receive function tells from whom a message is desired (including "all") and provides a buffer where the incoming message is to be stored.

Figure 7.10 suggests an implementation approach for message passing. Processes make use of the services of a message-passing module. Service requests can be expressed in terms of primitives and parameters. A primitive specifies the function to be performed, and the parameters are used to pass data and control information. The actual form of a primitive depends on the message-passing software. It may be a procedure call or it may itself be a message to a process that is part of the operating system.

The Send primitive is used by the process that desires to send the message. Its parameters are the identifier of the destination process and the contents of the message. The message-passing module constructs a data unit that includes these two elements. This data unit is sent to the machine that hosts the destination process, using some sort of communications facility, such as TCP/IP. When the data unit is received in the target system, it is routed by the communications facility to the

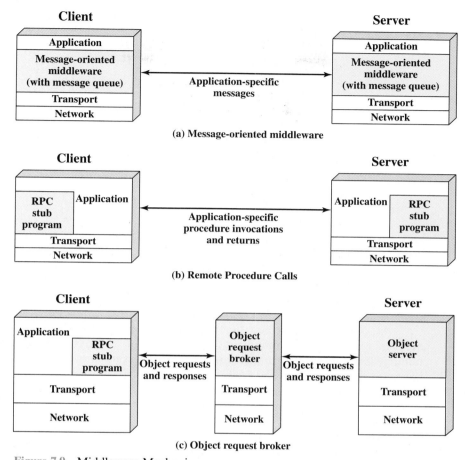

Figure 7.9   Middleware Mechanisms

message-passing module. This module examines the processId field and stores the message in the buffer for that process.

In this scenario, the receiving process must announce its willingness to receive messages by designating a buffer area and informing the message-passing module by a Receive primitive. An alternative approach does not require such an announcement. Instead, when the message-passing module receives a message, it signals the destination process with some sort of Receive signal and then makes the received message available in a shared buffer.

Several design issues are associated with distributed message passing, and these are addressed in the remainder of this subsection.

Reliability versus Unreliability   A reliable message-passing facility is one that guarantees delivery if possible. Such a facility would make use of a reliable transport protocol or similar logic to perform error checking, acknowledgment, retransmission,

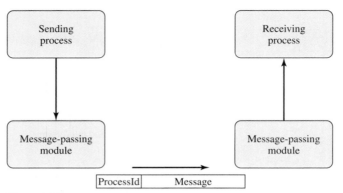

Figure 7.10   Basic Message-Passing Primitives

and reordering of misordered messages. Because delivery is guaranteed, it is not necessary to let the sending process know that the message was delivered. However, it might be useful to provide an acknowledgment back to the sending process so that it knows that delivery has already taken place. In either case, if the facility fails to achieve delivery (e.g., persistent network failure, crash of destination system), the sending process is notified of the failure.

At the other extreme, the message-passing facility may simply send the message out into the communications network but will report neither success nor failure. This alternative greatly reduces the processing and communications overhead of the message-passing facility. For those applications that require confirmation that a message has been delivered, the applications themselves may use request and reply messages to satisfy the requirement.

Blocking versus Nonblocking   With nonblocking, or asynchronous, primitives, a process is not suspended as a result of issuing a Send or Receive. Thus, when a process issues a Send primitive, the operating system returns control to the process as soon as the message has been queued for transmission or a copy has been made. If no copy is made, any changes made to the message by the sending process before or even while it is being transmitted are made at the risk of the process. When the message has been transmitted, or copied to a safe place for subsequent transmission, the sending process is interrupted to be informed that the message buffer may be reused. Similarly, a nonblocking Receive is issued by a process that then proceeds to run. When a message arrives, the process is informed by interrupt, or it can poll for status periodically.

Nonblocking primitives provide for efficient, flexible use of the message-passing facility by processes. The disadvantage of this approach is that it is difficult to test and debug programs that use these primitives. Irreproducible, timing-dependent sequences can create subtle and difficult problems.

The alternative is to use blocking, or synchronous, primitives. A blocking Send does not return control to the sending process until the message has been transmitted (unreliable service) or until the message has been sent and an acknowledgment received (reliable service). A blocking Receive does not return control until a message has been placed in the allocated buffer.

Remote Procedure Calls

A variation on the basic message-passing model is the remote procedure call. This is now a widely accepted and common method for encapsulating communication in a distributed system. The essence of the technique is to allow programs on different machines to interact using simple procedure call/return semantics, just as if the two programs were on the same machine. That is, the procedure call is used for access to remote services. The popularity of this approach is due to the following advantages:

1. The procedure call is a widely accepted, used, and understood abstraction.
2. The use of remote procedure calls enables remote interfaces to be specified as a set of named operations with designated types. Thus, the interface can be clearly documented and distributed programs can be statically checked for type errors.
3. Because a standardized and precisely defined interface is specified, the communication code for an application can be generated automatically.
4. Because a standardized and precisely defined interface is specified, developers can write client and server modules that can be moved among computers and operating systems with little modification and recoding.

The remote procedure call mechanism can be viewed as a refinement of reliable, blocking message passing. Figure 7.9b illustrates the general architecture, and Figure 7.11 provides a more detailed look. The calling program makes a normal procedure call with parameters on its machine. For example,

$$\text{CALL P}(X, Y)$$

where

$$P = \text{procedure name}$$
$$X = \text{passed arguments}$$
$$Y = \text{returned values}$$

It may or may not be transparent to the user that the intention is to invoke a remote procedure on some other machine. A dummy or stub procedure P must be included in the caller's address space or be dynamically linked to it at call time. This procedure creates a message that identifies the procedure being called and includes the parameters. It then sends this message to a remote system and waits for a reply. When a reply is received, the stub procedure returns to the calling program, providing the returned values.

At the remote machine, another stub program is associated with the called procedure. When a message comes in, it is examined and a local CALL P (X,Y) is generated. This remote procedure is thus called locally, so its normal assumptions about where to find parameters, the state of the stack, and so on, are identical to the case of a purely local procedure call.

Client/Server Binding Binding specifies how the relationship between a remote procedure and the calling program will be established. A binding is formed when two applications have made a logical connection and are prepared to exchange commands and data.

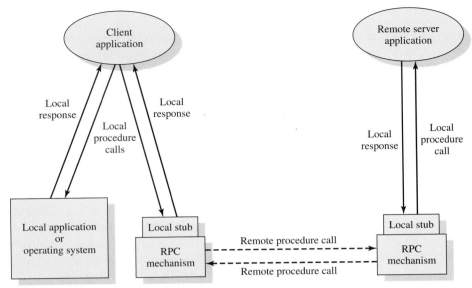

Figure 7.11   Remote Procedure Call Mechanism

Nonpersistent binding means that a logical connection is established between the two processes at the time of the remote procedure call and that as soon as the values are returned, the connection is dismantled. Because a connection requires the maintenance of state information on both ends, it consumes resources. The nonpersistent style is used to conserve those resources. On the other hand, the overhead involved in establishing connections makes nonpersistent binding inappropriate for remote procedures that are called frequently by the same caller.

With **persistent binding**, a connection that is set up for a remote procedure call is sustained after the procedure return. The connection can then be used for future remote procedure calls. If a specified period of time passes with no activity on the connection, the connection is terminated. For applications that make many repeated calls to remote procedures, persistent binding maintains the logical connection and allows a sequence of calls and returns to use the same connection.

Object-Oriented Mechanisms

As object-oriented technology becomes more prevalent in operating-system design, client/server designers have begun to embrace this approach. In this approach, clients and servers ship messages back and forth between objects. Object communications may rely on an underlying message or RPC structure or be developed directly on top of object-oriented capabilities in the operating system.

A client that needs a service sends a request to an object request broker, which acts as a directory of all the remote services available on the network (Figure 7.9c). The broker calls the appropriate object and passes along any relevant data. Then the remote object services the request and replies to the broker, which returns the response to the client.

The success of the object-oriented approach depends on standardization of the object mechanism. Unfortunately, there are several competing designs in this area. One is Microsoft's Common Object Model (COM), the basis for Object Linking and Embedding (OLE). This approach has the support of Digital Equipment Corporation, which has developed COM for UNIX. A competing approach, developed by the Object Management Group, is the Common Object Request Broker Architecture (CORBA), which has wide industry backing. IBM, Apple, Sun, and many other vendors support the CORBA approach.

7.4 INTRANETS

Intranet is a term used to refer to the implementation of Internet technologies within a corporate organization, rather than for external connection to the global Internet. This concept has resulted in the most rapid change of direction in the history of business data communications. By any measure, including product announcements by vendors, statements of intent by customers, actual deployment of products, and even books on the shelves of bookstores, intranets have enjoyed a more rapid penetration of the corporate consciousness than personal computers, client/server computing, or even the Internet and the World Wide Web.

What accounts for this growth is a long list of attractive features and advantages of an intranet-based approach to corporate computing, including the following:

* Rapid prototyping and deployment of new services (can be measured in hours or days)
* Scales effectively (start small, build as needed)
* Virtually no training required on the part of users and little training required of developers, because the services and user interfaces are familiar from the Internet
* Can be implemented on virtually all platforms with complete interoperability
* Open architecture means large and growing number of add-on applications available across many platforms
* Supports a range of distributed computing architectures (few central servers or many distributed servers)
* Structured to support integration of "legacy" information sources (databases, existing word processing documents, groupware databases)
* Supports a range of media types (audio, video, interactive applications)
* Inexpensive to start, requires little investment either in new software or infrastructure

The enabling technologies for the intranet are the high processing speed and storage capacity of personal computers together with the high data rates of LANs.

Although the term *intranet* refers to the whole range of Internet-based applications, including network news, e-mail, and FTP, it is Web technology that is responsible for the almost instant acceptance of intranets. Thus, the bulk of this section is devoted to a discussion of Web systems. At the close of the section, we briefly mention other intranet applications.

Intranet Web

The Web browser has become the universal information interface. An increasing number of employees have had experience using the Internet Web and are comfortable with the access model it provides. The intranet Web takes advantage of this experience base.

Web Content An organization can use the intranet Web to enhance management-employee communication and to provide job-related information easily and quickly. Figure 7.12 suggests, at a top level, the kinds of information that can be provided by a corporate Web. Typically, there is an internal corporate home page that serves as an entry point for employees into the corporate intranet. From this home page, there are links to areas of interest company-wide or to large groups of employees, including human resources, finance, and information system service. Other links are to areas of interest to groups of employees, such as sales and manufacturing.

Beyond these broad-based Web services, an intranet Web is ideal for providing departmental- and project-level information and services. A group can set up its own Web pages to disseminate information and to maintain project data. With the widespread availability of easy-to-use WYSIWYG page authoring tools, such as Adobe GoLive, it is relatively easy for employees outside the information services group to develop their own Web pages for specific needs.

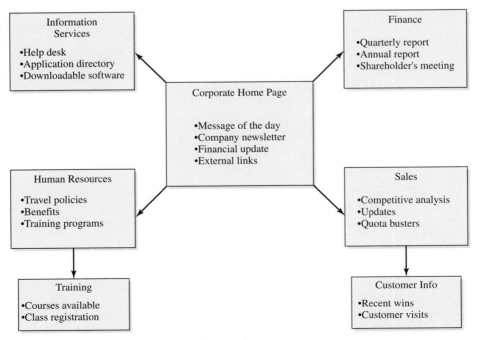

Figure 7.12   Example Corporate Web Page Structure

Web/Database Applications Although the Web is a powerful and flexible tool for supporting corporate requirements, the HTML used to construct Web pages provides a limited capability for maintaining a large, changing base of data. For an intranet to be truly effective, many organizations will want to connect the Web service to a database with its own database management system.

Figure 7.13 illustrates a general strategy for Web/database integration in simple terms. To begin, a client machine (running a Web browser) issues a request for information in the form of a URL reference. This reference triggers a program at the Web server that issues the correct database command to a database server. The output returned to the Web server is converted into HTML format and returned to the Web browser.

[WHET96] lists the following advantages of a Web/database system compared to a more traditional database approach:

- **Ease of administration:** The only connection to the database server is the Web server. The addition of a new type of database server does not require configuration of all the requisite drivers and interfaces at each type of client machine. Instead, it is only necessary for the Web server to be able to convert between HTML and the database interface.

- **Deployment:** Browsers are already available across almost all platforms, which relieves the developer of the need to implement graphical user interfaces across multiple customer machines and operating systems. In addition, developers can assume that customers already have and will be able to use browsers as soon as the intranet Web server is available, avoiding deployment issues such as installation and synchronized activation.

- **Development speed:** Large portions of the normal development cycle, such as deployment and client design, do not apply to Web-based projects. In addition, the text-based tags of HTML allow for rapid modification, making it easy to continually improve the look and feel of the application based on user feedback. By contrast, changing form or content of a typical graphical-based application can be a substantial task.

- **Flexible information presentation:** The hypermedia base of the Web enables the application developer to employ whatever information structure is best for a given application, including the use of hierarchical formats in which progressive levels of detail are available to the user.

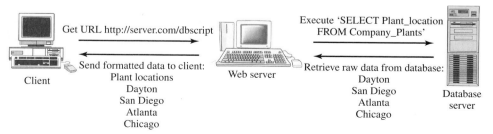

Figure 7.13   Web/Database Connectivity

These advantages are compelling in the decision to deploy a Web-based database interface. However, managers need to be aware of potential disadvantages, also listed in [WHET96]:

- **Functionality:** Compared to the functionality available with a sophisticated graphical user interface (GUI), a typical Web browser interface may be more limited.
- **Stateless operation:** The nature of HTTP is such that each interaction between a browser and a server is a separate transaction, independent of prior or future exchanges. Typically, the Web server keeps no information between transactions to track the state of the user. Such history information can be important. For example, consider an application that allows the user to query a database of parts for cars and trucks. Once the user has indicated that he or she is looking for a specific truck part, subsequent menus should show only parts that pertain to trucks. It is possible to work around this difficulty, but it is awkward.

Intranet Webs versus Traditional Client/Server Although traditional client/server systems have become increasingly widespread and popular, displacing older corporate computing models, their use is not without problems, such as the following:

- Long development cycles
- Difficulty of partitioning applications into client and server modules and the even greater difficulty in modifying the partition in response to user feedback
- Effort involved in distributing upgrades to clients
- Difficulty in scaling the servers to respond to increased load in a distributed environment
- Continuous requirement for increasingly powerful desktop machines

Much of this difficulty can be traced to the typical client/server design, which puts much of the load on the client; this fat client strategy corresponds to Figures 7.5c and d. As was mentioned earlier, this strategy may not scale well to corporate-wide applications. Thus, many companies opt for a fat server approach. An intranet Web can be viewed as one realization of the fat server.

Viewed as an alternative to other fat server schemes, the intranet Web has the advantages of ease of deployment, use of a small number of widely accepted standards, and integration with other TCP/IP-based applications. However, it is unlikely that the intranet Web will kill or even slow down traditional client/server deployment, at least in the near term. Longer term, the intranet Web may come to dominate corporate computing or it may simply be a widely used alternative to other client/server strategies that also flourish.

Other Intranet Technologies

The centerpiece of any intranet strategy is the intranet Web. However, other Internet technologies can also play a key role in the success of an intranet. Perhaps the two most important, after the Web, are electronic mail and network news.

Electronic Mail Electronic mail is already the most heavily used network application in the corporate world. However, traditional e-mail is generally limited and inflexible. Intranet mail products provide standard, simple methods for attaching documents, sound, images, and other multimedia to mail messages.

In addition to supporting multimedia, intranet mail systems generally make it easy to create and manage an **electronic mailing list.** A mailing list is really nothing more than an alias that has multiple destinations. Mailing lists are usually created to discuss specific topics. Anyone interested in that topic may join that list. Once a user has been added to a list, he or she receives a copy of every message posted to the list. A user can ask a question or respond to someone else's question by sending a message to the list address. The mailing list is thus an effective way of supporting project-level communication.

Network News Most readers of this book are familiar with **USENET,** otherwise known as network news. USENET is a collection of electronic bulletin boards that work in much the same way as the Internet mailing lists. If you subscribe to a particular news group, you receive all messages posted to that group, and you may post a message that is available to all subscribers. One difference between USENET and Internet mailing lists has to do with the mechanics of the systems. USENET is actually a distributed network of sites that collect and broadcast news group entries. To access a news group, for read or write, one must have access to a USENET node. Another, more significant, difference is the way in which messages are organized. With an electronic mailing list, each subscriber receives messages one at a time, as they are sent. With USENET, the messages are archived at each news site and organized by subject matter. Thus, it is easier to follow the thread of a particular discussion with USENET. This ability to organize and store messages in threads makes USENET ideal for collaborative work.

As with other Internet technologies, USENET is readily adapted to form an intranet news service. The news messages can be stored on a single news server, or multiple servers within the organization can act as news repositories. New groups are created as needed by departments and projects.

7.5 EXTRANETS

A concept similar to that of the intranet is the **extranet.** Like the intranet, the extranet makes use of TCP/IP protocols and applications, especially the Web. The distinguishing feature of the extranet is that it provides access to corporate resources by outside clients, typically suppliers and customers of the organization. This outside access can be through the Internet or through other data communications networks. An extranet provides more than the simple Web access for the public that virtually all companies now provide. Instead, the extranet provides more extensive access to corporate resources, usually in a fashion that enforces a security policy. As with the intranet, the typical model of operation for the extranet is client/server.

The essential feature of an extranet is that it enables the sharing of information among companies. [PFAF98] lists the following benefits of such sharing:

- **Reduced costs:** Information that must be shared is done in a highly automated fashion, with minimized paperwork and human involvement.

- **More marketable products:** Customers can be directly involved in the design process during the product design cycle, with rapid review of design specifications, automated tools for accepting requirements specifications from customers, and other tools for feedback and review. These capabilities help firms determine the optimum mix of product features.

- **Increased product quality:** Customer complaints reach suppliers faster and are easier to track, enabling corrections to be made to the product more quickly.

- **Enhanced profits for suppliers:** Up-to-the minute information on what is selling and what is not helps suppliers fine tune their marketplace response.

- **Reduced inventories and reduction of obsolete inventories:** Customer-driven just-in-time manufacturing techniques are enhanced, allowing more refined decision making in procurement.

- **Faster time to market:** Products reach the market more quickly when vendors, designers, marketers, and customers are electronically linked in a new product partnership.

An important consideration with extranets is security. Because corporate Web resources and database resources are made available to outside parties and transactions against these resources are allowed, privacy and authentication concerns must be addressed. This is typically done with the use of a virtual private network, which is discussed in Chapter 18. Here, we can simply list some of the communications options available for opening up the corporate intranet to outsiders to create an extranet:

- **Long-distance dial-up access:** This enables outsiders to access the intranet directly, using a logon procedure to authenticate the user. This approach may provide the weakest security because of the risk of impersonation, with few tools to counteract such risks.

- **Internet access to intranet with security:** Authentication of users and encryption of communications between user and intranet provide enhanced security. The encryption prevents eavesdropping, and authentication is intended to prevent unauthorized access. However, as with dial-up access, if a hacker is able to defeat the authentication mechanism, then the entire resources of the intranet become vulnerable.

- **Internet access to an external server that duplicates some of a company's intranet data:** This approach reduces the risk of hacker penetration but may also reduce the value of the extranet to external partners.

- **Internet access to an external server that originates database queries to internal servers:** The external server acts as a firewall to enforce the company's security policy. The firewall may employ encryption in communicating to external users, will authenticate external users, and filters the information flow to restrict access on the basis of user. If the firewall is itself secure from hacker attacks, this is a powerful approach.

- **Virtual private network:** The VPN in effect is a generalization of the firewall approach and takes advantage of IP security capabilities to allow secure communications between external users and the company's intranet. VPNs are discussed in Chapter 18.

APPLICATION NOTE
To be fat or thin—that is the question

Client configuration can have a significant effect on the performance of your network and the individual machines. Figure 7.2 illustrates the relationship between the client and the server. The different components required to perform a particular task can be separated in several ways. An organization can have a great deal of difficulty with their communication systems if there is no plan specifying the architecture or if the wrong choices are made.

For example, a company seeks to upgrade its aging network, servers, and desktop computers. The network is based on 10 Mbps Ethernet and consists of equipment supplied by several different vendors and is limited by older cabling and wiring closets. There are many servers each performing a separate task. This formula has been followed in every department so that there is a great deal of duplication of effort on the part of the servers. The desktop computers are of several different generations and manufacturers, making support very difficult.

The decision is made to upgrade the network, servers and computers. First the servers are migrated to a new operating system and the services consolidated. This can be a monumental task simply because there are many servers and no clear description as to what each one is doing and for whom. A survey of the machines must be made. Some decisions that must be made include the following:

- What services are required?
- What services can safely be run on a single server?
- What form should backup/redundancy take?
- What operating system best suits the needs?
- Should all user data be stored on the server?
- Where should the applications reside?
- What kind of machine should the server(s) be?
- How many users do we have?
- One set of servers or departmental servers?
- What are the performance expectations?

There are other questions, but these should suffice to get the process moving. While the new servers are being brought on line, old and new should run in parallel for a specified period of time.

The applications can be the tricky part. Depending on the size of the organization, some applications or services will probably run exclusively on the servers and some will run on the client machines. The following paragraphs outline some examples.

For a small company, individual printers may be appropriate. This is certainly something that becomes less feasible as the number of users increases. It is far more likely that the printers will be shared and that one of the servers will be operating as a print server, handling all of the printing requests. The number of printers and servers will depend on the number of users and their requirements.

Ordering software is one of those applications that will run on the server or mainframe. Clients may work via serial or network connections but very little processing or storage will occur on the clients. This is to ensure that the database information is accurate and up to date. The user keystrokes are passed to the mainframe or server and the information is sent back to the user after the crunching has been completed. With respect to this application, the clients may be considered "thin."

Applications such as word processors or spreadsheets can be either client or server based. In a fully distributed environment with fat clients, the users will have a complete set of applications that do not require any network connectivity. Even without the presence of a network connection the user can be very productive. It is also possible that the word processor exists entirely or in part on the server. In this case, the installation potentially saves space on the client machines. The user cannot work with these applications unless they are connected and possibly authenticated. This type of installation allows control of the use of the applications and the software licenses.

Software licenses can cost a great deal of money at purchase time, and there is always the possibility of fines if they are improperly administered. The server can act to control the number of users using the applications at any one time. This can also create problems if the number of licenses is not updated when new users are added. More than one user has been locked out of a network application because there were too many people already logged in.

Direct effects of running network applications in one form or another include an increase of network traffic and the extent to which users rely on the network to function. Depending on the type of network installed, performance can be dramatically reduced if everyone is required to use the network while they work. In the company example above, this was exactly the case and increased expenditures and installations were required as the network was effectively disabled by the network applications. These same users will have reduced effectiveness if all or even part of the network is down.

Storage of user data is another key component of any client/server discussion. With a large user population, the number of files generated can be staggering and the storage space required measured in the hundreds of gigabytes or even terabytes. Many companies require all users to store company data on servers for the purposes of security and backup. Add to this the advent of multimedia file types and the potential for high cost storage looms ever nearer. Specialized systems such as storage area networks (SAN), RAID arrays, and network attached storage (NAS) have been forwarded as solutions to the storage and backup problems, but all of these can be costly and require additional maintenance expertise. In the end, the value of the data determines the type of solution chosen. These are all examples of fat server storage.

There are some significant choices to be made when deciding on fat versus thin servers and clients. The choices made can have drastic effects on cost, security, performance, and the impact on end users. Both fat and thin clients (and servers) have particular areas to which they are well suited and every installation is different from the next. It is important to understand the requirements of the installed system, the services required, and the effect of being fat or thin.

7.6 SUMMARY

Client/server computing is the key to realizing the potential of information systems and networks to significantly improve productivity in organizations. With client/server computing, applications are distributed to users on single-user workstations and personal computers. At the same time, resources that can and should be shared are maintained on server systems that are available to all clients. Thus, the client/server architecture is a blend of decentralized and centralized computing.

Typically, the client system provides a graphical user interface (GUI) that enables a user to exploit a variety of applications with minimal training and relative ease. Servers support shared utilities, such as database management systems. The actual application is divided between client and server in a way intended to optimize ease of use and performance.

Because there are no generally accepted standards for client/server networking, a number of products have been developed to bridge the gap between client and server and to enable users to develop multivendor configurations. Such products generally are referred to as middleware. Middleware products are based on either a message-passing or a remote-procedure-call mechanism.

A more recent organizational model that competes with the client/server model is the intranet. An intranet leverages existing Internet applications, especially the Web, to provide an internal suite of applications suited to the needs of an organization. Intranets are easy to set up, involve standardized software, can be deployed on multiple platforms, and require virtually no user training.

7.7 RECOMMENDED READING AND WEB SITES

[BERS96] provides a good technical discussion of the design issues involved in allocating applications to client and server and in middleware approaches; the book also discusses products and standardization efforts. [RENA96] is oriented toward the management aspects of installing client/server systems and selecting applications for that environment. [SIMO95] describes the principles and mechanisms of client/server computing and middleware in the context of two detailed case studies, one for Windows and one for UNIX. [REAG00a] and [REAG00b] are more recent treatments of client/server computing and network design approaches for supporting client/server computing. A good short overview of middleware is [CAMP99].

[EVAN96] provides a practical, detailed how-to manual on setting up a corporate intranet; the book covers a wide spectrum of applications and gives concrete guidance for implementation. [ECKE96] is another good treatment, although somewhat less detailed. A more informal but very enlightening treatment is [BERN98]; this book provides a management-level discussion of the advantages of Web intranets and strategies for building and exploiting them. [PFAF98] is a thorough treatment of extranets.

BERN98   Bernard, R. *The Corporate Intranet.* New York: Wiley, 1998.

BERS96   Berson, A. *Client/Server Architecture.* New York: McGraw-Hill, 1996.

CAMP99   Campbell, A.; Coulson, G.; and Kounavis, M. "Managing Complexity: Middleware Explained." *IT Pro*, October 1999.

ECKE96   Eckel, G. *Intranet Working.* Indianapolis, IN: New Riders, 1996.

EVAN96   Evans, T. *Building an Intranet.* Indianapolis, IN: Sams, 1996.

PFAF98   Pfaffenberger, B. *Building a Strategic Extranet.* Foster City, CA: IDG Books, 1998.

REAG00a   Reagan, P. *Client/Server Computing.* Upper Saddle River, NJ: Prentice Hall, 2000.

REAG00b   Reagan, P. *Client/Server Network: Design, Operation, and Management.* Upper Saddle River, NJ: Prentice Hall, 2000.

RENA96   Renaud, P. *An Introduction to Client/Server Systems.* New York: Wiley, 1996.

SIMO95   Simon, A., and Wheeler, T. *Open Client/Server Computing and Middleware.* Chestnut Hill, MA: AP Professional Books, 1995.

Recomended Web Sites:

- **Complete Intranet Resource Site:** Wide range of resources useful in research, planning, design, and implementation of intranets
- **Intranet Journal:** Includes news and features, as well as links to intranet vendors and other intranet-related sites

7.8   KEY TERMS, REVIEW QUESTIONS, AND PROBLEMS

Key Terms

application programming interface (API)	extranet	network news
	graphical user interface (GUI)	object-oriented middleware
client	intranet	remote procedure call (RPC)
client/server	message	server
electronic mailing list	middleware	USENET

Review Questions

7.1. What is client/server computing?

7.2. What distinguishes client/server computing from any other form of distributed data processing?

7.3. Discuss the rationale for locating applications on the client, the server, or split between client and server.

7.4. What are four different ways processing can be divided between machines communicating with each other?

7.5. How are machines interacting in client/server based systems different from a typical laptop or desktop computer?

7.6. What are fat clients and fat servers, and what are the differences in philosophy of the two approaches?

7.7. Suggest pros and cons for fat client and fat server strategies.

7.8. What is middleware?

7.9. Middleware is often required for clients accessing data in different locations. Are telnet and ftp examples of applications requiring middleware?

7.10. Because we have standards such as TCP/IP and OSI, why is middleware needed?

7.11. What is an intranet?

7.12. What is the distinction between client/server and intranet?

7.13. What is an extranet?

7.14. List some benefits of the information sharing provided by an extranet.

7.15. What are the communications options available for converting an intranet into an extranet?

Problems

7.1 You have just been hired as the CIO of an organization that has been in business for a while and has recently acquired another smaller organizations in order to increase market share. The original organization operated a fleet of buses that conducted tours and travel packages along the northern portion of the U.S. eastern coast. All of their computer applications existed on a central mainframe at their headquarters in Baltimore, MD. The acquired organization conducted helicopter tours around New York City and Washington, DC. All of their systems were C/S based (primarily fat clients accessing thin DB servers) and they were based outside Baltimore, MD near the BWI airport. Due to the mergers, the organization's IT architecture is now a disparate combination of computer systems and manual procedures. Given the general description of the stakeholder groups below and using the general C/S classes defined in Figure 7.5, prepare a cohesive IT architectural plan for the new organization and present it to the CEO for approval. Address all potential advantages and disadvantages of the plan from the perspectives of the various groups of stakeholders.
- bus/helicopter maintenance workers and mechanics (10 employees)
  - system for ordering parts/supplies
- drivers/pilots (20 employees)
  - logs and route/schedule information
- administration/HR (5 employees)
  - employee records
  - financial records
- marketing (8 employees)
  - marketing activities
  - customer interactions (CRM)
- management (9 employees)
  - reports

7.2 The Java programming language is referred to by some as the language of the Web, due to its platform independent nature. Java uses a hybrid form of RPC and CORBA called RMI (Remote Method Invocation). How does RMI differ from these two technologies and for what type of environment might RMI be an acceptable (or even optimal) solution?
Reference:
> http://www.25hoursaday.com/DistributedComputingTechnologies Explained.html

7.3 A relatively new term that has been introduced to the web environment is that of the Web Service. What is a Web Service and how does it differ from the concept of a Web application?
Reference: http://www.w3.org/TR/2003/WD-ws-gloss-20030514/

7.4   What are the client/server based applications that are part of your operating system?

7.5   What are some of the servers on your local network operating within the client/server paradigm? Where are these servers located? What are the IP addresses of the servers? What are the names of the servers?

7.6   This chapter discusses "fat clients." There has been a good deal of work, past and present, in the area of thin clients. How would you characterize a thin client?

7.7   This chapter has introduced the term *intranet*. Previously the term *Internet* has also been introduced. Based on your understanding of these terms, draw a diagram depicting your local intranet (school network) and your organization's (school's) connection to the Internet.

- How big is your network?
- Who is your Internet service provider?
- How many networks comprise your school network?
- How many users does the network serve?
- What kind of network performance have you received?

Case Study III: ING Life

ING Life (formerly NN Financial) is a leading provider of life insurance products in Canada. The company is based in Ontario and operates out of three regional offices. Over 2000 brokerage partners market its products [BRUN99, IBM00]. In 1997 most of the brokers relied on fax, phone, and postal services to request policy information. Response times could sometimes be measured in hours. The company did have a 56-kbps frame relay wide area network, but that only connected the Ontario headquarters to 70 managing general agent offices (Figure III.1). The systems in Ontario converted the frame relay requests to SNA from TCP/IP and routed them to the corporate mainframe in Connecticut.

In December of 1997, ING decided it had to reduce response times to remain competitive and attract new brokers. The company wanted a cost-effective solution that could provide its brokers fast access to mainframe data and scale to accommodate new partners. ING investigated extending the existing frame relay network and estimated the cost at a prohibitive $3.3 million. Instead, the company decided to build an extranet and offer a Web-to-host service that would allow partners to access mainframe data directly via the Internet. ING estimated the annual cost of extranet services for 2000 brokers at $70,000. The annual cost of maintaining the existing WAN for 70 brokers was $750,000.

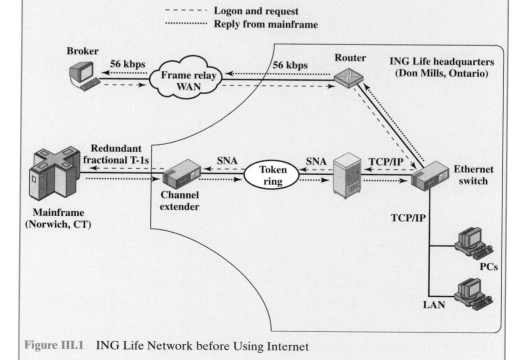

Figure III.1   ING Life Network before Using Internet

205

Besides reducing maintenance costs, the Web-to-host solution offered other benefits. The client software installed automatically as a browser applet, thereby reducing administrative costs. Also, using a browser as an interface meant that brokers were no longer tied to a specific workstation or PC.

The new solution would include two NT servers, a new SNA gateway, to translate between SNA and IP, and a Cisco Pix firewall connected to the Internet via a leased T-1 line (Figure III.2). The NT servers would run Lotus Notes, IBM Host on Demand (Web-to-host software), and Web server software. Because this service would send private data over the public Internet, security was a concern. The Pix firewall would prevent unauthorized access to the data. In addition, the Web-to-host software used an SSL (secure sockets layer) connection (described in Chapter 18). Before bringing the service on line, ING had security consultants probe the system for vulnerabilities.

By July of 1999, ING had 350 brokers connected to the extranet and plans to connect the remaining brokers by sometime in 2000. To use the new service, brokers connect to the Internet using dial-up and point their browser at the Web server. The Host on Demand client loads automatically as a browser applet. The applet provides TN3270 emulation services. After the applet has loaded, the broker can access the corporate mainframe as if he is using a directly connected TN3270 terminal. Response times for extranet requests are less than one minute.

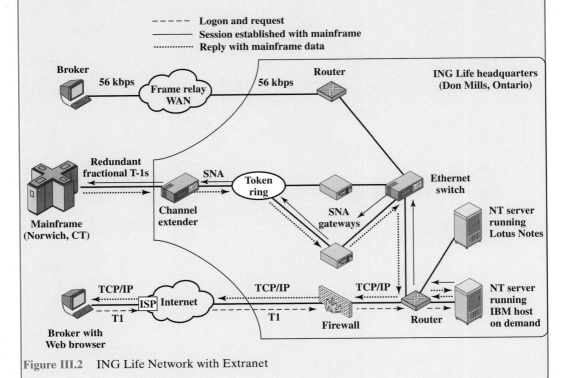

Figure III.2   ING Life Network with Extranet

Discussion Questions

1. What are the probable difficulties and risk associated with using public infrastructure, such as the Internet, as part of a private business solution?

2. Discuss the precautions taken by ING to ensure security. Were the measures adequate?

3. Comment on the extranet topology. Are there any potential bottlenecks?

CHAPTER 8

INTERNET OPERATION

After reading this chapter, you should be able to

- Describe Internet addressing and appreciate the key issues involved in address assignment.
- Understand the difference between an interior routing protocol and an exterior routing protocol.
- Explain the basic mechanisms in a routing protocol.
- Understand the concept of quality of service.
- Explain the difference between elastic traffic and inelastic traffic.
- Discuss the services provided by a differentiated services facility.

This chapter looks at some of the details "under the hood" of the Internet. We begin by examining the rather complicated issue of addressing in such a far-flung, massive, and dynamic configuration. Next the chapter provides an overview of routing protocols, by which routers cooperate to design routes, or paths, through the Internet from source to destination. Then we introduce the issue of quality of service. Finally, we look at the most important approach to providing quality of service on the Internet.

8.1 INTERNET ADDRESSING

The source and destination address fields in the IP header each contain a 32-bit global Internet address, generally consisting of a network identifier and a host identifier.

Network Classes

The address is coded to allow a variable allocation of bits to specify network and host, as depicted in Figure 8.1. This encoding provides flexibility in assigning addresses to hosts and allows a mix of network sizes on an internet. The three principal network classes are best suited to the following conditions:

- **Class A:** Few networks, each with many hosts
- **Class B:** Medium number of networks, each with a medium number of hosts
- **Class C:** Many networks, each with a few hosts

In a particular environment, it may be best to use addresses all from one class. For example, a corporate internetwork that consists of a large number of departmental local area networks may need to use Class C addresses exclusively. However, the format of the addresses is such that it is possible to mix all three classes of addresses on the same internetwork; this is what is done in the case of the Internet

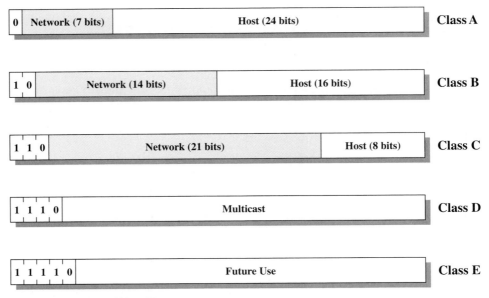

Figure 8.1   IPv4 Address Formats

itself. A mixture of classes is appropriate for an internetwork consisting of a few large networks, many small networks, plus some medium-sized networks.

IP addresses are usually written in what is called **dotted decimal notation,** with a decimal number representing each of the octets of the 32-bit address. For example, the IP address 11000000 11100100 00010001 00111001 is written as 192.228.17.57.

Note that all Class A network addresses begin with a binary 0. Network addresses with a first octet of 0 (binary 00000000) and 127 (binary 01111111) are reserved, so there are 126 potential Class A network numbers, which have a first dotted decimal number in the range 1 to 126. Class B network addresses begin with a binary 10, so that the range of the first decimal number in a Class B address is 128 to 191 (binary 10000000 to 10111111). The second octet is also part of the Class B address, so that there are $2^{14} = 16,384$ Class B addresses. For Class C addresses, the first decimal number ranges from 192 to 223 (11000000 to 11011111). The total number of Class C addresses is $2^{21} = 2,097,152$.

Subnets and Subnet Masks

The concept of subnet was introduced to address the following requirement. Consider an internet that includes one or more WANs and a number of sites, each of which has a number of LANs. We would like to allow arbitrary complexity of interconnected LAN structures within an organization while insulating the overall Internet against explosive growth in network numbers and routing complexity. One approach to this problem is to assign a single network number to all of the LANs at a site. From the point of view of the rest of the Internet, there is a single network at that site, which simplifies addressing and routing. To allow the routers within the site to function properly, each LAN is assigned a subnet number. The *host* portion of the Internet address is partitioned into a subnet number and a host number to accommodate this new level of addressing.

Within the subnetted network, the local routers must route on the basis of an extended network number consisting of the *network* portion of the IP address and the subnet number. The address mask indicates the bit positions containing this extended network number. The use of the address mask allows the host to determine whether an outgoing datagram is destined for a host on the same LAN (send directly) or another LAN (send datagram to router). It is assumed that some other means (e.g., manual configuration) are used to create address masks and make them known to the local routers.

Table 8.1a shows the calculations involved in the use of a subnet mask. Note that the effect of the subnet mask is to erase the portion of the host field that refers to an actual host on a subnet. What remain are the network number and the subnet number. Figure 8.2 shows an example of the use of subnetting. The figure shows a local complex consisting of three LANs and two routers. To the rest of the Internet, this complex is a single network with a Class C address of the form 192.228.17.*x*, where the leftmost three octets are the network number and the rightmost octet contains a host number *x*. Both routers R1 and R2 are configured with a subnet mask with the value 255.255.255.224 (see Table 8.1a). For example, if a datagram with the destination address 192.228.17.57 arrives at R1 from either the rest of the Internet or from LAN Y, R1 applies the subnet mask to determine that this address refers to subnet 1, which is LAN X, and so forwards the datagram to LAN X. Similarly, if a datagram with that destination address arrives at R2 from LAN Z, R2 applies the mask and then determines from its forwarding database that datagrams destined for subnet 1 should be forwarded to R1. Hosts must also employ a subnet mask to make routing decisions.

Table 8.1   IP Addresses and Subnet Masks

(a) Dotted decimal and binary representations of IP address and subnet masks		
	Binary Representation	**Dotted Decimal**
IP address	11000000.11100100.00010001.00111001	192.228.17.57
Subnet mask	11111111.11111111.11111111.11100000	255.255.255.224
Bitwise AND of address and mask (resultant network/subnet number)	11000000.11100100.00010001.00100000	192.228.17.32
Subnet number	11000000.11100100.00010001.001	1
Host number	00000000.00000000.00000000.00011001	25

(b) Default subnet masks		
	Binary Representation	**Dotted Decimal**
Class A default mask	11111111.00000000.00000000.00000000	255.0.0.0
Example Class A mask	11111111.11000000.00000000.00000000	255.192.0.0
Class B default mask	11111111.11111111.00000000.00000000	255.255.0.0
Example Class B mask	11111111.11111111.11111000.00000000	255.255.248.0
Class C default mask	11111111.11111111.11111111.00000000	255.255.255.0
Example Class C mask	11111111.11111111.11111111.11111100	255.255.255.252

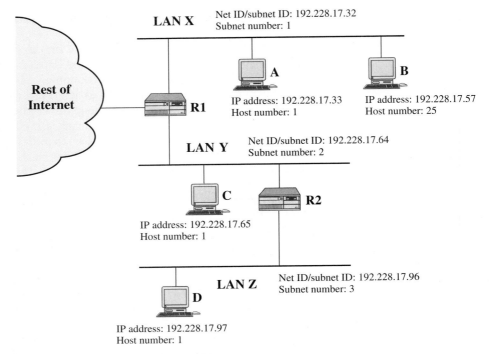

Figure 8.2   Example of Subnetworking

The default subnet mask for a given class of addresses is a null mask (Table 8.1b), which yields the same network and host number as the non-subnetted address.

8.2   INTERNET ROUTING PROTOCOLS

The routers in an internet are responsible for receiving and forwarding packets through the interconnected set of networks. Each router makes routing decisions based on knowledge of the topology and traffic/delay conditions of the internet. In a simple internet, a fixed routing scheme is possible, in which a single, permanent route is configured for each source-destination pair of nodes in the network. The routes are fixed, or at most only change when there is a change in the topology of the network. Thus, the link costs used in designing routes cannot be based on any dynamic variable such as traffic. They could, however, be based on estimated traffic volumes between various source-destination pairs or the capacity of each link.

In more complex internets, a degree of dynamic cooperation is needed among routers. In particular, routers must avoid portions of the network that have failed and should avoid portions of the network that are congested. To make such dynamic routing decisions, routers exchange routing information using a special routing protocol for that purpose. Information is needed about the status of the internet, in terms of which networks can be reached by which routes, and the delay characteristics of various routes.

In considering the routing function, it is important to distinguish two concepts:

- **Routing information:** Information about the topology and delays of the internet
- **Routing algorithm:** The algorithm used to make a routing decision for a particular datagram, based on current routing information

Autonomous Systems

To proceed with our discussion of routing protocols, we need to introduce the concept of an **autonomous system.** An autonomous system (AS) exhibits the following characteristics:

1. An AS is a set of routers and networks managed by a single organization.
2. An AS consists of a group of routers exchanging information via a common routing protocol.
3. Except in times of failure, an AS is connected (in a graph-theoretic sense); that is, there is a path between any pair of nodes.

A shared routing protocol, which we shall refer to as an **interior router protocol** (IRP), passes routing information between routers within an AS. The protocol used within the AS does not need to be implemented outside of the system. This flexibility allows IRPs to be custom tailored to specific applications and requirements.

It may happen, however, that an internet will be constructed of more than one AS. For example, all of the LANs at a site, such as an office complex or campus, could be linked by routers to form an AS. This system might be linked through a wide area network to other ASs. The situation is illustrated in Figure 8.3. In this case, the routing algorithms and information in routing tables used by routers in different ASs may differ. Nevertheless, the routers in one AS need at least a minimal level of information concerning networks outside the system that can be reached. We refer to the protocol used to pass routing information between routers in different ASs as an **exterior router protocol** (ERP).[1]

In general terms, IRPs and ERPs have a somewhat different flavor. An IRP needs to build up a rather detailed model of the interconnection of routers within an AS in order to calculate the least-cost path from a given router to any network within the AS. An ERP supports the exchange of summary reachability information between separately administered ASs. Typically, this use of summary information means that an ERP is simpler and uses less detailed information than an IRP.

In the remainder of this section, we look at what are perhaps the most important examples of these two types of routing protocols: BGP and OSPF.

Border Gateway Protocol

The Border Gateway Protocol (BGP) was developed for use in conjunction with internets that employ the TCP/IP suite, although the concepts are applicable to any internet. BGP has become the preferred exterior router protocol for the Internet.

---

[1]In the literature, the terms *interior gateway protocol* (IGP) and *exterior gateway protocol* (EGP) are often used for what are referred to here as IRP and ERP. However, because the terms *IGP* and *EGP* also refer to specific protocols, we avoid their use to define the general concepts.

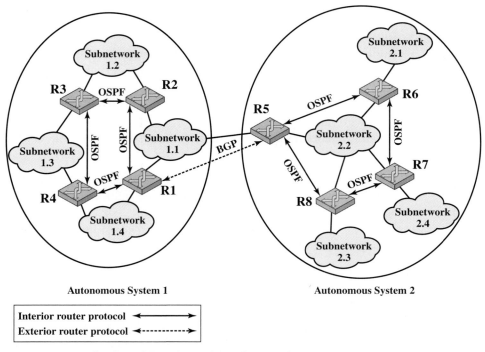

Figure 8.3   Application of Exterior and Interior Routing Protocols

BGP was designed to allow routers, called gateways in the standard, in different autonomous systems (ASs) to cooperate in the exchange of routing information. The protocol operates in terms of messages, which are sent over TCP connections. The current version of BGP is known as BGP-4.

Three functional procedures are involved in BGP:

- Neighbor acquisition
- Neighbor reachability
- Network reachability

Two routers are considered to be neighbors if they are attached to the same network. If the two routers are in different autonomous systems, they may wish to exchange routing information. For this purpose, it is necessary first to perform **neighbor acquisition.** The term *neighbor* refers to two routers that share the same network. In essence, neighbor acquisition occurs when two neighboring routers in different autonomous systems agree to exchange routing information regularly. A formal acquisition procedure is needed because one of the routers may not wish to participate. For example, the router may be overburdened and may not want to be responsible for traffic coming in from outside the AS. In the neighbor acquisition process, one router sends a request message to the other, which may either accept or refuse the offer. The protocol does not address the issue of how one router knows the address or even the existence of another router, nor how it decides that it needs to exchange routing information with that particular router. These issues must be dealt with at configuration time or by active intervention of a network manager.

To perform neighbor acquisition, one router sends an Open message to another. If the target router accepts the request, it returns a Keepalive message in response.

Once a neighbor relationship is established, the **neighbor reachability** procedure is used to maintain the relationship. Each partner needs to be assured that the other partner still exists and is still engaged in the neighbor relationship. For this purpose, the two routers periodically issue Keepalive messages to each other.

The final procedure specified by BGP is **network reachability.** Each router maintains a database of the networks that it can reach and the preferred route for reaching each network. Whenever a change is made to this database, the router issues an Update message that is broadcast to all other routers for which it has a neighbor relationship. Because the Update message is broadcast, all BGP routers can build up and maintain their routing information.

Open Shortest Path First (OSPF) Protocol

The OSPF protocol is widely used as an interior router protocol in TCP/IP networks. OSPF uses what is known as a link state routing algorithm. Each router maintains descriptions of the state of its local links to networks, and from time to time transmits updated state information to all of the routers of which it is aware. Every router receiving an update packet must acknowledge it to the sender. Such updates produce a minimum of routing traffic because the link descriptions are small and rarely need to be sent.

OSPF computes a route through the internet that incurs the least cost based on a user-configurable metric of cost. The user can configure the cost to express a function of delay, data rate, dollar cost, or other factors. OSPF is able to equalize loads over multiple equal-cost paths.

Each router maintains a database that reflects the known topology of the autonomous system of which it is a part. The topology is expressed as a directed graph. The graph consists of the following:

- Vertices, or nodes, of two types:
  - Router
  - Network, which is in turn of two types:
    — Transit, if it can carry data that neither originates nor terminates on an end system attached to this network
    — Stub, if it is not a transit network
- Edges, of two types:
  - A graph edge that connects two router vertices when the corresponding routers are connected to each other by a direct point-to-point link.
  - A graph edge that connects a router vertex to a network vertex when the router is directly connected to the network.

Figure 8.4 shows an example of an autonomous system, and Figure 8.5 is the resulting directed graph. The mapping is straightforward:

- Two routers joined by a point-to-point link are represented in the graph as being directly connected by a pair of edges, one in each direction (e.g., routers 6 and 10).

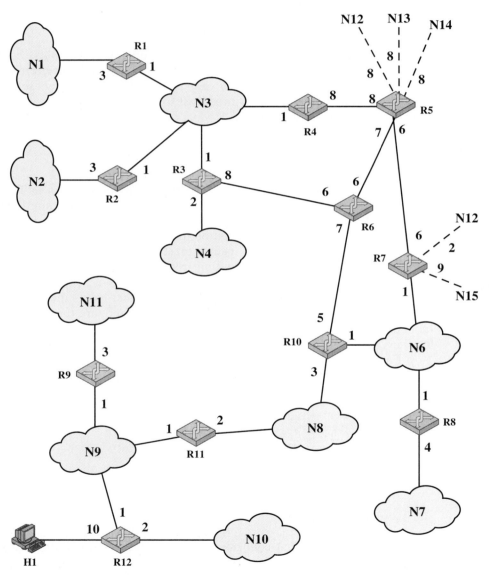

Figure 8.4 A Sample Autonomous System

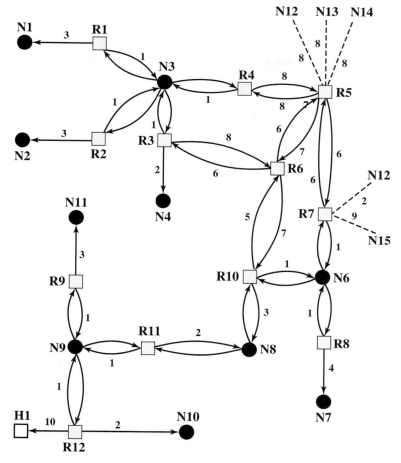

Figure 8.5   Directed Graph of Autonomous System of Figure 8.4

- When multiple routers are attached to a network (such as a LAN or packet-switching network), the directed graph shows all routers bidirectionally connected to the network vertex (e.g., routers 1, 2, 3, and 4 all connect to network 3).

- If a single router is attached to a network, the network will appear in the graph as a stub connection (e.g., network 7).

- An end system, called a host, can be directly connected to a router, in which case it is depicted in the corresponding graph (e.g., host 1).

- If a router is connected to other autonomous systems, then the path cost to each network in the other system must be obtained by some exterior routing protocol (ERP). Each such network is represented on the graph by a stub and an edge to the router with the known path cost (e.g., networks 12 through 15).

A cost is associated with the output side of each router interface. This cost is configurable by the system administrator. Arcs on the graph are labeled with the cost of the corresponding router output interface. Arcs having no labeled cost have a cost of 0. Note that arcs leading from networks to routers always have a cost of 0.

A database corresponding to the directed graph is maintained by each router. It is pieced together from link state messages from other routers in the internet. Using an algorithm explained in the next subsection, a router calculates the least-cost path to all destination networks. The results for router 6 of Figure 8.4 are shown as a tree in Figure 8.6, with R6 as the root of the tree. The tree gives the entire route to any destination network or host. However, only the next hop to the destination is used in the forwarding process. The resulting routing table for router 6 is shown in Table 8.2. The table includes entries for routers advertising external routes (routers 5 and 7). For external networks whose identity is known, entries are also provided.

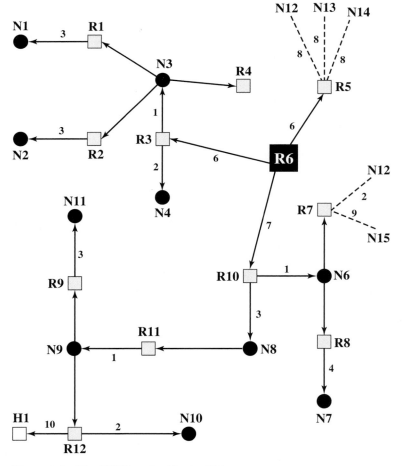

Figure 8.6 The SPF Tree for Router R6

Table 8.2   Routing Table for R6

Destination	Next Hop	Distance
N1	R3	10
N2	R3	10
N3	R3	7
N4	R3	8
N6	R10	8
N7	R10	12
N8	R10	10
N9	R10	11
N10	R10	13
N11	R10	14
H1	R10	21
R5	R5	6
R7	R10	8
N12	R10	10
N13	R5	14
N14	R5	14
N15	R10	17

8.3   THE NEED FOR SPEED AND QUALITY OF SERVICE

Momentous changes in the way corporations do business and process information have been driven by changes in networking technology and at the same time have driven those changes. It is hard to separate chicken and egg in this field. Similarly, the use of the Internet by both businesses and individuals reflects this cyclic dependency: The availability of new image-based services on the Internet (i.e., the Web) has resulted in an increase in the total number of users and the traffic volume generated by each user. This, in turn, has resulted in a need to increase the speed and efficiency of the Internet. On the other hand, it is only such increased speed that makes the use of Web-based applications palatable to the end user.

In this section, we survey some of the end-user factors that fit into this equation. We begin with the need for high-speed LANs in the business environment, because this need has appeared first and has forced the pace of networking development. Then we look at business WAN requirements. Then we offer a few words about the effect of changes in commercial electronics on network requirements. Finally, we relate the requirements for quality of service (QoS) to the Internet.

The Emergence of High-Speed LANs

Personal computers and microcomputer workstations began to achieve widespread acceptance in business computing in the early 1980s and have now achieved virtually the status of the telephone: an essential tool for office workers. Until relatively recently, office LANs provided basic connectivity services—connecting personal computers and terminals to mainframes and midrange systems that ran corporate applications and providing workgroup connectivity at the departmental or divisional level. In both cases, traffic patterns were relatively light, with an emphasis on file transfer and electronic mail. The LANs that were available for this type of workload, primarily Ethernet and token ring, are well suited to this environment.

In recent years, two significant trends altered the role of the personal computer and therefore the requirements on the LAN:

1. The speed and computing power of personal computers continued to enjoy explosive growth. These more powerful platforms support graphics-intensive applications and ever more elaborate graphical user interfaces to the operating system.

2. IT (information technology) organizations have recognized the LAN as a viable and essential computing platform, resulting in the focus on network computing. This trend began with client/server computing, which has become a dominant architecture in the business environment and the more recent Web-focused intranet trend. Both of these approaches involve the frequent transfer of potentially large volumes of data in a transaction-oriented environment.

The effect of these trends has been to increase the volume of data to be handled over LANs and, because applications are more interactive, to reduce the acceptable delay on data transfers. The earlier generation of 10-Mbps Ethernets and 16-Mbps token rings is simply not up to the job of supporting these requirements. The following are examples of requirements that call for higher-speed LANs:

- **Centralized server farms:** In many applications, there is a need for user, or client, systems to be able to draw huge amounts of data from multiple centralized servers, called server farms. An example is a color publishing operation, in which servers typically contain tens of gigabytes of image data that must be downloaded to imaging workstations. As the performance of the servers themselves has increased, the bottleneck has shifted to the network.

- **Power workgroups:** These groups typically consist of a small number of cooperating users who need to draw massive data files across the network. Examples are a software development group that runs tests on a new software version, or a computer-aided design (CAD) company that regularly runs simulations of new designs. In such cases, large amounts of data are distributed to several workstations, processed, and updated at very high speed for multiple iterations.

- **High-speed local backbone:** As processing demand grows, LANs proliferate at a site, and high-speed interconnection of these LANs is necessary.

Corporate Wide Area Networking Needs

As recently as the early 1990s, there was an emphasis in many organizations on a centralized data processing model. In a typical environment, there might be significant computing facilities at a few regional offices, consisting of mainframes or well-equipped midrange systems. These centralized facilities could handle most corporate applications, including basic finance, accounting, and personnel programs, as well as many of the business-specific applications. Smaller, outlying offices (e.g., a bank branch) could be equipped with terminals or basic personal computers linked to one of the regional centers in a transaction-oriented environment.

This model began to change in the early 1990s, and the change accelerated through the mid-1990s. Many organizations have dispersed their employees into multiple smaller offices. There is a growing use of telecommuting. Most significant, the nature of the application structure has changed. First client/server computing and, more recently, intranet computing have fundamentally restructured the organizational data processing environment. There is now much more reliance on personal computers, workstations, and servers and much less use of centralized mainframe and midrange systems. Furthermore, the virtually universal deployment of graphical user interfaces to the desktop enables the end user to exploit graphic applications, multimedia, and other data-intensive applications. In addition, most organizations require access to the Internet. Because a few clicks of the mouse can trigger huge volumes of data, traffic patterns have become more unpredictable while the average load has risen.

All of these trends mean that more data must be transported off premises and onto wide-area networks. It has long been accepted that in the typical business environment, about 80% of the traffic remains local and about 20% traverses wide area links. But this rule no longer applies to most companies, with a greater percentage of the traffic going into the WAN environment [COHE96]. This traffic flow shift places a greater burden on LAN backbones and, of course, on the WAN facilities used by a corporation. Thus, just as for LANs, changes in corporate data traffic patterns are driving the creation of high-speed WANs.

Digital Electronics

The rapid conversion of consumer electronics to digital technology is having an impact on both the Internet and corporate intranets. As these new gadgets come into view and proliferate, they dramatically increase the amount of image and video traffic carried by networks.

Two noteworthy examples of this trend are digital versatile discs and digital still cameras.

Digital Versatile Disc (DVD) With the capacious DVD, the electronics industry has at last found an acceptable replacement for the analog VHS videotape. The DVD will replace the videotape used in videocassette recorders (VCRs) and, more important for this discussion, replace the CD-ROM in personal computers and servers. The DVD takes video into the digital age. It delivers movies with picture quality that outshines laser discs, and it can be randomly accessed like audio CDs, which DVD machines can also play. Vast volumes of data can be crammed onto the disc, currently seven times as much as a CD-ROM. With DVD's huge storage capacity and vivid quality, PC games have become more realistic and educational software incorporates more video. Following in the wake of these developments is a new crest of traffic over the Internet and corporate intranets, as this material is incorporated into Web sites.

A related product development is the digital camcorder. This product will make it easier for individuals and companies to make digital video files to be placed on corporate and Internet Web sites, again adding to the traffic burden.

Digital Still Camera Although the digital still camera has been around for many years, it has only recently begun to take off because prices have dropped to reasonable levels. The convenience for use in networks is unsurpassed. An individual can take a picture of a loved one or pet and transfer it to a Web page. Companies can quickly develop online product catalogs with full-color pictures of every product. Thus, there has been a dramatic growth in the amount of online image and video traffic in recent years.

QoS on the Internet

As the Internet and private internets grow in scale, a host of new demands march steadily into view. Low-volume TELNET conversations are leapfrogged by high-volume client/server applications. To this has been added more recently the tremendous volume of Web traffic, which is increasingly graphics intensive. Now, real-time voice and video applications add to the burden.

To cope with these demands, it is not enough to increase internet capacity. Sensible and effective methods for managing the traffic and controlling congestion are needed.

The Internet and the Internet Protocol (IP) were designed to provide a **best-effort,** fair delivery service. Under a best-effort scheme, the Internet (or a private intranet) treats all packets equally. As the level of traffic on the network grows, and congestion occurs, all packet delivery is slowed down. If congestion becomes severe, packets are dropped more or less at random to ease the congestion. No distinction is made in terms of the relative importance of any traffic or of the timeliness requirements of any of the traffic.

With the tremendous increase in traffic volume and the introduction of new real-time, multimedia, and multicasting applications, the traditional Internet protocols and services are woefully inadequate. But the needs of users have changed. A company may have spent millions of dollars installing an IP-based internet designed to transport data among LANs but now finds that new real-time, multimedia, and multicasting applications are not well supported by such a configuration. The only networking scheme designed from day one to support both traditional TCP and UDP traffic and real-time traffic is ATM. However, reliance on ATM means either constructing a second networking infrastructure for real-time traffic or replacing the existing IP-based configuration with ATM, both of which are costly alternatives.

Traffic on a network or internet can be divided into two broad categories: elastic and inelastic. A consideration of their differing requirements clarifies the need for an enhanced internet architecture.

Elastic traffic can adjust, over wide ranges, to changes in delay and throughput across an internet and still meet the needs of its applications. This is the traditional type of traffic supported on TCP/IP-based internets and is the type of traffic for which internets were designed. With TCP, traffic on individual connections adjusts to congestion by reducing the rate at which data are presented to the network.

Elastic applications include common Internet-based applications, such as file transfer, electronic mail, remote logon, network management, and Web access. But there are differences among the requirements of these applications. For example,

- E-mail is generally quite insensitive to changes in delay.
- When file transfer is done online, as it frequently is, the user expects the delay to be proportional to the file size and so is sensitive to changes in throughput.

- With network management, delay is generally not a serious concern. However, if failures in an internet are the cause of congestion, then the need for network management messages to get through with minimum delay increases with increased congestion.

- Interactive applications, such as remote logon and Web access, are quite sensitive to delay.

So, even if we confine our attention to elastic traffic, a QoS-based internet service could be of benefit. Without such a service, routers are dealing evenhandedly with arriving IP packets, with no concern for the type of application and whether this packet is part of a large transfer or a small one. Under such circumstances, and if congestion develops, it is unlikely that resources will be allocated in such a way as to meet the needs of all applications fairly. When inelastic traffic is added to the mix, matters are even more unsatisfactory.

Inelastic traffic does not easily adapt, if at all, to changes in delay and throughput across an internet. The prime example is real-time traffic, such as voice and video. The requirements for inelastic traffic may include the following:

- **Throughput:** A minimum throughput value may be required. Unlike most elastic traffic, which can continue to deliver data with perhaps degraded service, many inelastic applications require a firm minimum throughput.

- **Delay:** An example of a delay-sensitive application is stock trading; someone who consistently receives later service will consistently act later, and with greater disadvantage.

- **Delay variation:** The larger the allowable delay, the longer the real delay in delivering the data and the greater the size of the delay buffer required at receivers. Real-time interactive applications, such as teleconferencing, may require a reasonable upper bound on delay variation.

- **Packet loss:** Real-time applications vary in the amount of packet loss, if any, that they can sustain.

These requirements are difficult to meet in an environment with variable queuing delays and congestion losses. Accordingly, inelastic traffic introduces two new requirements into the internet architecture. First, some means is needed to give preferential treatment to applications with more demanding requirements. Applications need to be able to state their requirements, either ahead of time in some sort of service request function, or on the fly, by means of fields in the IP packet header.

A second requirement in supporting inelastic traffic in an internet architecture is that elastic traffic must still be supported. Inelastic applications typically do not back off and reduce demand in the face of congestion, in contrast to TCP-based applications. Therefore, unless some control is imposed, in times of congestion inelastic traffic will continue to supply a high load and elastic traffic will be crowded off the internet.

Another way to look at the traffic requirements of an organization is shown in Figure 8.7 [CROL00]. Applications can be characterized by two broad categories. The requirement of delay sensitivity can be satisfied by a QoS that emphasizes timely delivery and/or provides a high data rate. The requirement of criticality can be satisfied by a QoS that emphasizes reliability.

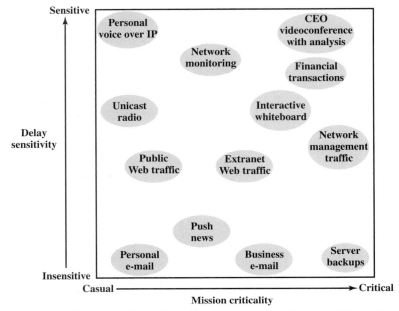

Figure 8.7   A Comparison of Application Delay Sensitivity and Criticality in an Enterprise

Several mechanisms for providing QoS services on the Internet have been proposed. The one that has received the broadest acceptance is known as differentiated services. We turn to this topic next.

8.4   DIFFERENTIATED SERVICES

As the burden on the Internet grows, and as the variety of applications grows, there is an immediate need to provide differing levels of QoS to different users. The differentiated services (DS) architecture is designed to provide a simple, easy-to-implement, low-overhead tool to support a range of network services that are differentiated on the basis of performance. In essence, **differentiated services** do not provide QoS on the basis of flows but rather on the basis of the needs of different groups of users. This means that all the traffic on the Internet is split into groups with different QoS requirements and that routers recognize different groups on the basis of a label in the IP header.

Several key characteristics of DS contribute to its efficiency and ease of deployment:

- IP packets are labeled for differing QoS treatment using the 6-bit DS field in the IPv4 and IPv6 headers (Figure 5.7). No change is required to IP.
- A service-level agreement (SLA) is established between the service provider (internet domain) and the customer prior to the use of DS. This avoids the need to incorporate DS mechanisms in applications. Thus, existing applications need not be modified to use DS.

- DS provides a built-in aggregation mechanism. All traffic with the same DS octet is treated the same by the network service. For example, multiple voice connections are not handled individually but in the aggregate. This provides for good scaling to larger networks and traffic loads.

- DS is implemented in individual routers by queuing and forwarding packets based on the DS octet. Routers deal with each packet individually and do not have to save state information on packet flows.

Today, DS is the most widely accepted QoS mechanism in enterprise networks.

Services

The DS type of service is provided within a DS domain, which is defined as a contiguous portion of the Internet over which a consistent set of DS policies are administered. Typically, a DS domain would be under the control of one administrative entity. The services provided across a DS domain are defined in a service-level agreement (SLA), which is a service contract between a customer and the service provider that specifies the forwarding service that the customer should receive for various classes of packets. A customer may be a user organization or another DS domain. Once the SLA is established, the customer submits packets with the DS octet marked to indicate the packet class. The service provider must assure that the customer gets at least the agreed QoS for each packet class. To provide that QoS, the service provider must configure the appropriate forwarding policies at each router (based on DS octet value) and must measure the performance being provided to each class on an ongoing basis.

If a customer submits packets intended for destinations within the DS domain, then the DS domain is expected to provide the agreed service. If the destination is beyond the customer's DS domain, then the DS domain will attempt to forward the packets through other domains, requesting the most appropriate service to match the requested service.

A DS framework document lists the following detailed performance parameters that might be included in an SLA:

- Service performance parameters, such as expected throughput, drop probability, and latency

- Constraints on the ingress and egress points at which the service is provided, indicating the scope of the service

- Traffic profiles that must be adhered to for the requested service to be provided

- Disposition of traffic submitted in excess of the specified profile

The framework document also gives some examples of services that might be provided:

1. Traffic offered at service level A will be delivered with low latency.

2. Traffic offered at service level B will be delivered with low loss.

3. Ninety percent of in-profile traffic delivered at service level C will experience no more than 50 ms latency.

4. Ninety-five percent of in-profile traffic delivered at service level D will be delivered.

5. Traffic offered at service level E will be allotted twice the bandwidth of traffic delivered at service level F.

6. Traffic with drop precedence X has a higher probability of delivery than traffic with drop precedence Y.

The first two examples are qualitative and are valid only in comparison to other traffic, such as default traffic that gets a best-effort service. The next two examples are quantitative and provide a specific guarantee that can be verified by measurement on the actual service without comparison to any other services offered at the same time. The final two examples are a mixture of quantitative and qualitative.

DS Field

Packets are labeled for service handling by means of the 6-bit DS field in the IPv4 header or the IPv6 header (Figure 5.7). The value of the DS field, referred to as the **DS codepoint,** is the label used to classify packets for differentiated services.

With a 6-bit codepoint, there are, in principle, 64 different classes of traffic that could be defined. These 64 codepoints are allocated across three pools of codepoints, as follows:

- Codepoints of the form xxxxx0, where x is either 0 or 1, are reserved for assignment as standards.
- Codepoints of the form xxxx11 are reserved for experimental or local use.
- Codepoints of the form xxxx01 are also reserved for experimental or local use, but may be allocated for future standards action as needed.

Within the first pool, the codepoint 000000 is the default packet class. The default class is the best-effort forwarding behavior in existing routers. Such packets are forwarded in the order that they are received as soon as link capacity becomes available. If other higher-priority packets in other DS classes are available for transmission, these are given preference over default best-effort packets.

Codepoints of the form xxx000 are reserved to provide backward compatibility with the IPv4 precedence service. To explain this requirement, we need to digress to an explanation of the IPv4 precedence service. The original IPv4 type of service (TOS) field includes two subfields: a 3-bit precedence subfield and a 4-bit TOS subfield. These subfields serve complementary functions. The TOS subfield provides guidance to the IP entity (in the source or router) on selecting the next hop for this datagram, and the precedence subfield provides guidance about the relative allocation of router resources for this datagram.

The precedence field is set to indicate the degree of urgency or priority to be associated with a datagram. If a router supports the precedence subfield, there are three approaches to responding:

- **Route selection:** A particular route may be selected if the router has a smaller queue for that route or if the next hop on that route supports network precedence or priority (e.g., a token ring network supports priority).

- **Network service:** If the network on the next hop supports precedence, then that service is invoked.
- **Queuing discipline:** A router may use precedence to affect how queues are handled. For example, a router may give preferential treatment in queues to datagrams with higher precedence.

RFC 1812, *Requirements for IP Version 4 Routers,* provides recommendations for queuing discipline that fall into two categories:

- **Queue service**
  (a) Routers SHOULD implement precedence-ordered queue service. Precedence-ordered queue service means that when a packet is selected for output on a (logical) link, the packet of highest precedence that has been queued for that link is sent.
  (b) Any router MAY implement other policy-based throughput management procedures that result in other than strict precedence ordering, but it MUST be configurable to suppress them (i.e., use strict ordering).
- **Congestion control.** When a router receives a packet beyond its storage capacity, it must discard it or some other packet or packets.
  (a) A router MAY discard the packet it has just received; this is the simplest but not the best policy.
  (b) Ideally, the router should select a packet from one of the sessions most heavily abusing the link, given that the applicable QoS policy permits this. A recommended policy in datagram environments using FIFO queues is to discard a packet randomly selected from the queue. An equivalent algorithm in routers using fair queues is to discard from the longest queue. A router MAY use these algorithms to determine which packet to discard.
  (c) If precedence-ordered queue service is implemented and enabled, the router MUST NOT discard a packet whose IP precedence is higher than that of a packet that is not discarded.
  (d) A router MAY protect packets whose IP headers request the maximize reliability TOS, except where doing so would be in violation of the previous rule.
  (e) A router MAY protect fragmented IP packets, on the theory that dropping a fragment of a datagram may increase congestion by causing all fragments of the datagram to be retransmitted by the source.
  (f) To help prevent routing perturbations or disruption of management functions, the router MAY protect packets used for routing control, link control, or network management from being discarded. Dedicated routers (i.e., routers that are not also general purpose hosts, terminal servers, etc.) can achieve an approximation of this rule by protecting packets whose source or destination is the router itself.

The DS codepoints of the form xxx000 should provide a service that at minimum is equivalent to that of the IPv4 precedence functionality.

DS Configuration and Operation

Figure 8.8 illustrates the type of configuration envisioned in the DS documents. A DS domain consists of a set of contiguous routers; that is, it is possible to get from any

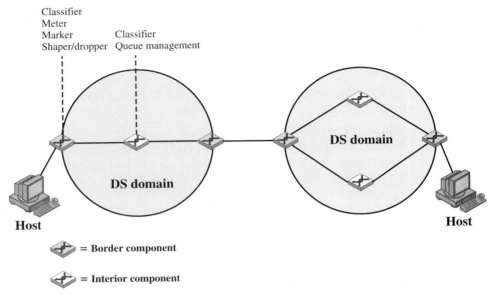

Figure 8.8   DS Domains

router in the domain to any other router in the domain by a path that does not include routers outside the domain. Within a domain, the interpretation of DS code-points is uniform, so that a uniform, consistent service is provided.

Routers in a DS domain are either boundary nodes or interior nodes. Typi-cally, the interior nodes implement simple mechanisms for handling packets based on their DS codepoint values. This includes a queuing discipline to give preferential treatment depending on codepoint value, and packet-dropping rules to dictate which packets should be dropped first in the event of buffer saturation. The DS specifications refer to the forwarding treatment provided at a router as per-hop behavior (PHB). This PHB must be available at all routers, and typically PHB is the only part of DS implemented in interior routers.

The boundary nodes include PHB mechanisms but also more sophisticated traffic conditioning mechanisms required to provide the desired service. Thus, inte-rior routers have minimal functionality and minimal overhead in providing the DS service, while most of the complexity is in the boundary nodes. The boundary node function can also be provided by a host system attached to the domain, on behalf of the applications at that host system.

The traffic conditioning function consists of five elements:

- **Classifier:** Separates submitted packets into different classes. This is the founda-tion of providing differentiated services. A classifier may separate traffic only on the basis of the DS codepoint (behavior aggregate classifier) or based on multiple fields within the packet header or even the packet payload (multifield classifier).

- **Meter:** Measures submitted traffic for conformance to a profile. The meter determines whether a given packet stream class is within or exceeds the ser-vice level guaranteed for that class.

- **Marker:** Re-marks packets with a different codepoint as needed. This may be done for packets that exceed the profile; for example, if a given throughput is guaranteed for a particular service class, any packets in that class that exceed the throughput in some defined time interval may be re-marked for best effort handling. Also, re-marking may be required at the boundary between two DS domains. For example, if a given traffic class is to receive the highest supported priority, and this is a value of 3 in one domain and 7 in the next domain, then packets with a priority 3 value traversing the first domain are remarked as priority 7 when entering the second domain.

- **Shaper:** Delays packets as necessary so that the packet stream in a given class does not exceed the traffic rate specified in the profile for that class.

- **Dropper:** Drops packets when the rate of packets of a given class exceeds that specified in the profile for that class.

Figure 8.9 illustrates the relationship between the elements of traffic conditioning. After a flow is classified, its resource consumption must be measured. The metering function measures the volume of packets over a particular time interval to determine a flow's compliance with the traffic agreement. If the host is bursty, a simple data rate or packet rate may not be sufficient to capture the desired traffic characteristics. A token bucket scheme is an example of a way to define a traffic profile to take into account both packet rate and burstiness.

A token bucket traffic specification consists of two parameters: a token replenishment rate R and a bucket size B. The token rate R specifies the continually sustainable data rate; that is, over a relatively long period of time, the average data rate to be supported for this flow is R. The bucket size B specifies the amount by which the data rate can exceed R for short periods of time. The exact

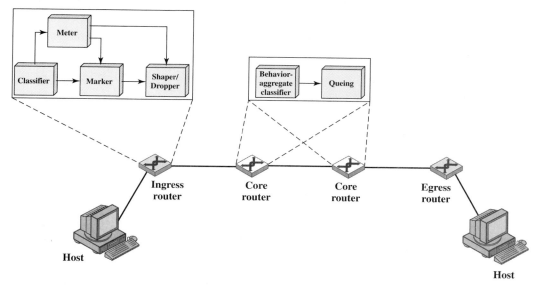

Figure 8.9 DS Functions

condition is as follows: During any time period T, the amount of data sent cannot exceed $RT + B$.

Figure 8.10 illustrates this scheme and explains the use of the term *bucket*. The bucket represents a counter that indicates the allowable number of octets of IP data that can be sent at any time. The bucket fills with *octet tokens* at the rate of R (i.e., the counter is incremented R times per second), up to the bucket capacity (up to the maximum counter value). IP packets arrive and are queued for processing. An IP packet may be processed if there are sufficient octet tokens to match the IP data size. If so, the packet is processed and the bucket is drained of the corresponding number of tokens. If a packet arrives and there are insufficient tokens available, then the packet exceeds the limit for this flow.

Over the long run, the rate of IP data allowed by the token bucket is R. However, if there is an idle or relatively slow period, the bucket capacity builds up, so that at most an additional B octets above the stated rate can be accepted. Thus, B is a measure of the degree of burstiness of the data flow that is allowed.

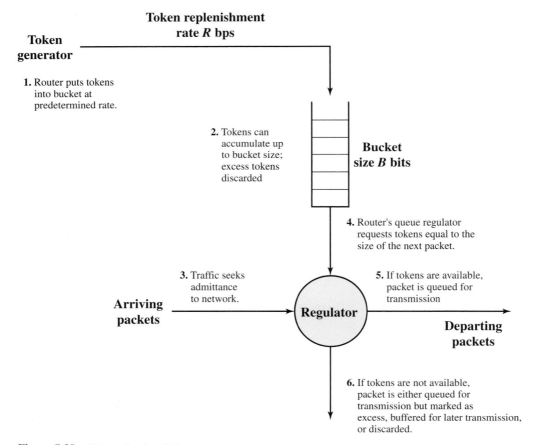

Figure 8.10   Token Bucket Scheme

If a traffic flow exceeds some profile, several approaches can be taken. Individual packets in excess of the profile may be re-marked for lower-quality handling and allowed to pass into the DS domain. A traffic shaper may absorb a burst of packets in a buffer and pace the packets over a longer period of time. A dropper may drop packets if the buffer used for pacing becomes saturated.

APPLICATION NOTE
Where does my network address come from?

Any network desiring connectivity to the rest of the world, regardless of its size, must get a network address from an Internet service provider (ISP). There are several approaches to assigning the addresses for the network and the network nodes. Network addresses are also closely linked to domain name registration (organization identity), which is also commonly handled by the ISP.

The two basic approaches can be described in terms of the number of computers that will have globally unique Internet addresses. Globally unique addresses are those that can only be used by one computer in the public Internet space. All communication interfaces connected to the Internet have globally unique addresses. These computers or interfaces are often referred to as the "visible" machines. *Visible* means that these computers are directly attached to the public Internet. This does not mean that "invisible" machines are barred from communicating over the Internet. Being visible also implies that the machines are more exposed to attack from hackers; this is true. Being invisible usually indicates that there is a firewall, specifically a network address translation firewall, between the computer and the Internet.

An organization may decide to have all of its machines use these globally unique addresses and be visible to the Internet. The reasons for this approach are related to concerns over connectivity and resource availability. In this case, the ISP must assign many addresses to the organization. This can be done by assigning a class address to the group. For example, a company having 200 nodes may request that a class C address be assigned to them. Class addressing is becoming less and less common. It is more likely that the ISP will assign addresses from within its own address space.

Large ISPs can control hundreds of thousands of IP addresses and, using the subnet mask, can assign a slice of this address space to their clients. For example, an ISP like Time Warner may control a large portion of the address space within a class A network. This address space constitutes millions of addresses. A small percentage of these addresses can be provided to an individual company. When this is done, it is also common to see the ISP handling a good number of services for the company like DNS, security and mail.

Another option is to have a small number of globally unique addresses assigned by the ISP and use these addresses as the outside connection to the company firewalls. In this type of configuration, the company computers would typically be invisible and the firewall would act as a communication proxy to the outside world. This process is called network address translation. All of the transmissions coming from the company network appear to have come from the outside interface of the company firewall. Thus, all of the inside machines are termed "invisible."

However, this presents the problem of addressing for the inside nodes. These are not coming from the ISP and so must be assigned by the local network administrator, either by static configuration or by DHCP. Care must be taken to avoid using standard Internet addressing internally. If internal machines are assigned the same addresses as external visible machines, the routers on the Internet will not be able to route traffic back to the internal company machines. This is because the addresses have potentially been allocated to other hosts that are located elsewhere.

For this reason, private IP addressing has been established. The Internet addresses

10.0.0.0 – 10.255.255.255 (10/8 prefix)

172.16.0.0 – 172.31.255.255 (172.16/12 prefix)

192.168.0.0 – 192.168.255.255 (192.168/16 prefix)

have been reserved for organizations wishing to deploy networks in this manner. Private addressing is described in detail in RFC 1918. Aside from the benefit of security for the internal machines, this scheme was introduced to alleviate the problem of increasing numbers of users on the Internet. With this tremendous growth, the number of globally unique addresses in IPv4 is insufficient for everyone to have their own public address.

There are benefits and drawbacks to each of the methods outlined above. Private addressing usually requires more management, at least in the form of a DHCP server, but does provide increased security and reduction in public address space used. Using public addressing throughout does ease the management and has the potential for easing connectivity concerns, as there are fewer firewall rules to contend with. However, it can make the organization dependent on the ISP for a large number of its concerns, including security.

8.5 SUMMARY

An essential element of the Internet is its addressing scheme. It is necessary that each attached host have a unique address to make routing and delivery possible. Internet standards define a 32-bit addressing scheme for this purpose.

An internet routing protocol is used to exchange information about reachability and traffic delays, allowing each router to construct a next-hop routing table for paths through the internet. Typically, relatively simple routing protocols are used between autonomous systems within a larger internet and more complex routing protocols are used within each autonomous system.

The increasing data rate (capacity) requirements of applications have spurred the development of higher speeds in data networks and the Internet. The higher available capacity has in turn encouraged ever more data-intensive applications. To cope with the varying demands on the Internet, the concept of quality of service has been introduced. A QoS facility allows the Internet to treat different classes of traffic differently in order to optimize the service to all customers.

The differentiated services architecture is designed to provide a simple, easy-to-implement, low-overhead tool to support a range of network services that are differentiated on the basis of performance. Differentiated services are provided on the basis of a 6-bit label in the IP header, which classifies traffic in terms of the type of service to be given by routers for that traffic.

8.6 RECOMMENDED READING

For the reader interested in a more in-depth discussion of IP addressing, [SPOR03] offers a wealth of detail. An excellent treatment of QoS is [CROL00].

[HUIT00], [BLAC00], and [PERL00] provide detailed coverage of various routing algorithms. [KESH98] provides an instructive look at present and future router functionality.

Perhaps the clearest and most comprehensive book-length treatment of Internet QoS is [ARMI00]. [XIAO99] provides an overview and overall framework for Internet QoS as well as integrated and differentiated services. [CLAR92] and [CLAR95] provide valuable surveys of the issues involved in internet service allocation for real-time and elastic applications, respectively. [SHEN95] is a masterful analysis of the rationale for a QoS-based internet architecture.

ARMI00 Armitage, G. *Quality of Service in IP Networks*. Indianapolis, IN: Macmillan Technical Publishing, 2000.

BLAC00 Black, U. *IP Routing Protocols: RIP, OSPF, BGP, PNNI & Cisco Routing Protocols*. Upper Saddle River, NJ: Prentice Hall, 2000.

CLAR92 Clark, D.; Shenker, S.; and Zhang, L. "Supporting Real-Time Applications in an Integrated Services Packet Network: Architecture and Mechanism" *Proceedings, SIGCOMM '92*, August 1992.

CLAR95 Clark, D. *Adding Service Discrimination to the Internet*. MIT Laboratory for Computer Science Technical Report, September 1995. Available at http://ana-www.lcs.mit.edu/anaweb/papers.html.

CROL00 Croll, A., and Packman, E. *Managing Bandwidth: Deploying QoS in Enterprise Networks*. Upper Saddle River, NJ: Prentice Hall, 2000.

HUIT00 Huitema, C. *Routing in the Internet*. Upper Saddle River, NJ: Prentice Hall, 2000.

KESH98 Keshav, S., and Sharma, R. "Issues and Trends in Router Design." *IEEE Communications Magazine*, May 1998.

PERL00 Perlman, R. *Interconnections: Bridges, Routers, Switches, and Internetworking Protocols*. Reading, MA: Addison-Wesley, 2000.

SHEN95 Shenker, S. "Fundamental Design Issues for the Future Internet." *IEEE Journal on Selected Areas in Communications*, September 1995.

SPOR03 Sportack, M. *IP Addressing Fundamentals*. Indianapolis, IN: Cisco Press, 2003.

XIAO99 Xiao, X., and Ni, L. "Internet QoS: A Big Picture." *IEEE Network*, March/April 1999.

8.7 KEY TERMS, REVIEW QUESTIONS, AND PROBLEMS

Key Terms

autonomous system (AS) best effort Border Gateway Protocol (BGP) differentiated services dotted decimal notation elastic traffic	exterior routing protocol inelastic traffic interior routing protocol neighbor Open Shortest Path First (OSPF) quality of service (QoS)	routing routing algorithm routing protocol subnet subnet mask token bucket

Review Questions

8.1. Describe the five classes of Internet addresses.

8.2. What is a subnet?

8.3. What is the purpose of the subnet mask?

8.4. What is an autonomous system?

8.5. What is the difference between an interior router protocol and an exterior router protocol?

8.6. List and briefly explain the three main functions of BGP.

8.7. OSPF uses what type of routing algorithm?

8.8. OSPF is designed as what type of routing protocol?

8.9. Define quality of service (QoS).

8.10. Explain the difference between elastic and inelastic traffic.

8.11. What are the four possible requirements for inelastic traffic?

8.12. What is the purpose of a DS codepoint?

8.13. List and briefly explain the five main functions of DS traffic conditioning.

8.14. What is a token bucket and how does it work?

Problems

8.1 Provide the following parameter values for each of the network classes A, B, and C. Be sure to consider any special or reserved addresses in your calculations.
  a. Number of bits in network portion of address
  b. Number of bits in host portion of address
  c. Number of distinct networks allowed
  d. Number of distinct hosts per network allowed
  e. Integer range of first octet

8.2 What percentage of the total IP address space does each of the network classes represent?

8.3 What is the difference between the subnet mask for a Class A address with 16 bits for the subnet ID and a class B address with 8 bits for the subnet ID?

8.4 Is the subnet mask 255.255.0.255 valid for a Class A address?

8.5 Given a network address of 192.168.100.0 and a subnet mask of 255.255.255.192,

    a. How many subnets are created?

    b. How many hosts are there per subnet?

8.6 Given a company with six individual departments and each department having ten computers or networked devices, what mask could be applied to the company network to provide the subnetting necessary to divide up the network equally?

8.7 In contemporary routing and addressing, the notation commonly used is called classless interdomain routing or CIDR. With CIDR, the number of bits in the mask is indicated in the following fashion: 192.168.100.0/24. This corresponds to a mask of 255.255.255.0. If this example would provide for 256 host addresses on the network, how many addresses are provided with the following?

    a. 192.168.100.0/23

    b. 192.168.100.0/25

8.8 Find out about your network. Using the command "ipconfig", "ifconfig", or "winipcfg", we can learn not only our IP address but other network parameters as well. Can you determine your mask, gateway, and the number of addresses available on your network?

8.9 Using your IP address and your mask, what is your network address? This is determined by converting the IP address and the mask to binary and then proceeding with a bitwise logical AND operation. For example, given the address 172.16.45.0 and the mask 255.255.224.0, we would discover that the network address would be 172.16.32.0.

8.10 Provide three examples (each) of elastic and inelastic Internet traffic. Justify each example's inclusion in their respective category.

8.11 Why does a Differentiated Services (DS) domain consist of a set of contiguous routers? How are the boundary node routers different from the interior node routers in a DS domain?

8.12 The token bucket scheme places a limit on the length of time at which traffic can depart at the maximum data rate. Let the token bucket be defined by a bucket size of B octets and a token arrival rate of R octets/s, and let the maximum output data rate be M octets/s.

    a. Derive a formula for S, which is the length of the maximum-rate burst. That is, for how long can a flow transmit at the maximum output rate when governed by a token bucket?

    b. What is the value of S for $B = 250$ KB, $R = 2$ MB/s, and $M = 25$ MB/s?

    Hint: The formula for S is not as simple as it might appear, because more tokens arrive while the burst is being output.

PART THREE

Local Area Networks

The trend in local area networks (LANs) involves the use of shared transmission media or shared switching capacity to achieve high data rates over relatively short distances. Several key issues present themselves. One is the choice of transmission medium. Whereas coaxial cable was commonly used in traditional LANs, contemporary LAN installations emphasize the use of twisted pair or optical fiber. In the case of twisted pair, efficient encoding schemes are needed to enable high data rates over the medium. Wireless LANs have also assumed increased importance. Another design issue is that of access control.

Chapter 9 LAN Architecture and Protocols

An essential element of any organization's data processing operation is a local area network (LAN). A LAN is needed to interconnect equipment on the user's premises and to provide a means to efficiently connect to outside services and other corporate sites. Chapter 9 provides an overview of LAN technology and standards, including a discussion of transmission media, medium access control, and standards.

Chapter 10 Ethernet and Fibre Channel

Chapter 10 looks in detail at the transmission media, and MAC protocols of the two most significant LAN systems in current use; both of these have been defined in standards documents. The most important of these is Ethernet, which has been deployed in versions at 10 Mbps, 100 Mbps, 1 Gbps, and 10 Gbps. Then the chapter looks at Fibre Channel, which is widely used for storage area networks and other high-speed applications.

Chapter 11 Wireless LANs

Wireless LANs use one of three transmission techniques: spread spectrum, narrowband microwave, and infrared. Chapter 11 provides an overview wireless LAN technology and applications. The most significant set of standards defining wireless LANs are those defined by the IEEE 802.11 committee. Another important wireless LAN standard is Bluetooth. Chapter 11 also examines both standards in some detail.

CHAPTER 9

LAN ARCHITECTURE AND PROTOCOI

Recent years have seen rapid changes in the technology, design, and commercial applications for local area networks (LANs). A major feature of this evolution is the introduction of a variety of new schemes for high-speed local networking. In this chapter we look at the underlying technology of LANs. Chapters 10 and 11 are devoted to a discussion of specific LAN systems.

9.1 BACKGROUND

The variety of applications for LANs is wide. To provide some insight into the types of requirements that LANs are intended to meet, this section discusses some of the most important general application areas for these networks. In the next section, we look at the implications for LAN configuration.

Personal Computer LANs

A common LAN configuration is one that supports personal computers. With the relatively low cost of PCs, managers within organizations often independently procure personal computers for departmental applications, such as spreadsheet and project management tools, and Internet access.

But a collection of department-level processors will not meet all of an organization's needs; central processing facilities are still required. Some programs, such as econometric forecasting models, are too big to run on a small computer. Corporate-wide data files, such as accounting and payroll, require a centralized facility but should be accessible to a number of users. In addition, there are other kinds of files that, although specialized, must be shared by a number of users. Further, there are sound reasons for connecting individual intelligent workstations not only to a central facility but to each other as well. Members of a project or organization team need to share work and information. By far the most efficient way to do so is digitally.

Certain expensive resources, such as a large disc system or a laser printer, can be shared by all users of the departmental LAN. In addition, the network can tie into larger corporate network facilities. For example, the corporation may have a building-wide LAN and a wide area private network. A communications server can provide controlled access to these resources.

LANs for the support of personal computers and workstations have become nearly universal in organizations of all sizes. Even those sites that still depend heavily on the mainframe have transferred much of the processing load to networks of personal computers. Perhaps the prime example of the way in which personal computers are being used is to implement client/server applications.

For personal computer networks, a key requirement is low cost. In particular, the cost of attachment to the network must be significantly less than the cost of the attached device. Thus, for the ordinary personal computer, an attachment cost in the tens of dollars is desirable. For more expensive, high-performance workstations, higher attachment costs can be tolerated. In any case, this suggests that the data rate of the network may be limited; in general, the higher the data rate, the higher the cost.

Backend Networks and Storage Area Networks

Backend networks are used to interconnect large systems such as mainframes, supercomputers, and mass storage devices. The key requirement here is for bulk data transfer among a limited number of devices in a small area. High reliability is generally also a requirement. Typical characteristics include the following:

- **High data rate:** To satisfy the high-volume demand, data rates of 100 Mbps or more are required.
- **High-speed interface:** Data transfer operations between a large host system and a mass storage device are typically performed through high-speed parallel I/O interfaces, rather than slower communications interfaces. Thus, the physical link between station and network must be high speed.
- **Distributed access:** Some sort of distributed medium access control (MAC) technique is needed to enable a number of devices to share the LAN with efficient and reliable access.
- **Limited distance:** Typically, a backend network will be employed in a computer room or a small number of contiguous rooms.
- **Limited number of devices:** The number of expensive mainframes and mass storage devices found in the computer room generally is in the tens of devices.

Typically, backend networks are found at sites of large companies or research installations with large data processing budgets. Because of the scale involved, a small difference in productivity can mean millions of dollars.

Consider a site that uses a dedicated mainframe computer. This implies a fairly large application or set of applications. As the load at the site grows, the existing mainframe may be replaced by a more powerful one, perhaps a multiprocessor system. At some sites, a single-system replacement will not be able to keep up; equipment performance growth rates will be exceeded by demand growth rates. The facility will eventually require multiple independent computers.

Again, there are compelling reasons for interconnecting these systems. The cost of system interrupt is high, so it should be possible, easily and quickly, to shift applications to backup systems. It must be possible to test new procedures and applications without degrading the production system. Large bulk storage files must be accessible from more than one computer. Load leveling should be possible to maximize utilization and performance.

It can be seen that some key requirements for backend networks differ from those for personal computer LANs. High data rates are required to keep up with the work, which typically involves the transfer of large blocks of data. The equipment for achieving high speeds is expensive. Fortunately, given the much higher cost of the attached devices, such costs are reasonable.

A concept related to that of the backend network is the **storage area network** (SAN). A SAN is a separate network to handle storage needs. The SAN decouples storage tasks from specific servers and creates a shared storage facility across a high-speed network. The collection of networked storage devices can include hard discs, tape libraries, and CD arrays. Most SANs use Fibre Channel, which is described in Chapter 10. In a typical large LAN installation, a number of servers and perhaps mainframes each has its own dedicated storage devices. If a client needs access to a particular storage device, it must go through the server that controls that device. In a SAN, no server sits between the storage devices and the network; instead, the storage devices and servers are linked directly to the network. The SAN arrangement improves client-to-storage access efficiency, as well as direct storage-to-storage communications for backup and replication functions.

Figure 9.1 suggests a typical SAN configuration. Users attached to the Internet send file requests (store, retrieve) to a bank of servers. These servers do not maintain the files locally but are connected to a SAN, which supports a number of mass storage devices. The SAN includes network devices optimized to handle storage tasks.

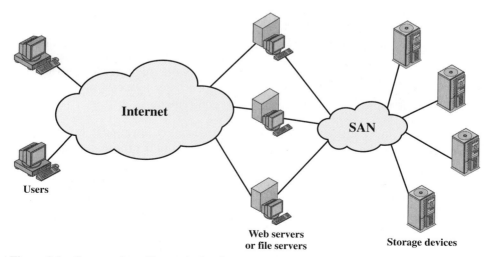

Figure 9.1   Storage Area Network Configuration

High-Speed Office Networks

Traditionally, the office environment has included a variety of devices with low- to medium-speed data transfer requirements. However, for newer applications in the office environment, the limited speeds (up to 10 Mbps) of the traditional LAN are inadequate. Desktop image processors have increased network data flow by an unprecedented amount. Examples of these applications include fax machines, document image processors, and graphics programs on personal computers and workstations. Consider that a typical page with 200 picture elements, or pels[1] (black or white points), per inch resolution (which is adequate but not high resolution) generates 3,740,000 bits (8.5 inches × 11 inches × 40,000 pels per square inch). Even with compression techniques, this will generate a tremendous load. In addition, disc technology and price/performance have evolved so that desktop storage capacities exceeding 1 Gbyte are common. These new demands require LANs with high speed that can support the larger numbers and greater geographic extent of office systems as compared to backend systems.

Backbone LANs

The increasing use of distributed processing applications and personal computers has led to a need for a flexible strategy for local networking. Support of premises-wide data communications requires a networking service that is capable of spanning the distances involved and that interconnects equipment in a single (perhaps large) building or a cluster of buildings. Although it is possible to develop a single LAN to interconnect all the data processing equipment of a premises, this is probably not a practical alternative in most cases. There are several drawbacks to a single-LAN strategy:

- **Reliability:** With a single LAN, a service interruption, even of short duration, could result in a major disruption for users.
- **Capacity:** A single LAN could be saturated as the number of devices attached to the network grows over time.
- **Cost:** A single LAN technology is not optimized for the diverse requirements of interconnection and communication. The presence of large numbers of low-cost microcomputers dictates that network support for these devices be provided at low cost. LANs that support very low cost attachment will not be suitable for meeting the overall requirement.

A more attractive alternative is to employ lower-cost, lower-capacity LANs within buildings or departments and to interconnect these networks with a higher-capacity LAN. This latter network is referred to as a backbone LAN. If confined to a single building or cluster of buildings, a high-capacity LAN can perform the backbone function.

---

[1]A *picture element*, or *pel*, is the smallest discrete scanning-line sample of a facsimile system, which contains only black-white information (no gray scales). A *pixel* is a picture element that contains gray-scale information.

Factory LANs

The factory environment is increasingly being dominated by automated equipment: programmable controllers, automated materials handling devices, time and attendance stations, machine vision devices, and various forms of robots. To manage the production or manufacturing process, it is essential to tie this equipment together. Indeed, the very nature of the equipment facilitates this. Microprocessor devices have the potential to collect information from the shop floor and accept commands. With the proper use of the information and commands, it is possible to improve the manufacturing process and to provide detailed machine control.

The more that a factory is automated, the greater is the need for communications. Only by interconnecting all of the devices and by providing mechanisms for their cooperation can the automated factory work effectively. The means for interconnection is the factory LAN. Key characteristics of a factory LAN include the following:

- High capacity
- Ability to handle a variety of data traffic
- Large geographic extent
- High reliability
- Ability to specify and control transmission delays

Factory LANs are a niche market requiring, in general, more flexible and reliable LANs than are found in the typical office environment.

9.2 LAN CONFIGURATION

Tiered LANs

Consider the kinds of data processing equipment to be supported in a typical organization. In rough terms, we can group this equipment into three categories:

- **Personal computers and workstations:** The workhorse in most office environments is the microcomputer, including personal computers and workstations. Most of this equipment is found at the departmental level, used by individual professionals and secretarial personnel. When used for network applications, the load generated tends to be rather modest.

- **Server farms:** Servers, used within a department or shared by users in a number of departments, can perform a variety of functions. Generic examples include supporting expensive peripherals such as mass storage devices, providing applications that require large amounts of processor resources, and maintaining databases accessible by many users. Because of this shared use, these machines may generate substantial traffic.

- **Mainframes:** For large database and scientific applications, the mainframe is often the machine of choice. When the machines are networked, bulk data transfers dictate that a high-capacity network be used.

The requirements indicated by this spectrum suggest that a single LAN will not, in many cases, be the most cost-effective solution. A single network would have to be rather high speed to support the aggregate demand. However, the cost of attachment to a LAN tends to increase as a function of the network data rate. Accordingly, a high-speed LAN would be very expensive for attachment of low-cost personal computers.

An alternative approach, which is becoming increasingly common, is to employ two or three tiers of LANs (Figure 9.2). Within a department, a low-cost, moderate-speed LAN supports a cluster of personal computers and workstations. These departmental LANs are lashed together with a backbone LAN of higher capacity. In addition, shared systems are also supported off of this backbone. If mainframes are also part of the office equipment suite, then a separate high-speed LAN supports these devices and may be linked, as a whole, to the backbone LAN to support a traffic between the mainframes and other office equipment. We will see that LAN standards and products address the need for all three types of LANs.

Evolution Scenario

One final aspect of the tiered architecture should be mentioned: the way in which such a networking implementation comes about in an organization. This will vary widely from one organization to the next, but two general scenarios can be defined. It is useful to be aware of these scenarios because of their implications for the selection and management of LANs.

In the first scenario, the LAN decisions are made from the bottom up, with each department making decisions more or less in isolation. In this scenario, the

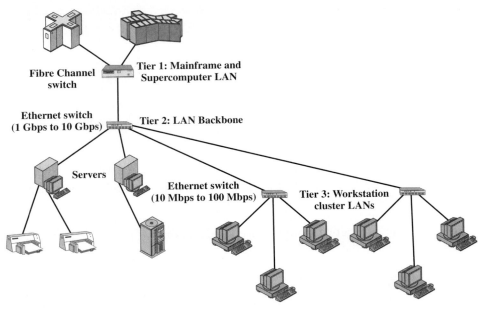

Figure 9.2 Tiered Local Area Networks

particular application requirements of a department are typically well known. For example, an engineering department has very high data rate requirements to support its CAD environment, whereas the sale department has low data rate requirements for its order entry and order inquiry needs. Because the applications are well known, a decision can be made quickly on which network to purchase. Departmental budgets usually can cover the costs of these networks, so approval of a higher authority is not required. The result is that each department will develop its own cluster network (tier 3). In the meantime, if this is a large organization, the central data processing organization may acquire a high-speed (tier 1) LAN to interconnect mainframes.

Over time, many departments will develop their own cluster tier; each department will realize it has a need to interconnect. For example, the marketing department may have to access cost information from the finance department as well as last month's order rate from sales. When cluster-to-cluster communication requirements become important, the company will make a conscious decision to provide interconnect capability. This interconnect capability is realized through the LAN backbone (tier 2).

The advantage of this scenario is that, since the department manager is closest to the department's needs, local interconnect strategies can be responsive to the specific applications of the department, and acquisition can be timely. There are several disadvantages to this approach. First, there is the problem of suboptimization. If procurement is made on a company-wide basis, perhaps less total equipment will be acquired to satisfy the total need. In addition, larger-volume purchases may result in more favorable terms. Second, the company is eventually faced with the need to interconnect all of these departmental LANs. If there are a wide variety of such LANs from many different vendors, the interconnection problem becomes more difficult.

For these reasons, an alternative scenario is becoming increasingly common: a top-down design of a LAN strategy. In this case, the company decides to map out a total local networking strategy. The decision is centralized because it impacts the entire operation or company. The advantage of this approach is built-in compatibility to interconnect the users. The difficulty with this approach is, of course, the need to be responsive and timely in meeting needs at the departmental level.

9.3 GUIDED TRANSMISSION MEDIA

In a data transmission system, the **transmission medium** is the physical path between transmitter and receiver. Transmission media can be classified as guided or unguided. In both cases, communication is in the form of electromagnetic waves. With **guided media,** the waves are guided along a solid medium, such as copper twisted pair, copper coaxial cable, or optical fiber. The atmosphere and outer space are examples of **unguided media,** which provide a means of transmitting electromagnetic signals but do not guide them; this form of transmission is usually referred to as **wireless transmission.**

The characteristics and quality of a data transmission system are determined both by the characteristics of the medium and the characteristics of the signal. In the case of guided media, the medium itself is more important in determining the limitations of transmission. For unguided media, the bandwidth of the signal produced by the transmitting antenna is more important than the medium in determining transmission characteristics. One key property of signals transmitted by antenna is directionality. In general, signals at lower frequencies are omnidirectional; that is, the signal propagates in all directions from the antenna. At higher frequencies, it is possible to focus the signal into a directional beam.

In considering the design of data transmission systems, key concerns are data rate and distance: The greater the data rate and distance capability the better. A number of design factors relating to the transmission medium and the signal determine the data rate and distance:

- **Bandwidth:** All other factors remaining constant, the wider the bandwidth of a signal, the higher the data rate that can be achieved.
- **Transmission impairments:** Impairments, such as attenuation, limit the distance. For guided media, twisted pair generally suffers more impairment than coaxial cable, which in turn suffers more than optical fiber.
- **Interference:** Interference from competing signals in overlapping frequency bands can distort or wipe out a signal. Interference is of particular concern for unguided media but is also a problem with guided media. For guided media, interference can be caused by emanations from nearby cables. For example, twisted pairs are often bundled together and conduits often carry multiple cables. Interference can also be experienced from unguided transmissions. Proper shielding of a guided medium can minimize this problem.
- **Number of receivers:** A guided medium can be used to construct a point-to-point link or a shared link with multiple attachments. In the latter case, each attachment introduces some attenuation and distortion on the line, limiting distance and/or data rate.

Figure 9.3 depicts the electromagnetic spectrum and indicates the frequencies at which various guided media and unguided transmission techniques operate. In this section, we look at the guided media alternatives for LANs; a discussion of wireless media alternatives for LANs is deferred to Chapter 11.

Twisted Pair

A twisted pair consists of two insulated copper wires arranged in a regular spiral pattern (Figure 9.4a). A wire pair acts as a single communication link. Typically, a number of these pairs are bundled together into a cable by wrapping them in a tough protective sheath. Over longer distances, cables may contain hundreds of pairs.

Twisted pair is much less expensive than the other commonly used guided transmission media (coaxial cable, optical fiber) and is easier to work with. Compared to other transmission media, twisted pair is limited in distance, bandwidth, and data rate. The medium is quite susceptible to interference and noise because of its potential for coupling with electromagnetic fields. For example, a wire run parallel to an ac power line will pick up 60-Hz energy. Impulse noise also easily intrudes into twisted pair. Several measures are taken to reduce impairments. Shielding the

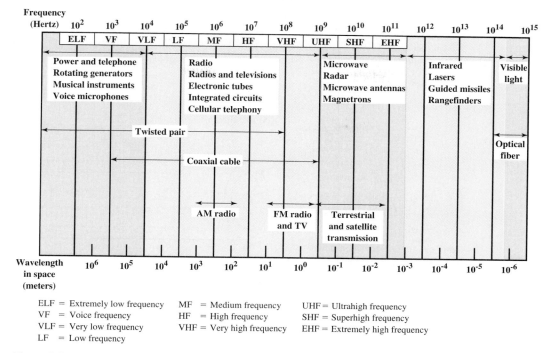

Figure 9.3   Electromagnetic Spectrum for Telecommunications

wire with metallic braid or sheathing reduces interference. The twisting of the wire reduces low-frequency interference, and the use of different twist lengths in adjacent pairs reduces crosstalk.

Unshielded and Shielded Twisted Pair Twisted pair comes in two varieties: unshielded and shielded. **Unshielded twisted pair** (UTP) is ordinary telephone wire. Office buildings, by universal practice, are prewired with excess unshielded twisted pair, more than is needed for simple telephone support. This is the least expensive of all the transmission media commonly used for LANs and is easy to work with and easy to install.

Unshielded twisted pair is subject to external electromagnetic interference, including interference from nearby twisted pair and from noise generated in the environment. A way to improve the characteristics of this medium is to shield the twisted pair with a metallic braid or sheathing that reduces interference. This **shielded twisted pair** (STP) provides better performance at lower data rates. However, it is more expensive and more difficult to work with than unshielded twisted pair.

Category 3 and Category 5 UTP Most office buildings are prewired with a type of twisted pair cable commonly referred to as voice grade. Because voice-grade twisted pair is already installed, it is an attractive alternative for use as a LAN medium. Unfortunately, the data rates and distances achievable with voice-grade twisted pair are limited.

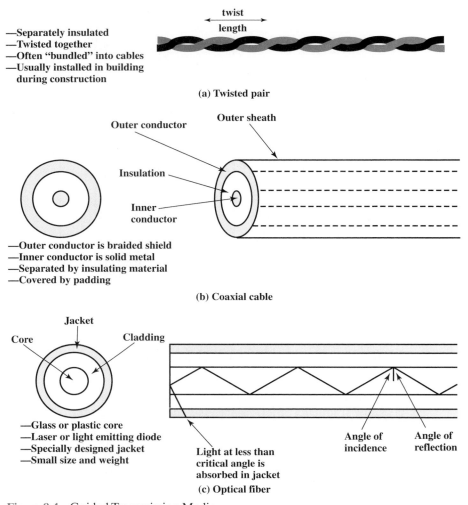

—Separately insulated
—Twisted together
—Often "bundled" into cables
—Usually installed in building
  during construction

twist
length

(a) Twisted pair

Outer conductor

Outer sheath

Insulation

Inner
conductor

—Outer conductor is braided shield
—Inner conductor is solid metal
—Separated by insulating material
—Covered by padding

(b) Coaxial cable

Jacket

Core

Cladding

—Glass or plastic core
—Laser or light emitting diode
—Specially designed jacket
—Small size and weight

Light at less than
critical angle is
absorbed in jacket

Angle of
incidence

Angle of
reflection

(c) Optical fiber

Figure 9.4   Guided Transmission Media

In 1991, the Electronic Industries Association published standard EIA-568, *Commercial Building Telecommunications Cabling Standard*, which specifies the use of voice-grade unshielded twisted pair as well as shielded twisted pair for inbuilding data applications. At that time, the specification was felt to be adequate for the range of frequencies and data rates found in office environments. Up to that time, the principle interest for LAN designs was in the range of data rates from 1 Mbps to 16 Mbps. Subsequently, as users migrated to higher-performance workstations and applications, there was increasing interest in providing LANs that could operate up to 100 Mbps over inexpensive cable. In response to this need, EIA-568-A was issued in 1995. The new standard reflects advances in cable and connector design and test methods. It covers shielded twisted pair and unshielded twisted pair.

EIA-568-A recognizes three categories of UTP cabling:

* **Category 3:** UTP cables and associated connecting hardware whose transmission characteristics are specified up to 16 MHz
* **Category 4:** UTP cables and associated connecting hardware whose transmission characteristics are specified up to 20 MHz
* **Category 5:** UTP cables and associated connecting hardware whose transmission characteristics are specified up to 100 MHz

Of these, Category 3 and Category 5 cable have received the most attention for LAN applications. Category 3 corresponds to the voice-grade cable found in abundance in most office buildings. Over limited distances, and with proper design, data rates of up to 16 Mbps should be achievable with Category 3. Category 5 is a data-grade cable that is becoming increasingly common for preinstallation in new office buildings. Over limited distances, and with proper design, data rates of up to 100 Mbps should be achievable with Category 5.

A key difference between Category 3 and Category 5 cable is the number of twists in the cable per unit distance. Category 5 is much more tightly twisted, with a typical twist length of 0.6 to 0.85 cm, compared to 7.5 to 10 cm for Category 3. The tighter twisting of Category 5 is more expensive but provides much better performance than Category 3.

Table 9.1 summarizes the performance of Category 3 and Category 5 UTP, as well as the STP specified in EIA-568-A. The first parameter used for comparison, attenuation, is fairly straightforward. The strength of a signal falls off with distance over any transmission medium. For guided media attenuation is generally exponential and therefore is typically expressed as a constant number of decibels per unit distance (see Appendix 9A). Attenuation introduces three considerations for the designer. First, a received signal must have sufficient magnitude so that the electronic circuitry in the receiver can detect and interpret the signal. Second, the signal must maintain a level sufficiently higher than noise to be received without error. Third, attenuation is an increasing function of frequency.

Near-end crosstalk as it applies to twisted pair wiring systems is the coupling of the signal from one pair of conductors to another pair. These conductors may be

Table 9.1   Comparison of Shielded and Unshielded Twisted Pair

Frequency (MHz)	Attenuation (dB per 100 m)			Near-End Crosstalk (dB)		
	Category 3 UTP	Category 5 UTP	STP	Category 3 UTP	Category 5 UTP	STP
1	2.6	2.0	1.1	41	62	58
4	5.6	4.1	2.2	32	53	58
16	13.1	8.2	4.4	23	44	50.4
25	—	10.4	6.2	—	41	47.5
100	—	22.0	12.3	—	32	38.5
300	—	—	21.4	—	—	31.3

Table 9.2   Twisted Pair Categories and Classes

	Category 3 Class C	Category 5 Class D	Category 5E	Category 6 Class E	Category 7 Class F
Bandwidth	16 MHz	100 MHz	100 MHz	200 MHz	600 MHz
Cable Type	UTP	UTP/FTP	UTP/FTP	UTP/FTP	SSTP
Link Cost (Cat 5 = 1)	0.7	1	1.2	1.5	2.2

UTP = Unshielded twisted pair
FTP = Foil twisted pair
SSTP = Shielded screen twisted pair

the metal pins in a connector or wire pairs in a cable. The near end refers to coupling that takes place when the transmit signal entering the link couples back to the receive conductor pair at that same end of the link (i.e., the near transmitted signal is picked up by the near receive pair).

Since the publication of EIA-568-A, there has been ongoing work on the development of standards for premises cabling. These are being driven by two issues. First, the Gigabit Ethernet specification requires the definition of parameters that are not specified completely in any published cabling standard. Second, there is a desire to specify cabling performance to higher levels, namely Enhanced Category 5 (Cat 5E), Category 6, and Category 7. Table 9.2 compares these schemes to the existing standards.

Coaxial Cable

Coaxial cable, like twisted pair, consists of two conductors but is constructed differently to permit it to operate over a wider range of frequencies. It consists of a hollow outer cylindrical conductor that surrounds a single inner wire conductor (Figure 9.4b). The inner conductor is held in place by either regularly spaced insulating rings or a solid dielectric material. The outer conductor is covered with a jacket or shield. A single coaxial cable has a diameter of from 1 to 2.5 cm. Because of its shielded, concentric construction, coaxial cable is much less susceptible to interference and crosstalk than is twisted pair. Coaxial cable can be used over longer distances and support more stations on a shared line than twisted pair.

Coaxial cable, like shielded twisted pair, provides good immunity from electromagnetic interference. Coaxial cable is more expensive than shielded twisted pair but provides greater capacity.

Traditionally, coaxial cable has been an important transmission medium for LANs, beginning with the early popularity of Ethernet. However, in recent years, the emphasis has been on low-cost limited distance LANs using twisted pair, and high-performance LANs using optical fiber. The effect is the gradual but steady decline in the use of coaxial cable for LAN implementation, to the point that it is rarely used today except in legacy LANs.

Optical Fiber

An optical fiber is a thin (2 to 125 μm), flexible medium capable of conducting an optical ray. Various glasses and plastics can be used to make optical fibers. The lowest losses have been obtained using fibers of ultrapure fused silica. Ultrapure fiber is difficult to manufacture; higher-loss multicomponent glass fibers are more economical and still provide good performance. Plastic fiber is even less costly and can be used for short-haul links, for which moderately high losses are acceptable.

An optical fiber has a cylindrical shape and consists of three concentric sections (Figure 9.4c). The two innermost are two types of glass with different indexes of refraction. The center one is called the core, and the next layer the cladding. These two sections of glass are covered by a protective, light-absorbing jacket. Optical fibers are grouped together into optical cables.

One of the most significant technological breakthroughs in information transmission has been the development of practical fiber optic communications systems. Optical fiber already enjoys considerable use in long-distance telecommunications, and its use in military applications is growing. The continuing improvements in performance and decline in prices, together with the inherent advantages of optical fiber, have made it increasingly attractive for local area networking. The following characteristics distinguish optical fiber from twisted pair or coaxial cable:

- **Greater capacity:** The potential bandwidth, and hence data rate, of optical fiber is immense; data rates of hundreds of Gbps over tens of kilometers have been demonstrated. Compare this to the practical maximum of hundreds of Mbps over about 1 km for coaxial cable and just a few Mbps over 1 km or up to 100 Mbps over a few tens of meters for twisted pair.

- **Smaller size and lighter weight:** Optical fibers are considerably thinner than coaxial cable or bundled twisted pair cable—at least an order of magnitude thinner for comparable information transmission capacity. For cramped conduits in buildings and underground along public rights-of-way, the advantage of small size is considerable. The corresponding reduction in weight reduces structural support requirements.

- **Lower attenuation:** Attenuation is significantly lower for optical fiber than for coaxial cable or twisted pair and is constant over a wider frequency range.

- **Electromagnetic isolation:** Optical fiber systems are not affected by external electromagnetic fields. Thus the system is not vulnerable to interference, impulse noise, or crosstalk. By the same token, fibers do not radiate energy, causing little interference with other equipment and providing a high degree of security from eavesdropping. In addition, fiber is inherently difficult to tap.

Optical fiber systems operate in the range of about 10^{14} to 10^{15} Hz; this covers portions of the infrared and visible spectrums. The principle of optical fiber transmission is as follows. Light from a source enters the cylindrical glass or plastic core. Rays at shallow angles are reflected and propagated along the fiber; other rays are absorbed by the surrounding material. This form of propagation is called **step-index multimode**, referring to the variety of angles that will reflect. With multimode transmission, multiple propagation paths exist, each with a different path length and hence time to traverse the fiber. This causes signal elements (light pulses) to spread out in time, which limits the rate at which data can be accurately received. Put another way, the need to leave spacing between the pulses limits data rate. This type of fiber is best suited for transmission over very short distances. When the fiber core radius is reduced, fewer angles will reflect. By reducing the radius of the core to the order of a wavelength, only a single angle or mode can pass: the axial ray. This **single-mode** propagation provides superior performance for the following reason. Because there is a single transmission path with single-mode transmission, the distortion found in multimode cannot occur. Single-mode is typically used for long-distance applications, including telephone and cable television. Finally, by varying the index of refraction of the core, a third type of transmission, known as **graded-index multimode**, is possible. This type is intermediate between the other two in characteristics. The higher refractive index at the center makes the light rays moving down the axis advance more slowly than those near the cladding. Rather than zigzagging off the cladding, light in the core curves helically because of the graded index, reducing its travel distance. The shortened path and higher speed allows light at the periphery to arrive at a receiver at about the same time as the straight rays in the core axis. Graded-index fibers are often used in LANs.

Two different types of light source are used in fiber optic systems: the light-emitting diode (LED) and the injection laser diode (ILD). Both are semiconductor devices that emit a beam of light when a voltage is applied. The LED is less costly, operates over a greater temperature range, and has a longer operational life. The ILD, which operates on the laser principle, is more efficient and can sustain greater data rates.

There is a relationship among the wavelength employed, the type of transmission, and the achievable data rate. Both single mode and multimode can support several different wavelengths of light and can employ laser or LED light source. In optical fiber, light propagates best in three distinct wavelength "windows," centered on 850, 1300, and 1550 nanometers (nm). These are all in the infrared portion of the frequency spectrum, below the visible-light portion, which is 400 to 700 nm. The loss is lower at higher wavelengths, allowing greater data rates over longer distances. Most local applications today use 850-nm LED light sources. Although this combination is relatively inexpensive, it is generally limited to data rates under 100 Mbps and distances of a few kilometers. To achieve higher data rates and longer distances, a 1300-nm LED or laser source is needed. The highest data rates and longest distances require 1500-nm laser sources.

Structured Cabling

As a practical matter, the network manager needs a cabling plan that deals with the selection of cable and the layout of the cable in a building. The cabling plan should be easy to implement and accommodate future growth.

To aid in the development of cabling plans, standards have been issued that specify the cabling types and layout for commercial buildings. These standards are referred to as *structured cabling systems*. A structured cabling system is a generic wiring scheme with the following characteristics:

- The scheme refers to the wiring within a commercial building.
- The scope of the system includes cabling to support of all types of information transfer, including voice, LANs, video and image transmission, and other forms of data transmission.

- The cabling layout and cable selection is independent of vendor and end-user equipment.
- The cable layout is designed to encompass distribution to all work areas within the building, so that relocation of equipment does not require rewiring but simply requires plugging the equipment into a preexisting outlet in the new location.

One advantage of such standards is that they provide guidance for preinstallation of cable in new buildings so that future voice and data networking needs can be met without the need to rewire the building. The standards also simplify cable layout design for network managers. Two standards for structured cabling systems have been issued: EIA/TIA-568, issued jointly by the Electronic Industries Association and the Telecommunications Industry Association, and ISO 11801, issued by the International Organization for Standardization. The two standards are quite similar; the details in this section are from the EIA/TIA-568 document.

A structured cabling strategy is based on the use of a hierarchical, star-wired cable layout. Figure 9.5 illustrates the key elements for a typical commercial building. External cables, from the local telephone company and from wide area networks, terminate in an equipment room that is generally on the ground floor or a basement level. Patch panel and cross-connect equipment in the equipment room connect the external cables to internal distribution cable. Typically, the first level of distribution consists of backbone cables. In the simplest implementation, a single backbone cable or set of cables run from the equipment room to telecommunications closets (called *wiring closets*) on each floor. A telecommunications closet differs from the equipment room only in that it is less complex; the telecommunications closet generally contains cross-connect

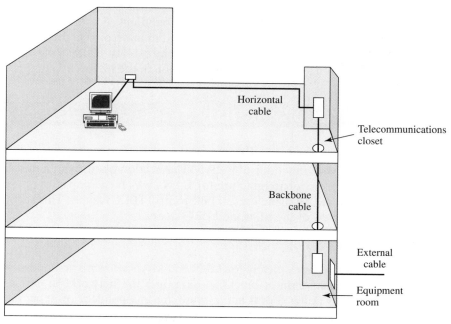

Figure 9.5   Elements of a Structured Cabling Layout

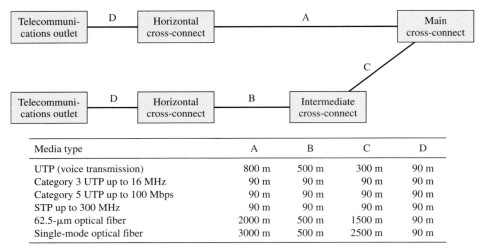

Figure 9.6   Cable Distances Specified in EIA-568-A

equipment for interconnecting cables on a single floor to the backbone. The cable distributed on a single floor is referred to as *horizontal cabling*. This cabling connects the backbone to wall outlets that service individual telephone and data equipment.

The use of a structured cabling plan enables an enterprise to use the transmission media appropriate for its requirements in a systematic and standardized fashion. Figure 9.6 indicates the recommended media for each portion of the structured cabling hierarchy. For horizontal cabling, a maximum distance of 90 m is recommended independent of media type. This distance is adequate to provide coverage for an entire floor for many commercial buildings. For buildings with very large floor space, backbone cable may be required to interconnect multiple telecommunications closets on a single floor. For backbone cabling, distances range from 90 m to 3000 m, depending on cable type and position in the hierarchy.

9.4   LAN PROTOCOL ARCHITECTURE

The architecture of a LAN is best described in terms of a layering of protocols that organize the basic functions of a LAN. This section opens with a description of the standardized protocol architecture for LANs, which encompasses physical, medium access control (MAC), and logical link control (LLC) layers. This section then provides an overview of the MAC and LLC layers.

IEEE 802 Reference Model

Protocols defined specifically for LAN and MAN transmission address issues relating to the transmission of blocks of data over the network. In OSI terms, higher-layer protocols (layer 3 or 4 and above) are independent of network architecture and are applicable to LANs, MANs, and WANs. Thus, a discussion of LAN protocols is concerned principally with lower layers of the OSI model.

Figure 9.7 relates the LAN protocols to the OSI architecture (Figure 5.15). This architecture was developed by the IEEE 802 committee and has been adopted by all organizations working on the specification of LAN standards. It is generally referred to as the IEEE 802 reference model.

Working from the bottom up, the lowest layer of the IEEE 802 reference model corresponds to the **physical layer** of the OSI model and includes such functions as encoding/decoding of signals and bit transmission/reception. In addition, the physical layer includes a specification of the transmission medium. Generally, the transmission medium is considered "below" the lowest layer of the OSI model. However, the choice of transmission medium is critical in LAN design, and so a specification of the medium is included.

Above the physical layer are the functions associated with providing service to LAN users. These include the following:

- On transmission, assemble data into a frame with address and error-detection fields.
- On reception, disassemble frame, and perform address recognition and error detection.
- Govern access to the LAN transmission medium.
- Provide an interface to higher layers and perform flow and error control.

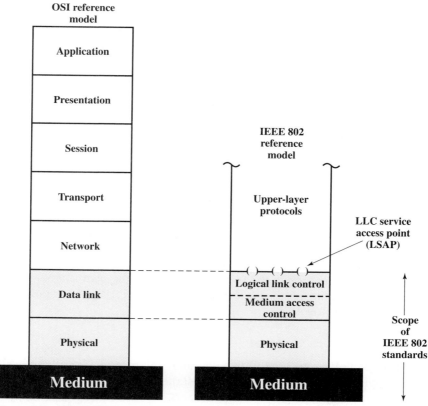

Figure 9.7   IEEE 802 Protocol Layers Compared to OSI Model

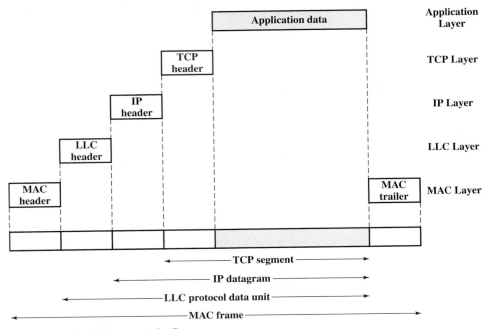

Figure 9.8 LAN Protocols in Context

These are functions typically associated with OSI layer 2. The functions in the last bullet item are grouped into a **Logical Link Control (LLC)** layer. The functions in the first three bullet items are treated as a separate layer, called **Medium Access Control (MAC)**. The separation is done for the following reasons:

- The logic required to manage access to a shared-access medium is not found in traditional layer 2 data link control.
- For the same LLC, several MAC options may be provided.

Figure 9.8 illustrates the relationship between the layers of the architecture (compare Figure 5.9). Higher-level data, such as an IP datagram, are passed down to LLC, which appends control information as a header, creating an **LLC protocol data unit (PDU)**. This control information is used in the operation of the LLC protocol. The entire LLC PDU is then passed down to the MAC layer, which appends control information at the front and back of the packet, forming a **MAC frame**. Again, control information in the frame is needed for the operation of the MAC protocol. For context, the figure also shows the use of TCP/IP and an application layer above the LAN protocols.

Logical Link Control

Logical link control (LLC) is a common link protocol for all the LANs. LLC specifies the mechanisms for addressing stations across the medium and for controlling the exchange of data between two users. Three services are provided as alternatives for attached devices using LLC:

- **Unacknowledged connectionless service:** This service is a datagram-style service. It is a very simple service that does not involve any of the flow control and error control mechanisms. Thus, the delivery of data is not guaranteed. However, in most devices there will be some higher layer of software that deals with reliability issues.

- **Connection-mode service:** This service is similar to that offered by HDLC. A logical connection is set up between two users exchanging data, and flow control and error control are provided.

- **Acknowledged connectionless service:** This is a cross between the previous two services. It provides that datagrams are to be acknowledged, but no prior logical connection is set up.

Typically, a vendor will provide these services as options that the customer can select when purchasing the equipment. Alternatively, the customer can purchase equipment that provides two or all three services and select a specific service based on application.

The **unacknowledged connectionless service** requires minimum logic and is useful in two contexts. First, it will often be the case that higher layers of software will provide the necessary reliability and flow-control mechanism, and it is efficient to avoid duplicating them. For example, TCP provides the mechanisms needed to ensure that data are delivered reliably. Second, there are instances in which the overhead of connection establishment and maintenance is unjustified or even counterproductive. One example is data collection activity that involves the periodic sampling of data sources, such as sensors and automatic self-test reports from security equipment or network components. In a monitoring application, the loss of an occasional data unit would not cause distress, as the next report should arrive shortly. Thus, in most cases, the unacknowledged connectionless service is the preferred option.

The **connection-mode service** could be used in very simple devices, such as terminal controllers, that have little software operating above this level. In these cases, it would provide the flow control and reliability mechanisms normally implemented at higher layers of the communications software.

The **acknowledged connectionless service** is useful in several contexts. With connection-mode service, the logical link control software must maintain some sort of table for each active connection, to keep track of the status of that connection. If the user needs guaranteed delivery, but there are a large number of destinations for data, connection-mode service may be impractical because of the large number of tables required. An example is a process control or automated factory environment where a central site may need to communicate with a large number of processors and programmable controllers. Another use of this is the handling of important and time-critical alarm or emergency control signals in a factory. Because of their importance, an acknowledgment is needed so that the sender can be assured that the signal got through. Because of the urgency of the signal, the user might not want to take the time to first establish a logical connection and then send the data.

The LLC PDU includes destination and source service access point (DSAP, SSAP) addresses. These refer to the next higher layer protocol that uses LLC (typically IP). The LLC PDU also includes a control field that provides a sequencing and flow control mechanism. Such a control field is typical for data link control protocols and is described in Chapter 17.

Medium Access Control

All LANs and MANs (metropolitan area networks) consist of collections of devices that must share the network's transmission capacity. Some means of controlling access to the transmission medium is needed to provide an orderly and efficient use of that capacity. This is the function of a **medium access control** (MAC) protocol.

The relationship between LLC and the MAC protocol can be seen by considering the transmission formats involved. User data are passed down to the LLC layer, which prepares a link-level frame, known as an LLC protocol data unit (PDU). This PDU is then passed down to the MAC layer. where it is enclosed in a MAC frame.

The exact format of the MAC frame differs somewhat for the various MAC protocols in use. In general, all of the MAC frames have a format similar to that of Figure 9.9. The fields of this frame are as follows:

- **MAC Control:** This field contains any protocol control information needed for the functioning of the MAC protocol. For example, a priority level could be indicated here.
- **Destination MAC Address:** The destination physical attachment point on the LAN for this frame.
- **Source MAC Address:** The source physical attachment point on the LAN for this frame.
- **LLC PDU:** The LLC data from the next higher layer. This includes the user data plus the source and destination service access point (SAPs), which indicate the user of LLC.

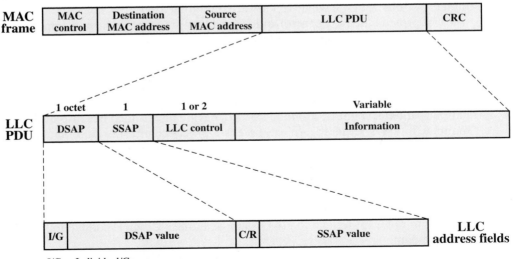

I/G = Individual/Group
C/R = Command/Response

Figure 9.9   LLC PDU in a Generic MAC Frame Format

- **CRC:** The cyclic redundancy check field (also known as the Frame Check Sequence, FCS, field). This is an error-detecting code, such as is used in other data link control protocols (Chapter 17). The CRC operates in the same fashion as the checksum described for TCP in Chapter 5. The CRC is calculated based on the bits in the entire frame. The sender calculates the CRC and adds it to the frame. The receiver performs the same calculation on the incoming frame and compares that calculation to the CRC field in that incoming frame. If the two values don't match, then one or more bits have been accidentally altered in transit.

In most data link control protocols, the data link protocol entity is responsible not only for detecting errors using the CRC, but for recovering from those errors by retransmitting damaged frames. In the LAN protocol architecture, these two functions are split between the MAC and LLC layers. The MAC layer is responsible for detecting errors and discarding any frames that contain errors. The LLC layer optionally keeps track of which frames have been successfully received and retransmits unsuccessful frames.

APPLICATION NOTE
Cabling Infrastructure

A solid cabling infrastructure is the basis for all reliable communications. Even with the advent of wireless communications, the cable plant is extremely important because wireless equipment is eventually connected to the wired backbone. It is easy to see where consideration for cabling is important on new installations, but on older systems it can be just as important for to network upgrades and understanding the system limitations.

There are several important components to the cabling infrastructure, of which cable selection is only a part. While most companies will use contractors for the installation of the network, having the local supervisor understand the issues can mean the difference between a well-built installation and a poor one.

The network will be an integral part of the building systems and so space must be allocated for the wiring closets and consideration given for the location of the data cables. This is similar in scope to the attention given to the electrical system. Wiring closets are the termination points for all of the cabling and where the networking equipment will be located. Wiring closets also include connections to the data center or the backbone, eventually leading to the Internet. Adequate space, cooling, drainage and cleanliness should be provided to ensure long life of the equipment and dependable connectivity. Often wiring closets are seen as an evil necessity and are relegated to the most inhospitable locations within the building. This can result in poor network performance as corrosion, heat, dirt, and interference all serve to degrade communications capability.

The wiring closet should also be located where distance limitations will not be violated. Every communication standard has its own maximum range. For example,

Ethernet requires that each segment be no more than 100 meters in length for 10-Mbps and 100-Mbps transmissions. The 100 meters includes the installed cabling and patch cables at either end. While many building are not 100 meters in length or width, going through floors, ceilings, and around obstacles can add distance quickly.

The quality of the cabling makes a huge difference as well. While there can be a cost savings between Category 5, 5e, and 6 cable, investment should be made in the best available wiring. This provides some longevity to the network, the best possible transmission rates and will usually save money in the long run as upgrades are less frequent. There is saying that goes, "Communication can be done over barbed wire; it's just not high quality."

Other cable installation issues include but are not limited to the following; proximity to power wiring, equipment installed near cable runs (motors, vent ducts, etc.), management of the cable in the run (cable trays, tie wraps, cable rings), proper cable used (plenum rated versus nonplenum), spares, damage during and after installation, enough cable pulled to allow modification of termination locations (office occupant desires a jack to be moved) and labels. All cabling should be labeled on both ends, at the jack, and in the wiring closet to facilitate troubleshooting and modification.

Termination equipment and quality are also important. Increasingly, modular equipment is being used on new networks. This means that connections can be easily moved and terminations completed quickly, but care must be taken to ensure that the correct components are purchased. Every type of cable and every type of application has a separate type of terminator. For example, a cat 6 solid cable will use a different jack than a cat 5 stranded cable. All terminations should be checked with the proper network test equipment such as a Fluke cable tester. This device will test the cable for crosstalk, return, attenuation, and wire mapping to ensure that all runs are within specification.

Inside the wiring closet a suitable amount of wire management should be used. Wire management are components used to organize and "tidy up" installations. Without it, a wiring closet can be an absolute mess that can make troubleshooting, maintenance, or additions all but impossible. Wire management includes items such as vertical and horizontal management, front/back pieces, covers, guides and cable rings for bundling.

Finally, the entire cable installation should be clean and neat. No one wants cables hanging out of the wall or a crooked wall plate in their office. No network technician wants to work in a closet that looks like a bad day at the spaghetti factory. A clean, well-done installation allows for faster troubleshooting, easier maintenance/modifications, and does not take up unnecessary room in the floor, ceiling, or closet.

9.5 SUMMARY

The requirement for networking capability within the individual building is just as strong as the requirement for wide area networking. Every business environment is populated with a large and growing collection of data processing equipment. Local area networks are needed to tie this equipment together, both for intraoffice communications and to provide a cost-effective link to wide area networks.

A LAN consists of a shared transmission medium and a set of hardware and software for interfacing devices to the medium and regulating the orderly access to the medium.

The transmission media that are used to convey information can be classified as guided or unguided. Guided media provide a physical path along which the signals are propagated; these include twisted pair, coaxial cable, and optical fiber. Unguided media employ an antenna for transmitting through air, vacuum, or water. Traditionally, twisted pair has been the workhorse for communications of all sorts. More recently, optical fiber has come to play a dominant role and has displaced other media in many applications. Of these two, optical fiber has the most promising future for the widest range of applications.

A set of standards has been defined for LANs that specifies a range of data rates and a variety of transmission media. These standards are widely accepted, and most of the products on the market conform to one of these standards.

9.6 RECOMMENDED READING AND WEB SITES

The material in this chapter is covered in much more depth in [STAL00]. [REGA04] also provides extensive coverage.

REGA04   Regan, P. *Local Area Networks*. Upper Saddle River, NJ: Prentice Hall, 2004.
STAL00   Stallings, W. *Local and Metropolitan Area Networks, Sixth Edition*. Upper Saddle River, NJ: Prentice Hall, 2000.

Recommended Web Site:

- **IEEE 802 LAN/MAN Standards Committee:** Status and documents for all of the working groups.

9.7 KEY TERMS, REVIEW QUESTIONS, AND PROBLEMS

Key Terms

backend network	Logical Link Control (LLC)	structured cabling
backbone LAN	Medium Access Control	tiered LAN
coaxial cable	(MAC)	transmission medium
decibel (dB)	optical fiber	twisted pair
guided media	server farm shielded twisted	unguided media
IEEE 802	pair (STP)	unshielded twisted pair (UTP)
local area network (LAN)	storage area network (SAN)	wireless transmission

Review Questions

9.1. How do the key requirements for computer room networks differ from those for personal computer local networks?

9.2. What are the differences among backend LANs, SANs, and backbone LANs?

9.3. Other than large storage capacity, what other advantage does a SAN provide?

9.4. What is the protocol typically used in storage area networks?

9.5. Differentiate between guided media and unguided media.

9.6. Why are the wires twisted in twisted-pair copper wire?

9.7. What are some major limitations of twisted-pair wire?

9.8. What is the difference between unshielded twisted pair and shielded twisted pair?

9.9. Describe the components of optical fiber cable.

9.10. What are the wavelengths used in fiber optic communication?

9.11. Arrange the following in order from highest to lowest regarding bandwidth: UTP, fiber, and coaxial cable.

9.12. Arrange the following in order from highest to lowest regarding cost: UTP, fiber, and coaxial cable.

9.13. What is the purpose of the IEEE 802 committee?

9.14. Why are there multiple LAN standards?

9.15. List and briefly define the services provided by LLC.

9.16. List and briefly define the types of operation provided by the LLC protocol.

9.17. List some basic functions performed at the MAC layer.

Problems

9.1 The semiconductor industry requires a large degree of automation in the processing of microelectronics devices. This is primarily due to the fact that extremely small tolerances are required in the manufacturing process of most semiconductor devices and therefore semiconductor fabrication plants must be many times "cleaner" than the average hospital surgical facility. For example, the conducting channel of a MOSFET (Metal Oxide Semiconductor Field Effect Transistor) is typically <1 micron in length. Conversely, a human hair is approximately 50 microns in diameter. Thus, seemingly minute biological contaminants (e.g., a single skin flake) can potentially render numerous transistors inoperable. Since the human process operator can be detrimental to the semiconductor fabrication process, robotics and automation must be instituted wherever possible. To facilitate this automation, the SEMI organization developed the SECS/GEM (Semiconductor Equipment Communication Standard/Generic Equipment Model) Protocol. Provide a basic overview of this standard and discuss the associated benefits relative to the design and operation of a factory LAN and its impact on general fabrication communications. Could this concept be useful in other scenarios outside the semiconductor industry?

9.2 Obtain a piece of category 3 and a piece of category 5 wiring. Strip back the outer insulation and count the number of twists. You should be able to observe three characteristics of twisted pair wiring. Discuss.

9.3 Develop, in general terms, a cost-effective cable plan (meeting minimal data integrity requirements) for a scientific R&D organization that is building a new five-story research facility. The first floor will contain the lobby and administrative offices. The second and third floors will contain labs that utilize fairly large pieces of heavy-power consumption equipment (e.g., small linear accelerators and reactive ion chambers). Numerous technicians and scientists will be working on this floor and data requirements include high-speed transmission of high bandwidth data (e.g., color video). The fourth floor will contain offices for the lab personnel and the fifth floor will contain executive offices.

9.4 Some organizations are implementing wide area networks as a high-speed backbone in order to increase communication efficiency and effectiveness of services throughout a particular region. One such example of this is Network Virginia, which delivers Internet and intranet services to organizations throughout the state of Virginia. Network Virginia also provides a regional interconnection point for Internet 2 members. Develop an overview of Network Virginia and discuss the importance of this concept in the evolution of networking strategy, with particular reference to LAN support.

9.5 Fill in the missing elements in the following table of approximate power ratios for various dB levels.

Decibels	1	2	3	4	5	6	7	8	9	10
Losses			0.5							0.1
Gains			2							10

9.6 If an amplifier has a 30 dB voltage gain, what voltage ratio does the gain represent?

9.7 Given a transmit power (P_{in}) of 5 watts and a received power (P_{out}) of 2.5 watts, what is the calculated loss in dB?

APPENDIX 9A DECIBELS AND SIGNAL STRENGTH

An important parameter in any transmission system is the signal strength. As a signal propagates along a transmission medium, there will be a loss, or *attenuation*, of signal strength. To compensate, amplifiers may be inserted at various points to impart a gain in signal strength. It is customary to express gains, losses, and relative levels in decibels because

- Signal strength often falls off exponentially, so loss is easily expressed in terms of the decibel, which is a logarithmic unit.

- The net gain or loss in a cascaded transmission path can be calculated with simple addition and subtraction.

The decibel is a measure of the ratio between two signal levels. The decibel gain is given by

$$G_{dB} = 10 \log_{10} \frac{P_{out}}{P_{in}}$$

where

$$G_{dB} = \text{gain, in decibels}$$
$$P_{in} = \text{input power level}$$
$$P_{out} = \text{output power level}$$
$$\log_{10} = \text{logarithm to the base 10}$$

Table 9.3 shows the relationship between decibel values and powers of 10.

There is some inconsistency in the literature over the use of the terms *gain* and *loss*. If the value of G_{dB} is positive, this represents an actual gain in power. For example, a gain of 3 dB means that the power has doubled. If the value of G_{dB} is negative, this represents an actual loss in power. For example a gain of -3 dB means that the power has halved, and this is a loss of power. Normally, this is expressed by saying there is a loss of 3 dB. However, some of the

Table 9.3   Decibel Values

Power Ratio	dB	Power Ratio	dB
10^1	10	10^{-1}	-10
10^2	20	10^{-2}	-20
10^3	30	10^{-3}	-30
10^4	40	10^{-4}	-40
10^5	50	10^{-5}	-50
10^6	60	10^{-6}	-60

literature would say that this is a loss of -3 dB. It makes more sense to say that a negative gain corresponds to a positive loss. Therefore, we define a decibel loss as

$$L_{dB} = -10 \log_{10} \frac{P_{out}}{P_{in}} = 10 \log_{10} \frac{P_{in}}{P_{out}}$$

EXAMPLE

If a signal with a power level of 10 mW is inserted onto a transmission line and the measured power some distance away is 5 mW, the loss can be expressed as

$$L_{dB} = 10 \log(10/5) = 10(0.3) = 3 \text{ dB}$$

Note that the decibel is a measure of relative, not absolute, difference. A loss from 1000 mW to 500 mW is also a loss of 3 dB. Thus, a loss of 3 dB halves the power level; a gain of 3 dB doubles the power.

The decibel is also used to measure the difference in voltage, taking into account that power is proportional to the square of the voltage:

$$P = \frac{V^2}{R}$$

where

$$P = \text{power dissipated across resistance } R$$

$$V = \text{voltage across resistance } R$$

Thus

$$L_{dB} = 10 \log \frac{P_{in}}{P_{out}} = 10 \log \frac{V_{in}^2/R}{V_{out}^2/R} = 20 \log \frac{V_{in}}{V_{out}}$$

EXAMPLE

Decibels are useful in determining the gain or loss over a series of transmission elements. Consider a series in which the input is at a power level of 4 mW, the first element is a transmission line with a 12-dB loss (-12-dB gain), the second element is an amplifier with a 35-dB gain, and the third element is a transmission line with a 10-dB loss. The net gain is $(-12 + 35 - 10) = 13$ dB. To calculate the output power P_{out},

$$G_{dB} = 13 = 10 \log(P_{out}/4 \text{ mW})$$
$$P_{out} = 4 \times 10^{1.3} \text{ mW} = 79.8 \text{ mW}$$

ETHERNET AND FIBRE CHANNEL

266

Recent years have seen rapid changes in the technology, design, and commercial applications for local area networks (LANs). A major feature of this evolution is the introduction of a variety of new schemes for high-speed local area networking. To keep pace with the changing local networking needs of business, a number of approaches to high speed LAN design have become commercial products. The most important of these are as follows:

- **Fast Ethernet and Gigabit Ethernet:** The extension of 10-Mbps CSMA/CD (carrier sense multiple access with collision detection) to higher speeds is a logical strategy, because it tends to preserve the investment in existing systems.
- **Fibre Channel:** This standard provides a low-cost, easily scalable approach to achieving very high data rates in local areas.
- **High-speed wireless LANs:** Wireless LAN technology and standards have at last come of age, and high-speed standards and products have been introduced.

Table 10.1 lists characteristics of these approaches. The remainder of this chapter fills in some of the details on Ethernet and Fibre Channel. Chapter 11 covers wireless LANs.

Table 10.1   Characteristics of Some High-Speed LANs

	Fast Ethernet	**Gigabit Ethernet**	**Fibre Channel**	**Wireless LAN**
Data Rate	100 Mbps	1 Gbps, 10 Gbps	100 Mbps–3.2 Gbps	1 Mbps–54 Mbps
Transmission Media	UTP, STP, optical fiber	UTP, shielded cable, optical fiber	Optical fiber, coaxial cable, STP	2.4-GHz, 5-GHz microwave
Access Method	CSMA/CD	Switched	Switched	CSMA/Polling
Supporting Standard	IEEE 802.3	IEEE 802.3	Fibre Channel Association	IEEE 802.11

10.1 THE EMERGENCE OF HIGH-SPEED LANS

Personal computers and microcomputer workstations began to achieve widespread acceptance in business computing in the early 1980s and have now achieved virtually the status of the telephone: an essential tool for office workers. Until relatively recently, office LANs provided basic connectivity services—connecting personal computers and terminals to mainframes and midrange systems that ran corporate applications, and providing workgroup connectivity at the departmental or divisional level. In both cases, traffic patterns were relatively light, with an emphasis on file transfer and electronic mail. The LANs that were available for this type of workload, primarily Ethernet and token ring, are well suited to this environment.

In the 1990s, two significant trends altered the role of the personal computer and therefore the requirements on the LAN:

- The speed and computing power of personal computers has continued to enjoy explosive growth.
- MIS organizations have recognized the LAN as a viable and indeed essential computing platform, resulting in the focus on network computing. This trend began with client/server computing, which has become a dominant architecture in the business environment and the more recent intranetwork trend. Both of these approaches, discussed in Chapter 7, involve the frequent transfer of potentially large volumes of data in a transaction-oriented environment.

The effect of these trends has been to increase the volume of data to be handled over LANs and, because applications are more interactive, to reduce the acceptable delay on data transfers. The earlier generation of 10-Mbps Ethernets and 16-Mbps token rings is simply not up to the job of supporting these requirements.

The following are examples of requirements that call for higher-speed LANs:

- **Centralized server farms:** In many applications, there is a need for user, or client, systems to be able to draw huge amounts of data from multiple centralized servers, called server farms. An example is a color publishing operation, in which servers typically contain tens of gigabytes of image data that must be downloaded to imaging workstations. As the performance of the servers themselves has increased, the bottleneck has shifted to the network. Switched Ethernet alone would not solve this problem because of the limit of 10 Mbps on a single link to the client.
- **Power workgroups:** These groups typically consist of a small number of cooperating users who need to draw massive data files across the network. Examples are a software development group that runs tests on a new software version, or a computer-aided design (CAD) company that regularly runs simulations of new designs. In such cases, large amounts of data are distributed to several workstations, processed, and updated at very high speed for multiple iterations.
- **High-speed local backbone:** As processing demand grows, LANs proliferate at a site, and high-speed interconnection is necessary.

10.2 TRADITIONAL ETHERNET

Within the IEEE 802 LAN standards committee, the 802.3 group has issued a set of standards with a common medium access control technique known as CSMA/CD. This set of standards grew out of the commercial product **Ethernet**, and the term *Ethernet* is still often used to refer to all the specifications. Collectively, the Ethernet-like LANs are the dominant force in the LAN market.

The original commercial Ethernet, as well as the original IEEE 802.3 standard, operated at 10 Mbps, and there are still a number of 10-Mbps Ethernet LANs in use. In recent years, standards have been developed for 802.3 systems operating at 100 Mbps, 1 Gbps, and 10 Gbps. Before looking at these high-speed LANs, we provide a brief overview of the original 10-Mbps Ethernet and introduce the concept of switched LANs.

Classical Ethernet operates at 10 Mbps over a bus topology LAN using the CSMA/CD (carrier sense multiple access with collision detection) medium access control protocol. In this section, we introduce the concepts of bus LANs and CSMA/CD operation, and then briefly discuss transmission medium options

Bus Topology LAN

In a bus topology LAN, all stations attach, through appropriate hardware interfacing known as a tap, directly to a linear transmission medium, or bus. Full-duplex operation between the station and the tap allows data to be transmitted onto the bus and received from the bus. A transmission from any station propagates the length of the medium in both directions and can be received by all other stations. At each end of the bus is a terminator, which absorbs any signal, removing it from the bus.

Two problems present themselves in this arrangement. First, because a transmission from any one station can be received by all other stations, there needs to be some way of indicating for whom the transmission is intended. Second, a mechanism is needed to regulate transmission. To see the reason for this, consider that if two stations on the bus attempt to transmit at the same time, their signals will overlap and become garbled. Or consider that one station decides to transmit continuously for a long period of time, blocking the access of other users.

To solve these problems, stations transmit data in small blocks, known as **frames**. Each frame consists of a portion of the data that a station wishes to transmit, plus a frame header that contains control information. Each station on the bus is assigned a unique address, or identifier, and the destination address for a frame is included in its header.

Figure 10.1 illustrates the scheme. In this example, station C wishes to transmit a frame of data to A. The frame header includes A's address. As the frame propagates along the bus, it passes B. B observes the address and ignores the frame. A, on the other hand, sees that the frame is addressed to itself and therefore copies the data from the frame as it goes by.

So the frame structure solves the first problem mentioned previously: It provides a mechanism for indicating the intended recipient of the data. It also provides

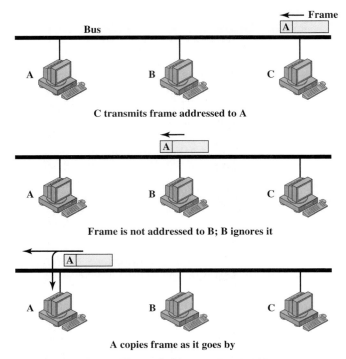

Figure 10.1   Frame Transmission on a Bus LAN

the basic tool for solving the second problem, the regulation of access. In particular, the stations take turns sending frames in some cooperative fashion, as explained in the next subsection.

Medium Access Control

For CSMA/CD, a station wishing to transmit first listens to the medium to determine if another transmission is in progress (carrier sense). If the medium is idle, the station may transmit. It may happen that two or more stations attempt to transmit at about the same time. If this happens, there will be a **collision**; the data from both transmissions will be garbled and not received successfully. The following procedure specifies what a station should do if the medium is found busy and what it should do if a collision occurs:

1. If the medium is idle, transmit; otherwise, go to step 2.
2. If the medium is busy, continue to listen until it is idle, then transmit immediately.
3. If a collision is detected during transmission, transmit a brief jamming signal to assure that all stations know that there has been a collision and then cease transmission.
4. After transmitting the jamming signal, wait a random amount of time, referred to as the **backoff**, then attempt to transmit again (repeat from step 1).

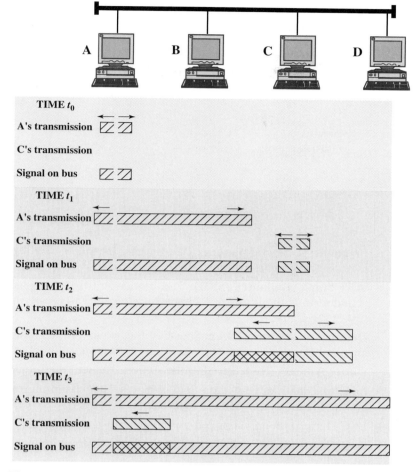

Figure 10.2   CSMA/CD Operation

Figure 10.2 illustrates the technique. The upper part of the figure shows a bus LAN layout. The remainder of the figure depicts activity on the bus at four successive instants in time. At time t_0, station A begins transmitting a packet addressed to D. At t_1, both B and C are ready to transmit. B senses a transmission and so defers. C, however, is still unaware of A's transmission and begins its own transmission. When A's transmission reaches C, at t_2, C detects the collision and ceases transmission. The effect of the collision propagates back to A, where it is detected some time later, t_3, at which time A ceases transmission.

The advantage of CSMA/CD is its simplicity. It is easy to implement the logic required for this protocol. Furthermore, there is little to go wrong in the execution of the protocol. For example, if for some reason a station fails to detect a collision, the worst that can happen is that it continues to transmit its frame, wasting some time on the medium. Once the transmission is over, the algorithm continues to function as before.

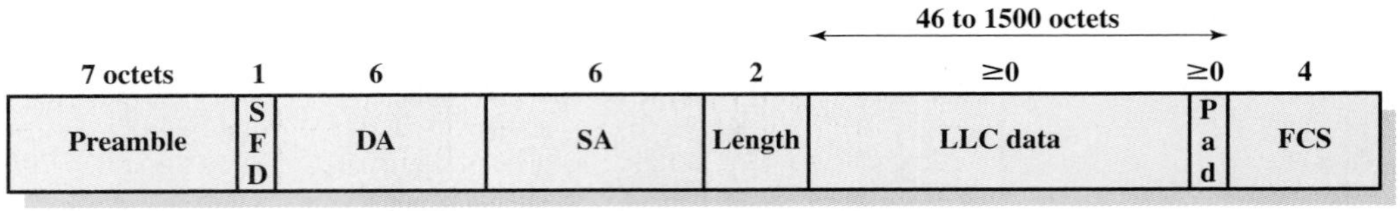

7 octets	1	6	6	2	≥0	≥0	4
Preamble	S F D	DA	SA	Length	LLC data	P a d	FCS

46 to 1500 octets

SFD = Start of frame delimiter
DA = Destination address
SA = Source address
FCS = Frame check sequence

Figure 10.3 IEEE 802.3 Frame Format

MAC Frame

Figure 10.3 depicts the frame format for the 802.3 protocol. It consists of the following fields:

- **Preamble:** A 7-octet pattern of alternating 0s and 1s used by the receiver to establish bit synchronization.
- **Start Frame Delimiter (SFD):** The sequence 10101011, which indicates the actual start of the frame and enables the receiver to locate the first bit of the rest of the frame.
- **Destination Address (DA):** Specifies the station(s) for which the frame is intended. It may be a unique physical address, a group address, or a global address.
- **Source Address (SA):** Specifies the station that sent the frame.
- **Length:** Length of LLC data field in octets. The maximum frame size, excluding the Preamble and SFD, is 1518 octets.
- **LLC Data:** Data unit supplied by LLC.
- **Pad:** Octets added to ensure that the frame is long enough for proper CD operation.
- **Frame Check Sequence (FCS):** A 32-bit CRC, based on all fields except preamble, SFD, and FCS.

IEEE 802.3 Medium Options at 10 Mbps

The IEEE 802.3 committee has defined a number of alternative physical configurations. This is both good and bad. On the good side, the standard has been responsive to evolving technology. On the bad side, the customer, not to mention the potential vendor, is faced with a bewildering array of options. However, the committee has been at pains to ensure that the various options can be easily integrated into a configuration that satisfies a variety of needs. Thus, the user who has a complex set of requirements may find the flexibility and variety of the 802.3 standard to be an asset.

To distinguish the various implementations that are available, the committee has developed a concise notation:

<data rate in Mbps> <signaling method>
<maximum segment length in hundreds of meters>

Table 10.2   IEEE 802.3 10-Mbps Physical Layer Medium Alternatives

	10BASE5	**10BASE2**	**10BASE-T**	**10BASE-F**
Transmission Medium	Coaxial cable	Coaxial cable	Unshielded twisted pair	850-nm optical fiber pair
Topology	Bus	Bus	Star	Star
Maximum Segment Length (m)	500	185	100	500
Nodes per Segment	100	30	—	33
Cable Diameter	10 mm	5 mm	0.4 to 0.6 mm	62.5/125 μm

Table 10.2 summarizes these options. Note that 10BASE-T and 10BASE-F do not quite follow the notation: "T" stands for twisted pair and "F" stands for optical fiber.

10.3 BRIDGES, HUBS, AND SWITCHES

Before continuing our discussion of Ethernet, we need to take a detour and examine the concepts of bridges, hubs, and switches.

Bridges

In virtually all cases, there is a need to expand beyond the confines of a single LAN, to provide interconnection to other LANs and to wide area networks. Two general approaches are used for this purpose: bridges and routers. The **bridge** is the simpler of the two devices and provides a means of interconnecting similar LANs. The router is a more general-purpose device, capable of interconnecting a variety of LANs and WANs. We explore bridges in this section; routers are discussed in Part Two.

The bridge is designed for use between local area networks (LANs) that use identical protocols for the physical and link layers (e.g., all conforming to IEEE 802.3). Because the devices all use the same protocols, the amount of processing required at the bridge is minimal. More sophisticated bridges are capable of mapping from one MAC format to another (e.g., to interconnect an Ethernet and a Fibre Channel LAN).

Because the bridge is used in a situation in which all the LANs have the same characteristics, the reader may ask, why not simply have one large LAN? Depending on circumstance, there are several reasons for the use of multiple LANs connected by bridges:

- **Reliability:** The danger in connecting all data processing devices in an organization to one network is that a fault on the network may disable communication for all devices. By using bridges, the network can be partitioned into self-contained units.

- **Performance:** In general, performance on a LAN declines with an increase in the number of devices or the length of the wire. A number of smaller LANs will often give improved performance if devices can be clustered so that intranetwork traffic significantly exceeds internetwork traffic.

- **Security:** The establishment of multiple LANs may improve security of communications. It is desirable to keep different types of traffic (e.g., accounting, personnel, strategic planning) that have different security needs on physically separate media. At the same time, the different types of users with different levels of security need to communicate through controlled and monitored mechanisms.

- **Geography:** Clearly, two separate LANs are needed to support devices clustered in two geographically distant locations. Even in the case of two buildings separated by a highway, it may be far easier to use a microwave bridge link than to attempt to string coaxial cable between the two buildings.

Figure 10.4 shows the action of a bridge connecting two LANs, A and B, using the same MAC protocol. In this example, a single bridge attaches to both LANs; frequently, the bridge function is performed by two "half-bridges," one on each LAN. The functions of the bridge are few and simple:

- Read all frames transmitted on A and accept those addressed to any station on B.

- Using the medium access control protocol for B, retransmit each frame on B.

- Do the same for B-to-A traffic.

Several design aspects of a bridge are worth highlighting:

- The bridge makes no modification to the content or format of the frames it receives, nor does it encapsulate them with an additional header. Each frame to be transferred is simply copied from one LAN and repeated with exactly the same bit pattern as the other LAN. Because the two LANs use the same LAN protocols, it is permissible to do this.

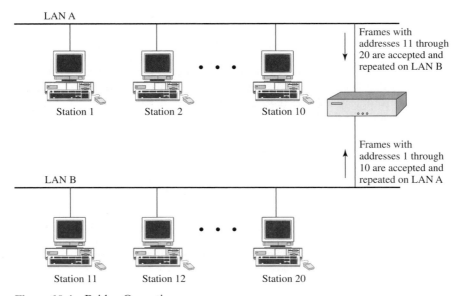

Figure 10.4   Bridge Operation

- The bridge should contain enough buffer space to meet peak demands. Over a short period of time, frames may arrive faster than they can be retransmitted.
- The bridge must contain addressing and routing intelligence. At a minimum, the bridge must know which addresses are on each network to know which frames to pass. Further, there may be more than two LANs interconnected by a number of bridges. In that case, a frame may have to be routed through several bridges in its journey from source to destination.
- A bridge may connect more than two LANs.

In summary, the bridge provides an extension to the LAN that requires no modification to the communications software in the stations attached to the LANs. It appears to all stations on the two (or more) LANs that there is a single LAN on which each station has a unique address. The station uses that unique address and need not explicitly discriminate between stations on the same LAN and stations on other LANs; the bridge takes care of that.

Hubs

In recent years, there has been a proliferation of types of devices for interconnecting LANs that goes beyond bridges and the routers. These devices can conveniently be grouped into the categories of layer 2 switches and layer 3 switches. We begin with a discussion of hubs and then explore these two concepts.

A hub is an alternative to the bus topology. Each station is connected to the hub by two lines (transmit and receive). The hub acts as a repeater: When a single station transmits, the hub repeats the signal on the outgoing line to each station. Ordinarily, the line consists of two unshielded twisted pairs. Because of the high data rate and the poor transmission qualities of unshielded twisted pair, the length of a line is limited to about 100 m. As an alternative, an optical fiber link may be used. In this case, the maximum length is about 500 m.

Note that although this scheme is physically a star, it is logically a bus: A transmission from any one station is received by all other stations, and if two stations transmit at the same time there will be a collision.

Multiple levels of hubs can be cascaded in a hierarchical configuration. Figure 10.5 depicts a two-level configuration. There is one **header hub** (HHUB) and one or more **intermediate hubs** (IHUB). Each hub may have a mixture of stations and other hubs attached to it from below. This layout fits well with building wiring practices. Typically, there is a wiring closet on each floor of an office building, and a hub can be placed in each one. Each hub could service the stations on its floor.

Layer 2 Switches

In recent years, the layer 2 switch, has replaced the hub in popularity, particularly for high-speed LANs. The layer 2 switch is also sometimes referred to as a switching hub.

To clarify the distinction between hubs and switches, Figure 10.6a shows a typical bus layout of a traditional 10-Mbps LAN. A bus is installed that is laid out so that all the devices to be attached are in reasonable proximity to a point on the bus. In the figure, station B is transmitting. This transmission goes from B, across the link from B to the bus, along the bus in both directions, and along the access lines of each

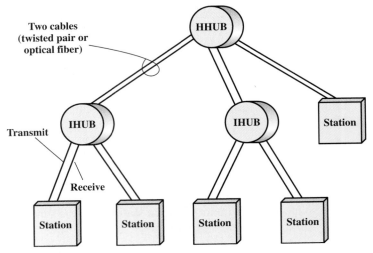

Figure 10.5 Two-Level Configuration

of the other attached stations. In this configuration, all the stations must share the total capacity of the bus, which is 10 Mbps.

A hub, often in a building wiring closet, uses a star wiring arrangement to attach stations to the hub. In this arrangement, a transmission from any one station is received by the hub and retransmitted on all of the outgoing lines. Therefore, to avoid collisions, only one station should transmit at a time. Again, the total capacity of the LAN is 10 Mbps. The hub has several advantages over the simple bus arrangement. It exploits standard building wiring practices in the layout of cable. In addition, the hub can be configured to recognize a malfunctioning station that is jamming the network and to cut that station out of the network. Figure 10.6b illustrates the operation of a hub. Here again, station B is transmitting. This transmission goes from B, across the transmit line from B to the hub, and from the hub along the receive lines of each of the other attached stations.

We can achieve greater performance with a layer 2 switch. In this case, the central hub acts as a switch, similar to a packet switch. An incoming frame from a particular station is switched to the appropriate output line to be delivered to the intended destination. At the same time, other unused lines can be used for switching other traffic. Figure 10.6c shows an example in which B is transmitting a frame to A and at the same time C is transmitting a frame to D. So, in this example, the current throughput on the LAN is 20 Mbps, although each individual device is limited to 10 Mbps. The layer 2 switch has several attractive features:

1. No change is required to the software or hardware of the attached devices to convert a bus LAN or a hub LAN to a switched LAN. In the case of an Ethernet LAN, each attached device continues to use the Ethernet medium access control protocol to access the LAN. From the point of view of the attached devices, nothing has changed in the access logic.

2. Each attached device has a dedicated capacity equal to that of the entire original LAN, assuming that the layer 2 switch has sufficient capacity to keep up with all

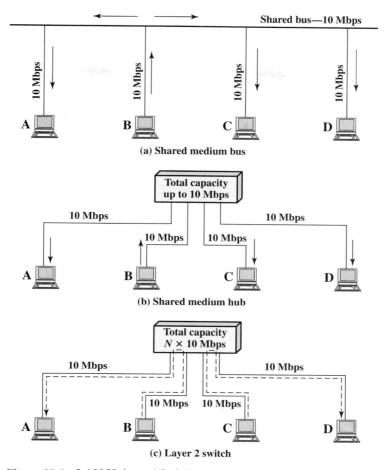

Figure 10.6   LAN Hubs and Switches

attached devices. For example, in Figure 10.6c, if the layer 2 switch can sustain a throughput of 20 Mbps, each attached device appears to have a dedicated capacity for either input or output of 10 Mbps.

3. The layer 2 switch scales easily. Additional devices can be attached to the layer 2 switch by increasing the capacity of the layer 2 switch correspondingly.

Two types of layer 2 switches are available as commercial products:

- **Store-and-forward switch:** The layer 2 switch accepts a frame on an input line, buffers it briefly, and then routes it to the appropriate output line.
- **Cut-through switch:** The layer 2 switch takes advantage of the fact that the destination address appears at the beginning of the MAC (medium access control) frame. The layer 2 switch begins repeating the incoming frame onto the appropriate output line as soon as the layer 2 switch recognizes the destination address.

The cut-through switch yields the highest possible throughput but at some risk of propagating bad frames, because the switch is not able to check the cyclic redundancy check (CRC, described in Chapter 9) prior to retransmission. The store-and-forward switch involves a delay between sender and receiver but boosts the overall integrity of the network.

A layer 2 switch can be viewed as a full-duplex version of the hub. It can also incorporate logic that allows it to function as a multiport bridge. [BREY99] lists the following differences between layer 2 switches and bridges:

- Bridge frame handling is done in software. A layer 2 switch performs the address recognition and frame forwarding functions in hardware.

- A bridge can typically only analyze and forward one frame at a time, whereas a layer 2 switch has multiple parallel data paths and can handle multiple frames at a time.

- A bridge uses store-and-forward operation. With a layer 2 switch, it is possible to have cut-through instead of store-and-forward operation.

Because a layer 2 switch has higher performance and can incorporate the functions of a bridge, the bridge has suffered commercially. New installations typically include layer 2 switches with bridge functionality rather than bridges.

Layer 3 Switches

Layer 2 switches provide increased performance to meet the needs of high-volume traffic generated by personal computers, workstations, and servers. However, as the number of devices in a building or complex of buildings grows, layer 2 switches reveal some inadequacies. Two problems in particular present themselves: broadcast overload and the lack of multiple links.

A set of devices and LANs connected by layer 2 switches is considered to have a flat address space. The term *flat* means that all users share a common MAC broadcast address. Thus, if any device issues a MAC frame with a broadcast address, that frame is to be delivered to all devices attached to the overall network connected by layer 2 switches and/or bridges. In a large network, frequent transmission of broadcast frames can create tremendous overhead. Worse, a malfunctioning device can create a *broadcast storm*, in which numerous broadcast frame clog the network and crowd out legitimate traffic.

A second performance-related problem with the use of bridges and/or layer 2 switches is that the current standards for bridge protocols dictate that there be no closed loops in the network. That is, there can only be one path between any two devices. Thus, it is impossible, in a standards-based implementation, to provide multiple paths through multiple switches between devices. This restriction limits both performance and reliability.

To overcome these problems, it seems logical to break up a large local network into a number of **subnetworks** connected by routers. A MAC broadcast frame is then limited to only the devices and switches contained in a single subnetwork. Furthermore, IP-based routers employ sophisticated routing algorithms that allow the use of multiple paths between subnetworks going through different routers.

However, the problem with using routers to overcome some of the inadequacies of bridges and layer 2 switches is that routers typically do all of the IP-level processing involved in the forwarding of IP traffic in software. High-speed LANs and high-performance layer 2 switches may pump millions of packets per second whereas a software-based router may only be able to handle well under a million packets per second. To accommodate such a load, a number of vendors have developed layer 3 switches, which implement the packet-forwarding logic of the router in hardware.

There are various layer 3 schemes on the market, but fundamentally they fall into two categories: packet by packet and flow based. The packet-by-packet switch operates in the identical fashion as a traditional router. Because the forwarding logic is in hardware, the packet-by-packet switch can achieve an order of magnitude increase in performance compared to the software-based router. A flow-based switch tries to enhance performance by identifying flows of IP packets that have the same source and destination. This can be done by observing ongoing traffic or by using a special flow label in the packet header (allowed in IPv6 but not in IPv4; see Figure 5.7). Once a flow is identified, a predefined route can be established through the network to speed up the forwarding process. Again, huge performance increases over a pure software-based router are achieved.

Figure 10.7 is a typical example of the approach taken to local networking in an organization with a large number of PCs and workstations (thousands to tens of thousands). Desktop systems have links of 10 Mbps to 100 Mbps into a LAN controlled by a layer 2 switch. Wireless LAN connectivity is also likely to be available for mobile users. Layer 3 switches are at the local network's core, forming a local backbone. Typically, these switches are interconnected at 1 Gbps and connect to layer 2 switches at from 100 Mbps to 1 Gbps. Servers connect directly to layer 2 or layer 3 switches at 1 Gbps or possibly 100 Mbps. A lower-cost software-based router provides WAN connection. The circles in the figure identify separate LAN subnetworks; a MAC broadcast frame is limited to its own subnetwork.

10.4 HIGH-SPEED ETHERNET

Fast Ethernet

If one were to design a high-speed (100 Mbps or more) LAN from scratch, one would not choose CSMA/CD as the basis for the design. CSMA/CD is simple to implement and robust in the face of faults. However, it does not scale well. As the load on a bus increases, the number of collisions increases, degrading performance. Furthermore, as the data rate for a given system increases, performance also decreases. The reason for this is that at a higher data rate, a station can transmit more bits before it recognizes a collision, and therefore more wasted bits are transmitted.

These problems can be overcome. To accommodate higher loads, a system can be designed to have a number of different segments, interconnected with hubs. The hubs can act as barriers, separating the LAN into collision domains, so that a collision in one domain does not spread to other domains. The use

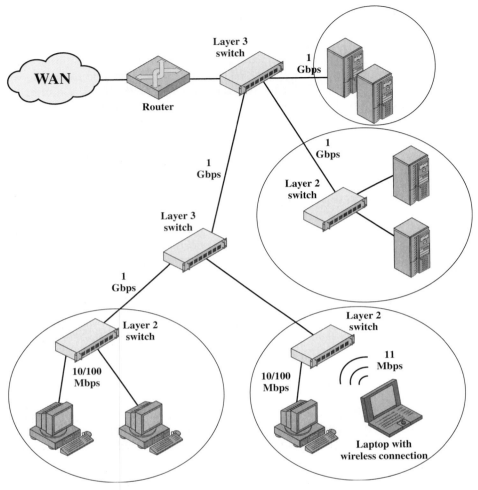

Figure 10.7   Typical Premises Network Configuration

of switched Ethernet hubs in effect eliminates collisions, further increasing efficiency.

Despite some drawbacks to its use, Ethernet-style LANs have been developed that operate at 100 Mbps, 1 Gbps, and 10 Gbps. The reasons for this are instructive. From the vendor's point of view, the CSMA/CD protocol is well understood and vendors have experience building the hardware, firmware, and software for such systems. Scaling the system up to 100 Mbps or more may be easier than implementing an alternative protocol and topology. From the customer's point of view, it is relatively easy to integrate older systems running at 10 Mbps with newer systems running at higher speeds if all the systems use the same frame format and the same access protocol. In other words, the continued use of Ethernet-style systems is attractive because Ethernet is already there. This same situation is encountered in other areas of data communications. Vendors and customers do not always, or even in the majority of cases, choose the technically superior solution. Cost, ease of management, and other factors relating to the already-existing base of equipment are more important factors in the selection. This is the reason that Ethernet-style systems continue to dominate the LAN market long after most observers predicted the demise of Ethernet.

Fast Ethernet refers to a set of specifications developed by the IEEE 802.3 committee to provide a low-cost, Ethernet-compatible LAN operating at 100 Mbps. The blanket designation for these standards is 100BASE-T. The committee defined a number of alternatives to be used with different transmission media.

Table 10.3 summarizes key characteristics of the 100BASE-T options. All of the 100BASE-T options use the IEEE 802.3 MAC protocol and frame format. 100BASE-X refers to a set of options that use the physical medium specifications. All of the 100BASE-X schemes use two physical links between nodes; one for transmission and one for reception. 100BASE-TX makes use of shielded twisted pair (STP) or high-quality (Category 5) unshielded twisted pair (UTP).[1] 100BASE-FX uses optical fiber.

In many buildings, any of the 100BASE-X options requires the installation of new cable. For such cases, 100BASE-T4 defines a lower-cost alternative that can use Category 3, voice-grade UTP in addition to the higher-quality Category 5 UTP. To achieve the 100-Mbps data rate over lower-quality cable, 100BASE-T4 dictates the use of four twisted-pair lines between nodes, with the data transmission making use of three pairs in one direction at a time.

For all of the 100BASE-T options, the topology is similar to that of 10BASE-T, namely a star-wire topology.

A traditional Ethernet is half duplex: A station can either transmit or receive a frame, but it cannot do both simultaneously. With full-duplex operation, a station can transmit and receive simultaneously. If a 100-Mbps Ethernet ran in full duplex mode, the theoretical transfer rate becomes 200 Mbps.

Several changes are needed to operate in full-duplex mode. The attached stations must have full-duplex rather than half-duplex adapter cards. The central point is a switch. In this case, each station constitutes a separate collision domain. In fact, there are no collisions and the CSMA/CD algorithm is no longer needed. However, the same 802.3 MAC frame format is used and the attached stations can

Table 10.3   IEEE 802.3 100-Mbps Physical Layer Medium Alternatives

	100BASE-TX		**100BASE-FX**	**100BASE-T4**
Transmission Medium	2 pair, STP	2 pair, Category 5 UTP	2 optical fibers	4 pair, Category 3, 4, or 5 UTP
Maximum Segment Length	100 m	100 m	100 m	100 m
Network Span	200 m	200 m	400 m	200 m

---

[1]See Chapter 9 for a discussion of Category 3 and Category 5 cable.

continue to execute the CSMA/CD algorithm, even though no collisions can ever be detected.

Gigabit Ethernet

The strategy for Gigabit Ethernet is the same as that for Fast Ethernet. While defining a new medium and transmission specification, Gigabit Ethernet retains the CSMA/CD protocol and frame format of its 10-Mbps and 100-Mbps predecessors. It is compatible with 100BASE-T and 10BASE-T, preserving a smooth migration path. As more organizations move to 100BASE-T, putting huge traffic loads on backbone networks, demand for Gigabit Ethernet has intensified.

Figure 10.8 shows a typical application of Gigabit Ethernet. A 1-Gbps LAN switch provides backbone connectivity for central servers and high-speed workgroup switches. Each workgroup LAN switch supports both 1-Gbps links, to connect to the backbone LAN switch and to support high-performance workgroup servers, and 100-Mbps links, to support high-performance workstations, servers, and 100-Mbps LAN switches.

The current 1-Gbps specification for IEEE 802.3 includes the following physical layer alternatives (Figure 10.9):

- **1000BASE-LX:** This long-wavelength option supports duplex links of up to 550 m of 62.5-μm or 50-μm multimode fiber or up to 5 km of 10-μm single-mode fiber. Wavelengths are in the range of 1270 to 1355 nm.

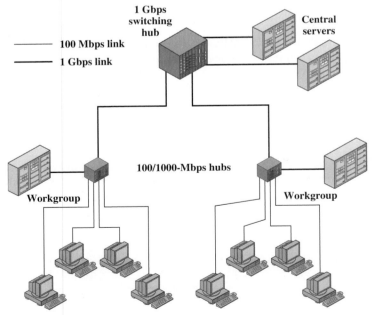

Figure 10.8   Example Gigabit Ethernet Configuration

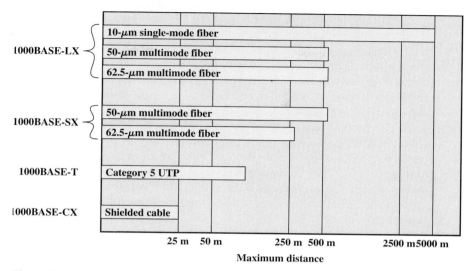

Figure 10.9 Gigabit Ethernet Medium Options (log scale)

- **1000BASE-SX:** This short-wavelength option supports duplex links of up to 275 m using 62.5-μm multimode or up to 550 m using 50-μm multimode fiber. Wavelengths are in the range of 770 to 860 nm.
- **1000BASE-CX:** This option supports 1-Gbps links among devices located within a single room or equipment rack, using copper jumpers (specialized shielded twisted pair cable that spans no more than 25 m). Each link is composed of a separate shielded twisted pair running in each direction.
- **1000BASE-T:** This option makes use of four pairs of Category 5 unshielded twisted pair to support devices over a range of up to 100 m.

10–Gbps Ethernet

With gigabit products still fairly new, attention has turned in the past several years to a 10-Gbps Ethernet capability. The principal driving requirement for 10-Gigabit Ethernet is the increase in Internet and intranet traffic. A number of factors contribute to the explosive growth in both Internet and intranet traffic:

- An increase in the number of network connections
- An increase in the connection speed of each end-station (e.g., 10 Mbps users moving to 100 Mbps, analog 56-kbps users moving to DSL and cable modems)
- An increase in the deployment of bandwidth-intensive applications such as high-quality video
- An increase in Web hosting and application hosting traffic

Initially, network managers will use 10-Gbps Ethernet to provide high-speed, local backbone interconnection between large-capacity switches. As the demand for bandwidth increases, 10-Gbps Ethernet will be deployed throughout the entire network and will include server farm, backbone, and campuswide connectivity. This technology enables Internet service providers (ISPs) and network service providers (NSPs) to create very high-speed links at a low cost, between co-located, carrier-class switches and routers.

The technology also allows the construction of metropolitan area networks (MANs) and WANs that connect geographically dispersed LANs between campuses or points of presence (PoPs). Thus, Ethernet begins to compete with ATM and other wide area transmission/networking technologies. In most cases where the customer requirement is data and TCP/IP transport, 10-Gbps Ethernet provides substantial value over ATM transport for both network end users and service providers:

- No expensive, bandwidth-consuming conversion between Ethernet packets and ATM cells is required; the network is Ethernet, end to end.
- The combination of IP and Ethernet offers quality of service and traffic policing capabilities that approach those provided by ATM, so that advanced traffic engineering technologies are available to users and providers.
- A wide variety of standard optical interfaces (wavelengths and link distances) have been specified for 10-Gbps Ethernet, optimizing its operation and cost for LAN, MAN, or WAN applications.

The goal for maximum link distances cover a range of applications: from 300 m to 40 km. The links operate in full-duplex mode only, using a variety of optical fiber physical media.

Four physical layer options are defined for 10-Gbps Ethernet (Figure 10.10):

- **10GBASE-S (short):** Designed for 850-nm transmission on multimode fiber. This medium can achieve distances up to 300 m.
- **10GBASE-L (long):** Designed for 1310-nm transmission on single-mode fiber. This medium can achieve distances up to 10 km.
- **10GBASE-E (extended):** Designed for 1550-nm transmission on single-mode fiber. This medium can achieve distances up to 40 km.
- **10GBASE-LX4:** Designed for 1310-nm transmission on single-mode or multimode fiber. This medium can achieve distances up to 10 km. This medium uses wavelength-division multiplexing (WDM) to multiplex the bit stream across four light waves.

The success of Fast Ethernet, Gigabit Ethernet, and 10-Gbps Ethernet highlights the importance of network management concerns in choosing a network technology. Both ATM and Fiber Channel, explored later, may be technically superior choices for a high-speed backbone, because of their flexibility and scalability. However, the Ethernet alternatives offer compatibility with existing installed

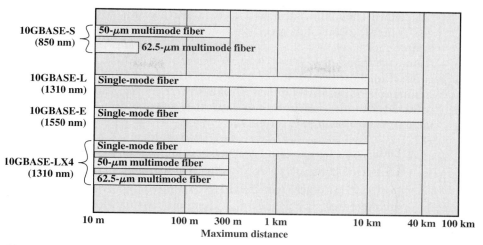

Figure 10.10   10-Gbps Ethernet Distance Options (log scale)

LANs, network management software, and applications. This compatibility has accounted for the survival of a nearly 30-year-old technology (CSMA/CD) in today's fast-evolving network environment.

10.5 FIBRE CHANNEL

As the speed and memory capacity of personal computers, workstations, and servers have grown, and as applications have become ever more complex with greater reliance on graphics and video, the requirement for greater speed in delivering data to the processor has grown. This requirement affects two methods of data communications with the processor: I/O channel and network communications.

An I/O channel is a direct point-to-point or multipoint communications link, predominantly hardware based and designed for high speed over very short distances. The I/O channel transfers data between a buffer at the source device and a buffer at the destination device, moving only the user contents from one device to another, without regard to the format or meaning of the data. The logic associated with the channel typically provides the minimum control necessary to manage the transfer plus hardware error detection. I/O channels typically manage transfers between processors and peripheral devices, such as discs, graphics equipment, CD-ROMs, and video I/O devices.

A network is a collection of interconnected access points with a software protocol structure that enables communication. The network typically allows many different types of data transfer, using software to implement the networking protocols and to provide flow control, error detection, and error recovery. As we have discussed in this book, networks typically manage transfers between end systems over local, metropolitan, or wide area distances.

Fibre Channel is designed to combine the best features of both technologies—the simplicity and speed of channel communications with the flexibility and interconnectivity that characterize protocol-based network communications. This fusion of approaches allows system designers to combine traditional peripheral connection, host-to-host internetworking, loosely coupled processor clustering, and multimedia applications in a single multiprotocol interface. The types of channel-oriented facilities incorporated into the Fibre Channel protocol architecture include the following:

* Data-type qualifiers for routing frame payload into particular interface buffers
* Link-level constructs associated with individual I/O operations
* Protocol interface specifications to allow support of existing I/O channel architectures, such as the Small Computer System Interface (SCSI)

The types of network-oriented facilities incorporated into the Fibre Channel protocol architecture include the following:

* Full multiplexing of traffic between multiple destinations
* Peer-to-peer connectivity between any pair of ports on a Fibre Channel network
* Capabilities for internetworking to other communication technologies

Depending on the needs of the application, either channel or networking approaches can be used for any data transfer. The Fibre Channel Industry Association, which is the industry consortium promoting Fibre Channel, lists the following ambitious requirements that Fibre Channel is intended to satisfy [FCIA01]:

* Full duplex links with two fibers per link
* Performance from 100 Mbps to 800 Mbps on a single line (full-duplex 200 Mbps to 1600 Mbps per link)
* Support for distances up to 10 km
* Small connectors
* High-capacity utilization with distance insensitivity
* Greater connectivity than existing multidrop channels
* Broad availability (i.e., standard components)
* Support for multiple cost/performance levels, from small systems to supercomputers
* Ability to carry multiple existing interface command sets for existing channel and network protocols

The solution was to develop a simple generic transport mechanism based on point-to-point links and a switching network. This underlying infrastructure supports a simple encoding and framing scheme that in turn supports a variety of channel and network protocols.

Fibre Channel Elements

The key elements of a Fibre Channel network are the end systems, called *nodes*, and the network itself, which consists of one or more switching elements. The collection of switching elements is referred to as a *fabric*. These elements are interconnected by point-to-point links between ports on the individual nodes and switches. Communication consists of the transmission of frames across the point-to-point links.

Each node includes one or more ports, called N_ports, for interconnection. Similarly, each fabric-switching element includes multiple ports, called F_ports. Interconnection is by means of bidirectional links between ports. Any node can communicate with any other node connected to the same fabric using the services of the fabric. All routing of frames between N_ports is done by the fabric. Frames may be buffered within the fabric, making it possible for different nodes to connect to the fabric at different data rates.

A fabric can be implemented as a single fabric element with attached nodes (a simple star arrangement) or as a more general network of fabric elements, as shown in Figure 10.11. In either case, the fabric is responsible for buffering and for routing frames between source and destination nodes.

Because it is based on a switching network, the Fibre Channel scales easily in terms of N_ports, data rate, and distance covered. This approach provides great flexibility. Fibre Channel can readily accommodate new transmission media and data rates by adding new switches and F_ports to an existing fabric. Thus, an existing investment is not lost with an upgrade to new technologies and equipment. Further, the layered protocol architecture accommodates existing I/O interface and networking protocols, preserving the preexisting investment.

Fibre Channel Protocol Architecture

The Fibre Channel standard is organized into five levels. Each level defines a function or set of related functions. The standard does not dictate a correspondence

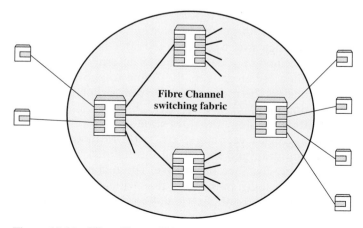

Figure 10.11 Fibre Channel Network

between levels and actual implementations, with a specific interface between adjacent levels. Rather, the standard refers to the level as a "document artifice" used to group related functions. The layers are as follows:

- **FC-0 Physical Media:** Includes optical fiber for long-distance applications, coaxial cable for high speeds over short distances, and shielded twisted pair for lower speeds over short distances
- **FC-1 Transmission Protocol:** Defines the signal encoding scheme
- **FC-2 Framing Protocol:** Deals with defining topologies, frame format, flow and error control, and grouping of frames into logical entities called sequences and exchanges
- **FC-3 Common Services:** Includes multicasting
- **FC-4 Mapping:** Defines the mapping of various channel and network protocols to Fibre Channel, including IEEE 802, ATM, IP, and the Small Computer System Interface (SCSI)

Fibre Channel Physical Media and Topologies

One of the major strengths of the Fibre Channel standard is that it provides a range of options for the physical medium, the data rate on that medium, and the topology of the network.

Transmission Media   The transmission media options that are available under Fibre Channel include shielded twisted pair, coaxial cable, and optical fiber. Standardized data rates range from 100 Mbps to 3.2 Gbps. Point-to-point link distances range from 33 m to 10 km.

Topologies   The most general topology supported by Fibre Channel is referred to as a fabric or switched topology. This is an arbitrary topology that includes at least one switch to interconnect a number of end systems. The fabric topology may also consist of a number of switches forming a switched network, with some or all of these switches also supporting end nodes.

Routing in the fabric topology is transparent to the nodes. Each port in the configuration has a unique address. When data from a node are transmitted into the fabric, the edge switch to which the node is attached uses the destination port address in the incoming data frame to determine the destination port location. The switch then either delivers the frame to another node attached to the same switch or transfers the frame to an adjacent switch to begin routing the frame to a remote destination.

The fabric topology provides scalability of capacity: As additional ports are added, the aggregate capacity of the network increases, thus minimizing congestion and contention and increasing throughput. The fabric is protocol independent and largely distance insensitive. The technology of the switch itself and of the transmission links connecting the switch to nodes may be changed without affecting the overall configuration. Another advantage of the fabric topology is that the burden on nodes is minimized. An individual Fibre Channel node (end

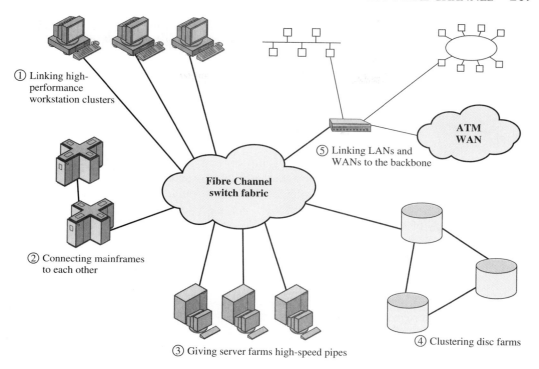

① Linking high-
performance
workstation clusters

⑤ Linking LANs and
WANs to the backbone

**Fibre Channel
switch fabric**

**ATM
WAN**

② Connecting mainframes
to each other

③ Giving server farms high-speed pipes

④ Clustering disc farms

Figure 10.12   Five Applications of Fibre Channel

system) is only responsible for managing a simple point-to-point connection between itself and the fabric; the fabric is responsible for routing between ports and error detection.

In addition to the fabric topology, the Fibre Channel standard defines two other topologies. With the point-to-point topology there are only two ports, and these are directly connected, with no intervening fabric switches. In this case there is no routing. The arbitrated loop topology is a simple, low-cost topology for connecting up to 126 nodes in a loop.

Topologies, transmission media, and data rates may be combined to provide an optimized configuration for a given site. Figure 10.12 is an example that illustrates the principal applications of Fibre Channel.

Prospects for Fibre Channel

Fibre Channel is backed by an industry interest group known as the Fibre Channel Association and a variety of interface cards for different applications are available. Fibre Channel has been most widely accepted as an improved peripheral device interconnect, providing services that can eventually replace such schemes as SCSI. It is a technically attractive solution to general high-speed

LAN requirements but must compete with Ethernet and ATM LANs. Cost and performance issues should dominate the manager's consideration of these competing technologies.

APPLICATION NOTE
Networking with Ethernet

There is a wide variety of networking systems currently installed in companies and organizations. Several of these networking protocols are being relegated to the ranks of legacy systems. Examples of this trend include Token Ring, FDDI, and LocalTalk. Some versions of Ethernet are also joining this group, specifically 10BASE5, 10BASE2, and stand-alone 10BASE-T. The vast majority of networks currently deployed are based on faster forms of Ethernet such as 10/100 Ethernet, 100BASE-TX, 100BASE-FX, Gigabit and 10-Gbps Ethernet.

Today, and for the foreseeable future, Ethernet is the dominant local area network protocol. It is even beginning to make inroads into the last mile market. The strength of Ethernet lies in its backward compatibility and simplicity. Setting up an Ethernet network is nearly as simple as taking the equipment out of the box and plugging it in. In addition, common Ethernet components are becoming very inexpensive. In contrast, maintaining or installing any of the previously mentioned legacy systems can be very costly.

The question now becomes, "Which Ethernet to invest in?" While the "under the hood" operation of Ethernet makes for good engineering reading, there are some very practical aspects of Ethernet that are important to know before deciding. An organization must analyze its requirements and decide how much bandwidth is required for present and future use, what applications will be running over the network (the network architecture) and how much money will be spent.

Like Microsoft Windows, Ethernet has many varieties. Some basic facts about networking speeds can provide some illumination. With the advance in technology, almost all new equipment marries 10 and 100 Mbps speeds. Network cards are referred to as 10/100 and will "auto-sense" the network conditions and determine what speed is available. This is also true of the ports on networking equipment such as hubs and switches.

Many vendors advertise the availability of gigabit speeds to the desktop. While this sounds very attractive, this purchase may be unnecessary. It is possible that the network may outstrip the computer's ability to process the information. Computer bus clock rates and operating system delays represent barriers to actually making use of the huge amounts of data a gigabit network can send. In addition, there are not very many computers that need to send data measured in gigabytes. For most applications, the cost of this high-speed equipment does not justify itself.

In addition to the cost of the equipment, gigabit speeds may require the installation of fiber to the desktop. Gigabit over UTP is available but has a shorter range. Fiber can significantly increase installation costs. Thus, Gigabit Ethernet is well suited to fiber backbone connections such as those between wiring closets, connections going off site, and to hard-working servers. For standard machines, the 100-Mbps or 10/100 cards are usually sufficient and this is not likely to change in the near future. The networking equipment connected to the end nodes can also be selected to support 10/100 speeds. Finally, if the network cards and equipment support it, 100-Mbps links can be set for full duplex operation, effectively increasing the maximum bandwidth to 200 Mbps. Even some 10-Mbps links can be set for 20 Mbps at full duplex.

While virtually no new networks will be installed at 10 Mbps, older networks will often be 10-Mbps systems and have a mix of technologies. Where possible, all systems should be migrated to UTP except where excessive interference makes this inappropriate. Any new equipment that is purchased should be of the 10/100 models to ensure compatibility with both the old system and any newer equipment purchased. However, new equipment will only transmit as fast as is permitted by the wiring. Old Category 3 wiring will not facilitate 100 Mbps speeds. Even Category 5 wiring may not support the higher speeds depending on distance.

Hubs are another item that seem destined for extinction. Not to long ago, the cost per port for bridges and switches made the transition to them painfully expensive. However, in the last few years the cost reduction of these components more than justifies their purchase. Switches today have learning algorithms and require no complicated setup. Simply connect them to the network and they automatically learn network topologies and node locations. The advanced features offered by switches over hubs can add significant management and security for the price. For example, many switches come with built in statistics, virtual local area networks and firewall filtering. Lastly, switches (and bridges) offer filtering and fault isolation as part of their standard operation.

For any new installation, the following should be part of the shopping list: the best quality UTP cabling (Category 6), network cards capable of 10/100 full-duplex operation, and switches with ports capable of 10/100 full duplex operation. When upgrading the old system, network administrators should follow these guidelines with the understanding that the equipment will be running on an older infrastructure.

10.6 SUMMARY

High-speed LANs have emerged as a critical element of corporate information systems. Such LANs are needed not only to provide an on-premises backbone for linking departmental LANs, but also to support the high-performance requirements of graphics-based client/server and intranet applications.

For most applications, Fast Ethernet and the emerging Gigabit Ethernet technologies dominate corporate high-speed LAN choices. These systems involve the least risk and cost for managers for a number of reasons, including compatibility with the existing large Ethernet installed base, maturity of the basic technology, and compatibility with existing network management and configuration software.

In most cases, an organization will have multiple LANs that need to be interconnected. The simplest approach to meeting this requirement is the bridge.

Another approach to LAN implementation is Fibre Channel, which supports the storage area network (SAN) concept and is intended for high-speed workstations and servers as well as direct connection of some high-speed I/O devices.

10.7 RECOMMENDED READING AND WEB SITES

[SPUR00] provides a concise but thorough overview of all of the 10-Mbps through 1-Gbps 802.3 systems, including configuration guidelines for a single segment of each media type, as well as guidelines for building multisegment Ethernets using a variety of media types. [NORR03] provides a good overview of Gigabit Ethernet, with an extended discussion of applications of the technology. Two somewhat more technical treatments of both 100-Mbps and Gigabit Ethernet are [SEIF98] and [KADA98]. A good survey article on Gigabit Ethernet is [FRAZ99]. [10GE02] is a white paper providing a useful introduction to 10-Gbps Ethernet.

[SACH96] is a good survey of Fibre Channel. A short but worthwhile treatment is [FCIA01].

10GE02   10 Gigabit Ethernet Alliance. *10 Gigabit Ethernet Technology Overview*. White paper, May 2002.

FCIA01   Fibre Channel Industry Association. *Fibre Channel Storage Area Networks*. San Francisco: Fibre Channel Industry Association, 2001.

FRAZ99   Frazier, H., and Johnson, H. "Gigabit Ethernet: From 100 to 1,000 Mbps." *IEEE Internet Computing*, January/February 1999.

KADA98   Kadambi, J.; Crayford, I.; and Kalkunte, M. *Gigabit Ethernet*. Upper Saddle River, NJ: Prentice Hall, 1998.

NORR03   Norris, M. *Gigabit Ethernet Technology and Applications*. Norwood, MA: Artech House, 2003.

SACH96   Sachs. M., and Varma, A. "Fibre Channel and Related Standards." *IEEE Communications Magazine*, August 1996.

SEIF98   Seifert, R. *Gigabit Ethernet*. Reading, MA: Addison-Wesley, 1998.

SPUR00   Spurgeon, C. *Ethernet: The Definitive Guide*. Cambridge, MA: O'Reilly and Associates, 2000.

Recommended Web Sites:

- **Interoperability Lab:** University of New Hampshire site for equipment testing for high-speed LANs.
- **Charles Spurgeon's Ethernet Web Site:** Provides extensive information about Ethernet, including links and documents.
- **10 Gigabit Ethernet Alliance:** This group promotes the 10-Gbps Ethernet standard.
- **Fibre Channel Industry Association:** Includes tutorials, white papers, links to vendors, and descriptions of Fibre Channel applications.
- **Storage Network Industry Association:** An industry forum of developers, integrators, and IT professionals who evolve and promote storage networking technology and solutions.

10.8 KEY TERMS, REVIEW QUESTIONS, AND PROBLEMS

Key Terms

bridge	Ethernet	layer 2 switch
carrier sense multiple access	Fast Ethernet	layer 3 switch
with collision detection	frame	store-and-forward switch
(CSMA/CD)	frame check sequence (FCS)	switch
cut-through switch	Fibre Channel	
cyclic redundancy check (CRC)	Hub	

Review Questions

10.1. What is a server farm?

10.2. Explain why a data rate of 10 Mbps on all LAN segments is increasingly inadequate for many businesses.

10.3. What is CSMA/CD?

10.4. What functions are performed by a bridge?

10.5. What is the difference between a hub and a layer 2 switch?

10.6. What is the difference between a store-and forward switch and a cut-through switch?

10.7. What are the differences between a bridge and a switch?

10.8. What is meant by the phrase *flat address space*?

10.9. What are the transmission medium options for Fast Ethernet?

10.10. What are the transmission medium options for Gigabit Ethernet?

10.11. What are the transmission medium options for 10-Gbps Ethernet?

10.12. List the levels of Fibre Channel and the functions of each level.

10.13. What are the topology options for Fibre Channel?

Problems

10.1 Can you determine the type of network interface card installed in your computer? Describe this card in terms of the speed, layer 2 protocol and the type of medium you are using (for example, 10-Mbps Ethernet over UTP).

10.2 Using capture programs such as Ethereal and built in programs like ping, nslookup and ipconfig, can you find the following information?
- **a.** With ipconfig or ifconfig, find your MAC address.
- **b.** Capture traffic from your own computer and examine your MAC address—does it match the previous question?
- **c.** Can you determine the code value for IP in the frames you have been captured? This can be found in the control field of the Ethernet frame.

10.3 An argument that has been ongoing for some time now involves the question as to whether ATM or Gigabit Ethernet is the best choice for a high-speed networking solution. Compare these two technologies and formulate a position paper outlining a potential scenario for each technology where it might constitute the optimal solution.

10.4 Broadband Integrated Services Digital Network (BISDN) is an optical broadband version of ISDN (which provides digital transmission over POTS). BISDN services incorporate several technologies, including Asynchronous Transfer Mode (ATM) and

Synchronous Optical Network (SONET). Provide a basic overview of SONET. Can SONET be used to extend the reach of the Fibre Channel data center protocol for international data traffic?

10.5   Token Ring is an alternative (but largely considered obsolete) technology to Ethernet. Provide a basic overview of Token-Ring and explain why it has largely been effaced by Ethernet as a LAN technology alternative.

10.6   When a collision occurs, IEEE 802.3 systems use an algorithm called *binary exponential backoff* to calculate the random amount of time the sender must wait before attempting to retransmit the frame. For each of the retransmissions, the algorithm doubles the range of the random delay. Thus, after n collisions, the sender will wait for a random amount of time, in the range from 0 to $2^n - 1$ units of time, before attempting to retransmit the frame. Analyze the advantages of this design decision.

10.7   Analyze the advantages of having the FCS field of IEEE 802.3 frames in the trailer of the frame rather than the header of the frame.

Case Study IV: Carlson Companies

Carlson Companies is one of the largest privately held companies in the United States, with more than 180,000 employees in more than 140 countries. Carlson enterprises include a presence in marketing, business and leisure travel, and hospitality industries.

Its Information Technology (IT) division, Carlson Shared Services, acts as a service provider to its internal clients and consequently must support a spectrum of user applications and services. The IT division uses a centralized data processing model to meet business operational requirements. The central computing environment includes an IBM mainframe and over 50 networked Hewlett-Packard and Sun servers [CLAR02, HIGG02]. The mainframe supports a wide range of applications, including Oracle financial database, e-mail, Microsoft Exchange, Web, PeopleSoft, and a data warehouse application.

In 2002, the IT division established six goals for assuring that IT services continued to meet the needs of a growing company with heavy reliance on data and applications:

1. Implement an enterprise data warehouse.
2. Build a global network.
3. Move to enterprise-wide architecture.
4. Establish six-sigma quality for Carlson clients.
5. Facilitate outsourcing and exchange.
6. Leverage existing technology and resources.

The key to meeting these goals was to implement a storage area network (SAN) with a consolidated, centralized database to support mainframe and server applications. Carlson needed a SAN and data center approach that provided a reliable, highly scalable facility to accommodate the increasing demands of its users.

Storage Requirements

Until recently, the central DP shop included separate disc storage for each server, plus that of the mainframe. This dispersed data storage scheme had the advantage of responsiveness; that is, the access time from a server to its data was minimal. However, the data management cost was high. There had to be backup procedures for the storage on each server, as well as management controls to reconcile data distributed throughout the system. The mainframe included an efficient disaster recovery plan to preserve data in the event of major system crashes or other incidents and to get data back online with little or no disruption to the users. No comparable plan existed for the many servers.

As Carlson's databases grow beyond 10 terabytes (TB) of business-critical data, the IT team determined that a comprehensive network storage strategy would be required to manage future growth.

Solution Concept

The existing Carlson server complex made use of Fibre Channel links to achieve communication and backup capabilities among servers. Carlson considered extending this capability to a full-blown Fibre Channel SAN that would encompass the servers, the mainframe, and massive centralized storage facilities. The IT team concluded that further expansion using Fibre Channel technologies alone would be difficult and costly to manage. At the same time, in supporting the many offsite client systems that accessed data center servers, the IT shop already had a substantial investment in IP network products and staff training. Accordingly, Carlson sought a solution that would leverage this IP investment, provide scalability as additional local and remote services are added, and require minimal traffic engineering of the storage transport network.

Thus, Carlson settled on a solution based on a core IP SAN that would meet both data-center and wide area storage requirements and seamlessly integrate new storage technologies.

The Carlson SAN

The core of the Carlson SAN is an IP-based scheme in which Gigabit Ethernet switches carry IP traffic among servers and between servers and the central storage. Attached to the Gigabit switches are Nishan IP storage switches, which provide a Fibre Channel interface for the servers and storage and an IP traffic switch into the Ethernet core (Figure IV.1). The Ethernet switches enjoy a considerable cost advantage over comparable Fibre Channel switches and require lower-cost management and maintenance.

For redundancy, servers are dual-homed to the IP storage switches, which in turn connect to redundant Ethernet switches. The ratio of servers to storage interconnect is determined by the throughput requirements of each server group. Similarly, multiple IP storage switches connect the Ethernet switch core to the SAN storage system. This configuration can be scaled to support additional servers and storage arrays by adding additional IP storage switches. The network core of Ethernet switches also expands easily by adding additional switches.

The focus of the Carlson SAN is a 13-TB HP StorageWorks Disc array. A major consideration in planning the transition was the migration of data from the mainframe's storage to the central storage. The mainframe hosts several mission-critical applications in a round-the-clock fashion. Thus, an offline data migration was not feasible. The migration of all common data to this array proceeded in two phases. In the first phase, each server was taken offline and a simple copy was performed to transfer the application data on the server systems to the new storage system. The second phase involved the transfer of 1.2 TB of data from the mainframe's legacy storage to the new storage system. Carlson contracted this task out to HP storage experts who made use of proprietary data migration and

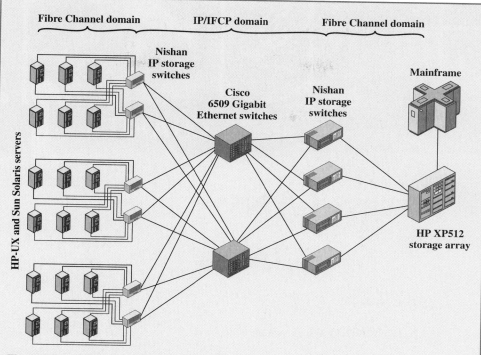

Figure IV.1   Carlson's Data Center SAN

network management tools to enable the transfer to occur during production processing hours. End users were unaffected during the migration.

Carlson's IP SAN helps reduce the ongoing administration and management of storage networking by taking advantage of well-established and well-understood IP networking technologies. In addition, putting storage data over IP facilitates integration of more efficient storage services for Carlson's enterprise-wide network, including centralized backup of remote sites to the data center SAN.

Discussion Questions

1. Discuss how the Carlson SAN approach addresses the IT goals the company is trying to achieve.

2. Discuss the pros and cons of consolidating data on a SAN central data facility versus the dispersed arrangement it replaces.

3. The Carlson SAN mixes equipment from a number of vendors. What problems does this raise and what are some management options for dealing with them?

CHAPTER 11

WIRELESS LANS

11.1 Overview

11.2 IEEE 802.11 Wireless Lan Standard

11.3 Bluetooth

11.4 Summary

11.5 Recommended Reading and Web Sites

11.6 Key Terms, Review Questions, and Problems

298

In just the past few years, wireless LANs have become a significant segment of the LAN market. Increasingly, organizations are finding that wireless LANs are an indispensable adjunct to traditional wired LANs, to satisfy requirements for mobility, relocation, ad hoc networking, and coverage of locations difficult to wire.

This chapter provides a survey of wireless LANs. We begin with an overview that looks at the motivations for using wireless LANs and summarizes the various approaches in current use. Then, the two most widely used wireless LAN schemes, IEEE 802.11 and Bluetooth, are examined.

11.1 OVERVIEW

As the name suggests, a wireless LAN is one that makes use of a wireless transmission medium. Until relatively recently, wireless LANs were little used. The reasons for this included high prices, low data rates, occupational safety concerns, and licensing requirements. As these problems have been addressed, the popularity of wireless LANs has grown rapidly.

Wireless LAN Applications

[PAHL95] lists four application areas for wireless LANs: LAN extension, cross-building interconnect, nomadic access, and ad hoc networks. Let us consider each of these in turn.

LAN Extension Early wireless LAN products, introduced in the late 1980s, were marketed as substitutes for traditional wired LANs. A wireless LAN saves the cost of the installation of LAN cabling and eases the task of relocation and other modifications to network structure. However, this motivation for wireless LANs was overtaken by events. First, as awareness of the need for LANs became greater, architects designed new buildings to include extensive prewiring for data

299

applications. Second, with advances in data transmission technology, there is an increasing reliance on twisted-pair cabling for LANs and, in particular, Category 3 and Category 5 unshielded twisted pair. Most older buildings are already wired with an abundance of Category 3 cable, and many newer buildings are prewired with Category 5. Thus, the use of a wireless LAN to replace wired LANs has not happened to any great extent.

However, in a number of environments, there is a role for the wireless LAN as an alternative to a wired LAN. Examples include buildings with large open areas, such as manufacturing plants, stock exchange trading floors, and warehouses; historical buildings with insufficient twisted pair and where drilling holes for new wiring is prohibited; and small offices where installation and maintenance of wired LANs is not economical. In all of these cases, a wireless LAN provides an effective and more attractive alternative. In most of these cases, an organization will also have a wired LAN to support servers and some stationary workstations. For example, a manufacturing facility typically has an office area that is separate from the factory floor but that must be linked to it for networking purposes. Therefore, typically, a wireless LAN will be linked into a wired LAN on the same premises. Thus, this application area is referred to as LAN extension.

Figure 11.1 indicates a simple wireless LAN configuration that is typical of many environments. There is a backbone wired LAN, such as Ethernet, that supports

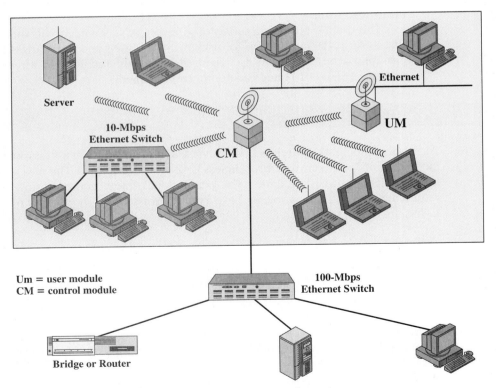

Figure 11.1   Example Single-Cell Wireless LAN Configuration

servers, workstations, and one or more bridges or routers to link with other networks. In addition, there is a control module (CM) that acts as an interface to a wireless LAN. The control module includes either bridge or router functionality to link the wireless LAN to the backbone. It includes some sort of access control logic, such as a polling or token-passing scheme, to regulate the access from the end systems. Note that some of the end systems are standalone devices, such as a workstation or a server. Hubs or other user modules (UMs) that control a number of stations off a wired LAN may also be part of the wireless LAN configuration.

The configuration of Figure 11.1 can be referred to as a single-cell wireless LAN; all of the wireless end systems are within range of a single control module. Another common configuration, suggested by Figure 11.2, is a multiple-cell wireless LAN. In this case, there are multiple control modules interconnected by a wired LAN. Each control module supports a number of wireless end systems within its transmission range. For example, with an infrared LAN, transmission is limited to a single room; therefore, one cell is needed for each room in an office building that requires wireless support.

Cross-Building Interconnect Another use of wireless LAN technology is to connect LANs in nearby buildings, be they wired or wireless LANs. In this case, a point-to-point wireless link is used between two buildings. For example, two microwave or infrared transmitter/receiver units can be placed on the rooftops of two buildings within the line of sight of each other. The devices so connected are

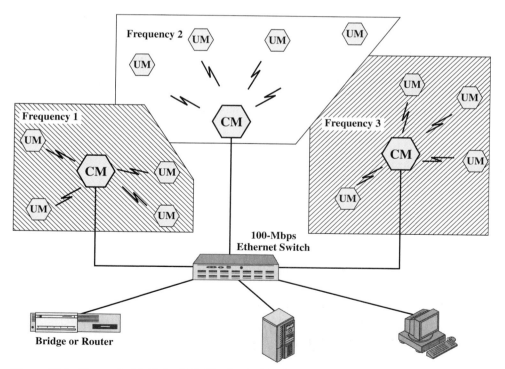

Figure 11.2 Example Multiple-Cell Wireless LAN Configuration

typically bridges or routers. This single point-to-point link is not a LAN per se, but it is usual to include this application under the heading of wireless LAN.

Nomadic Access Nomadic access provides a wireless link between a LAN hub and a mobile data terminal equipped with an antenna, such as a laptop computer or notepad computer. One example of the utility of such a connection is to enable an employee returning from a trip to transfer data from a personal portable computer to a server in the office. Nomadic access is also useful in an extended environment such as a campus or a business operating out of a cluster of buildings. In both of these cases, users may move around with their portable computers and may wish access to the servers on a wired LAN from various locations.

Ad Hoc Networking An ad hoc network is a peer-to-peer network (no centralized server) set up temporarily to meet some immediate need. For example, a group of employees, each with a laptop or palmtop computer, may convene in a conference room for a business or classroom meeting. The employees link their computers in a temporary network just for the duration of the meeting.

Figure 11.3 suggests the differences between a wireless LAN that supports LAN extension and nomadic access requirements and an ad hoc wireless LAN. In the former case, the wireless LAN forms a stationary infrastructure consisting of one or more cells with a control module for each cell. Within a cell, there may be a number of stationary end systems. Nomadic stations can move from one cell to another. In contrast, there is no infrastructure for an ad hoc network. Rather, a peer collection of stations within range of each other may dynamically configure themselves into a temporary network.

Wireless LAN Requirements

A wireless LAN must meet the same sort of requirements typical of any LAN, including high capacity, ability to cover short distances, full connectivity among attached stations, and broadcast capability. In addition, there are a number of requirements specific to the wireless LAN environment. The following are among the most important requirements for wireless LANs:

- **Throughput:** The medium access control protocol should make as efficient use as possible of the wireless medium to maximize capacity.
- **Number of nodes:** Wireless LANs may need to support hundreds of nodes across multiple cells.
- **Connection to backbone LAN:** In most cases, interconnection with stations on a wired backbone LAN is required. For infrastructure wireless LANs, this is easily accomplished through the use of control modules that connect to both types of LANs. There may also need to be accommodation for mobile users and ad hoc wireless networks.
- **Service area:** A typical coverage area for a wireless LAN has a diameter of 100 to 300 m.
- **Battery power consumption:** Mobile workers use battery-powered workstations that need to have a long battery life when used with wireless adapters. This suggests that a MAC protocol that requires mobile nodes to monitor access points constantly or engage in frequent handshakes with a base station

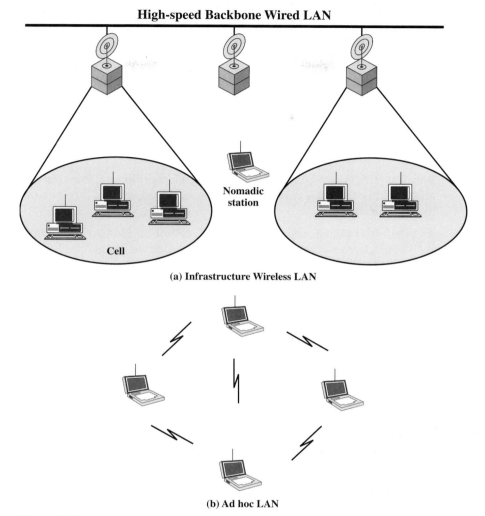

Figure 11.3   Wireless LAN Configurations

is inappropriate. Typical wireless LAN implementations have features to reduce power consumption while not using the network, such as a sleep mode.

- **Transmission robustness and security:** Unless properly designed, a wireless LAN may be interference prone and easily eavesdropped. The design of a wireless LAN must permit reliable transmission even in a noisy environment and should provide some level of security from eavesdropping.

- **Collocated network operation:** As wireless LANs become more popular, it is quite likely for two or more wireless LANs to operate in the same area or in some area where interference between the LANs is possible. Such interference may thwart the normal operation of a MAC algorithm and may allow unauthorized access to a particular LAN.

- **License-free operation:** Users would prefer to buy and operate wireless LAN products without having to secure a license for the frequency band used by the LAN.
- **Handoff/roaming:** The MAC protocol used in the wireless LAN should enable mobile stations to move from one cell to another.
- **Dynamic configuration:** The MAC addressing and network management aspects of the LAN should permit dynamic and automated addition, deletion, and relocation of end systems without disruption to other users.

Wireless LAN Technology

Wireless LANs are generally categorized according to the transmission technique that is used. All current wireless LAN products fall into one of the following categories:

- **Infrared (IR) LANs:** An individual cell of an IR LAN is limited to a single room, because infrared light does not penetrate opaque walls.
- **Spread spectrum LANs:** This type of LAN makes use of spread spectrum transmission technology. In most cases, these LANs operate in the ISM (Industrial, Scientific, and Medical) bands so that no FCC licensing is required for their use in the United States.
- **Narrowband microwave:** These LANs operate at microwave frequencies but do not use spread spectrum. Some of these products operate at frequencies that require FCC licensing, while others use one of the unlicensed ISM bands.

Table 11.1 summarizes some of the key characteristics of these three technologies; the details are explored in the next three sections.

11.2 IEEE 802.11 WIRELESS LAN STANDARD

The IEEE 802.11 committee has developed a set of wireless LAN standards. This section provides an overview.

IEEE 802.11 Architecture

Figure 11.4 illustrates the model developed by the 802.11 working group. The smallest building block of a wireless LAN is a basic service set (BSS), which consists of some number of stations executing the same MAC protocol and competing for access to the same shared wireless medium. A BSS may be isolated or it may connect to a backbone distribution system (DS) through an access point (AP). The access point functions as a bridge. The MAC protocol may be fully distributed or controlled by a central coordination function housed in the access point. The BSS generally corresponds to what is referred to as a cell in the literature. The DS can be a switch, a wired network, or a wireless network.

The simplest configuration is shown in Figure 11.4, in which each station belongs to a single BSS; that is, each station is within wireless range only of other stations within the same BSS. It is also possible for two BSSs to overlap geographi-

Table 11.1 Comparison of Wireless LAN Technologies

	Infrared		Spread Spectrum		Radio
	Diffused Infrared	Directed Beam Infrared	Frequency Hopping	Direct Sequence	Narrowband Microwave
Data Rate (Mbps)	1 to 4	1 to 10	1 to 3	2 to 50	10 to 20
Mobility	Stationary/mobile	Stationary with LOS	Mobile	Stationary/mobile	Stationary/mobile
Range (m)	15 to 60	25	30 to 100	30 to 250	10 to 40
Detectability	Negligible		Little		Some
Wavelength/ Frequency	λ: 800 to 900 nm		902 to 928 MHz 2.4 to 2.4835 GHz 5.725 to 5.85 GHz		902 to 928 MHz 5.2 to 5.775 GHz 18.825 to 19.205 GHz
Modulation Technique	ASK		FSK	QPSK	FSK/QPSK
Radiated Power	—		<1 W		25 mW
Access Method	CSMA	Token ring, CSMA	CSMA		Reservation ALOHA, CSMA
License Required	No		No		Yes unless ISM

305

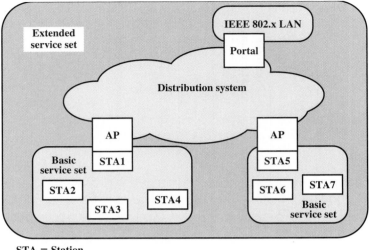

STA = Station
AP = Access point

Figure 11.4   IEEE 802.11 Architecture

cally, so that a single station could participate in more than one BSS. Further, the association between a station and a BSS is dynamic. Stations may turn off, come within range, and go out of range.

An extended service set (ESS) consists of two or more basic service sets interconnected by a distribution system. Typically, the distribution system is a wired backbone LAN but can be any communications network. The extended service set appears as a single logical LAN to the logical link control (LLC) level.

Figure 11.4 indicates that an access point (AP) is implemented as part of a station; the AP is the logic within a station that provides access to the DS by providing DS services in addition to acting as a station. To integrate the IEEE 802.11 architecture with a traditional wired LAN, a portal is used. The portal logic is implemented in a device, such as a bridge or router, that is part of the wired LAN and that is attached to the DS.

IEEE 802.11 Services

IEEE 802.11 defines a number of services that need to be provided by the wireless LAN to provide functionality equivalent to that which is inherent to wired LANs. The most important services are as follows:

- **Association:** Establishes an initial association between a station and an access point. Before a station can transmit or receive frames on a wireless LAN, its identity and address must be known. For this purpose, a station must establish an association with an access point. The access point can then communicate this information to other access points to facilitate routing and delivery of addressed frames.
- **Reassociation:** Enables an established association to be transferred from one access point to another, allowing a mobile station to move.

- **Disassociation:** A notification from either a station or an access point that an existing association is terminated. A station should give this notification before leaving an area or shutting down. However, the MAC management facility protects itself against stations that disappear without notification.

- **Authentication:** Used to establish the identity of stations to each other. In a wired LAN, it is generally assumed that access to a physical connection conveys authority to connect to the LAN. This is not a valid assumption for a wireless LAN, in which connectivity is achieved simply by having an attached antenna that is properly tuned. The authentication service is used by stations to establish their identity with stations they wish to communicate with. The standard does not mandate any particular authentication scheme, which could range from relatively unsecure handshaking to public-key encryption schemes.

- **Privacy:** Used to prevent the contents of messages from being read by other than the intended recipient. The standard provides for the optional use of encryption to assure privacy.

IEEE 802.11 Medium Access Control

The IEEE 802.11 MAC layer covers three functional areas: reliable data delivery, access control, and security. In this section we examine reliable data delivery and access control; the security area is beyond our scope.

Reliable Data Delivery As with any wireless network, a wireless LAN using the IEEE 802.11 physical and MAC layers is subject to considerable unreliability. Noise, interference, and other propagation effects may result in the loss of a significant number of frames. Even with error-correction codes, a number of MAC frames may not successfully be received. This situation can be dealt with by reliability mechanisms at a higher layer, such as TCP. However, timers used for retransmission at higher layers are typically on the order of seconds. It is therefore more efficient to deal with errors at the MAC level. For this purpose, IEEE 802.11 includes a frame exchange protocol. When a station receives a data frame from another station, it returns an acknowledgment (ACK) frame to the source station. This exchange is treated as an atomic unit, not to be interrupted by a transmission from any other station. If the source does not receive an ACK within a short period of time, either because its data frame was damaged or because the returning ACK was damaged, the source retransmits the frame.

Thus, the basic data transfer mechanism in IEEE 802.11 involves an exchange of two frames. To further enhance reliability, a four-frame exchange may be used. In this scheme, a source first issues a Request to Send (RTS) frame to the destination. The destination then responds with a Clear to Send (CTS). After receiving the CTS, the source transmits the data frame, and the destination responds with an ACK. The RTS alerts all stations that are within reception range of the source that an exchange is under way; these stations refrain from transmission in order to avoid a collision between two frames transmitted at the same time. Similarly, the CTS alerts all stations that are within reception range of the destination that an exchange is under way. The RTS/CTS portion of the exchange is a required function of the MAC but may be disabled.

Access Control   The 802.11 working group considered two types of proposals for a MAC algorithm: distributed access protocols, which, like Ethernet, distribute the decision to transmit among all the nodes using a carrier-sense mechanism; and centralized access protocols, which involve regulation of transmission by a centralized decision maker. A distributed access protocol makes sense for an ad hoc network of peer workstations and may also be attractive in other wireless LAN configurations that consist primarily of bursty traffic. A centralized access protocol is natural for configurations in which a number of wireless stations are interconnected with each other and some sort of base station that attaches to a backbone wired LAN; it is especially useful if some of the data are time sensitive or high priority.

The end result for 802.11 is a MAC algorithm called DFWMAC (distributed foundation wireless MAC) that provides a distributed access control mechanism with an optional centralized control built on top of that. Figure 11.5 illustrates the architecture. The lower sublayer of the MAC layer is the distributed coordination function (DCF). DCF uses an Ethernet-style contention algorithm to provide access to all traffic. Ordinary asynchronous traffic directly uses DCF. The point coordination function (PCF) is a centralized MAC algorithm used to provide contention-free service; this is done by polling stations in turn. Higher-priority traffic, or traffic with greater timing requirements, makes use of the PCF. PCF is built on top of DCF and exploits features of DCF to assure access for its users. Finally, the logical link control (LLC) layer provides an interface to higher layers and performs basic link layer functions such as error control.

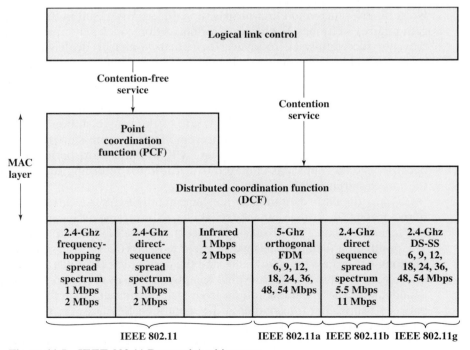

Figure 11.5   IEEE 802.11 Protocol Architecture

IEEE 802.11 Physical Layer

The physical layer for IEEE 802.11 has been issued in four stages; the first part was issued in 1997, two additional parts in 1999, and the most recent in 2002. The first part, simply called IEEE 802.11, includes the MAC layer and three physical layer specifications, two in the 2.4-GHz band and one in the infrared, all operating at 1 and 2 Mbps. IEEE 802.11a operates in the 5-GHz band at data rates up to 54 Mbps. IEEE 802.11b operates in the 2.4-Ghz band at 5.5 and 11 Mbps. IEEE 802.g extends IEEE 802.11b to higher data rates. We look at each of these in turn.

Three physical media are defined in the original 802.11 standard:

- Direct-sequence spread spectrum (DSSS) operating in the 2.4 GHz ISM band, at data rates of 1 Mbps and 2 Mbps
- Frequency-hopping spread spectrum (FHSS) operating in the 2.4 GHz ISM band, at data rates of 1 Mbps and 2 Mbps
- Infrared at 1 Mbps and 2 Mbps, operating at a wavelength between 850 and 950 nm

The infrared option never gained market support. The other two schemes use spread spectrum approaches. In essence, spread spectrum involves the use of a much wider bandwidth than is actually necessary to support a given data rate. The purpose of using a wider bandwidth is to minimize interference and drastically reduce the error rate. In the case of FHSS, spread spectrum is achieved by frequently jumping from one carrier frequency to another; thus, if there is interference or performance degradation at a given frequency, it only affects a small fraction of the transmission. DSSS effectively increases the data rate of a signal by mapping each data bit into a string of bits, with one string used for binary 1 and another used for binary 0. The higher data rate uses a greater bandwidth. The effect is to spread each bit out over time, which minimizes the effects of interference and degradation. FHSS, which is simpler, was employed in most early 802.11 networks. Products using DSSS, which is more effective in the 802.11 scheme, followed. However, all of the original 802.11 products were of limited utility because of the low data rates.

IEEE 802.11b is an extension of the IEEE 802.11 DSSS scheme, providing data rates of 5.5 and 11 Mbps. A higher data rate is achieved by using a more complex modulation technique. The 802.11b specification quickly led to product offerings, including chipsets, PC cards, access points, and systems. Apple Computer was the first company to offer 802.11b products, with its iBook portable computer using the AirPort wireless network option. Other companies, including Cisco, 3Com, and Dell, have followed. Although these new products are all based on the same standard, there is always a concern whether products from different vendors will successfully interoperate. To meet this concern, the Wireless Ethernet Compatibility Alliance (WECA) created a test suite to certify interoperability for 802.11b products. Inter-operability tests have been conducted and a number of products have achieved certification.

One other concern for both the original 802.11 and the 802.11b products is interference with other systems that operate in the 2.4-GHz band, such as Bluetooth, HomeRF, and many other devices that use the same portion of the spectrum (including baby monitors and garage door openers). A coexistence study group (IEEE 802.15) is examining this issue and so far the prospects are encouraging.

Although 802.11b is achieving a certain level of success, its limited data rate results in limited appeal. To meet the needs for a truly high-speed LAN, IEEE 802.11a has been developed. The IEEE 802.11a specification makes use of the 5-GHz band. Unlike the 2.4-GHz specifications, IEEE 802.11a does not use a spread spectrum scheme but rather uses orthogonal frequency division multiplexing (OFDM). OFDM, also called multicarrier modulation, uses multiple carrier signals (up to 52) at different frequencies, sending some of the bits on each channel. The possible data rates for IEEE 802.11a are 6, 9, 12, 18, 24, 36, 48, and 54 Mbps.

IEEE 802.11g is a higher-speed extension to IEEE 802.11b. This scheme combines a variety of physical layer encoding techniques used in 802.11a and 802.11b to provide service at a variety of data rates.

11.3 BLUETOOTH

Bluetooth is an always-on, short-range radio hookup that resides on a microchip. It was initially developed by Swedish mobile-phone maker Ericsson in 1994 as a way to let laptop computers make calls over a mobile phone. Since then, several thousand companies have signed on to make Bluetooth the low-power short-range wireless standard for a wide range of devices.

The Bluetooth standards are published by an industry consortium known as the Bluetooth SIG (special interest group).

The concept behind Bluetooth is to provide a universal short-range wireless capability. Using the 2.4-GHz band, available globally for unlicensed low-power uses, two Bluetooth devices within 10 m of each other can share up to 720 kbps of capacity. Bluetooth is intended to support an open-ended list of applications, including data (e.g., schedules and telephone numbers), audio, graphics, and even video. For example, audio devices can include headsets, cordless and standard phones, home stereos, and digital MP3 players. Examples of some of the capabilities Bluetooth can provide consumers are as follows:

- Make calls from a wireless headset connected remotely to a cell phone.
- Eliminate cables linking computers to printers, keyboards, and the mouse.
- Hook up MP3 players wirelessly to other machines to download music.
- Set up home networks so that the users can remotely monitor air conditioning, the oven, and children's Internet surfing.
- Call home from a remote location to turn appliances on and off, set the alarm, and monitor activity.

Bluetooth Applications

Bluetooth is designed to operate in an environment of many users. Up to eight devices can communicate in a small network called a **piconet.** Ten of these piconets can coexist in the same coverage range of the Bluetooth radio. To provide security, each link is encoded and protected against eavesdropping and interference.

Bluetooth provides support for three general application areas using short-range wireless connectivity:

- **Data and voice access points:** Bluetooth facilitates real-time voice and data transmissions by providing effortless wireless connection of portable and stationary communications devices.
- **Cable replacement:** Bluetooth eliminates the need for numerous, often proprietary, cable attachments for connection of practically any kind of communication device. Connections are instant and are maintained even when devices are not within line of sight. The range of each radio is approximately 10 m but can be extended to 100 m with an optional amplifier.
- **Ad hoc networking:** A device equipped with a Bluetooth radio can establish instant connection to another Bluetooth radio as soon as it comes into range.

Bluetooth Standards Documents

The Bluetooth standards present a formidable bulk: well over 1500 pages, divided into two groups: core and profile. The **core specifications** describe the details of the various layers of the Bluetooth protocol architecture, from the radio interface to link control. Related topics are covered, such as interoperability with related technologies, testing requirements, and a definition of various Bluetooth timers and their associated values.

The **profile specifications** are concerned with the use of Bluetooth technology to support various applications. Each profile specification discusses the use of the technology defined in the core specifications to implement a particular usage model. The profile specification includes a description of which aspects of the core specifications are mandatory, optional, and not applicable. The purpose of a profile specification is to define a standard of interoperability, so that products from different vendors that claim to support a given usage model will work together. In general terms, profile specifications fall into one of two categories: cable replacement or wireless audio. The cable replacement profiles provide a convenient means for logically connecting devices in proximity to one another and for exchanging data. For example, when two devices first come within range of one another, they can automatically query each other for a common profile. This might then cause the end users of the device to be alerted, or cause some automatic data exchange to take place. The wireless audio profiles are concerned with establishing short-range voice connections.

The Bluetooth developer must wade through the many documents with a particular application in mind. The reading list begins with coverage of some essential core specifications plus the general access profile. This profile is one of a number of profiles that serve as a foundation for other profiles and do not specify independently usable functionality. The general access profile specifies how the Bluetooth baseband architecture, defined in the core specifications, is to be used between devices that implement one or multiple profiles. Following a basic set of documents, the reading list splits along two lines, depending on whether the reader's interest is in cable replacement or wireless audio.

Protocol Architecture

Bluetooth is defined as a layered protocol architecture consisting of core protocols, cable replacement and telephony control protocols, and adopted protocols.

The **core protocols** form a five-layer stack consisting of the following elements:

- **Radio:** Specifies details of the air interface, including frequency, the use of frequency hopping, modulation scheme, and transmit power.

- **Baseband:** Concerned with connection establishment within a piconet, addressing, packet format, timing, and power control.

- **Link manager protocol (LMP):** Responsible for link setup between Bluetooth devices and ongoing link management. This includes security aspects such as authentication and encryption, plus the control and negotiation of baseband packet sizes.

- **Logical link control and adaptation protocol (L2CAP):** Adapts upper-layer protocols to the baseband layer. L2CAP provides both connectionless and connection-oriented services.

- **Service discovery protocol (SDP):** Device information, services, and the characteristics of the services can be queried to enable the establishment of a connection between two or more Bluetooth devices.

RFCOMM is the **cable replacement protocol** included in the Bluetooth specification. RFCOMM presents a virtual serial port that is designed to make replacement of cable technologies as transparent as possible. Serial ports are one of the most common types of communications interfaces used with computing and communications devices. Hence, RFCOMM enables the replacement of serial port cables with the minimum of modification of existing devices. RFCOMM provides for binary data transport and emulates EIA-232 control signals over the Bluetooth baseband layer. EIA-232 (formerly known as RS-232) is a widely used serial port interface standard.

Bluetooth specifies a **telephony control protocol**. TCS BIN (telephony control specification—binary) is a bit-oriented protocol that defines the call control signaling for the establishment of speech and data calls between Bluetooth devices. In addition, it defines mobility management procedures for handling groups of Bluetooth TCS devices.

The **adopted protocols** are defined in specifications issued by other standards-making organizations and incorporated into the overall Bluetooth architecture. The Bluetooth strategy is to invent only necessary protocols and use existing standards whenever possible. The adopted protocols include the following:

- **PPP:** The point-to-point protocol is an Internet standard protocol for transporting IP datagrams over a point-to-point link.

- **TCP/UDP/IP:** These are the foundation protocols of the TCP/IP protocol suite.

- **OBEX:** The object exchange protocol is a session-level protocol developed by the Infrared Data Association (IrDA) for the exchange of objects. OBEX provides functionality similar to that of HTTP, but in a simpler fashion. It also provides a model for representing objects and operations. Examples of content formats transferred by OBEX are vCard and vCalendar, which provide the format of an electronic business card and personal calendar entries and scheduling information, respectively.

- **WAE/WAP:** Bluetooth incorporates the wireless application environment and the wireless application protocol into its architecture.

Usage Models

A number of usage models are defined in Bluetooth profile documents. In essence, a usage model is a set of protocols that implement a particular Bluetooth-based application. Each profile defines the protocols and protocol features supporting a particular usage model. The most important usage models are as follows:

- **File transfer:** The file transfer usage model supports the transfer of directories, files, documents, images, and streaming media formats. This usage model also includes the capability to browse folders on a remote device.
- **Internet bridge:** With this usage model, a PC is wirelessly connected to a mobile phone or cordless modem to provide dial-up networking and fax capabilities. For dial-up networking, AT commands are used to control the mobile phone or modem, and another protocol stack (e.g., PPP over RFCOMM) is used for data transfer. For fax transfer, the fax software operates directly over RFCOMM.
- **LAN access:** This usage model enables devices on a piconet to access a LAN. Once connected, a device functions as if it were directly connected (wired) to the LAN.
- **Synchronization:** This model provides a device-to-device synchronization of PIM (personal information management) information, such as phone book, calendar, message, and note information. IrMC (infrared mobile communications) is an IrDA protocol that provides a client/server capability for transferring updated PIM information from one device to another.
- **Three-in-one phone:** Telephone handsets that implement this usage model may act as a cordless phone connecting to a voice base station, as an intercom device for connecting to other telephones, and as a cellular phone.
- **Headset:** The headset can act as a remote device's audio input and output interface.

Piconets and Scatternets

The basic unit of networking in Bluetooth is a **piconet,** consisting of a master and from one to seven active slave devices. The radio designated as the master makes the determination of the channel (frequency-hopping sequence) and phase (timing offset, i.e., when to transmit) that shall be used by all devices on this piconet. The radio designated as master makes this determination using its own device address as a parameter, while the slave devices must tune to the same channel and phase. A slave may only communicate with the master and may only communicate when granted permission by the master. A device in one piconet may also exist as part of another piconet and may function as either a slave or master in each piconet (Figure 11.6). This form of overlapping is called a **scatternet.** Figure 11.7 contrasts the piconet/scatternet architecture with other forms of wireless networks.

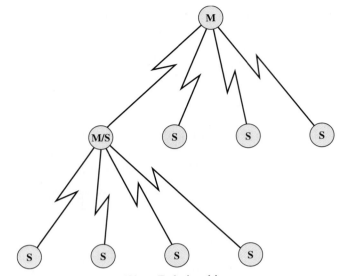

Figure 11.6   Master/Slave Relationships

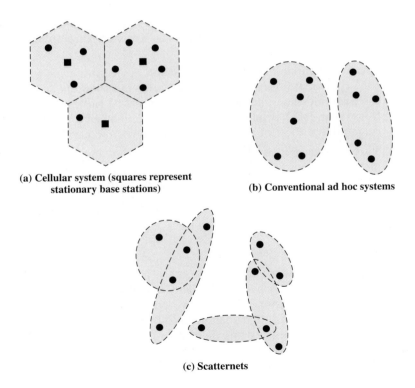

**(a) Cellular system (squares represent
stationary base stations)**

(b) Conventional ad hoc systems

(c) Scatternets

Figure 11.7   Wireless Network Configurations

The advantage of the piconet/scatternet scheme is that it allows many devices to share the same physical area and make efficient use of the bandwidth. A Bluetooth system uses a frequency-hopping scheme with a carrier spacing of 1 MHz. Typically, up to 80 different frequencies are used for a total bandwidth of 80 MHz. If frequency hopping were not used, then a single channel would correspond to a single 1-MHz band. With frequency hopping a logical channel is defined by the frequency-hopping sequence. At any given time, the bandwidth available is 1 MHz, with a maximum of eight devices sharing the bandwidth. Different logical channels (different hopping sequences) can simultaneously share the same 80-MHz bandwidth. Collisions will occur when devices in different piconets, on different logical channels, happen to use the same hop frequency at the same time. As the number of piconets in an area increases, the number of collisions increases, and performance degrades. In summary, the physical area and total bandwidth are shared by the scatternet. The logical channel and data transfer are shared by a piconet.

APPLICATION NOTE
Deploying Wireless LANs

Many organizations are faced with the problem of deciding whether or not to deploy a wireless local area network or WLAN. This problem is exacerbated by several issues regarding WLANs, such as security, management of deployed devices, and a confusing array of standards. Finally, deployment of a WLAN increases the responsibility of the support staff without necessarily providing them with the training or expertise to manage it.

There are a couple of reasons for deploying a wireless LAN: mobility, reducing the cost of an installation, ad hoc networking, and connecting geographically remote nodes. Probably the first thing that an organization should probably ask itself is if a WLAN is a requirement or is the WLAN something that, while cool and interesting, really doesn't add any value. Many companies are taking this approach because of the security hole that the wireless network represents. It is understandable that it may simply be too much of a risk or management nightmare to deploy. This approach does come with some danger, especially if the company also decides not to bother with wireless training. This is because employees, students, and visitors will deploy wireless equipment without the company knowing about it. This is not usually to attack the company network; it is simply a fact of life that more and more devices come equipped with wireless capability. New laptops are a very good example of this.

Wireless devices also have the annoying ability to automatically find connections. This is made worse with operating systems like Windows XP, which handles many wireless issues transparently and has the functionality of connection sharing. Connection sharing will allow multiple users to access the network through a single computers' network connection. If you decide not to deploy a wireless network, you still should prepare for someone else deploying one within your organization.

Choosing the right standard can be very difficult. The 802.11 family has had several generations, with 802.11b being the most successful. However, there have been significant problems with the 802.11b standard, including relatively low bandwidth, a small number of access points that can occupy an area, and interference from other devices sharing the 2.4-GHz portion of the spectrum.

The next generation standards, 802.11a and 802.11g, both attempt to address these problems, with 802.11a being the more successful because it has moved up to 5 GHz. If you have a wireless network already, then your decision may be slightly different than if you are deploying one from scratch. In order to be compatible with an existing 802.11b network, you may opt for 802.11g, which has higher data capacity but still can communicate directly with 802.11b nodes. This is becoming less of a consideration because many vendors are producing devices capable of bridging the barrier between the standards.

Depending on the intended use, new installations may decide on one of the new standards exclusively. We must remember that there is a tremendous amount on preexisting 802.11b equipment and more is being deployed daily so the decision must be made about its support. For many, 802.11a will be the best choice because of its high data rates, low interference and the number of available channels. The strength of 802.11a is also its weakness. A basic rule of thumb for radio based communication is that the higher the frequency, the shorter the transmission distance. Because it uses higher frequencies, 802.11a has a shorter range than 802.11b. Another rule of thumb it that the higher the frequency, the easier it is to disrupt the signal. This last problem is highly dependent on your operating environment.

Our last discussion point concerns security. While there is never a silver bullet regarding security measures, there are some basic practices that will help reduce exposure and vulnerability:

- Placing access points outside the company firewall to ensure that company data is not broadcast.
- Turn on WEP. It does have its problems, but it will stop most casual eavesdroppers.
- Run access points back to switches instead of hubs, to provide increased traffic filtering.
- Complete a wireless site survey to determine your level of exposure.
- Use a VPN for wireless nodes.
- Deploy some basic layer 2 or 3 filters for securing access.
- When in doubt, use encryption on your data.
- Understand that most problems do not come from external hackers, most problems (both malicious and accidental) come from internal users.

The real problem with wireless communication is that very few network administrators have spent much time with it. As a result, there is a tremendous lack of understanding and experience with the issues. While this short discussion is not meant to be the ultimate guide to wireless networking, it should help you understand some of the larger problems and thought processes associated with WLANs.

11.4 SUMMARY

In recent years, a whole new class of local area networks has arrived to provide an alternative to LANs based on twisted pair, coaxial cable, and optical fiber: wireless LANs. The key advantages of the wireless LAN are that it eliminates the wiring cost, which is often the most costly component of a LAN, and that it accommodates mobile workstations.

Wireless LANs use one of three transmission techniques: spread spectrum, narrowband microwave, and infrared. The most significant set of standards defining wireless LANs are those defined by the IEEE 802.11 committee. Bluetooth is an open specification for wireless communication and networking among PCs, mobile phones, and other wireless devices. Bluetooth is one of the fastest growing technology standards ever. It is intended for use within a local area.

11.5 RECOMMENDED READING AND WEB SITES

[OHAR99] is an excellent technical treatment of IEEE 802.11. Another good treatment is [LARO02]. [GEIE99] also provides detailed coverage of the IEEE 802.11 standards, and numerous case studies. [CROW97] is a good survey article on the 802.11 standards. Neither of the last two references covers IEEE 802.11a and IEEE 802.11b. [GEIE01] has a good discussion of IEEE 802.11a. [SHOE02] provides an overview of IEEE 802.11b.

[HAAR00a] and [HAAR00b] provide good overviews of Bluetooth. Two other surveys, both multipart, are also of interest: [WILS00] and [RODB00]. There are two good book-length technical treatments: [BRAY01] and [MILL01]; the former provides somewhat more technical detail than the latter.

BRAY01 Bray, J., and Sturman, C. *Bluetooth: Connect without Cables.* Upper Saddle River, NJ: Prentice Hall, 2001.

CROW97 Crow, B., et al. "IEEE 802.11 Wireless Local Area Networks." *IEEE Communications Magazine*, September 1997.

GEIE99 Geier, J. *Wireless LANs.* New York: Macmillan Technical Publishing, 1999.

GEIE01 Geier, J. "Enabling Fast Wireless Networks with OFDM." *Communications System Design*, February 2001. (www.csdmag.com)

HAAR00a Haartsen, J. "The Bluetooth Radio System." *IEEE Personal Communications*, February 2000.

HAAR00b Haartsen, J., and Mattisson, S. "Bluetooth—A New Low-Power Radio Interface Providing Short-Range Connectivity." *Proceedings of the IEEE*, October 2000.

LARO02 LaRocca, J., and LaRocca, R. *802.11 Demystified.* New York: McGraw-Hill, 2002.

MILL01 Miller, B., and Bisdikian, C. *Bluetooth Revealed.* Upper Saddle River, NJ: Prentice Hall, 2001.

OHAR99 Ohara, B., and Petrick, A. *IEEE 802.11 Handbook: A Designer's Companion.* New York: IEEE Press, 1999.

RODB00 Rodbell, M. "Bluetooth: Wireless Local Access, Baseband and RF Interfaces, and Link Management." *Communications System Design*, March, April, May 2000. (www.csdmag.com)

SHOE02   Shoemake, M. "IEEE 802.11g Jells as Applications Mount." *Communications System Design*, April 2002. (www.commsdesign.com)

WILS00   Wilson, J., and Kronz, J. "Inside Bluetooth: Part I and Part II." *Dr. Dobb's Journal*, March, April 2000.

Recommended Web Sites:

- **Wireless LAN Association:** Gives an introduction to the technology, including a discussion of implementation considerations and case studies from users. Links to related sites.
- **The IEEE 802.11 Wireless LAN Working Group:** Contains working group documents plus discussion archives.
- **Wi-Fi Alliance:** An industry group promoting the interoperability of 802.11 products with each other and with Ethernet.
- **Bluetooth SIG:** Contains all the standards, numerous other documents, and news and information on Bluetooth companies and products.
- **Infotooth:** An excellent supplementary source of information on Bluetooth.

11.6 KEY TERMS, REVIEW QUESTIONS, AND PROBLEMS

Key Terms

ad hoc networking Bluetooth IEEE 802.11 infrared LAN	narrowband microwave LAN nomadic access piconet scatternet	service area spread spectrum LAN usage model wireless LAN

Review Questions

11.1. List and briefly define four application areas for wireless LANs.

11.2. List and briefly define key requirements for wireless LANs.

11.3. What is the difference between a single-cell and a multiple-cell wireless LAN?

11.4. What is the basic building block of an 802.11 WLAN?

11.5. Define an extended service set.

11.6. List and briefly define IEEE 802.11 services.

11.7. What is the difference between an access point and a portal?

11.8. Is a distribution system a wireless network?

11.9. How is the concept of an association related to that of mobility?

11.10. In general terms, what application areas are supported by Bluetooth?

11.11. What is the difference between a core specification and a profile specification?

11.12. What is a usage model?

11.13. What type of network do Bluetooth nodes form?

11.14. How may nodes can a piconet support?

11.15. What is the relationship between master and slave in a piconet?

Problems

11.1 How much do you know about your wireless network?
   a. What is the SSID?
   b. Who is the equipment vendor?
   c. What standard are you using?
   d. What is the size of the network?

11.2 Using what you know about wired and wireless networks, draw the topology of your network.

11.3 There are many free tools and applications available for helping decipher wireless networks. One of the most popular is Netstumbler. Obtain the software at www.netstumbler.com and follow the links for downloads. The site has a list of supported wireless cards. Using the Netstumbler software, determine the following:
   a. How many access points in your network have the same SSID?
   b. What is your signal strength to your access point?
   c. How many other wireless networks and access points can you find?

11.4 Most wireless cards come with a small set of applications that can perform tasks similar to Netstumbler. Using your own client software, determine the same items you did with Netstumbler. Do they agree?

11.5 Try this experiment: How far can you go and still be connected to your network? This will depend to a large extent on your environment.

11.6 Compare and contrast wired and wireless LANs. What unique concerns must be addressed by the designer of a wireless LAN network?

11.7 Two documents related to safety concerns associated with wireless media are the FCC OET-65 Bulletin and the ANSI/IEEE C95.1-1999. Briefly describe the purpose of these documents and briefly outline the safety concerns associated with wireless LAN technology.

11.8 Another competitor to Bluetooth (in addition to 802.11) is the Infrared Development Association (IrDA). Compare and contrast these two wireless media and characterize a scenario where each may be an optimal solution.

Case Study V: St. Luke's Episcopal Hospital

Hospitals have been some of the earliest adopters of wireless local area networks (WLANs). The user population is typically mobile and spread out across a number of buildings, with a need to enter and access data in real time. St. Luke's Episcopal Hospital in Houston, Texas is a good example of a hospital that has made effective use of a WLAN. Their wireless network is distributed throughout several hospital buildings and used in many different applications. Examples include the following:

- **Diagnosing patients and charting their progress:** Doctors and nurses use carts equipped with wireless laptops for instant access to an application that manages patient data.

- **Prescriptions:** Medications are dispensed from a cart that is wheeled from room to room. Clinicians use a wireless scanner to scan the patient's ID bracelet, their own ID, and the bar code on the medicine. If a prescription order has been changed or cancelled, the clinician will know immediately because the mobile device displays current patient data.

- **Critical care units:** These areas use the WLAN because running hard wires would mean moving ceiling panels. The dust and microbes that such work stirs up would pose a threat to patients.

- **Case management:** The case managers in the Utilization Management Department use the WLAN to document patient reviews, insurance calls/authorization information, and denial information. The wireless session enables real time access to information that ensures the correct level of care for a patient and/or timely discharge.

- **Blood pressure carts:** These carts are moved from one patient to another as the hospital staff collects and records blood pressure information.

- **Nutrition and diet:** Dietary service representatives collect patient menus at each nursing unit and enter them as they go. This allows more menus to be submitted before the cutoff time, giving more patients more choice. The dietitian can also see current patient information, such as supplement or tube feeding data, and view what the patient actually received for a certain meal.

The hospital spans three buildings and treats over 500,000 patients each year.

Original WLAN

St. Luke's first WLAN was deployed in January 1998 in a single building using access points (APs) made by Proxim (www.proxim.com). The AP is a standalone device that functions as an interface between a local IEEE 802.11 cell (basic service set) and other cells, conforming to the

IEEE 802.11 architecture of Figure 11.4. A principal goal of this initial installation was to improve efficiency. However, it sometimes had the opposite effect. The main problem was dropped connections. As a user moved about the building, there was a tendency for the WLAN to drop the connection, rather than performing the desired handoff to another access point. As a result, a user had to reestablish the connection, log into the application again, and reenter whatever data might have been lost.

There were physical problems as well. The walls in part of the building were constructed around chicken wire, which interfered with radio waves. Some patients' rooms were located in pockets with weak radio signals. For these rooms, a nurse or doctor would sometimes lose a connection and have to step out into the hallway to reconnect. Microwave ovens in the kitchenettes on each floor were also a source of interference.

Finally, as more users were added to the system, the Proxim APs, with a capacity of 1.2 Mbps, became increasingly inadequate, causing ongoing performance issues.

Enhanced LAN

To overcome the problems with their original WLAN and reap the potential benefits listed earlier in this case study, St. Luke's made two changes [CONR03]. First, the hospital phased out the Proxim APs and replaced them with Cisco Aironet (www.aironet.com) APs. The Cisco APs, using IEEE 802.11b, operate at 11 Mbps. Also, the Cisco APs use direct sequence spread spectrum (DSSS), which is more reliable than the frequency-hopping technique used in the Proxim APs.

The second measure taken by St Luke's was to acquire a software solution from NetMotion Wireless (netmotionwireless.com) called Mobility. The basic layout of the Mobility solution is shown in Figure V.1. Mobility software is installed in each wireless client device (typically a laptop or handheld) and in two NetMotion servers whose task is to maintain connections. The two servers provide a backup capability in case one server fails. The Mobility software maintains the state of an application even if a wireless device moves out of range, experiences interference, or switches to standby mode. When a user comes back into range or switches into active mode, the user's application resumes where it left off.

In essence, Mobility works as follows. Upon connecting, each Mobility client is assigned a virtual IP address by the Mobility server on the wired network. The Mobility server manages network traffic on behalf of the client, intercepting packets destined for the client's virtual address and forwarding them to the client's current POP (point of presence) address. While the POP address may change when the device moves to a different subnet, from one coverage area to another, or even from one network to another, the virtual address remains constant while any connections are

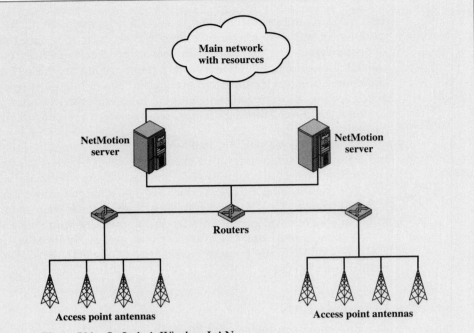

Figure V.1   St. Luke's Wireless LAN

active. Thus, the Mobility server is a proxy device inserted between a client device and an application server.

As of early 2003, about one-third of the patient care area (21 floors) is covered by the WLAN, consisting of approximately 270 wireless devices. The other floors are still using paper charts. The transition to a wireless, paperless operation has taken longer than expected. One reason is simply a matter of staff members accepting a more computerized working environment and training them to use the devices properly.

Discussion Questions

1. Visit the NetMotion Web site and learn more about the technical approach of the Mobility architecture. Discuss how this approach provides the mobility features of the product.

2. Discuss potential problems that can occur in a WLAN environment at St. Luke's.

PART FOUR

Wide Area Networks

P art Four examines the internal mechanisms and user-network interfaces that have been developed to support voice, data, and multimedia communications over long-distance networks. The traditional technologies of packet switching and circuit switching are examined, as well as the more recent ATM and wireless WANs.

Chapter 12 Circuit Switching and Packet Switching

Chapter 12 introduces the concept of network switching techniques. The chapter then introduces the two traditional approaches to wide area networking: circuit switching and packet switching. With circuit switching, a key design issue is that of control signaling, and this area is explored. The remainder of Chapter 12 introduces packet-switching technology. The chapter covers the basic principles of packet switching and analyzes datagram and virtual circuit approaches.

Chapter 13 Frame Relay and ATM

Frame relay is in essence a packet-switching technology, but it is more streamlined and efficient than traditional packet switching and is designed to support higher data rates. ATM, also known as cell relay, is also a packet-switching technology; it is even more streamlined than frame relay and is designed for very high data rates. Chapter 13 looks at the protocols and design issues involved in both frame relay and ATM.

Chapter 14 Wireless WANs

Chapter 14 begins with a discussion of the important design issues related to cellular wireless networks. The chapter then looks at issues of multiple access, with a special emphasis on code-division multiple access (CDMA), which is becoming the dominant cellular transmission technology. Chapter 14 next looks at issues related to third-generation cellular networks. The remainder of Chapter 14 deals with satellite communications.

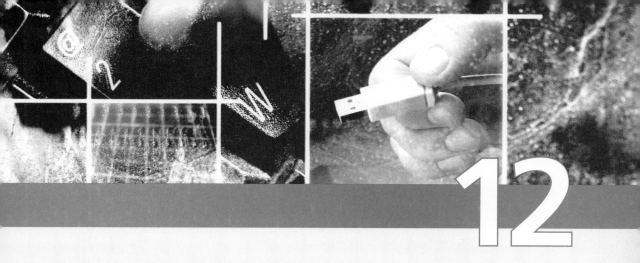

CHAPTER 12

CIRCUIT SWITCHING AND PACKET SWITCHING

After reading this chapter, you should be able to

- Explain the need for a communications network for wide area voice and data communications.
- Define circuit switching and describe the key elements of circuit-switching networks.
- Discuss the important applications of circuit switching, including public networks, private networks, and software-defined networks.
- Define packet switching and describe the key elements of packet-switching technology.
- Discuss the important applications of packet switching, including public and private networks.
- Discuss the relative merits of circuit switching and packet switching and analyze the circumstances for which each is most appropriate.

This chapter begins with a general discussion of switched communications networks. The remainder of the chapter focuses on wide area networks and, in particular, on traditional approaches to wide area network design: circuit switching and packet switching.

12.1 SWITCHING TECHNIQUES

For transmission of data[1] beyond a local area, communication is typically achieved by transmitting data from source to destination through a network of intermediate switching nodes; this switched network design is typically used to implement LANs as well. The switching nodes are not concerned with the content of the data; rather, their purpose is to provide a switching facility that will move the data from node to node until they reach their destination. Figure 12.1 illustrates a simple network. The end devices that wish to communicate may be referred to as *stations*. The stations may be computers, terminals, telephones, or other communicating devices. We shall refer to the switching devices whose purpose is to provide communication as *nodes*. The nodes are connected to one another in some topology by transmission links. Each station attaches to a node, and the collection of nodes is referred to as a *communications network*.

In a *switched communication network,* data entering the network from a station are routed to the destination by being switched from node to node. For example, in

---

[1]We use this term here in a very general sense, to include audio, image, and video, as well as ordinary data (e.g., numerical, text).

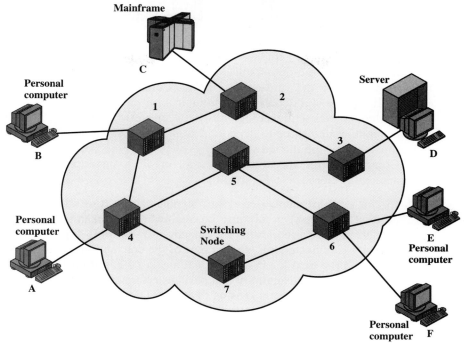

Figure 12.1 Simple Switching Network

Figure 12.1, data from station A intended for station F are sent to node 4. They may then be routed via nodes 5 and 6 or nodes 7 and 6 to the destination. Several observations are in order:

1. Some nodes connect only to other nodes (e.g., 5 and 7). Their sole task is the internal (to the network) switching of data. Other nodes have one or more stations attached as well; in addition to their switching functions, such nodes accept data from and deliver data to the attached stations.

2. Node-station links are generally dedicated point-to-point links. Node-node links are usually multiplexed links, using either frequency division multiplexing (FDM) or some form of time division multiplexing (TDM).

3. Usually, the network is not fully connected; that is, there is not a direct link between every possible pair of nodes. However, it is always desirable to have more than one possible path through the network for each pair of stations. This enhances the reliability of the network.

Two different technologies are used in wide area switched networks: circuit switching and packet switching. These two technologies differ in the way the nodes switch information from one link to another on the way from source to destination. In the remainder of this chapter, we look at the details of both of these technologies.

12.2 CIRCUIT-SWITCHING NETWORKS

Basic Operation

Circuit switching is the dominant technology for voice communications today and will remain so for the foreseeable future. Communication via circuit switching implies that there is a dedicated communication path between two stations. That path is a connected sequence of links between network nodes. On each physical link, a channel is dedicated to the connection. The most common example of circuit switching is the telephone network.

Communication via circuit switching involves three phases, which can be explained with reference to Figure 12.1.

1. **Circuit establishment.** Before any signals can be transmitted, an end-to-end (station-to-station) circuit must be established. For example, station A sends a request to node 4 requesting a connection to station E. Typically, the link from A to 4 is a dedicated line, so that part of the connection already exists. Node 4 must find the next leg in a route leading to E. Based on routing information and measures of availability and perhaps cost, node 4 selects the link to node 5, allocates a free channel (using FDM or TDM) on that link and sends a message requesting connection to E. So far, a dedicated path has been established from A through 4 to 5. Because a number of stations may attach to 4, it must be able to establish internal paths from multiple stations to multiple nodes. How this is done is discussed later in this section. The remainder of the process proceeds similarly. Node 5 allocates a channel to node 6 and internally ties that channel to the channel from node 4. Node 6 completes the connection to E. In completing the connection, a test is made to determine if E is busy or is prepared to accept the connection.

2. **Data transfer.** Data can now be transmitted from A through the network to E. The transmission may be analog voice, digitized voice, or binary data, depending on the nature of the network. As the carriers evolve to fully integrated digital networks, the use of digital (binary) transmission for both voice and data is becoming the dominant method. The path is as follows: A-4 link, internal switching through 4, 4-5 channel, internal switching through 5, 5-6 channel, internal switching through 6, 6-E link. Generally, the connection is full duplex, and signals may be transmitted in both directions simultaneously.

3. **Circuit disconnect.** After some period of data transfer, the connection is terminated, usually by the action of one of the two stations. Signals must be propagated to nodes 4, 5, and 6 to deallocate the dedicated resources.

Note that the connection path is established before data transmission begins. Thus, channel capacity must be reserved between each pair of nodes in the path and each node must have available internal switching capacity to handle the requested connection. The switches must have the intelligence to make these allocations and to devise a route through the network.

Circuit switching can be rather inefficient. Channel capacity is dedicated for the duration of a connection, even if no data are being transferred. For a voice connection, utilization may be rather high, but it still does not approach 100%. For a terminal-to-computer connection, the capacity may be idle during most of the time of the connection. In terms of performance, there is a delay prior to signal transfer for call establishment. However, once the circuit is established, the network is effectively transparent to the users. Information is transmitted at a fixed data rate with no delay other than the propagation delay through the transmission links. The delay at each node is negligible.

Circuit switching was developed to handle voice traffic but is now also used for data traffic. Some of the key applications of circuit switching are summarized in Table 12.1. The best-known example of a circuit-switching network is the public telephone network (Figure 12.2). This is actually a collection of national networks interconnected to form the international service. Although originally designed and implemented to service analog telephone subscribers, it handles substantial data traffic via modem and is well on its way to being converted to a digital network. Another well-known application of circuit switching is the private branch exchange (PBX), used to interconnect telephones within a building or office. Circuit switching is also used in private networks. Typically, such a network is set up by a corporation or other large organization to interconnect its various sites. Such a network usually consists of PBX systems at each site interconnected by dedicated, leased lines obtained from a carrier, such as AT&T. A final common example of the application

Table 12.1   Applications of Circuit Switching and Packet Switching

Circuit Switching	Packet Switching
Public Telephone Network Provide interconnection for two-way voice exchange between attached telephones. Calls can be placed between any two subscribers on a national and international basis. This type of network handles an increasing volume of data traffic.	**Public Data Network (PDN)/Value-Added Network (VAN)** Provide a wide area data communications facility for computers and terminals. The network is a shared resource, owned by a provider who sells the capacity to others. Thus, it functions as a utility service for a number of subscriber communities.
Private Branch Exchange Provide a telephone and data exchange capability within a single building or cluster of buildings. Calls can be placed between any two subscribers within the local site; interconnection is also provided to public or private wide area circuit-switched networks.	**Private Packet-Switching Network** Provide a shared resource for one organization's computers and terminals. A private packet-switching network is justified if there are a substantial number of devices with a substantial amount of traffic in one organization.
Private Wide Area Network Provide interconnection among a number of sites. Generally used to interconnect PBXs that are part of the same organization.	
Data Switch Provide for the interconnection of terminals and computers within a local site.	

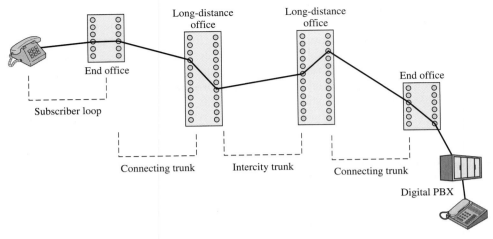

Figure 12.2 Example Connection over a Public Circuit-Switching Network

of circuit switching is the data switch. The data switch is similar to the PBX but is designed to interconnect digital data processing devices, such as terminals and computers.

A public telecommunications network can be described using four generic architectural components:

- **Subscribers:** The devices that attach to the network. It is still the case that most subscriber devices to public telecommunications networks are telephones, but the percentage of data traffic increases year by year.

- **Subscriber line:** The link between the subscriber and the network, also referred to as the *subscriber loop* or *local loop*. Almost all local loop connections use twisted-pair wire. The length of a local loop is typically in a range from a few kilometers to a few tens of kilometers.

- **Exchanges:** The switching centers in the network. A switching center that directly supports subscribers is known as an end office. Typically, an end office will support many thousands of subscribers in a localized area. There are over 19,000 end offices in the United States, so it is clearly impractical for each end office to have a direct link to each of the other end offices; this would require on the order of 2×10^8 links. Rather, intermediate switching nodes are used.

- **Trunks:** The branches between exchanges. Trunks carry multiple voice-frequency circuits using either FDM or synchronous TDM. These are also referred to as *carrier systems*.

Subscribers connect directly to an end office, which switches traffic between subscribers and between a subscriber and other exchanges. The other exchanges are responsible for routing and switching traffic between end offices. This distinction is shown in Figure 12.3. To connect two subscribers attached to the same end office, a circuit is set up between them in the same fashion as described before. If two subscribers connect to different end offices, a circuit between them consists of

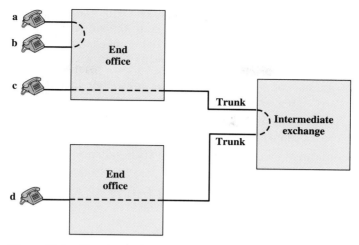

Figure 12.3   Circuit Establishment

a chain of circuits through one or more intermediate offices. In the figure, a connection is established between lines a and b by simply setting up the connection through the end office. The connection between c and d is more complex. In c's end office, a connection is established between line c and one channel on a TDM trunk to the intermediate switch. In the intermediate switch, that channel is connected to a channel on a TDM trunk to d's end office. In that end office, the channel is connected to line d.

Circuit-switching technology has been driven by its use to carry voice traffic. One of the key requirements for voice traffic is that there must be virtually no transmission delay and certainly no variation in delay. A constant signal transmission rate must be maintained, because transmission and reception occur at the same signal rate. These requirements are necessary to allow normal human conversation. Further, the quality of the received signal must be sufficiently high to provide, at a minimum, intelligibility.

Circuit switching achieved its widespread, dominant position because it is well suited to the analog transmission of voice signals. In today's digital world, its inefficiencies are more apparent. However, despite the inefficiency, circuit switching is and will remain an attractive choice for both local area and wide area networking. One of its key strengths is that it is transparent. Once a circuit is established, it appears like a direct connection to the two attached stations; no special networking logic is needed at the station.

Control Signaling

Control signals are the means by which the network is managed and by which calls are established, maintained, and terminated. Both call management and overall network management require that information be exchanged between subscriber and switch, among switches, and between switch and network management center. For a large public telecommunications network, a relatively complex control signaling scheme is required.

Signaling Functions Control signals affect many aspects of network behavior, including both network services visible to the subscriber and internal mechanisms. As networks become more complex, the number of functions performed by control signaling necessarily grows. The following functions are among the most important:

1. Audible communication with the subscriber, including dial tone, ringing tone, busy signal, and so on.
2. Transmission of the number dialed to switching offices that will attempt to complete a connection.
3. Transmission of information between switches indicating that a call cannot be completed.
4. Transmission of information between switches indicating that a call has ended and that the path can be disconnected.
5. A signal to make a telephone ring.
6. Transmission of information used for billing purposes.
7. Transmission of information giving the status of equipment or trunks in the network. This information may be used for routing and maintenance purposes.
8. Transmission of information used in diagnosing and isolating system failures.
9. Control of special equipment such as satellite channel equipment.

As an example of the use of control signaling, consider a typical telephone connection sequence from one line to another in the same central office:

1. Prior to the call, both telephones are not in use (on-hook). The call begins when one subscriber lifts the receiver (off-hook); this action is automatically signaled to the end office switch.
2. The switch responds with an audible dial tone, signaling the subscriber that the number may be dialed.
3. The caller dials a number, which is communicated as a called address to the switch.
4. If the called subscriber is not busy, the switch alerts that subscriber to an incoming call by sending a ringing signal, which causes the telephone to ring.
5. Feedback is provided to the calling subscriber by the switch:
   a. If the called subscriber is not busy, the switch returns an audible ringing tone to the caller while the ringing signal is being sent to the called subscriber.
   b. If the called subscriber is busy, the switch sends an audible busy signal to the caller.
   c. If the call cannot be completed through the switch, the switch sends an audible "reorder" message to the caller.
6. The called party accepts the call by lifting the receiver (off-hook), which is automatically signaled to the switch.
7. The switch terminates the ringing signal and the audible ringing tone, and establishes a connection between the two subscribers.
8. The connection is released when either subscriber hangs up.

When the called subscriber is attached to a different switch than the calling subscriber, the following switch-to-switch trunk signaling functions are required:

1. The originating switch seizes an idle interswitch trunk, sends an off-hook indication on the trunk, and requests a digit register at the far end, so that the address may be communicated.

2. The terminating switch sends an off-hook followed by an on-hook signal, known as a "wink." This indicates a register-ready status.

3. The originating switch sends the address digits to the terminating switch.

This example illustrates some of the functions performed using control signals. Signaling can also be classified functionally as supervisory, address, call information, and network management.

The term **supervisory** is generally used to refer to control functions that have a binary character (true/false; on/off), such as request for service, answer, alerting, and return to idle. They deal with the availability of the called subscriber and of the needed network resources. Supervisory control signals are used to determine if a needed resource is available and, if so, to seize it. They are also used to communicate the status of requested resources.

Address signals identify a subscriber. Initially, an address signal is generated by a calling subscriber when dialing a telephone number. The resulting address may be propagated through the network to support the routing function and to locate and ring the called subscriber's phone.

The term **call information** refers to those signals that provide information to the subscriber about the status of a call. This is in contrast to internal control signals between switches used in call establishment and termination. Such internal signals are analog or digital electrical messages. In contrast, call information signals are audible tones that can be heard by the caller or an operator with the proper phone set.

Supervisory, address, and call information control signals are directly involved in the establishment and termination of a call. **Network management** signals are used for the maintenance, troubleshooting, and overall operation of the network. Such signals may be in the form of messages, such as a list of preplanned routes being sent to a station to update its routing tables. These signals cover a broad scope, and it is this category that will expand most with the increasing complexity of switched networks.

Location of Signaling Control signaling needs to be considered in two contexts: signaling between a subscriber and the network, and signaling within the network. Typically, signaling operates differently within these two contexts.

Signaling between a telephone or other subscriber device and the switching office to which it attaches is, to a large extent, determined by the characteristics of the subscriber device and the needs of the human user. Signals within the network are entirely computer-to-computer. Internal signaling is concerned not only with the management of subscriber calls but also with the management of the network itself. Thus, for internal signaling, a more complex repertoire of commands, responses, and set of parameters is needed.

Because two different signaling techniques are used, the local switching office to which the subscriber is attached must provide a mapping between the relatively less complex signaling technique used by the subscriber and the more complex technique used within the network. For intranetwork signaling, Signaling System Number 7 (SS7) is used on most digital networks.

Common Channel Signaling Traditional control signaling in circuit-switching networks has been on a per-trunk or **inchannel** basis. With inchannel signaling, the same channel is used to carry control signals as is used to carry the call to which the control signals relate. Such signaling begins at the originating subscriber and follows the same path as the call itself. This has the merit that no additional transmission facilities are needed for signaling; the facilities for voice transmission are shared with control signaling.

As public telecommunications networks become more complex and provide a richer set of services, the drawbacks of inchannel signaling become more apparent. The information transfer rate is quite limited with inchannel signaling because the same capacity is shared with the information being transmitted. With such limits, it is difficult to accommodate, in a timely fashion, any but the simplest form of control messages. To take advantage of the potential services and to cope with the increasing complexity of evolving network technology, a richer and more powerful control signal repertoire is needed.

A second drawback of inchannel signaling is the amount of delay from the time a subscriber enters an address (dials a number) and the connection is established. The requirement to reduce this delay is becoming more important as the network is used in new ways. For example, computer-controlled calls, such as with transaction processing, use relatively short messages; therefore, the call setup time represents an appreciable part of the total transaction time.

Both of these problems can be addressed with common channel signaling, in which control signals are carried over paths completely independent of the voice channels. One independent control signal path can carry the signals for a number of subscriber channels and hence is a common control channel for these subscriber channels.

Internal to the network, common channel signals are transmitted on paths that are logically distinct from those that carry the subscriber information. In some cases, these may be physically distinct transmission facilities; in other cases, separate logical channels on shared trunks are used. The common channel can be configured with the bandwidth required to carry control signals for a rich variety of functions. Thus, both the signaling protocol and the network architecture to support that protocol are more complex than inchannel signaling. However, the continuing drop in computer hardware costs makes common channel signaling increasingly attractive. The control signals are messages that are passed between switches and between a switch and the network management center. Thus, the control signaling portion of the network is in effect a distributed computer network carrying short messages.

With inchannel signaling, control signals from one switch are originated by a control processor and switched onto the outgoing channel. On the receiving end, the control signals must be switched from the voice channel into the control processor. With common channel signaling, the control signals are transferred directly from one control processor to another, without being tied to a voice signal. This is a simpler procedure and one that is less susceptible to accidental or intentional interference between subscriber and control signals. This is one of the main motivations for common channel signaling. Another key motivation for common channel signaling is that call setup time is reduced. Consider the sequence of events for call setup with inchannel signaling when more than one switch is involved. A control signal will be sent from one switch to the next in the intended path. At each switch, the control signal cannot be transferred through the switch to the next leg of the route until the associated circuit is established through that switch. With common channel signaling, forwarding of control information can overlap the circuit-setup process.

Common channel techniques can also be used external to the network, at the interface between the subscriber and the network. This is the case with ISDN (Integrated Digital Services Network) and many other digital networks. For external signaling, a logically distinct channel on the subscriber-network link is devoted to control signaling, used for setting up and tearing down connections on other logical channels on that link. Thus, a multiplexed link is controlled by a single channel over that link.

Softswitch Architecture

The latest trend in the development of circuit-switching technology is generally referred to as the softswitch. In essence, a softswitch is a general-purpose computer running specialized software that turns it into a smart phone switch. Softswitches cost significantly less than traditional circuit switches and can provide more functionality. In particular, in addition to handling the traditional circuit-switching functions, a softswitch can convert a stream of digitized voice bits into packets. This opens up a number of options for transmission, including the increasingly popular voice over IP (Internet Protocol) approach.

In any telephone network switch, the most complex element is the software that controls call processing. This software performs call routing and implements call-processing logic for hundreds of custom calling features. Typically, this software runs on a proprietary processor that is integrated with the physical circuit-switching hardware. A more flexible approach is to physically separate the call processing function from the hardware switching function. In softswitch terminology, the physical switching function is performed by a **media gateway** (MG) and the call processing logic resides is a **media gateway controller** (MGC).

Figure 12.4 contrasts the architecture of a traditional telephone network circuit switch with the softswitch architecture. In the latter case, the MG and MGC are distinct entities and may be provided by different vendors. To facilitate interoperability, a standard has been issued for a media gateway control protocol between the MG and MGC (RFC 3015).

12.3 PACKET-SWITCHING NETWORKS

Around 1970, research began on a new form of architecture for long-distance digital data communications: **packet switching.** Although the technology of packet switching has evolved substantially since that time, it is remarkable that (1) the basic technology of packet switching is fundamentally the same today as it was in the early-1970s networks and (2) packet switching remains one of the few effective technologies for long-distance data communications. The two newest WAN technologies, frame relay

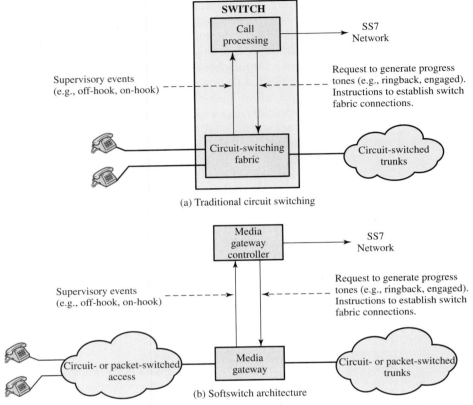

Figure 12.4   Comparison between Traditional Circuit Switching and Softswitch

and ATM, are essentially variations on the basic packet-switching approach. In this chapter, we provide an overview of traditional packet switching, which is still in use; frame relay and ATM are discussed in Chapter 13.

Basic Operation

The long-haul circuit-switching telecommunications network was originally designed to handle voice traffic, and the majority of traffic on these networks continues to be voice. A key characteristic of circuit-switching networks is that resources within the network are dedicated to particular calls. For voice connections, the resulting circuit will enjoy a high percentage of utilization because, most of the time, one party or the other is talking. However, as the circuit-switching network began to be used increasingly for data connections, two shortcomings became apparent:

- In a typical user/host data connection (e.g., personal computer user logged on to a database server), much of the time the line is idle. Thus, with data connections, a circuit-switching approach is inefficient.
- In a circuit-switching network, the connection provides for transmission at a constant data rate. Thus, each of the two devices that are connected must

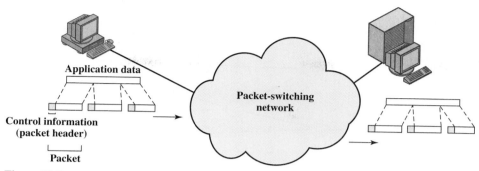

Figure 12.5   The Use of Packets

transmit and receive at the same data rate as the other. This limits the utility of the network in interconnecting a variety of host computers and workstations.

To understand how packet switching addresses these problems, let us briefly summarize packet-switching operation. Data are transmitted in short packets. A typical upper bound on packet length is 1000 octets (bytes). If a source has a longer message to send, the message is broken up into a series of packets (Figure 12.5). Each packet contains a portion (or all for a short message) of the user's data plus some control information. The control information, at a minimum, includes the information that the network requires to be able to route the packet through the network and deliver it to the intended destination. At each node en route, the packet is received, stored briefly, and passed on to the next node.

Figure 12.6 illustrates the basic operation. A transmitting computer or other device sends a message as a sequence of packets (a). Each packet includes control information indicating the destination station (computer, terminal, etc.). The packets are initially sent to the node to which the sending station attaches. As each packet arrives at this node, it stores the packet briefly, determines the next leg of the route, and queues the packet to go out on that link. When the link is available, each packet is transmitted to the next node (b). All of the packets eventually work their way through the network and are delivered to the intended destination.

The packet-switching approach has a number of advantages over circuit switching:

- Line efficiency is greater, because a single node-to-node link can be dynamically shared by many packets over time. The packets are queued up and transmitted as rapidly as possible over the link. By contrast, with circuit switching, time on a node-to-node link is preallocated using synchronous time-division multiplexing. Much of the time, such a link may be idle because a portion of its time is dedicated to a connection that is idle.

- A packet-switching network can carry out data-rate conversion. Two stations of different data rates can exchange packets, because each connects to its node at its proper data rate.

- When traffic becomes heavy on a circuit-switching network, some calls are blocked; that is, the network refuses to accept additional connection requests

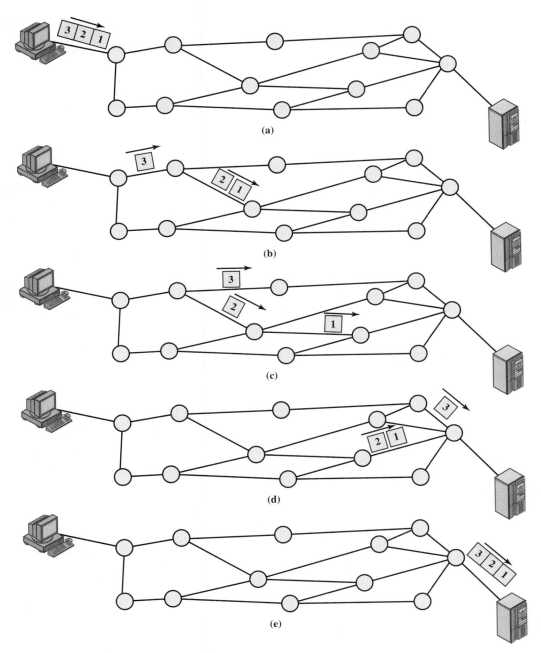

Figure 12.6   Packet Switching: Datagram Approach

until the load on the network decreases. On a packet-switching network, packets are still accepted, but delivery delay increases.

- Priorities can be used. If a node has a number of packets queued for transmission, it can transmit the higher-priority packets first. These packets will therefore experience less delay than lower-priority packets.

Packet switching also has disadvantages relative to circuit switching:

- When a packet passes through a packet-switching node, it incurs a delay not experienced in circuit switching. At a minimum, it incurs a transmission delay equal to the length of the packet in bits divided by the incoming channel rate in bits per second; this is the time it takes to absorb the packet into an internal buffer. In addition, there may be a variable delay due to processing and queuing in the node.

- Because the packets between a given source and destination may vary in length, may take different routes, and may be subject to varying delay in the switches they encounter, the overall packet delay can vary substantially. This phenomenon, called **jitter**, may not be desirable for some applications (for example, in real-time applications including telephone voice and real-time video).

- To route packets through the network, overhead information including the address of the destination and often sequencing information must be added to each packet, which reduces the communication capacity available for carrying user data. This is not needed in circuit switching once the circuit is set up.

- More processing is involved in the transfer of information using packet switching than in circuit switching at each node. In the case of circuit switching, there is virtually no processing at each switch once the circuit is set up.

Switching Technique

A station has a message to send through a packet-switching network that is of greater length than the maximum packet size. It therefore breaks the message into packets and sends these packets, one at a time, to the network. A question arises as to how the network will handle this stream of packets as it attempts to route them through the network and deliver them to the intended destination. Two approaches are used in contemporary networks: datagram and virtual circuit.

In the **datagram** approach, each packet is treated independently, with no reference to packets that have gone before. This approach is illustrated in Figure 12.6. Each node chooses the next node on a packet's path, taking into account information received from neighboring nodes on traffic, line failures, and so on. So the packets, each with the same destination address, do not all follow the same route, and they may arrive out of sequence at the exit point. In this example, the exit node restores the packets to their original order before delivering them to the destination. In some datagram networks, it is up to the destination rather than the exit node to do the reordering. Also, it is possible for a packet to be damaged in the network. For example, if a packet-switching node crashes momentarily, all of its queued packets may be lost. Again, it is up to either the exit node or the destination to detect the loss of a packet and decide how to recover it. In this technique, each packet, treated independently, is referred to as a datagram.

In the **virtual-circuit** approach, a preplanned route is established before any packets are sent. Once the route is established, all the packets between a pair of communicating parties follow this same route through the network. This is illustrated in Figure 12.7. Because the route is fixed for the duration of the logical connection, it is somewhat similar to a circuit in a circuit-switching network and is referred to as a virtual circuit. Each packet now contains a virtual circuit identifier as well as data. Each node on the preestablished route knows where to direct such packets; no routing decisions are required. At any time, each station can have more than one virtual circuit to any other station and can have virtual circuits to more than one station.

So the main characteristic of the virtual-circuit technique is that a route between stations is set up prior to data transfer. Note that this does not mean that this is a dedicated path, as in circuit switching. A packet is still buffered at each node and queued for output over a line. The difference from the datagram approach is that, with virtual circuits, the node need not make a routing decision for each packet. It is made only once for all packets using that virtual circuit.

If two stations wish to exchange data over an extended period of time, there are certain advantages to virtual circuits. First, the network may provide services related to the virtual circuit, including sequencing and error control. Sequencing refers to the fact that, because all packets follow the same route, they arrive in the original order. Error control is a service that assures not only that packets arrive in proper sequence but also that all packets arrive correctly. For example, if a packet in a sequence from node 4 to node 6 fails to arrive at node 6, or arrives with an error, node 6 can request a retransmission of that packet from node 4. Another advantage is that packets should transit the network more rapidly with a virtual circuit; it is not necessary to make a routing decision for each packet at each node.

One advantage of the datagram approach is that the call setup phase is avoided. Thus, if a station wishes to send only one or a few packets, datagram delivery will be quicker. Another advantage of the datagram service is that, because it is more primitive, it is more flexible. For example, if congestion develops in one part of the network, incoming datagrams can be routed away from the congestion. With the use of virtual circuits, packets follow a predefined route, and thus it is more difficult for the network to adapt to congestion. A third advantage is that datagram delivery is inherently more reliable. With the use of virtual circuits, if a node fails, all virtual circuits that pass through that node are lost. With datagram delivery, if a node fails, subsequent packets may find an alternate route that bypasses that node.

12.4 TRADITIONAL WIDE AREA NETWORK ALTERNATIVES

As Table 12.1 indicates, packet switching adds several new alternatives for wide area networking, in addition to those that can be provided using circuit-switching technology. Just as there are public and private circuit-switching networks, there are also public and private packet-switching networks. A public packet-switching network works much like a public telephone network. In this case, the network provides a packet transmission service to a variety of subscribers. Typically, the network provider owns a set of packet-switching nodes and links these together with leased lines provided by a carrier such as AT&T. Such a network is called a **value-added**

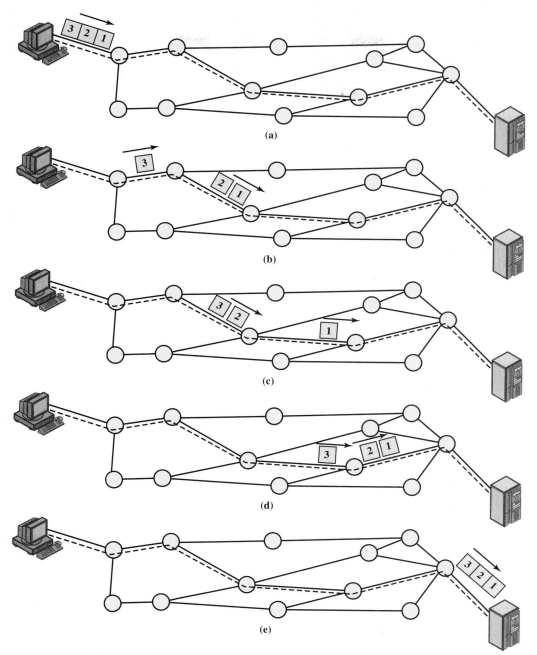

Figure 12.7   Packet Switching: Virtual-Circuit Approach

network (VAN), reflecting the fact that the network adds value to the underlying transmission facilities. In a number of countries, there is a single public network owned or controlled by the government and referred to as a **public data network** (PDN). The other packet-switching alternative is a network dedicated to the needs of a single organization. The organization may own the packet-switching nodes or lease an entire dedicated packet-switching network from a network provider. In either case, the links between nodes are again leased telecommunications lines.

Thus, a business is faced with an array of choices for meeting wide area networking needs. These choices include a number of high-speed options, such as frame relay and ATM. In this section, we explore the various traditional WAN options, to get some feel for the types of tradeoffs involved. The issues are revisited in Chapter 13.

Before beginning our evaluation of these alternatives, it is useful to consider the overview of circuit switching and packet switching provided in Table 12.2. While

Table 12.2   Relative Merits of Circuit Switching and Packet Switching of Data

Circuit Switching	
Advantages	**Disadvantages**
Compatible with voice. Economies of scale can be realized by using the same network for voice and data. Commonality of calling procedures for voice and data. No special user training or communication protocols are needed to handle data traffic. Predictable, constant rate for data traffic.	Subject to blocking. This makes it difficult to size the network properly. The problem is less severe with the use of dynamic nonhierarchical routing techniques. Requires subscriber compatibility. The devices at each end of a circuit must be compatible in terms of protocol and data rate, since the circuit is a transparent connection. Large processing and signal burden. For transaction-type applications, data calls are of short duration and need to be set up rapidly. This proportionally increases the overhead burden on the network.
Packet Switching	
Advantages	**Disadvantages**
Provides speed conversion. Two attached devices with different data rates may exchange data; the network buffers the data and delivers them at the appropriate data rate. Appears nonblocking. As the network load increases, the delay increases, but new exchanges are usually permitted. Efficient utilization. Switches and trunks are used on demand rather than dedicating capacity to a particular call. Logical multiplexing. A host system can have simultaneous conversations with a number of terminals over a single line.	Complex routing and control. To achieve efficiency and resilience, a packet-switched network must employ a complex set of routing and control algorithms. Delay. Delay is a function of load. It can be long and it is variable.

both circuit switching and packet switching can be used for data transmission, each has its particular strengths and weaknesses for a given application.

Wide Area Networks for Voice

Traditionally, the preferred business alternatives for wide area voice communications all employ circuit switching. With the increasing competition and advancing technology of recent years, this still leaves the manager with many choices, including private networks, software-defined networks, ordinary telephone service, and a variety of special services such as toll-free numbers. Further complicating the choice is the introduction of services related to ISDN.

With all of these choices, and with the constantly changing prices attached to the various choices, it is difficult to generalize. What can be said is that business relies heavily on the public telephone networks and related services. Private networks are appropriate for an organization with a number of sites and with a substantial amount of voice traffic between them.

A new entry in the competition is voice over IP (VoIP), mentioned in Chapter 6. VoIP uses a packet transmission approach over Internets and intranets. VoIP is enjoying gradually growing acceptance as an alternative.

Wide Area Networks for Data

For data traffic, the number of wide area networking choices is even broader. Roughly, we can list the following categories as alternatives:

- **Public packet-switching networks:** There are a number of such networks in the United States and at least one in most industrialized countries. Typically, the user must lease a line from the user's computing equipment to the nearest packet-switching node.

- **Private packet-switching networks:** In this case, the user owns or leases the packet-switching nodes, which are generally collocated with the user's data processing equipment. Leased lines, typically 56- or 64-kbps digital lines, interconnect the nodes.

- **Private leased lines:** Dedicated lines can be used between sites. No switching is involved, so a leased line is needed between any pair of sites that wish to exchange data.

- **Public circuit-switching networks:** With the use of modems or switched digital service, the user can employ dial-up telephone lines for data communications.

- **Private circuit-switching networks:** If the user has an interconnected set of digital PBXs, either by leased 56-kbps lines or T-1 lines, then this network can carry data as well as voice.

- **ISDN:** ISDN offers both packet switching and traditional circuit switching in an integrated service.

The last two alternatives are likely to be justified on the basis of the voice traffic, with data traffic being a sort of bonus that comes with the network. Because this approach is therefore not directly comparable to the others, we do not consider it further in this chapter.

As with voice, the choice of approach for data networking is complex and depends on current prices. In comparing the alternatives for wide area data networks, we look first at the cost and performance considerations, which are more easily quantified and analyzed. Then we consider some other issues that are also important in selecting a network.

Cost/Performance Considerations Data communications traffic can be roughly classified into two categories: stream and bursty. Stream traffic is characterized by lengthy and fairly continuous transmission. Examples are file transfer, telemetry, other sorts of batch data processing applications, and digitized voice communication. Bursty traffic is characterized by short, sporadic transmissions. Interactive client/server traffic, such as transaction processing, data entry, and time sharing, fits this description. Facsimile transmission is also bursty.

The public circuit-switching network approach makes use of dial-up lines. The cost is based on data rate, connection time, and distance. As we have said, this is quite inefficient for bursty traffic. However, for occasional stream-oriented requirements, this may be the most appropriate choice. For example, a corporation may have distributed offices. At the close of the day, each office transfers a file to headquarters summarizing the activities for that day. A dial-up line used for the single transfer from each office appears to be the most cost-effective solution. When there is a high volume of stream traffic among a few sites, the most economical solution is to obtain dedicated circuits among sites. These circuits, also known as leased lines or semipermanent circuits, may be leased from a telecommunications provider, such as a telephone company, or from a satellite provider. The dedicated circuit carries a constant fixed cost based on data rate and, in some cases, distance. If the traffic volume is high enough, then the utilization will be high enough to make this approach the most attractive.

On the other hand, if the traffic is primarily bursty, then packet switching has the advantage. Furthermore, packet switching permits terminals and computer ports of various data rates to be interconnected. If the traffic is primarily bursty but is of relatively modest volume for an organization, a public packet-switching network provides the best solution. In this case, the network provides a packet transmission service to a variety of subscribers, each of which has moderate traffic requirements. If there is a number of different subscribers, the total traffic should be great enough to result in high utilization. Hence, the public network is cost effective from the provider's point of view. The subscriber gets the advantages of packet switching without the fixed cost of implementing and maintaining the network. The cost to the subscriber is based on both connection time and traffic volume but not distance.

If the volume of an organization's bursty traffic is high and is concentrated among a small number of sites, a private packet-switching network is the best solution. With a lot of bursty traffic among sites, the private packet-switching network provides much better utilization and hence lower cost than using circuit switching or simple dedicated lines. The cost of a private network (other than the initial fixed cost of the packet switching nodes) is based solely on distance. Thus, it combines the efficiencies of public packet switching with the time and volume independence of dedicated circuits.

Other Considerations In addition to the issues of cost and performance, the choice of network should also take into account control, reliability, and security.

An organization large enough to need a wide area data network will come to rely heavily on that network. Accordingly, it is vital that management be able to maintain proper control of the network to provide an efficient and effective service to users. We will explore this topic at some length in Chapter 19. For our purposes here, we can say that three aspects of control are significant in comparing various network approaches: strategic control, growth control, and day-to-day operation of the network.

Strategic control involves the process of designing and implementing the network to meet the organization's unique requirements. With public packet switching, the subscriber has virtually no strategic control over service levels, reliability, or maintenance. The network is intended as a public utility to serve the average customer. With either dedicated lines or a private packet-switching network, the user organization can decide on the capacity and level of redundancy that it is willing to pay for. **Growth control** allows users to plan for network expansion and modifications arising as their needs change. A private packet-switching network provides the most flexibility in accommodating needs for growth. Additional packet switching nodes, more trunks, and higher-capacity trunks can be added as needed. These raise the overall capacity and reliability of the network. Although the user has control over the number and capacity of lines in a dedicated-line design, there is less flexibility for incrementally expanding the network. Again, with a public packet-switching network, the user has no control over growth. The user's needs are satisfied only if they happen to be within the capabilities of the public network. With respect to **day-to-day operation**, the user is concerned with accommodating peaks of traffic and with quickly diagnosing and repairing faults. Packet-switching networks can be designed with effective centralized network control that allows the network to be adjusted to changing conditions. Of course, in the case of the public network, the user is dependent on the network provider. As in any public utility, such as a transportation system, there tend to be "rush hours" in public networks when service levels decline. Day-to-day control is more difficult to automate in the case of dedicated lines; available tools are comparatively few and crude because we are not dealing with a unified network.

The inherent reliability of a packet-switching network is higher than that of a collection of dedicated lines. The network consists of a set of shared facilities and is equipped with centralized, automated network control facilities. Faults can be easily located and isolated and the traffic shifted to the healthy part of the network. A public network may be able to afford a greater investment in redundancy and control tools, because the cost is spread over many users. Further, the user is relieved of the burden of developing the expertise required to keep a large data communications network operational.

Finally, data security is vital to most corporations. We explore this topic in detail in Chapter 18. For purposes of the present discussion, we can say that use of a private network or dedicated lines will clearly afford greater security than a public packet-switching network. Public networks can use various access control mechanisms to limit the ways in which users can obtain data across the network. Those same control mechanisms are useful in private networks, because an organization may wish to segregate various communities of users.

Table 12.3 summarizes the difference among the various communications approaches.

Table 12.3   Features of Wide Area Networks

Feature	Dedicated (leased lines)	Public Packet	Private Packet
Strategic control	Network design, service, and maintenance can be given priority and controlled by user.	Service limited to that which suits average customer.	Network design, service, and maintenance can be given priority and controlled by user.
Growth control and operation control	Not integrated; decentralized fault detection may be expensive.	Provided by service supplier to satisfy average requirements.	Integrated into all equipment; centrailzed fault isolation and detection.
Reliability	Manual and user-visible recovery from failure.	Transparent and automatic recovery from failure.	Transparent and automatic recovery from failure.
Security	Private users only.	Public users, network access control.	Private users only, network access control.

APPLICATION NOTE
Switching

Discussions about switching can be confusing because there are so many protocols and because switching can be described as operating at several different layers of our networking model. For many organizations, the type of switching used to send data from the local site to external destinations can be a complete mystery due to the complexity of wide area networks and a reduced level of local control. Once the data leave the home network, there is little that a local network administrator can do to affect the data's travel. Usually the local network staff influence is limited to the customer premises equipment and the type of connection going off site.

To make things more difficult, next generation networks will make use of multilayer switching techniques such as layer 2 routing, layer 3 switching, optical switching and application layer switching. In the next couple of paragraphs we will try to provide some guidance into the switching terms that a typical network administrator is likely to run into and some of the terms used to describe external connectivity.

Most local area networks run the Internet Protocol (IP) over some form of Ethernet. Ethernet nodes are usually connected to each other via a layer 2 switch that examines layer 2 addresses in the frame prior to forwarding. The traffic encapsulated within the Ethernet frame is the IP-based data. The IP packet header includes all the information necessary for getting the packet from source to destination. This means that we are using a datagram approach. While upper-layer protocols like the Transmission Control Protocol (TCP) can control the flow of data to a certain extent, they do not change the type of switching used. If we include the idea that any routers involved are processing the IP packets flowing between networks, we could classify this type of transmission as a packet switching network with a datagram approach. Both packet switching and circuit switching are described in this chapter.

When the traffic must travel off site, it will be transferred to the network of the Internet service provider (ISP) for processing. Essentially, this is the beginning of the Internet. The Internet is actually a huge collection of networks, most of which belong to the ISPs. Web sites or Web servers are also attached to these networks. The ISP networks can vary quite a bit in terms of protocols used, speeds available, and the type of switching used. One consistent item is that all networks attached to the Internet transmit and receive IP packets. As a packet travels from source to destination, it is probable that it will cross several different networks before arriving.

Upon entering the ISP network, routing decisions need to be made. If the network utilizes a datagram approach, no further action is taken as the IP packets contain all of the necessary information and no circuit is required. However, if the network utilizes virtual circuits for establishing a pathway from one end of the ISP network to the other, this circuit must be established before any data can be forwarded. Examples of protocols utilizing virtual circuits are Frame Relay and Asynchronous Transfer Mode or ATM.

Once the circuit has been established, the data are forwarded, with each network node making forwarding decisions based on the connection setup. Thus, a routing decision (typically layer 3) is made upon entrance to the network and then lower-layer switching decisions are made as the data cross the network. This virtual circuit is only valid to the border of the provider's network. At the edge, another routing decision must be made and a hand-off completed to the following network. At this point, the process starts again for each network until the destination is reached.

For example, a dial-up user connects over the same sort of line that a telephone call does and the data are handled in the exact same fashion—circuit switching. The only difference is that the data started out as digital and were converted before transmission. Once the circuit switched telephone call to the ISP is made, data can be transferred. The packets all follow the same path to the ISP. The ISP may have a standard IP network running over Ethernet that simply forwards the data to the correct router output interface. This interface may subsequently be connected to another, larger ISP using T carriers, a Frame Relay, or an ATM network. The packet passes through a router and is forwarded to the ATM network in preparation for travel over a virtual circuit connection. This virtual circuit was set up in the same fashion as a circuit-switched telephone call. Note that at no time are the contents of the layer 3 IP datagrams manipulated. They are simply being carried over an ATM network instead of Ethernet.

The type of external switching that an organization selects is a decision that is often dependent upon factors such as bandwidth requirements, cost, and availability. There are a large number of protocols that can be used for connecting to the outside world, but choosing the correct type requires a survey of available products and an understanding of local requirements.

12.5 SUMMARY

The use of a direct point-to-point link for information communications is impractical for all but the most limited requirements. For cost-effective, practical information communications, some sort of communications network is needed. For communications outside the range of a single building or a cluster of building, a wide area network (WAN) is employed. Two basic technologies are employed: circuit switching and packet switching.

Circuit switching is used in public telephone networks and is the basis for private networks built on leased lines and using on-site circuit switches. Circuit switching was developed to handle voice traffic but can also handle digital data, although this latter use is often inefficient. With circuit switching, a dedicated path is established between two stations for communication. Switching and transmission resources within the network are reserved for the exclusive use of the circuit for the duration of the connection. The connection is transparent: Once it is established, it appears to attached devices as if there were a direct connection.

Packet switching is employed to provide an efficient means of using the shared facilities in a data communications network. With packet switching, a station transmits data in small blocks, called packets. Each packet contains some portion of the user data plus control information needed for proper functioning of the network. Public packet-switching networks are available, to be shared by a number of separate subscriber communities. The technology may also be employed to build a private packet-switching network.

The choice between circuit and packet switching depends on a host of considerations, including cost, performance, reliability, and flexibility. Both technologies will continue to be important in wide area networking.

12.6 RECOMMENDED READING AND WEB SITES

As befits its age, circuit switching has inspired a voluminous literature. Two good books on the subject are [BELL00] and [FREE96].

The literature on packet switching is also enormous. Books with good treatments of this subject include [SPOH02] and [BERT92].

BELL00 Bellamy, J. *Digital Telephony*. New York: Wiley, 2000.

BERT92 Bertsekas, D., and Gallager, R. *Data Networks*. Englewood Cliffs, NJ: Prentice Hall, 1992.

FREE96 Freeman, R. *Telecommunication System Engineering*. New York: Wiley, 1996.

SPOH02 Spohn, D. *Data Network Design*. New York: McGraw-Hill, 2002.

Recommended Web Sites:

- **International Packet Communications Consortium:** News, technical information, and vendor information on softswitch technology and products.
- **Media Gateway Control Working Group:** Chartered by IETF to develop the media gateway control protocol and related standards.

12.7 KEY TERMS, REVIEW QUESTIONS, AND PROBLEMS

Key Terms

circuit switching	local loop	subscriber loop
common channel signaling	packet	trunk value-added network
control signaling	packet switching	(VAN)
datagram	public data network	virtual circuit
exchange	(PDN)	
inchannel signaling	softswitch	
integrated services digital net-	subscriber	
work (ISDN)	subscriber line	

Review Questions

12.1. Why is it useful to have more than one possible path through a network for each pair of stations?

12.2. Concerning a switched communications network, answer the following as either true or false.
  a. All switching nodes are connected to every other node.
  b. Links between switching nodes utilize some sort of multiplexing technique.
  c. Switching nodes provide connectivity for a single end station.

12.3. What are the four generic architectural components of a public communications network? Define each term.

12.4. Answer the following as either true or false regarding circuit switching.
  a. A complete connection from end to end must be completed before data transmission can occur.
  b. There are three basic stages; connection setup, data transfer, and connection termination.
  c. Circuit switching is very efficient.

12.5. What is the principal application that has driven the design of circuit-switching networks?

12.6. Distinguish between static and alternate routing in a circuit-switching network.

12.7. What is the difference between inchannel and common channel signaling?

12.8. The control signals used in the public switched telephone network are part of what architecture?

12.9. Explain the difference between datagram and virtual circuit operation.

12.10. What are some advantages of private networks?

12.11. What are some of the limitations of using a circuit-switching network for data transmission?

12.12. What is a value-added network (VAN)?

12.13. Why is packet switching impractical for digital voice transmission?

Problems

12.1 How far away from your local switching center is your business or home?

12.2 In the public switched telephone network, your call is set up and switched based on the numbers that you dial. These numbers actually provide different frequency sounds or tones to the switching center. What is this signaling called?

12.3   Define the following parameters for a switching network:

N = number of hops between two given end systems

L = message length in bits

B = data rate, in bits per second (bps), on all links

P = fixed packet size, in bits

H = overhead (header) bits per packet

S = call setup time (circuit switching or virtual circuit) in seconds

D = propagation delay per hop in seconds

a.   For $N = 4$, $L = 3200$, $B = 9600$, $P = 1024$, $H = 16$, $S = 0.2$, $D = 0.001$, compute the end-to-end delay for circuit switching, virtual circuit packet switching, and datagram packet switching. Assume that there are no acknowledgments. Ignore processing delay at the nodes.

b.   Derive general expressions for the three techniques of part (a), taken two at a time (three expressions in all), showing the conditions under which the delays are equal.

12.4   Consider a simple telephone network consisting of two end offices and one intermediate switch with a 1-MHz full-duplex trunk between each end office and the intermediate switch. The average telephone is used to make four calls per 8-hour workday, with a mean call duration of six minutes. Ten percent of the calls are long distance. What is the maximum number of telephones an end office can support?

12.5   Explain the flaw in the following reasoning: Packet switching requires control and address bits to be added to each packet. This introduces considerable overhead in packet switching. In circuit switching, a transparent circuit is established. No extra bits are needed.

a.   Therefore, there is no overhead in circuit switching.

b.   Because there is no overhead in circuit switching, line utilization must be more efficient than in packet switching.

12.6   Assuming no malfunction in any of the stations or nodes of a network, is it possible for a packet to be delivered to the wrong destination?

12.7   Consider a packet-switching network of N nodes, connected by the following topologies:

a.   Star: one central node with no attached station; all other nodes attach to the central node.

b.   Loop: Each node connects to two other nodes to form a closed loop.

c.   Fully connected: Each node is directly connected to all other nodes.

For each case, give the average number of hops between stations.

Case Study VI: Staten Island University Hospital

One of the basic Information Age truths is that every business depends on quick, efficient movement of data within and beyond the enterprise. Nowhere is this more evident than in the healthcare industry. While hospitals may ostensibly be in the business of snipping, stitching, and medicating human beings, their ability to do so for the maximum number of patients—and with acceptable profits—is largely contingent on their ability to effectively process and exchange a wide range of data among internal departments and outside partners. This need is becoming even more evident as the dynamics of the healthcare industry change. One healthcare facility that has found itself right in the middle of all these technology and business changes is Staten Island University Hospital (SIUH) in Staten Island, New York [LIEB98, LIEB99, KEEN99]. "It used to be that hospitals could operate in a very self-contained manner," explains Richard Jerothe, SIUH's director of PC LAN services. "Now, however, the healthcare process revolves around the primary care physician, which requires extensive connectivity between the network of doctors associated with the hospital." According to Jerothe, as cost recovery becomes a more complex issue, government regulations concerning Medicare and Medicaid have also put additional requirements on healthcare information management. Jerothe says these factors make the healthcare field a very exciting one for information technology professionals. As he sees it, for many years most hospitals lagged behind other industries in their IT implementations. But competitive pressures and the advent of electronic medical imaging technologies have caused many hospitals to leapfrog non-healthcare organizations in their networking uses. "This industry is one of the most aggressive when it comes to pushing the technology envelope," he says.

Staten Island University Hospital is a 620-bed facility with a level-1 trauma center and a wide range of specialized practices, including advanced coronary care, radiation oncology, geriatrics, and obstetrics/gynecology. It is housed on two major campus sites, with administrative functions occupying a third. Additionally, SIUH operates dozens of satellite clinics throughout New York City and a Community Wellness Center in the Staten Island Mall. It also has extensive working relationships with doctors and medical practices throughout the surrounding area. Up until 1995, the hospital's computing environment had centered on AS/400 hosts—which ran the organization's core purchasing, registration, and health data systems—and an SNA network that connected approximately 900 terminals. Desktop PCs were brought online over time, but they still connected to the backend systems via terminal emulation. In 1995, however, the IT department under Patrick Carney's leadership formulated its strategic plan. Among other considerations, the plan recognized two realities about the future of the hospital's network. First, external connectivity would become increasingly important over time. The second reality that Carney and Jerothe acknowledged was that there was no way to predict accurately how much bandwidth would be required for this planned network. "We knew it would have to be able to scale; with medical imaging, you can easily end up with 30-Mbyte files moving over the wire," notes Jerothe. Thus, as they went to area network providers for proposals, they had more of a requirements vision to share than a set of concrete technical specifications. That wasn't something that SIUH's local exchange carrier, Nynex (now known as Bell Atlantic), was especially prepared to handle. "Nynex's attitude was 'You have to tell us what you want,'" says Carney. "But we didn't know exactly what we wanted. We were looking for them to add value, and they couldn't.' "They had a pre-canned service that they wanted to sell us," Jerothe recalls.

Based in Staten Island, Teleport Communications Group (TCG) is one of the country's first and largest Competitive Local Exchange Carriers (CLECs). Back in 1994, TCG began providing private line and other dedicated access services for the New York–New Jersey metropolitan area. Today, the company boasts over 8700 route-miles of fiber optics, as well as broadband wireless networking facilities. It operates in 57 major markets nationwide, with that number continuing to rise as it acquires additional local operations. TCG had already won SIUH's local voice business in 1994. In addition to being significantly less expensive than the incumbent local exchange carrier, Nynex, "The people at the hospital were looking for a carrier that would respond faster to service requests and give them a faster mean time to repair," says Rob Westervelt, vice president of sales at TCG New York and the account representative for SIUH prior to his promotion.

According to Westervelt, TCG recommended that SIUH retain Nynex for inbound service and keep their outbound ports available as a failover precaution. "We don't really try to sell ourselves as a complete replacement for the incumbent carrier," he explains. "We offer customers diversity so they can eliminate potential single points of failure in their business." Jerothe comments, "They came to us with the idea of 'dark' fiber, which would have given us a lot of bandwidth at a very aggressive price," recalls Jerothe. "But again, we didn't see the management there." Dark fiber refers to situations where the communications vendor directly leases the customer its own optical fibers, without provisioning any services on that fiber. Customers are therefore responsible for installing their own electronics at each termination point and for managing the traffic on the specific fibers they lease.

TCG was left with a solid shot at SIUH's networking business. The proposal included providing the hospital with a fully integrated backbone-and-spoke network that could link all the affiliated offices throughout the New York metropolitan area with enough bandwidth to share medical imaging files and other critical data. Today, TCG, which is now part of AT&T, handled 99% of SIUH's local calling, with Bell Atlantic serving as the overflow backup. One year after moving its traffic to TCG, the hospital saves at least 50% on local calling [KING99].

According to Carney, the new network has already begun paying huge dividends in enabling SIUH to respond to ever-evolving business requirements. "For one thing, we can bring up new sites in just a few weeks," he says. "Also, we have a single network infrastructure that can support all of our 'new age' applications, from teleradiology to enterprise scheduling."

Discussion Questions

1. Explain why telecommunications is vital to the healthcare industry and in particular to SIUH.

2. Who are CLECs? Explain the reasons why SIUH preferred a CLEC to its Incumbent Local Exchange Carrier for its networking needs.

3. Discuss the advantages and disadvantages of AT&T's acquisition of TCG on this project and hence on SIUH.

CHAPTER 13

FRAME RELAY AND ATM

CHAPTER OBJECTIVES

After reading this chapter, you should be able to

- Discuss the reasons for the growing interest in and availability of high-speed alternatives for wide area networking.
- Describe the features and characteristics of frame relay networks.
- Describe the features and characteristics of ATM networks.
- Assess the pros and cons of alternative high-speed services.

As the speed and number of local area networks (LANs) continue their relentless growth, increasing demand is placed on wide area packet-switching networks to support the tremendous throughput generated by these LANs. In the early days of wide area networking, X.25 was designed to support direct connection of terminals and computers over long distances. At speeds of up to 64 kbps, X.25 copes well with these demands. As LANs have come to play an increasing role in the local environment, X.25, with its substantial overhead, is an inadequate tool for wide area networking. Fortunately, several new generations of high-speed switched services for wide area networking have moved rapidly from the research lab and the draft standard stage to the commercially available, standardized-product stage. There are a number of such high-speed WAN services available.

Indeed, the network manager may now be faced with too many choices for solving capacity problems. In this chapter, we begin with an overview of various wide area networking alternatives, and show where the strengths and weaknesses lie. We then focus on perhaps the two most important WAN technologies: frame relay and ATM.

One approach that is not addressed in this chapter is the use of the Internet. The Internet is often used as a secondary or even primary WAN infrastructure for connecting computers at multiple sites. This topic, as well as the related topics of intranets, extranets, and virtual private networks, is best addressed separately and is dealt with elsewhere in this book.

13.1 WIDE AREA NETWORKING ALTERNATIVES

In considering wide area networking strategies for business and other organizations, two distinct but related trends need to be analyzed. The first is the distributed processing architecture used to support applications and to meet an organization's needs, and the second is the wide area networking technologies and services available to meet those needs.

WAN Offerings

To meet the demands of the new corporate computing paradigm, service and equipment providers have developed a variety of high-speed services. These include faster multiplexed line schemes, such as T-3 and SONET/SDH, as well as faster switched networks schemes, including frame relay and ATM.

Figure 13.1 lays out the primary alternatives available from public U.S. carriers; a similar mix is available in other countries. A nonswitched, or dedicated, line is a transmission link leased for a fixed price. Such lines can be leased from a carrier and used to link offices of an organization. Common offerings include the following:

- **Analog:** The least expensive option is to lease a twisted-pair analog link. With dedicated private line modems, data rates of 4.8 to 56 kbps are common.
- **Digital data service:** High-quality digital lines that require digital signaling units rather than modems are more expensive but can be leased at higher data rates.

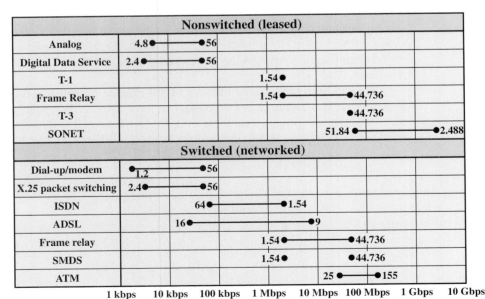

Figure 13.1 U.S. Carriers' Communications Services

- **T-1, T-3:** For many years, the most common leased line for high-traffic voice and data needs was the T-1 line, which is still quite popular. For greater needs, the T-3 is widely available.

- **Frame relay:** Although frame relay is a switched network technology, the frame relay protocol can be used over a dedicated line to provide a convenient and flexible multiplexing technique. Frame relay devices are required at the customer's premises for this approach.

- **Sonet:** The highest-speed leased lines that are available use SONET/SDH, discussed in Chapter 17.

Public switched services include the following:

- **Dial-up/modem:** Modems connected to the public telephone network provide a relatively inexpensive way to obtain low-speed data services. The modems themselves are inexpensive, and the telephone rates are reasonable for modest connect times. This is the near-universal access technique for residential users. In organizations, many LANs and PBXs are equipped with modem banks to provide low-cost, supplemental data transmission service.

- **X.25 packet switching:** This elderly standby is still used to provide a switched data transfer service. With the increasing use of graphic and multimedia applications, X.25 at its traditional data rates is becoming increasingly inadequate. Typically, network charges are based on the volume of data transferred.

- **ISDN:** The Integrated Services Digital Network provides both circuit switching and X.25 packet switching over 64-kbps B channels. Higher data rates are also achievable. Typically, network charges are based on the duration of the call regardless of the amount of data transferred.

- **Frame relay:** Provides switched capability at speeds equivalent to the leased T-1 rate and, in some offerings, higher rates up to T-3. Its low overhead makes it suitable for interconnecting LANs and high-speed stand-alone systems.

- **ATM:** Asynchronous transfer mode is widely viewed as a universal networking technology, destined to replace many of the current offerings.

Choosing among the various leased and switched alternatives is no easy task, and the proliferation of alternatives has increased the difficulty. Table 13.1 indicates common pricing practices in the United States; comparable practices are used in other countries. As can be seen, the pricing structures of the various services are not directly comparable. This is one complication. Other issues that complicate the selection process include the difficulty of forecasting future traffic volumes by organizations with wide area networking requirements, and difficulty in forecasting traffic distributions given the flexibility of applications and the mobility of users.

Evolution of WAN Architectures

Figure 13.2a shows the type of architecture that was dominant in business networks until recently and continues to be a popular model. In a typical configuration, all the devices at a customer's premises are fed through a synchronous time division

Table 13.1 WAN Alternatives (U.S. pricing)

Service	Usage Rate	Distance Rate
Leased line	Fixed price per month for a specific capacity (e.g., T-1 or T-3) and no additional fee for usage.	More for greater distance.
ISDN	Fixed price per month for service plus a usage charge based on amount of connect time.	Long-distance charges apply.
Frame relay	Fixed price per month for a port connection and a flat rate for a permanent virtual circuit (PVC) based on the capacity of the link.	Not distance sensitive.
ATM	Pricing policies vary.	Not distance sensitive.

multiplexer onto a high-speed subscriber line to a carrier. This includes a PBX that controls phone and fax machines for voice and fax traffic as well as an interface to a LAN. Typically, the LAN is interfaced by means of a router, discussed in Chapter 4. There may also be a number of dumb terminals connected to a controller that interfaces to the multiplexer. The line itself can be either T-1 or T-3; as demand rises, SONET links will become more common.

At the carrier end, the multiplexed traffic can be split up into a number of leased circuits. These enable the creation of a private network linking to PBXs, LANs, and mainframe hosts at other locations for this customer. In addition, for data traffic, the carrier can provide an interface to a public high-speed switched network. Most commonly today, that network is frame relay, but ATM networks are also offered. Finally, a link to the Internet may be provided.

The configuration of Figure 13.2a is an attractive one. It integrates all of the customer's voice and data traffic onto a single external line, which simplifies network management and configuration. One drawback is its relative lack of flexibility. The capacity on the synchronous TDM line is divided into fixed partitions allocated to the various elements at the customer site, such as PBX, LAN, and terminal controller. This makes it difficult if not impossible to allocate capacity dynamically as needed.

With the advent of faster and faster public switched networks, a more flexible solution is now possible, an example of which is shown in Figure 13.2b. In this arrangement, the high-speed external line connects directly to a public switched network, such as frame relay or ATM. Although frame relay was initially offered as a data network, some recent offerings have sufficient capacity to handle voice as well, and ATM is quite capable of handling voice traffic. Thus, it is possible to link all of the site equipment onto this single line into the switched network. Virtual connections can be used to set up temporary "pipes" to various destinations. In addition, most frame relay and ATM suppliers offer what are called permanent virtual connections; these provide the equivalent of dedicated synchronous TDM channels and can be used to set up private networks. However, the permanent virtual connections can be changed from time to time to alter capacity. For maximum flexibility, the customer can rely on switched virtual connections that are set up and torn down dynamically. Each time a connection is set up, the customer can configure that connection to carry a particular capacity of traffic. Thus, as the mix of traffic

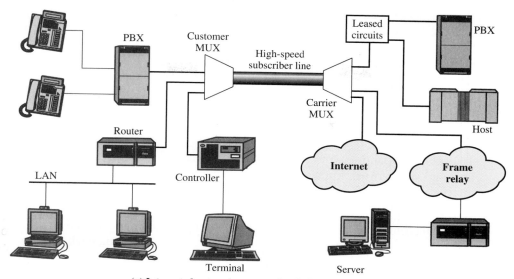

(a) **Integrated network access using dedicated channels**

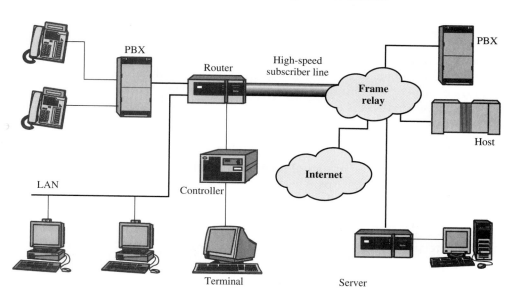

(b) **Integrated network access using public switched WAN**

Figure 13.2   Integrated Network Strategies

into and out of the site changes, the customer can dynamically change the capacity mix to provide optimum performance.

For high-speed wide area networking, the frame relay and ATM offerings have become increasingly the methods of choice. Although ATM is considered technically superior, frame relay has a greater market share because it has been available for longer, allowing the development of a large installed base [WEXL03].

13.2 FRAME RELAY

Frame relay is designed to provide a more efficient transmission scheme than traditional packet switching. The standards for frame relay matured earlier than those for ATM, and commercial products also arrived earlier. Accordingly, there is a large installed base of frame relay products.

Background

The traditional approach to packet switching makes use of a protocol between the user and the network known as X.25. X.25 not only determines the user-network interface but also influences the internal design of the network. Several key features of the X.25 approach are as follows:

- Call control packets, used for setting up and terminating virtual circuits, are carried on the same channel and same virtual circuit as data packets. In effect, inband signaling is used.
- Multiplexing of virtual circuits takes place at layer 3.
- Both layer 2 and layer 3 include flow control and error control mechanisms.

The X.25 approach results in considerable overhead. At each hop through the network, the data link control protocol involves the exchange of a data frame and an acknowledgment frame. Furthermore, at each intermediate node, state tables must be maintained for each virtual circuit to deal with the call management and flow control/error control aspects of the X.25 protocol. All of this overhead may be justified when there is a significant probability of error on any of the links in the network. This approach is not the most appropriate for modern digital communication facilities. Today's networks employ reliable digital transmission technology over high-quality, reliable transmission links, many of which are optical fiber. In addition, with the use of optical fiber and digital transmission, high data rates can be achieved. In this environment, the overhead of X.25 is not only unnecessary but degrades the effective utilization of the available high data rates.

Frame relay is designed to eliminate much of the overhead that X.25 imposes on end user systems and on the packet-switching network. The key differences between frame relaying and a conventional X.25 packet-switching service are as follows:

- Call control signaling is carried on a separate logical connection from user data. Thus, intermediate nodes need not maintain state tables or process messages relating to call control on an individual per-connection basis.
- Multiplexing and switching of logical connections takes place at layer 2 instead of layer 3, eliminating one entire layer of processing.
- There is no hop-by-hop flow control and error control. End-to-end flow control and error control are the responsibility of a higher layer, if they are employed at all.

Thus, with frame relay, a single user data frame is sent from source to destination, and an acknowledgment, generated at a higher layer, may be carried back in a frame. There are no hop-by-hop exchanges of data frames and acknowledgments.

Let us consider the advantages and disadvantages of this approach. The principal potential disadvantage of frame relaying, compared to X.25, is that we have lost the ability to do link-by-link flow and error control. (Although frame relay does not provide end-to-end flow and error control, this is easily provided at a higher layer.) In X.25, multiple virtual circuits are carried on a single physical link, and the link-layer protocol provides reliable transmission from the source to the packet-switching network and from the packet-switching network to the destination. In addition, at each hop through the network, the link control protocol can be used for reliability. With the use of frame relaying, this hop-by-hop link control is lost. However, with the increasing reliability of transmission and switching facilities, this is not a major disadvantage.

The advantage of frame relaying is that we have streamlined the communications process. The protocol functionality required at the user-network interface is reduced, as is the internal network processing. As a result, lower delay and higher throughput can be expected. Studies indicate an improvement in throughput using frame relay, compared to X.25, of an order of magnitude or more [HARB92]. The ITU-T Recommendation I.233 indicates that frame relay is to be used at access speeds up to 2 Mbps. However, frame relay service at even higher data rates is now available.

Frame Relay Protocol Architecture

Figure 13.3 depicts the protocol architecture to support the frame relay. We need to consider two separate planes of operation: a control (C) plane, which is involved in the establishment and termination of logical connections, and a user (U) plane, which is responsible for the transfer of user data between subscribers. Thus, C-plane protocols are between a subscriber and the network, while U-plane protocols provide end-to-end functionality.

Control Plane The control plane for frame relay is similar to that for common channel signaling for circuit-switching services, in that a separate logical channel is

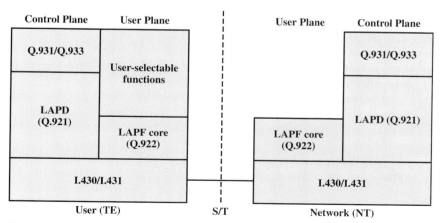

Figure 13.3   Frame Relay User-Network Interface Protocol Architecture

used for control information. At the data link layer, LAPD (Q.921) provides a reliable data link control service, with error control and flow control, between user (TE) and network (NT). This data link service is used for the exchange of Q.933 control signaling messages.

User Plane For the actual transfer of information between end users, the user-plane protocol is LAPF (Link Access Procedure for Frame Mode Bearer Services), which is defined in Q.922. Only the core functions of LAPF are used for frame relay:

- Frame delimiting, alignment, and transparency
- Frame multiplexing/demultiplexing using the address field
- Inspection of the frame to ensure that it consists of an integral number of octets prior to zero bit insertion or following zero bit extraction
- Inspection of the frame to ensure that it is neither too long nor too short
- Detection of transmission errors
- Congestion control functions

The last function listed is new to LAPF. The remaining functions listed are also functions of LAPD.

The core functions of LAPF in the user plane constitute a sublayer of the data link layer. This provides the bare service of transferring data link frames from one subscriber to another, with no flow control or error control. Above this, the user may choose to select additional data link or network-layer end-to-end functions. These are not part of the frame relay service. Based on the core functions, a network offers frame relaying as a connection-oriented link layer service with the following properties:

- Preservation of the order of frame transfer from one edge of the network to the other
- A small probability of frame loss

As with X.25, frame relay involves the use of logical connections, in this case called data link connections rather than virtual circuits. Figure 13.4b emphasizes that the frames transmitted over these data link connections are not protected by a data link control pipe with flow and error control.

Another difference between X.25 and frame relay is that the latter devotes a separate data link connection to call control. The setting up and tearing down of data link connections is done over this permanent control-oriented data link connection.

The frame relay architecture significantly reduces the amount of work required of the network. User data are transmitted in frames with virtually no processing by the intermediate network nodes, other than to check for errors and to route based on connection number. A frame in error is simply discarded, leaving error recovery to higher layers.

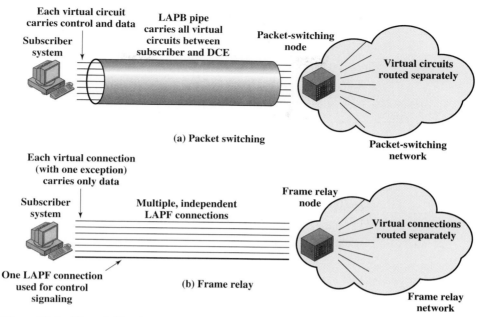

Figure 13.4 Virtual Circuits and Frame Relay Virtual Connections

User Data Transfer

The operation of frame relay for user data transfer is best explained by beginning with the frame format, illustrated in Figure 13.5. The format is similar to that of other data link control protocols, such as HDLC (described in Chapter 17), with one omission: There is no control field. In traditional data link control protocols, the control field is used for the following functions:

- Part of the control field identifies the frame type. In addition to a frame for carrying user data, there are various control frames. These carry no user data but are used for various protocol control functions, such as setting up and tearing down logical connections.

- The control field for user data frames includes send and receive sequence numbers. The send sequence number is used to sequentially number each transmitted frame. The receive sequence number is used to provide a positive or negative acknowledgment to incoming frames. The use of sequence numbers allows the receiver to control the rate of incoming frames (flow control) and to report missing or damaged frames which can then be retransmitted (error control).

The lack of a control field in the frame relay format means that the process of setting up and tearing down connections must be carried out on a separate channel at a higher layer of software. It also means that it is not possible to perform flow control and error control at the data link layer.

The flag and frame check sequence (FCS) fields function as in HDLC. The flag field is a unique pattern that delimits the start and end of the frame. The FCS field is

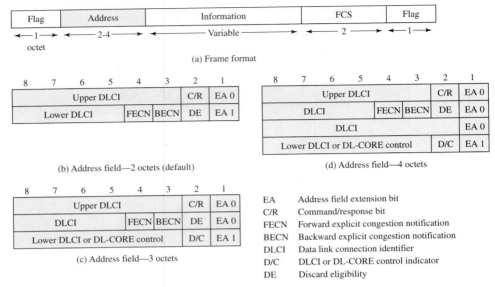

Figure 13.5   LAPF-Core Formats

used for error detection. On transmission, the FCS checksum is calculated and stored in the FCS field. On reception, the checksum is again calculated and compared to the value stored in the incoming FCS field. If there is a mismatch, then the frame is assumed to be in error and is discarded.

The information field carries higher-layer data. The higher-layer data may be either user data or call control messages, as explained later.

The address field has a default length of 2 octets and may be extended to 3 or 4 octets. It carries a data link connection identifier (DLCI) of 10, 16, or 23 bits. The DLCI allows multiple logical frame relay connections to be multiplexed over a single channel.

The length of the address field, and hence of the DLCI, is determined by the address field extension (EA) bits. The C/R bit is application specific and not used by the standard frame relay protocol. The remaining bits in the address field have to do with congestion control and are explained later.

Frame Relay Call Control

The actual details of the call control procedure for frame relay depend on the context of its use. Here, we summarize the essential elements of frame relay call control.

Frame relay supports multiple connections over a single link, and each has a locally unique DLCI. Data transfer involves the following stages:

1. Establish a logical connection between two endpoints, and assign a unique DLCI to the connection.

2. Exchange information in data frames. Each frame includes a DLCI field to identify the connection.

3. Release the logical connection.

The establishment and release of a logical connection is accomplished by the exchange of messages over a connection dedicated to call control, with DLCI = 0. A frame with DLCI = 0 contains a call control message in the information field. At a minimum, four message types are needed: SETUP, CONNECT, RELEASE, and RELEASE COMPLETE.

Either side may request the establishment of a logical connection by sending a SETUP message. The other side, upon receiving the SETUP message, must reply with a CONNECT message if it accepts the connection; otherwise it responds with a RELEASE COMPLETE message. The side sending the SETUP message may assign the DLCI by choosing an unused value and including this value in the SETUP message. Otherwise, the DLCI value is assigned by the accepting side in the CONNECT message.

Either side may request to clear a logical connection by sending a RELEASE message. The other side, upon receipt of this message, must respond with a RELEASE COMPLETE message.

Congestion Control

Congestion control for a frame relay network is challenging because of the limited tools available to the frame handlers. The frame relay protocol has been streamlined to maximize throughput and efficiency. A consequence of this is that a frame handler cannot control the flow of frames coming from a subscriber or an adjacent node using the typical flow control mechanism of other data link control protocols.

Congestion control is the joint responsibility of the network and the end users. The network (i.e., the collection of frame handling nodes) is in the best position to monitor the degree of congestion, while the end users are in the best position to control congestion by limiting the flow of traffic. With this in mind, two general congestion control strategies are supported in frame relay: congestion avoidance and congestion recovery.

Congestion avoidance procedures are used at the onset of congestion to minimize the effect on the network. At a point at which the network detects a build-up of queue lengths and the danger of congestion, there would be little evidence available to end users that congestion is increasing. Thus, there must be some explicit signaling mechanism from the network that will trigger the congestion avoidance.

Congestion recovery procedures are used to prevent network collapse in the face of severe congestion. These procedures are typically initiated when the network has begun to drop frames due to congestion. Such dropped frames will be reported by some higher layer of software and serve as an implicit signaling mechanism.

For explicit signaling, two bits in the address field of each frame are provided. Either bit may be set by the frame handler that detects congestion. If a frame handler forwards a frame in which one or both of these bits are set, it must not clear the bits. Thus, the bits constitute signals from the network to the end user. The two bits are as follows:

- **Backward explicit congestion notification (BECN):** Notifies the user that congestion avoidance procedures should be initiated where applicable for traffic in the opposite direction of the received frame. It indicates that the frames that the user transmits on this logical connection may encounter congested resources.

- **Forward explicit congestion notification (FECN):** Notifies the user that congestion avoidance procedures should be initiated where applicable for traffic in the same direction as the received frame. It indicates that this frame, on this logical connection, has encountered congested resources.

Implicit signaling occurs when the network discards a frame, and this fact is detected by the end user at a higher layer. The network role, of course, is to discard frames as necessary. One bit in the address field of each frame can be used to provide guidance:

- **Discard eligibility (DE):** Indicates a request that a frame should be discarded, instead of other frames in which this bit is not set, when it is necessary to discard frames.

The DE capability makes it possible for the user temporarily to send more frames than it is allowed to on average. In this case, the user sets the DE bit on the excess frames. The network will forward these frames if it has the capacity to do so.

The DE bit also can be set by a frame handler. The network can monitor the influx of frames from the user and use the DE bit to protect the network. That is, if the frame handler to which the user is directly connected decides that the input is potentially excessive, it sets the DE bit on each frame and then forwards it further into the network.

The DE bit can be used in such a way as to provide guidance for the discard decision and at the same time as a tool for providing a guaranteed level of service. This tool can be used on a per data link connection basis to ensure that heavy users can get the throughput they need without penalizing lighter users. The mechanism works as follows: each user can negotiate a **committed information rate (CIR)** (in bits per second) at connection setup time. The requested CIR represents the user's estimate of its "normal" traffic during a busy period; the granted CIR, which is less than or equal to the requested CIR, is the network's commitment to deliver data at that rate in the absence of errors. The frame handler to which the user's station attaches then performs a metering function (Figure 13.6). If the user is sending data at less than the CIR, the incoming frame handler does not alter the

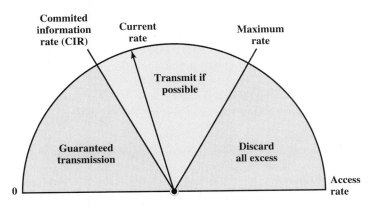

Figure 13.6   Operation of the CIR

DE bit. If the rate exceeds the CIR, the incoming frame handler will set the DE bit on the excess frames and then forward them; such frames may get through or may be discarded if congestion is encountered. Finally, a maximum rate is defined, such that any frames above the maximum are discarded at the entry frame handler.

13.3 ASYNCHRONOUS TRANSFER MODE (ATM)

Frame relay is designed to support access speeds up to 2 Mbps. But now, even the streamlined design of frame relay is faltering in the face of a requirement for wide area access speeds in the tens and hundreds of megabits per second. To accommodate these gargantuan requirements, a new technology has emerged: **asynchronous transfer mode** (ATM), also known as **cell relay**.

Cell relay is similar in concept to frame relay. Both frame relay and cell relay take advantage of the reliability and fidelity of modern digital facilities to provide faster packet switching than X.25. Cell relay is even more streamlined than frame relay in its functionality and can support data rates several orders of magnitude greater than frame relay.

Virtual Channels and Virtual Paths

ATM is a packet-oriented transfer mode. Like frame relay and X.25, it allows multiple logical connections to be multiplexed over a single physical interface. The information flow on each logical connection is organized into fixed-size packets, called **cells**. As with frame relay, there is no link-by-link error control or flow control.

Logical connections in ATM are referred to as **virtual channels**. A virtual channel is analogous to a virtual circuit in X.25 or a frame relay data link connection. It is the basic unit of switching in an ATM network. A virtual channel is set up between two end users through the network and a variable-rate, full-duplex flow of fixed-size cells is exchanged over the connection. Virtual channels are also used for user-network exchange (control signaling) and network-network exchange (network management and routing).

For ATM, a second sublayer of processing has been introduced that creates and manages virtual paths (Figure 13.7). A **virtual path** is a bundle of virtual channels that have the same endpoints. Thus, all of the cells flowing over all of the virtual channels in a single virtual path are switched together.

Figure 13.7   ATM Connection Relationships

Several advantages can be listed for the use of virtual paths:

- **Simplified network architecture:** Network transport functions can be separated into those related to an individual logical connection (virtual channel) and those related to a group of logical connections (virtual path).
- **Increased network performance and reliability:** The network deals with fewer, aggregated entities.
- **Reduced processing and short connection setup time:** Much of the work is done when the virtual path is set up. The addition of new virtual channels to an existing virtual path involves minimal processing.
- **Enhanced network services:** The virtual path is used internal to the network but is also visible to the end user. Thus, the user may define closed user groups or closed networks of virtual-channel bundles.

Virtual Path/Virtual Channel Characteristics   ITU-T Recommendation I.150 lists the following as characteristics of virtual channel connections:

- **Quality of service:** A user of a virtual channel is provided with a quality of service specified by parameters such as cell loss ratio (ratio of cells lost to cells transmitted) and cell delay variation.
- **Switched and semipermanent virtual channel connections:** Both switched connections, which require call-control signaling, and dedicated channels (called semipermanent) can be provided.
- **Cell sequence integrity:** The sequence of transmitted cells within a virtual channel is preserved.
- **Traffic parameter negotiation and usage monitoring:** Traffic parameters can be negotiated between a user and the network for each virtual channel. The input of cells to the virtual channel is monitored by the network to ensure that the negotiated parameters are not violated.

The types of traffic parameters that can be negotiated include average rate, peak rate, burstiness, and peak duration. The network may need a number of strategies to deal with congestion and to manage existing and requested virtual channels. At the crudest level, the network may simply deny new requests for virtual channels to prevent congestion. Additionally, cells may be discarded if negotiated parameters are violated or if congestion becomes severe. In an extreme situation, existing connections might be terminated.

I.150 also lists characteristics of virtual paths. The first four characteristics listed are identical to those for virtual channels. That is, quality of service, switched and semipermanent virtual paths, cell sequence integrity, and traffic parameter negotiation and usage monitoring are all characteristics of a virtual path. There are a number of reasons for this duplication. First, this provides some flexibility in how the network manages the requirements placed upon it. Second, the network must be concerned with the overall requirements for a virtual path, and within a virtual path may negotiate the establishment of virtual circuits with given characteristics. Finally, once a virtual path is set up, it is possible for the end users to negotiate the creation of new virtual channels. The virtual path characteristics impose a discipline on the choices that the end users may make.

In addition, a fifth characteristic is listed for virtual paths:

- **Virtual channel identifier restriction within a virtual path:** One or more virtual channel identifiers, or numbers, may not be available to the user of the virtual path but may be reserved for network use. Examples would be virtual channels used for network management.

Control Signaling In ATM, a mechanism is needed for the establishment and release of virtual paths and virtual channels. The exchange of information involved in this process is referred to as control signaling and takes place on separate connections from those that are being managed.

For virtual channels, I.150 specifies four methods for providing an establishment/release facility. One or a combination of these methods will be used in any particular network:

1. **Semipermanent virtual channels** may be used for user-to-user exchange. In this case, no control signaling is required.
2. If there is no preestablished call control signaling channel, one must be set up. For that purpose, a control signaling exchange must take place between the user and the network on some channel. Hence we need a permanent channel, probably of low data rate, that can be used to set up a virtual channel that can be used for call control. Such a channel is called a **meta-signaling channel**, because the channel is used to set up signaling channels.
3. The meta-signaling channel can be used to set up a virtual channel between the user and the network for call control signaling. This user-to-network signaling virtual channel can than be used to set up virtual channels to carry user data.
4. The meta-signaling channel can also be used to set up a user-to-user signaling virtual channel. Such a channel must be set up within a preestablished virtual path. It can then be used to allow the two end users, without network intervention, to establish and release user-to-user virtual channels to carry user data.

For virtual paths, three methods are defined in I.150:

1. A virtual path can be established on a **semipermanent basis** by prior agreement. In this case, no control signaling is required.
2. Virtual path establishment/release may be **customer controlled**. In this case, the customer uses a signaling virtual channel to request the virtual path from the network.
3. Virtual path establishment/release may be **network controlled**. In this case, the network establishes a virtual path for its own convenience. The path may be network to network, user to network, or user to user.

ATM Cells

The asynchronous transfer mode makes use of fixed-size cells, consisting of a 5-octet header and a 48-octet information field. There are several advantages to the use of small, fixed-size cells. First, the use of small cells may reduce queuing delay for a high-priority cell, because it waits less if it arrives slightly behind a lower-priority cell that has gained access to a resource (e.g., the transmitter). Second, it appears that fixed-size cells can be switched more efficiently, which is important for the very high data rates of ATM. With fixed-size cells, it is easier to implement the switching mechanism in hardware.

Figure 13.8a shows the header format at the user-network interface. Figure 13.8b shows the cell header format internal to the network.

The **Generic Flow Control** (GFC) field does not appear in the cell header internal to the network, but only at the user-network interface. Hence, it can be used for control of cell flow only at the local user-network interface. The field could be used to assist the customer in controlling the flow of traffic for different qualities of service. In any case, the GFC mechanism is used to alleviate short-term overload conditions in the network.

I.150 lists as a requirement for the GFC mechanism that all terminals be able to get access to their assured capacities. This includes all constant-bit-rate (CBR) terminals as well as the variable-bit-rate (VBR) terminals that have an element of guaranteed capacity (CBR and VBR are explained subsequently).

The **Virtual Path Identifier** (VPI) field constitutes a routing field for the network. It is 8 bits at the user-network interface and 12 bits at the network-network interface, allowing for more virtual paths to be supported within the network. The

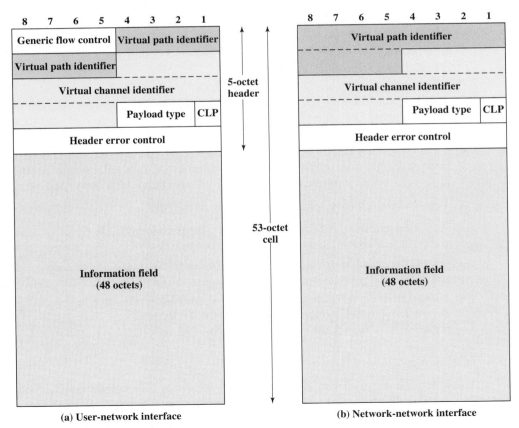

Figure 13.8 ATM Cell Format

Table 13.2   Payload Type (PT) Field Coding

PT Coding	Interpretation	
0 0 0	User data cell, congestion not experienced	SDU-type = 0
0 0 1	User data cell, congestion not experienced	SDU-type = 1
0 1 0	User data cell, congestion experienced	SDU-type = 0
0 1 1	User data cell, congestion experienced	SDU-type = 1
1 0 0	OAM segment associated cell	
1 0 1	OAM end-to-end associated cell	
1 1 0	Resource management cell	
1 1 1	Reserved for future function	

SDU = Service data unit
OAM = Operations, administration, and maintenance

Virtual Channel Identifier (VCI) field is used for routing to and from the end user. Thus, it functions much as a service access point.

The **Payload Type** (PT) field indicates the type of information in the information field. Table 13.2 shows the interpretation of the PT bits. A value of 0 in the first bit indicates user information (that is, information from the next higher layer). In this case, the second bit indicates whether congestion has been experienced; the third bit, known as the service data unit (SDU)[1] type bit, is a one-bit field that can be used to discriminate two types of ATM SDUs associated with a connection. The term *SDU* refers to the 48-octet payload of the cell. A value of 1 in the first bit of the payload type field indicates that this cell carries network management or maintenance information. This indication allows the insertion of network-management cells onto a user's virtual channel without impacting the user's data. Thus, the PT field can provide inband control information.

The **cell loss priority** (CLP) bit is used to provide guidance to the network in the event of congestion. A value of 0 indicates a cell of relatively higher priority, which should not be discarded unless no other alternative is available. A value of 1 indicates that this cell is subject to discard within the network. The user might employ this field so that extra cells (beyond the negotiated rate) may be inserted into the network, with a CLP of 1, and delivered to the destination if the network is not congested. The network may set this field to 1 for any data cell that is in violation of the agreement concerning traffic parameters between the user and the network. In this case, the switch that does the setting realizes that the cell exceeds the agreed traffic parameters but that the switch is capable of handling the cell. At a later point in the network, if congestion is encountered, this cell has been marked for discard in preference to cells that fall within agreed traffic limits.

---

[1]This is the term used in ATM Forum documents. In ITU-T documents, this bit is referred to as the ATM-user-to-ATM-user (AAU) indication bit. The meaning is the same.

The **Header Error Control** (HEC) field is an 8-bit error code that can be used to correct single-bit errors in the header and to detect double-bit errors. In the case of most existing data link layer protocols, such as LAPD and HDLC, the data field that serves as input to the error code calculation is in general much longer than the size of the resulting error code. This allows for error detection. In the case of ATM, the input to the calculation is only 32 bits, compared to 8 bits for the code. The fact that the input is relatively short allows the code to be used not only for error detection but also, in some cases, for actual error correction. This is because there is sufficient redundancy in the code to recover from certain error patterns.

The error protection function provides both recovery from single-bit header errors and a low probability of the delivery of cells with errored headers under bursty error conditions. The error characteristics of fiber-based transmission systems appear to be a mix of single-bit errors and relatively large burst errors. For some transmission systems, the error correction capability, which is more time-consuming, might not be invoked.

ATM Service Categories

An ATM network is designed to be able to transfer many different types of traffic simultaneously, including real-time flows such as voice, video, and bursty TCP flows. Although each such traffic flow is handled as a stream of 53-octet cells traveling through a virtual channel, the way in which each data flow is handled within the network depends on the characteristics of the traffic flow and the QoS requirements of the application. For example, real-time video traffic must be delivered within minimum variation in delay.

In this subsection, we summarize ATM service categories, which are used by an end system to identify the type of service required. The following service categories have been defined by the ATM Forum:

- **Real-Time Service**
  - Constant bit rate (CBR)
  - Real-time variable bit rate (rt-VBR)

- **Non-Real-Time Service**
  - Non-real-time variable bit rate (nrt-VBR)
  - Available bit rate (ABR)
  - Unspecified bit rate (UBR)
  - Guaranteed frame rate (GFR)

Real-Time Services The most important distinction among applications concerns the amount of delay and the variability of delay, referred to as jitter, that the application can tolerate. Real-time applications typically involve a flow of information to a user that is intended to reproduce that flow at a source. For example, a user expects a flow of audio or video information to be presented in a continuous, smooth fashion. A lack of continuity or excessive loss results in significant loss of quality. Applications that involve interaction between people have tight constraints on delay. Typically, any delay above a few hundred milliseconds becomes noticeable and annoying. Accordingly, the demands in the ATM network for switching and delivery of real-time data are high.

The **Constant Bit Rate (CBR)** service is perhaps the simplest service to define. It is used by applications that require a fixed data rate that is continuously available during the connection lifetime and a relatively tight upper bound on transfer delay. CBR is commonly used for uncompressed audio and video information. Examples of CBR applications include the following:

- Videoconferencing
- Interactive audio (e.g., telephony)
- Audio/video distribution (e.g., television, distance learning, pay per view)
- Audio/video retrieval (e.g., video on demand, audio library)

The **Real-Time Variable Bit Rate (rt-VBR)** category is intended for time-sensitive applications; that is, those requiring tightly constrained delay and delay variation. The principal difference between applications appropriate for rt-VBR and those appropriate for CBR is that rt-VBR applications transmit at a rate that varies with time. Equivalently, an rt-VBR source can be characterized as somewhat bursty. For example, the standard approach to video compression results in a sequence of image frames of varying sizes. Because real-time video requires a uniform frame transmission rate, the actual data rate varies.

The rt-VBR service allows the network more flexibility than CBR. The network is able to statistically multiplex a number of connections over the same dedicated capacity and still provide the required service to each connection.

Non–Real-Time Services Non-real-time services are intended for applications that have bursty traffic characteristics and do not have tight constraints on delay and delay variation. Accordingly, the network has greater flexibility in handling such traffic flows and can make greater use of statistical multiplexing to increase network efficiency.

For some non-real-time applications, it is possible to characterize the expected traffic flow so that the network can provide substantially improved quality of service (QoS) in the areas of loss and delay. Such applications can use the **Non-Real-Time Variable Bit Rate (nrt-VBR)** service. With this service, the end system specifies a peak cell rate, a sustainable or average cell rate, and a measure of how bursty or clumped the cells may be. With this information, the network can allocate resources to provide relatively low delay and minimal cell loss.

The nrt-VBR service can be used for data transfers that have critical response-time requirements. Examples include airline reservations, banking transactions, and process monitoring.

At any given time, a certain amount of the capacity of an ATM network is consumed in carrying CBR and the two types of VBR traffic. Additional capacity is available for one or both of the following reasons: (1) Not all of the total resources have been committed to CBR and VBR traffic, and (2) the bursty nature of VBR traffic means that at some times less than the committed capacity is being used. All of this unused capacity could be made available for the **Unspecified Bit Rate (UBR)** service. This service is suitable for applications that can tolerate variable delays and some cell losses, which is typically true of TCP-based traffic. With UBR, cells are forwarded on a first-in, first-out (FIFO) basis using the capacity not consumed by other services; both delays and variable losses are possible. No initial commitment is made to a UBR source and no feedback concerning congestion is provided; this is referred to as a **best-effort service.** Examples of UBR applications include the following:

- Text/data/image transfer, messaging, distribution, retrieval
- Remote terminal (e.g., telecommuting)

Bursty applications that use a reliable end-to-end protocol such as TCP can detect congestion in a network by means of increased round-trip delays and packet discarding. However, TCP has no mechanism for causing the resources within the network to be shared fairly among many TCP connections. Further, TCP does not minimize congestion as efficiently as is possible using explicit information from congested nodes within the network.

To improve the service provided to bursty sources that would otherwise use UBR, the **Available Bit Rate (ABR)** service has been defined. An application using ABR specifies a peak cell rate (PCR) that it will use and a minimum cell rate (MCR) that it requires. The network allocates resources so that all ABR applications receive at least their MCR capacity. Any unused capacity is then shared in a fair and controlled fashion among all ABR sources. The ABR mechanism uses explicit feedback to sources to assure that capacity is fairly allocated. Any capacity not used by ABR sources remains available for UBR traffic.

An example of an application using ABR is LAN interconnection. In this case, the end systems attached to the ATM network are routers.

The most recent addition to the set of ATM service categories is **Guaranteed Frame Rate (GFR),** which is designed specifically to support IP backbone subnetworks. GFR provides better service than UBR for frame-based traffic, including IP and Ethernet. A major goal of GFR is to optimize the handling of frame-based traffic that passes from a LAN through a router onto an ATM backbone network. Such ATM networks are increasingly being used in large enterprise, carrier, and Internet service provider networks to consolidate and extend IP services over the wide area. While ABR is also an ATM service meant to provide a greater measure of guaranteed packet performance over ATM backbones, ABR is relatively difficult to implement between routers over an ATM network. With the increased emphasis on using ATM to support IP-based traffic, especially traffic that originates on Ethernet LANs, GFR may offer the most attractive alternative for providing ATM service.

One of the techniques used by GFR to provide improved performance compared to UBR is to require that network elements be aware of frame or packet boundaries. Thus, when congestion requires the discard of cells, network elements must discard all of the cells that comprise a single frame. GFR also allows a user to reserve capacity for each GFR VC. The user is guaranteed that this minimum capacity will be supported. Additional frames may be transmitted if the network is not congested.

APPLICATION NOTE
Newer Solutions for Getting Offsite

Increasingly we see organizations exchanging data with offsite locations as part of their normal business routine. As a result, traditional low bandwidth solutions are not sufficient to handle the load. In addition to the protocols and services already mentioned in this chapter, there are newer transport systems that have emerged recently. While originally viewed as solutions for the home, they are showing promise for businesses as well. Cable and digital subscriber systems (DSL) have shown that they are appropriate for certain types of installations and so should be part of any site analysis.

Like ATM and frame relay, cable and DSL can be "throttled." This means that the data transmission rate can be modified to suit a particular need. DSL also has several different types of service available. Cable has also come up with different service plans for businesses.

As with most services, there is the question of regional availability. Geographic offerings vary quite a bit. The pricing from area to area can also be significantly different. For example, in the Northeast U.S., frame relay is very popular while ISDN and ATM remain available but expensive solutions. Cable and DSL services are both available and in fact directly compete with each other in advertising campaigns.

Cable simply means that the data is being sent down the same cabling infrastructure that provides cable television. Another channel (like the television channels) is allocated for this transmission. All of the channels are allocated 6 MHz, and the data channel is no different. The upstream and downstream data transmissions are provided with different carriers and the modems simply modulate or demodulate the signal. Cable is capable of long-range transmission because of the coaxial cable. This medium serves to protect the signal from outside interference.

The problem that most people complain about with cable is the number of users that may be on a particular segment. Cable distribution is a shared media and because of this, all of the users in a local area are often on the same segment, competing for bandwidth. Because of this, cable often starts to behave like shared Ethernet, the higher the number of users, the lower the bandwidth allocated to each individual. Even with this drawback, cable offers a higher-speed (usually up to 1 Mbps) alternative worth considering.

DSL runs over the same line that your telephone uses. Like cable, DSL providers advertise that you can use your telephone while transmitting data. While cable transmissions use a completely different system, DSL requires a mechanism for "stepping around" a telephone conversation. DSL transmissions use different frequencies than that of voice. Because your voice output is low frequency, DSL modems transmit at frequencies above this to prevent interference. It is interesting to note that the two systems use the same modulation technique—QAM.

Unlike cable, DSL users do not share a line with others. However, DSL has other restrictions. The most prominent problem is distance. This, coupled with the quality of the copper connecting a site to the central office, can eliminate DSL as a viable solution. DSL does not perform well beyond a few kilometers, and the farther the distance, the greater the noise and therefore the lower the data rate. Even with the best UTP, the maximum distance is limited to 5.5 km.

While neither cable nor DSL are currently capable of very high-speed connections (10–100 Mbps), they represent successful alternatives to traditional services. Depending on the organization needs and service availability, they are definitely worth considering.

This discussion wouldn't be complete without noting another last mile connectivity solution that has appeared very recently—10-gigabit Ethernet. Targeted specifically for this particular market, it leverages a well-known technology (Ethernet) and runs exclusively over fiber. The result is an extremely high-speed alternative to other services that is able to transmit over long distances. To compare, a high data transfer site like a university that might purchase an expensive OC-3 at 155 Mbps, could get a comparably priced 10-gigabit connection that is more than 60 times faster.

13.4 SUMMARY

A major change has occurred in the provision of wide area telecommunications services. The increasing capacity requirements of distributed computing systems, coupled with the introduction of transmission facilities of high speed and high reliability, have led to the introduction of a variety of WAN services that far outstrip the capabilities of traditional packet-switching networks.

The most widely available such service is frame relay. Frame relay is offered by a wide variety of providers for both public and private network configurations. Frame relay makes use of variable-sized packets, called frames, and a processing scheme that is considerably simpler than traditional packet-switching networks. Data rates of up to 2 Mbps are readily achievable.

Asynchronous transfer mode (ATM) is even more streamlined than frame relay and is intended to provide capacity in the 100s of Mbps and into the Gbps range. ATM technology is finding use in a wide variety of offerings for both wide area and local area networking.

13.5 RECOMMENDED READING AND WEB SITES

A more in-depth treatment of frame relay can be found in [STAL99]. An excellent book-length treatment is [BUCK00]. [MCDY99], [BLAC99], and [STAL02] provide good coverage of ATM.

BLAC99   Black, U. *ATM Volume I: Foundation for Broadband Networks.* Upper Saddle River, NJ: Prentice Hall, 1992.

BUCK00   Buckwalter, J. *Frame Relay: Technology and Practice.* Reading, MA: Addison-Wesley, 2000.

MCDY99   McDysan, D., and Spohn, D. *ATM: Theory and Application.* New York: McGraw-Hill, 1999.

STAL99   Stallings, W. *ISDN and Broadband ISDN, with Frame Relay and ATM.* Upper Saddle River, NJ: Prentice Hall, 1999.

STAL02   Stallings, W. *High-Speed Networks and Internets.* Upper Saddle River, NJ: Prentice Hall, 2002.

Recommended Web Sites:

- **Frame Relay Alliance:** An association of corporate members comprised of vendors, carriers, users, and consultants committed to the implementation of frame relay in accordance with national and international standards. Site includes list of technical and implementation documents for sale.
- **Frame Relay Resource Center:** Good source of information on frame relay.
- **ATM Hot Links:** Excellent collection of white papers and links maintained by the University of Minnesota.
- **ATM Forum:** Contains technical specifications and white papers.
- **Cell Relay Retreat:** Contains archives of the cell-relay mailing list, links to numerous ATM-related documents, and links to many ATM-related Web sites.

13.6 KEY TERMS, REVIEW QUESTIONS, AND PROBLEMS

Key Terms

asynchronous transfer mode (ATM)	guaranteed frame rate (GFR)	unspecified bit rate (UBR)
available bit rate (ABR)	integrated services digital network (ISDN)	variable bit rate (VBR)
cell	SONET	virtual channel
constant bit rate (CBR)	T-1	virtual path
frame relay	T-3	wide area network (WAN)

Review Questions

13.1. What are the key high-speed networking services available for wide area networking?

13.2. How does frame relay differ from packet switching?

13.3. What are the relative advantages and disadvantages of frame relay compared to packet switching?

13.4. Why is all of the error checking used by an X.25 system not required on modern communication facilities?

13.5. How is congestion control handled in a frame relay network?

13.6. How does ATM differ from frame relay?

13.7. What are the relative advantages and disadvantages of ATM compared to frame relay?

13.8. What is the difference between a virtual channel and a virtual path?

13.9. What are the advantages of using virtual paths?

13.10. What are the characteristics of a virtual channel?

13.11. What are the characteristics of a virtual path?

13.12. List and briefly explain the fields in an ATM cell.

13.13. List and briefly define the ATM service categories.

Problems

13.1 In every area of the country, the services available from carriers can vary. Determine the following for your area:

    a. What types of service are the most prevalent?

    b. What would be the cost of these services for 256 kbps? 512 kbps? 1 Mbps?

    c. In addition to the cost of the service, what other costs might be incurred?

13.2 List all 16 possible values of the GFC field and the interpretation of each value (some values are illegal).

13.3 One key design decision for ATM was whether to use fixed- or variable-length cells. Let us consider this decision from the point of view of efficiency. We can define transmission efficiency as

$$N = \frac{\text{Number of information octets}}{\text{Number of information octets } + \text{ Number of overhead octets}}$$

    a. Consider the use of fixed length packets. In this case the overhead consists of the header octets. Define

        L = Data field size of the cell in octets

        H = Header size of the cell in octets

        X = Number of information octets to be transmitted as a single message

    Derive an expression for N. *Hint:* The expression will need to use the operator $\lceil \cdot \rceil$, where $\lceil Y \rceil$ = the smallest integer greater than or equal to Y.

    b. If cells have variable length, then overhead is determined by the header, plus the flags to delimit the cells or an additional length field in the header. Let Hv = additional overhead octets required to enable the use of variable-length cells. Derive an expression for N in terms of X, H, and Hv.

    c. Let $L = 48$, $H = 5$, and $Hv = 2$. Plot N versus message size for fixed- and variable-length cells. Comment on the results.

13.4 Another key design decision for ATM is the size of the data field for fixed-size cells. Let us consider this decision from the point of view of efficiency and delay.

    a. Assume that an extended transmission takes place, so that all cells are completely filled. Derive an expression for the efficiency N as a function of H and L.

    b. Packetization delay is the delay introduced into a transmission stream by the need to buffer bits until an entire packet is filled before transmission. Derive an expression for this delay as a function of L and the data rate R of the source.

    c. Common data rates for voice coding are 32 kbps and 64 kbps. Plot packetization delay as a function of L for these two data rates; use a left-hand y-axis with a maximum value of 2 ms. On the same graph, plot transmission efficiency as a function of L; use a right-hand y axis with a maximum value of 100%. Comment on the results.

13.5 Consider the following applications. In each case indicate whether you would use X.25, frame relay, or ATM facilities. Assume that the facilities are available and "competitively" priced (i.e., determine, in each case, whether the functional characteristics of the service offering match well the requirements of the application). Explain in each case the reasons for your choice.

    a. You have a large number of locations in a metropolitan area. At each location there is a large number of real time data transactions processed. Information about the transactions must be sent independently and more or less randomly among the locations. That is, the transaction are not batched or do not occur in bunches. Performance requirements are such that the delay must be short. Volumes at each location are modest but in total range up to few megabits per second in total.

    b. You now have a national WAN with about a half dozen locations in relatively remote areas. The transmission facilities are varied and include radio links, satellite links, and phone links using modems. The data rates are relatively modest.

c. In this case, you have multimedia applications. These include image communication and significant real-time video and audio services. These are interspersed with a multitude of other data services. The number of locations is small, but with the image and video applications, the volume is quite large, nearing gigabit per second ranges. There is also a large number of users and applications involved so that a large number of virtual circuits are needed even though the number of locations is small.

13.6 Consider compressed video transmission in an ATM network. Suppose standard ATM cells must be transmitted through 5 switches. The data rate is 43 Mbps.
   a. What is the transmission time for one cell through one switch?
   b. Each switch may be transmitting a cell from other traffic all of which we assume to have lower (non-preemptive for the cell) priority. If the switch is busy transmitting a cell, our cell has to wait until the other cell completes transmission. If the switch is free our cell is transmitted immediately. What is the maximum time from when a typical video cell arrives at the first switch (and possibly waits) until it is finished being transmitted by the fifth and last one? Assume that you can ignore propagation time, switching time, and everything else but the transmission time and the time spent waiting for another cell to clear a switch.
   c. Now suppose we know that each switch is utilized 60% of the time with the other low priority traffic. By this we mean that with probability 0.6 when we look at a switch it is busy. Suppose that if there is a cell being transmitted by a switch, the average delay spent waiting for a cell to finish transmission is one-half a cell transmission time. What is the average time from the input of the first switch to clearing the fifth?
   d. However, the measure of most interest is not delay but jitter, which is the variability in the delay. Use parts (b) and (c) calculate the maximum and average variability, respectively, in the delay.

   In all cases assume that the various random events are independent of one another; for example, we ignore the burstiness typical of such traffic.

13.7 A widely used set of standards employed in local ATM environments is called ATM LAN Emulation (LANE). Provide a basic overview of LANE and describe its place in an organization's network strategy.

Case Study VII: Olsten Staffing Services

Olsten Staffing Services is a world leader in the temporary employment industry. In order to better serve its hundreds of thousands of full-time employees and temporary workers, Olsten overhauled its local and wide area networks, as well as the applications running on them. The network redesign, begun in 1996, took three years to implement and deploy [DESM99, SULL99, HOLD99].

The problem that Olsten faced in 1996 was the result of its dramatic growth. At that time, Olsten was a $2 billion company, having grown from revenues of less than $100 million in 1980. Yet Olsten remained a primarily paper-driven company. The company has 625 field offices, but its paper-based systems made cooperation difficult. If one office could not quickly fill a need, searching for candidates in nearby offices meant numerous phone calls, faxes, and culling through mounds of paper files. The localization of staffing data made it especially difficult to service large corporate accounts. Thus, big accounts such as Chase Manhattan maintained separate accounts at different field offices. This made it difficult for either Chase or Olsten to generate reports detailing how many temporary employees were used and in what positions over a given time frame.

Olsten's IT department saw only one way for the company to maintain its industry position and to grow: throw out its mainframe and AS/400 machines and build a network infrastructure of UNIX servers and high-speed networks from scratch. Olsten had two main goals for the project: provide centralized information that would quickly identify employees available for a specific assignment, and provide rapid, complete information to customers. From the networking point of view, the need to centralize data resulted in two requirements: a reliable WAN and a headquarters LAN complex to support the data and applications for the entire organization.

For vendors, Olsten chose 3Com for the network equipment and AT&T for the WAN services. Olsten chose 3Com because it had competitively priced equipment and because Olsten had low-end 3Com gear installed in its field offices and wanted to stay with a single vendor. Olsten already had a contract with AT&T and was able to renegotiate it to address the new requirements.

Figure VII.1 shows the highlights of Olsten's solution. A nationwide frame relay network is used to connect all of Olsten's offices. The largest offices have multiple T-1 links (1.544 Mbps per link) and the remaining field offices have 256-kbps links into the frame relay network. All of the frame relay traffic is merged into a single T-3 (44.7 Mbps) ATM connection to the data center at the company's headquarters in Melville, New York. The T-3 connects to AT&T's Accu-Ring service, which uses self-healing fiber rings to provide a high level of redundancy in the subscriber loop. A second T-3 link over a different physical path provides a redundant backup. At the data center, the traffic feeds into a LAN complex consisting of a number of interconnected high-speed Ethernet systems operating at 100 Mbps and 1 Gbps.

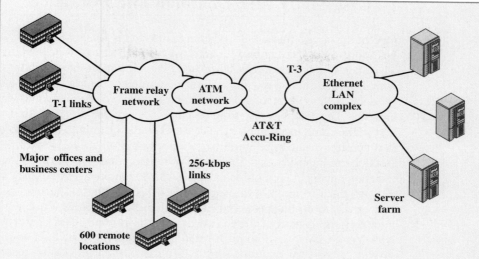

Figure VII.1   Olsten's Network Configuration

This infrastructure supports a huge collection of servers (known in the industry as a "server farm") consisting of 14 Sun Solaris servers and 75 Windows NT servers, as well as over 500 end-user machines.

Discussion Questions

1. What sorts of applications do you expect that Olsten could effectively implement on the new network infrastructure?

2. Does the new network infrastructure appear to provide a reasonable growth path for the future?

Case Study VIII: Guardian Life Insurance

One of the largest mutual life insurance firms in the United States, Guardian has more than 5500 employees and over 2800 financial representatives in 94 agencies. Guardian and its subsidiaries provide almost three million people with life and disability income insurance, retirement services, and investment products such as mutual funds, securities, variable life insurance, and variable annuities. The company also supplies employee benefits programs to five million participants, including life, health, and dental insurance, as well as qualified pension plans. In addition to regional home offices in New York City; Bethlehem, Pennsylvania; Spokane, Washington; and Appleton, Wisconsin, the company has 55 remote sales offices and 80 remote agency offices.

In the aftermath of the September 11, 2001 attack, Guardian became concerned about business continuity issues. Guardian had four significant data centers, at its four home offices, but the primary data center was in New York City. Guardian performed an assessment of its data centers to provide a basis for planning on the location of data processing resources. One surprising outcome of this assessment had to do with utilization. The assessment revealed that the four data centers had about 1000 UNIX and NT servers, with an average capacity utilization of 10%. Even at peak demand, only 25% of the processing power of the servers was being used [CLAR03, MUSI02]. Guardian responded to this assessment with a plan that included the following objectives:

1. Move the primary data center from New York City to Bethlehem, Pennsylvania.

2. Improve the efficiency of its data centers, including server and storage utilization. Specifically, Guardian set a goal of reducing the number of servers supporting Guardian's applications and databases by 40% and reducing the server support staff by 60%.

3. Ensure a smooth transition to the new primary data center.

Although it has considerable information technology (IT) expertise, Guardian felt that it needed outside assistance for such a massive undertaking. Warren Jones, VP of IT operations, cited three reasons for seeking outside assistance:

1. Partnering gives you the ability to address a stand-alone project and get it done in a specific time from without being influenced by day-to-day activities.

2. Partnering brings in an outside perspective. The partner provides an independent assessment of the strengths and weaknesses of the plan.

The company chose IT consulting firm Greenwich Technology Partners (GTP) to help it design and carry out the transition. Four of the nine bids submitted for the outsourcing contract were financially competitive with GTP's. Guardian decided on GTP because of its promptness in

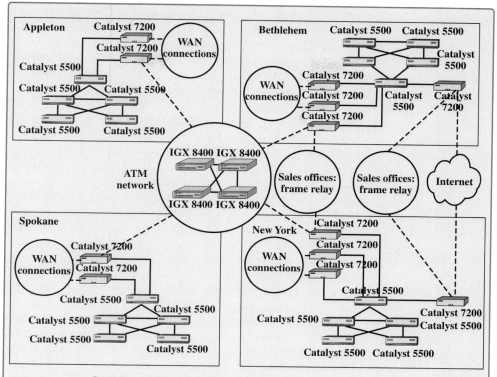

Figure VIII.1 Guardian's Network Infrastructure

responding to the RFP, its track record of flexibility on difficult jobs, and its commitment to supply any resources required to execute the project, without any hidden costs.

GTP began with an assessment of the company's IT environment and looked at the impact of moving the data center from New York to Bethlehem. A major issue related to the move was that the largest number of data center users was located in the New York area. Thus, the new deployment needed to provide for sufficient data transmission capacity to meet users' needs. Fortunately, the network infrastructure already in place was fairly standard and easily scalable (Figure VIII.1). An ATM WAN backbone links the four regional home offices. Frame relay connections link the remote sales offices and remote agency offices, and 100-Mbps and 1-Gbps Ethernet LANs provide connectivity within campuses. The Cisco Catalyst 5500 and 7200 series routers provide Ethernet support combined with a modular, easily scalable design. The Cisco IGX 8400 ATM switches can be scaled to support an ATM network service at any desired capacity. With three widely used networking technologies in place, some of the problems that might have been encountered in a more convoluted networking environment are avoided.

GTP also looked at the application and database patterns. They determined which servers were application, database, and file and print servers, and analyzed the data in each. In addition to traditional applications such as file and print services, PeopleSoft, and Lotus Notes, Guardian also uses a collection of applications to support its intranet Web site. The site includes marketing materials and sales tools for the firm's agents, account profiling, and customer data. The company had also invested in a number of financial services applications, including applications for supporting its trading and securities functions. Due to their complexity and the amount of resource required to support them, many of Guardian's applications require dedicated servers.

The transition team, consisting of Guardian and GTP personnel, did extensive validation work and benchmarking to make sure the data they had gathered during the initial assessment was accurate. They measured network utilization at granular levels and modeled various consolidation scenarios for reducing server hardware.

From this analysis, GTP proceeded to develop a plan for consolidating the servers, looking at both business and technology issues. For example, the team considered the criticality of the applications supported by the servers, as well as which business units they belonged to. Some servers were good candidates for consolidation; others were not; and others were out of warranty, which made them too expensive to keep. After the migration plan was devised and the new architecture developed, more testing was conducted to ensure their viability.

The team devoted much thought and analysis to the migration to the new architecture, so as not to disrupt day-to-day operations. The plan targeted the least complex opportunities first, starting with file and print services. Guardian initially had more than 30 servers providing file and print services. These were consolidated into just two servers clustered in a high-availability, fault-tolerant configuration. For more complex parts of the plan, the team opted to do some of the consolidation in New York, and only then move the servers to Bethlehem after the consolidation had settled down.

The ongoing consolidation and relocation project has yielded tangible benefits to Guardian in terms of reduced hardware and personnel requirements. But the benefits extend beyond these initial objectives. The mindset of solving new problems efficiently and in the context of the existing infrastructure has taken hold. Guardian no longer automatically takes orders for new servers as most of the operations and infrastructure world did throughout the 1990s. Instead, Guardian analyzes each new application requirement and attempt to support it with the existing hardware/software suite or with minimal upgrades and extensions.

The total cost of the project is $4.5 million, with GTP's services making up about 40% of the total. But the company saved more than $3 million in 2002, offsetting much of that cost. The company projects annual savings of over $5 million over the next two years.

Discussion Questions

1. Guardian initially decided to tackle the two key elements of its project simultaneously, namely the consolidation of its servers and the relocation of the primary data center. The alternatives would have been to first consolidate and then relocate, or to first relocate and then consolidate. As the preceding discussion indicates, Guardian ended up using a mix of the first and second strategies. Discuss pros and cons of all three alternatives.

2. Discuss the pros and cons of outsourcing Guardian's project.

CHAPTER 14

WIRELESS WANS

CHAPTER OBJECTIVES

After reading this chapter, you should be able to

- Identify the advantages and disadvantages of unguided (wireless communication) relative to guided communication.
- Distinguish among three generations of mobile telephony.
- Understand the relative merits of time division multiple access (TDMA) and code division multiple access (CDMA) approaches to mobile telephony.
- Describe the possibilities of personal communications systems (PCSs).
- Understand the properties and applications of LEOS, MEOS, and GEOS satellites.

As electronic information systems affect every aspect of our lives, it becomes increasingly bothersome to be tethered to these systems by wires. Wireless communications offers us mobility and much else. Wireless communications should be considered when

- Mobile communication is needed.
- Communication must take place in a hostile or difficult terrain that makes wired communication difficult or impossible.
- A communication system must be deployed quickly.
- Communication facilities must be installed at low initial cost.
- The same information must be broadcast to many locations.

On the other hand, wireless communication has disadvantages compared to guided media such as twisted pair, coaxial cable, or optical fiber:

- Wireless communication operates in a less controlled environment and is therefore more susceptible to interference, signal loss, noise, and eavesdropping.
- Generally, wireless facilities have lower data rates than guided facilities.
- Frequencies can be more easily reused with guided media than with wireless media.

In this chapter we consider wide-area wireless systems, including mobile telephony, third-generation wireless systems, and satellite communications. Wireless LANs are discussed in Chapter 11.

14.1 CELLULAR WIRELESS NETWORKS

Of all the tremendous advances in data communications and telecommunications, perhaps the most revolutionary is the development of cellular networks. Cellular technology is the foundation of mobile wireless communications and supports users in locations that are not easily served by wired networks. Cellular technology is the underlying technology for mobile telephones, personal communications systems, wireless Internet and wireless Web applications, and much more.

Cellular radio is a technique that was developed to increase the capacity available for mobile radio telephone service. Prior to the introduction of cellular radio, mobile radio telephone service was only provided by a high-power transmitter/receiver. A typical system would support about 25 channels with an effective radius of about 80 km. The way to increase the capacity of the system is to use lower-power transmitters with shorter radius and to use numerous transmitters/receivers.

Cellular Network Organization

The essence of a cellular network is the use of multiple low-power transmitters, on the order of 100 W or less. Because the range of such a transmitter is small, an area can be divided into cells, each one served by its own antenna. Each cell is allocated a band of frequencies and is served by a **base station,** consisting of transmitter, receiver, and control unit. Adjacent cells are assigned different frequencies to avoid interference or crosstalk. However, cells sufficiently distant from each other can use the same frequency band.

The first design decision to make is the shape of cells to cover an area. A matrix of square cells would be the simplest layout to define (Figure 14.1a). However, this geometry is not ideal. If the width of a square cell is d, then a cell has four neighbors at a distance d and four neighbors at a distance $\sqrt{2}d$. As a mobile user within a cell moves toward the cell's boundaries, it is best if all of the adjacent antennas are equidistant. This simplifies the task of determining when to switch the user to an adjacent antenna and which antenna to choose. A hexagonal pattern provides

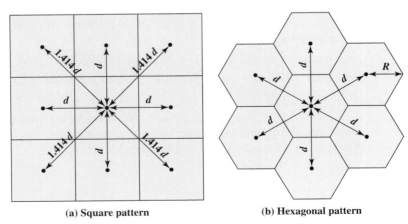

(a) Square pattern   (b) Hexagonal pattern

Figure 14.1 Cellular Geometries

for equidistant antennas (Figure 14.1b). The radius of a hexagon is defined to be the radius of the circle that circumscribes it (equivalently, the distance from the center to each vertex; also equal to the length of a side of a hexagon). For a cell radius R, the distance between the cell center and each adjacent cell center is $d = \sqrt{3}R$.

In practice, a precise hexagonal pattern is not used. Variations from the ideal are due to topographical limitations, local signal propagation conditions, and practical limitation on siting antennas.

With a wireless cellular system, you are limited in how often you can use the same frequency for different communications because the signals, not being constrained, can interfere with one another even if geographically separated. Systems supporting a large number of communications simultaneously need mechanisms to conserve spectrum.

Frequency Reuse In a cellular system, each cell has a base transceiver. The transmission power is carefully controlled (to the extent that it is possible in the highly variable mobile communication environment) to allow communication within the cell using a given frequency while limiting the power at that frequency that escapes the cell into adjacent ones. The objective is to use the same frequency in other nearby (but not adjacent) cells, thus allowing the frequency to be used for multiple simultaneous conversations. Generally, 10 to 50 frequencies are assigned to each cell, depending on the traffic expected.

The essential issue is to determine how many cells must intervene between two cells using the same frequency so that the two cells do not interfere with each other. Various patterns of frequency reuse are possible. Figure 14.2 shows some examples. If the pattern consists of N cells and each cell is assigned the same number of frequencies, each cell can have K/N frequencies, where K is the total number of frequencies allotted to the system. For AMPS (Advanced Mobile Phone Service, a widely used first-generation cellular scheme), $K = 395$, and $N = 7$ is the smallest pattern that can provide sufficient isolation between two uses of the same frequency. This implies that there can be at most 57 frequencies per cell on average.

In characterizing frequency reuse, the following parameters are commonly used:

D = minimum distance between centers of cells that use
      same band of frequencies (called cochannels)

R = radius of a cell

d = distance between centers of adjacent cells ($d = \sqrt{3}R$)

N = number of cells in a repetitive pattern (each cell in the pattern
      uses a unique band of frequencies), termed the **reuse factor**

In a hexagonal cell pattern, only the following values of N are possible:

$$N = I^2 + J^2 + (I \times J), \quad I, J = 0, 1, 2, 3, \ldots$$

Hence, possible values of N are 1, 3, 4, 7, 9, 12, 13, 16, 19, 21, and so on. The following relationship holds:

$$\frac{D}{R} = \sqrt{3N}$$

This can also be expressed as $D/d = \sqrt{N}$.

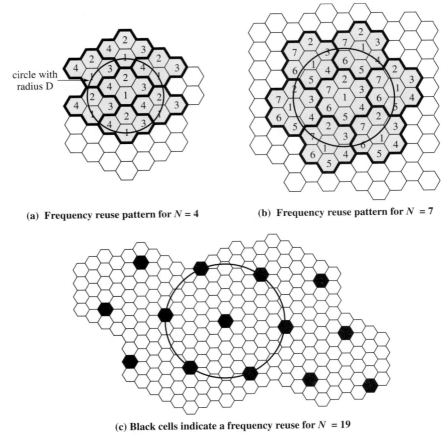

(a) Frequency reuse pattern for $N = 4$

(b) Frequency reuse pattern for $N = 7$

(c) Black cells indicate a frequency reuse for $N = 19$

Figure 14.2 Frequency Reuse Patterns

Increasing Capacity In time, as more customers use the system, traffic may build up so that there are not enough frequencies assigned to a cell to handle its calls. A number of approaches have been used to cope with this situation, including the following:

- **Adding new channels:** Typically, when a system is set up in a region, not all of the channels are used, and growth and expansion can be managed in an orderly fashion by adding new channels.

- **Frequency borrowing:** In the simplest case, frequencies are taken from adjacent cells by congested cells. The frequencies can also be assigned to cells dynamically.

- **Cell splitting:** In practice, the distribution of traffic and topographic features is not uniform, and this presents opportunities for capacity increase. Cells in areas of high usage can be split into smaller cells. Generally, the original cells are about 6.5 to 13 km in size. The smaller cells can themselves be split; however, 1.5-km cells are close to the practical minimum size as a general solution (but see the subsequent discussion of microcells). To use a smaller cell, the power level used must be reduced to keep the signal within the cell. Also, as the mobile units move, they pass from cell to cell, which requires transferring of the call from one base transceiver to another. This process is called a *handoff*. As the cells get smaller, these handoffs become more frequent. A radius reduction by a factor of F reduces the coverage area and increases the required number of base stations by a factor of F^2.

- **Cell sectoring:** With cell sectoring, a cell is divided into a number of wedge-shaped sectors, each with its own set of channels, typically 3 or 6 sectors per cell. Each sector is assigned a separate subset of the cell's channels, and directional antennas at the base station are used to focus on each sector.

- **Microcells:** As cells become smaller, antennas move from the tops of tall buildings or hills, to the tops of small buildings or the sides of large buildings, and finally to lamp posts, where they form microcells. Each decrease in cell size is accompanied by a reduction in the radiated power levels from the base stations and the mobile units. Microcells are useful in city streets, in congested areas along highways, and inside large public buildings.

Table 14.1 suggests typical parameters for traditional cells, called macrocells, and microcells with current technology. The average delay spread refers to multipath delay spread (i.e., the same signal follows different paths and there is a time delay between the earliest and latest arrival of the signal at the receiver). As indicated, the use of smaller cells enables the use of lower power and provides superior propagation conditions.

EXAMPLE.   Assume a system of 32 cells with a cell radius of 1.6 km, a total of 32 cells, a total frequency bandwidth that supports 336 traffic channels, and a reuse factor of $N = 7$. If there are 32 total cells, what geographic area is covered, how many channels are there per cell, and what is the total number of concurrent calls that can be handled? Repeat for a cell radius of 0.8 km and 128 cells.

Figure 14.3a shows an approximately square pattern. The area of a hexagon of radius R is $1.5 R^2\sqrt{3}$. A hexagon of radius 1.6 km has an area of 6.65 km², and the total area covered is $6.65 \times 32 = 213$ km². For $N = 7$, the number of channels per cell is $336/7 = 48$, for a total channel capacity of $48 \times 32 = 1536$ channels. For the layout of Figure 14.3b, the area covered is $1.66 \times 128 = 213$ km². The number of channels per cell is $336/7 = 48$, for a total channel capacity of $48 \times 128 = 6144$ channels.

Table 14.1   Typical Parameters for Macrocells and Microcells

	Macrocell	**Microcell**
Cell radius	1 to 20 km	0.1 to 1 km
Transmission power	1 to 10 W	0.1 to 1 W
Average delay spread	0.1 to 10 μs	10 to 100 ns
Maximum bit rate	0.3 Mbps	1 Mbps

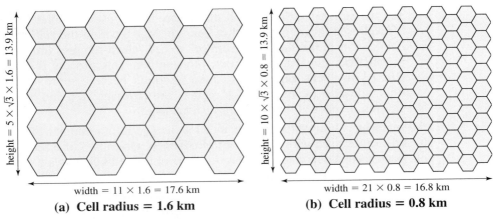

(a) **Cell radius = 1.6 km**   (b) **Cell radius = 0.8 km**

Figure 14.3   Frequency Reuse Example

Operation of Cellular Systems

Figure 14.4 shows the principal elements of a cellular system. In the approximate center of each cell is a base station (BS). The BS includes an antenna, a controller, and a number of transceivers, all of which are used for communicating on the channels assigned to that cell. The controller is used to handle the call process between the mobile unit and the rest of the network. At any time, a number of mobile user units may be active and moving about within a cell, communicating with the BS. Each BS is connected to a mobile telecommunications switching office (MTSO), with one MTSO serving multiple BSs. Typically, the link between an MTSO and a BS is by a wire line, although a wireless link is also possible. The MTSO connects calls between mobile units. The MTSO is also connected to the public telephone or telecommunications network and can make a connection between a fixed subscriber to the public network and a mobile subscriber to the cellular network. The MTSO assigns the voice channel to each call, performs handoffs, and monitors the call for billing information.

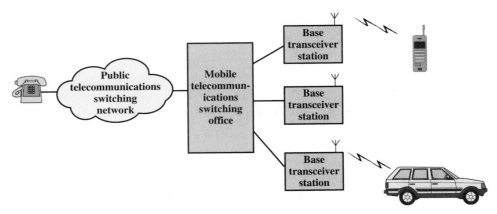

Figure 14.4   Overview of Cellular System

The use of a cellular system is fully automated and requires no action on the part of the user other than placing or answering a call. Two types of channels are available between the mobile unit and the base station (BS): control channels and traffic channels. **Control channels** are used to exchange information having to do with setting up and maintaining calls and with establishing a relationship between a mobile unit and the nearest BS. **Traffic channels** carry a voice or data connection between users. Figure 14.5 illustrates the steps in a typical call between two mobile users within an area controlled by a single MTSO:

- **Mobile unit initialization:** When the mobile unit is turned on, it scans for setup control channels (Figure 14.5a). Cells with different frequency bands repetitively

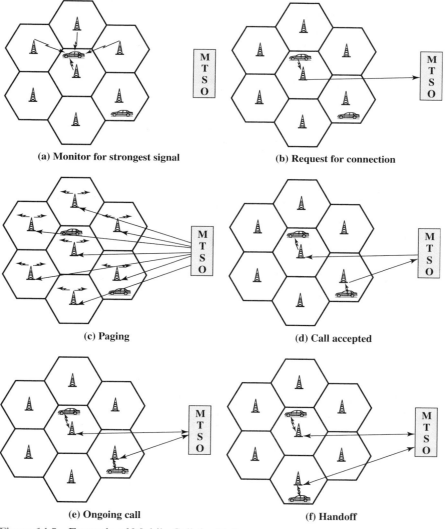

(a) Monitor for strongest signal

(b) Request for connection

(c) Paging

(d) Call accepted

(e) Ongoing call

(f) Handoff

Figure 14.5   Example of Mobile Cellular Call

broadcast on different setup channels. The receiver selects the strongest setup channel and monitors that channel. The effect of this procedure is that the mobile unit has automatically selected the BS antenna of the cell within which it will operate.[1] Then a handshake takes place between the mobile unit and the MTSO controlling this cell, through the BS in this cell. The handshake is used to identify the user and register its location. As long as the mobile unit is on, this scanning procedure is repeated periodically to account for the motion of the unit. If the unit enters a new cell, then a new BS is selected. In addition, the mobile unit is monitoring for pages, discussed subsequently.

- **Mobile-originated call:** A mobile unit originates a call by sending the number of the called unit on the preselected setup channel (Figure 14.5b). The receiver at the mobile unit first checks that the setup channel is idle by examining information in the forward (from the BS) channel. When an idle is detected, the mobile may transmit on the corresponding reverse (to BS) channel. The BS sends the request to the MTSO.

- **Paging:** The MTSO then attempts to complete the connection to the called unit. The MTSO sends a paging message to certain BSs depending on the called mobile number (Figure 14.5c). Each BS transmits the paging signal on its own assigned setup channel.

- **Call accepted:** The called mobile unit recognizes its number on the setup channel being monitored and responds to that BS, which sends the response to the MTSO. The MTSO sets up a circuit between the calling and called BSs. At the same time, the MTSO selects an available traffic channel within each BS's cell and notifies each BS, which in turn notifies its mobile unit (Figure 14.5d). The two mobile units tune to their respective assigned channels.

- **Ongoing call:** While the connection is maintained, the two mobile units exchange voice or data signals, going through their respective BSs and the MTSO (Figure 14.5e).

- **Handoff:** If a mobile unit moves out of range of one cell and into the range of another during a connection, the traffic channel has to change to one assigned to the BS in the new cell (Figure 14.5f). The system makes this change without either interrupting the call or alerting the user.

Other functions performed by the system but not illustrated in Figure 14.5 include the following:

- **Call blocking:** During the mobile-initiated call stage, if all the traffic channels assigned to the nearest BS are busy, then the mobile unit makes a preconfigured number of repeated attempts. After a certain number of failed tries, a busy tone is returned to the user.

- **Call termination:** When one of the two users hangs up, the MTSO is informed and the traffic channels at the two BSs are released.

---

[1]Usually, but not always, the antenna and therefore the base station selected is the closest one to the mobile unit. However, because of propagation anomalies, this is not always the case.

- **Call drop:** During a connection, because of interference or weak signal spots in certain areas, if the BS cannot maintain the minimum required signal strength for a certain period of time, the traffic channel to the user is dropped and the MTSO is informed.

- **Calls to/from fixed and remote mobile subscriber:** The MTSO connects to the public switched telephone network (PSTN). Thus, the MTSO can set up a connection between a mobile user in its area and a fixed subscriber via the telephone network. Further, the MTSO can connect to a remote MTSO via the telephone network or via dedicated lines and set up a connection between a mobile user in its area and a remote mobile user.

14.2 MULTIPLE ACCESS

One can categorize mobile telephone systems into generations. The first-generation systems are based on analog voice communication using frequency modulation. A widely used first-generation system was the Advanced Mobile Phone System (AMPS), which is used in North and South America, Australia, and China. Due to the overwhelming popularity of the first-generation systems, systems that use the spectrum more efficiently became necessary to reduce congestion. This requirement was addressed by the second generation, which uses digital techniques and time division multiple access (TDMA) or code division multiple access (CDMA) for channel access. Advanced call processing features are present as well. The third generation is evolving from a number of second-generation wireless systems.

In this section, we describe the basic concept of multiple access, which is a key design element of any cellular system.

The primary motivation for the transition from the first-generation cellular telephones to the second was the need to conserve spectrum. The first-generation systems were extremely successful and the number of subscribers had been growing exponentially for years. However, use (and profit) is constrained by spectrum capacity. Hence there is a premium on the efficient use of spectrum. In the United States this interest has not been decreased by the recent policy of the FCC to auction spectrum (for very large sums of money) rather than give it away. For these reasons, it is of interest to examine how the spectrum is divided among users in current and planned systems. There are basically four ways to divide the spectrum among active users: frequency division multiple access (FDMA), time division multiple access (TDMA), code division multiple access (CDMA), and space division multiple access (SDMA).[2] The first two types are discussed in Chapter 17; the remaining two we treat here.

Space division multiplexing is simply the idea of using the same spectral band in two physically disjoint places. A simple example is the idea of frequency reuse in cells, as discussed in this chapter. The same frequency can be used in two different cells as long as the cells are sufficiently far apart so that their signals do not interfere. Another form of space division that has been proposed for cellular telephony is to

---

[2]The terms FDMA, TDMA, CDMA, and SDMA are essentially equivalent to the terms FDM, TDM, CDM, and SDM, respectively. The phrase *multiple access* emphasizes that a single channel is being shared (accessed by) multiple users.

use highly directional antennas so that the same frequency may be used for two communications. This idea can be carried further by using steered beam antennas; these antennas can actually be aimed electronically and dynamically at a specific user. The ideas behind code division multiplexing are a little more complex, but because of their importance, we discuss them next.

Code Division Multiple Access (CDMA)

CDMA is based on direct sequence spread spectrum (DSSS). DSSS, which was briefly introduced in Chapter 11, is based on the following rather counterintuitive notion. We take a signal that we wish to communicate that has a data rate of, say, D bits per second and we convert it for transmission into a longer message and transmit it at a higher rate say, kD, where k is called the *spreading factor*. It might be about 100. Several things can be gained from this apparent waste of spectrum. For example, we can gain immunity from various kinds of noise and multipath distortion. The earliest applications of spread spectrum were military, where it was used for its immunity to jamming. It can also be used for hiding and encrypting signals. However, of interest to us is that several users can independently use the same (higher) bandwidth with very little interference.

Let us sketch how this works. We start with a data signal with rate D, which we call the bit data rate. We break each bit into k *chips* according to a fixed pattern that is specific to each user, called the user's code. The new channel has a chip data rate of kD chips per second. As an illustration we consider a simple example[3] with $k = 6$. It is simplest to characterize a code as a sequence of 1s and -1s. Figure 14.6 shows the codes for three users, A, B, and C, each of which is communicating with the same base

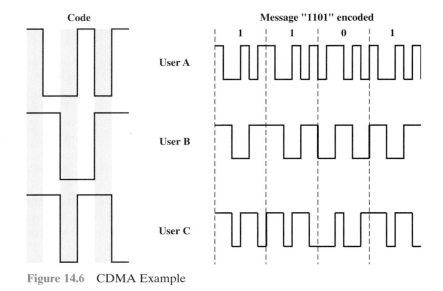

Figure 14.6 CDMA Example

---

[3]This example was provided by Professor Richard Van Slyke of the Polytechnic University of Brooklyn.

station receiver, R. Thus, the code for user A is $c_A = (1, -1, -1, 1, -1, 1)$. Similarly, user B has code $c_B = (1, 1, -1, -1, 1, 1)$, and user C has $c_C = (1, 1, -1, 1, 1, -1)$.

Consider the case of user A communicating with the base station. The base station is assumed to know A's code. For simplicity, assume that communication is already synchronized so that the base station knows when to look for codes. If A wants to send a 1 bit, A transmits its code as a chip pattern $(1, -1, -1, 1, -1, 1)$. To send a 0 bit, A transmits the complement (1s and -1 s reversed) of its code, $(-1, 1, 1, -1, 1, -1)$. At the base station the receiver decodes the chip patterns. If the receiver R receives a chip pattern $d = (d1, d2, d3, d4, d5, d6)$, and the receiver is seeking to communicate with a user u so that it has at hand u's code, $(c1, c2, c3, c4, c5, c6)$, the receiver performs the following decoding function:

$$S_u(d) = d1 \times c1 + d2 \times c2 + d3 \times c3 + d4 \times c4 + d5 \times c5 + d6 \times c6$$

The subscript u on S simply indicates that u is the user that we are interested in. Let's suppose the user u is actually A and see what happens. If A sends a 1 bit, then d is $(1, -1, -1, 1, -1, 1)$ and the preceding computation using S_A becomes

$$s_A(1, -1, -1, 1, -1, 1) = 1 \times 1 + (-1) \times (-1) + (-1) \times (-1)$$
$$+ 1 \times 1 + (-1) \times (-1) + 1 \times 1 = 6$$

If A sends a 0 bit that corresponds to $d = (-1, 1, 1, -1, 1, -1)$, we get

$$S_A(-1, 1, 1, -1, 1, -1) = -1 \times 1 + 1 \times (-1) + 1 \times (-1)$$
$$+ (-1) \times 1 + 1 \times (-1) + (-1) \times 1 = -6$$

Note that it is always the case that $-6 \leq S_A(d) \leq 6$ no matter what sequence of -1s and 1s that d is, and that the only d's resulting in the extreme values of 6 and -6 are A's code and its complement, respectively. So if S_A produces a $+6$, we say that we have received a 1 bit from A; if S_A produces a -6, we say that we have received a 0 bit from user A; otherwise, we assume that someone else is sending information or there is an error. So why go through all this? The reason becomes clear if we see what happens if user B is sending and we try to receive it with S_A, that is, we are decoding with the wrong code, A's. If B sends a 1 bit, then $d = (1, 1, -1, -1, 1, 1)$. Then

$$S_A(1, 1, -1, -1, 1, 1) = 1 \times 1 + 1 \times (-1) + (-1) \times (-1)$$
$$+ (-1) \times 1 + 1 \times (-1) + 1 \times 1 = 0$$

Thus, the unwanted signal (from B) does not show up at all. You can easily verify that if B had sent a 0 bit, the decoder would produce a value of 0 for S_A again. This means that if the decoder is linear and if A and B transmit signals s_A and s_B, respectively, at the same time, then $S_A(s_A + s_B) = S_A(s_A) + S_A(s_B) = S_A(s_A)$ since the decoder ignores B when it is using A's code. The codes of A and B that have the property that $S_A(c_B) = S_B(c_A) = 0$ are called *orthogonal*. Such codes are very nice to have but there are not all that many of them. More common is the case when $S_X(c_Y)$ is small in absolute value when $X \neq Y$. Then it is easy to distinguish between the two cases when $X = Y$ and when $X \neq Y$. In our example $S_A(c_C) = S_C(c_A) = 0$, but $S_B(c_C) = S_C(c_B) = 2$. In the latter case the C signal would make a small contribution to the decoded signal instead of 0. Using the decoder, S_u, the receiver can sort out transmission from u even when there may be other users broadcasting in the same cell.

In practice, the CDMA receiver can filter out the contribution from unwanted users or they appear as low-level noise. However, if there are many users competing for the channel with the user the receiver is trying to listen to, or if the signal power of one or more competing signals is too high, perhaps because it is very near the receiver (the "near/far" problem), the system breaks down. The coding gain we get, which is 6 in our simple example, may be greater than 100 in practical systems, so that the ability of our decoder to filter out unwanted codes can be quite effective.

Which Access Method to Use

Figure 14.7 illustrates the differences among FDMA, TDMA, and CDMA. In summary, with FDMA, each user communicates with the base station on its own narrow frequency band. For TDMA, the users share a wider frequency band and take turns communicating with the base station. For CDMA, many users can simultaneously use the same wide frequency band. Each user's signal is scrambled using a unique code so that it resembles random background noise to other users. The base station uses the same codes to unscramble the different user signals. CDMA allows more users to share a given bandwidth than does FDMA or TDMA.

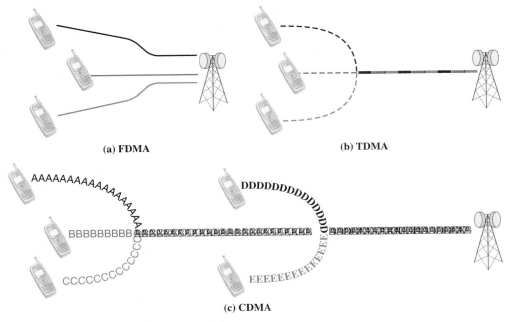

(a) FDMA

(b) TDMA

(c) CDMA

Figure 14.7   Cellular Multiple Access Schemes

Besides the pure forms of splitting the channel (FDMA, TDMA, CDMA, SDMA), hybrids are also possible. For example, the second-generation system known as GSM uses FDM to divide the allotted spectrum into 124 carriers. Each carrier is then split in up to eight parts using TDMA. The number of potential users in any one cell is potentially enormous. Any subscriber in the area could enter the cell; in addition, a whole world of roamers could show up. Fortunately, the number of customers who are in a given cell at one time and are using their units for calls is usually quite modest. The problem is how to determine which users are active in a cell and how to assign them to vacant subchannels. Mobiles/subscribers entering a cell by a handoff can be allocated a channel directly through the mobile switching office. The question remains what to do about mobiles/subscribers that are just becoming active. A common answer is to use a random access channel, in which any user can transmit at any time. If two users transmit at approximately the same time, their signals interfere and each must retransmit. Since the message from a mobile/subscriber announcing its presence is quite short and infrequent, the poor utilization that is characteristic of random access channels is not a problem. Similarly, control information originating from a mobile/subscriber can be carried in the same random access mode. One control message is to assign the mobile/subscriber a dedicated channel when a conversation or data transfer is necessary.

So the assignment of channels and other control functions that are relatively short and rare can be initiated using a random access method, while the higher-traffic activities can be carried out in dedicated conversation subchannels derived by a multiple access scheme.

The primary multiple access schemes used in cellular telephony (and satellite communications as well) are FDMA (e.g., the first-generation system AMPS), TDMA (e.g., Digital AMPS, the digital successor to AMPS, and GSM, which also uses FDM), and CDMA, pioneered by Qualcomm. This listing is in order of increasing complexity of implementation and also of increasing spectral efficiency. In Digital AMPS the 30-kHz channels of AMPS are divided into subchannels using TDM, giving about a 3 : 1 improvement in spectrum utilization. Qualcomm claims a tenfold improvement for CDMA systems over AMPS. CDMA uses *soft handoff*, wherein the power from the codes in the old and new cells is summed by the mobile. In the other direction, the two signals received by the two base transceivers can be compared to make better communication.

In the United States there has been debate over the access method to use. FDMA is clearly too wasteful of spectrum for contemporary systems. Moreover, with the development of inexpensive, high-performance digital signal processing chips, FDMA is no longer necessarily easier to implement than TDMA. But the choice between TDMA and CDMA is a matter debated. Adherents of TDMA argue that the theoretical advantages of the CDMA scheme are hard to realize in practice and that there is a lot more successful experience with TDMA. CDMA proponents argue that the theoretical advantages can be realized and that CDMA offers additional features as well, such as increased range. The TDMA systems have achieved an early lead in actual implementations worldwide. But large wireless providers are beginning to sign up with CDMA vendors, and CDMA seems to be the access method of choice for third-generation systems.

14.3 THIRD-GENERATION WIRELESS COMMUNICATION

The objective of the third generation of wireless communication is to provide fairly high speed wireless communications to support multimedia, data, and video in addition to voice. The ITU's International Mobile Telecommunications for the year 2000 (IMT-2000) initiative has defined the ITU's view of third-generation capabilities as follows:

- Voice quality comparable to the public switched telephone network
- 144 kbps data rate available to users in high-speed motor vehicles over large areas
- 384 kbps available to pedestrians standing or moving slowly over small areas
- Support (to be phased in) for 2.048 Mbps for office use
- Support for both packet switched and circuit switched data services
- An adaptive interface to the Internet to reflect efficiently the common asymmetry between inbound and outbound traffic
- More efficient use of the available spectrum in general
- Support for a wide variety of mobile equipment
- Flexibility to allow the introduction of new services and technologies

More generally, one of the driving forces of modern communication technology is the trend toward universal personal telecommunications and universal communications access. The first concept refers to the ability of a person to identify himself or herself easily and use conveniently any communication system in an entire country, over a continent, or even globally, in terms of a single account. The second refers to the capability of using one's terminal in a wide variety of environments to connect to information services (e.g., to have a portable terminal that will work in the office, on the street, and on airplanes equally well). This revolution in personal computing will obviously involve wireless communication in a fundamental way. The GSM cellular telephony with its subscriber identity module, for example, is a large step toward these goals.

Personal communication services (PCSs) and personal communication networks (PCNs) are names attached to these concepts of global wireless communications, and they also form objectives for third-generation wireless.

Generally, the technology planned is digital using time division multiple access or code division multiple access to provide efficient use of the spectrum and high capacity.

PCS handsets are designed to be low power and relatively small and light. Efforts are being made internationally to allow the same terminals to be used worldwide. Worldwide frequency allocations have been made for second-generation cordless telephones (CT-2) in the 800-MHz region and for more advanced personal communications in the 1.7- to 2.2-GHz band of the spectrum.

The 1992 World Administrative Radio Conference (WARC 92) resulted in worldwide allocations for future public land mobile telecommunications systems (FPLMTS). This concept includes both terrestrial and satellite-based services. In addition, allocations were made for low-earth-orbiting (LEO) satellite services that can be used to support personal communications.

Some proposed technologies that come under the umbrella of PCS are American Digital Cellular System, Japanese Digital Cellular System, second-generation cordless telephones (CT-2), the European community's Global System for Mobile communications (GSM) for digital cellular service, and Digital European Cordless Telephone (DECT). These involve advanced wireless telephony, which may be supported by LEO satellites and geostationary satellites, as well as by terrestrial antennas. The technology is developing rapidly. One desirable third-generation capability is mobile telephone and mobile terminals that can access Web services.

Wireless Application Protocol (WAP)

The Wireless Application Protocol (WAP) is a universal, open standard developed by the WAP Forum to provide mobile users of wireless phones and other wireless terminals such as pagers and personal digital assistants (PDAs) access to telephony and information services including the Internet and the Web. WAP is designed to work with all wireless network technologies (e.g., GSM, CDMA, and TDMA). It is also based on existing Internet standards, such as IP, XML, HTML, and HTTP, as much as possible. It also includes security facilities. Ericsson, Motorola, Nokia, and Phone.com established the WAP Forum in 1997, which now has several hundred members. The WAP Forum released v1.1 of WAP in June 1999.

Strongly affecting the use of mobile phones and terminals for data services are the significant limitations of the devices and the networks that connect them. The devices have limited processors, memory, and battery life. The user interface is also limited, and the displays small. The wireless networks are characterized by relatively low bandwidth, high latency, and unpredictable availability and stability compared to wired connections. Moreover, all these features vary widely from terminal device to terminal device and from network to network. Finally, mobile, wireless users have different expectations and needs from other information systems users. For instance, mobile terminals must be extremely easy to use, much easier than workstations and personal computers. WAP is designed to deal with these challenges.

The WAP specification includes the following:

- A programming model based on the WWW Programming Model
- A markup language, the Wireless Markup Language, adhering to XML
- A specification of a small browser suitable for a mobile, wireless terminal
- A lightweight communications protocol stack
- A framework for wireless telephony applications (WTAs)

The WAP Programming Model

The WAP Programming Model is based on three elements: the *client*, the *gateway*, and the *original server* (Figure 14.8). HTTP is used between the gateway and the original server to transfer content. The gateway acts as a proxy server for the wireless domain. Its processor(s) provide services that offload the limited capabilities of the hand-held, mobile, wireless terminals. For example, the gateway provides DNS services, converts between WAP protocol stack and the WWW stack (HTTP and TCP/IP), encodes information from the Web into a more compact form that

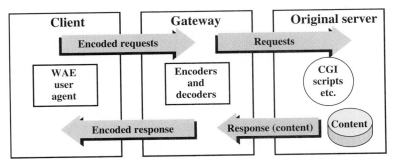

Figure 14.8 The WAP Programming Model

minimizes wireless communication, and, in the other direction, decodes the compacted form into standard Web communication conventions. The gateway also caches frequently requested information.

The Wireless Markup Language (WML)

WML does not assume a standard keyboard or a mouse as an input device. It is designed to work with telephone keypads, styluses, and other input devices common to mobile, wireless communication. WML documents are subdivided into small, well-defined units of user interaction called *cards*. Users navigate by moving back and forth between cards. WML uses a small set of markup tags appropriate to telephony-based systems.

The Microbrowser

The microbrowser is based on a user interface model appropriate for mobile, wireless devices. A traditional 12-key phone keypad is used to enter alphanumeric characters. Users navigate among the WML cards using up and down scroll keys rather than a mouse. Navigation features familiar from the Web (e.g., Back, Home, and Bookmark) are provided as well.

Wireless Telephony Applications (WTAs)

WTA provides an interface to the local and wide-area telephone systems. Thus, using WTA, applications developers can use the microbrowser to originate telephone calls and to respond to events from the telephone network.

A Sample Configuration

Figure 14.9 represents schematically a possible WAP configuration. There are three networks: the Internet (excluding the wireless net), the public switched telephone network (PSTN), and a wireless network based on, for example, GSM. The client could be a hand-held, mobile terminal in the wireless network. It communicates, in this example, with two gateways; one is the WAP Proxy to the Internet. The WAP Proxy communicates on the terminal's behalf with servers on the Internet. The Proxy translates HTML information to WML and sends it to the terminal. Material

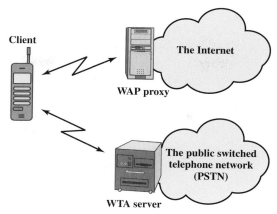

Figure 14.9 WAP Network Schematic

on the Internet already in WML format is passed directly to the terminal without translation. The other gateway, the WTA Server, is a gateway to the PSTN so that the WAP terminal can access telephony-based functionality such as call control, phone book access, and messaging through the microbrowser.

14.4 SATELLITE COMMUNICATIONS

Satellite communications is comparable in importance to optical fiber in the evolution of telecommunications and data communications.

The heart of a satellite communications system is a satellite-based antenna in a stable orbit above the earth. In a satellite communications system, two or more stations on or near the earth communicate via one or more satellites that serve as relay stations in space. The antenna systems on or near the earth are referred to as **earth stations**. A transmission from an earth station to the satellite is referred to as **uplink**, whereas transmissions from the satellite to the earth station are **downlink**. The electronics in the satellite that takes an uplink signal and converts it to a downlink signal is called a **transponder**.

Satellite Orbits

Geostationary Satellites The most common type of communications satellite today is the geostationary (GEO) satellite, first proposed by the science fiction author Arthur C. Clarke in 1945. If the satellite is in a circular orbit 35,863 km above the earth's surface and rotates in the equatorial plane of the earth, it will rotate at exactly the same angular speed as the earth and will remain above the same spot on the equator as the earth rotates.[4] Figure 14.10 depicts the

---

[4]The term *geosynchronous* is often used in place of *geostationary*. For purists, the difference is that a geosynchronous orbit is any circular orbit at an altitude of 35,863 km, and a geostationary orbit is a geosynchronous orbit with zero inclination, so the satellite hovers over one spot on the earth's equator.

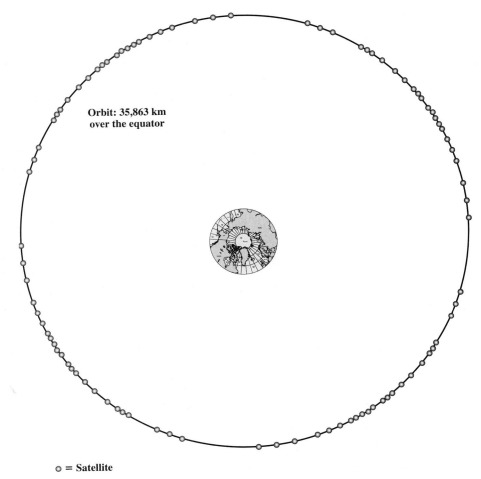

Figure 14.10   Geostationary Earth Orbit (GEO)

GEO orbit in scale with the size of the earth; the satellite symbols are intended to suggest that there are many satellites in GEO orbit, some of which are quite close to each other.

The GEO orbit has several advantages to recommend it:

- Because the satellite is stationary relative to the earth, there is no problem with frequency changes due to the relative motion of the satellite and antennas on earth (Doppler effect).
- Tracking of the satellite by its earth stations is simplified.
- At 35,863 km above the earth the satellite can communicate with roughly a fourth of the earth; three satellites in geostationary orbit separated by 120 cover most of the inhabited portions of the entire earth excluding only the areas near the north and south poles.

On the other hand, there are problems:

- The signal can get quite weak after traveling over 35,000 km.
- The polar regions and the far northern and southern hemispheres are poorly served by geostationary satellites.
- Even at the speed of light, about 300,000 km/s, the delay in sending a signal from a point on the equator beneath the satellite to the satellite and back is substantial.

The delay of communication between two locations on earth directly under the satellite is in fact $(2 \times 35{,}863)/300{,}000 \approx 0.24$ s. For other locations not directly under the satellite, the delay is even longer. If the satellite link is used for telephone communication, the added delay between when one person speaks and the other responds is increased twofold, to almost 0.5 s. This is definitely noticeable. Another feature of geostationary satellites is that they use their assigned frequencies over a very large area. For point-to-multipoint applications such as broadcasting TV programs, this can be desirable, but for point-to-point communications it is very wasteful of spectrum. Special spot and steered beam antennas, which restrict the area covered by the satellite's signal, can be used to control the "footprint" or signaling area. To solve some of these problems, orbits other than geostationary have been designed for satellites. *Low-earth-orbiting satellites (LEOS)* and *medium-earth-orbiting satellites (MEOS)* are important for third-generation personal communications.

LEO Satellites   LEOs (Figure 14.11a) have the following characteristics:

- Circular or slightly elliptical orbit at less than 2000 km. Proposed and actual systems are in the range 500 to 1500 km.
- The orbit period is in the range of 1.5 to 2 hours.
- The diameter of coverage is about 8000 km.
- Round-trip signal propagation delay is less than 20 ms.
- The maximum time that the satellite is visible from a fixed point on earth (above the radio horizon) is up to 20 minutes.
- Because the motion of the satellite relative to a fixed point on earth is high, the system must be able to cope with large Doppler shifts, which change the frequency of the signal.
- The atmospheric drag on a LEO satellite is significant, resulting in gradual orbital deterioration.

Practical use of this system requires that multiple orbital planes be used, each with multiple satellites in orbit. Communication between two earth stations typically will involve handing off the signal from one satellite to another.

LEO satellites have a number of advantages over GEO satellites. In addition to the reduced propagation delay mentioned previously, a received LEO signal is much stronger than that of GEO signals for the same transmission power. LEO coverage can be better localized so that spectrum can be better conserved. For this reason, this technology is currently being proposed for communicating with mobile terminals and with personal terminals that need stronger signals to function. On the other hand, to provide broad coverage over 24 hours, many satellites are needed.

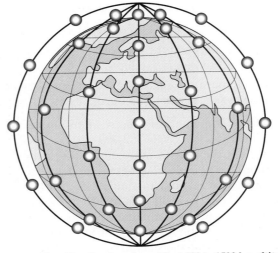

(a) Low earth orbit: often in polar orbit at 500 to 1500 km altitude

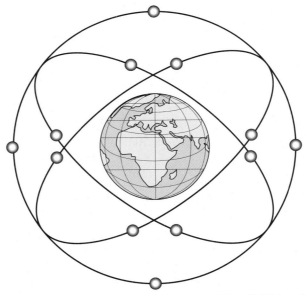

(b) Medium earth orbit: inclined to the equator, at 5000 to 12,000 km altitude

Figure 14.11   LEO and MEO Orbits

A number of commercial proposals have been made to use clusters of LEOs to provide communications services. These proposals can be divided into two categories:

- **Little LEOs:** Intended to work at communication frequencies below 1 GHz using no more than 5 MHz of bandwidth and supporting data rates up to 10 kbps. These systems are aimed at paging, tracking, and low-rate messaging.

Orbcomm is an example of such a satellite system. It was the first (little) LEO in operation; its first two satellites were launched in April of 1995. It is designed for paging and burst communication and is optimized for handling small bursts of data from 6 to 250 bytes in length. It is used by businesses to track trailers, railcars, heavy equipment, and other remote and mobile assets. It can also be used to monitor remote utility meters, oil and gas storage tanks, wells, and pipelines. It can be used to stay in touch with remote workers anywhere in the world as well. It uses frequencies in the range of 148.00 to 150.05 MHz to the satellites, and in the range of 137.00 to 138.00 MHz from the satellites. It has well over 30 satellites in low earth orbit. It supports subscriber data rates of 2.4 kbps to the satellite and 4.8 kbps down.

- **Big LEOs:** Work at frequencies above 1 GHz and support data rates up to a few megabits per second. These systems tend to offer the same services as those of small LEOs, with the addition of voice and positioning services. Globalstar is one example of a Big LEO system. Its satellites are fairly rudimentary. Unlike some of the little LEO systems, it has no onboard processing or communications between satellites. Most processing is done by the system's earth stations. It uses CDMA as in the CDMA cellular standard. It uses the S-Band (about 2 GHz) for the downlink to mobile users. Globalstar is tightly integrated with traditional voice carriers. All calls must be processed through earth stations. The satellite constellation consists of 48 operating satellites and 8 spares. They are in 1413-km-high orbits.

MEO Satellites

MEOs (Figure 14.11b) have the following characteristics:

- Circular orbit at an altitude in the range 5000 to 12,000 km.
- The orbit period is about 6 hours.
- The diameter of coverage is from 10,000 to 15,000 km.
- Round-trip signal propagation delay is less than 50 ms.
- The maximum time that the satellite is visible from a fixed point on earth (above the radio horizon) is a few hours.

MEO satellites require much fewer handoffs than LEO satellites. While propagation delay to earth from such satellites and the power required are greater than for LEOs, they are still substantially less than for GEO satellites. New ICO, established in January 1995, proposed a MEO system. Launches began in 2000. Twelve satellites, including two spares, are planned in 10,400-km-high orbits. The satellites will be divided equally between two planes tilted 45° to equator. Proposed applications are digital voice, data, facsimile, high-penetration notification, and messaging services.

Satellite Network Configurations

Figure 14.12 depicts in a general way two common configurations for satellite communication. In the first, the satellite is being used to provide a point-to-point link between two distant ground-based antennas. In the second, the satellite provides communications between one ground-based transmitter and a number of ground-based receivers.

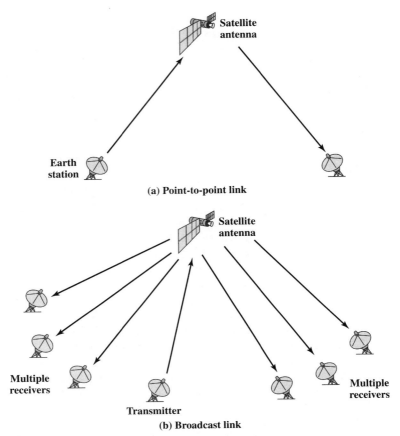

Figure 14.12 Satellite Communication Configurations

Applications

The communications satellite is a technological revolution as important as fiber optics. Among the most important applications for satellites are the following:

- Television distribution
- Long-distance telephone transmission
- Private business networks

Because of their broadcast nature, satellites are well suited to television distribution and are being used extensively for this purpose in the United States and throughout the world. In its traditional use, a network provides programming from a central location. Programs are transmitted to the satellite and then broadcast down to a number of stations, which then distribute the programs to individual viewers. A more recent application of satellite technology to television distribution is direct broadcast satellite (DBS), in which satellite video signals are transmitted directly to the home user.

Satellite transmission is also used for point-to-point trunks between telephone exchange offices in public telephone networks. It is a useful medium for high-usage

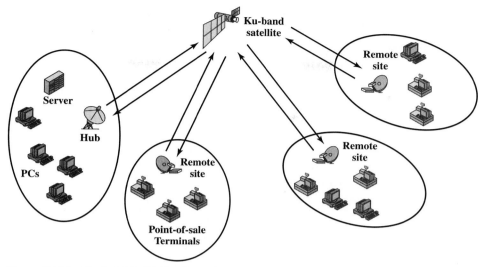

Figure 14.13   Typical VSAT Configuration

international trunks and is competitive with terrestrial systems for many long-distance intranational links, particularly in remote and undeveloped areas.

Finally, there are a number of business data applications for satellite. The satellite provider can divide the total capacity into a number of channels and lease these channels to individual business users. A user equipped with antennas at a number of sites can use a satellite channel for a private network. Traditionally, such applications have been quite expensive and limited to larger organizations with high-volume requirements. Today, the very small aperture terminal (VSAT) system provides a low-cost alternative. Figure 14.13 depicts a typical VSAT configuration. A number of subscriber stations are equipped with low-cost VSAT antennas. Using some discipline, these stations share a satellite transmission capacity for transmission to a hub station. The hub station can exchange messages with each of the subscribers and can relay messages between subscribers.

APPLICATION NOTE
PDAs, Cell Phones, and Laptops — Oh My!

Businesses are faced with several questions regarding computing resources. While it is common for an organization to purchase dozens or even hundreds of desktop computers, occasionally organizations must also make mobile computing decisions. The choices really depend on the application or use for which the device is intended. More than one company has stretched its budget by buying devices that are over powered for the application or left to gather dust because they are unsatisfactory for the defined tasks. In order to make the right decision, some analysis for the right device must be undertaken.

Laptops are probably the first option that comes to mind when we think of mobile devices. Laptops have a great deal of processing power, memory, and hard drive capacity. Most laptops now come with built in wireless connectivity that makes them even more attractive. Combined with a docking station, this type of computer can double as a desktop station. As attractive as they are, laptops do have a darker side. Many users opt to have larger monitors, extended keyboards, and an extra mouse when working in desktop mode. This indicates that laptops are sometimes more difficult to use because of the keyboard style and type of built in mouse. Another possible downside to laptop purchases, if the laptop is actually used as mobile station, is that batteries rarely behave as advertised. Every activity drains the battery further, and the true mobile user must become familiar with power-saving settings. In the end, for a user who requires processing and storage capacity and easy access to all of his or her files when moving from home to the office, the laptop may represent the best solution.

Handhelds or personal data assistants (PDAs) are another solution to mobile connectivity. Palm Pilots, Handspring Visors, and Blackberries are among the most popular. All handhelds boast a wide variety of tools, including e-mail, image viewing, and calendaring. General use PDA applications seem to pop up daily in addition to those developed locally by an organization. Connectivity to PDA is usually accomplished via a packet radio system (that runs over a local cellular provider network) like the general packet radio service or GPRS.

PDAs represent a compact, highly portable data access device that can upload data from or download data to a computer. PDAs can be a solid asset where a limited number of applications are needed and document generation is not required. A good example is the legal industry, where lawyers previously outfitted with laptops had them replaced with handheld devices. This was a good match because the attorneys did not need to generate their own documents. Their real requirement was staying in contact with the office via e-mail. As a result, the firms realized significant savings and the lawyers were not burdened with the heavier laptop.

A PDA is not a replacement for a laptop as it does not have the required processing capability or storage capacity. While this is improving, there is also the question of usability. Working with a stylus or miniature keyboard can be a frustrating experience. However, for the determined PDA user, folding keyboards are also available. In fact, PDAs can be equipped with an impressive array of add-on devices, including wireless or wired local area network connection modules.

Cell phones are our third mobile connectivity option and are beginning to provide some value-added services, such as messaging or two-way radio. While the services offered in the United States are nowhere near the level of those offered in other countries, they are improving. The real strength of the cell phone lies in its anywhere, anytime voice connectivity. While a PDA can connect over the same network, the packet data service is not always available and support for voice is not at its best. The same is true for laptop voice support. In addition to the value-added services, cell phones are also beginning to show signs of applications for the end user; however, the applications currently seem to be more geared toward entertainment than a business model. Examples of additional cell phone capabilities include games, video, still images, and push technologies such as sporting news and weather.

As is often the case, we must first ask ourselves, "What are we trying to do?" or "What do we need to do?" Once these questions are answered it is usually easier to find a solution that fits the needs of the organization. PDAs and cell phones, while often considered necessary tools, are not usually a replacement for a laptop or desktop computer. For sheer portability, it is often much more feasible to carry around a wallet-size device rather than a tablet-size one. On the other hand, there is a big difference between wanting and needing, especially where the bottom line is concerned. Companies would be well advised to look at usage patterns before and after PDA or cell phone purchases to determine if they are indeed necessary. Even if the power of a laptop is currently the best solution, improvements in cell phones and PDAs can have us pondering which device we will use for the next generation of connectivity.

14.5 SUMMARY

Cellular wireless networks have traditionally supported mobile telephony but now also support wireless Internet access and other wireless data networking applications. Cellular networks are becoming pervasive worldwide and carry an increasing portion of long-distance voice and data traffic. A cellular system is based on the principle of using a large number of relatively small geographic areas, called cells, to cover a large area. Each cell is allocated a band of frequencies and is served by a base station, consisting of transmitter, receiver, and control unit. Adjacent cells are assigned different frequencies to avoid interference or crosstalk. However, cells sufficiently distant from each other can use the same frequency band.

The capacity available within each cell is shared among a number of users by means of some sort of multiple access scheme. For a given system, multiple access is based on TDMA, FDMA, CDMA, or some combination of these.

Another important form of wireless communications is satellite communications. The bulk of satellite traffic has traditionally been carried by geostationary satellites. Recently, networks using LEO and MEO satellites have been introduced.

14.6 RECOMMENDED READING AND WEB SITES

The topics in this chapter are covered in greater depth in [STAL02a]. An excellent survey text is [RAPP02]. For a detailed technical treatment of wireless transmission and communications, see [FREE97].

FREE97 Freeman, R. *Radio System Design for Telecommunications.* New York: Wiley, 1997.

RAPP02 Rappaport, T., *Wireless Communications: Principles and Practice.* Upper Saddle River, NJ: Prentice Hall, 2002.

STAL02a Stallings, W. *Wireless Communications and Networks.* Upper Saddle River, NJ: Prentice Hall, 2002.

Recommended Web Sites:

- **Cellular Telecommunications and Internet Association:** An industry consortium that provides information on successful applications of wireless technology.
- **3G Americas:** A trade group of Western Hemisphere companies supporting a variety of second and third-generation schemes. Includes industry news, white papers, and other technical information.
- **Lloyd Wood's satellite Web page:** An excellent overview of satellite communications, with lots of links.
- **Satellite Industry Association:** Trade organization representing U.S. space and communications companies in the commercial satellite arena. Lots of links.

14.7 KEY TERMS, REVIEW QUESTIONS, AND PROBLEMS

Key Terms

base station	frequency division multiple	space division multiple
cell sectoring	access (FDMA)	access (SDMA)
cell splitting	frequency reuse	time division multiple access
cellular wireless network	geostationary satellite	(TDMA)
code division multiple access	low-earth-orbiting (LEO)	transponder
(CDMA)	satellite	uplink
communications satellite	medium-earth-orbiting	wireless application protocol
direct sequence spread spec-	(MEO) satellite	(WAP)
trum (DSSS)	microcells	wireless markup language
downlink	multiple access	(WML)
earth station	reuse factor	

Review Questions

14.1. What geometric shape is used in cellular system design?

14.2. What is the principle of frequency reuse in the context of a cellular network?

14.3. List five ways of increasing the capacity of a cellular system.

14.4. Explain the paging function of a cellular system.

14.5. What is cellular handoff?

14.6. For a cellular system, describe the function of the following: control channels and traffic channels.

14.7. Describe what is meant by the term *multiple access* as it applies to cellular communication.

14.8. Briefly explain the principle behind CDMA.

14.9. What is the wireless application protocol (WAP)?

14.10. Explain what GEOS, LEOS, and MEOS satellites are (including what the acronyms stand for). Compare the three types with respect to factors such as size and shape of orbits, signal power, frequency reuse, propagation delay, number of satellites for global coverage, and handoff frequency.

14.11. Under what circumstances would you use GEOS, LEOS, and MEOS, respectively?

Problems

14.1 There are many cellular providers serving each geographic area and each one may use a different technology.
  a. Who are the providers in your area and what are the multiple access technologies used?
  b. What are the technologies behind the cellular phones you or your family and friends use?

14.2 Consider four different cellular systems that share the following characteristics. The frequency bands are 825 to 845 MHz for mobile unit transmission and 870 to 890 MHz for base station transmission. A duplex circuit consists of one 30-kHz channel in each direction. The systems are distinguished by the reuse factor, which is 4, 7, 12, and 19, respectively.
  a. Suppose that in each of the systems, the cluster of cells (4, 7, 12, 19) is duplicated 16 times. Find the number of simultaneous communications that can be supported by each system.
  b. Find the number of simultaneous communications that can be supported by a single cell in each system.
  c. What is the area covered, in cells, by each system?
  d. Suppose the cell size is the same in all four systems and a fixed area of 100 cells is covered by each system. Find the number of simultaneous communications that can be supported by each system.

14.3 Describe a sequence of events similar to that of Figure 14.5 for
  a. a call from a mobile unit to a fixed subscriber
  b. a call from a fixed subscriber to a mobile unit

14.4 An analog cellular system has a total of 33 MHz of bandwidth and uses two 25-kHz simplex (one-way) channels to provide full-duplex voice and control channels.
  a. What is the number of channels available per cell for a frequency reuse factor of (1) 4 cells, (2) 7 cells, and (3) 12 cells?
  b. Assume that 1 MHz is dedicated to control channels but that only one control channel is needed per cell. Determine a reasonable distribution of control channels and voice channels in each cell for the three frequency reuse factors of part (a).

14.5 A cellular system uses FDMA with a spectrum allocation of 12.5 MHz in each direction, a guard band at the edge of the allocated spectrum of 10 kHz, and a channel bandwidth of 30 kHz. What is the number of available channels?

14.6 For a cellular system, FDMA spectral efficiency is defined as $\eta_a = \dfrac{B_c N_T}{B_w}$, where

  B_c = channel bandwidth

  B_w = total bandwidth in one direction

  N_T = total number of voice channels in the covered area

  What is an upper bound on η_a?

14.7 Global System for Mobile communications (GSM) is an international standard for digital cellular communication. Provide a basic overview of GSM, focusing on the three primary functional entities of a GSM network. Is the GSM strategy a superior or inferior alternative to CDMA? Support your answer.

14.8   Some concern has been expressed regarding potential health hazards related to cellular phone use. Discuss potential health risks related to cellular phone technology. What precautions can be taken to minimize potential dangers involved in cell phone use?

Case Study IX: Choice Hotels International

Within the hospitality industry, there has traditionally been a division between networks that serve guest functions and those that serve operations and administration, both with respect to data transmission and voice transmission. In recent years, most hotel and motel chains have moved in the direction of consolidating multiple functions on networks that used to be dedicated to one use. Tighter integration of voice and data and of guest and operations/administration networking is a fast-growing trend. Choice Hotels International is a good example of this trend [HARL02, DORN01, UHLA00].

Choice Hotels International is the world's second largest hotel franchise, with enough beds for about a million people. The company franchises more than 5000 hotels, inns, all-suite hotels, and resorts open and under development in 48 countries under the Comfort Inn, Comfort Suites, Quality, Clarion, Sleep Inn, Rodeway Inn, Econo Lodge, and MainStay Suites brands.

Choice supports two distinct networking functions. A central Web site enables customers to reserve rooms at any Choice franchise accommodation. The central reservation system, known as Profit Manager, automatically finds the most appropriate hotel based on location, price range, or standard. Individual hotels also take bookings, so there needs to be a way for hotels and the central system to remain synchronized.

Choice networks also support its franchisees. Choice is in fact a relatively small company in terms of personnel (about 2000 employees) and does not own or operate any hotels. All of the establishments under its brand names are independently own and pay Choice licensing fees and a royalty on all sales. In return, they receive a variety of services, including marketing, quality control, and inventory management. Many of these services are offered via network, such as allowing managers to order supplies online and check booking status. This support network is similar to a corporate intranet but has a higher reliability requirement. The 5000 hotel managers are, in effect, Choice's customers, not employees. Thus, the standards for reliability and performance of the network are high.

In the late 1990s, Choice began to focus on providing a state-of-the-art global reservation system. At this point, the synchronization of local and online reservations was done manually. Each hotel provided Choice with a fixed block of inventory to sell over the central reservation system, with an average of 30% of capacity. Once that 30% was sold, Profit Manager listed the hotel as fully booked, even though there might be plenty of rooms available from the other 70%. The reverse problem also occurred: If the local reservation system had sold all available rooms except those assigned to Choice, the local staff had to refuse additional customers or overbook. Thus, the system was inherently inefficient.

Around this time, Choice moved from a purely telephone-based central reservation system to a Web-based system. Choice found, as did many companies, that letting customers serve themselves online saved time and money. Further, unlike many industries burned in the move to e-commerce, the travel sector is an ideal match for Web-based services. Booking a hotel room has always been done remotely, via telephone. There are none of the fulfillment problems that have plagued the online mail-order business, because there are no shipping costs and no shipping and delivery hassles. And the benefits are striking. Customers can get an instant list of every room available with their chosen criteria. They can also view the hotel and, in some cases, the individual room. In addition, hotel rooms are a typical example of "distressed" products; like airline seats and theater tickets, they can't be stockpiled if left unsold. Thus, they are ideal for using last-minute special offers and promotions, which can be posted online or e-mailed to interested customers.

But all of these benefits require full integration between local reservation systems and the central reservation system. Choice decided to implement a franchise-wide IP network that provided every American hotel with a permanent connection to the central Profit Manager database. The most important criteria for this network were coverage and reliability. The network needed to reach every franchise and needed to be highly available. Capacity was not a particular concern, because updates and reservations use little capacity.

To meet its needs, Choice decided to go with a satellite network. Even within the United States, reliable universal coverage requires expensive leased lines or dependence on switched networks that may not always deliver. The situation is far worse internationally. Satellite networks provide the universal coverage and are in fact more reliable than the competition. Satellites that use fixed dishes are a mature, dependable technology. Downtime averages only minutes each year.

For its initial effort, Choice went to Hughes Network Systems, who set up a dedicated IP network using two geostationary satellites based at separate hubs (Figure IX.1). The hub is a ground-based control center that includes a number of switches and routers. At the hub, Hughes separates Choice's traffic from that of its other customers and routes it accordingly. The Los Angeles hub covers the entire United States via a broad-beam satellite service. The Germantown hub controls a number of narrower spot beams that service Alaska, Hawaii, and provides extra capacity for major cities. Each hotel is equipped with a VSAT dish.

The satellite system has worked well, and Choice has gradually transition operational and administrative functions to the network. For example, data for settling accounts with travel agents and tracking the Choice Privilege frequent-stayer program are sent on the satellite network.

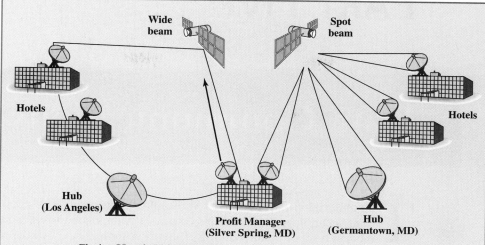

Figure IX.1 Choice Hotels U.S. Network

Discussion Questions

1. Perhaps the major drawback to a satellite-based system is latency. The delays can be noticeable on some online applications. Discuss what issues this might raise for the Choice suite of applications.

2. What issues would you expect to arise as Choice moves to expand the network to full global reach?

PART FIVE

Data Communications

The material in Part Five deals with fundamental aspects of communications technology. In a business context it is important to have at least a modest level of understanding of these technologies to be able to assess various products and services. However, in most cases, the choices facing the decision maker do not boil down to a simple selection of a technology but rather to a product or service that exploits a variety of technologies. Thus, it is only in other chapters (Part Four onward) of this book that we are able to relate effectively the concepts being discussed to the needs of the business.

Chapter 15 Data Transmission

The principles of data transmission underlie all of the concepts and techniques presented in this book. To understand the need for encoding, multiplexing, switching, error control, and so on, the reader should understand the behavior of data signals propagated through a transmission medium. Chapter 15 discusses the distinction between digital and analog data and digital and analog transmission. Concepts of attenuation and noise are also examined.

Chapter 16 Data Communication Fundamentals

The transmission of information across a transmission medium involves more than simply inserting a signal on the medium. Chapter 16 discusses a number of data communications concepts, including analog versus digital transmission, data encoding techniques, and the distinction between asynchronous and synchronous transmission. This chapter also deals with the topic of error detection.

Chapter 17 Data Link Control and Multiplexing

True cooperative exchange of digital data between two devices requires some form of data link control. Chapter 17 examines the fundamental techniques common to all data link control protocols, including flow control and error control, and then examines the most commonly used protocol, HDLC. Chapter 17 discusses the two most common types of multiplexing techniques. The first, frequency division multiplexing (FDM), is the most widespread and is familiar to anyone who has ever used a radio or television set. The second is a particular case of time division multiplexing (TDM) often known as synchronous TDM. This is commonly used for multiplexing digitized voice streams.

CHAPTER 15

DATA TRANSMISSION

In this book we are concerned with one particular means for communicating information: the transmission of electromagnetic waves. All of the forms of information that we have discussed (audio, data, image, video) can be represented by electromagnetic signals and transmitted over a suitable transmission medium.

We first look at the types of electromagnetic signals that are used to convey information. In doing so we describe the most straightforward way in which each of the four types of information can be represented. Then we discuss the sad fact that such transmission is subject to impairments that can introduce errors and inefficiencies. Following this discussion, we can arrive at an understanding of the concept of channel capacity.

15.1 SIGNALS FOR CONVEYING INFORMATION

Electromagnetic Signals

Information is transmitted by means of electromagnetic signals. An electromagnetic signal is a function of time, but it can also be expressed as a function of frequency; that is, the signal consists of components of different frequencies. It turns out that the frequency domain view of a signal is far more important to an understanding of data transmission than a time domain view. Both views are introduced here.

Time Domain Concepts Viewed as a function of time, an electromagnetic signal can be either analog or digital. An **analog signal** is one in which the signal intensity varies in a smooth fashion over time. In other words, there are no breaks or discontinuities in the signal. A **digital signal** is one in which the signal intensity maintains a constant level for some period of time and then changes to another constant level. Figure 15.1 shows examples of both kinds of signals. The analog signal might represent speech, and the digital signal might represent binary 1s and 0s.

The simplest sort of signal is a **periodic signal,** in which the same signal pattern repeats over time. Figure 15.2 shows an example of a periodic analog signal (sine wave) and a periodic digital signal (square wave). The sine wave is the fundamental analog signal. A general sine wave can be represented by three parameters: peak amplitude (A), frequency (f), and phase (ϕ). The **peak amplitude** is the maximum

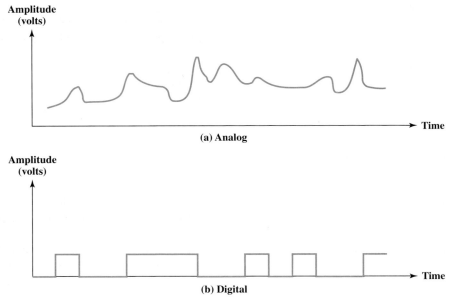

Figure 15.1   Analog and Digital Waveforms

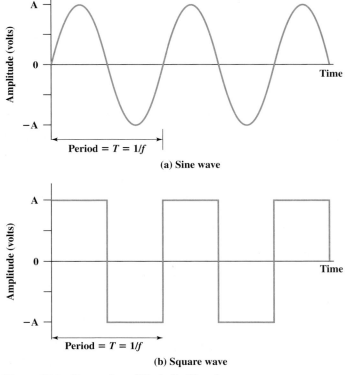

Figure 15.2   Examples of Periodic Signals

value or strength of the signal over time; typically, this value is measured in volts. The **frequency** is the rate [in cycles per second, or hertz (Hz)] at which the signal repeats. An equivalent parameter is the **period** (T) of a signal, which is the amount of time it takes for one repetition; therefore, $T = 1/f$. **Phase** is a measure of the relative position in time within a single period of a signal, as illustrated later.

The general sine wave can be written

$$s(t) = A \sin(2\pi ft + \phi)$$

Figure 15.3 shows the effect of varying each of the three parameters. In part (a) of the figure, the frequency is 1 Hz; thus the period is $T = 1$ second. Part (b) has the same frequency and phase but a peak amplitude of 0.5. In part (c) we have $f = 2$, which is equivalent to $T = 1/2$. Finally, part (d) shows the effect of a phase shift of $\pi/4$ radians, which is 45 degrees (2π radians $= 360° = 1$ period).

In Figure 15.3 the horizontal axis is time; the graphs display the value of a signal at a given point in space as a function of time. These same graphs, with a change of scale, can apply with horizontal axes in space. In this case the graphs display the value of a signal at a given point in time as a function of distance. For example, for a sinusoidal transmission (say, an electromagnetic radio wave some distance from a radio antenna or a sound some distance from loudspeaker) at a particular instant of time, the intensity of the signal varies in a sinusoidal way as a function of distance from the source.

There is a simple relationship between the two sine waves, one in time and one in space. The **wavelength** (λ) of a signal is defined as the distance occupied by a sin-

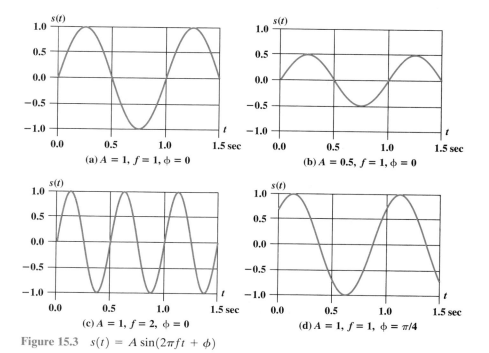

Figure 15.3 $s(t) = A \sin(2\pi ft + \phi)$

gle cycle, or put another way, the distance between two points of corresponding phase of two consecutive cycles. Assume that the signal is traveling with a velocity v. Then the wavelength is related to the period as follows: $\lambda = vT$. Equivalently, $\lambda f = v$. Of particular relevance to this discussion is the case where $v = c$, the speed of light in free space, which is approximately 3×10^8 m/s.

Frequency Domain Concepts In practice, an electromagnetic signal will be made up of many frequencies. For example, the signal

$$s(t) = (4/\pi) \times (\sin(2\pi ft) + (1/3)\sin(2\pi(3f)t))$$

is shown in Figure 15.4c. The components of this signal are just sine waves of frequencies f and $3f$; parts (a) and (b) of the figure show these individual components. There are two interesting points that can be made about this figure:

- The second frequency is an integer multiple of the first frequency. When all of the frequency components of a signal are integer multiples of one frequency, the latter frequency is referred to as the **fundamental frequency.**

- The period of the total signal is equal to the period of the fundamental frequency. The period of the component $\sin(2\pi ft)$ is $T = 1/f$, and the period of $s(t)$ is also T, as can be seen from Figure 15.4c.

By adding together enough sinusoidal signals, each with the appropriate amplitude, frequency, and phase, any electromagnetic signal can be constructed. Put another way, any electromagnetic signal can be shown to consist of a collection of periodic analog signals (sine waves) at different amplitudes, frequencies, and phases. The importance of being able to look at a signal from the frequency perspective (frequency domain) rather than a time perspective (time domain) should become clear as the discussion proceeds.

The **spectrum** of a signal is the range of frequencies that it contains. For the signal of Figure 15.4c, the spectrum extends from f to $3f$. The absolute bandwidth of a signal is the width of the spectrum. In the case of Figure 15.4c, the bandwidth is $3f - f = 2f$. Many signals have an infinite bandwidth. However, most of the energy in the signal is contained in a relatively narrow band of frequencies. This band is referred to as the effective bandwidth, or just **bandwidth.**

There is a direct relationship between the information-carrying capacity of a signal and its bandwidth: The greater the bandwidth, the higher the information-carrying capacity. As a very simple example, consider the square wave of Figure 15.2b. Suppose that we let a positive pulse represent binary 0 and a negative pulse represent binary 1. Then the waveform represents the binary stream 0101. ... The duration of each pulse is $1/(2f)$; thus the data rate is $2f$ bits per second (bps). What are the frequency components of this signal? To answer this question, consider again Figure 15.4. By adding together sine waves at frequencies f and $3f$, we get a waveform that begins to resemble the original square wave. Let us continue this process by adding a sine wave of frequency $5f$, as shown in Figure 15.5a, and then adding a sine wave of frequency $7f$, as shown in Figure 15.5b. As we add additional odd multiples of f, suitably scaled, the resulting waveform approaches that of a square wave more and more closely.

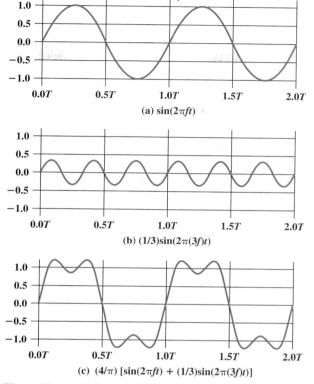

Figure 15.4   Addition of Frequency Components $(T = 1/f)$

Indeed, it can be shown that the frequency components of the square wave with amplitudes A and $-A$ can be expressed as follows:

$$s(t) = A \times \frac{4}{\pi} \times \sum_{k \text{ odd},k=1}^{\infty} \frac{\sin(2\pi k f t)}{k}$$

Thus, this waveform has an infinite number of frequency components and hence an infinite bandwidth. However, the peak amplitude of the kth frequency component, kf, is only $1/k$, so most of the energy in this waveform is in the first few frequency components. What happens if we limit the bandwidth to just the first three frequency components? We have already seen the answer, in Figure 15.5a. As we can see, the shape of the resulting waveform is reasonably close to that of the original square wave.

We can use Figures 15.4 and 15.5 to illustrate the relationship between data rate and bandwidth. Suppose that we are using a digital transmission system that is capable of transmitting signals with a bandwidth of 4 MHz. Let us attempt to transmit a sequence of alternating 1s and 0s as the square wave of Figure 15.5c. What data rate can be achieved? We look at three cases.

Case I. Let us approximate our square wave with the waveform of Figure 15.5a. Although this waveform is a "distorted" square wave, it is sufficiently close to

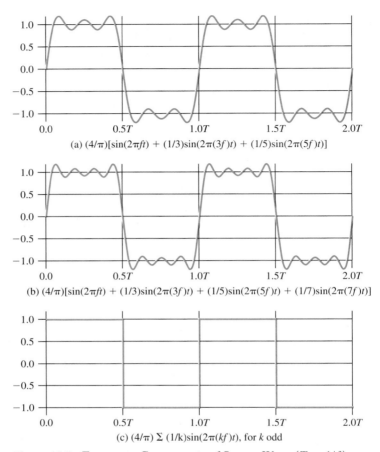

(a) $(4/\pi)[\sin(2\pi ft) + (1/3)\sin(2\pi(3f)t) + (1/5)\sin(2\pi(5f)t)]$

(b) $(4/\pi)[\sin(2\pi ft) + (1/3)\sin(2\pi(3f)t) + (1/5)\sin(2\pi(5f)t) + (1/7)\sin(2\pi(7f)t)]$

(c) $(4/\pi)\ \Sigma\ (1/k)\sin(2\pi(kf)t)$, for k odd

Figure 15.5   Frequency Components of Square Wave $(T = 1/f)$

the square wave that a receiver should be able to discriminate between a binary 0 and a binary 1. If we let $f = 10^6$ cycles/second $= 1$ MHz, then the bandwidth of the signal

$$s(t) = \frac{4}{\pi} \times \left[\sin((2\pi \times 10^6)t) + \frac{1}{3}\sin((2\pi \times 3 \times 10^6)t) \right.$$
$$\left. + \frac{1}{5}\sin((2\pi \times 5 \times 10^6)t) \right]$$

is $(5 \times 10^6) - 10^6 = 4$ MHz. Note that for $f = 1$ MHz, the period of the fundamental frequency is $T = 1/10^6 = 10^{-6} = 1\ \mu$s. If we treat this waveform as a bit string of 1s and 0s, one bit occurs every 0.5 μs, for a data rate of $2 \times 10^6 = 2$ Mbps. Thus, for a bandwidth of 4 MHz, a data rate of 2 Mbps is achieved.

Case II.   Now suppose that we have a bandwidth of 8 MHz. Let us look again at Figure 15.5a, but now with $f = 2$ MHz. Using the same line of reasoning as before, the bandwidth of the signal is $(5 \times 2 \times 10^6) - (2 \times 10^6) = 8$ MHz. But in this case $T = 1/f = 0.5\,\mu$s. As a result, one bit occurs every $0.25\,\mu$s for a data rate of 4 Mbps. Thus, other things being equal, by doubling the bandwidth, we double the potential data rate.

Case III. Now suppose that the waveform of Figure 15.4c is considered adequate for approximating a square wave. That is, the difference between a positive and negative pulse in Figure 15.4c is sufficiently distinct that the waveform can be successfully used to represent a sequence of 1s and 0s. Assume as in Case II that $f = 2$ MHz and $T = 1/f = 0.5\,\mu$s, so that one bit occurs every $0.25\,\mu$s for a data rate of 4 Mbps. Using the waveform of Figure 15.4c, the bandwidth of the signal is $(3 \times 2 \times 10^6) - (2 \times 10^6) = 4$ MHz. Thus, a given bandwidth can support various data rates depending on the ability of the receiver to discern the difference between 0 and 1 in the presence of noise and other impairments.

To summarize,

- **Case I:** Bandwidth = 4 MHz; data rate = 2 Mbps
- **Case II:** Bandwidth = 8 MHz; data rate = 4 Mbps
- **Case III:** Bandwidth = 4 MHz; data rate = 4 Mbps

We can draw the following conclusions from the preceding discussion. In general, any digital waveform will have infinite bandwidth. If we attempt to transmit this waveform as a signal over any medium, the transmission system will limit the bandwidth that can be transmitted. Furthermore, for any given medium, the greater the bandwidth transmitted, the greater the cost. Thus, on the one hand, economic and practical reasons dictate that digital information be approximated by a signal of limited bandwidth. On the other hand, limiting the bandwidth creates distortions, which makes the task of interpreting the received signal more difficult. The more limited the bandwidth, the greater the distortion and the greater the potential for error by the receiver.

Analog Signals

Audio Signals Just as an analog signal is one whose value varies in a continuous fashion, we can say that analog information is information that takes on continuous values. The most familiar example of analog information is audio, or acoustic, information, which, in the form of sound waves, can be perceived directly by human beings. One form of acoustic information, of course, is human speech, which has frequency components in the range 20 Hz to 20 kHz. This form of information is easily converted to an electromagnetic signal for transmission (Figure 15.6). In essence, all of the sound frequencies, whose amplitude is measured in terms of loudness, are converted into electromagnetic frequencies, whose amplitude is measured in volts. The telephone handset contains a simple mechanism for making such a conversion.

Thus, the voice sound wave can be represented directly by an electromagnetic signal occupying the same spectrum. However, there is a need to compromise between the fidelity of the sound as transmitted electromagnetically and the cost of transmission, which increases with increasing bandwidth. Although, as mentioned, human speech has a spectrum of 20 Hz to 20 kHz, tests have shown that a much

In this graph of a typical analog signal, the variations in amplitude and frequency convey the gradations of loudness and pitch in speech or music. Similar signals are used to transmit television pictures, but at much higher frequencies.

Figure 15.6   Conversion of Voice Input to Analog Signal

narrower bandwidth, the range 300 to 3400 Hz, will produce acceptable voice reproduction. That is, if the frequency components outside that range are subtracted, the remainder sounds quite natural. For this reason, telephone networks are able to use communication facilities that limit the transmission of sound to that narrower bandwidth (Figure 15.7). This reduction in the capacity requirement for the transmission of speech results in a corresponding reduction in the cost of the facility.

Note from Figure 15.7 that the actual bandwidth used by the telephone transmission facility is 4 kHz, not 3.1 kHz. The extra bandwidth serves the purpose of isolating the audio signal from interference from signals in adjacent bandwidths.[1] For transmission, then, the telephone handset converts the incoming voice-produced sound wave into an analog electromagnetic signal over the range 300 to 3400 Hz. This signal is then transmitted over the telephone system to a telephone receiver, which reproduces a sound wave from the incoming electromagnetic signal.

Video Signals   To produce a video signal, a TV camera, which performs similar functions to the TV receiver, is used. One component of the camera is a photosensitive plate, upon which a scene is optically focused. An electron beam sweeps across

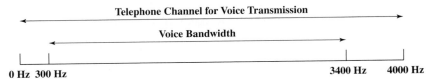

The human voice creates waves of many frequencies, but natural-sounding speech can be limited to a frequency range, or band, of 300 to 3400 Hz. Telephone equipment allows voice a bandwidth of 4000 Hz, which includes a guardband at each end of the frequency range to prevent interference from adjacent voice channels when a number of voice channels are multiplexed.

Figure 15.7   The Voice Band

---

[1]We show in Chapter 17 that it is common to have a number of signals occupy the same transmission medium at different portions of the spectrum, a process known as multiplexing. The extra bandwidth, or guardbands, prevent adjacent signals from interfering with one another.

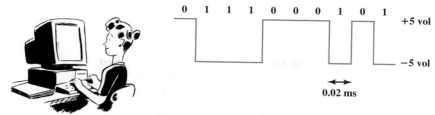

0 1 1 1 0 0 0 1 0 1

+5 vol

−5 vol

0.02 ms

User input at a PC is converted into a stream of binary
digits (1s and 0s). In this graph of a typical digital signal,
binary one is represented by −5 volts and binary zero is
represented by +5 volts. The signal for each bit has a duration
of 0.02 ms, giving a data rate of 50,000 bits per second (50 kbps

Figure 15.8   Conversion of PC Input to Digital Signal

the plate from left to right and top to bottom, in the same fashion as depicted in
Figure 2.4 for the receiver. As the beam sweeps, an analog electric signal is developed proportional to the brightness of the scene at a particular spot. A total of 483
lines are scanned at a rate of 30 complete scans per second. This is an approximate
number taking into account the time lost during the vertical retrace interval. The
actual U.S. standard is 525 lines, but of these about 42 are lost during vertical retrace.
Thus the horizontal scanning frequency is (525 lines)×(30 scans/s) = 15,750 lines
per second, or 63.5 μs/line. Of this 63.5 μs, about 11 μs are allowed for horizontal
retrace, leaving a total of 52.5 μs per video line.

To transmit analog video information at the necessary rate, a bandwidth of
about 4 MHz is needed. As with voice transmission over the telephone network,
video signaling over cable TV or via broadcast involves the use of extra bandwidth
or guardbands to isolate video signals. With these guardbands, the standard bandwidth for color video signaling is 6 MHz.

Digital Signals

The term *digital signaling* usually refers to the transmission of electromagnetic
pulses that represent the two binary digits, 1 and 0. For example, a constant positive
voltage pulse could represent binary 0 and a constant negative voltage pulse could
represent binary 1. Another alternative is to have one binary digit represented by a
constant voltage pulse and the other represented by the absence of any voltage. In
either case, what is being represented is binary information. Binary information is
generated by terminals, computers, and other data processing equipment and then
converted into digital voltage pulses for transmission, as illustrated in Figure 15.8. In
the context of this book, the data in which we are interested are in the form of numbers or text. In either case, we must convert this information into binary form; in
binary form, it can then be converted into a digital signal.

For humans, numbers are represented in decimal form. In the decimal system,
10 different digits are used to represent numbers. The position of each digit in a
number determines its value. Thus, the decimal number 83 means eight tens plus
three:

$$83 = (8 \times 10) + 3$$

and the number 4728 means

$$4728 = (4 \times 1000) + (7 \times 100) + (2 \times 10) + 8$$

The decimal system is said to have a base of 10. This means that each digit in the number is multiplied by 10 raised to a power corresponding to that digit's position. Thus,

$$83 = (8 \times 10^1) + 3$$
$$4728 = (4 \times 10^3) + (7 \times 10^2) + (2 \times 10^1) + 8$$

In the binary system, we have only two digits, 1 and 0. Thus, numbers in the binary system are represented to the base 2. As with decimal notation, each digit in a binary number has a value depending on its position:

$$10 = (1 \times 2) + 0 = \text{decimal } 2$$
$$11 = (1 \times 2) + 1 = \text{decimal } 3$$
$$100 = (1 \times 2^2) + (0 \times 2) + 0 = \text{decimal } 4$$

where the first number on each line is a binary number. The binary notation can be extended to represent fractional values and negative numbers. The details are not of concern here.

15.2 TRANSMISSION IMPAIRMENTS AND CHANNEL CAPACITY

With any communications system, the signal that is received will differ from the signal that is transmitted, due to various transmission impairments. For analog signals, these impairments introduce various random modifications that degrade the signal quality. For digital signals, bit errors are introduced: A binary 1 is transformed into a binary 0, and vice versa. In this section we examine the various impairments and comment on their effect on the information-carrying capacity of a communications link; Chapter 16 looks at measures that can be taken to compensate for these impairments.

For guided media such as twisted pair, coaxial cable, and optical fiber, the most significant impairments are as follows:

- Attenuation and attenuation distortion
- Delay distortion
- Noise

With wireless transmission, the concerns are as follows:

- Free-space loss
- Atmospheric absorption
- Multipath
- Refraction
- Thermal noise

Guided Media

Attenuation When an electromagnetic signal is transmitted along any medium, it gradually becomes weaker at greater distances; this is referred to as attenuation. Attenuation introduces three considerations for the transmission engineer:

1. A received signal must have sufficient strength so that the electronic circuitry in the receiver can detect and interpret the signal.

2. The signal must maintain a level sufficiently higher than noise to be received without error.

3. Attenuation is greater at higher frequencies, and this causes distortion.

The first and second considerations are dealt with by attention to signal strength and the use of amplifiers or repeaters. In the simplest sort of link between transmitter and receiver, data transmission occurs between a *transmitter* and a *receiver* over a *transmission medium*. For a very short link, no measures may need to be taken to compensate for attenuation. For distances at which the attenuation becomes significant, one or more intermediate devices may be used to compensate. In the case of analog signals, an amplifier is used; the amplifier boosts the amplitude, or strength, of the signal. In the ideal case, the amplifier will not alter the information content of the signal. In practice, however, the amplifier will introduce some distortion to the signal. This distortion will be cumulative if multiple amplifiers are used along the path between the transmitter and receiver. In the case of digital signals, the intermediate devices are one or more repeaters. The repeater receives the incoming signal on one side, recovers the binary data, and transmits a new digital signal on the other side (Figure 15.9). Thus, there is not an accumulation of distortion. However, any error made in recovering the binary data from the incoming signal persists for the remainder of the transmission path.

The third consideration, known as attenuation distortion, is particularly noticeable for analog signals. Because attenuation is different for different frequencies, and the signal is made up of a number of components at different

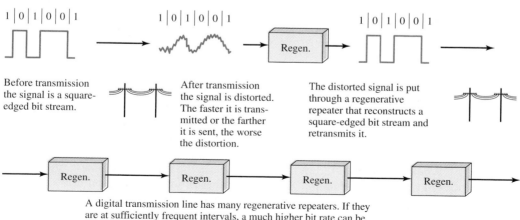

A digital transmission line has many regenerative repeaters. If they are at sufficiently frequent intervals, a much higher bit rate can be transmitted than with analog transmission.

Figure 15.9 Regenerative Repeaters

frequencies, the received signal is not only reduced in strength but is also distorted. To overcome this problem, techniques are available for equalizing attenuation across a band of frequencies. This is commonly done for telephone lines by using loading coils that change the electrical properties of the line to smooth out attenuation effects.

Digital signals are also made up of a number of frequencies. However, most of the energy in a digital signal is concentrated in a reasonably narrow band. Hence, attenuation distortion is less of a problem than it is for analog signals.

Delay Distortion Delay distortion is a phenomenon that occurs in transmission cables (such as twisted pair, coaxial cable, and optical fiber); it does not occur when signals are transmitted through the air by means of antennas. Delay distortion is caused by the fact that the velocity of propagation of a signal through a cable is different for different frequencies. For a signal with a given bandwidth, the velocity tends to be highest near the center frequency of the signal and to fall off toward the two edges of the band. Thus, various components of a signal will arrive at the receiver at different times.

This effect is referred to as delay distortion because the received signal is distorted due to a variable delay in its frequency components. Delay distortion is particularly critical for digital data. Because of delay distortion, some of the signal energy in one bit position will spill over into other bit positions, which may cause errors on reception; this is a major limitation to the data rate for digital data.

Noise When information is transmitted in the form of an electromagnetic signal, the received signal will consist of the transmitted signal, modified by attenuation and the various distortions imposed by the transmission system, plus the addition of unwanted electromagnetic energy that is inserted somewhere between the transmitter and the receiver. The latter, undesired signals are referred to as **noise.** It is noise that is the major limiting factor in communications system performance.

Noise may be divided into four categories:

- Thermal noise
- Intermodulation noise
- Crosstalk
- Impulse noise

Thermal noise is due to thermal agitation of electrons in a conductor. It is present in all electronic devices and transmission media and is a function of temperature. Thermal noise is uniformly distributed across the frequency spectrum and hence is often referred to as **white noise.** Thermal noise cannot be eliminated and therefore places an upper bound on communications system performance.

When signals of different frequencies share the same transmission medium, the result may be *intermodulation noise.* The effect of intermodulation noise is to produce signals at a frequency that is the sum or difference of the two original frequencies or multiples of those frequencies. For example, if two signals, one at 4000 Hz and one at 8000 Hz, share the same transmission facility, they might produce energy at 12,000 Hz. This noise could interfere with an intended signal at 12,000 Hz.

Intermodulation noise is produced when there is some nonlinearity in the transmitter, receiver, or intervening transmission system. Normally, these components behave as linear systems; that is, the output is equal to the input times a constant. In a nonlinear system, the output is a more complex function of the input. Such nonlinearity can be caused by component malfunction or the use of excessive signal strength. It is under these circumstances that the sum and difference terms occur.

Crosstalk has been experienced by anyone who, while having a telephone conversation, has been able to hear another telephone conversation; it is an unwanted coupling between signal paths. It can occur by electrical coupling between nearby cables or by the overlap of signals transmitted by antennas. Typically, crosstalk is of the same order of magnitude as, or less than, thermal noise.

All of the types of noise discussed so far have reasonably predictable and reasonably constant magnitudes. Thus, it is possible to engineer a transmission system to cope with them. *Impulse noise*, however, is noncontinuous, consisting of irregular pulses or noise spikes of short duration and of relatively high amplitude. It is generated from a variety of causes, including external electromagnetic disturbances, such as lightning, and faults and flaws in the communications system.

Impulse noise is generally only a minor annoyance for analog data. For example, voice transmission may be corrupted by short clicks and crackles with no loss of intelligibility. However, impulse noise is the primary source of error in digital data communication. For example, a sharp spike of energy of 0.01 sec duration would not destroy any voice information but would wash out about 500 bits of data being transmitted at 56 kbps. Figure 15.10 is an example of the effect on a digital signal. Here the noise consists of a relatively modest level of thermal noise plus occasional spikes of impulse noise. The digital data are recovered from the signal by sampling the received waveform once per bit time. As can be seen, the noise is occasionally sufficient to change a 1 to a 0 or a 0 to a 1.

Unguided Media

Free-Space Loss For any type of wireless communication the signal disperses with distance. Therefore, an antenna with a fixed area will receive less signal power the farther it is from the transmitting antenna. For satellite communication this is the primary mode of signal loss. Under idealized conditions, the ratio of the power P_r received by the antenna to the radiated power P_t is given by

$$\frac{P_r}{P_t} = \frac{A_r A_t f^2}{(cd)^2}$$

where A_r is the area of the receiving antenna, A_t the area of the transmitting antenna, d the distance between the antennas, f the carrier frequency, $\lambda = c/f$ the wavelength, and $c = 300{,}000$ km/s the speed of the electromagnetic wave. Thus, for the same antenna dimensions and separation, the higher the carrier frequency f, the lower is the free-space path loss.

Atmospheric Absorption An additional loss between the transmitting and receiving antennas is atmospheric absorption. Water vapor and oxygen contribute

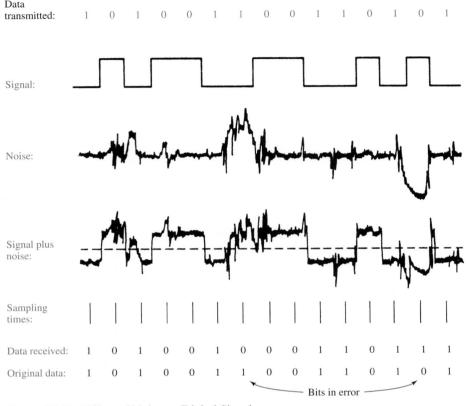

Figure 15.10 Effect of Noise on Digital Signal

most to attenuation. A peak attenuation occurs in the vicinity of 22 GHz due to water vapor. At frequencies below 15 GHz, the attenuation is less. The presence of oxygen results in an absorption peak in the vicinity of 60 GHz but contributes less at frequencies below 30 GHz. Rain and fog (suspended water droplets) cause scattering of radio waves that results in attenuation. This can be a major cause of signal loss. Thus, in areas of significant precipitation, either path lengths have to be kept short or lower-frequency bands should be used.

Multipath For wireless facilities where there is a relatively free choice of where antennas are to be located, they can be placed so that if there are no nearby interfering obstacles, there is a direct line-of-sight path from transmitter to receiver. This is generally the case for many satellite facilities and for point-to-point microwave. In other cases, such as mobile telephony, there are obstacles in abundance. The signal can be reflected by such obstacles so that multiple copies of the signal with varying delays can be received. In fact, in extreme cases, there may be no direct signal. Depending on the differences in the path lengths of the direct and reflected waves, the composite signal can be either larger or smaller than the direct signal. Reinforcement and cancellation of the signal resulting from the signal following multiple paths can be controlled for communication between fixed, well-sited antennas, and between satellites and fixed ground stations, but for mobile telephony and communication to antennas that are not well sited, multipath considerations can be paramount.

Refraction Radio waves are refracted (or bent) when they propagate through the atmosphere. The refraction is caused by changes in the speed of the signal with altitude or by other spatial changes in the atmospheric conditions. Normally, the speed of the signal increases with altitude, causing radio waves to bend downward. However, on occasion, weather conditions may lead to variations in speed with height that differ significantly from the typical variations. This may result in a situation in which only a fraction or no part of the line-of-sight wave reaches the receiving antenna.

Thermal Noise Thermal or white noise is inescapable. It arises from the thermal activity of the devices and media of the communication system. Because of the weakness of the signal received by satellite earth stations, thermal noise is particularly important for satellite communication.

Channel Capacity

We have seen that there are a variety of impairments that distort or corrupt a signal. For digital data, the question that then arises is to what extent these impairments limit the data rate that can be achieved. The rate at which data can be transmitted over a given communication path, or channel, under given conditions, is referred to as the **channel capacity.**

There are four concepts here that we are trying to relate to one another:

- **Data rate:** This is the rate, in bits per second (bps), at which data can be communicated.

- **Bandwidth:** This is the bandwidth of the transmitted signal as constrained by the transmitter and the nature of the transmission medium, expressed in cycles per second, or Hertz.

- **Noise:** This is the average level of noise over the communications path.

- **Error rate:** This is the rate at which errors occur, where an error is the reception of a 1 when a 0 was transmitted or the reception of a 0 when a 1 was transmitted.

The problem we are addressing is this: Communications facilities are expensive, and in general, the greater the bandwidth of a facility, the greater the cost. Furthermore, all transmission channels of any practical interest are of limited bandwidth. The limitations arise from the physical properties of the transmission medium or from deliberate limitations at the transmitter on the bandwidth to prevent interference from other sources. Accordingly, we would like to make as efficient use as possible of a given bandwidth. For digital data, this means that we would like to get as high a data rate as possible at a particular limit of error rate for a given bandwidth. The main constraint on achieving this efficiency is noise.

We have already shown the relationship between bandwidth and data rate in Figure 15.4. All other things being equal, doubling the bandwidth doubles the data rate. Now consider the relationship among data rate, noise, and error rate. This can be explained intuitively by again considering Figure 15.10. The presence of noise can corrupt one or more bits. If the data rate is increased, the bits become "shorter," so that more bits are affected by a given pattern of noise. Thus, at a given noise level, the higher the data rate, the higher the error rate.

All of these concepts can be tied together neatly in a formula developed by the mathematician Claude Shannon. As we have just illustrated, the higher the data rate, the more damage that unwanted noise can do. For a given level of noise, we would expect that a greater signal strength would improve the ability to receive data correctly in the presence of noise. The key parameter involved in this reasoning is the signal-to-noise ratio (SNR, or S/N), which is the ratio of the power in a signal to the power contained in the noise that is present at a particular point in the transmission. Typically, this ratio is measured at a receiver, because it is at this point that an attempt is made to process the signal and eliminate the unwanted noise. The signal-to-noise ratio is important in the transmission of digital data because it sets the upper bound on the achievable data rate. Shannon's result is that the maximum channel capacity, in bits per second, obeys the equation

$$C = B \log_2(1 + \text{SNR})$$

where C is the capacity of the channel in bits per second and B is the bandwidth of the channel in Hertz. The Shannon formula represents the theoretical maximum that can be achieved. In practice, however, lower rates are achieved. One reason for this is that the formula assumes white noise (thermal noise). Impulse noise is not accounted for, nor are attenuation distortion or delay distortion.

Several observations concerning the Shannon equation can be made. The measure of efficiency of a digital transmission is the ratio C/B, which is the bps per hertz value that is achieved. For a given level of noise, it would appear that the data rate could be increased by increasing the signal strength or bandwidth. However, as the signal strength increases, so do nonlinearities in the system, leading to an increase in intermodulation noise. Note also that because noise is assumed to be white, the wider the bandwidth, the more noise is admitted to the system. Thus, as B increases, SNR decreases.

APPLICATION NOTE
Analog Signals

We are surrounded by signals from a wide variety of sources. Understanding these signals can often help us get through basic problems with communications equipment. For example, cellular telephone users often learn to stand by windows to improve their reception. When we are responsible for communications systems, understanding the signals around us can mean the difference between success and failure of daily business operations.

It is interesting to note the differences between digital and analog systems. Analog communications have certainly been around for a much longer period of time. With the digital revolution in the 1970s and 1980s, analog systems were believed to be inferior. And now with advances in cellular technology and other communications systems, we all want digital communication. What is interesting is that most communication is in fact, still analog. What is really meant by the terms *digital cellular communication* or *digital subscriber lines* is that we are converting digital information for conveyance over an analog network.

Communication in many systems, and especially communication through the air, requires an analog carrier. Even high-speed communications over fiber optics use analog based signals. Digital cellular phones still use an analog carrier to carry the digitally encoded messages from one place to another. Even digital local area network signals can be broken down into their component analog parts.

For this reason, understanding analog signals and the effect of installing a communication system within a certain environment can be extremely beneficial to an organization. Understanding the issues makes us better able to make appropriate choices during design phases as well as facilitating troubleshooting should problems occur after installation.

For guided media, problems are easier to track down and eliminate. As we discussed in the Application Note in Chapter 9, the best defense against communication problems in guided media systems is a solid installation. This is true not only for copper based systems like Ethernet over UTP, but fiber as well. For wireless systems, even the finest quality system can be rendered inoperable by uncontrollable, outside forces. These forces do not have to be significant events like hurricanes. Even small changes to the environment can create problems. Cellular telephone providers know this only too well as they have experienced the difference even a tree can make depending on whether or not it is wet. Local construction of a new building or fountain can create reflections or even eliminate line of sight between source and destination.

What can be worse than the obvious problem of a skyscraper popping up are unseen obstacles such as other sources of electromagnetic radiation. Cellular towers, radio stations, police and fire channels, XM radio, and many others can, individually or together, create problems for a local wireless system. In the case of wireless optical communications, radio interference is not a problem, but line of sight and weather conditions certainly are. Probably the worst problem in terms of weather is mist or fog, but other problems such as heating/cooling of the transceiver platform, wind, dust, and even large trucks, can cause misalignment problems or reduce performance.

XM radio presents an interesting case of radio interference. XM radio is a satellite-based service offering primarily radio music and news channels over the satellite frequencies. The frequencies happen to be very close to those used by WiFi or wireless local area networks. Wireless "hotspots" have been installed in increasing numbers over the last two years, and these hotspots cause interference with the XM radio receiver. Because the XM radio providers paid for the license to operate in this portion of the spectrum, it was felt that their signals were improperly interfered with from an unlicensed source. Unfortunately, the vast proliferation of wireless networking equipment made it difficult to fix.

> The problems experienced by wireless analog systems are many and varied. Understanding how analog signals propagate and interact and the effect of local conditions can vastly improve our chances for successful communications. It is also interesting to note that what we are learning because of our increased reliance on wireless communication HAM radio operators have known for years.

15.3 SUMMARY

All of the forms of information that are discussed in this book (audio, data, image, video) can be represented by electromagnetic signals and transmitted over a suitable transmission medium. Depending on the transmission medium and the communications environment, either analog or digital signals can be used to convey information. Any electromagnetic signal, analog or digital, is made up of a number of constituent frequencies. A key parameter that characterizes the signal is bandwidth, which is the width of the range of frequencies that comprise the signal. In general, the greater the bandwidth of the signal, the greater its information-carrying capacity.

A major problem in designing a communications facility is transmission impairment. The most significant impairments are attenuation, attenuation distortion, delay distortion, and the various types of noise. The various forms of noise include thermal noise, inter-modulation noise, crosstalk, and impulse noise. For analog signals, transmission impairments introduce random modifications that degrade the quality of the received information and may affect intelligibility. For digital signals, transmission impairments may cause bit errors.

The designer of a communications facility must deal with four factors: the bandwidth of the signal, the data rate that is used for digital information, the amount of noise and other impairments, and the level of error rate that is acceptable. The bandwidth is limited by the transmission medium and the desire to avoid interference with other nearby signals. Because bandwidth is a scarce resource, we would like to maximize the data rate that is achieved in a given bandwidth. The data rate is limited by the bandwidth, the presence of impairments, and the error rate that is acceptable. The efficiency of a transmission system is measured by the ratio of data rate (in bps) to bandwidth (in Hz). Efficiencies of between 1 and 5 bps/Hz are considered good.

15.4 RECOMMENDED READING

[STAL04] covers all of the topics in this chapter in greater detail. [FREE99] is also a readable and rigorous treatment of the topics of this chapter. A thorough treatment of both analog and digital communication is provided in [COUC01].

COUC01 Couch, L. *Digital and Analog Communication Systems.* Upper Saddle River, NJ: Prentice Hall, 2001.

FREE99 Freeman, R. *Fundamentals of Telecommunications.* New York: Wiley, 1999.

STAL04 Stallings, W. *Data and Computer Communications,* 7th edition. Upper Saddle River: NJ: Prentice Hall, 2004.

15.5 KEY TERMS, REVIEW QUESTIONS, AND PROBLEMS

Key Terms

amplitude	frequency	phase
analog signal	fundamental frequency	radian
attenuation	Hertz	sine wave
bandwidth	noise	spectrum
channel capacity	peak amplitude	square wave
delay distortion	period	wavelength
digital signal	periodic signal	white noise

Review Questions

15.1. Differentiate between an analog and a digital electromagnetic signal.

15.2. What are three important characteristics of a periodic signal?

15.3. How many radians are there in a complete circle of 360 degrees?

15.4. What is the relationship between the wavelength and frequency of a sine wave?

15.5. Define fundamental frequency.

15.6. What is the relationship between a signal's spectrum and its bandwidth?

15.7. How can telephone networks use communication facilities that limit the transmission of sound to a narrow bandwidth?

15.8. What is attenuation?

15.9. How does delay distortion place a limitation on the data rate for digital data?

15.10. What is noise?

15.11. What is white noise?

15.12. Why does thermal noise place an upper bound on communication system performance?

15.13. What is intermodulation noise?

15.14. Describe the phenomenon known as multipath.

15.15. Define channel capacity.

15.16. What key factors affect channel capacity?

Problems

15.1 A signal has a fundamental frequency of 1000 Hz. What is its period?

15.2 Express the following in the simplest form you can:

  a. $\sin(2\pi ft - \pi) + \sin(2\pi ft + \pi)$
  b. $\sin 2\pi ft + \sin(2\pi ft - \pi)$

15.3 Sound may be modeled as sinusoidal functions. Compare the relative frequency and wavelength of musical notes. Use 330 m/s as the speed of sound and the following frequencies for the musical scale.

Note	C	D	E	F	G	A	B	C
Frequency	264	297	330	352	396	440	495	528

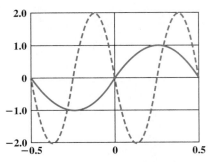

Figure 15.11   Figure for Problem 15.4

15.4   If the solid curve in Figure 15.11 represents $sin(2\pi t)$ what does the dotted curve represent? That is, the dotted curve can be written in the form $A \sin(2\pi + \phi)$; what are $A, f,$ and ϕ?

15.5   Decompose the signal $(1 + 0.1 \cos 5t) \cos 100t$ into a linear combination of sinusoidal functions, and find the amplitude, frequency, and phase of each component. *Hint:* Use the identity for $\cos a \cos b$

15.6   Find the period of the function $f(t) = (10 \cos t)^2$

15.7   Figure 15.4 shows the effect of eliminating higher-harmonic components of a square wave and retaining only a few lower harmonic components. What would the signal look like in the opposite case; that is, retaining all higher harmonics and eliminating a few lower harmonics?

15.8   Given the narrow (usable) audio bandwidth of a telephone transmission facility, a nominal SNR of 56 dB (400,000), and a distortion level of <0.2%:

   a.   What is the theoretical maximum channel capacity (Kbps) of traditional telephone lines (POTS)?

   b.   What is the actual maximum channel capacity?

DATA COMMUNICATION FUNDAMENTALS

After reading this chapter, you should be able to

- Explain the differences between analog and digital transmission.
- Describe how digital data can be encoded by means of a modem so that they can be transmitted over analog telephone lines.
- Describe how analog data, such as voice, can be encoded by means of a codec so that it can be transmitted over digital facilities.
- Explain the differences between asynchronous and synchronous transmission and when each technique is used.
- Describe the process of error detection.

The transmission of data across a transmission medium involves more than simply inserting a signal on the medium. A considerable degree of cooperation between the two sides is needed. This chapter and the next explore the essential mechanisms involved in the successful transmission of data between two devices across a transmission medium. First, we discuss the distinction between analog and digital transmission. Then we discuss the ways in which signals can be encoded for effective and efficient communication. Next, we look at the issue of synchronization: The receiver, to interpret correctly the incoming signal, must know when each arriving bit begins and ends so that it can keep pace with the transmitter. Several common techniques for synchronizing the receiver with the transmitter are described. Finally, this chapter introduces the concept of error detection.

16.1 ANALOG AND DIGITAL DATA COMMUNICATIONS

Electromagnetic signals, which are capable of propagation on a variety of transmission media, can be used to convey data. The exact way in which these signals are encoded to convey data will determine the efficiency and reliability of the transmission. This section introduces some basic concepts that are essential to the discussion.

The terms *analog* and *digital* correspond, roughly, to *continuous* and *discrete*, respectively. These two terms are frequently used in data communications in at least three contexts: data, signaling, and transmission.

The use of these terms in different contexts is often the source of confusion in articles and books. In this section, we clarify the various uses of these two terms. Briefly, we define **data** as entities that convey meaning, or information. **Signals** are electric or electromagnetic representations of data. **Signaling** is the physical propagation of the signal along a suitable medium. **Transmission** is the communication of data by the propagation and processing of signals.

We have already had occasion to use these terms in the first two contexts. **Analog data** take on continuous values on some interval. For example, voice and video are continuously varying patterns of intensity. Most data collected by sensors, such as temperature and pressure, are continuous valued. **Digital data** take on discrete values; examples are text, integers, and binary data.

In a communications system, data are propagated from one point to another by means of electromagnetic signals. An **analog signal** is a continuously varying electromagnetic wave that may be transmitted over a variety of media, depending on frequency. A **digital signal** is a sequence of voltage pulses that may be transmitted over a wire medium; for example, a constant positive voltage may represent binary 0, and a constant negative value may represent binary 1. The principal advantages of digital signaling are that it is generally cheaper than analog signaling and is less susceptible to noise interference. The principal disadvantage is that digital signals suffer more from attenuation than do analog signals. Note that digital signaling is possible only on copper media and cannot be used on optical fiber or wireless media.

Both analog and digital data can be represented, and hence propagated, by either analog or digital signals; this is illustrated in Figure 16.1. Generally, analog data are a function of time and occupy a limited frequency spectrum. Such data can

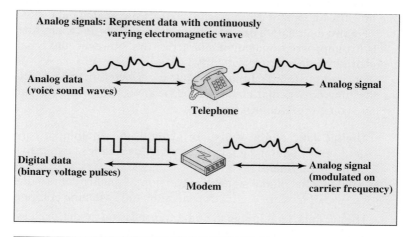

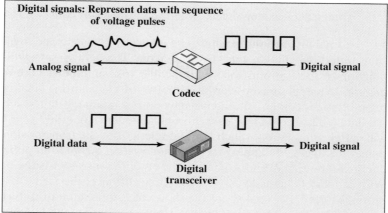

Figure 16.1   Analog and Digital Signaling of Analog and Digital Data

be directly represented by an electromagnetic signal occupying the same spectrum (e.g., voice data in the telephone voice band). In addition, we shall see that various forms of encoding can be used to provide an analog signal at a different portion of the spectrum. This is done to improve signal quality or transmission efficiency.

Digital data can also be represented by analog signals, by use of a **modem** (modulator/demodulator). The modem converts a series of binary voltage pulses into an analog signal by modulating a *carrier frequency*. The resulting signal occupies a certain spectrum of frequency centered about the carrier and may be propagated across a medium suitable for that carrier. The most common modems represent digital data in the voice spectrum and hence enable digital data to be propagated over ordinary voice-grade telephone lines. At the other end of the line, a modem demodulates the signal to recover the original data. Various modulation techniques are discussed in this section.

In an operation very similar to that performed by a modem, analog data can be represented by a digital signal. The device that performs this function is a **codec** (coder/decoder). In essence, the codec takes an analog signal that directly represents the voice data and approximates that signal by a bit stream. At the other end of a line, the bit stream is used to reconstruct the analog data.

Finally, digital data can be represented directly, in binary form, by two voltage levels. To improve propagation characteristics, however, the binary data are often encoded, as explained subsequently.

Each of the four combinations just described is in widespread use. The reasons for choosing a particular combination for any given communications task vary. We list here some representative reasons:

- **Digital data, digital signal:** In general, the equipment for encoding digital data into a digital signal is less complex and less expensive than digital-to-analog equipment.
- **Analog data, digital signal:** Conversion of analog data to digital form permits the use of modern digital transmission and switching equipment.
- **Digital data, analog signal:** Some transmission media, such as optical fiber and satellite, will only propagate analog signals.
- **Analog data, analog signal:** Analog data are easily converted to an analog signal.

A final distinction remains to be made. Both analog and digital signals may be transmitted on suitable transmission media. The way these signals are treated is a function of the transmission system. Table 16.1 summarizes the methods of transmission. **Analog transmission** is a means of transmitting analog signals without regard to their content; the signals may represent analog data (such as voice) or digital data (such as data that pass through a modem). In either case, the analog signal will suffer attenuation, which limits the length of the transmission link. To achieve longer distances, the analog transmission system includes amplifiers that boost the energy in the signal. Unfortunately, the amplifier also boosts the noise components. With amplifiers cascaded to achieve long distance, the signal becomes more and more distorted. For analog data, such as voice, quite a bit of distortion can be tolerated and the data remain intelligible. However, for digital data transmitted as analog signals, cascaded amplifiers will increase the number of errors.

Table 16.1   Analog and Digital Transmission

(a) Data and Signals		
	Analog Signal	**Digital Signal**
Analog Data	Two alternatives: (1) signal occupies the same spectrum as the analog data; (2) analog data are encoded to occupy a different portion of spectrum.	Analog data are encoded using a codec to produce a digital bit stream.
Digital Data	Digital data are encoded using a modem to produce analog signal.	Two alternatives: (1) signal consists of a two voltage levels to represent the two binary values; (2) digital data are encoded to produce a digital signal with desired properties.
(b) Treatment of Signals		
	Analog Transmission	**Digital Transmission**
Analog Signal	Is propagated through amplifiers; same treatment whether signal is used to represent analog data or digital data.	Assumes that the analog signal represents digital data. Signal is propagated through repeaters; at each repeater, digital data are recovered from inbound signal and used to generate a new analog outbound signal.
Digital Signal	Not used	Digital signal represents a stream of 1s and 0s, which may represent digital data or may be an encoding of analog data. Signal is propagated through repeaters; at each repeater, stream of 1s and 0s is recovered from inbound signal and used to generate a new digital outbound signal.

Digital transmission, in contrast, is concerned with the content of the signal. We have mentioned that a digital signal can be propagated only a limited distance before attenuation endangers the integrity of the data. To achieve greater distances, repeaters are used. A repeater receives the digital signal, recovers the pattern of ones and zeros, and retransmits a new signal. Thus the attenuation is overcome.

The same technique may be used with an analog signal if it is assumed that the signal carries digital data. At appropriately spaced points, the transmission system has retransmission devices rather than amplifiers. The retransmission device recovers the digital data from the analog signal and generates a new, clean analog signal. Thus noise is not cumulative.

The question naturally arises as to which is the preferred method of transmission. The answer being supplied by the telecommunications industry and its customers is digital, this despite an enormous investment in analog communications facilities. Both long-haul telecommunication facilities and intrabuilding services are gradually

Table 16.2   Advantages of Digital Transmission

Cost

The advent of large-scale integration (LSI) and very-large-scale integration (VLSI) has caused a continuing drop in the cost and size of digital circuitry. Analog equipment has not shown a similar drop. Further, maintenance costs for digital circuitry are a fraction of those for analog circuitry.

Data Integrity

With the use of digital repeaters rather than analog amplifiers, the effects of noise and other signal impairments are not cumulative. Thus it is possible to transmit data longer distances and over lesser-quality lines by digital means while maintaining the integrity of the data.

Capacity Utilization

It has become economical to build transmission links of very high bandwidth, including satellite channels and optical fiber. A high degree of multiplexing is needed to effectively utilize such capacity, and this is more easily and cheaply achieved with digital (time division) rather than analog (frequency division) techniques (see Chapter 17).

Security and Privacy

Encryption techniques can be readily applied to digital data and to analog data that have been digitized.

Integration

By treating both analog and digital information digitally, all signals have the same form and can be treated similarly. Thus economies of scale and convenience can be achieved by integrating voice, video, image, and digital data.

being converted to digital transmission and, where possible, digital signaling techniques. The most important reasons for this are summarized in Table 16.2.

We now turn to an examination of each of the four signal encoding options.

16.2 DATA ENCODING TECHNIQUES

As we have pointed out, data, either analog or digital, must be converted into a signal for purposes of transmission.

In the case of digital data, different signal elements are used to represent binary 1 and binary 0. The mapping from binary digits to signal elements is the *encoding scheme* for transmission. Encoding schemes are designed to minimize errors in determining the start and end of each bit and errors in determining whether each bit is a 1 or a 0.

For analog data, the encoding scheme is designed to enhance the quality, or fidelity, of transmission. That is, we would like the received analog data to be as close as possible to the transmitted data.

Analog Encoding of Digital Information

The basis for analog encoding is a continuous constant-frequency signal known as the *carrier signal*. Digital information is encoded by means of a **modem** that modulates one of the three characteristics of the carrier: amplitude, frequency, or phase, or some combination of these. Figure 16.2 illustrates the three basic forms of modulation of analog signals for digital data:

- Amplitude-shift keying
- Frequency-shift keying
- Phase-shift keying

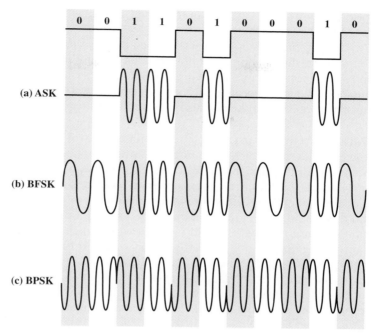

Figure 16.2   Modulation of Analog Signals for Digital Data

In all these cases, the resulting signal contains a range of frequencies on both sides of the carrier frequency; this range is the bandwidth of the signal.

In **amplitude-shift keying (ASK),** the two binary values are represented by two different amplitudes of the carrier frequency. In some cases, one of the amplitudes is zero; that is, one binary digit is represented by the presence, at constant amplitude, of the carrier, the other by the absence of the carrier. Amplitude-shift keying is susceptible to sudden gain changes and is a rather inefficient modulation technique. On voice-grade lines, it is typically used only up to 1200 bps.

The ASK technique is also commonly used to transmit digital data over optical fiber. For LED transmitters, binary 1 is represented by a short pulse of light and binary 0 by the absence of light. Laser transmitters normally have a fixed "bias" current that causes the device to emit a low light level. This low level represents binary 0, while a higher-amplitude lightwave represents binary 1.

In **frequency-shift keying (FSK),** the two binary values are represented by two different frequencies near the carrier frequency. This scheme is less susceptible to error than amplitude-shift keying. On voice-grade lines, it is typically used up to 1200 bps. It is also commonly used for high-frequency (4 to 30 MHz) radio transmission.

In **phase-shift keying (PSK),** the phase of the carrier signal is shifted to encode data. Figure 16.2c is an example of a two-phase system. In this system, a 0 is represented by sending a signal burst of the same phase as the preceding signal burst sent. A 1 is represented by sending a signal burst of opposite phase to the preceding one. Phase-shift keying can use more then two phase shifts. A four-phase system would encode two bits with each signal burst. The phase-shift keying technique is more noise resistant and efficient than frequency-shift keying; on a voice-grade line, rates up to 9600 bps are achieved.

Finally, the techniques just discussed may be combined. A common combination is phase-shift keying and amplitude-shift keying, where some or all of the phase shifts may occur at one or two amplitudes. These techniques are referred to as *multilevel* signaling because each signal element represents multiple bits. Note that four-phase phase-shift keying also falls into this category.

Data Rate and Signaling Rate With multilevel signaling, we must distinguish between data rate, which is the rate, in bits per second, that bits are transmitted, and modulation rate, or signaling rate, which is the rate at which signal elements are transmitted. This latter rate is expressed in *baud*, or signal elements per second.

Four-phase PSK illustrates the difference between the data rate R (in bps) and the modulation rate D (in baud) of a signal. Let us assume that this scheme is being employed with digital input in which each bit is represented by a constant voltage pulse, one level for binary one and one level for binary zero. The data rate is $R = 1/T_b$, where T_b is the duration of one bit. However, the encoded signal contains $L = 4$ bits in each signal element using $M = 16$ different combinations of amplitude and phase. The modulation rate can be seen to be $R/4$, because each change of signal element communicates four bits. Thus the line signaling speed is 2400 baud, but the data rate is 9600 bps. This is the reason that higher bit rates can be achieved over voice-grade lines by employing more complex modulation schemes.

In general,

$$D = \frac{R}{L} = \frac{R}{\log_2 M}$$

where

D = modulation rate, baud
R = data rate, bps
M = number of different signal elements = 2^L
L = number of bits per signal element

Modems Although both public and private telecommunications facilities are becoming increasingly digital, the use of analog facilities for data transmission will be substantial for many years to come. Thus, the modem is one of the most widely used pieces of communications gear.

Modems are offered in several different forms for use in different applications. Stand-alone modems, for instance, are self-contained, with internal power supplies, and are used with separate information products. Where a number of circuits come together—as at the interface to a large computer system—rack-mounted modems are often used, sharing power supplies and packaging. Modems can also be packaged inside another system (such as personal computer). Such integrated modems usually lower overall cost but increase the complexity of the information product and the cost of designing it. Integrated modems are usually offered as an option, because to standardize on a particular modem type with a product might restrict the usefulness of the

Table 16.3   Modem Specifications

ITU-T Recommendation	Data Rate (bps)	Dial-Up	Half Duplex	Full Duplex
V.29	9600		X	X
V.32	9600	X		X
V.32bis	14,400	X		X
V.33	14,400			X
V.34	33,600	X	X	X
V.90	33,600 (send) 56,000 (receive)	X	X	X

product. In this subsection, we provide a brief introduction to three popular types of modems: voice-grade, cable, and ADSL.

Voice-grade modems are designed for the transmission of digital data over ordinary telephone lines. Thus, the modems make use of the same 4-kHz bandwidth available for voice signals. Because modems are used in pairs for communications, and because this use often occurs over the public telephone network, allowing many different modems to be paired, standards are essential. Table 16.3 lists the most popular voice-grade modem types, as designated by the ITU-T Recommendation that defines them.[1]

The **cable modem** permits Internet access over cable television networks. The cable television industry has been the early leader in providing high-speed access to the home. Figure 16.3 shows a typical layout for cable delivery. At the cable central location, or linked by a high-speed line, is the Internet service provider (ISP). Typically, the cable company offers its own ISP but may also provide links to other ISPs. From the central location, the cable company lays out a network of underground fiber and coaxial cable lines that can reach every home and office in its region of operation. Traditionally, this system has been used to deliver one-way transmission of television channels, using 6 MHz per channel. The same cable layout, with appropriate electronics at both ends, can also be used to deliver a data channel to the subscriber and to provide a reverse channel from subscriber to the central location. Both upstream and downstream channels used for data transmission are shared among a number of subscribers, using a time division multiplexing technique, described in Chapter 17. Within the subscriber's home or office, a splitter is employed to direct ordinary television signals to a television and the data channel to a cable modem, which can serve one or a network of PCs.

In the implementation and deployment of a high-speed wide area public digital network, the most challenging part is the link between subscriber and network: the digital subscriber line. With billions of potential endpoints worldwide, the prospect of installing new cable for each new customer is daunting. Instead, network designers have sought ways of exploiting the installed base of twisted-pair wire that

---

[1]A discussion of ITU-T and other standards bodies is contained in a supporting document at this book's Web site.

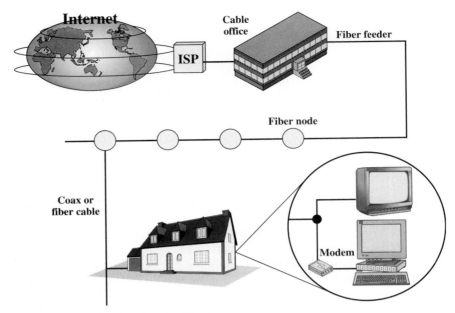

Figure 16.3   Cable Modem Application

links virtually all residential and business customers to telephone networks. These links were installed to carry voice-grade signals in a bandwidth from 0 to 4 kHz. However, the wires are capable of transmitting signals over a far broader spectrum—1 MHz or more. The **asymmetric digital subscriber line** (ADSL) is the most widely publicized of a family of new modem technologies designed to provide high-speed digital data transmission over ordinary telephone wire. ADSL is now being offered by a number of carriers.

Figure 16.4 depicts the ADSL configuration for Internet access. The telephone central office can provide support for a number of ISPs, each of which must support the ADSL modem technology. At the central office, the ISP data signal is combined with a voice signal from the ordinary telephone voice switch. The combined signal can then be transmitted to/from a local subscriber over the subscriber line. At the subscriber's site, the twisted pair is split and routed to both a PC and a telephone. At the PC, an ADSL modem demodulates the data signal for the PC. At the telephone, a microfilter passes the 4-kHz voice signal. The data and voice signals are combined on the twisted pair line using frequency division multiplexing techniques, as described in Chapter 17.

Table 16.4 compares the performance of the various modems we have discussed with each other and with ISDN access, which uses a digital signaling technique.

Digital Encoding of Analog Information

The evolution of public telecommunications networks and private branch exchanges to digital transmission and switching requires that voice data be represented in digital form. The best-known technique for voice digitization is **pulse-code modulation** (PCM). PCM is based on the sampling theorem, which states that if a signal is sampled

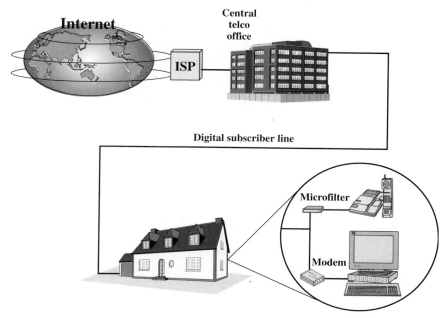

Figure 16.4 ADSL Modem Application

at regular intervals of time and at a rate higher than twice the highest significant signal frequency, then the samples contain all the information of the original signal.

If voice data were limited to frequencies below 4000 Hz, as is done in the analog telephone network, then 8000 samples per second would be sufficient to characterize completely the voice signal. Note, however, that these are analog samples. To convert to digital, each of these analog samples must be assigned a binary code. Figure 16.5 shows an example in which the original signal is assumed to be bandlimited with a bandwidth of B. Analog samples are taken at a rate of $2B$, or once every $T_s = 1/2B$ seconds. Each analog sample is approximated by being *quantized* into one of 16 different levels. Each sample can then be represented by 4 bits. But because the quantized values are only approximations, it is impossible to recover the original signal exactly. By using an 8-bit sample, which allows 256 quantizing levels, the quality of the recovered voice signal is comparable with that achieved via analog

Table 16.4 Speeds for Internet Access Methods

Access Method	Upload Speed	Download Speed	Download Time (10-megabit file)
Dial-up modem	33.6 kbps	56 kbps	3 minutes
ISDN basic rate (two channels)	128 kbps	128 kbps	1.3 minutes
ADSL	16 to 640 kbps	1.5 to 9 Mbps	1.1 to 6.7 seconds
Cable modem	400 kbps	10 to 30 Mbps	0.3 to 1 second

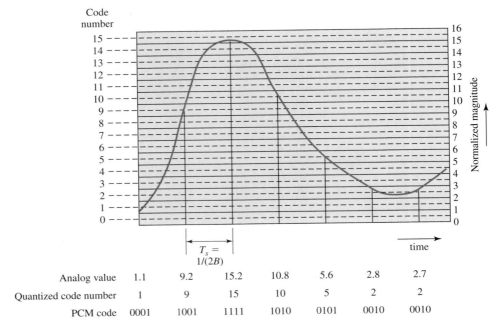

		Analog value	1.1	9.2	15.2	10.8	5.6	2.8	2.7
	Quantized code number		1	9	15	10	5	2	2
		PCM code	0001	1001	1111	1010	0101	0010	0010

Figure 16.5 Pulse-Code Modulation Example

transmission. Note that this implies that a data rate of 8000 samples per second $\times$ 8 bits per sample = 64 kbps is needed for a single voice signal.

PCM can, of course, be used for other than voice signals. For example, a color TV signal has a useful bandwidth of 4.6 MHz, and reasonable quality can be achieved with 10-bit samples, for a data rate of 92 Mbps.

In recent times, variations on the PCM technique, as well as other encoding techniques, have been used to reduce the digital data rate required to carry voice. Good-quality voice transmission can be achieved with a data rate of 8 kbps. With video, advantage can be taken of the fact that from frame to frame most picture elements will not change. Interframe coding techniques should allow the video requirement to be reduced to about 15 Mbps, and for slowly changing scenes, such as those in a video teleconference, down to 1.5 Mbps or less. Indeed, recent advances have resulted in commercial videoconference products with data rates as low as 64 kbps.

Digital Encoding of Digital Data

The most common, and easiest, way to transmit digital signals is to use two different voltage levels for the two binary digits. Typically, a negative voltage represents binary 1 and a positive voltage represents binary 0 (Figure 16.6a). This code is known as **Nonreturn-to-Zero-Level (NRZ-L)** (meaning the signal never returns to zero voltage, and the value during a bit time is a level voltage). NRZ-L is often used for very short connections, such as between a personal computer and an external modem or a terminal and a nearby computer.

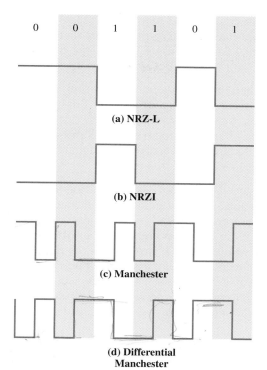

Figure 16.6 Examples of Digital Signal Encoding Schemes

A variation of NRZ is **NRZI (NRZ, Invert on Ones).** As with NRZ-L, NRZI maintains a constant-voltage pulse for the duration of a bit time. The data themselves are encoded as the presence or absence of a signal transition at the beginning of the bit time. A transition (low-to-high or high-to-low) at the beginning of a bit time denotes a binary 1 for that bit time; no transition indicates a binary 0 (Figure 16.6b). NRZI is used on low-speed (64 kbps) ISDN connections.

NRZI is an example of *differential encoding*. In differential encoding, the signal is decoded by comparing the polarity of adjacent signal elements rather than determining the absolute value of a signal element. One benefit of this scheme is that it may be more reliable to detect a transition in the presence of noise than to compare a value to a threshold. Another benefit is that, with a complex cabling layout, it is easy to lose the sense of the polarity of the signal. For example, if the leads from an attached device to a twisted-pair cable are accidentally inverted, all ones and zeros will be inverted for NRZ-L. This does not happen with differential encoding.

A significant disadvantage of NRZ transmission is that it is difficult to determine where one bit ends and another begins. To picture the problem, consider that with a long string of ones or zeros for NRZ-L, the output is a constant voltage over a long period of time. Under these circumstances, any drift between the timing of transmitter and receiver will result in the loss of synchronization between the two.

There is a set of alternative coding techniques, grouped under the term *biphase*, that overcomes this problem. Two of these techniques, Manchester and Differential Manchester, are in common use. All of the biphase techniques require at least one transition per bit time and may have as many as two transitions. Thus, the maximum modulation rate is twice that for NRZ; this means that the bandwidth required is correspondingly greater. To compensate for this, the biphase schemes have two advantages:

- **Synchronization:** Because there is a predictable transition during each bit time, the receiver can synchronize on that transition. For this reason, the biphase codes are known as self-clocking codes.
- **Error detection:** The absence of an expected transition can be used to detect errors. Noise on the line would have to invert both the signal before and after the expected transition to cause an undetected error.

In the **Manchester** code (Figure 16.6c), there is a transition at the middle of each bit period. The midbit transition serves as a clocking mechanism and also as data: A high-to-low transition represents a 0, and a low-to-high transition represents a 1. Manchester coding is used in Ethernet and a number of other local area networks (LANs). In **Differential Manchester** (Figure 16.6d), the midbit transition is used only to provide clocking. The encoding of a 0 is represented by the presence of a transition at the beginning of a bit period, and a 1 is represented by the absence of a transition at the beginning of a bit period. Differential Manchester is used in token ring LANs. Differential Manchester has the added advantage of employing differential encoding.

Analog Encoding of Analog Information

Analog information can be converted directly into an analog signal that occupies the same bandwidth. The best example of this is voice. Voice-generated sound wave in the range of 300 to 3400 Hz can be represented by an electromagnetic signal with the same frequency components. This signal can then be directly transmitted on a voice-grade telephone line.

It is also possible to use an analog signal to modulate a carrier to produce a new analog signal that conveys the same information but occupies a different frequency band. There are two principal reasons for doing this:

- A higher frequency may be needed for effective transmission. For unguided media, it is virtually impossible to transmit low-frequency signals; the required antennas would be many kilometers in diameter. Guided media also have constraints on frequency range. Optical fiber, for example, requires that the frequency be on the order of 10^{14} Hz.
- Analog-to-analog modulation permits frequency-division multiplexing, an important technique explored in Chapter 17.

As with digital-to-analog modulation, analog-to-analog modulation involves an information source that is used to modulate one of the three principal characteristics of a carrier signal: amplitude, frequency, or phase.

Figure 16.7 illustrates the three possibilities. With amplitude modulation (AM), the amplitude of the carrier varies with the pattern of the modulating signal. Similarly, frequency modulation (FM) and phase modulation (PM) modulate the frequency and phase of a carrier, respectively.

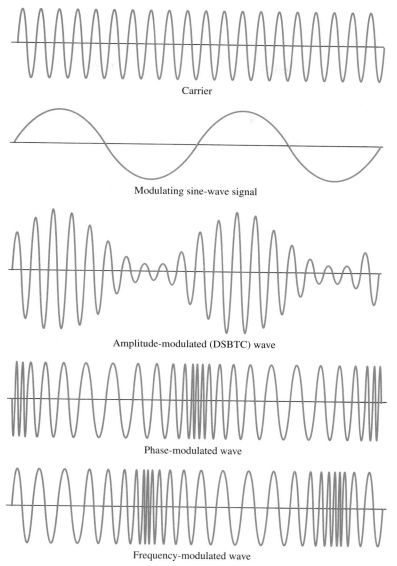

Figure 16.7 Amplitude, Phase, and Frequency Modulation of a Sine-Wave Carrier by a Sine-Wave Signal

16.3 ASYNCHRONOUS AND SYNCHRONOUS TRANSMISSION

Recall from Figure 15.10 that the reception of digital data involves sampling the incoming signal once per bit time to determine the binary value. One of the difficulties encountered in such a process is that various transmission impairments will corrupt the signal so that occasional errors will occur. This problem is compounded by a timing difficulty: In order for the receiver to sample the incoming bits properly, it must know the arrival time and duration of each bit that it receives.

Suppose that the sender simply transmits a stream of data bits. The sender has a clock that governs the timing of the transmitted bits. For example, if data are to be transmitted at one million bits per second (1 Mbps), then one bit will be transmitted every $1/10^6 = 1$ microsecond (μs), as measured by the sender's clock. Typically, the receiver will attempt to sample the medium at the center of each bit time. The receiver will time its samples at intervals of one bit time. In our example, the sampling would occur once every 1 μs. If the receiver times its samples based on its own clock, then there will be a problem if the transmitter's and receiver's clocks are not precisely aligned. If there is a drift of 1% (the receiver's clock is 1% faster or slower than the transmitter's clock), then the first sampling will be 0.01 of a bit time (0.01 μs) away from the center of the bit (center of bit is 0.5 μs from beginning and end of bit). After 50 or more samples, the receiver may be in error because it is sampling in the wrong bit time ($50 \times .01 = 0.5 \mu s$). For smaller timing differences, the error would occur later, but eventually the receiver will be out of step with the transmitter if the transmitter sends a sufficiently long stream of bits and if no steps are taken to synchronize the transmitter and receiver.

Asynchronous Transmission

Two approaches are common for achieving the desired synchronization. The first is called, oddly enough, **asynchronous transmission.** The strategy with this scheme is to avoid the timing problem by not sending long, uninterrupted streams of bits. Instead, data are transmitted one character at a time, where each character is 5 to 8 bits in length.[2] Timing or synchronization must only be maintained within each character; the receiver has the opportunity to resynchronize at the beginning of each new character.

Figure 16.8 illustrates this technique. When no character is being transmitted, the line between transmitter and receiver is in an *idle* state. The definition of *idle* is equivalent to the signaling element for binary 1. Thus, for NRZ-L signaling (see Figure 16.6), which is common for asynchronous transmission, idle would be the presence of a negative voltage on the line. The beginning of a character is signaled by a *start bit* with a value of binary 0. This is followed by the 5 to 8 bits that actually make up the character. The bits of the character are transmitted beginning with the least significant bit. For example, for IRA characters, the data bits are usually followed by a parity bit, which therefore is in the most significant bit position. The parity bit is set by the transmitter such that the total number of ones in the character, including the parity bit, is even (even parity) or odd (odd parity), depending on the convention being used. This bit is used by the receiver for error detection, as discussed in Section 16.4. The final element is a *stop element*, which is a binary 1. A minimum length for the stop element is specified, and this is usually 1, 1.5, or 2 times the duration of an ordinary bit. No maximum value is specified. Because the stop element is the same as

---

[2]The number of bits that comprise a character depends on the code used. We have already seen one common example, the IRA code, which uses 7 bits per character (Chapter 2). Another common code is the Extended Binary Coded Decimal Interchange Code (EBCDIC), which is an 8-bit character code used on all IBM machines except for IBM's personal computers.

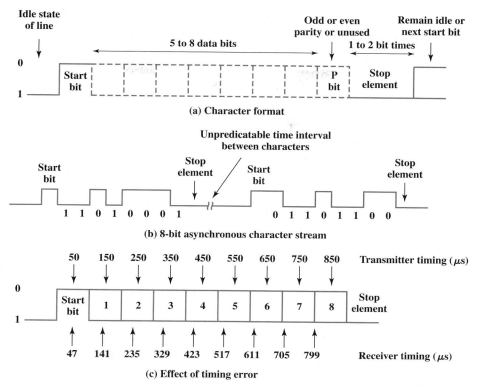

Figure 16.8 Asynchronous Transmission

the idle state, the transmitter will continue to transmit the stop element until it is ready to send the next character.

If a steady stream of characters is sent, the interval between two characters is uniform and equal to the stop element. For example, if the stop element is one bit time and the IRA characters ABC are sent (with even parity bit), the pattern is 01000001010010000101011000011111 . . . 111.[3] The start bit (0) starts the timing sequence for the next nine elements, which are the 7-bit IRA code, the parity bit, and the stop element. In the idle state, the receiver looks for a transition from 1 to 0 to signal the beginning of the next character and then samples the input signal at 1-bit intervals for seven intervals. It then looks for the next 1-to-0 transition, which will occur no sooner than one more bit time.

The timing requirements for this scheme are modest. For example, IRA characters are typically sent as 8-bit units, including the parity bit. If the receiver is 5% slower or faster than the transmitter, the sampling of the eighth character bit will be displaced by 45% and still be correctly sampled. Figure 16.8c shows the effects of a timing error of sufficient magnitude to cause an error in reception. In this example we assume a data rate of 10,000 bits per second (10 kbps); therefore, each bit is of 0.1 millisecond (ms), or

---

[3]In the text, the transmission is shown from left (first bit transmitted) to right (last bit transmitted).

100 μs, duration. Assume that the receiver is fast by 6%, or 6 μs per bit time. Thus, the receiver samples the incoming character every 94 μs (based on the transmitter's clock). As can be seen, the last sample is erroneous.

Asynchronous transmission is simple and cheap but requires an overhead of 2 to 3 bits per character. For example, for an 8-bit character with no parity bit, using a 1-bit-long stop element, 2 out of every 10 bits convey no information but are there merely for synchronization; thus the overhead is 20%. Of course, the percentage overhead could be reduced by sending larger blocks of bits between the start bit and stop element. However, as Figure 16.8c suggests, the larger the block of bits, the greater the cumulative timing error. To achieve greater efficiency, a different form of synchronization, known as synchronous transmission, is used.

Synchronous Transmission

With **synchronous transmission,** a block of bits is transmitted in a steady stream without start and stop codes. The block may be many characters in length. To prevent timing drift between transmitter and receiver, their clocks must somehow be synchronized. One possibility is to provide a separate clock line between transmitter and receiver. One side (transmitter or receiver) pulses the line regularly with one short pulse per bit time. The other side uses these regular pulses as a clock. This technique works well over short distances, but over longer distances the clock pulses are subject to the same impairments as the data signal, and timing errors can occur. The other alternative is to embed the clocking information in the data signal. For digital signals, this can be accomplished with Manchester or Differential Manchester encoding, as explained in Section 16.2. For analog signals, a number of techniques can be used; for example, the carrier frequency itself can be used to synchronize the receiver based on the phase of the carrier.

With synchronous transmission, there is another level of synchronization required, to allow the receiver to determine the beginning and end of a block of data. To achieve this, each block begins with a *preamble* bit pattern and generally ends with a *postamble* bit pattern. In addition, other bits added to the block convey control information used in the data link control procedures discussed in Chapter 17. The data plus preamble, postamble, and control information are called a **frame.** The exact format of the frame depends on which data link control procedure is being used.

For sizable blocks of data, synchronous transmission is far more efficient than asynchronous. Asynchronous transmission requires 20% or more overhead. The control information, preamble, and postamble in synchronous transmission are typically less than 100 bits. For example, one of the more common schemes, HDLC, contains 48 bits of control, preamble, and postamble. Thus, for a 1000-character block of data, each frame consists of 48 bits of overhead and $1000 \times 8 = 8{,}000$ bits of data, for a percentage overhead of only $48/8048 \times 100\% = 0.6\%$.

For applications involving low-speed terminals or personal computers, asynchronous transmission is the most common technique. The technique is inexpensive, and its inefficiency is not a problem in most interactive applications, where more time is spent in looking at the screen and thinking than in transmission. However, the overhead of asynchronous transmission would be a heavy price to pay in more communications-intensive applications.

For large systems and computer networks, the efficiency of synchronous transmission is needed, even though it introduces the technical problem of synchronizing the clocks of transmitter and receiver.

In addition to the requirement for efficiency, large transfers introduce a requirement for error checking. The interactive user checks his or her own input and output for errors by looking at the screen and rekeying or asking for retransmission of portions that contain errors. Such a procedure is clearly impractical for long file transfers that occur at fast rates and often without an operator present. As we will see, synchronous transmission involves the use of a data link control procedure, which will automatically detect transmission errors and cause a frame in error to be retransmitted.

16.4 ERROR DETECTION

The Need for Error Control

As discussed in Chapter 15, any transmission facility has the potential of introducing errors. The ability to control those errors is an increasingly important task of a data communications system. This is partly because the issue of data integrity is becoming increasingly important. There is downward pressure on the allowable error rates for communication and mass storage systems as bandwidths and volumes of data increase. Certain data cannot be wrong; for example, consider the effect of an undetected data error on an electronic funds transfer. More generally, in any system that handles large amounts of data, uncorrected and undetected errors can degrade performance, response time, and possibly increase the need for intervention by human operators.

The process of **error control** involves two elements:

- **Error detection:** Redundancy is introduced into the data stream so that the occurrence of an error will be detected.
- **Error correction:** Once an error is detected by the receiver, the receiver and the transmitter cooperate to cause the frames in error to be retransmitted.

In this section, we look at the error detection process. We examine error correction in Chapter 17.

Parity Checks

The simplest approach to error detection is to append a parity bit to the end of a block of data. A typical example is IRA transmission, in which a parity bit is attached to each 7-bit IRA character. The value of this bit is selected so that the character has an even number of 1s (even parity) or an odd number of 1s (odd parity). So, for example, if the transmitter is transmitting the character G (1110001) and using odd parity, it will append a 1 and transmit 11100011. The receiver examines the received character and, if the total number of 1s is odd, assumes that no error has occurred. If one bit (or any odd number of bits) is erroneously inverted during transmission (for example, 11000011), then the receiver will detect an error. Note, however, that if two (or any even number) of bits are inverted due to error, an undetected error occurs. Typically, even parity is used for synchronous transmission and odd parity for asynchronous transmission.

The use of the parity bit is not foolproof, because noise impulses are often long enough to destroy more than one bit, particularly at high data rates.

Cyclic Redundancy Check

When synchronous transmission is used, it is possible to employ an error detection technique that is both more efficient (lower percentage of overhead bits) and more powerful (more errors detected) than the simple parity bit. This technique requires the addition of a **frame check sequence (FCS), or error-detecting code,** to each synchronous frame. The use of an FCS is illustrated in Figure 16.9, using the CRC code described in this subsection. On transmission, a calculation is performed on the bits of the frame to be transmitted; the result is inserted as an additional field in the frame. On reception, the same calculation is performed on the received bits and the calculated result is compared to the value stored in the incoming frame. If there is a discrepancy, the receiver assumes that an error has occurred.

One of the most common, and one of the most powerful, of the error-detecting codes is the **cyclic redundancy check (CRC).** For this technique, the message to be transmitted is treated as one long binary number. This number is divided by a unique prime binary number (a number divisible only by itself and 1), and the remainder is attached to the frame to be transmitted. When the frame is received, the receiver performs the same division, using the same divisor, and compares the calculated remainder with the remainder received in the frame. The most commonly used divisors are a 17-bit divisor, which produces a 16-bit remainder, and a 33-bit divisor, which produces a 32-bit remainder.

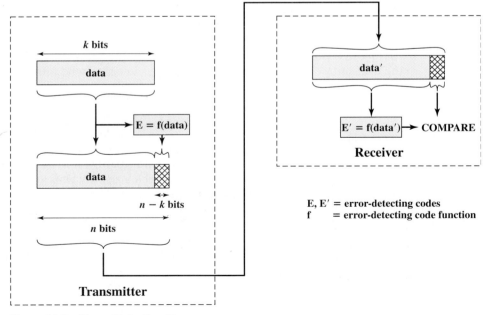

Figure 16.9 Error Detection Process

The measure of effectiveness of any error-detecting code is what percentage of errors it detects. For a CRC of length N, the rate of undetected errors is on the order of 2^{-N} (see [STAL04] for details). In summary, the CRC is a very powerful means of error detection and requires very little overhead. As an example, if a 16-bit FCS is used with frames of 1000 bits, then the overhead is only 1.6%. With a 32-bit FCS, the overhead is 3.2%.

APPLICATION NOTE
Devices, Encoding, Communication Parameters and Protocols

Encoding schemes, protocols and errors are not normally a part of our everyday lives. From an end user perspective, all we know is whether or not the network (or computer) is working. Even if we are on the front lines where communication systems are concerned, we do not often have to give them much thought. However, during installation, maintenance, and troubleshooting, understanding the mechanisms used by data transmission equipment and the standards involved can make a big difference.

Today's computers have a number of methods they can use to communicate with other machines. USB, EIA232 (A.K.A. COM or serial port), Firewire, parallel ports, network cards, video, and interfaces for mice and keyboards all represent some form of data transmission. What adds to the confusion is that organizations often wind up with several different computing platforms. As a result, the protocols and encoding schemes used by one device can be markedly different from the next. As an example, a company may have a variety or Macintosh computers alongside Windows-based machines. This can create an environment wherein peripherals must be purchased for both Fire wire and USB. In addition, the local area network protocol could be older LocalTalk or Ethernet.

Terminal emulation programs can also be a source of difficulty in terms of communication parameters. Computers connected via a serial connection must be configured to "speak the same language." This amounts to determining the speed of the link, number of data bits used, and the parity. This is a manual configuration that must be done on both ends of the link. If any one of these is not correct, the communication cannot proceed. Even operating systems and device drivers can create problems because they expose settings that users can change. An example can be found in Ethernet speed configurations. Ports on network equipment and the network interface card can be configured for a particular speed and full or half duplex. Normally left to "auto sense" the network, manually changing these can stop the network connection. In this case, different settings will make it impossible for the two ends to understand each other because not only are the speeds different, but the encoding schemes have completely changed. Another example can be seen in faster forms of Ethernet. Gigabit Ethernet comes in several versions, both in copper and optics. The optical versions vary based on wavelength, and the different wavelengths are not compatible.

Part of every successful transmission is error control. Error control can mean error detection or error detection *and* correction. Contemporary networks have extremely low error rates. Having a single bit in error for a billion transmitted would be excessive. The most common forms of error detection today are single parity bits, cyclical redundancy checks and checksums. These are used primarily by lower layer protocols and file systems. Some lower-level protocols have many error checking and testing functions built in. Protocols like the Point-to-Point Protocol (PPP) have provided extra tools, although they are not often used today. Supplementing these mechanisms are those used in the upper-layer protocols such as the sequence numbers and retransmission in TCP.

With the advent of wireless networks, the error rates have increased and additional problems such as lost connections can occur. Generally the throughput of wireless local area networks is less than that of wired networks. This is because the wireless network is a shared medium and the nodes must contend for bandwidth with each other. The access method used is similar to Ethernet but can take even longer. In addition, the overall bandwidth is less (for 802.11b the nodes are sharing an 11Mbps link) and so the throughput has already suffered. Finally, each frame in a wireless LAN is acknowledged (ACK), which further slows things down. Other local area network protocols do not use acknowledgments. While some of this delay will be alleviated with the newer, faster wireless standards, the media will remain shared and still require ACKs. For these reasons it may be necessary to modify communication parameters to ensure the successful completion of wireless transmissions.

The end users or network administrators cannot modify many of the components in a communication system. However, understanding the interrelated nature of encoding schemes, settings, and protocol operation can help improve efficiency, speed troubleshooting efforts, and assist in the design phases so that many problems can be avoided. In many cases, getting back to basics is the only way to solve a problem.

16.5 SUMMARY

Both analog and digital information can be encoded as either analog or digital signals. The particular encoding that is chosen depends on the specific requirements to be met and the media and co mmunications facilities available. For example, to transmit digital information over an analog telephone line, a modem is used to convert the digital data into analog form. Similarly, there is an increasing use of digital facilities, and voice information must be encoded in digital form to be transmitted on these digital facilities.

The transmission of a stream of bits from one device to another across a transmission link involves a great deal of cooperation and agreement between the two sides. One of the most fundamental requirements is **synchronization.** The receiver must know the rate at which bits are being received so that it can sample the line at regular intervals to determine the value of each received bit. Two techniques are in common use for this purpose. In asynchronous transmission, each character of data is treated independently. Each byte begins with a start bit that alerts the receiver that a character is arriving. The receiver samples each bit in the character and then looks for the beginning of the next character. This technique would not work well for long blocks of data because the receiver's clock might eventually drift out of synchronization with the transmitter's clock. However, sending data in large blocks is more efficient than sending data one character at a time. For large blocks, synchronous transmission is used. Each block of data is formatted as a frame that includes a starting and ending flag. Some form of synchronization, such as the use of Manchester encoding, is employed to maintain synchronization.

Error detection techniques are an important part of data transmission. The most widely used algorithm for error detection is the cyclic redundancy check.

16.6 RECOMMENDED READING AND WEB SITES

[STAL04] covers the topics of this chapter in greater detail. Another comprehensive treatment is [FREE98].

FREE98   Freeman, R. *Telecommunication Transmission Handbook*. New York: Wiley, 1998.
STAL04   Stallings, W. *Data and Computer Communications*, 7th edition. Upper Saddle River, NJ: Prentice Hall, 2004.

Recommended Web Sites:

- **DSL Forum:** Includes a FAQ and technical information about ADSL Forum specifications
- **Cable Datacom News:** Good collection of information on cable modems

16.7 KEY TERMS, REVIEW QUESTIONS, AND PROBLEMS

Key Terms

amplitude modulation	cyclic redundancy check (CRC)	modem
amplitude-shift keying	digital data	parity bit
analog data	digital signal	phase modulation
analog signal	digital transmission	phase-shift keying
analog transmission	error-detecting code	pulse-code modulation (PCM)
asynchronous transmission	error detection	synchronous transmission
baud	frequency modulation	
codec	frequency shift keying	

Review Questions

16.1.   Distinguish among analog data, analog signaling, and analog transmission.
16.2.   Distinguish among digital data, digital signaling, and digital transmission.
16.3.   What is the difference between amplification and retransmission?
16.4.   What is differential encoding?
16.5.   What function does a modem perform?

16.6.   Are the modem and the codec functional inverses (i.e., could an inverted modem function as a codec, or vice versa)?

16.7.   Indicate three major advantages of digital transmission over analog transmission.

16.8.   How are binary values represented in amplitude shift keying, and what is the limitation of this approach?

16.9.   Indicate the major categories into which modems may be classified based on their data rates.

16.10.   What is NRZ-L? What is a major disadvantage of this data encoding approach?

16.11.   Match the device or system with the correct type of signal and data.

Device/System	Data/Signal
Modem transmissions	A. Digital data/digital encoding
Ethernet	B. Digital data/analog encoding
AM/FM radio	C. Analog data/digital encoding
PCM	D. Analog data/analog encoding

16.12.   How is the transmission of a single character differentiated from the transmission of the next character in asynchronous transmission?

16.13.   What is a major disadvantage of asynchronous transmission?

Problems

16.1   Given the bit pattern 01100, encode this data using ASK, FSK, and PSK. For these problems you may assume that a digital zero is the base value and that a digital one requires an increase in amplitude, frequency, or a phase change. You may also assume transmission from left to right with the first digital zero being the leftmost bit.

16.2   Using Manchester encoding, encode the bit pattern 0100.

16.3   Suppose a file of 10,000 bytes is to be sent over a line at 2400 bps.

a.   Calculate the overhead in bits and time in using asynchronous communication. Assume one start bit and a stop element of length one bit, and 8 bits to send the byte itself for each character. The 8-bit character consists of all data bits, with no parity bit.

b.   Calculate the overhead in bits and time using synchronous communication. Assume that the data are sent in frames. Each frame consists of 1000 characters = 8000 bits and an overhead of 48 control bits per frame.

c.   What would the answers to parts (a) and (b) be for a file of 100,000 characters?

d.   What would the answers to parts (a) and (b) be for the original file of 10,000 characters except at a data rate of 9600 bps?

16.4   A data source produces 7-bit IRA characters. Derive an expression of the maximum effective data rate (rate of IRA data bits) over a x-bps line for the following:

a.   Asynchronous transmission, with a 1.5-unit stop element and a parity bit.

b.   Synchronous transmission, with a frame consisting of 48 control bits and 128 information bits. The information field contains 8-bit (parity included) IRA characters.

c.   Same as part (b) except that the information field is 1024 bits.

16.5   Demonstrate by example (write down a few dozen arbitrary bit patterns; assume one start bit and a stop element of length 1 bit) that a receiver that suffers a framing error on asynchronous transmission will eventually become realigned.

16.6   Suppose that a sender and receiver use asynchronous transmission and agree not to use any stop elements. Could this work? If so, explain any necessary conditions.

16.7   An asynchronous transmission scheme uses 8 data bits, an even parity bit, and a stop element of length 2 bits. What percentage of clock inaccuracy can be tolerated at the receiver with respect to the framing error? Assume that the bit samples are taken at the middle of the clock period. Also assume that at the beginning of the start bit the clock and incoming bits are in phase.

16.8 Suppose that a synchronous serial data transmission is clocked by two clocks (one at the sender and one at the receiver) that each has a drift of 1 minute in one year. How long a sequence of bits can be sent before possible clock drift could cause a problem? Assume that a bit waveform will be good if it is sampled within 40% of its center and that the sender and receiver are resynchronized at the beginning of each frame. Note that the transmission rate is not a factor, as both the bit period and the absolute timing error decrease proportionately at higher transmission rates.

16.9 When President Franklin Delano Roosevelt gave his first inaugural speech—"the only thing we have to fear is fear itself. . . ."—it lasted about 23 minutes. In printed form it takes about 4 pages. The part that is printed on a page is about $4\frac{1}{2}$ inches wide and $7\frac{3}{8}$ inches vertically. There are about 77 characters per line, and there are about $5\frac{1}{3}$ lines per vertical inch. Suppose you wished to represent the speech in a CD-ROM encyclopedia.

a. How many 8-bit bytes would it take to store a recording of FDR giving the speech using PCM without compression assuming a bandwidth of 22,000 Hz, monaural? Ignore any overhead. You wish to pick a sample discretization that can encode about 64,000 amplitude levels. Use the minimum sampling rate implied by the sampling theorem.

b. Suppose the speech was stored as text, one text character per byte without compression. How much space, in bytes, is on the CD-ROM now?

c. Suppose the speech was stored as an image of the text as specified previously. That is, you only scan the area with text. Suppose the image is scanned at 1200 pixels per inch in both the horizontal and vertical directions, and that the image is stored as black and white (no color or gray scale). Again ignore overhead and assume no compression. How much CD-ROM storage in bytes is needed for this representation?

Note: The relative size of the results of (a), (b), and (c) make qualitative sense. The reading carries the most information, including inflection and pacing, in addition to the text itself. This representation takes the most space. The image carries more information than the text, such as fonts and page layout, but less information than the reading. The text as an ASCII string carries no additional information beyond the text itself but is the most compact.

16.10 Two communicating devices are using a single-bit even-parity check for error detection. The transmitter sends the byte 10101010, and (because of channel noise) the receiver gets the byte 10011010. Will the receiver detect the error? Why or why not?

DATA LINK CONTROL AND MULTIPLEXING

CHAPTER OBJECTIVES

After reading this chapter, you should be able to

- Explain the need for a data link control protocol.
- Describe the basic operation of a data link control protocol such as the widely used HDLC.
- Explain the need for transmission efficiency and list the two major approaches used to achieve efficiency.
- Discuss the use of frequency division multiplexing in video distribution and in voice networks.
- Describe the use of multiplexing in digital carrier systems.
- Discuss the T-1 service and describe its importance and the applications that are using it.
- Discuss the SONET standard and its significance for wide area networking.

This chapter examines two important data communications concepts: data link control and multiplexing.

A data link control protocol includes techniques for regulating the flow of data over a communications link and for compensating for transmission errors. We first examine the concepts of flow control and error control and then illustrate their use in the data link control protocol HDLC. This protocol is one of the most commonly used ones, and it illustrates the techniques used in such protocols.

A major source of expense in any distributed or networked environment is transmission cost. Because of the critical nature of transmission in such environments and their potentially high cost, it is important to maximize the amount of information that can be carried over a given resource or, alternatively, to minimize the transmission capacity needed to satisfy a given business information communications requirement. The latter part of the chapter looks at key approach to achieving transmission efficiency: multiplexing.

17.1 FLOW CONTROL AND ERROR CONTROL

Physical interface standards provide a means by which a stream of data can be transmitted, either synchronously or asynchronously, onto a transmission medium. However, these interfaces do not include all of the required functions for data communication. Among the most important items lacking are flow control and error control.

To provide these needed functions, a data link control protocol is used. Such protocols are generally only used for synchronous transmission. The basic scheme is as follows. The data to be transmitted by an application are sent to the data link module, which organizes the data into a set of frames. Each frame is supplemented with control bits that allow the two sides to cooperate to deliver the data reliably. The control bits are added by the sender of the frame. When the frame arrives, the receiver examines the control bits and, if the data arrive successfully, strips off the control bits and then delivers the pure data to the intended destination point within the system. Figure 17.1 illustrates the process.

With the use of control bits, a number of functions can be performed, including flow control and error control. In this section, we introduce these functions. The next section looks specifically at one data link control protocol, known as High-Level Data Link Control (HDLC).

Flow Control

Suppose that we wish to write a program, called a printer driver, to pass data from a computer to a printer. We connect the two with the appropriate cable to a port on the host machine. The host port is programmable to match the peripheral device. In this case, let us say that the printer is set up for IRA 7-bit characters, odd parity, a stop of 1-bit length, and a data rate of 9600 bps. We use these parameters on the host port, write the program, and try to send a page of text to the printer. The result is that, after the first few lines of text, there are a number of missing characters; in fact more missing characters than are printed.

What is the problem? First, let's calculate the character transfer rate. We have 7 bits for the character, 1 for the start bit, 1 for parity, and 1 for stop, for a total of 10 bits per character. Because the computer is transmitting at 9600 bps, the character rate is 960 characters per second. Checking the printer manual, we find that the printer can print at a maximum rate of 80 characters per second. This means that

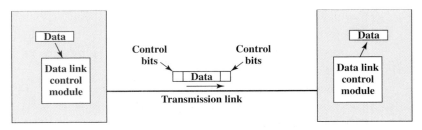

Figure 17.1 Operation of a Data Link Control Module

we are sending 12 times as much data as the printer can accept. No wonder that data are lost.

It may seem odd that the printer is equipped with a higher data rate capability than printing capability, but this is common. The printer includes a small buffer (perhaps 200 characters) so that it can accept characters in a burst of speed, print those characters, and then accept another burst. This allows the printer to be used on a shared line that is running at a sufficiently high speed to service a number of printers and terminals. For example, a 9600-bps line could easily accommodate 5 or 10 such printers. However, because the data rate is higher than the printing rate, it is possible for the overrun condition previously described to occur.

Flow control is a technique for assuring that a transmitting entity does not overwhelm a receiving entity with data. In the case of an electromagnetic device, such as a printer or disc drive, a fixed buffer is provided, as described previously. In the case of data being transmitted to a computer, it is typically destined for some application or system program. The receiving computer allocates a data buffer of some maximum length for that application or system program. When data are received, the computer must do a certain amount of processing before passing the data to the higher-level software. In the absence of flow control, the receiver's buffer may fill up and overflow while it is processing old data.

For data link control protocols, flow control is achieved by numbering each frame sequentially (e.g., 0, 1, 2, ...). Initially, a buffer is allocated at the receiver of an agreed size. As frames arrive and are processed, the receiver returns an acknowledgment indicating which frames have been received and implicitly indicating that more frames may be sent. This should be clearer when HDLC is discussed subsequently.

Error Control

In Chapter 16, we discussed techniques that enable a receiver to detect errors that occur in the transmission and reception process. To correct these errors, data link control provides mechanisms by which the two sides cooperate in the retransmission of frames that suffer from errors on the first try. These mechanisms extend the flow control techniques discussed previously. Again, data are sent as a sequence of frames. In addition, we consider two types of errors:

- **Lost frame:** A frame fails to arrive at the other side. In the case of a network, the network may simply fail to deliver a frame. In the case of a direct point-to-point data link, a noise burst may damage a frame to the extent that the receiver is not aware that a frame has been transmitted.

- **Damaged frame:** A recognizable frame does arrive, but some of the bits are in error (have been altered during transmission).

The most common techniques for error control are based on some or all of the following ingredients:

- **Error detection:** The destination detects frames that are in error, using the techniques described in the preceding chapter, and discards those frames.

- **Positive acknowledgment:** The destination returns a positive acknowledgment to successfully received, error-free frames.

- **Retransmission after timeout:** The source retransmits a frame that has not been acknowledged after a predetermined amount of time.
- **Negative acknowledgment and retransmission:** The destination returns a negative acknowledgment to frames in which an error is detected. The source retransmits such frames.

Collectively, these mechanisms are all referred to as **automatic repeat request (ARQ).** The effect of ARQ is to turn a potentially unreliable data link into a reliable one. The precise mechanism of ARQ is described in the next section as part of our discussion of HDLC.

17.2 HIGH-LEVEL DATA LINK CONTROL

The most important data link control protocol is HDLC. HDLC is widely used and is the basis for many other important data link control protocols, which use the same or similar formats and the same mechanisms as employed in HDLC.

HDLC Frame Structure

Perhaps the best way to begin an explanation of HDLC is to look at the frame structure. The operation of HDLC involves the exchange of two sorts of information between the two connected stations. First, HDLC accepts user data from some higher layer of software and delivers that user data across the link to the other side. On the other side, HDLC accepts the user data and delivers it to a higher layer of software on that side. Second, the two HDLC modules exchange control information to provide for flow control, error control, and other control functions. The method by which this is done is to format the information that is exchanged into a **frame**. A frame is a predefined structure that provides a specific location for various kinds of control information and for user data.

Figure 17.2 depicts the format of the HDLC frame. The frame has the following fields:

- **Flag:** Used for synchronization. It appears at the beginning and end of the frame and always contains the pattern 01111110.
- **Address:** Indicates the secondary station for this transmission. It is needed in the case of a multidrop line, where a primary may send data to one of a number of secondaries, and one of a number of secondaries may send data to the primary. This field is usually 8 bits long but can be extended (Figure 17.2b).
- **Control:** Identifies the purpose and functions of the frame. It is described later in this subsection.
- **Information:** Contains the user data to be transmitted.
- **Frame Check Sequence:** Contains a 16- or 32-bit cyclic redundancy check, used for error detection.

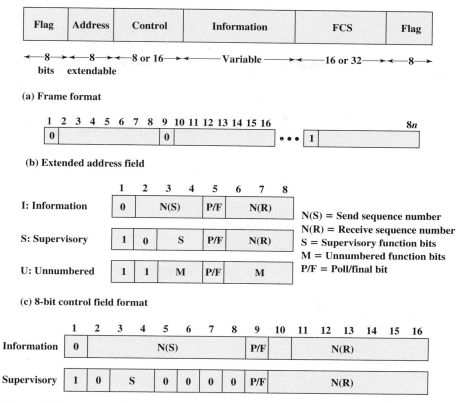

Figure 17.2 HDLC Frame Structure

HDLC defines three types of frames, each with a different control field format. Information frames (I frames) carry the user data to be transmitted for the station. Additionally, the information frames contain control information for flow control and error control. Supervisory frames (S frames) provide another means of exercising flow control and error control. Unnumbered frames (U frames) provide supplemental link control functions.

The first one or two bits of the control field serve to identify the frame type. The remaining bit positions are organized into subfields, as indicated in Figures 17.2c and 17.2d. Their use is explained in the discussion of HDLC operation, which follows. Note that the basic control field for S and I frames uses 3-bit sequence numbers. With the appropriate set-mode commands, an extended control field can be used that employs 7-bit sequence numbers.

All of the control field formats contain the poll/final (P/F) bit. Its use depends on context. Typically, in command frames, it is referred to as the P bit and is set to 1 to solicit (poll) a response frame from the peer HDLC entity. In response frames, it is referred to as the F bit and is set to 1 to indicate the response frame transmitted as a result of a soliciting command.

HDLC Operation

HDLC operation consists of the exchange of I frames, S frames, and U frames between two stations. The various commands and responses defined for these frame types are listed in Table 17.1. In describing HDLC operation, we will discuss these three types of frames.

The operation of HDLC involves three phases. First, one side or another initializes the data link so that frames may be exchanged in an orderly fashion. During this phase, the options that are to be used are agreed upon. After initialization, the two sides exchange user data and the control information to exercise flow and error control. Finally, one of the two sides signals the termination of the operation.

Table 17.1   HDLC Commands and Responses

Name	Command/Response	Description
Information (I)	C/R	**Exchange user data**
Supervisory (S)		
Receive ready (RR)	C/R	Positive acknowledgment; ready to receive I frame
Receive not ready (RNR)	C/R	Positive acknowledgment; not ready to receive
Reject (REJ)	C/R	Negative acknowledgment; go back N
Selective reject (SREJ)	C/R	Negative acknowledgment; selective reject
Unnumbered (U)		
Set normal response/extended mode (SNRM/SNRME)	C	Set mode; extended = 7-bit sequence numbers
Set asynchronous response/extended mode (SARM/SARME)	C	Set mode; extended = 7-bit sequence numbers
Set asynchronous balanced/extended mode (SABM, SABME)	C	Set mode; extended = 7-bit sequence numbers
Set initialization mode (SIM)	C	Initialize link control functions in addressed station
Disconnect (DISC)	C	Terminate logical link connection
Unnumbered acknowledgment (UA)	R	Acknowledge acceptance of one of the set-mode commands
Disconnected mode (DM)	R	Responder is in disconnected mode
Request disconnect (RD)	R	Request for DISC command
Request initialization mode (RIM)	R	Initialization needed; request for SIM command
Unnumbered information (UI)	C/R	Used to exchange control information
Unnumbered poll (UP)	C	Used to solicit control information
Reset (RSET)	C	Used for recovery; resets N(R), N(S)
Exchange identification (XID)	C/R	Used to request/report status
Test (TEST)	C/R	Exchange identical information fields for testing
Frame reject (FRMR)	R	Report receipt of unacceptable frame

Initialization Either side may request initialization by issuing one of the six set-mode commands. This command serves three purposes:

1. It signals the other side that initialization is requested.

2. It specifies which of three modes is requested; these modes have to do with whether one side acts as a primary and controls the exchange or whether the two sides are peers and cooperate in the exchange.

3. It specifies whether 3- or 7-bit sequence numbers are to be used.

If the other side accepts this request, then the HDLC module on that end transmits an Unnumbered Acknowledgment (UA) frame back to the initiating side. If the request is rejected, then a Disconnected Mode (DM) frame is sent.

Data Transfer When initialization has been requested and accepted, a logical connection is established. Both sides may begin to send user data in I frames, starting with sequence number 0. The N(S) and N(R) fields of the I frame are sequence numbers that support flow control and error control. An HDLC module sending a sequence of I frames will number them sequentially, modulo 8 or 128, depending on whether 3- or 7-bit sequence numbers are used, and place the sequence number in N(S). N(R) is the acknowledgment for I frames received; it enables the HDLC module to indicate which number I frame it expects to receive next.

S frames are also used for flow control and error control. The Receive Ready (RR) frame is used to acknowledge the last I frame received by indicating the next I frame expected. The RR is used when there is no reverse user data traffic (I frames) to carry an acknowledgment. Receive Not Ready (RNR) acknowledges an I frame, as with RR, but also asks the peer entity to suspend transmission of I frames. When the entity that issued RNR is again ready, it sends an RR. REJ initiates the go-back-N ARQ. It indicates that the last I frame received has been rejected and that retransmission of all I frames beginning with number N(R) is required. Selective reject (SREJ) is used to request retransmission of a single frame.

Disconnect Either HDLC module can initiate a disconnect, either on its own initiative if there is some sort of fault or at the request of its higher-layer user. HDLC issues a disconnect by sending a Disconnect (DISC) frame. The other side must accept the disconnect by replying with a UA.

Examples of Operation To better understand HDLC operation, several examples are presented in Figure 17.3. In the example diagrams, each arrow includes a legend that specifies the frame type, the setting of the P/F bit, and, where appropriate, the values of N(R) and N(S). The setting of the P or F bit is 1 if the designation is present and 0 if absent.

Figure 17.3a shows the frames involved in link setup and disconnect. The HDLC entity for one side issues an SABM command[1] to the other side and starts a

---

[1]This stands for Set Asynchronous Mode Balanced. The SABM command is a request to start an exchange. The ABM part of the acronym refers to the mode of transfer, a detail that need not concern us here.

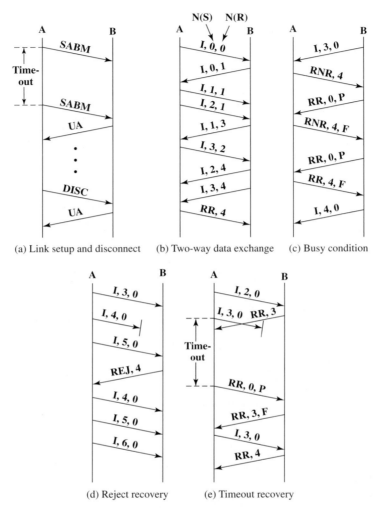

Figure 17.3 Examples of HDLC Operation

timer. The other side, upon receiving the SABM, returns a UA response and sets local variables and counters to their initial values. The initiating entity receives the UA response, sets its variables and counters, and stops the timer. The logical connection is now active, and both sides may begin transmitting frames. Should the timer expire without a response, the originator will repeat the SABM, as illustrated. This would be repeated until a UA or DM is received or until, after a given number of tries, the entity attempting initiation gives up and reports failure to a management entity. In such a case, higher-layer intervention is necessary. The same figure (Figure 17.3a) shows the disconnect procedure. One side issues a DISC command, and the other responds with a UA response.

Figure 17.3b illustrates the full-duplex exchange of I frames. When an entity sends a number of I frames in a row with no incoming data, then the receive sequence number, N(R), is simply repeated (e.g., I,1,1; I,2,1 in the A-to-B direction). When an entity receives a number of I frames in a row with no outgoing frames, then the receive sequence number in the next outgoing frame must reflect the cumulative activity (e.g., I,1,3 in the B-to-A direction). Note that, in addition to I frames, data exchange may involve supervisory frames.

Figure 17.3c shows an operation involving a busy condition. Such a condition may arise because an HDLC entity is not able to process I frames as fast as they are arriving, or the intended user is not able to accept data as fast as they arrive in I frames. In either case, the entity's receive buffer fills up and it must halt the incoming flow of I frames, using an RNR command. In this example, station A issues an RNR, which requires the other side to halt transmission of I frames. The station receiving the RNR will usually poll the busy station at some periodic interval by sending an RR with the P bit set. This requires the other side to respond with either an RR or an RNR. When the busy condition has cleared, A returns an RR, and I frame transmission from B can resume.

An example of error recovery using the REJ command is shown in Figure 17.3d. In this example, A transmits I frames numbered 3, 4, and 5. Frame 4 suffers an error. B detects the error and discards the frame. When B receives I frame 5, it discards this frame because it is out of order and sends an REJ with an N(R) of 4. This causes A to initiate retransmission of all I frames sent, beginning with frame 4. It may continue to send additional frames after the retransmitted frames.

An example of error recovery using a timeout is shown in Figure 17.3e. In this example, A transmits I frame number 3 as the last in a sequence of I frames. The frame suffers an error. B detects the error and discards it. However, B cannot send an REJ. This is because there is no way to know if this was an I frame. If an error is detected in a frame, all of the bits of that frame are suspect, and the receiver has no way to act upon it. A, however, started a timer as the frame was transmitted. This timer has a duration long enough to span the expected response time. When the timer expires, A initiates recovery action. This is usually done by polling the other side with an RR command with the P bit set, to determine the status of the other side. Because the poll demands a response, the entity will receive a frame containing an N(R) field and be able to proceed. In this case, the response indicates that frame 3 was lost, which A retransmits.

These examples are not exhaustive. However, they should give the reader a good feel for the behavior of HDLC.

17.3 MOTIVATION FOR MULTIPLEXING

Typically, two communicating stations will not utilize the full capacity of a data link. For efficiency, it should be possible to share that capacity. A generic term for such sharing is *multiplexing*.

A common application of multiplexing is in long-haul communications. Trunks on long-haul networks are high-capacity fiber, coaxial, or microwave links. These links can carry large numbers of voice and data transmissions simultaneously using multiplexing.

Figure 17.4 depicts the multiplexing function in its simplest form. There are *n* inputs to a multiplexer. The multiplexer is connected by a single data link to a

Figure 17.4   Multiplexing

demultiplexer. The link is able to carry n separate channels of data. The multiplexer combines (multiplexes) data from the n input lines and transmits over a higher-capacity data link. The demultiplexer accepts the multiplexed data stream, separates (demultiplexes) the data according to channel, and delivers them to the appropriate output lines.

The widespread use of multiplexing in data communications can be explained by the following:

- The higher the data rate, the more cost-effective the transmission facility. That is, for a given application and over a given distance, the cost per kbps declines with an increase in the data rate of the transmission facility. Similarly, the cost of transmission and receiving equipment, per kbps, declines with increasing data rate.

- Most individual data communicating devices require relatively modest data rate support. For example, for many terminal and personal computer applications that do not involve Web access or intensive graphics, a data rate of between 9600 bps and 64 kbps is generally adequate.

The preceding statements were phrased in terms of data communicating devices. Similar statements apply to voice communications. That is, the greater the capacity of a transmission facility, in terms of voice channels, the less the cost per individual voice channel, and the capacity required for a single voice channel is modest.

The remainder of this chapter concentrates on two types of multiplexing techniques. The first, frequency division multiplexing (FDM), is the most heavily used and is familiar to anyone who has ever used a radio or television set. The second is a particular case of time division multiplexing (TDM) known as synchronous TDM. This is commonly used for multiplexing digitized voice streams and data streams.

17.4 FREQUENCY DIVISION MULTIPLEXING

Frequency division multiplexing (FDM) is a familiar and widely used form of multiplexing. A simple example is its use in cable TV systems, which carry multiple video channels on a single cable. FDM is possible when the useful bandwidth of the transmission medium exceeds the required bandwidth of signals to be transmitted. A number of signals can be carried simultaneously if each signal is modulated onto a different carrier frequency and the carrier frequencies are sufficiently separated that the bandwidths of the signals do not overlap. A general case of FDM is shown

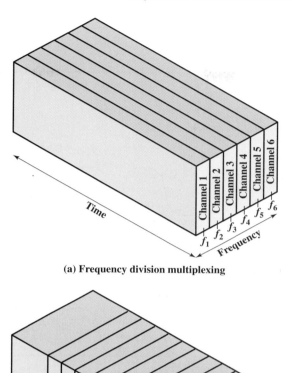

(a) Frequency division multiplexing

(b) Time division multiplexing

Figure 17.5   FDM and TDM

in Figure 17.5a. Six signal sources are fed into a multiplexer, which modulates each signal onto a different frequency ($f_1, \ldots, f_6$). Each modulated signal requires a certain bandwidth centered on its carrier frequency, referred to as a *channel*. To prevent interference, the channels are separated by guard bands, which are unused portions of the spectrum.

   The composite signal transmitted across the medium is analog. Note, however, that the input signals may be either digital or analog. In the case of digital input, the input signals must be passed through modems to be converted to analog. In either case, each analog input signal must then be modulated to move it to the appropriate frequency band.

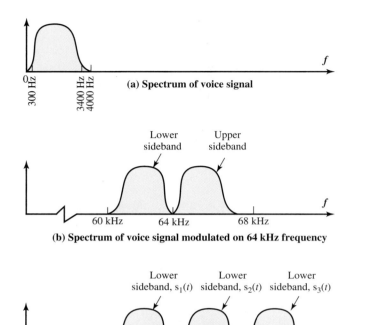

Figure 17.6   FDM of Three Voiceband Signals

A simple example of FDM is illustrated in Figure 17.6, which shows the transmission of three voice signals simultaneously over a transmission medium. As was mentioned, the bandwidth of a voice signal is generally taken to be 4 kHz, with an effective spectrum of 300 to 3400 Hz (Figure 17.6a). If such a signal is used to amplitude modulate a 64-kHz carrier, the spectrum of Figure 17.6b results. The modulated signal has a bandwidth of 8 kHz, extending from 60 to 68 kHz. To make efficient use of bandwidth, we elect to transmit only the lower half of the spectrum, called the lower sideband. Similarly, the two other voice signals can be modulated to fit into the ranges 64 to 68 kHz and 68 to 72 kHz, respectively. These signals are then combined in the multiplexer to produce a single signal with a range of 60 to 72 kHz. At the receiving end, the demultiplexing process involves splitting the received signal into three frequency bands and then demodulating each signal back to the original voice band (0 to 4 kHz). Note that there is only a minor amount of overlap between the multiplexed signals. Because the effective bandwidth of each signal is actually less than 4 kHz, no noticeable interference results.

FDM was the mainstay of telephone transmission for many years; it is actually more efficient in terms of bandwidth than digital systems. The problem is that noise is amplified along with the voice signal. This fact, and the great decrease in the cost of digital electronics, has led to the widespread replacement of FDM systems with TDM systems in telephone networks.

Although the use of FDM for voice transmission is declining rapidly, it is still used almost exclusively for television distribution systems, including broadcast television and cable TV. The analog television signal discussed in Chapter 2 fits comfortably into a 6-MHz bandwidth. Figure 17.7 depicts the transmitted video signal and its bandwidth. The black-and-white video signal is amplitude modulated on a carrier signal. The resulting signal has a bandwidth of about 5 MHz, most of which is above the carrier signal. A separate color subcarrier is used to transmit color information. This is spaced far enough from the main carrier that there is essentially no interference. Finally, the audio portion of the signal is modulated on a third carrier, outside the effective bandwidth of the other two signals. The composite signal fits into a 6-MHz bandwidth with the video, color, and audio signal carriers at 1.25 MHz, 4.799545 MHz, and 5.75 MHz above the lower edge of the band, respectively. Thus, multiple TV signals can be frequency division multiplexed on a cable, each with a bandwidth of 6 MHz. Given the enormous bandwidth of

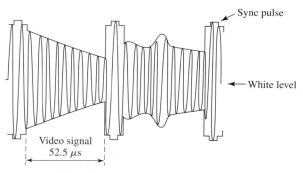

(a) Amplitude modulation with video signal

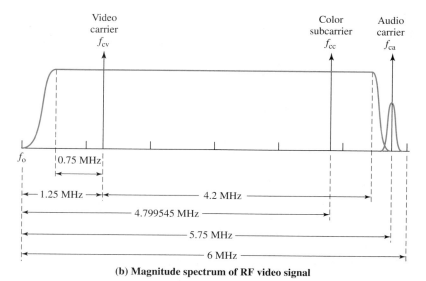

(b) Magnitude spectrum of RF video signal

Figure 17.7   Transmitted TV Signal

coaxial cable (as much a 500 MHz), dozens of video signals can be simultaneously carried using FDM.

Wavelength Division Multiplexing

The true potential of optical fiber is fully exploited when multiple beams of light at different frequencies are transmitted on the same fiber. This is a form of frequency division multiplexing (FDM) but is commonly called wavelength division multiplexing (WDM). With WDM, the light streaming through the fiber consists of many colors, or wavelengths, each carrying a separate channel of data. In 1997, a landmark was reached when Bell Laboratories was able to demonstrate a WDM system with 100 beams each operating at 10 Gbps, for a total data rate of 1 trillion bits per second (also referred to as 1 terabit per second or 1 Tbps). Commercial systems with 160 channels of 10 Gbps are now available. In a lab environment, Alcatel has carried 256 channels at 39.8 Gbps each, a total of 10.1 Tbps, over a 100-km span.

A typical WDM system has the same general architecture as other FDM systems. A number of sources generate a laser beam at different wavelengths. These are sent to a multiplexer, which consolidates the sources for transmission over a single fiber line. Optical amplifiers, typically spaced tens of kilometers apart, amplify all of the wavelengths simultaneously. Finally, the composite signal arrives at a demultiplexer, where the component channels are separated and sent to receivers at the destination point.

Most WDM systems operate in the 1550-nm range. In early systems, 200 GHz was allocated to each channel, but today most WDM systems use 50-GHz spacing. The channel spacing defined in ITU-T G.692, which accommodates 80 50-GHz channels, is summarized in Table 17.2.

The term **dense wavelength division multiplexing** (DWDM) is often seen in the literature. There is no official or standard definition of this term. The term connotes

Table 17.2   ITU WDM Channel Spacing (G.692)

Frequency (THz)	Wavelength in Vacuum (nm)	50 GHz	100 GHz	200 GHz
196.10	1528.77	X	X	X
196.05	1529.16	X		
196.00	1529.55	X	X	
195.95	1529.94	X		
195.90	1530.33	X	X	X
195.85	1530.72	X		
195.80	1531.12	X	X	
195.75	1531.51	X		
195.70	1531.90	X	X	X
195.65	1532.29	X		
195.60	1532.68	X	X	
. . .	. . .			
192.10	1560.61	X	X	X

the use of more channels, more closely spaced, than ordinary WDM. In general, a channel spacing of 200 GHz or less could be considered dense.

ADSL

The asymmetric digital subscriber line provides an interesting example of the use of FDM. In this section, we provide a brief overview of the method.

ADSL Design The term *asymmetric* is used because ADSL provides more capacity downstream (from the carrier's central office to the customer's site) than upstream (from customer to carrier). ADSL was originally targeted at the expected need for video on demand and related services. This application has not materialized. However, since the introduction of ADSL technology, the demand for high-speed access to the Internet has grown. Typically, the user requires far higher capacity for downstream than for upstream transmission. Most user transmissions are in the form of keyboard strokes or transmission of short e-mail messages, whereas incoming traffic, especially Web traffic, can involve large amounts of data and include images or even video. Thus, ADSL provides a perfect fit for the Internet requirement.

ADSL uses frequency division modulation (FDM) in a novel way to exploit the 1-MHz capacity of twisted pair. There are three elements of the ADSL strategy (Figure 17.8):

- Reserve lowest 25 kHz for voice, known as POTS (plain old telephone service). The voice is carried only in the 0- to 4-kHz band; the additional bandwidth is to prevent crosstalk between the voice and data channels.
- Use either echo cancellation[2] or FDM to allocate two bands, a smaller upstream band and a larger downstream band.
- Use FDM within the upstream and downstream bands. In this case, a single bit stream is split into multiple parallel bit streams and each portion is carried in a separate frequency band. A commonly used technique is known as discrete multitone, explained subsequently.

When echo cancellation is used, the entire frequency band for the upstream channel overlaps the lower portion of the downstream channel. This has two advantages compared to the use of distinct frequency bands for upstream and downstream.

- The higher the frequency, the greater the attenuation. With the use of echo cancellation, more of the downstream bandwidth is in the "good" part of the spectrum.
- The echo cancellation design is more flexible for changing upstream capacity. The upstream channel can be extended upward without running into the downstream; instead, the area of overlap is extended.

The disadvantage of the use of echo cancellation is the need for echo cancellation logic on both ends of the line.

---

[2]Echo cancellation is a signal processing technique that allows transmission of signals in both directions in the same frequency band on a single transmission line simultaneously. In essence, a transmitter must subtract the echo of its own transmission from the incoming signal to recover the signal sent by the other side.

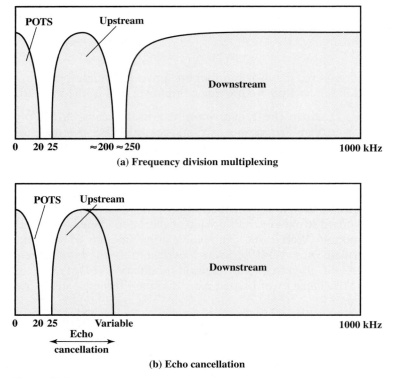

Figure 17.8   ADSL Channel Configuration

The ADSL scheme provides a range of up to 5.5 km, depending on the diameter of the cable and its quality. This is sufficient to cover about 95% of all U.S. subscriber lines and should provide comparable coverage in other nations.

Discrete Multitone   Discrete multitone (DMT) uses multiple carrier signals at different frequencies, sending some of the bits on each channel. The available transmission band (upstream or downstream) is divided into a number of 4-kHz subchannels. On initialization, the DMT modem sends out test signals on each subchannel to determine the signal-to-noise ratio. The modem then assigns more bits to channels with better signal transmission qualities and less bits to channels with poorer signal transmission qualities. Figure 17.9 illustrates this process. Each subchannel can carry a data rate of from 0 to 60 kbps. The figure shows a typical situation in which there is

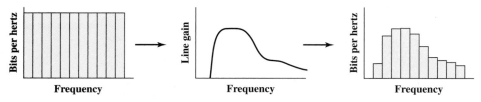

Figure 17.9   DMT Bits per Channel Allocation

increasing attenuation and hence decreasing signal-to-noise ratio at higher frequencies. As a result, the higher-frequency subchannels carry less of the load.

Present ADSL/DMT designs employ 256 downstream subchannels. In theory, with each 4-kHz subchannel carrying 60 kbps, it would be possible to transmit at a rate of 15.36 Mbps. In practice, transmission impairments prevent attainment of this data rate. Current implementations operate at from 1.5 to 9 Mbps, depending on line distance and quality.

17.5 SYNCHRONOUS TIME DIVISION MULTIPLEXING

The TDM Mechanism

The other major form of multiplexing is **time division multiplexing** (TDM). In this section we examine **synchronous TDM,** which is often simply referred to as TDM.

Time division multiplexing is possible when the data rate of the transmission medium exceeds the required data rate of signals to be transmitted. A number of digital signals, or analog signals carrying digital data, can be carried simultaneously by interleaving portions of each signal in time. A general case of TDM is shown in Figure 17.5b. Six signal sources are fed into a multiplexer, which interleaves the bits from each signal by taking turns transmitting bits from each of the signals in a round-robin fashion. For example, the multiplexer in Figure 17.5b has six inputs that might be, say, 9.6 kbps each. A single line with a capacity of at least 57.6 kbps accommodates all six sources.

A simple example of TDM is illustrated in Figure 17.10, which shows the transmission of three data signals simultaneously over a transmission medium. In this example, each source operates at 64 kbps. The output from each source is briefly buffered. Each buffer is typically one bit or one character in length. The buffers are scanned in round-robin fashion to form a composite digital data stream. The scan

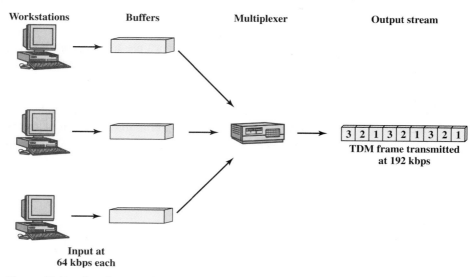

Figure 17.10   Synchronous TDM of Three Data Channels

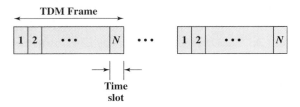

Figure 17.11   TDM Frame Structure

operations are sufficiently rapid so that each buffer is emptied before more data can arrive. The scanned data are combined by the multiplexer into a composite data stream. Thus, the data rate transmitted by the multiplexer must at least equal the sum of the data rates of the three inputs ($3 \times 64 = 192$ kbps). The digital signal produced by the multiplexer may be transmitted digitally or passed through a modem so that an analog signal is transmitted. In either case, transmission is typically synchronous (as opposed to asynchronous). At the receiving end , the demultiplexing process involves distributing the incoming data among three destination buffers.

The data transmitted by a synchronous TDM system have a format like that of Figure 17.11. The data are organized into **frames,** each of which contains a cycle of time slots. In each frame, one or more slots are dedicated to each data source. Transmission consists of the transmission of a sequence of frames. The set of time slots dedicated to one source, from frame to frame, is called a **channel.** Note that this is the same term used for FDM. The two uses of the term *channel* are logically equivalent. In both cases, a portion of the transmission capacity is dedicated to signals from a single source; that source sees a constant-data-rate or constant-bandwidth channel for transmission.

The slot length equals the transmitter buffer length, typically a bit or a byte (character). The byte-interleaving technique is used with both asynchronous and synchronous sources. Each time slot contains one byte of data. Typically, the start and stop bits of each character are eliminated before transmission and reinserted by the receiver, thus improving efficiency. The bit-interleaving technique is used with synchronous sources.

Synchronous TDM is called synchronous not because synchronous transmission is used but because the time slots are preassigned to sources and are fixed. The time slots for a given source are transmitted whether or not the source has data to send. This is, of course, also the case with FDM: A frequency band is dedicated to a particular source whether or not the source is transmitting at any given time. In both cases, capacity is wasted to achieve simplicity of implementation. Even when fixed assignment is used, however, it is possible for a synchronous TDM device to handle sources of different data rates. For example, the slowest input devices could be assigned one slot per frame, while faster devices are assigned multiple slots per frame.

Digital Carrier Systems

The long-distance carrier system provided in the United States and throughout the world was designed to transmit voice signals over high-capacity transmission links, such as optical fiber, coaxial cable, and microwave. Part of the evolution of these telecommunications networks to digital technology has been the adoption of synchronous

Table 17.3   North American and International TDM Carrier Standards

North American			International (ITU-T)		
Designation	Number of Voice Channels	Data Rate (Mbps)	Level	Number of Voice Channels	Data Rate (Mbps)
DS-1	24	1.544	1	30	2.048
DS-1C	48	3.152	2	120	8.448
DS-2	96	6.312	3	480	34.368
DS-3	672	44.736	4	1920	139.264
DS-4	4032	274.176	5	7680	565.148

TDM transmission structures. In the United States, AT&T developed a hierarchy of TDM structures of various capacities; this structure is used in Canada and Japan as well as the United States. A similar, but unfortunately not identical, hierarchy has been adopted internationally under the auspices of ITU-T (Table 17.3).

The basis of the TDM hierarchy (in North America and Japan) is the DS-1 transmission format (Figure 17.12), which multiplexes 24 channels. Each frame contains 8 bits per channel plus a framing bit for a total of $24 \times 8 + 1 = 193$ bits. For voice transmission, the following rules apply. Each channel contains one word of digitized voice data. The original analog voice signal is digitized using pulse code modulation (PCM) at a rate of 8000 samples per second. Therefore, each channel slot and hence each frame must repeat 8000 times per second. With a frame length of 193 bits, we have a data rate of $8000 \times 193 = 1.544$ Mbps. For five of every six frames, 8-bit PCM samples are used. For every sixth frame, each channel contains a

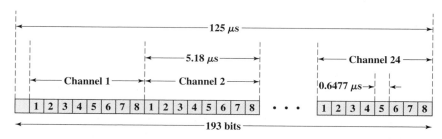

Notes:

1. The first bit is a framing bit, used for synchronization.
2. Voice channels:
    •8-bit PCM used on five of six frames.
    •7-bit PCM used on every sixth frame; bit 8 of each channel is a signaling bit.
3. Data channels:
    •Channel 24 is used for signaling only in some schemes.
    •Bits 1–7 used for 56-kbps service.
    •Bits 2–7 used for 9.6-, 4.8-, and 2.4-kbps service.

Figure 17.12   DS-1 Transmission Format

7-bit PCM word plus a signaling bit. The signaling bits form a stream for each voice channel that contains network control and routing information. For example, control signals are used to establish a connection or terminate a call.

The same DS-1 format is used to provide digital data service. For compatibility with voice, the same 1.544-Mbps data rate is used. In this case, 23 channels of data are provided. The twenty-fourth channel position is reserved for a special sync byte, which allows faster and more reliable reframing following a framing error. Within each channel, 7 bits per frame are used for data, with the eighth bit used to indicate whether the channel, for that frame, contains user data or system control data. With 7 bits per channel, and because each frame is repeated 8000 times per second, a data rate of 56 kbps can be provided per channel. Lower data rates are provided using a technique known as subrate multiplexing. For this technique, an additional bit is robbed from each channel to indicate which subrate multiplexing rate is being provided. This leaves a total capacity per channel of $6 \times 8000 = 48$ kbps. This capacity is used to multiplex five 9.6-kbps channels, ten 4.8-kbps channels, or twenty 2.4-kbps channels. For example, if channel 2 is used to provide 9.6-kbps service, then up to five data subchannels share this channel. The data for each subchannel appear as six bits in channel 2 every fifth frame.

Finally, the DS-1 format can be used to carry a mixture of voice and data channels. In this case, all 24 channels are utilized; no sync byte is provided.

Above this basic data rate of 1.544 Mbps, higher-level multiplexing is achieved by interleaving bits from DS-1 inputs. For example, the DS-2 transmission system combines four DS-1 inputs into a 6.312-Mbps stream. Data from the four sources are interleaved 12 bits at a time. Note that $1.544 \times 4 = 6.176$ Mbps. The remaining capacity is used for framing and control bits.

The designations DS-1, DS-1C, and so on refer to the multiplexing scheme used for carrying information. AT&T and other carriers supply transmission facilities that support these various multiplexed signals, referred to as carrier systems. These are designated with a "T" label. Thus, the T-1 carrier provides a data rate of 1.544 Mbps and is thus capable of supporting the DS-1 multiplex format, and so on for higher data rates.

T-1 Facilities

The T-1 facility is widely used by companies as a way of supporting networking capability and controlling costs. The most common external use (not part of the telephone network) of T-1 facilities is for leased dedicated transmission between customer premises. These facilities allow the customer to set up private networks to carry traffic throughout an organization. Examples of applications for such private networks include the following:

- **Private voice networks:** When there is a substantial amount of intersite voice traffic, a leased private network can provide significant savings over using dialup facilities.
- **Private data network:** Similarly, high data volumes between two or more sites can be supported by T-1 lines.
- **Video teleconferencing:** Allows high-quality video to be transmitted. As the bandwidth requirement for video declines, private video conferencing links can share T-1 facilities with other applications.

- **High-speed digital facsimile:** Permits rapid transmission of facsimile images and, depending on the facsimile load, may be able to share the T-1 link with other applications.

- **Internet access:** If a high volume of traffic between the site and the Internet is anticipated, then a high-capacity access line to the local Internet service provider is needed.

For users with substantial data transmission needs, the use of private T-1 networking is attractive for two reasons. First, T-1 permits simpler configurations than the use of a mix of lower-speed offerings, and second, T-1 transmission services are less expensive.

Another popular use of T-1 is to provide high-speed access from the customer's premises to the telephone network. In this application, a local area network or telephone exchange on the customer's premises supports a number of devices that generate sufficient off-site traffic to require the use of a T-1 access line to the public network.

SONET/SDH

SONET (Synchronous Optical Network) is an optical transmission interface originally proposed by BellCore and standardized by ANSI. A compatible version, referred to as Synchronous Digital Hierarchy (SDH), has been published by ITU-T in Recommendations G.707, G.708, and G.709.[3] SONET is intended to provide a specification for taking advantage of the high-speed digital transmission capability of optical fiber.

Signal Hierarchy The SONET specification defines a hierarchy of standardized digital data rates (Table 17.4). The lowest level, referred to as STS-1 (Synchronous

Table 17.4 SONET/SDH Signal Hierarchy

SONET Designation	ITU-T Designation	Data Rate	Payload Rate (Mbps)
STS-1/OC-1	STM-0	51.84 Mbps	50.112 Mbps
STS-3/OC-3	STM-1	155.52 Mbps	150.336 Mbps
STS-9/OC-9		466.56 Mbps	451.008 Mbps
STS-12/OC-12	STM-4	622.08 Mbps	601.344 Mbps
STS-18/OC-18		933.12 Mbps	902.016 Mbps
STS-24/OC-24		1.24416 Gbps	1.202688 Gbps
STS-36/OC-36		1.86624 Gbps	1.804032 Gbps
STS-48/OC-48	STM-16	2.48832 Gbps	2.405376 Gbps
STS-96/OC-96		4.87664 Gbps	4.810752 Gbps
STS-192/OC-192	STM-64	9.95328 Gbps	9.621504 Gbps
STS-768	STM-256	39.81312 Gbps	38.486016 Gbps
STS-3072		159.25248 Gbps	1.53944064 Gbps

---

[3]In what follows, we will use the term *SONET* to refer to both specifications. Where differences exist, these will be addressed.

Transport Signal level 1) or OC-1 (Optical Carrier level 1),[4] is 51.84 Mbps. This rate can be used to carry a single DS-3 signal or a group of lower-rate signals, such as DS1, DS1C, DS2, plus ITU-T rates (e.g., 2.048 Mbps).

Multiple STS-1 signals can be combined to form an STS-N signal. The signal is created by interleaving bytes from N STS-1 signals that are mutually synchronized. For the ITU-T Synchronous Digital Hierarchy, the lowest rate is 155.52 Mbps, which is designated STM-1. This corresponds to SONET STS-3.

Frame Format The basic SONET building block is the STS-1 frame, which consists of 810 octets and is transmitted once every 125 μs, for an overall data rate of 51.84 Mbps (Figure 17.13a). The frame can logically be viewed as a matrix of 9 rows of 90 octets each, with transmission being one row at a time, from left to right and top to bottom.

The first three columns (3 octets $\times$ 9 rows = 27 octets) of the frame are devoted to overhead octets, called section overhead and line overhead, which relate to different levels of detail in describing a SONET transmission. These octets not only convey synchronization information but network management information.

The remainder of the frame is payload, which is provided by the logical layer of SONET called the path layer. The payload includes a column of path overhead, which is not necessarily in the first available column position; the line overhead contains a pointer that indicates where the path overhead starts.

Figure 17.13b shows the general format for higher-rate frames, using the ITU-T designation.

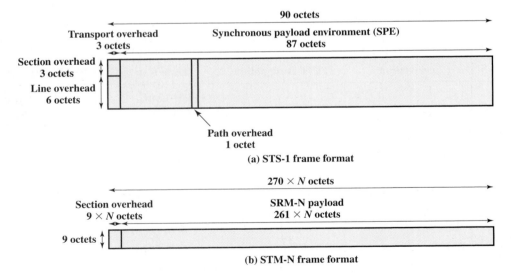

Figure 17.13 SONET/SDH Frame Formats

---

[4]An OC-N rate is the optical equivalent of an STS-N electrical signal. End user devices transmit and receive electrical signals; these must be converted to and from optical signals for transmission over optical fiber.

APPLICATION NOTE
Changing Communications

It is interesting to note the changes to the mechanisms we use in data communications. Of special interest is how data gets from place to place compared to how it did ten or even five years ago. Mechanisms that we put in place to ensure successful transmissions go out of date only to be replaced by other fault eliminating tools. These changes are not always a result of advances in technology; many of them come about because of changes in *what* we communicate and with whom.

Technology certainly does advance and create new ways to get things done. When we examine wide area networks, and in particular the protocols used, we see many changes to the quality of the connections. For example, X.25 is a protocol used to connect sites to the WAN. It has several functions built in to ensure error-free connectivity. All of the nodes that are part of the network perform these checks. With improvements in data transmission, both in the transmitting equipment and the media used, this amount of error checking is no longer necessary and is now considered unnecessary overhead.

However, this overhead may not have been an issue had it not been for the huge demand for offsite connectivity. There has been a fundamental change in the way that we exchange information. More and more we see people and organizations sending data to sites "beyond the horizon." At one time, network designers used what was called the "80/20" rule. This rule described what some call the "locality of reference," which simply means, to whom do we talk? With the 80/20 rule, 80% of our data stayed on the home network. The 20% represented the traffic that might flow to external nodes. This means that most of the time, individual nodes did not require offsite connections.

With the advent of distributed processing, secure connections between business sites, Web sites, hotmail, adult sites, search engines, and significant research resources available online, this rule has been almost completely reversed. Now we need significant increases in speed and accuracy to prevent clogging the outgoing lines with retransmissions. New applications can add to this need for external connectivity. The gaming industry is spending tremendous sums of money developing powerful virtual worlds that are engaging enough to secure their percentage of users moving online. The online game "Everquest" is a perfect example of this trend. We have seen migrations from X.25 to frame relay, T carriers, and ATM, which were followed by SONET. The next generation may accomplish all information transfer via 10-Gbps Ethernet links or something even faster.

Universities are potentially the best illustrations of organizations affected by this trend. One listing that universities compete for is "most wired" as can be seen in the Yahoo! Internet Life reports. Constant upgrades to improve desktop link speeds, router capability, protocol support, wireless mobility, and offsite links are all part of this drive to be superwired. This list also includes a host of new policies for acceptable use and security for campus networks. Students can place very high demands on the infrastructure. Most professors would probably agree that anytime there are new tools or mechanisms to facilitate communication and file sharing over the network, students find them and implement them.

But links to the external world are not the only changes to the way we exchange information. Wireless communication is another area of demand for university and noneducational networks alike. Wireless has wide-ranging effects in terms of support, security, and management. People now want to be connected on the go and wherever they move. This means that the applications will require what is called persistence. Persistence refers to a connections ability to weather changes to topology, protocol, and speed as a user moves. The most obvious technology to be put in use is 802.11, but the list must also include MobileIP (to ensure roaming connectivity) and IPv6 to accommodate the larger number of users and the quality of service they will expect. Major changes to telephony will also be part of this migration as we move to a more IP based existence.

Moving to wireless also means increased performance difficulties as users familiar with dedicated 10- or 100-Mbps connections now must share slower, more error prone links. This places demands on the providers to ensure some level of quality, increasing levels of access for individual nodes and radio interference control. While it is not one of the familiar error control methods, staying away from or eliminating sources of interference will improve throughput and reduce errors on wireless links.

As we move from one architecture to the next and from one set of protocols to another, the methods of flow and error control may change but the goals remain the same. Links must be managed to reduce errors and ensure connectivity. In addition to understanding the new protocols, it is important for providers to follow the flow of information as users take different pathways and change system requirements.

17.6 SUMMARY

Because of the possibility of transmission errors, and because the receiver of data may need to regulate the rate at which data arrive, the synchronization and interfacing techniques are insufficient by themselves. It is necessary to impose a layer of control in each communicating device that provides functions such as flow control, error detection, and error control. This layer of control is known as a **data link control protocol.** The most common of these is HDLC. Other similar data link control protocols are also in use.

Multiplexing allows several transmission sources to share a larger transmission capacity. Two forms of multiplexing are frequency division multiplexing (FDM) and time division multiplexing (TDM).

17.7 RECOMMENDED READING AND WEB SITES

A discussion of FDM and TDM carrier systems can be found in [FREE98] and [CARN99]. SONET is treated in greater depth in [STAL04].

CARN99 Carne, E. *Telecommunications Primer: Data, Voice, and Video Communications.* Upper Saddle River, NJ: Prentice Hall, 1999.

FREE98 Freeman, R. *Telecommunications Transmission Handbook.* New York: Wiley, 1998.

STAL04 Stallings, W. *Data and Computer Communications,* 7th edition. Upper Saddle River, NJ: Prentice Hall, 2004.

Recommended Web Sites:

- **Network Services and Integration Forum:** Discusses current SONET products, technology, and standards
- **SONET Home Page:** Useful links, tutorials, white papers, FAQs (frequently asked questions)

17.8 KEY TERMS, REVIEW QUESTIONS, AND PROBLEMS

Key Terms

asymmetric digital subscriber line (ADSL)	error control	synchronous TDM
automatic repeat request (ARQ)	flow control	TDM channel
data link control protocol	frame	TDM frame
dense wavelength-division multiplexing (DWDM)	frequency division multiplexing (FDM)	time division multiplexing (TDM)
digital subscriber line (DSL)	High-Level Data Link Control (HDLC)	wavelength-division multiplexing (WDM)
discrete multitone (DMT)	multiplexing	
	synchronous digital hierarchy (SDH)	
	synchronous optical network (SONET)	

Review Questions

17.1. Define *flow control.*

17.2. Define *error control.*

17.3. List common ingredients for error control for a link control protocol.

17.4. What is the purpose of the flag field in HDLC?

17.5. What type of error detection is used in the HDLC frame check sequence field?

17.6. What are the three frame types supported by HDLC? Describe each.

17.7. What is multiplexing?

17.8. The set of time slots or the frequency allocated to a single source is called what?

17.9. Why is multiplexing so cost-effective?

17.10. How is interference avoided by using frequency division multiplexing?

17.11. What is echo cancellation?

17.12. Define *upstream* and *downstream* with respect to subscriber lines.

17.13. Explain how synchronous time division multiplexing (TDM) works.

17.14. What are some of the major uses of T-1 lines?

17.15. Why is the use of private T-1 lines attractive to companies?

Problems

17.1 Consider that several physical links connect two stations. We would like to use a "multilink HDLC" that makes efficient use of these links by sending frames on a FIFO (first-in, first-out) basis on the next available link. What enhancements to HDLC are needed?

17.2 How do we achieve a data rate of 56 kbps in 23 channels using a DS-1 format?

17.3 To get some indication of the relative demands of voice and data traffic, consider the following:
a. Calculate the number of bits used to send a 3-minute telephone call using standard PCM.
b. How many pages of IRA text with an average of 65 characters a line and 55 lines a page corresponds to one 3-minute telephone call?
c. How many pages of facsimile at standard resolution, that is, 200 dpi (dots per inch) horizontally and 100 dpi vertically, correspond to one 3-minute phone call? Assume that the effective page is 8 inches wide and 10.5 inches long. Moreover, assume an effective compression ratio of 10 to 1.

17.4 Recently a new scanner was announced that provided 1200 dpi resolution and over 1 billion colors.
a. How much memory in bytes would it take to store a bit map of an 8×10 inch monochrome picture at 1200 dpi with a 10-bit gray scale?
b. Suppose the colors are represented as a combination of three colors—red, blue, green—each with n bits to represent its intensity. What is the least value of n that will provide over 1 billion colors?
c. How long would it take to send a gray scale representation of an 8×10 inch picture at 1200 dpi over a T-1 line (1.544 Mbps)?

17.5 To paraphrase Lincoln, all of the channel some of the time, some of the channel all of the time. Refer to Figure 17.5 and relate the preceding to the figure.

17.6 Assume that you are to design a TDM carrier, say T-489, to support 30 voice channels using 6 bit samples and a structure similar to T-1. Determine the required bit rate.

17.7 Statistical (or asynchronous) TDM is an alternative to synchronous TDM. Describe how STDM is different from (synchronous) TDM. What advantages and disadvantages does STDM exhibit?

17.8 T-3 and OC-3 lines are alternatives to the T-1 line. What are the maximum data rates for these two media? Describe a scenario where each media (T-1, T-3, and OC-3) would constitute an optimal solution. Consider capacity and cost considerations in your response.

Case Study X: Haukeland University Hospital

Haukeland University Hospital is one of the largest hospitals in Norway. The hospital offers almost every form of medical diagnosis and treatment. Haukeland University Hospital is the regional hospital for the Western Area Health Region, offering services to the region's 900,000 inhabitants. With 200 admissions and 1000 outpatients a day, it is one of the busiest hospitals in Scandinavia. With its total of 6000 employees, the hospital is also the largest employer in Western Norway. More than 500 physicians and 2000 nurses provide round-the-clock health services to more than 67,000 inpatients and 314,000 outpatients a year. The hospital has 1100 beds. Haukeland University Hospital is a teaching hospital with close links to the University of Bergen. Every year, 180 medical students receive their clinical training at the hospital, which is also an important teaching and training centre for other groups of health care and other students. At the hospital's own training center, more than 100 nurses a year specialize in intensive care, anesthesia, pediatrics, and theater nursing. The hospital also offers 100 nursing specialists additional education every year.

Haukeland is the principal member of a health care network of treatment centers, local hospitals, psychiatric institutions, and dental facilities throughout southwestern Norway; the network is known as iHelse.net. The sparse population density and mountainous terrain make this region an ideal candidate for telemedicine. The hospital recognized a need to create a network and image transfer infrastructure such that location did not limit the availability of medical specialists. Without such an infrastructure, specialists have to travel to look at every individual patient, wasting valuable time traveling throughout the region. Thus, a telemedicine facility significantly enhances specialist productivity. Further, if patients move from one hospital to another, their treatment isn't delayed, because the hospital they choose can immediately access the patient's medical history, including past radiology scans. Finally, doctors working at any location, have access to all the records and information services as at the central hospital because of the computer interconnections.

Central to the hospital's telemedicine strategy was the installation of the Picture Archiving and Communications System (PACS), which can produce digital images of radiology scans and other medical documents. PACS requires considerable storage and, equally important, the support of a high capacity WAN that could serve the hospital's region [KIRB01].

When Haukeland decided to develop PACS, a key part of the planning was to look at the current WAN infrastructure that served iHelse.net. At the time, iHelse.net relied on a 256-kbps frame relay network, at a cost of $600 per month per connection. The iHelse.net WAN served 70 locations in the region, with 10,000 users and over 5000 workstations. While the coverage of the WAN was satisfactory for the then-current day-to-day operations, it could not support PACS. The hospital needed to significantly increase capacity, and initially project leaders set their sights on upgrading the WAN to 10 Mbps or 100 Mbps using frame relay or ATM.

To their surprise and delight, the hospital found that they could do better than they had hoped, and save money in the bargain. The reason for this has to do with the economics of providing long-distance fiber links. Competitive local exchange carriers (CLECs) typically install fiber optic cable with enormous amounts of capacity. The principal costs in long-distance fiber installation are land costs and labor; the fiber itself is an incidental expense. Thus, the strategy is to put down lots of cable while you've got the dirt excavated and the trench open, and make back the investment selling low-cost capacity. With such capacity available, Haukeland was able to put together a deal that involved not just 100 Mbps but 1-Gbps connection capacity at a price of $500 per month per connection. This is today's economics in long-distance capacity: Haukeland got a 400,000% increase in connection capacity at a reduced price.

The networking technology used to support this WAN service was Gigabit Ethernet. Although Ethernet is generally thought of as a LAN technology, it has in fact become a competitive player for modest distances in the WAN market—a niche often called metropolitan area network (MAN). For Gigabit Ethernet, links between Ethernet switches, using single-mode fiber, on the order of tens of kilometers are feasible. With a diameter of about 200 km, the hospital's region lends itself to a switched Ethernet MAN.

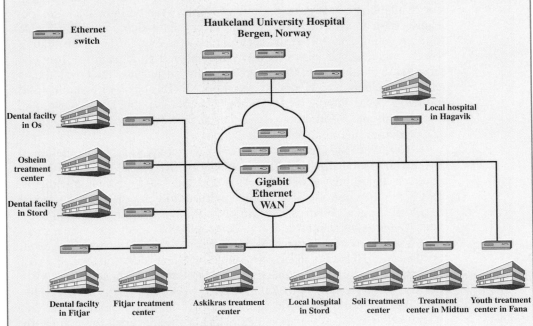

Figure X.1   Haukeland Network Configuration

One of the most attractive features of the Ethernet solution for the hospital is that it already was using Gigabit Ethernet on its LAN. Thus, the hospitals IT staff required no training to be able to incorporate the Ethernet MAN into the facility. Figure X.1 gives an overview of the current configuration.

Discussion Questions

1. Research current offerings for frame relay, ATM, and Ethernet MANs, and discuss the relative advantages of each.

2. What transition issues would you expect Haukeland to face in going from the frame relay WAN to the Ethernet WAN?

PART SIX

Management Issues

As the networks used in an organization and the distributed applications they support grow in scale and complexity, management issues become increasingly difficult and important. In this final part, we look at the issues involved in including the Internet in the corporate computing environment and the operational management of computer networks.

Chapter 18 Network Security

Network security has become increasingly important with the growth in the number and importance of networks. Chapter 18 provides a survey of security techniques and services. The chapter begins with a look at encryption techniques for ensuring confidentiality, which include the use of conventional and public-key encryption. Then the area of authentication and digital signatures is explored. The two most important encryption algorithms, AES and RSA, are examined, as well as SHA-1, a one-way hash function important in a number of security applications. Chapter 18 also discusses SSL and the set of IP security standards.

Chapter 19 Network Management

A vital element for any business network is network management. Chapter 19 lays out the requirements for network management and then looks at the key elements of network management systems. The important Simple Network Management Protocol (SNMP) is examined in detail.

NETWORK SECURITY

The requirements of **information security** within an organization have undergone two major changes in the last several decades. Before the widespread use of data processing equipment, the security of information felt to be valuable to an organization was provided primarily by physical and administrative means. An example of the former is the use of rugged filing cabinets with combination locks for storing sensitive documents. An example of the latter is personnel screening procedures used during the hiring process.

With the introduction of the computer, the need for automated tools for protecting files and other information stored on the computer became evident. This is especially the case for a shared system, such as a time-sharing system, and the need is even more acute for systems that can be accessed over a public telephone or data network. The generic name for the collection of tools designed to protect data and to thwart hackers is **computer security.** Although this is an important topic, it is beyond the scope of this chapter.

The second major change that affected security is the introduction of distributed systems and the use of networks and communications facilities for carrying data between user terminal and computer and between computer and computer. **Network security** measures are needed to protect data during their transmission and to guarantee that data transmissions are authentic.

The essential technology underlying virtually all automated network and computer security applications is encryption. Two fundamental approaches are in use: symmetric encryption and public-key encryption, also known as asymmetric encryption. As we look at the various approaches to network security, these two types of encryption will be explored.

This chapter begins with an overview of the requirements for network security. Next, we look at symmetric encryption and its use to provide confidentiality. This is followed by a discussion of message authentication. We then look at the use of public-key encryption and digital signatures. The chapter closes with an examination of security features in IPSec.

18.1 SECURITY REQUIREMENTS AND ATTACKS

To understand the types of threats to security that exist, we need to have a definition of security requirements. Computer and network security address four requirements:

- **Confidentiality:** Requires that data be accessible only by authorized parties. This type of access includes printing, displaying, and other forms of disclosure, including simply revealing the existence of an object.
- **Integrity:** Requires that only authorized parties can modify data. Modification includes writing, changing, changing status, deleting, and creating.
- **Availability:** Requires that data be available to authorized parties.
- **Authenticity:** Requires that a host or service be able to verify the identity of a user.

A useful means of classifying security attacks (RFC 2828) is in terms of *passive attacks* and *active attacks*. A passive attack attempts to learn or make use of information from the system but does not affect system resources. An active attack attempts to alter system resources or affect their operation.

Passive Attacks

Passive attacks are in the nature of eavesdropping on, or monitoring of, transmissions. The goal of the opponent is to obtain information that is being transmitted. Two types of passive attacks are release of message contents and traffic analysis.

The **release of message contents** is easily understood. A telephone conversation, an electronic mail message, or a transferred file may contain sensitive or confidential information. We would like to prevent an opponent from learning the contents of these transmissions.

A second type of passive attack, **traffic analysis,** is subtler. Suppose that we masked the contents of messages or other information traffic so that opponents, even if they captured the message, could not extract the information from the message. The common technique for masking contents is encryption. Even with encryption protection in place, an opponent might still be able to observe the pattern of these messages. The opponent could determine the location and identity of communicating hosts and could observe the frequency and length of messages being exchanged. This information might be useful in guessing the nature of the communication that was taking place.

Passive attacks are very difficult to detect because they do not involve any alteration of the data. Typically, the message traffic is sent and received in an apparently normal fashion and neither the sender nor receiver is aware that a third party has read the messages or observed the traffic pattern. However, it is feasible to prevent the success of these attacks, usually by means of encryption. Thus, the emphasis in dealing with passive attacks is on prevention rather than detection.

Active Attacks

Active attacks involve some modification of the data stream or the creation of a false stream and can be subdivided into four categories: masquerade, replay, modification of messages, and denial of service.

A **masquerade** takes place when one entity pretends to be a different entity. A masquerade attack usually includes one of the other forms of active attack. For example, authentication sequences can be captured and replayed after a valid authentication sequence has taken place, thus enabling an authorized entity with few privileges to obtain extra privileges by impersonating an entity that has those privileges.

Replay involves the passive capture of a data unit and its subsequent retransmission to produce an unauthorized effect.

Modification of messages simply means that some portion of a legitimate message is altered, or that messages are delayed or reordered, to produce an unauthorized effect. For example, a message meaning "Allow John Smith to read confidential file *accounts*" is modified to mean "Allow Fred Brown to read confidential file *accounts.*"

The **denial of service** prevents or inhibits the normal use or management of communications facilities. This attack may have a specific target; for example, an entity may suppress all messages directed to a particular destination (e.g., the security audit service). Another form of service denial is the disruption of an entire network or a server, either by disabling the network server, or by overloading it with messages so as to degrade performance.

Active attacks present the opposite characteristics of passive attacks. Whereas passive attacks are difficult to detect, measures are available to prevent their success. On the other hand, it is quite difficult to prevent active attacks absolutely, because to do so would require physical protection of all communications facilities and paths at all times. Instead, the goal is to detect them and to recover from any disruption or delays caused by them. Because the detection has a deterrent effect, it may also contribute to prevention.

18.2 CONFIDENTIALITY WITH SYMMETRIC ENCRYPTION

The universal technique for providing confidentiality for transmitted data is symmetric encryption. This section looks first at the basic concept of symmetric encryption, followed by a discussion of the two most important symmetric encryption algorithms: the Data Encryption Standard (DES) and the Advanced Encryption Standard (AES). We then examine the application of symmetric encryption to achieve confidentiality.

Symmetric Encryption

Symmetric encryption, also referred to as conventional encryption or single-key encryption, was the only type of encryption in use prior to the introduction of public-key encryption in the late 1970s. Countless individuals and groups, from Julius Caesar to the German U-boat force to present-day diplomatic, military, and commercial users, have used symmetric encryption for secret communication. It remains by far the more widely used of the two types of encryption.

A symmetric encryption scheme has five ingredients (Figure 18.1):

- **Plaintext:** This is the original message or data that is fed into the algorithm as input.

- **Encryption algorithm:** The encryption algorithm performs various substitutions and transformations on the plaintext.

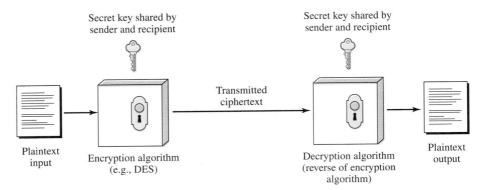

Secret key shared by
sender and recipient

Secret key shared by
sender and recipient

Transmitted
ciphertext

Plaintext
input

Encryption algorithm
(e.g., DES)

Decryption algorithm
(reverse of encryption
algorithm)

Plaintext
output

Figure 18.1   Simplified Model of Symmetric Encryption

- **Secret key:** The secret key is also input to the encryption algorithm. The exact substitutions and transformations performed by the algorithm depend on the key.
- **Ciphertext:** This is the scrambled message produced as output. It depends on the plaintext and the secret key. For a given message, two different keys will produce two different ciphertexts.
- **Decryption algorithm:** This is essentially the encryption algorithm run in reverse. It takes the ciphertext and the secret key and produces the original plaintext.

There are two requirements for secure use of symmetric encryption:

1. We need a strong encryption algorithm. At a minimum, we would like the algorithm to be such that an opponent who knows the algorithm and has access to one or more ciphertexts would be unable to decipher the ciphertext or figure out the key. This requirement is usually stated in a stronger form: The opponent should be unable to decrypt ciphertext or discover the key even if he or she is in possession of a number of ciphertexts together with the plaintext that produced each ciphertext.

2. Sender and receiver must have obtained copies of the secret key in a secure fashion and must keep the key secure. If someone can discover the key and knows the algorithm, all communication using this key is unsecure.

There are two general approaches to attacking a symmetric encryption scheme. The first attack is known as **cryptanalysis.** Cryptanalytic attacks rely on the nature of the algorithm plus perhaps some knowledge of the general characteristics of the plaintext or even some sample plaintext-ciphertext pairs. This type of attack exploits the characteristics of the algorithm to attempt to deduce a specific plaintext or to deduce the key being used. If the attack succeeds in deducing the key, the effect is catastrophic: All future and past messages encrypted with that key are compromised.

The second method, known as the **brute-force** attack, is to try every possible key on a piece of ciphertext until an intelligible translation into plaintext is obtained. On average, half of all possible keys must be tried to achieve success. Table 18.1 shows how much time is involved for various key sizes. The table shows results for

Table 18.1 Average Time Required for Exhaustive Key Search

Key Size (bits)	Number of Alternative Keys	Time required at 1 encryption/μs	Time required at 10^6 encryptions/μs
32	$2^{32} = 4.3 \times 10^9$	2^{31} μs = 35.8 minutes	2.15 milliseconds
56	$2^{56} = 7.2 \times 10^{16}$	2^{55} μs = 1142 years	10.01 hours
128	$2^{128} = 3.4 \times 10^{38}$	2^{127} μs = 5.4×10^{24} years	5.4×10^{18} years
168	$2^{168} = 3.7 \times 10^{50}$	2^{167} μs = 5.9×10^{36} years	5.9×10^{30} years

each key size, assuming that it takes 1 μs to perform a single decryption, a reasonable order of magnitude for today's computers. With the use of massively parallel organizations of microprocessors, it may be possible to achieve processing rates many orders of magnitude greater. The final column of the table considers the results for a system that can process 1 million keys per microsecond. As one can see, at this performance level, a 56-bit key can no longer be considered computationally secure.

Encryption Algorithms

The most commonly used symmetric encryption algorithms are block ciphers. A block cipher processes the plaintext input in fixed-size blocks and produces a block of ciphertext of equal size for each plaintext block. The two most important symmetric algorithms, both of which are block ciphers, are the Data Encryption Standard (DES) and the Advanced Encryption Standard (AES).

Data Encryption Standard DES has been the dominant encryption algorithm since its introduction in 1977. However, because DES uses only a 56-bit key, it was only a matter of time before computer processing speed made DES obsolete. In 1998, the Electronic Frontier Foundation (EFF) announced that it had broken a DES challenge using a special-purpose "DES cracker" machine that was built for less than $250,000. The attack took less than three days. The EFF has published a detailed description of the machine, enabling others to build their own cracker [EFF98]. And, of course, hardware prices will continue to drop as speeds increase, making DES worthless.

The life of DES was extended by the use of triple DES (3DES), which involves repeating the basic DES algorithm three times, using either two or three unique keys, for a key size of 112 or 168 bits.

The principal drawback of 3DES is that the algorithm is relatively sluggish in software. A secondary drawback is that both DES and 3DES use a 64-bit block size. For reasons of both efficiency and security, a larger block size is desirable.

Advanced Encryption Standard Because of these drawbacks, 3DES is not a reasonable candidate for long-term use. As a replacement, the National Institute of Standards and Technology (NIST) in 1997 issued a call for proposals for a new Advanced Encryption Standard (AES), which should have a security strength equal to or better than 3DES and significantly improved efficiency. In addition to these general requirements, NIST specified that AES must be a symmetric block cipher with a block length of 128 bits and support for key lengths of 128, 192, and 256 bits. Evaluation criteria include security, computational efficiency, memory requirements, hardware and software suitability, and flexibility. In 2001, NIST issued AES as a federal information processing standard (FIPS 197).

In the description of this section, we assume a key length of 128 bits, which is likely to be the one most commonly implemented.

Figure 18.2 shows the overall structure of AES. The input to the encryption and decryption algorithms is a single 128-bit block. In FIPS 197, this block is depicted as a square matrix of bytes. This block is copied into the **State** array, which is modified at

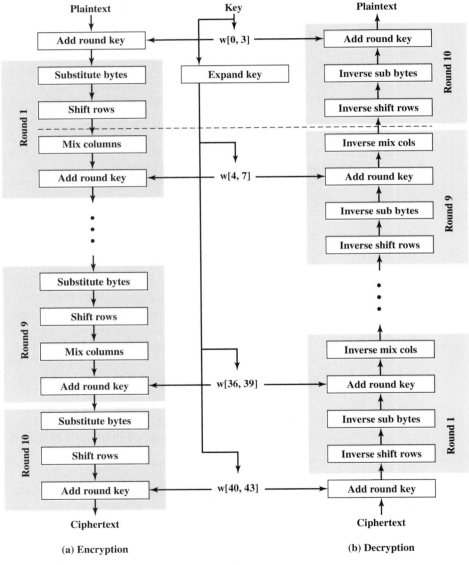

Figure 18.2 AES Encryption and Decryption

each stage of encryption or decryption. After the final stage, **State** is copied to an output matrix. Similarly, the 128-bit key is depicted as a square matrix of bytes. This key is then expanded into an array of key schedule words; each word is four bytes and the total key schedule is 44 words for the 128-bit key. The ordering of bytes within a matrix is by column. So, for example, the first four bytes of a 128-bit plaintext input to the encryption cipher occupy the first column of the **in** matrix, the second four bytes occupy the second column, and so on. Similarly, the first four bytes of the expanded key, which form a word, occupy the first column of the **w** matrix.

The following comments give some insight into AES:

1. The key that is provided as input is expanded into an array of forty-four 32-bit words, $\mathbf{w}[i]$. Four distinct words (128 bits) serve as a round key for each round.

2. Four different stages are used, one of permutation and three of substitution:
   - **Substitute bytes:** Uses a table, referred to as an S-box,[1] to perform a byte-by-byte substitution of the block
   - **Shift rows:** A simple permutation that is performed row by row
   - **Mix columns:** A substitution that alters each byte in a column as a function of all of the bytes in the column
   - **Add round key:** A simple bitwise XOR of the current block with a portion of the expanded key

3. The structure is quite simple. For both encryption and decryption, the cipher begins with an Add Round Key stage, followed by nine rounds that each includes all four stages, followed by a tenth round of three stages. Figure 18.3 depicts the structure of a full encryption round.

4. Only the Add Round Key stage makes use of the key. For this reason, the cipher begins and ends with an Add Round Key stage. Any other stage, applied at the beginning or end, is reversible without knowledge of the key and so would add no security.

5. The Add Round Key stage by itself would not be formidable. The other three stages together scramble the bits, but by themselves would provide no security because they do not use the key. We can view the cipher as alternating operations of XOR encryption (Add Round Key) of a block, followed by scrambling of the block (the other three stages), followed by XOR encryption, and so on. This scheme is both efficient and highly secure.

6. Each stage is easily reversible. For the Substitute Byte, Shift Row, and Mix Columns stages, an inverse function is used in the decryption algorithm. For the Add Round Key stage, the inverse is achieved by XORing the same round key to the block, using the equality $A \oplus A \oplus B = B$.

7. As with most block ciphers, the decryption algorithm makes use of the expanded key in reverse order. However, the decryption algorithm is not identical to the encryption algorithm. This is a consequence of the particular structure of AES.

---

[1]The term *S-box*, or substitution box, is commonly used in the description of symmetric ciphers to refer to a table used for a table-lookup type of substitution mechanism.

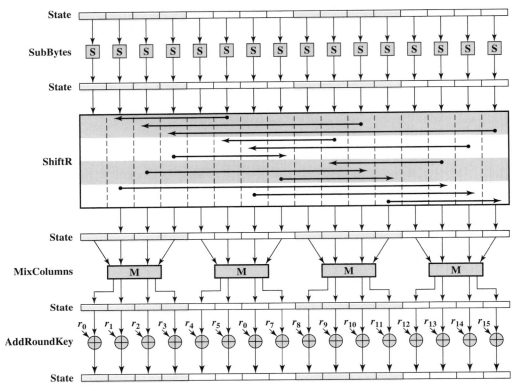

Figure 18.3   AES Encryption Round

8. Once it is established that all four stages are reversible, it is easy to verify that decryption does recover the plaintext. Figure 18.2 lays out encryption and decryption going in opposite vertical directions. At each horizontal point (e.g., the dashed line in the figure), **State** is the same for both encryption and decryption.

9. The final round of both encryption and decryption consists of only three stages. Again, this is a consequence of the particular structure of AES and is required to make the cipher reversible.

Location of Encryption Devices

The most powerful, and most common, approach to countering the threats to network security is encryption. In using encryption, we need to decide what to encrypt and where the encryption gear should be located. As Figure 18.4 indicates, there are two fundamental alternatives: link encryption and end-to-end encryption.

With link encryption, each vulnerable communications link is equipped on both ends with an encryption device. Thus, all traffic over all communications links is secured. Although this requires a lot of encryption devices in a large network, it provides a high level of security. One disadvantage of this approach is that the message

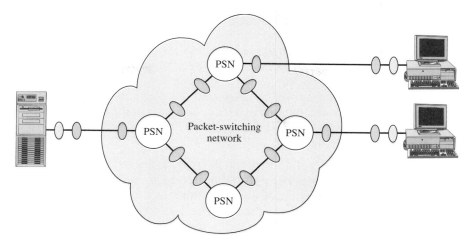

( ) = End-to-end encryption device

( ) = Link encryption device

PSN = Packet-switching node

Figure 18.4   Encryption across a Packet-Switching Network

must be decrypted each time it enters a packet switch; this is necessary because the switch must read the address (virtual circuit number) in the packet header to route the packet. Thus, the message is vulnerable at each switch. If this is a public packet-switching network, the user has no control over the security of the nodes.

With end-to-end encryption, the encryption process is carried out at the two end systems. The source host or terminal encrypts the data. The data, in encrypted form, are then transmitted unaltered across the network to the destination terminal or host. The destination shares a key with the source and so is able to decrypt the data. This approach would seem to secure the transmission against attacks on the network links or switches. There is, however, still a weak spot.

Consider the following situation. A host connects to an X.25 packet-switching network, sets up a virtual circuit to another host, and is prepared to transfer data to that other host using end-to-end encryption. Data are transmitted over such a network in the form of packets, consisting of a header and some user data. What part of each packet will the host encrypt? Suppose that the host encrypts the entire packet, including the header. This will not work because, remember, only the other host can perform the decryption. The packet-switching node will receive an encrypted packet and be unable to read the header. Therefore, it will not be able to route the packet. It follows that the host may only encrypt the user data portion of the packet and must leave the header in the clear, so that the network can read it.

Thus, with end-to-end encryption, the user data are secure. However, the traffic pattern is not, because packet headers are transmitted in the clear. To achieve greater security, both link and end-to-end encryption are needed, as is shown in Figure 18.4.

To summarize, when both forms are employed, the host encrypts the user data portion of a packet using an end-to-end encryption key. The entire packet is then encrypted using a link encryption key. As the packet traverses the network, each switch decrypts the packet using a link encryption key to read the header and then encrypts the entire packet again for sending it out on the next link. Now the entire packet is secure except for the time that the packet is actually in the memory of a packet switch, at which time the packet header is in the clear.

Key Distribution

For symmetric encryption to work, the two parties to a secure exchange must have the same key, and that key must be protected from access by others. Furthermore, frequent key changes are usually desirable to limit the amount of data compromised if an attacker learns the key. Therefore, the strength of any cryptographic system rests with the key distribution technique, a term that refers to the means of delivering a key to two parties that wish to exchange data, without allowing others to see the key. Key distribution can be achieved in a number of ways. For two parties A and B,

1. A key could be selected by A and physically delivered to B.
2. A third party could select the key and physically deliver it to A and B.
3. If A and B have previously and recently used a key, one party could transmit the new key to the other, encrypted using the old key.
4. If A and B each have an encrypted connection to a third party C, C could deliver a key on the encrypted links to A and B.

Options 1 and 2 call for manual delivery of a key. For link encryption, this is a reasonable requirement, because each link encryption device is only going to be exchanging data with its partner on the other end of the link. However, for end-to-end encryption, manual delivery is awkward. In a distributed system, any given host or terminal may need to engage in exchanges with many other hosts and terminals over time. Thus, each device needs a number of keys, supplied dynamically. The problem is especially difficult in a wide area distributed system.

Option 3 is a possibility for either link encryption or end-to-end encryption, but if an attacker ever succeeds in gaining access to one key, then all subsequent keys are revealed. Even if frequent changes are made to the link encryption keys, these should be done manually. To provide keys for end-to-end encryption, option 4 is preferable.

Figure 18.5 illustrates an implementation of option 4 for end-to-end encryption. In the figure, link encryption is ignored. This can be added, or not, as required. For this scheme, two kinds of keys are identified:

- **Session key:** When two end systems (hosts, terminals, etc.) wish to communicate, they establish a logical connection (e.g., virtual circuit). For the duration of that logical connection, all user data are encrypted with a one-time session key. At the conclusion of the session, or connection, the session key is destroyed.
- **Permanent key:** A permanent key is a key used between entities for the purpose of distributing session keys.

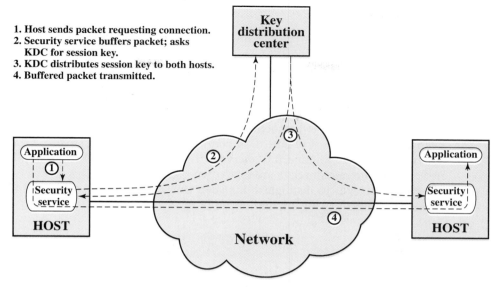

1. Host sends packet requesting connection.
2. Security service buffers packet; asks
   KDC for session key.
3. KDC distributes session key to both hosts.
4. Buffered packet transmitted.

Figure 18.5   Automatic Key Distribution for Connection-Oriented Protocol

The configuration consists of the following elements:

- **Key distribution center:** The key distribution center determines which systems are allowed to communicate with each other. When permission is granted for two systems to establish a connection, the key distribution center provides a one-time session key for that connection.

- **Security service module (SSM):** This module, which may consist of functionality at one protocol layer, performs end-to-end encryption and obtains session keys on behalf of users.

The steps involved in establishing a connection are shown in the figure. When one host wishes to set up a connection to another host, it transmits a connection-request packet (step 1). The SSM saves that packet and applies to the KDC for permission to establish the connection (step 2). The communication between the SSM and the KDC is encrypted using a master key shared only by this SSM and the KDC. If the KDC approves the connection request, it generates the session key and delivers it to the two appropriate SSMs, using a unique permanent key for each SSM (step 3). The requesting SSM can now release the connection request packet, and a connection is set up between the two end systems (step 4). All user data exchanged between the two end systems are encrypted by their respective SSMs using the one-time session key.

The automated key distribution approach provides the flexibility and dynamic characteristics needed to allow a number of terminal users to access a number of hosts and for the hosts to exchange data with each other.

Another approach to key distribution uses public-key encryption, which is discussed in Section 18.4.

Traffic Padding

We mentioned that, in some cases, users are concerned about security from traffic analysis. With the use of link encryption, packet headers are encrypted, reducing the opportunity for traffic analysis. However, it is still possible in those circumstances for an attacker to assess the amount of traffic on a network and to observe the amount of traffic entering and leaving each end system. An effective countermeasure to this attack is traffic padding.

Traffic padding is a function that produces ciphertext output continuously, even in the absence of plaintext. A continuous random data stream is generated. When plaintext is available, it is encrypted and transmitted. When input plaintext is not present, the random data are encrypted and transmitted. This makes it impossible for an attacker to distinguish between true data flow and noise and therefore impossible to deduce the amount of traffic.

18.3 MESSAGE AUTHENTICATION AND HASH FUNCTIONS

Encryption protects against passive attack (eavesdropping). A different requirement is to protect against active attack (falsification of data and transactions). Protection against such attacks is known as message authentication.

Approaches to Message Authentication

A message, file, document, or other collection of data is said to be authentic when it is genuine and came from its alleged source. Message authentication is a procedure that allows communicating parties to verify that received messages are authentic. The two important aspects are to verify that the contents of the message have not been altered and that the source is authentic. We may also wish to verify a message's timeliness (it has not been artificially delayed and replayed) and sequence relative to other messages flowing between two parties.

Authentication Using Symmetric Encryption It is possible to perform authentication simply by the use of symmetric encryption. If we assume that only the sender and receiver share a key (which is as it should be), then only the genuine sender would be able successfully to encrypt a message for the other participant. Furthermore, if the message includes an error-detection code and a sequence number, the receiver is assured that no alterations have been made and that sequencing is proper. If the message also includes a timestamp, the receiver is assured that the message has not been delayed beyond that normally expected for network transit.

Message Authentication without Message Encryption In this section, we examine several approaches to message authentication that do not rely on message encryption. In all of these approaches, an authentication tag is generated and appended to each message for transmission. The message itself is not encrypted and can be read at the destination independent of the authentication function at the destination.

Because the approaches discussed in this section do not encrypt the message, message confidentiality is not provided. Because symmetric encryption will provide authentication, and because it is widely used with readily available products, why not simply use such an approach, which provides both confidentiality and authentication? [DAVI89] suggests three situations in which message authentication without confidentiality is preferable:

1. There are a number of applications in which the same message is broadcast to a number of destinations. For example, notification to users that the network is now unavailable or an alarm signal in a control center. It is cheaper and more reliable to have only one destination responsible for monitoring authenticity. Thus, the message must be broadcast in plaintext with an associated message authentication tag. The responsible system performs authentication. If a violation occurs, the other destination systems are alerted by a general alarm.

2. Another possible scenario is an exchange in which one side has a heavy load and cannot afford the time to decrypt all incoming messages. Authentication is carried out on a selective basis, with messages chosen at random for checking.

3. Authentication of a computer program in plaintext is an attractive service. The computer program can be executed without having to decrypt it every time, which would be wasteful of processor resources. However, if a message authentication tag were attached to the program, it could be checked whenever assurance is required of the integrity of the program.

Thus, there is a place for both authentication and encryption in meeting security requirements.

Message Authentication Code One authentication technique involves the use of a secret key to generate a small block of data, known as a message authentication code, that is appended to the message. This technique assumes that two communicating parties, say A and B, share a common secret key K_{AB}. When A has a message M to send to B, it calculates the message authentication code as a function of the message and the key: $MAC_M = F(K_{AB}, M)$. The message plus code are transmitted to the intended recipient. The recipient performs the same calculation on the received message, using the same secret key, to generate a new message authentication code. The received code is compared to the calculated code (Figure 18.6). If we assume that only the receiver and the sender know the identity of the secret key, and if the received code matches the calculated code, then

1. The receiver is assured that the message has not been altered. If an attacker alters the message but does not alter the code, then the receiver's calculation of the code will differ from the received code. Because the attacker is assumed not to know the secret key, the attacker cannot alter the code to correspond to the alterations in the message.

2. The receiver is assured that the message is from the alleged sender. Because no one else knows the secret key, no one else could prepare a message with a proper code.

3. If the message includes a sequence number (such as is used with X.25, HDLC, and TCP), then the receiver can be assured of the proper sequence, because an attacker cannot successfully alter the sequence number.

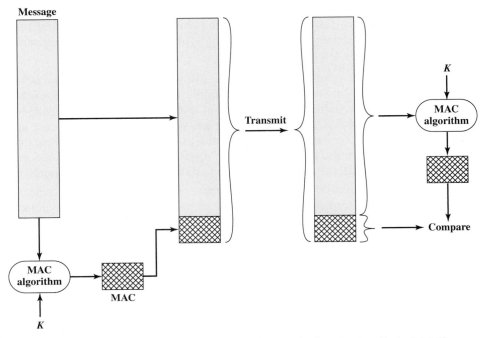

Figure 18.6 Message Authentication Using a Message Authentication Code (MAC)

A number of algorithms could be used to generate the code. The National Bureau of Standards, in its publication *DES Modes of Operation*, recommends the use of DES. DES is used to generate an encrypted version of the message, and the last number of bits of ciphertext are used as the code. A 16- or 32-bit code is typical.

The process just described is similar to encryption. One difference is that the authentication algorithm need not be reversible, as it must for decryption. It turns out that because of the mathematical properties of the authentication function, it is less vulnerable to being broken than encryption.

One–Way Hash Function A variation on the message authentication code that has received much attention is the one-way hash function. As with the message authentication code, a hash function accepts a variable-size message M as input and produces a fixed-size message digest $H(M)$ as output. Unlike the MAC, a hash function does not also take a secret key as input. To authenticate a message, the message digest is sent with the message in such a way that the message digest is authentic.

Figure 18.7 illustrates three ways in which the message can be authenticated. The message digest can be encrypted using symmetric encryption (part a); if it is assumed that only the sender and receiver share the encryption key, then authenticity is assured. The message digest can also be encrypted using public-key encryption (part b); this is explained in Section 18.4. The public-key approach has two advantages: It provides a digital signature as well as message authentication, and it does not require the distribution of keys to communicating parties.

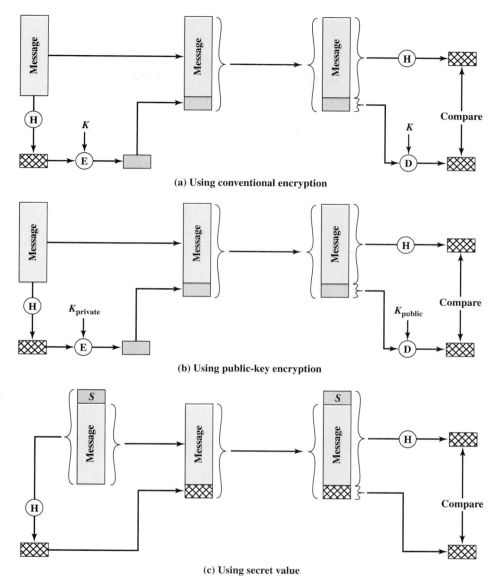

(a) Using conventional encryption

(b) Using public-key encryption

(c) Using secret value

Figure 18.7   Message Authentication Using a One-Way Hash Function

These two approaches have an advantage over approaches that encrypt the entire message in that less computation is required. Nevertheless, there has been interest in developing a technique that avoids encryption altogether. Several reasons for this interest are pointed out in [TSUD92]:

- Encryption software is somewhat slow. Even though the amount of data to be encrypted per message is small, there may be a steady stream of messages into and out of a system.

- Encryption hardware costs are nonnegligible. Low-cost chip implementations of DES are available, but the cost adds up if all nodes in a network must have this capability.
- Encryption hardware is optimized toward large data sizes. For small blocks of data, a high proportion of the time is spent in initialization/invocation overhead.
- Encryption algorithms may be covered by patents and must be licensed, adding a cost.
- Encryption algorithms may be subject to export control.

Figure 18.7c shows a technique that uses a hash function but no encryption for message authentication. This technique assumes that two communicating parties, say A and B, share a common secret value S_{AB}. When A has a message to send to B, it calculates the hash function over the concatenation of the secret value and the message: $MD_M = H(S_{AB}\|M)$.[2] It then sends $[M\|MD_M]$ to B. Because B possesses S_{AB}, it can recompute $H(S_{AB}\|M)$ and verify MD_M. Because the secret value itself is not sent, it is not possible for an attacker to modify an intercepted message. As long as the secret value remains secret, it is also not possible for an attacker to generate a false message.

This third technique, using a shared secret value, is the one adopted for IP security; it has also been specified for SNMPv3, discussed in Chapter 19.

Secure Hash Functions

The one-way hash function, or secure hash function, is important not only in message authentication but in digital signatures. In this section, we begin with a discussion of requirements for a secure hash function. Then we look at one of the most important hash functions, SHA-1.

Hash Function Requirements The purpose of a hash function is to produce a "fingerprint" of a file, message, or other block of data. To be useful for message authentication, a hash function H must have the following properties:

1. H can be applied to a block of data of any size.
2. H produces a fixed-length output.
3. $H(x)$ is relatively easy to compute for any given x, making both hardware and software implementations practical.
4. For any given code h, it is computationally infeasible to find x such that $H(x) = h$.
5. For any given block x, it is computationally infeasible to find $y \neq x$ with $H(y) = H(x)$.
6. It is computationally infeasible to find any pair (x, y) such that $H(x) = H(y)$.

The first three properties are requirements for the practical application of a hash function to message authentication.

---

[2]$\|$ denotes concatenation.

The fourth property is the one-way property: It is easy to generate a code given a message but virtually impossible to generate a message given a code. This property is important if the authentication technique involves the use of a secret value (Figure 18.7c). The secret value itself is not sent; however, if the hash function is not one way, an attacker can easily discover the secret value: If the attacker can observe or intercept a transmission, the attacker obtains the message M and the hash code $MD_M = H(S_{AB}\|M)$. The attacker then inverts the hash function to obtain $S_{AB}\|M = H^{-1}(MD_M)$. Because the attacker now has both M and $S_{AB}\|M$, it is a trivial matter to recover S_{AB}.

The fifth property guarantees that it is impossible to find an alternative message with the same hash value as a given message. This prevents forgery when an encrypted hash code is used (Figures 18.7a and b). If this property were not true, an attacker would be capable of the following sequence: First, observe or intercept a message plus its encrypted hash code; second, generate an unencrypted hash code from the message; third, generate an alternate message with the same hash code.

A hash function that satisfies the first five properties in the preceding list is referred to as a weak hash function. If the sixth property is also satisfied, then it is referred to as a strong hash function. The sixth property protects against a sophisticated class of attack known as the birthday attack.[3]

In addition to providing authentication, a message digest also provides data integrity. It performs the same function as a frame check sequence: If any bits in the message are accidentally altered in transit, the message digest will be in error.

18.4 PUBLIC-KEY ENCRYPTION AND DIGITAL SIGNATURES

Of equal importance to symmetric encryption is public-key encryption, which finds use in message authentication and key distribution. This section looks first at the basic concept of public-key encryption, followed by a discussion of digital signatures. Then we discuss the most widely used public-key algorithm: RSA. We then look at the problem of key distribution.

Public-Key Encryption

Public-key encryption, first publicly proposed by Diffie and Hellman in 1976 [DIFF76], is the first truly revolutionary advance in encryption in literally thousands of years. For one thing, public-key algorithms are based on mathematical functions rather than on simple operations on bit patterns. More important, public-key cryptography is asymmetric, involving the use of two separate keys, in contrast to symmetric encryption, which uses only one key. The use of two keys has profound consequences in the areas of confidentiality, key distribution, and authentication.

Before proceeding, we should first mention several common misconceptions concerning public-key encryption. One is that public-key encryption is more secure

---
[3]See [STAL03] for a discussion of birthday attacks.

from cryptanalysis than symmetric encryption. In fact, the security of any encryption scheme depends on (1) the length of the key and (2) the computational work involved in breaking a cipher. There is nothing in principle about either symmetric or public-key encryption that makes one superior to another from the viewpoint of resisting cryptanalysis. A second misconception is that public-key encryption is a general-purpose technique that has made symmetric encryption obsolete. On the contrary, because of the computational overhead of current public-key encryption schemes, there seems no foreseeable likelihood that symmetric encryption will be abandoned. Finally, there is a feeling that key distribution is trivial when using public-key encryption, compared to the rather cumbersome handshaking involved with key distribution centers for symmetric encryption. In fact, some form of protocol is needed, often involving a central agent, and the procedures involved are no simpler or any more efficient than those required for symmetric encryption.

A public-key encryption scheme has six ingredients (Figure 18.8):

- **Plaintext:** This is the readable message or data that is fed into the algorithm as input.
- **Encryption algorithm:** The encryption algorithm performs various transformations on the plaintext.
- **Public and private key:** This is a pair of keys that have been selected so that if one is used for encryption the other is used for decryption. The exact transformations performed by the encryption algorithm depend on the public or private key that is provided as input.
- **Ciphertext:** This is the scrambled message produced as output. It depends on the plaintext and the key. For a given message, two different keys will produce two different ciphertexts.
- **Decryption algorithm:** This algorithm accepts the ciphertext and the matching key and produces the original plaintext.

As the names suggest, the public key of the pair is made public for others to use, while the private key is known only to its owner. A general-purpose public-key cryptographic algorithm relies on one key for encryption and a different but related key for decryption. Furthermore, these algorithms have the following important characteristics:

- It is computationally infeasible to determine the decryption key given only knowledge of the cryptographic algorithm and the encryption key.
- For most public-key schemes, either of the two related keys can be used for encryption, with the other used for decryption.

The essential steps are the following:

1. Each user generates a pair of keys to be used for the encryption and decryption of messages.
2. Each user places one of the two keys in a public register or other accessible file. This is the public key. The companion key is kept private. As Figure 18.8 suggests, each user maintains a collection of public keys obtained from others.

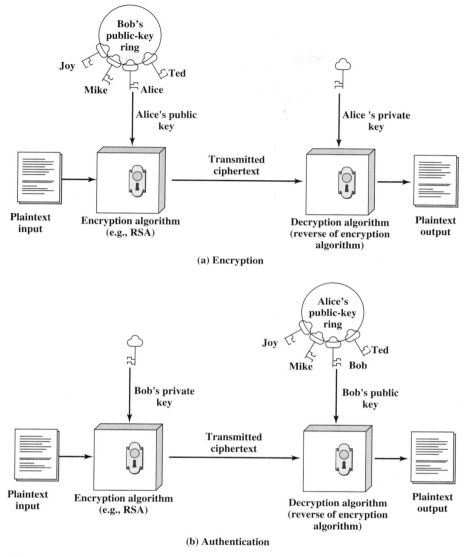

Figure 18.8 Public-Key Cryptography

3. If Bob wishes to send a private message to Alice, Bob encrypts the message using Alice's public key.

4. When Alice receives the message, she decrypts it using her private key. No other recipient can decrypt the message because only Alice knows Alice's private key.

With this approach, all participants have access to public keys, and private keys are generated locally by each participant and therefore need never be distributed. As long as a user protects his or her private key, incoming communication is secure.

At any time, a user can change the private key and publish the companion public key to replace the old public key.

Digital Signature

Public-key encryption can be used in another way, as illustrated in Figure 18.8b. Suppose that Bob wants to send a message to Alice and, although it is not important that the message be kept secret, he wants Alice to be certain that the message is indeed from him. In this case Bob uses his own private key to encrypt the message. When Alice receives the ciphertext, she finds that she can decrypt it with Bob's public key, thus proving that the message must have been encrypted by Bob. No one else has Bob's private key and therefore no one else could have created a ciphertext that could be decrypted with Bob's public key. Therefore, the entire encrypted message serves as a **digital signature.** In addition, it is impossible to alter the message without access to Bob's private key, so the message is authenticated both in terms of source and in terms of data integrity.

In the preceding scheme, the entire message is encrypted, which, although validating both author and contents, requires a great deal of storage. Each document must be kept in plaintext to be used for practical purposes. A copy also must be stored in ciphertext so that the origin and contents can be verified in case of a dispute. A more efficient way of achieving the same results is to encrypt a small block of bits that is a function of the document. Such a block, called an authenticator, must have the property that it is infeasible to change the document without changing the authenticator. If the authenticator is encrypted with the sender's private key, it serves as a signature that verifies origin, content, and sequencing. A secure hash code such as SHA-1 can serve this function.

It is important to emphasize that the digital signature does not provide confidentiality. That is, the message being sent is safe from alteration but not safe from eavesdropping. This is obvious in the case of a signature based on a portion of the message, because the rest of the message is transmitted in the clear. Even in the case of complete encryption, there is no protection of confidentiality because any observer can decrypt the message by using the sender's public key.

The RSA Public-Key Encryption Algorithm

One of the first public-key schemes was developed in 1977 by Ron Rivest, Adi Shamir, and Len Adleman at MIT and first published in 1978 [RIVE78]. The RSA scheme has since that time reigned supreme as the only widely accepted and implemented approach to public-key encryption. RSA is a block cipher in which the plaintext and ciphertext are integers between 0 and $n - 1$ for some n.

Encryption and decryption are of the following form, for some plaintext block M and ciphertext block C:

$$C = M^e \bmod n$$
$$M = C^d \bmod n = (M^e)^d \bmod n = M^{ed} \bmod n$$

Both sender and receiver must know the values of n and e, and only the receiver knows the value of d. This is a public-key encryption algorithm with a public key of $KU = \{e, n\}$ and a private key of $KR = \{d, n\}$. For this algorithm to be satisfactory for public-key encryption, the following requirements must be met:

1. It is possible to find values of e, d, n such that $M^{ed} = M \bmod n$ for all $M < n$.
2. It is relatively easy to calculate M^e and C^d for all values of $M < n$.
3. It is infeasible to determine d given e and n.

The first two requirements are easily met. The third requirement can be met for large values of e and n.

Figure 18.9 summarizes the RSA algorithm. Begin by selecting two prime numbers, p and q, and calculating their product n, which is the modulus for encryption and decryption. Next, we need the quantity $\phi(n)$, referred to as the Euler totient of n, which is the number of positive integers less than n and relatively prime to n.[4] Then select an integer e that is relatively prime to $\phi(n)$ [i.e., the greatest common divisor of e and $\phi(n)$ is 1]. Finally, calculate d such that $de \bmod \phi(n) = 1$. It can be shown that d and e have the desired properties.

Suppose that user A has published its public key and that user B wishes to send the message M to A. Then B calculates $C = M^e \pmod n$ and transmits C. On receipt of this ciphertext, user A decrypts by calculating $M = C^d \pmod n$.

Key Generation	
Select p, q	p and q both prime, $p \neq q$
Calculate $n = p \times q$	
Calculate $\phi(n) = (p - 1)(q - 1)$	
Select integer e	$\gcd(\phi(n), e) = 1; \ 1 < e < \phi(n)$
Calculate d	$de \bmod \phi(n) = 1$
Public key	$KU = \{e, n\}$
Private key	$KR = \{d, n\}$

Encryption	
Plaintext:	$M < n$
Ciphertext:	$C = M^e \pmod n$

Decryption	
Ciphertext:	C
Plaintext:	$M = C^d \pmod n$

Figure 18.9   The RSA Algorithm

---

[4]It can be shown that when n is a product of two primes, p and q, then $\phi(n) = (p - 1)(q - 1)$.

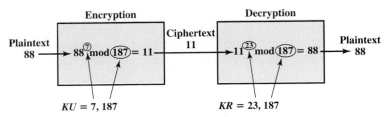

Figure 18.10 Example of RSA Algorithm

An example, from [SING99], is shown in Figure 18.10. For this example, the keys were generated as follows:

1. Select two prime numbers, $p = 17$ and $q = 11$.
2. Calculate $n = pq = 17 \times 11 = 187$.
3. Calculate $\phi(n) = (p - 1)(q - 1) = 16 \times 10 = 160$.
4. Select e such that e is relatively prime to $\phi(n) = 160$ and less than $\phi(n)$; we choose $e = 7$.
5. Determine d such that de mod $160 = 1$ and $d < 160$. The correct value is $d = 23$, because $23 \times 7 = 161 = 10 \times 160 + 1$.

The resulting keys are public key $KU = \{7, 187\}$ and private key $KR = \{23, 187\}$. The example shows the use of these keys for a plaintext input of $M = 88$. For encryption, we need to calculate $C = 88^7$ mod 187. Exploiting the properties of modular arithmetic, we can do this as follows:

88^7 mod $187 = [(88^4$ mod $187) \times (88^2$ mod $187) \times (88^1$ mod $187)]$ mod 187

88^1 mod $187 = 88$

88^2 mod $187 = 7744$ mod $187 = 77$

88^4 mod $187 = 59,969,536$ mod $187 = 132$

88^7 mod $187 = (88 \times 77 \times 132)$ mod $187 = 894,432$ mod $187 = 11$

For decryption, we calculate $M = 11^{23}$ mod 187:

11^{23} mod $187 = [(11^1$ mod $187) \times (11^2$ mod $187) \times (11^4$ mod $187)$
$\times (11^8$ mod $187) \times (11^8$ mod $187)]$ mod 187

11^1 mod $187 = 11$

11^2 mod $187 = 121$

11^4 mod $187 = 14,641$ mod $187 = 55$

11^8 mod $187 = 214,358,881$ mod $187 = 33$

11^{23} mod $187 = (11 \times 121 \times 55 \times 33 \times 33)$
$\quad$ mod $187 = 79,720,245$ mod $187 = 88$

There are two possible approaches to defeating the RSA algorithm. The first is the brute force approach: Try all possible private keys. Thus, the larger the number of bits in e and d, the more secure the algorithm. However, because the calculations involved, both in key generation and in encryption/decryption, are complex, the larger the size of the key, the slower the system will run.

Most discussions of the cryptanalysis of RSA have focused on the task of factoring n into its two prime factors. For a large n with large prime factors, factoring is a hard problem, but not as hard as it used to be. A striking illustration of this is the following. In 1977, the three inventors of RSA dared *Scientific American* readers to decode a cipher they printed in Martin Gardner's "Mathematical Games" column. They offered a $100 reward for the return of a plaintext sentence, an event they predicted might not occur for some 40 quadrillion years. In April of 1994, a group working over the Internet and using over 1600 computers claimed the prize after only eight months of work [LEUT94]. This challenge used a public-key size (length of n) of 129 decimal digits, or around 428 bits. This result does not invalidate the use of RSA; it simply means that larger key sizes must be used. Currently, a 1024-bit key size (about 300 decimal digits) is considered strong enough for virtually all applications.

Key Management

With symmetric encryption, a fundamental requirement for two parties to communicate securely is that they share a secret key. Suppose Bob wants to create a messaging application that will enable him to exchange e-mail securely with anyone who has access to the Internet or to some other network that the two of them share. Suppose Bob wants to do this using only symmetric encryption. With symmetric encryption, Bob and his correspondent, say, Alice, must come up with a way to share a unique secret key that no one else knows. How are they going to do that? If Alice is in the next room from Bob, Bob could generate a key and write it down on a piece of paper or store it on a diskette and hand it to Alice. But if Alice is on the other side of the continent or the world, what can Bob do? Well, he could encrypt this key using symmetric encryption and e-mail it to Alice, but this means that Bob and Alice must share a secret key to encrypt this new secret key. Furthermore, Bob and everyone else who uses this new e-mail package faces the same problem with every potential correspondent: Each pair of correspondents must share a unique secret key.

How to distribute secret keys securely is the most difficult problem for symmetric encryption. This problem is wiped away with public-key encryption by the simple fact that the private key is never distributed. If Bob wants to correspond with Alice and other people, he generates a single pair of keys, one private and one public. He keeps the private key secure and broadcasts the public key to all and sundry. If Alice does the same, then Bob has Alice's public key, Alice has Bob's public key, and they can now communicate securely. When Bob wishes to communicate with Alice, Bob can do the following:

1. Prepare a message.
2. Encrypt that message using symmetric encryption with a one-time symmetric session key.
3. Encrypt the session key using public-key encryption with Alice's public key.
4. Attach the encrypted session key to the message and send it to Alice.

Only Alice is capable of decrypting the session key and therefore of recovering the original message.

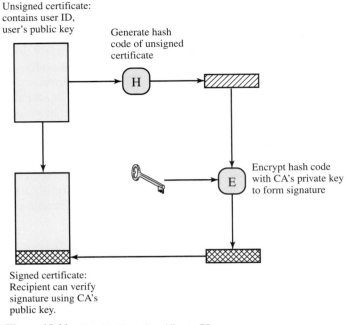

Figure 18.11   Public-Key Certificate Use

It is only fair to point out, however, that we have replaced one problem with another. Alice's private key is secure because she need never reveal it; however, Bob must be sure that the public key purporting to be Alice's is in fact Alice's public key. Someone else could have broadcast a public key and said it was Alice's.

The solution to this problem is the **public-key certificate.** In essence, a certificate consists of a public key plus a User ID of the key owner, with the whole block signed by a trusted third party. Typically, the third party is a certificate authority (CA) that is trusted by the user community, such as a government agency or a financial institution. A user can present his or her public key to the authority in a secure manner and obtain a certificate. The user can then publish the certificate. Anyone needing this user's public key can obtain the certificate and verify that it is valid by way of the attached trusted signature. Figure 18.11 illustrates the process.

18.5 VIRTUAL PRIVATE NETWORKS AND IPSEC

In today's distributed computing environment, the **virtual private network** (VPN) offers an attractive solution to network managers. In essence, a VPN consists of a set of computers that interconnect by means of a relatively unsecure network and that make use of encryption and special protocols to provide security. At each corporate site, workstations, servers, and databases are linked by one or more local area networks (LANs). The LANs are under the control of the network manager and can be configured and tuned for cost-effective performance. The Internet or some other public network can be used to interconnect sites, providing a cost savings over the use of a private network and offloading the wide area network management task to the public network provider. That same public network provides an access path for telecommuters and other mobile employees to log on to corporate systems from remote sites.

But the manager faces a fundamental requirement: security. Use of a public network exposes corporate traffic to eavesdropping and provides an entry point for unauthorized users. To counter this problem, the manager may choose from a variety of encryption and authentication packages and products. Proprietary solutions raise a number of problems. First, how secure is the solution? If proprietary encryption or authentication schemes are used, there may be little reassurance in the technical literature as to the level of security provided. Second is the question of compatibility. No manager wants to be limited in the choice of workstations, servers, routers, firewalls, and so on by a need for compatibility with the security facility. This is the motivation for the IP Security (IPSec) set of Internet standards.

IPSec

In 1994, the Internet Architecture Board (IAB) issued a report titled "Security in the Internet Architecture" (RFC 1636). The report stated the general consensus that the Internet needs more and better security, and identified key areas for security mechanisms. Among these were the need to secure the network infrastructure from unauthorized monitoring and control of network traffic and the need to secure end-user-to-end-user traffic using authentication and encryption mechanisms.

These concerns are fully justified. As confirmation, the 2002 annual report from the Computer Emergency Response Team (CERT) lists over 82,000 reported security incidents [CERT03]. The most serious types of attacks included IP spoofing, in which intruders create packets with false IP addresses and exploit applications that use authentication based on IP; and various forms of eavesdropping and packet sniffing, in which attackers read transmitted information, including logon information and database contents.

To provide security, the IAB included authentication and encryption as necessary security features in the next-generation IP, which has been issued as IPv6. Fortunately, these security capabilities were designed to be usable both with the current IPv4 and the future IPv6. This means that vendors can begin offering these features now, and many vendors do now have some IPSec capability in their products. The IPSec specification now exists as a set of Internet standards.

Applications of IPSec

IPSec provides the capability to secure communications across a LAN, across private and public WANs, and across the Internet. Examples of its use include the following:

- **Secure branch office connectivity over the Internet:** A company can build a secure virtual private network over the Internet or over a public WAN. This enables a business to rely heavily on the Internet and reduce its need for private networks, saving costs and network management overhead.

- **Secure remote access over the Internet:** An end user whose system is equipped with IP security protocols can make a local call to an Internet service provider

(ISP) and gain secure access to a company network. This reduces the cost of toll charges for traveling employees and telecommuters.

- **Establishing extranet and intranet connectivity with partners:** IPSec can be used to secure communication with other organizations, ensuring authentication and confidentiality and providing a key exchange mechanism.
- **Enhancing electronic commerce security:** Even though some Web and electronic commerce applications have built-in security protocols, the use of IPSec enhances that security. IPSec guarantees that all traffic designated by the network administrator is both encrypted and authenticated, adding an additional layer of security to whatever is provided at the application layer.

The principal feature of IPSec that enables it to support these varied applications is that it can encrypt and/or authenticate *all* traffic at the IP level. Thus, all distributed applications, including remote logon, client/server, e-mail, file transfer, Web access, and so on, can be secured.

Figure 18.12 is a typical scenario of IPSec usage. An organization maintains LANs at dispersed locations. Nonsecure IP traffic is conducted on each LAN. For traffic offsite, through some sort of private or public WAN, IPSec protocols are used. These protocols operate in networking devices, such as a router or firewall, that connect each LAN to the outside world. The IPSec networking device will typically encrypt and compress all traffic going into the WAN, and decrypt and decompress traffic coming from the WAN; these operations are transparent to workstations and servers on the LAN. Secure transmission is also possible with individual users who dial into the WAN. Such user workstations must implement the IPSec protocols to provide security.

Benefits of IPSec

Some of the benefits of IPSec are as follows:

- When IPSec is implemented in a firewall or router, it provides strong security that can be applied to all traffic crossing the perimeter. Traffic within a company or workgroup does not incur the overhead of security-related processing.
- IPSec in a firewall is resistant to bypass if all traffic from the outside must use IP and the firewall is the only means of entrance from the Internet into the organization.
- IPSec is below the transport layer (TCP, UDP) and so is transparent to applications. There is no need to change software on a user or server system when IPSec is implemented in the firewall or router. Even if IPSec is implemented in end systems, upper-layer software, including applications, is not affected.
- IPSec can be transparent to end users. There is no need to train users on security mechanisms, issue keying material on a per-user basis, or revoke keying material when users leave the organization.
- IPSec can provide security for individual users if needed. This is useful for offsite workers and for setting up a secure virtual subnetwork within an organization for sensitive applications.

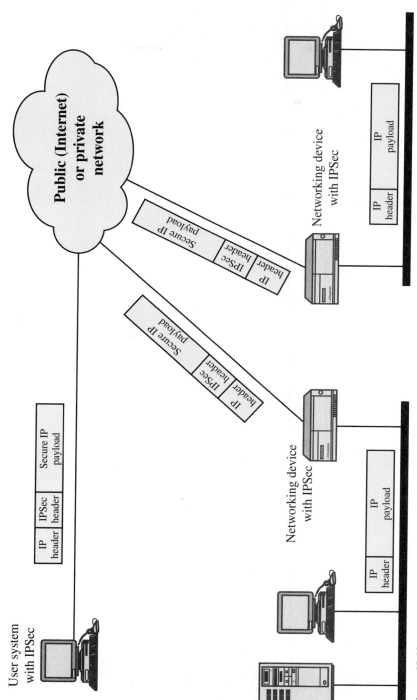

Figure 18.12 An IP Security Scenario

IPSec Functions

IPSec provides three main facilities: an authentication-only function referred to as Authentication Header (AH), a combined authentication/encryption function called Encapsulating Security Payload (ESP), and a key exchange function. For VPNs, both authentication and encryption are generally desired, because it is important both to (1) assure that unauthorized users do not penetrate the virtual private network and (2) assure that eavesdroppers on the Internet cannot read messages sent over the virtual private network. Because both features are generally desirable, most implementations are likely to use ESP rather than AH. The key exchange function allows for manual exchange of keys as well as an automated scheme.

The current specification requires that IPSec support the Data Encryption Standard (DES) for encryption, but a variety of other encryption algorithms may also be used. Because of concern about the strength of DES, it is likely that other algorithms, such as triple DES, will be widely used. For authentication, a relatively new scheme, known as HMAC, is required.

Transport and Tunnel Modes

ESP supports two modes of use: transport and tunnel mode.

Transport mode provides protection primarily for upper-layer protocols. That is, transport mode protection extends to the payload of an IP packet. Typically, transport mode is used for end-to-end communication between two hosts (e.g., a client and a server, or two workstations). ESP in transport mode encrypts and optionally authenticates the IP payload but not the IP header (Figure 18.13b). This configuration is useful for relatively small networks, in which each host and server is equipped with IPSec. However, for a full-blown VPN, tunnel mode is far more efficient.

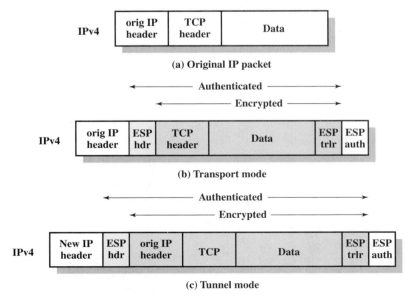

Figure 18.13 Scope of ESP Encryption and Authentication

Tunnel mode provides protection to the entire IP packet. To achieve this, after the ESP fields are added to the IP packet, the entire packet plus security fields is treated as the payload of new "outer" IP packet with a new outer IP header. The entire original, or inner, packet travels through a "tunnel" from one point of an IP network to another; no routers along the way are able to examine the inner IP header. Because the original packet is encapsulated, the new, larger packet may have totally different source and destination addresses, adding to the security. Tunnel mode is used when one or both ends is a security gateway, such as a firewall or router that implements IPSec. With tunnel mode, a number of hosts on networks behind firewalls may engage in secure communications without implementing IPSec. The unprotected packets generated by such hosts are tunneled through external networks by using tunnel mode set up by the IPSec software in the firewall or secure router at the boundary of the local network.

Here is an example of how tunnel-mode IPSec operates. Host A on a network generates an IP packet with the destination address of host B on another network. This packet is routed from the originating host to a firewall or secure router at the boundary of A's network. The firewall filters all outgoing packets to determine the need for IPSec processing. If this packet from A to B requires IPSec, the firewall performs IPSec processing and encapsulates the packet in an outer IP header. The source IP address of this outer IP packet is this firewall, and the destination address may be a firewall that forms the boundary to B's local network. This packet is now routed to B's firewall, with intermediate routers examining only the outer IP header. At B's firewall, the outer IP header is stripped off, and the inner packet is delivered to B.

ESP in tunnel mode encrypts and optionally authenticates the entire inner IP packet, including the inner IP header.

Key Management

The key management portion of IPSec involves the determination and distribution of secret keys. The IPSec Architecture document mandates support for two types of key management:

- **Manual:** A system administrator (SA) manually configures each system with its own keys and with the keys of other communicating systems. This is practical for small, relatively static environments.

- **Automated:** An automated system enables the on-demand creation of keys and facilitates the use of keys in a large distributed system with an evolving configuration. An automated system is the most flexible but requires more effort to configure and requires more software, so smaller installations are likely to opt for manual key management.

IPSec and VPNs

The driving force for the acceptance and deployment of secure IP is the need for business and government users to connect their private WAN/LAN infrastructure to the Internet for (1) access to Internet services and (2) use of the Internet as a component of the WAN transport system. Users need to secure their networks and at the same time send and receive traffic over the Internet. The authentication and privacy mechanisms of secure IP provide the basis for a security strategy.

Because IP security mechanisms have been defined independent of their use with either the current IP or IPv6, deployment of these mechanisms does not depend on deployment of IPv6. Indeed, it is likely that we will see widespread use of secure IP features long before IPv6 becomes popular, because the need for IP-level security is greater than the need for the added functions that IPv6 provides compared to the current IP.

With the arrival of IPSec, managers have a standardized means of implementing security for VPNs. Further, all of the encryption and authentication algorithms, and security protocols, used in IPSec are well studied and have survived years of scrutiny. As a result, the user can be confident that the IPSec facility indeed provides strong security.

IPSec can be implemented in routers or firewalls owned and operated by the organization. This gives the network manager complete control over security aspects of the VPN, which is much to be desired. However, IPSec is a complex set of functions and modules and the management and configuration responsibility is formidable. The alternative is to seek a solution from a service provider. A service provider can simplify the job of planning, implementing, and maintaining Internet-based VPNs for secure access to network resources and secure communication between sites.

APPLICATION NOTE
Security Layers

Security regarding computers and networks can be very confusing business. In addition to the large number of threats, the wide variety of systems and technologies that need to be protected can make the job of security guru seem all but impossible. It can be helpful to divide up the tasks or areas and find the best security approach. One method is to divide the domain into system and network security groups.

Perhaps one of the first rules of security, no matter what area you are focusing on, is to understand the nature of the threat. Companies spend millions of dollars on equipment and personnel protecting things that don't need protection. Most organizations agree that their own users, whether accidentally or with intent, become their worst security problem. The range of difficulties includes downloaded viruses, improper use of company resources, and misuse of passwords (their own and the passwords of others). The cracker burrowing through corporate firewalls in order to steal valuable company research isn't the typical case. From the outside, the bad guys are usually trying to shut things down with some sort of denial of service attack.

When working with system security, the group is usually focused on end user computers and servers. These are the most common devices to be attacked. Examine any recent attack and we see that most problems end up being solved or blocked with a variety of upgrades, system patches or personal firewalls. Every time a server or service is brought on line, it must be up to date regarding the operating system and only the required communication ports opened.

With network security we are trying to prevent unauthorized traffic. The problem is that there are dozens of protocols used today and the services that are open are myriad. Thus, blocking a certain type of traffic may cause a desired service to be disrupted. As a result, network administrators must have a deep understanding of not only initial configuration but of how protocols operate as well.

Often we refer to the programs and techniques used in security as our toolbox. With the network security analyst, one of the easiest ways to think of this toolbox is as a series of layers that correspond to the layers of the TCP/IP networking model. A sample of the tools for the various layers follows:

1—physical   The problem here is with the actual signal and so the approaches are very straightforward—locking doors, minimizing access to ports, antenna locations, and low-level encryption such as WEP.

2—network   Moving up the stack, we are now dealing with increased intelligence in the networking devices and can start to apply low-level firewalls such as MAC address-based filters. Additional tools include VLANs and 802.1x.

3—internetwork   At layer 3 the IP header is now exposed and so filtering or firewalls can be applied to IP addresses. Other valuable methods include VPNs and NAT.

4—transport   At layer 4 the TCP and UDP ports are the main focus and so our filters now target particular streams of communication. At layer 3 the filters are called standard ACLs. More complex ACL are called extended ACLs and are usually applied to layer 4.

5—application   The tools available to us here are usually focused at the user with passwords and authentication. These can be combined with other tools mentioned earlier, like 802.1x and VPNs. In addition, other forms of encryption exist like those used in SSH and SSL.

It is important to note that this is only a partial list and no single approach can be said to work against all threats. In fact, most security techniques can be defeated if applied individually. However, taken together as a layered approach, they represent a formidable barrier to would-be interlopers.

Whatever your area of focus, system or network, of great importance is a policy regarding safe and acceptable use. Education for users is also very important. Many times users defeat security practices by unintentionally going around them, and viruses provide an excellent example. Policies and some basic education for best practices can go a long way in protecting the network and system assets.

18.6 SUMMARY

The reliance by business on the use of data processing systems and the increasing use of networks and communications facilities to build distributed systems have resulted in a strong requirement for computer and network security. Computer security relates to mechanisms inside and related to a single computer system. The principal object is to protect the data resources of that system. Network security deals with the protection of data and messages that are communicated. This chapter deals with network security.

The requirements for security are best assessed by examining the various security threats faced by an organization. We can organize these threats into two main categories. Passive threats, sometimes referred to as wiretapping or eavesdropping, involve attempts by an attacker to obtain information relating to a communication. In most cases, the most serious such threat is the disclosure of files, messages, or documents in transit to an unauthorized party. The other category of threats includes a variety of active threats. These involve some modification of the transmitted data or the creation of false transmissions.

By far the most important automated tool for network and communications security is encryption. Encryption is a process that conceals meaning by changing intelligible messages into unintelligible messages. Most commercially available encryption equipment makes use of conventional encryption, in which the two parties share a single encryption/decryption key. The principal challenge with conventional encryption is the distribution and protection of the keys. The alternative is a public-key encryption scheme, in which the process involves two keys, one for encryption and a paired key for decryption. One of the keys is kept private by the party that generated the key pair, and the other is made public.

Conventional encryption and public-key encryption are often combined in secure networking applications to provide a spectrum of security services. Conventional encryption is used to encrypt transmitted data, often using a one-time or short-term session key. The session key can be distributed by a trusted key distribution center or transmitted in encrypted form using public-key encryption. Public-key encryption also is used to create digital signatures, which authenticate the source of transmitted messages.

18.7 RECOMMENDED READING AND WEB SITES

The topics in this chapter are covered in greater detail in [STAL03]. For coverage of cryptographic algorithms, [SCHN96] is an essential reference work; it contains descriptions of numerous cryptographic algorithms and protocols.

SCHN96   Schneier, B. *Applied Cryptography.* New York: Wiley, 1996.

STAL03   Stallings, W. *Cryptography and Network Security: Principles and Practice,* 3rd edition. Upper Saddle River, NJ: Prentice Hall, 2003.

Recommended Web Sites:

- **COAST:** Comprehensive set of links related to cryptography and network security
- **IETF Security Area:** Provides up-to-date information on Internet security standardization efforts
- **IEEE Technical Committee on Security and Privacy:** Provides copies of IEEE's newsletter and information on IEEE-related activities

18.8 KEY TERMS, REVIEW QUESTIONS, AND PROBLEMS

Key Terms

active attack	decryption algorithm	plaintext
authenticity	digital signature	private key
availability	encryption algorithm	public key
Advanced Encryption Stan-	integrity	public-key encryption
dard (AES)	IP security (IPSec)	secret key
brute-force attack	key distribution	secure hash function
ciphertext	key management	session key
confidentiality	message authentication	symmetric encryption
cryptanalysis	one-way hash function	traffic padding
Data Encryption Standard	passive attack	virtual private networks
(DES)	permanent key	

Review Questions

18.1.   Name and describe the four basic security requirements.

18.2.   What is the difference between passive and active security threats?

18.3.   List and briefly define categories of passive and active security threats.

18.4.   What are DES and triple DES?

18.5.   How is the AES expected to be an improvement over triple DES?

18.6.   Explain traffic padding.

18.7.   List and briefly define various approaches to message authentication.

18.8.   What is a secure hash function?

18.9.   Explain the difference between symmetric encryption and public-key encryption.

18.10.   What are the distinctions among the terms *public key, private key*, and *secret key*?

18.11.   What is a digital signature?

18.12.   What is a public-key certificate?

18.13.   What services are provided by IPSec?

Problems

18.1   Give some examples where traffic analysis could jeopardize security. Describe situations where end-to-end encryption combined with link encryption would still allow enough traffic analysis to be dangerous.

18.2   Key distribution schemes using an access control center and/or a key distribution center have central points vulnerable to attack. Discuss the security implications of such centralization.

18.3   Suppose that someone suggests the following way to confirm that the two of you are both in possession of the same secret key. You create a random bit string the length of the key, XOR it with the key, and send the result over the channel. Your partner XORs the incoming block with the key (which should be the same as your key) and sends it back. You check, and if what you receive is your original random string, you have verified that your partner has the same secret key, yet neither of you has ever transmitted the key. Is there a flaw in this scheme?

18.4   Oscar wants to send a message to Minerva that only Minerva can interpret. Oscar also wants Minerva to be assured that the message came from him and not from some imposter. Describe a scenario (and/or devise a diagram) that illustrates the use of public-key cryptography to successfully enable this transaction.

18.5   Prior to the discovery of any specific public-key schemes, such as RSA, an existence proof was developed whose purpose was to demonstrate that public-key encryption is possible in theory. Consider the functions $f_1(x_1) = z_1$; $f_2(x_2, y_2) = z_2$; $f_3(x_3, y_3) = z_3$, where all values are integers with $1 \leq x_i, y_i, z_i \leq N$. Function f_1 can be represented by a vector M1 of length N, in which the kth entry is the value of $f_1(k)$. Similarly, f_2 and f_3 can be represented by $N \times N$ matrices M2 and M3. The intent is to represent the encryption/decryption process by table lookups for tables with very large values of N. Such tables would be impractically huge but could, in principle, be constructed. The scheme works as follows: Construct M1 with a random permutation of all integers between 1 and N; that is, each integer appears exactly once in M1. Construct M2 so that each row contains a random permutation of the first N integers. Finally, fill in M3 to satisfy the following condition:

$$f_3(f_2(f_1(k), p), k) = p \text{ for all } k, p \text{ with } 1 \leq k, p \leq N$$

In words,

1. M1 takes an input k and produces an output x.
2. M2 takes inputs x and p giving output z.
3. M3 takes inputs z and k and produces p.

The three tables, once constructed, are made public.

a.   It should be clear that it is possible to construct M3 to satisfy the preceding condition. As an example, fill in M3 for the following simple case:

$$M1 = \begin{array}{|c|} \hline 5 \\ \hline 4 \\ \hline 2 \\ \hline 3 \\ \hline 1 \\ \hline \end{array} \quad M2 = \begin{array}{|c|c|c|c|c|} \hline 5 & 2 & 3 & 4 & 1 \\ \hline 4 & 2 & 5 & 1 & 3 \\ \hline 1 & 3 & 2 & 4 & 5 \\ \hline 3 & 1 & 4 & 2 & 5 \\ \hline 2 & 5 & 3 & 4 & 1 \\ \hline \end{array} \quad M3 = \begin{array}{|c|c|c|c|c|} \hline & & & & \\ \hline & & & & \\ \hline & & & & \\ \hline & & & & \\ \hline & & & & \\ \hline \end{array}$$

Convention: The ith element of M1 corresponds to $k = i$. The ith row of M2 corresponds to $x = i$; the jth column of M2 corresponds to $p = j$. The ith row of M3 corresponds to $z = i$; the jth column of M3 corresponds to $k = j$.

b.   Describe the use of this set of tables to perform encryption and decryption between two users.

c.   Argue that this is a secure scheme.

18.6   Perform encryption and decryption using the RSA algorithm, as in Figure 18.10, for the following:

a. $p = 3$; $q = 11$, $d = 7$; $M = 5$
b. $p = 5$; $q = 11$, $e = 3$; $M = 9$
c. $p = 7$; $q = 11$, $e = 17$; $M = 8$
d. $p = 11$; $q = 13$, $e = 11$; $M = 7$
e. $p = 17$; $q = 31$, $e = 7$; $M = 2$. *Hint:* Decryption is not as hard as you think; use some finesse.

18.7   In a public-key system using RSA, you intercept the ciphertext $C = 10$ sent to a user whose public key is $e = 5$, $n = 35$. What is the plaintext M?

18.8   In an RSA system, the public key of a given user is $e = 31$, $n = 3599$. What is the private key of this user?

18.9 Suppose we have a set of blocks encoded with the RSA algorithm and we don't have the private key. Assume $n = pq$, e is the public key. Suppose also someone tells us that she knows that one of the plaintext blocks has a common factor with n. Does this help us in any way?

18.10 Show how RSA can be represented by matrices M1, M2, and M3 of Problem 18.4.

18.11 Consider the following scheme:

1. Pick an odd number, E.
2. Pick two prime numbers, P and Q, where $(P - 1)(Q - 1) - 1$ is evenly divisible by E.
3. Multiply P and Q to get N.
4. Calculate $D = \dfrac{(P - 1)(Q - 1)(E - 1) + 1}{E}$.

Is this scheme equivalent to RSA? Show why or why not.

18.12 Consider using RSA with a known key to construct a one-way hash function. Then process a message consisting of a sequence of blocks as follows: Encrypt the first block, XOR the result with the second block and encrypt again, and so on. Show that this scheme is not secure by solving the following problem. Given a two-block message B1, B2, and its hash

$$RSAH(B1,B2) = RSA(RSA(B1) \oplus B2)$$

Given an arbitrary block C1, choose C2 so that $RSAH(C1, C2) = RSAH(B1, B2)$.

18.13 This book's Web site includes a link to a site from which PGP public-key encryption software is available free for download. Download and install this software and try the following after creating your own public/private-key pair. Before you proceed, there are a few important things to remember. No one will be able to decrypt what you send unless you post your public key. The recipients will also need PGP software. Finally, remember your passwords.

Encrypt a single file.
Encrypt several files together (also called an archive).
Encrypt your e-mail.
As a more advanced project, you can install the PGP VPN. You must ensure that another machine can decode your tunnel at the other end.

18.14 Test the vulnerability of a machine at the following site: http://grc.com/default.htm. Follow the *ShieldsUP!* link for a series of free tests listed midway down the page.

Case Study XI: The Hacker in All of Us[1]

"How do you spell pillage?" asks Fred Norwood, manager of information infrastructure technology at El Paso Energy Corp. in Houston. Twelve of us had just hacked Microsoft Corp.'s crown jewel — a Windows NT box — and were copying passwords to our hard drives. From across the room, a quick-witted Sam Gerard, data security manager at Motorola Inc., spells out the answer for us: "F-U-N!" Thus goes Day 2 of Extreme Hacking, a course taught by security whiz kids at Ernst and Young LLP's towering Houston offices.

For four days, network managers, auditors and security specialists from companies such as Motorola, Electronic Data Systems Corp. and State Farm Insurance switched to the dark side. In so doing, they learned just what they're up against in their fight to keep crackers out of their networks.

The truth is, hacking is easy. And, well, fun. We pushed open server doors and helped ourselves to whatever data we wanted — all without any feeling of culpability.

"This course gives me a lot more insight into the mentality and capability of attackers," says John McGraw, a security technology planner at a large computing services company. "We know all these vulnerabilities, but there are probably so many more that no one knows about."

So fun was it that I was sorry to leave the capture-the-flag game at the end of Day 3. But my cab to the airport was waiting 20 floors below. By then, I had leapfrogged to the fourth and final victim Unix server and was closing in on that flag. But I had a plane to catch.

Day 1: Finding the Goods

On Day 1, we case out our victim. Our instructor, Stuart McClure, prefers the more sanitized term "discovery." We begin discovery by finding publicly available information on the Internet. McClure talks about searching the Securities and Exchange Commission (SEC) Web site to get a thumbnail sketch of a company and its affiliates, laboratories and acquisitions. We could use this information to break in to a company by hacking its acquisitions or subsidiaries because those subnetworks aren't usually as well monitored or secure as networks at the home office. But for expediency's sake we bypass the SEC and go straight to the InterNic Registrar, the service that assigns domain names. By querying InterNic with a simple "whois" command, we get all the IP addresses of our victim's Web servers — along with company nicknames — and auxiliary domain name servers (DNS) in affiliates and laboratories. We even find out what type of servers they are (the main DNS is a Sun-3/180 running Unix), along with the names and phone numbers of the server administrators.

---

[1]Reprinted with permission from *Computer World*, October 11, 1999, by Deborah Radcliff.

534

I flash to the infamous cracker, Kevin Mitnick, who loved this little InterNic feature. He'd call those network administrators and try to "social engineer" (sweet-talk) them out of network information. "It's amazing the amount of information you can get from the Internet. You don't realize you're hanging out there as exposed as you are," says El Paso Energy's Norwood.

We deploy a few common network-troubleshooting tools (like zone transfers—normally used to correlate data between the backup and primary servers, and Name Service lookup—a utility used to look up the IP address of a name like www.microsoft.com) against some of the IP addresses we've just gleaned. We soon have a list of domain names and IP addresses of all the machines connected to our victim network.

Next, we use traceroute (another administrative tool, which traces the route between a source and destination) to view the network topology and identify potential access control devices like routers and firewalls, which we'll steer clear of.

Time to rattle some doors and look in some windows. McClure calls this "port-scanning"—using administration and downloadable hacking tools to find out what ports are open and what services are running on those ports. I'm particularly taken with the stealthy Nmap, a utility for network mapping available for free off the Web. We deploy Nmap against our primary target to get a road map of open ports, along with the network protocols and application services they support. At the top of our list, for example, we see: "Port 7: Open; protocol TCP; service Telnet." And so it goes for 10 other open ports on that machine alone. The classroom buzzes with excitement.

I realize how removed I feel from the victim. It's chilling to think that there are hundreds, nay thousands, of other crackers from underground groups such as Global Hell who probably feel the same way.

Day 2: The NT Root Dance

We're introduced to Eric Schultze, affectionately called a "Hoover" by his cronies. A Hoover can really suck the guts out of a victim machine, and Schultze, 31, proves he's worthy of his name. We start by picking our target. Test servers are notorious for lax password controls and monitoring. Or we could sniff the mail server for user names and passwords. We decide to go for the backup domain controller—a separate physical server—where user names are stored and security is often forgotten because it's a backup.

We establish a null session (a Microsoft utility that allows services to communicate with one another without a user identification) with the victim server. I feel like a ghost inside someone else's house. I can see everything—network services, password files, user accounts, even payroll. But I can't touch anything because null is only designed for interprocess communication.

For the victim, "the sad thing about Microsoft is it doesn't log any of this," Schultze explains.

We're itching to gain root access (the most privileged level of access). But first, we must log off and then back on as legitimate users in order to grab the password hashes (encoded passwords) and submit them to our ace password-cracking tools. We get back in under the user name "backup" by guessing the password (which is also "backup"). "Command completed successfully," the machine responds.

I ask Schultze whether raised awareness has pushed administrators to better monitor passwords. No, he says. Most networks are still chock-full of such easy-to-guess passwords.

Once in, we copy user files and encrypted password hashes onto our hard drive. We log off and hit the hashes with L0phtcrack and the even faster John the Ripper. Available on the Web, both tools test passwords against a dictionary of common passwords until they break open. The tougher passwords may take a day, though, as they must be cracked one character at a time. Within minutes, we've got more than 70% of plain-text passwords in our greasy little paws.

Microsoft's LAN Manager hashes are the worst from a victim stand-point because LAN Manager splits passwords into seven-character halves and uses a known constant to encrypt each half, says Schultze. Our cracking tools are programmed for this, so they kick out passwords much faster than they would in Unix. And if the administrator disables LAN Manager, the NT box won't talk to any Windows 95 or 98 boxes, so it's a tough problem to solve.

Armed with our newfound passwords, we finally reach our goal for the day and hack back into the machine at administrator level and get root control of our machine. "What's the first thing you do when you gain root? You do the root dance," explains Ron Nguyen, another instructor. Push one arm up, jiggle your hips, put the other arm up, jiggle your hips and repeat until you get it out of your system.

For our reward, Nguyen hands out a red wallet card titled "18 Things to Do After You've Hacked Admin" (Table XI.1). But for the final slap to our victims' faces, we hide our hacking tools in an alternate data stream behind a readme.txt file on the victim server. You could easily hide 10M bytes of hacker tools behind such a file without changing the file size, according to Schultze. The only way administrators can catch this is to set up audit logs that would alert them when disk space changes significantly.

Day 3: Capturing the Unix Flag

"Hacking root is a state of mind." Thus begins our syllabus for Day 3. And we really are getting into this "state." We arrive at the class rubbing our hands in anticipation of breaking the venerable Unix. Our instructor, former Air Force geek Chris Prosise, doesn't let us down.

Table XI.1   Things to Do after You've Hacked Admin

1.   Disable auditing
2.   Grab the password file
3.   Create an "adminkit" (hacker tools)
4.   Enumerate server information
5.   Enumerate secrets of LSA (Windows NT's Local Security Authority in the registry where password hashes are kept)
6.   Dump registry info
7.   Use Nltest (a tool that queries NT servers remotely)
8.   Pilfer the box
9.   Add an administrator account
10. Grab a remote command shell
11. Hijack the graphical user interface
12. Disable Passprop (NT's password policy settings)
13. Install a back door
14. Install Trojan horses and sniffers
15. Repeat
16. Hide the adminkit (so you can use the machine as a launch point to attack others)
17. Enable auditing
18. Eat a nice meal

We begin by repeating discovery and gaining entry in much the same way we did on NT. But Prosise wants to have a little fun. He's showing us how to corrupt the DNS server to reroute traffic to a phony IP address on an "evil.com" server where he can: a) grab information or b) reroute the message into oblivion.

He also shows us how to conduct common HTTP attacks like test-Common Gateway Interface, which forces the victim to give up files and directories with a simple "get" command, and how to execute remote commands that would disable access controls. We install Trojan horses (executable code to do our bidding remotely) and punch open back doors so we can get back in using a Telnet terminal session without needing identifications or passwords.

Then we play capture the flag by leapfrogging among four Unix boxes. And this, I'm afraid, is where I was so rudely interrupted by my awaiting taxi.

Suffice it to say, we learned our lessons. Network and security managers have a tough row to hoe. Bullet-proof security is a misnomer. And managing security risk is the best anyone can hope for. We also learned that there's a little bit of hacker in all of us. And by cultivating this hacker within, information security professionals can better fight the cracker without.

Discussion Points

1. How vulnerable do you think the typical computer site is?

2. What is the magnitude of the risk? That is, if security is compromised, what is the potential cost to the victim?

3. What policies and procedures can you suggest to counter the types of threats illustrated in this case study?

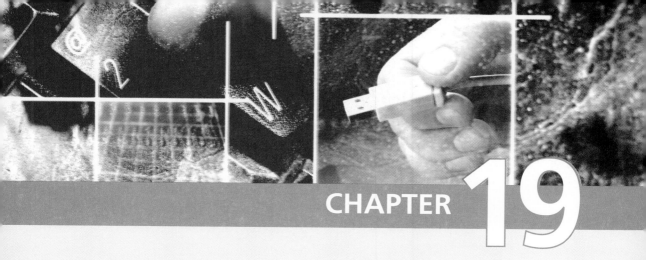

CHAPTER 19

NETWORK MANAGEMENT

CHAPTER OBJECTIVES

After reading this chapter, you should be able to

- List and define the key requirements that a network management system should satisfy.
- Give an overview of the architecture of a network management system, and explain each of its key elements.
- Describe SNMP and list the differences among versions 1, 2, and 3.

Networks and distributed processing systems are of critical and growing importance in enterprises of all sorts. The trend is toward larger, more complex networks supporting more applications and more users. As these networks grow in scale, two facts become painfully evident:

- The network and its associated resources and distributed applications become indispensable to the organization.
- More things can go wrong, disabling the network or a portion of the network or degrading performance to an unacceptable level.

A large network cannot be put together and managed by human effort alone. The complexity of such a system dictates the use of automated network management tools. The urgency of the need for such tools is increased, and the difficulty of supplying such tools is also increased, if the network includes equipment from multiple vendors. Moreover, the increasing decentralization of network services as exemplified by the increasing importance of workstations and client/server computing makes coherent and coordinated network management increasingly difficult. In such complex information systems, many significant network assets are dispersed far from network management personnel.

This chapter provides an overview of network management. We begin by looking at the requirements for network management. This should give some idea of the scope of the task to be accomplished. To manage a network, it is fundamental to know something about the current status and behavior of that network.

For either LAN management alone, or for a combined LAN/WAN environment, what is needed is a network management system that includes a comprehensive set of data gathering and control tools and that is integrated with the network hardware and software. We look at the general architecture of a network management system and then examine the most widely used standardized software package for supporting network management: SNMP.

19.1 NETWORK MANAGEMENT REQUIREMENTS

Table 19.1 lists key areas of network management as suggested by the International Organization for Standardization (ISO). These categories provide a useful way of organizing our discussion of requirements.

Fault Management

Overview To maintain proper operation of a complex network, care must be taken that systems as a whole, and each essential component individually, are in proper working order. When a fault occurs, it is important, as rapidly as possible, to

- Determine exactly where the fault is.
- Isolate the rest of the network from the failure so that it can continue to function without interference.
- Reconfigure or modify the network in such a way as to minimize the impact of operation without the failed component or components.
- Repair or replace the failed components to restore the network to its initial state.

Central to the definition of fault management is the fundamental concept of a fault. Faults are to be distinguished from errors. A **fault** is an abnormal condition that requires management attention (or action) to repair. A fault is usually indicated by failure to operate correctly or by excessive errors. For example, if a communications line is physically cut, no signals can get through. Or a crimp in the cable may cause wild distortions so that there is a persistently high bit error rate. Certain errors (e.g., a single bit error on a communication line) may occur occasionally and are not normally considered to be faults. It is usually possible to compensate for errors using the error control mechanisms of the various protocols.

Table 19.1   ISO Management Functional Areas

Fault management

The facilities that enable the detection, isolation, and correction of abnormal operation of the OSI environment.

Accounting management

The facilities that enable charges to be established for the use of managed objects and costs to be identified for the use of those managed objects.

Configuration and name management

The facilities that exercise control over, identify, collect data from, and provide data to managed objects for the purpose of assisting in providing for continuous operation of interconnection services.

Performance management

The facilities needed to evaluate the behavior of managed objects and the effectiveness of communication activities.

Security management

Those aspects of OSI security essential to operate OSI network management correctly and to protect managed objects.

User Requirements   Users expect fast and reliable problem resolution. Most end users will tolerate occasional outages. When these infrequent outages do occur, however, the user generally expects to receive immediate notification and expects that the problem will be corrected almost immediately. To provide this level of fault resolution requires very rapid and reliable fault detection and diagnostic management functions. The impact and duration of faults can also be minimized by the use of redundant components and alternate communication routes, to give the network a degree of fault tolerance. The fault management capability itself should be redundant to increase network reliability.

Users expect to be kept informed of the network status, including both scheduled and unscheduled disruptive maintenance. Users expect reassurance of correct network operation through mechanisms that use confidence tests or analyze dumps, logs, alerts, or statistics. After correcting a fault and restoring a system to its full operational state, the fault management service must ensure that the problem is truly resolved and that no new problems are introduced. This requirement is called problem tracking and control.

As with other areas of network management, fault management should have minimal effect on network performance.

Accounting Management

Overview   In many enterprise networks, individual divisions or cost centers, or even individual project accounts, are charged for the use of network services. These are internal accounting procedures rather than actual cash transfers, but they are important to the participating users nevertheless. Furthermore, even if no such internal charging is employed, the network manager needs to be able to track the use of network resources by user or user class for a number of reasons, including the following:

- A user or group of users may be abusing their access privileges and burdening the network at the expense of other users.
- Users may be making inefficient use of the network, and the network manager can assist in changing procedures to improve performance.
- The network manager is in a better position to plan for network growth if user activity is known in sufficient detail.

User Requirements   The network manager needs to be able to specify the kinds of accounting information to be recorded at various nodes, the desired interval between successive sendings of the recorded information to higher-level management nodes, and the algorithms to be used in calculating the charging. Accounting reports should be generated under network manager control.

To limit access to accounting information, the accounting facility must provide the capability to verify users' authorization to access and manipulate that information.

Configuration and Name Management

Overview   Modern data communication networks are composed of individual components and logical subsystems (e.g., the device driver in an operating system) that can be configured to perform many different applications. The same device, for example, can be configured to act either as a router or as an end system node or both. Once it is decided how a device is to be used, the configuration manager can choose the appropriate software and set of attributes and values (e.g., a transport layer retransmission timer) for that device.

Configuration management is concerned with initializing a network and gracefully shutting down part or all of the network. It is also concerned with maintaining, adding, and updating the relationships among components and the status of components themselves during network operation.

User Requirements Startup and shutdown operations on a network are the specific responsibilities of configuration management. It is often desirable for these operations on certain components to be performed unattended (e.g., starting up or shutting down a network interface unit). The network manager needs the capability to identify initially the components that comprise the network and to define the desired connectivity of these components. Those who regularly configure a network with the same or a similar set of resource attributes need ways to define and modify default attributes and to load these predefined sets of attributes into the specified network components. The network manager needs the capability to change the connectivity of network components when users' needs change. Reconfiguration of a network is often desired in response to performance evaluation or in support of network upgrade, fault recovery, or security checks.

Users often need to, or want to, be informed of the status of network resources and components. Therefore, when changes in configuration occur, users should be notified of these changes. Configuration reports can be generated either on some routine periodic basis or in response to a request for such a report. Before reconfiguration, users often want to inquire about the upcoming status of resources and their attributes.

Network managers usually want only authorized users (operators) to manage and control network operation (e.g., software distribution and updating).

Performance Management

Overview Modern data communications networks are composed of many and varied components, which must intercommunicate and share data and resources. In some cases, it is critical to the effectiveness of an application that the communication over the network be within certain performance limits. Performance management of a computer network comprises two broad functional categories—monitoring and controlling. Monitoring is the function that tracks activities on the network. The controlling function enables performance management to make adjustments to improve network performance. Some of the performance issues of concern to the network manager:

- What is the level of capacity utilization?
- Is there excessive traffic?
- Has throughput been reduced to unacceptable levels?
- Are there bottlenecks?
- Is response time increasing?

To deal with these concerns, the network manager must focus on some initial set of resources to be monitored to assess performance levels. This includes associating appropriate metrics and values with relevant network resources as indicators of different levels of performance. For example, what count of retransmissions on a transport connection is considered to be a performance problem requiring attention? Performance management, therefore, must monitor many resources to provide information in determining network operating level. By collecting this information, analyzing it, and then using the resultant analysis as feedback to the prescribed set of values, the network manger can become more and more adept at recognizing situations indicative of present or impending performance degradation.

User Requirements Before using a network for a particular application, a user may want to know such things as the average and worst case response times and the reliability of network services. Thus, performance must be known in sufficient detail to respond to specific user queries. End users expect network services to be managed in such a way as to afford their applications consistently good response time.

Network managers need performance statistics to help them plan, manage, and maintain large networks. Performance statistics can be used to recognize potential bottlenecks before they cause problems to end users. Appropriate corrective action can then be taken. This action can take the form of changing routing tables to balance or redistribute traffic load during times of peak use or when a bottleneck is identified by a rapidly growing load in one area. Over the long term, capacity planning based on such performance information can indicate the proper decisions to make, for example, with regard to expansion of lines in that area.

Security Management

Overview Security management is concerned with generating, distributing, and storing encryption keys. Passwords and other authorization or access control information must be maintained and distributed. Security management is also concerned with monitoring and controlling access to computer networks and access to all or part of the network management information obtained from the network nodes. Logs are an important security tool, and therefore security management is very much involved with the collection, storage, and examination of audit records and security logs, as well as with the enabling and disabling of these logging facilities.

User Requirements Security management provides facilities for protection of network resources and user information. Network security facilities should be available for authorized users only. Users want to know that the proper security policies are in force and effective and that the management of security facilities is itself secure.

19.2 NETWORK MANAGEMENT SYSTEMS

Architecture of a Network Management System

A **network management system** is a collection of tools for network monitoring and control that is integrated in the following senses:

- A single operator interface with a powerful but user-friendly set of commands for performing most or all network management tasks.

- A minimal amount of separate equipment. That is, most of the hardware and software required for network management is incorporated into the existing user equipment.

A network management system consists of incremental hardware and software additions implemented among existing network components. The software used in accomplishing the network management tasks resides in the host computers and communications processors (e.g., front-end processors, terminal cluster controllers, bridges, routers). A network management system is designed to view the entire network as a unified architecture, with addresses and labels assigned to each point and the specific attributes of each element and link known to the system. The active elements of the network provide regular feedback of status information to the network control center.

Figure 19.1 suggests the architecture of a network management system. Each network node contains a collection of software devoted to the network management task, referred to in the diagram as a network management entity (NME). Each NME performs the following tasks:

- Collect statistics on communications and network-related activities.
- Store statistics locally.
- Respond to commands from the network control center, including commands to
  1. Transmit collected statistics to the network control center.
  2. Change a parameter (e.g., a timer used in a transport protocol).

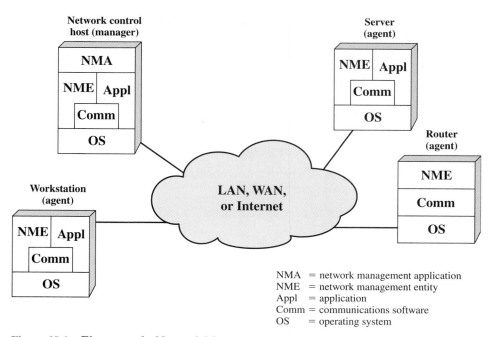

Figure 19.1 Elements of a Network Management System

3. Provide status information (e.g., parameter values, active links).

4. Generate artificial traffic to perform a test.

- Send messages to the NCC when local conditions undergo a significant change.

At least one host in the network is designated as the network control host, or **manager.** In addition to the NME software, the network control host includes a collection of software called the network management application (NMA). The NMA includes an operator interface to allow an authorized user to manage the network. The NMA responds to user commands by displaying information and/or by issuing commands to NMEs throughout the network. This communication is carried out using an application-level network management protocol that employs the communications architecture in the same fashion as any other distributed application.

Each other node in the network that is part of the network management system includes a NME and, for purposes of network management, is referred to as an **agent.** Agents include end systems that support user applications as well as nodes that provide a communications service, such as front-end processors, cluster controllers, bridges, and routers.

As depicted in Figure 19.1, the network control host communicates with and controls the NMEs in other systems. For maintaining high availability of the network management function, two or more network control hosts are used. In normal operation, one of the centers is used for control, while the other centers are idle or simply collecting statistics. If the primary network control host fails, the backup system can be used.

19.3 SIMPLE NETWORK MANAGEMENT PROTOCOL (SNMP)

Simple Network Management Protocol Version 1 (SNMPv1)

SNMP was developed for use as a network management tool for networks and internetworks operating TCP/IP. It has since been expanded for use in all types of networking environments. The term *simple network management protocol (SNMP)* is actually used to refer to a collection of specifications for network management that include the protocol itself, the definition of a database, and associated concepts.

Basic Concepts The model of network management that is used for SNMP includes the following key elements:

- Management station, or manager
- Agent
- Management information base
- Network management protocol

The **management station** is typically a standalone device but may be a capability implemented on a shared system. In either case, the management station serves as the interface between the human network manager and the network management system. The management station will have, at minimum,

- A set of management applications for data analysis, fault recovery, and so on
- A user interface by which the network manager may monitor and control the network
- The capability of translating the network manager's requirements into the actual monitoring and control of remote elements in the network
- A database of network management information extracted from the databases of all the managed entities in the network

Only the last two elements are the subject of SNMP standardization.

The other active element in the network management system is the **management agent.** Key platforms, such as hosts, bridges, routers, and hubs, may be equipped with agent software so that they may be managed from a management station. The agent responds to requests for information from a management station, responds to requests for actions from the management station, and may from time to time provide the management station with important but unsolicited information.

To manage resources in the network, each resource is represented as an object. An object is, essentially, a data variable that represents one aspect of the managed agent. The collection of objects is referred to as a **management information base** (MIB). The MIB functions as a collection of access points at the agent for the management station. These objects are standardized across systems of a particular class (e.g., all bridges support the same management objects). A management station performs the monitoring function by retrieving the value of MIB objects. A management station can cause an action to take place at an agent or can change the configuration settings of an agent by modifying the value of specific variables.

The management station and agents are linked by a **network management protocol.** The protocol used for the management of TCP/IP networks is the Simple Network Management Protocol (SNMP). An enhanced version of SNMP, known as SNMPv2, is intended for both TCP/IP- and OSI-based networks. Each of these protocols includes the following key capabilities:

- **Get:** Enables the management station to retrieve the value of objects at the agent
- **Set:** Enables the management station to set the value of objects at the agent
- **Notify:** Enables an agent to send unsolicited notifications to the management station of significant events

In a traditional centralized network management scheme, one host in the configuration has the role of a network management station; there may be one or two other management stations in a backup role. The remainder of the devices on the network contain agent software and a MIB, to allow monitoring and control from the management station. As networks grow in size and traffic load, such a centralized system is unworkable. Too much burden is placed on the management station, and there is too much traffic, with reports from every single agent having to wend their way across the entire network to headquarters. In such circumstances, a decentralized, distributed approach works best (e.g., Figure 19.2). In a decentralized network management scheme, there may be multiple top-level management stations,

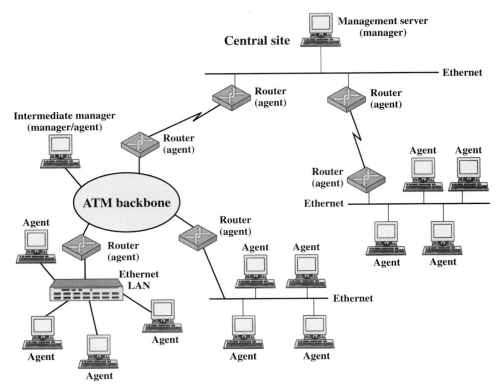

Figure 19.2 Example Distributed Network Management Configuration

which might be referred to as management servers. Each such server might directly manage a portion of the total pool of agents. However, for many of the agents, the management server delegates responsibility to an intermediate manager. The intermediate manager plays the role of manager to monitor and control the agents under its responsibility. It also plays an agent role to provide information and accept control from a higher-level management server. This type of architecture spreads the processing burden and reduces total network traffic.

Network Management Protocol Architecture SNMP is an application-level protocol that is part of the TCP/IP protocol suite. It is intended to operate over the user datagram protocol (UDP). Figure 19.3 suggests the typical configuration of protocols for SNMPv1. For a standalone management station, a manager process controls access to a central MIB at the management station and provides an interface to the network manager. The manager process achieves network management by using SNMP, which is implemented on top of UDP, IP, and the relevant network-dependent protocols (e.g., Ethernet, ATM, frame relay).

Each agent must also implement SNMP, UDP, and IP. In addition, there is an agent process that interprets the SNMP messages and controls the agent's MIB. For an agent device that supports other applications, such as FTP, TCP as well as UDP is required. In Figure 19.3, the shaded portions depict the operational

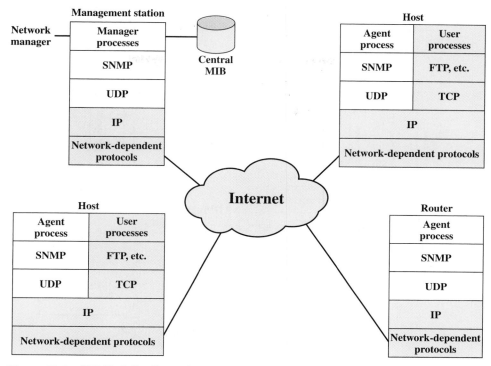

Figure 19.3 SNMPv1 Configuration

environment: that which is to be managed. The unshaded portions provide support to the network management function.

Figure 19.4 provides a somewhat closer look at the protocol context of SNMP. From a management station, three types of SNMP messages are issued on behalf of management applications: GetRequest, GetNextRequest, and SetRequest. The first two are two variations of the get function. All three messages are acknowledged by the agent in the form of a GetResponse message, which is passed up to the management application. In addition, an agent may issue a Trap message in response to an event that affects the MIB and the underlying managed resources. Management requests are sent to UDP port 161, while the agent sends traps to UDP port 162.

Because SNMP relies on UDP, which is a connectionless protocol, SNMP is itself connectionless. No ongoing connections are maintained between a management station and its agents. Instead, each exchange is a separate transaction between a management station and an agent.

Simple Network Management Protocol Version 2 (SNMPv2)

In August of 1988, the specification for SNMP was issued and rapidly became the dominant network management standard. A number of vendors offer standalone network management workstations based on SNMP, and most vendors of bridges,

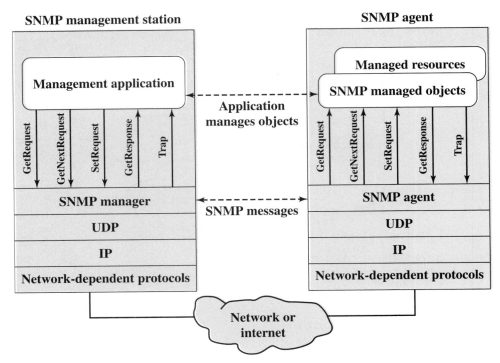

Figure 19.4 The Role of SNMPv1

routers, workstations, and PCs offer SNMP agent packages that allow their products to be managed by an SNMP management station.

As the name suggests, SNMP is a simple tool for network management. It defines a limited, easily implemented management information base (MIB) of scalar variables and two-dimensional tables, and it defines a streamlined protocol to enable a manager to get and set MIB variables and to enable an agent to issue unsolicited notifications, called *traps*. This simplicity is the strength of SNMP. SNMP is easily implemented and consumes modest processor and network resources. Also, both the protocol and the MIB structures are sufficiently straightforward that it is not difficult to achieve interoperability among management stations and agent software from a mix of vendors.

With its widespread use, the deficiencies of SNMP became increasingly apparent; these include both functional deficiencies and a lack of a security facility. As a result, an enhanced version, known as SNMPv2, was issued (RFCs 1901, 1905 through 1909, and 2578 through 2580). SNMPv2 quickly gained support, and a number of vendors announced products within months of the issuance of the standard.

The Elements of SNMPv2 As with SNMPv1, SNMPv2 provides a framework on which network management applications can be built. Those applications, such as fault management, performance monitoring, and accounting, are outside the scope of the standard.

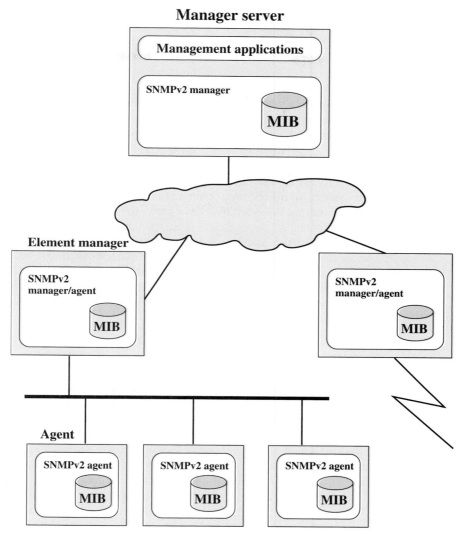

Figure 19.5 SNMPv2-Managed Configuration

SNMPv2 provides the infrastructure for network management. Figure 19.5 is an example of a configuration that illustrates that infrastructure.

The essence of SNMPv2 is a protocol that is used to exchange management information. Each "player" in the network management system maintains a local database of information relevant to network management, known as the management information base (MIB). The SNMPv2 standard defines the structure of this information and the allowable data types; this definition is known as the structure of management information (SMI). We can think of this as the language for defining management information. The standard also supplies a number of MIBs that are generally useful for network management.[1] In addition, new MIBs may be defined by vendors and user groups.

At least one system in the configuration must be responsible for network management. It is here that any network management applications are hosted. There may be more than one of these management stations, to provide redundancy or simply to split up the duties in a large network. Most other systems act in the role of agent. An agent collects information locally and stores it for later access by a manager. The information includes data about the system itself and may also include traffic information for the network or networks to which the agent attaches.

SNMPv2 supports either a highly centralized network management strategy or a distributed one. In the latter case, some systems operate both in the role of manager and of agent. In its agent role, such a system will accept commands from a superior management system. Some of those commands relate to the local MIB at the agent. Other commands require the agent to act as a proxy for remote devices. In this case, the proxy agent assumes the role of manager to access information at a remote agent, and then assumes the role of an agent to pass that information on to a superior manager.

All of these exchanges take place using the SNMPv2 protocol, which is a simple request/response type of protocol. Typically, SNMPv2 is implemented on top of the user datagram protocol (UDP), which is part of the TCP/IP suite. Because SNMPv2 exchanges are in the nature of discrete request-response pairs, an ongoing reliable connection is not required.

Structure of Management Information   The structure of management information (SMI) defines the general framework within which a MIB can be defined and constructed. The SMI identifies the data types that can be used in the MIB, and how resources within the MIB are represented and named. The philosophy behind SMI is to encourage simplicity and extensibility within the MIB. Thus, the MIB can store only simple data types: scalars and two-dimensional arrays of scalars, called tables. The SMI does not support the creation or retrieval of complex data structures. This philosophy is in contrast to that used with OSI systems management, which provides for complex data structures and retrieval modes to support greater functionality. SMI avoids complex data types and structures to simplify the task of implementation and to enhance interoperability. MIBs will inevitably contain vendor-created data types and, unless tight restrictions are placed on the definition of such data types, interoperability will suffer.

There are three key elements in the SMI specification. At the lowest level, the SMI specifies the data types that may be stored. Then the SMI specifies a formal technique for defining objects and tables of objects. Finally, the SMI provides a scheme for associating a unique identifier with each actual object in a system, so that data at an agent can be referenced by a manager.

Table 19.2 shows the data types that are allowed by the SMI. This is a fairly restricted set of types. For example, real numbers are not supported. However, it is rich enough to support most network management requirements.

---

[1]There is a slight fuzziness about the term *MIB*. In its singular form, the term *MIB* can be used to refer to the entire database of management information at a manager or an agent. It can also be used in singular or plural form to refer to a specific defined collection of management information that is part of an overall MIB. Thus, the SNMPv2 standard includes the definition of several MIBs and incorporates, by reference, MIBs defined in SNMPv1.

Table 19.2   Allowable Data Types in SNMPv2

Data Type	Description
INTEGER	Integers in the range of -2^{31} to $2^{31} - 1$.
UInteger32	Integers in the range of 0 to $2^{32} - 1$.
Counter32	A nonnegative integer that may be incremented modulo 2^{32}.
Counter64	A nonnegative integer that may be incremented modulo 2^{64}.
Gauge32	A nonnegative integer that may increase or decrease, but shall not exceed a maximum value. The maximum value can not be greater than $2^{32} - 1$.
TimeTicks	A nonnegative integer that represents the time, modulo 2^{32}, in hundredths of a second.
OCTET STRING	Octet strings for arbitrary binary or textual data; may be limited to 255 octets.
IpAddress	A 32-bit internet address.
Opaque	An arbitrary bit field.
BIT STRING	An enumeration of named bits.
OBJECT IDENTIFIER	Administratively assigned name to object or other standardized element. Value is a sequence of up to 128 nonnegative integers.

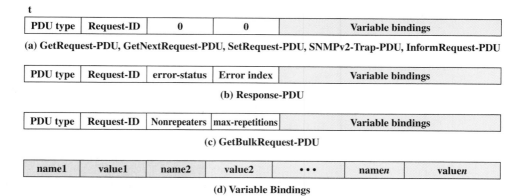

t

PDU type	Request-ID	0	0	Variable bindings

(a) GetRequest-PDU, GetNextRequest-PDU, SetRequest-PDU, SNMPv2-Trap-PDU, InformRequest-PDU

PDU type	Request-ID	error-status	Error index	Variable bindings

(b) Response-PDU

PDU type	Request-ID	Nonrepeaters	max-repetitions	Variable bindings

(c) GetBulkRequest-PDU

name1	value1	name2	value2	•••	name*n*	value*n*

(d) Variable Bindings

Figure 19.6   SNMPv2 PDU Format

Protocol Operation The heart of the SNMPv2 framework is the protocol itself. The protocol provides a straightforward, basic mechanism for the exchange of management information between manager and agent.

The basic unit of exchange is the message, which consists of an outer message wrapper and an inner protocol data unit (PDU). The outer message header deals with security and is discussed later in this section.

Seven types of PDUs may be carried in an SNMP message. The general formats for these are illustrated informally in Figure 19.6. Several fields are common to a number of PDUs. The Request-ID field is an integer assigned such that each outstanding request can be uniquely identified. This enables a manager to correlate incoming responses with outstanding requests. It also enables an agent to cope with duplicate PDUs generated by an unreliable transport service. The Variable-Bindings field contains a list of object identifiers; depending on the PDU, the list may also include a value for each object.

The GetRequest-PDU, issued by a manager, includes a list of one or more object names for which values are requested. If the get operation is successful, then the responding agent will send a Response-PDU. The variable-bindings list will contain the identifier and value of all retrieved objects. For any variables that are not in the relevant MIB view, its identifier and an error code are returned in the variable-bindings list. Thus, SNMPv2 permits partial responses to a GetRequest, which is a significant improvement over SNMP. In SNMP, if one or more of the variables in a GetRequest is not supported, the agent returns an error message with a status of noSuchName. To cope with such an error, the SNMP manager must either return no values to the requesting application, or it must include an algorithm that responds to an error by removing the missing variables, resending the request, and then sending a partial result to the application.

The GetNextRequest-PDU also is issued by a manager and includes a list of one or more objects. In this case, for each object named in the Variable-Bindings field, a value is to be returned for the object that is next in lexicographic order, which is equivalent to saying next in the MIB in terms of its position in the tree structure of object identifiers. As with the GetRequest-PDU, the agent will return values for as many variables as possible. One of the strengths of the GetNextRequest-PDU is that it enables a manager entity to discover the structure of a MIB view dynamically. This is useful if the manager does not know a priori the set of objects that are supported by an agent or that are in a particular MIB view.

One of the major enhancements provided in SNMPv2 is the GetBulkRequest PDU. The purpose of this PDU is to minimize the number of protocol exchanges required to retrieve a large amount of management information. The GetBulkRequest PDU allows an SNMPv2 manager to request that the response include as many requested variables as possible given the constraints on message size.

The SetRequest-PDU is issued by a manager to request that the values of one or more objects be altered. The receiving SNMPv2 entity responds with a Response-PDU containing the same Request-ID. The SetRequest operation is atomic: Either all of the variables are updated or none are. If the responding entity is able to set values for all of the variables listed in the incoming variable-bindings list, then the Response-PDU includes the Variable-Bindings field, with a value supplied for each variable. If at least one of the variable values cannot be supplied, then no values are returned, and no values are updated. In the latter case, the error-status code indicates the reason for the failure, and the error-index field indicates the variable in the variable-bindings list that caused the failure.

The SNMPv2-Trap-PDU is generated and transmitted by an SNMPv2 entity acting in an agent role when an unusual event occurs. It is used to provide the management station with an asynchronous notification of some significant event. The variable-bindings list is used to contain the information associated with the trap message. Unlike the GetRequest, GetNextRequest, GetBulkRequest, SetRequest, and InformRequest-PDUs, the SNMPv2-Trap-PDU does not elicit a response from the receiving entity; it is an unconfirmed message.

The InformRequest-PDU is sent by an SNMPv2 entity acting in a manager role, on behalf of an application, to another SNMPv2 entity acting in a manager role, to provide management information to an application using the latter entity. As with the SNMPv2-Trap-PDU, the Variable-Bindings field is used to convey the associated information. The manager receiving an InformRequest acknowledges receipt with a Response-PDU.

For both the SNMPv2-Trap and the InformRequest, various conditions can be defined that indicate when the notification is generated; the information to be sent is also specified.

Simple Network Management Protocol Version 3 (SNMPv3)

Many of the functional deficiencies of SNMP were addressed in SNMPv2. To correct the security deficiencies of SNMPv1/v2, SNMPv3 was issued as a set of Proposed Standards in January 1998 (currently RFCs 3410 through 3415). This set of documents does not provide a complete SNMP capability but rather defines an overall SNMP architecture and a set of security capabilities. These are intended to be used with the existing SNMPv2 or with SNMPv1.

SNMPv3 provides three important services: authentication, privacy, and access control. The first two are part of the User-Based Security Model (USM), and the last is defined in the View-Based Access Control Model (VACM). Security services are governed by the identity of the user requesting the service; this identity is expressed as a principal, which may be an individual or an application or a group of individuals or applications.

The authentication mechanism in USM assures that a received message was transmitted by the principal whose identifier appears as the source in the message header. This mechanism also assures that the message has not been altered in transit and has not been artificially delayed or replayed. The sending principal provides authentication by including a message authentication code with the SNMP message it is sending. This code is a function of the contents of the message, the identity of the sending and receiving parties, the time of transmission, and a secret key that should be known only to sender and receiver. The secret key must be set up outside of USM as a configuration function. That is, the configuration manager or network manager is responsible for distributing secret keys to be loaded into the databases of the various SNMP managers and agents. This can be done manually or using some form of secure data transfer outside of USM. When the receiving principal gets the message, it uses the same secret key to calculate the message authentication code once again. If the receiver's version of the code matches the value appended to the incoming message, then the receiver knows that the message can only have originated from the authorized manager and that the message was not altered in transit. The shared secret key between sending and receiving parties must be pre-configured. The actual authentication code used is known as HMAC, which is an Internet-standard authentication mechanism.

The privacy facility of USM enables managers and agents to encrypt messages. Again, manager principal and agent principal must share a secret key. In this case, if the two are configured to use the privacy facility, all traffic between them is encrypted using the Data Encryption Standard (DES). The sending principal encrypts the message using the DES algorithm and its secret key and sends the message to the receiving principal, which decrypts it using the DES algorithm and the same secret key.

The access control facility makes it possible to configure agents to provide different levels of access to the agent's management information base (MIB) to different managers. An agent principal can restrict access to its MIB for a particular manager principal in two ways. First, it can restrict access to a certain portion of its MIB. For example, an agent may restrict most manager parties to viewing performance-related statistics and only allow a single designated manager principal to view and update configuration parameters. Second, the agent can limit the operations that a manager can use on that portion of the MIB. For example, a particular manager principal could be limited to read-only access to a portion of an agent's MIB. The access control policy to be used by an agent for each manager must be preconfigured and essentially consists of a table that detail the access privileges of the various authorized managers.

APPLICATION NOTE
How Much Management?

Managing systems and networks has one thing in common with managing children—sometimes it is very difficult to let them be themselves. With today's communication software and hardware, there is a tremendous amount of management capability built in. If this isn't enough, you can install additional software and hardware for the express purpose of more management. While it is clear that some level of management is vital, it is easy to get carried away and spend the day managing devices that are working just fine.

There are literally dozens of management "items." The following is a brief list of the information that can be reported from most networking devices:

- Track statistics for the network
- Status of machinery
- Enable/disable ports
- Graphically display information (ports)
- Security (users, login, block traffic from unknown device, scrambling)
- Resilience
- Messaging/polling
- Software upgrades
- Traffic/topology control
- Configure IP address
- Set to defaults
- Monitor other devices
- Messaging (to monitor)
- View faults

In addition to being able to determine a great deal regarding the network, this information can be sent to the administrator via e-mail, SNMP messages, pagers, and cell phones. A common mistake is to set the management parameters and alarm limits prior to understanding the normal operation of the network. It is the inexperienced manager that decides to be notified of any and all network events. As an example, we might set an alarm to e-mail us when the number of frames transmitted in error on the wireless network exceeds 10 when the normal level of retransmissions per hour is 300. This results in a whole bunch of e-mail.

With small networks (including home networks), the amount of management required is usually very small. However, there are instances where a certain amount of configuration and notification may be desired. These instances include initial setup, security alerts, and network-specific items such as billing or authorization. At home we may have additional requirements, such as parental monitoring for children using the Web or software configuration for browsers. In either case, the level of involvement is usually small and there is not much call for expensive servers or days spent configuring the management system.

As networks grow, decisions need to be made regarding the appropriate level of sophistication regarding the Network Management System (NMS). Remember, the time you spend managing the network is time away from other tasks. The NMS can also degrade network performance. Earlier in this book, the concepts of in-band and out-of-band have been introduced. Most devices are initially configured via a console or serial link. This is a separate physical pathway for the management traffic and is called out-of-band management. Once the administrator starts using Telnet, HTTP, or SNMP to run the network, the messages compete with standard data traffic. This is called in-band management. There are some instances where the topology or configuration can effectively disable a portion of the network because of management inspired messaging. For example, a suspect link can be told to mirror all of its traffic to another location for analysis. Once this is done, the link receiving the new information can be over subscribed if there are other processes running. Thus, care must be taken not only in the amount of management deployed, but how it is used.

Management of computing resources and a network can be costly and time consuming. The keys to running successful management schemes include understanding the normal operating conditions of the network, implementing only those management items that are required, understanding the conditions that will result in alarm conditions, and understanding the effect of implementing your NMS and only program alerts for items you really want to know about.

19.4 RECOMMENDED READING AND WEB SITES

[STAL99] provides a comprehensive and detailed examination of SNMP, SNMPv2, and SNMPv3; the book also provides an overview of network management technology. One of the few textbooks on the subject of network management is [SUBR00].

STAL99   Stallings, W. *SNMP, SNMPv2, SNMPv3, and RMON 1 and 2.* Reading, MA: Addison-Wesley, 1999.

> **SUBR00**   Subranamian, M. *Network Management: Principles and Practice.* Reading, MA:
> Addison-Wesley, 2000.

Recommended Web Site:

- **Simple Web Site:** Maintained by the University of Twente. It is a good source of information on SNMP, including pointers to many public-domain implementations and lists of books and articles.

19.5 KEY TERMS, REVIEW QUESTIONS, AND PROBLEMS

Key Terms

accounting management
agent
configuration and name
    management
fault
fault management
	management information base
	    (MIB)
	management station
	manager
	network management
	network management protocol
		network management system
		performance management
		security management
		Simple Network Management
		    Protocol (SNMP)
		Structure of Management
		    Information (SMI)

Review Questions

19.1. List and briefly define the key areas that comprise network management.

19.2. Define *fault* as it applies to network management.

19.3. List two ways in which a network management system may be characterized as integrated.

19.4. List and briefly define the key elements of SNMP.

19.5. What functions are provided by SNMP?

19.6. What lower-layer protocol encapsulates SNMP messages?

19.7. Describe two different interpretations of the term *MIB*.

19.8. What are the differences among SNMPv1, SNMPv2, and SNMPv3?

Problems

19.1 Because SNMP uses two different port numbers (UDP ports 161 and 162), a single system can easily run both a manager and an agent. What would happen if the same port number were used for both?

19.2 The original (version 1) specification of SNMP has the following definition of a new type:

Gauge ::= [APPLICATION 2] IMPLICIT INTEGER (0..4294967295)

The standard includes the following explanation of the semantics of this type:

> This application-wide type represents a non-negative integer, which may increase or decrease, but which latches at a maximum value. This standard specifies a maximum value of $2^{32} - 1$ (4294967295 decimal) for gauges.

Unfortunately, the word *latch* is not defined, and this has resulted in two different interpretations. The SNMPv2 standard cleared up the ambiguity with the following definition:

> The value of a Gauge has its maximum value whenever the information being modeled is greater than or equal to that maximum value; if the information being modeled subsequently decreases below the maximum value, the Gauge also decreases.

    a. What is the alternative interpretation?
    b. Discuss the pros and cons of the two interpretations.

19.3 One of the first steps in configuring a device to be managed is to give it an IP address. Why?

19.4 Many network administrators use the ping program as a primary management tool.
    a. Why would you "ping" a network device?
    b. Why would you "ping" yourself?

19.5 We have seen that SNMP uses UDP as its transport protocol. Why was UDP chosen over TCP?

19.6 What is the disadvantage of having the network management system operate at the application layer?

GLOSSARY

Amplitude The size or magnitude of a voltage or current waveform.

Amplitude-shift keying Modulation in which the two binary values are represented by two different amplitudes of the carrier frequency.

Analog data Data represented by a physical quantity that is considered to be continuously variable and whose magnitude is made directly proportional to the data or to a suitable function of the data.

Analog signal A continuously varying electromagnetic wave that may be propagated over a variety of media.

Analog transmission The transmission of analog signals without regard to content. The signal may be amplified, but there is no intermediate attempt to recover the data from the signal.

Application layer Layer 7 of the OSI model. This layer determines the interface of the system with the user and provides useful application-oriented services.

Asynchronous transfer mode (ATM) A form of packet switching in which fixed-size cells of 53 octets are used. There is no network layer and many of the basic functions have been streamlined or eliminated to provide for greater throughput.

Asynchronous transmission Transmission in which each information character is individually synchronized, usually by the use of start elements and stop elements.

Attenuation A decrease in magnitude of current, voltage, or power of a signal in transmission between points.

Automatic repeat request (ARQ) A feature that automatically initiates a request for retransmission when an error in transmission is detected.

Availability The percentage of time that a particular function or application is available for users.

Bandwidth The difference between the limiting frequencies of a continuous frequency band.

Band A unit of signaling speed equal to the number of discrete conditions or signal events per second, or the reciprocal of the time of the shortest signal element.

Best effort A network or internet delivery technique that does not guarantee delivery of data and treats all packets equally. All packets are forwarded on a first-come-first-served basis. Preferential treatment based on priority or other concerns is not provided.

Bit Binary digit. A unit of information represented by either a zero or a one.

Bridge An internetworking device that connects two similar local area networks that use the same LAN protocols.

Byte A binary bit string operated on as a unit and usually eight bits long and capable of holding one character in the local character set.

Cellular network A wireless communications network in which fixed antennas are arranged in a hexagonal pattern and mobile stations communicate through nearby fixed antennas.

Checksum An error-detecting code based on a summation operation performed on the bits to be checked.

Central office (CO) The place where telephone companies terminate customer lines and locate switching equipment to interconnect those lines with other networks.

Ciphertext The output of an encryption algorithm; the encrypted form of a message or data.

Circuit switching A method of communicating in which a dedicated communications path is established between two devices through one or more intermediate switching nodes. Unlike with packet switching, digital data are sent as a continuous stream of bits. Data rate is guaranteed, and delay is essentially limited to propagation time.

Coaxial cable A cable consisting of one conductor, usually a small copper tube or wire, within and insulated from another conductor of larger diameter, usually copper tubing or copper braid.

Code division multiple access A multiplexing technique used with spread spectrum.

Codec Coder-decoder. Transforms analog data into a digital bit stream (coder) and digital signals into analog data (decoder).

Common channel signaling Technique in which network control signals (e.g., call request) are separated from the associated voice or data path by placing the signaling from a group of voice or data paths on a separate channel dedicated to signaling only.

Customer premises equipment (CPE) Telecommunications equipment that is located on the customer's premises (physical location) rather than on the provider's premises or in between.

Cyclic redundancy check (CRC) An error-detecting code in which the code is the remainder resulting from dividing the bits to be checked by a predetermined binary number.

Database A collection of interrelated data, often with controlled redundancy, organized to serve multiple applications. The data are stored so that they can be used by different programs without concern for the internal data structure or organization.

Datagram In packet switching, a self-contained packet, independent of other packets, that carries information sufficient for routing from the originating data terminal equipment (DTE) to the destination DTE without relying on earlier exchanges between the DTEs and the network.

Data link layer Layer 2 of the OSI model. Converts an unreliable transmission channel into a reliable one.

Decibel A measure of the relative strength of two signals. The number of decibels is 10 times the log of the ratio of the power of two signals, or 20 times the log of the ratio of the voltage of two signals.

Decryption The translation of encrypted text or data (called ciphertext) into original text or data (called plaintext). Also called deciphering.

Differentiated services Functionality in the Internet and private internets to support specific QoS requirements for a group of users, all of whom use the same service label in IP packets.

Digital data Data represented by discrete values or conditions.

Digital signal A discrete or discontinuous signal, such as a sequence of voltage pulses.

Digital signature An authentication mechanism that enables the creator of a message to attach a code that acts as a signature. The signature guarantees the source and integrity of the message.

Digital transmission The transmission of digital data or analog data that have been digitized, using either an analog or digital signal, in which the digital content is recovered and repeated at intermediate points to reduce the effects of impairments, such as noise, distortion, and attenuation.

Direct sequence spread spectrum A form of spread spectrum in which each bit in the original signal is represented by multiple bits in the transmitted signal, using a spreading code.

Distributed database A database that is not stored in a single location but is dispersed over a network of interconnected computers.

Distributed data processing Data processing in which some or all of the processing, storage, and control functions, in addition to input/output functions, are dispersed among data processing stations.

Domain A group of networks that are part of the Internet and that are under the administrative control of a single entity, such as a company or government agency.

Domain Name System (DNS) A directory lookup service that provides a mapping between the name of a host on the Internet and its numerical address.

Downlink The communications link from satellite to earth station.

Electronic mail Correspondence in the form of messages transmitted between workstations over a network. The most common protocol used to support electronic mail is the Simple Mail Transfer Protocol (SMTP).

Encryption To convert plain text or data into unintelligible form by means of a reversible mathematical computation.

Error control A technique for detecting and correcting errors.

Error-detecting code A code in which each data signal conforms to specific rules of construction, so that departures from this construction in the received signal can be automatically detected.

Extranet The extension of a company's intranet out onto the Internet to allow selected customers, suppliers, and mobile workers to access the company's private data and applications via the World Wide Web. This is in contrast to, and usually in addition to, the company's public web site, which is accessible to everyone. The difference can be somewhat blurred, but generally an extranet implies real-time access through a firewall of some kind.

Frame A group of bits that includes data plus one or more addresses and other protocol control information. Generally refers to a link layer (OSI layer 2) protocol data unit.

Frame check sequence (FCS) An error-detecting code inserted as a field in a block of data to be transmitted. The code serves to check for errors upon reception of the data.

Frame relay A form of packet switching based on the use of variable-length link layer frames. There is no network layer, and many of the basic functions have been streamlined or eliminated to provide for greater throughput.

Frequency Rate of signal oscillation in cycles per second (Hertz).

Frequency division multiplexing (FDM) Division of a transmission facility into two or more channels by splitting the frequency band transmitted by the facility into narrower bands, each of which is used to constitute a distinct channel.

Frequency-shift keying Modulation in which the two binary values are represented by two different frequencies near the carrier frequency.

Guided medium A transmission medium in which electromagnetic waves are guided along a solid medium, such as copper twisted pair, copper coaxial cable, or optical fiber.

Header System-defined control information that precedes user data in a protocol data unit.

Host Any end system, such as a PC, workstation, or server, that connects to the Internet.

Internet A worldwide internetwork based on TCP/IP that interconnects thousands of public and private networks and millions of users.

Internet Protocol (IP) A standardized protocol that executes in hosts and routers to interconnect a number of independent networks.

Internetworking Communication among devices across multiple networks.

Internet service provider (ISP) A company that provides other companies or individuals with access to, or presence on, the Internet.

Intranet A corporate internetwork that provides the key Internet applications, especially the World Wide Web. An intranet operates within the organization for internal purposes and can exist as an isolated, self-contained internet, or may have links to the Internet. The most common example is the use by a company of one or more World-Wide Web servers on an internal TCP/IP network for distribution of information within the company.

Local area network (LAN) A data communications network that is geographically limited to a single building or a cluster of buildings.

Local loop A transmission path, generally twisted pair, between the individual subscriber and the nearest switching center of a public telecommunications network. Also referred to as a subscriber loop.

Medium Access Control (MAC) For a communications network, the method of determining which station has access to the transmission medium at any time.

Modem Modulator/demodulator. A device that converts digital data to an analog signal that can be transmitted on a telecommunication line and converts the received analog signal to digital data.

Multiplexing   In data transmission, a function that permits two or more data sources to share a common transmission medium such that each data source has its own channel.

Network access point (NAP)   In the United States, a network access point (NAP) is one of several major Internet interconnection points that serve to tie all the ISPs together.

Network layer   Layer 3 of the OSI model. Responsible for routing data through a communication network.

Network service provider (NSP)   A company that provides backbone services to an Internet service provider (ISP), the company that most Web users use for access to the Internet.

Noise   Unwanted signals that combine with and hence distort the signal intended for transmission and reception.

Octet   A group of eight adjacent bits, usually operated upon as a unit.

Open Systems Interconnection (OSI) reference Model   A model of communications between cooperating devices. It defines a seven-layer architecture of communication functions.

Optical fiber   A thin filament of glass or other transparent material through which a signal-encoded light beam may be transmitted by means of total internal reflection.

Packet   A group of bits that includes data plus control information. Generally refers to a network layer (OSI layer 3) protocol data unit.

Packet switching   A method of transmitting messages through a communications network, in which long messages are subdivided into short packets. Each packet is passed from source to destination through intermediate nodes. At each node, the entire message is received, stored briefly, and then passed on to the next node.

Parity bit   A check bit appended to an array of binary digits to make the sum of all the binary digits, including the check bit, always odd or always even.

Period   The absolute value of the minimum interval after which the same characteristics of a periodic waveform recur.

Periodic signal   A signal $f(t)$ that satisfies $f(t) = f(t + nk)$ for all integers n, with k being a constant.

Phase   For a periodic signal $f(t)$, the fractional part t/P of the period P through which t has advanced relative to an arbitrary origin. The origin is usually taken at the last previous passage through zero from the negative to the positive direction.

Phase-shift keying   Modulation in which the phase of the carrier signal is shifted to represent digital data.

Physical layer   Layer 1 of the OSI model. Concerned with the electrical, mechanical, and timing aspects of signal transmission over a medium.

Plaintext   The input to an encryption function or the output of a decryption function.

Point of presence (POP)   A site that has a collection of telecommunications equipment, usually refers to ISP or telephone company sites. An ISP POP is the edge of the ISP's network; connections from users are accepted and authenticated here. An Internet access provider may operate several POPs distributed throughout their area of operation to increase the chance that their subscribers will be able to reach one with a local telephone call.

Point-to-point   A configuration in which two and only two stations share a transmission path.

Port   A transport-layer address that identifies a user of a transport-layer protocol.

Presentation layer   Layer 6 of the OSI model. Concerned with data format and display.

Protocol   A set of semantic and syntactic rules that describe how to transmit data, especially across a network. Low-level protocols define the electrical and physical standards to be observed, bit- and byte-ordering, and the transmission and error detection and correction of the bit stream. High-level protocols deal with the data formatting, including the syntax of messages, the terminal to computer dialogue, character sets, and sequencing of messages.

Protocol architecture   The software structure that implements the communications function. Typically, the protocol architecture consists of a layered set of protocols, with one or more protocols at each layer.

Protocol data unit (PDU)   Information that is delivered as a unit between peer entities of a network. A PDU typically contains control information and address information in a header. The PDU may also contain data.

Public-key encryption   A form of cryptosystem in which encryption and decryption are performed using two different keys, one of which is referred to as the public key and one of which is referred to as the private key.

Pulse code modulation (PCM)   A process in which a signal is sampled, and the magnitude of each sample with respect to a fixed reference is quantized and converted by coding to a digital signal.

Quality of service (QoS)   A set of parameters that describe the quality (e.g., data rate, timeliness, buffer usage, priority) of a specific stream of data. The minimum QoS is best effort, which treats all packets equally on a first-come-first-served basis. QoS may dictate the path chosen for delivery by a router, the network service requested by the router of the next network on that path, and the order in which waiting packets are forwarded from the router.

Router   An internetworking device that connects two computer networks. It makes use of an internet protocol and assumes that all attached devices on the networks use the same protocol architecture at the internet layer and above.

Routing   The determination of a path that a data unit (frame, packet, message) will traverse from source to destination.

Service access point (SAP)   A means of identifying a user of the services of a protocol entity. A protocol entity provides one or more SAPs, for use by higher-level entities.

Session layer   Layer 5 of the OSI model. Manages a logical connection (session) between two communicating processes or applications.

Signal   An electromagnetic wave used to convey information.

Signaling   The production of an electromagnetic signal that represents analog or digital data and its propagation along a transmission medium.

Spectrum   Refers to an absolute, contiguous range of frequencies.

Symmetric encryption   A form of cryptosystem in which encryption and decryption are performed using the same key. Also known as conventional encryption.

Synchronous time division multiplexing   A method of TDM in which time slots on a shared transmission line are assigned to devices on a fixed, predetermined basis.

Synchronous transmission   Data transmission in which the time of occurrence of each signal representing a bit is related to a fixed time frame.

Time division multiplexing (TDM)   The division of a transmission facility into two or more channels by allotting the common channel to several different information channels, one at a time.

Transmission   The communication of data by the propagation and processing of signals. In the case of digital signals or of analog signals that encode digital data, repeaters may be used. For analog signals, amplifiers may be used.

Transmission medium   The physical medium that conveys data between data stations.

Transport layer   Layer 4 of the OSI model. Provides reliable, sequenced transfer of data between endpoints.

Twisted pair   A transmission medium that consists of two insulated conductors twisted together to reduce noise.

Unguided medium   A transmission medium, such as the atmosphere or outer space, used for wireless transmission.

Uplink   The communications link from earth station to satellite.

Virtual circuit   A packet-switching mechanism in which a logical connection (virtual circuit) is established between two stations at the start of transmission. All packets follow the same route, need not carry a complete address, and arrive in sequence.

Virtual private network (VPN)   The use of encryption and authentication in the lower protocol layers to provide a secure connection through an otherwise insecure network, typically the Internet. VPNs are generally cheaper than real private networks using private lines but rely on having the same encryption and authentication system at both ends. The encryption may be performed by firewall software or possibly by routers.

White noise   Noise that has a flat, or uniform, frequency spectrum in the frequency range of interest.

Wireless transmission   Electromagnetic transmission through air, vacuum, or water by means of an antenna.

World Wide Web (WWW)   A networked, graphically oriented hypermedia system. Information is stored on servers, exchanged between servers and browsers, and displayed on browsers in the form of pages of text and images.

REFERENCES

ABBREVIATIONS

ACM   Association for Computing Machinery
IEEE   Institute of Electrical and Electronics Engineers

10GE02   10 Gigabit Ethernet Alliance. *10 Gigabit Ethernet Technology Overview.* White paper, May 2002.

ANDE95   Anderson, J.; Rappaport, T.; and Yoshida, S. "Propagation Measurements and Models for Wireless Communications Channels." *IEEE Communications Magazine*, January 1995.

ARMI00   Armitage, G. *Quality of Service in IP Networks.* Indianapolis, IN: Macmillan Technical Publishing, 2000.

BELL00   Bellamy, J. *Digital Telephony.* New York: Wiley, 2000.

BERN98   Bernard, R. *The Corporate Intranet.* New York: Wiley, 1998.

BERS96a   Berson, A. *Client/Server Architecture.* New York: McGraw-Hill, 1996.

BERN96b   Bernstein, P. "Middleware: A Model for Distributed System Services." *Communications of the ACM*, February 1996.

BERT92   Bertsekas, D., and Gallager, R. *Data Networks.* Englewood Cliffs, NJ: Prentice Hall, 1992.

BLAC99   Black, U. *ATM Volume I: Foundation for Broadband Networks.* Upper Saddle River, NJ: Prentice Hall, 1992.

BLAC00   Black, U. *IP Routing Protocols: RIP, OSPF, BGP, PNNI & Cisco Routing Protocols.* Upper Saddle River, NJ: Prentice Hall, 2000.

BORT02   Borthick, S. "SIP Services: Slowly Rolling Forward." *Business Communications Review*, June 2002.

BORT03   Borthick, S. "SIP for the Enterprise: Work in Progress." *Business Communications Review*, February 2003.

BRAY01   Bray, J., and Sturman, C. *Bluetooth: Connect without Cables.* Upper Saddle River, NJ: Prentice Hall, 2001.

BREY99   Breyer, R., and Riley, S. *Switched, Fast, and Gigabit Ethernet.* New York: Macmillan Technical Publishing, 1999.

BRUN99   Bruno, L. " Extranet Indemnity." *Data Communications*, July 1999.

BUCK00   Buckwalter, J. *Frame Relay: Technology and Practice.* Reading, MA: Addison-Wesley, 2000.

CAMP99   Campbell, A.; Coulson, G.; and Kounavis, M. "Managing Complexity: Middleware Explained." *IT Pro*, October 1999.

CARN99   Carne, E. *Telecommunications Primer: Data, Voice, and Video Communications.* Upper Saddle River, NJ: Prentice Hall, 1999.

CERF74   Cerf, V., and Kahn, R. "A Protocol for Packet Network Interconnection." *IEEE Transactions on Communications,* May 1974.

CERT03   CERT Coordination Center. *CERT Coordination Center 2002 Annual Report.* Carnegie-Mellon University, 2003. http://www.cert.org/annual_rpts/cert_rpt_01.html.

CLAR92   Clark, D.; Shenker, S.; and Zhang, L. "Supporting Real-Time Applications in an Integrated Services Packet Network: Architecture and Mechanism" *Proceedings, SIGCOMM '92*, August 1992.

CLAR95   Clark, D. *Adding Service Discrimination to the Internet.* MIT Laboratory for Computer Science Technical Report, September 1995. Available at http://ana-www.lcs.mit.edu/anaweb/papers.html.

CLAR02   Clark, E. "Carlson Companies Trades up to an IP SAN." *Network Magazine*, December 2002.

CLAR03   Clark, E. "Guardian Life Insurance Shapes Up With Server Consolidation." *Communications Convergence Magazine*, February 4, 2003. www.cconvergence.com.

COHE96   Cohen, J. "Rule Reversal: Old 80/20 LAN Traffic Model is Getting Turned on Its Head." *Network World*, December 16, 1996.

COME00   Comer, D. *The Internet Book.* Upper Saddle River, NJ: Prentice Hall, 2000.

CONN99   Connor, D. "Data Replication Helps Prevent Potential Problems." *Network World*, December 13, 1999.

CONR03   Conery-Murray, A. "Hospital Cures Wireless LAN of Dropped Connections." *Network Magazine*, January 2003.

COUC01   Couch, L. *Digital and Analog Communication Systems.* Upper Saddle River, NJ: Prentice Hall, 2001.

COUL02   Coulouris, G.; Dollimore, J.; and Kindberg, T. *Distributed Systems: Concepts and Design.* Reading, MA: Addison-Wesley, 2002.

CROL00   Croll, A., and Packman, E. *Managing Bandwidth: Deploying QoS in Enterprise Networks.* Upper Saddle River, NJ: Prentice Hall, 2000.

CROW97   Crow, B., et al. "IEEE 802.11 Wireless Local Area Networks." *IEEE Communications Magazine*, September 1997.

DAVI89   Davies, D., and Price, W. *Security for Computer Networks.* New York: Wiley, 1989.

DESM99   Desmond, P. "Top-Notch Network Overhaul." *Network World*, November 15, 1999.

DIAN02   Dianda, J.; Gurbani, V.; and Jones, M. "Session Initiation Protocol Services Architecture." *Bell Labs Technical Journal*, Volume 7, Number 1, 2002.

DIFF76   Diffie, W., and Hellman, M. "Multiuser Cryptographic Techniques." *IEEE Transactions on Information Theory*, November 1976.

DORN01   Dornan, A. "Hotel Chain Reserves Room on Space Network." *Network Magazine*, January 1001.

DWYE92   Dwyer, S., et al. "Teleradiology Using Switched Dialup Networks." *IEEE Journal on Selected Areas in Communications*, September 1992.

ECKE95   Eckerson, W. "Client Server Architecture." *Network World Collaboration*, Winter 1995.

ECKE96   Eckel, G. *Intranet Working.* Indianapolis, IN: New Riders, 1996.

EFF98   Electronic Frontier Foundation. *Cracking DES: Secrets of Encryption Research, Wiretap Politics, and Chip Design.* Sebastopol, CA: O'Reilly, 1998

ELSA02   El-Sayed, M., and Jaffe, J. "A View of Telecommunications Network Evolution." *IEEE Communications Magazine*, December 2002.

EVAN96   Evans, T. *Building an Intranet.* Indianapolis, IN: Sams, 1996.

FCIA01   Fibre Channel Industry Association. *Fibre Channel Storage Area Networks.* San Francisco: Fibre Channel Industry Association, 2001.

FRAZ99   Frazier, H., and Johnson, H. "Gigabit Ethernet: From 100 to 1,000 Mbps." *IEEE Internet Computing*, January/February 1999.

FREE96   Freeman, R. *Telecommunication System Engineering*. New York: Wiley, 1996.

FREE97   Freeman, R. *Radio System Design for Telecommunications*. New York: Wiley, 1997.

FREE98   Freeman, R. *Telecommunication Transmission Handbook*. New York: Wiley, 1998.

FREE99   Freeman, R. *Fundamentals of Telecommunications*. New York: Wiley, 1999.

GEIE99   Geier, J. *Wireless LANs*. New York: Macmillan Technical Publishing, 1999.

GEIE01   Geier, J. "Enabling Fast Wireless Networks with OFDM." *Communications System Design*, February 2001. (www.csdmag.com)

GOLI99   Golick, J. "Distributed Data Replication." *Network Magazine*, December 1999.

GOOD02   Goode, B. "Voice Over Internet Protocol (VoIP)." *Proceedings of the IEEE*, September 2002.

GOUR02   Gourley, D., et al. *HTTP: The Definitive Guide*. Sebastopol, CA: O'Reilly, 2002.

GUYN88   Guynes, J. 1988. "Impact of System Response Time on State Anxiety." *Communications of the ACM,* March, 1988.

HAAR00a   Haartsen, J. "The Bluetooth Radio System." *IEEE Personal Communications*, February 2000.

HAAR00b   Haartsen, J., and Mattisson, S. "Bluetooth—A New Low-Power Radio Interface Providing Short-Range Connectivity." *Proceedings of the IEEE*, October 2000.

HAFN96   Hafner, K., and Lyon, M. *Where Wizards Stay up Late*, New York: Simon and Schuster, 1996.

HAIG92   Haight, T. "The Dynamic Desktop." *Network Computing*, June 1992.

HARB92   Harbison, R. "Frame Relay: Technology for Our Time." *LAN Technology*, December 1992.

HARL02   Harler, C. "Bring It On!" *Hospitality Technology Magazine*, January/February 2002.

HETT03   Hettick, L. "Building Blocks for Converged Applications." *Business Communications Review*, June 2003.

HIGG02   Higgins, K. "T.G.I. Friday's Owner Serves up an IP SAN." *Network Computing*, September 15, 2002.

HIGG03   Higgins, K. "Warehouse Data Earns its Keep." *Network Computing*, May 1, 2003.

HOFF00   Hoffman, P. "Overview of Internet Mail Standards." *The Internet Protocol Journal*, June 2000. (www.cisco.com/warp/public/759)

HOFF02   Hoffer, J.; Prescott, M.; and McFadden, F. *Modern Database Management*. Upper Saddle River, NJ: Prentice Hall, 2002.

HOLD99   Hold, D. "Building Business Networks." *Business Week*, July 12, 1999.

HUIT00   Huitema, C. *Routing in the Internet*. Upper Saddle River, NJ: Prentice Hall, 2000.

IBM00   IBM Corp. "ING Life Develops Extranet Using Domino and Host On-Demand with VSE/ESA." *VM and VSE Solutions Journal*, July 2000. (www1.ibm.com/servers/eserver/zseries/library/casestudies)

JOHN96   Johnson, J. "Tech Team." *Data Communications*, February 1996.

KADA98   Kadambi, J.; Crayford, I.; and Kalkunte, M. *Gigabit Ethernet*. Upper Saddle River, NJ: Prentice Hall, 1998.

KANE98   Kanel, J.; Givler, J.; Leiba, B.; and Segmuller, W. "Internet Messaging Frameworks." *IBM Systems Journal*, No. 1, 1998.

KESH98   Keshav, S., and Sharma, R. "Issues and Trends in Router Design." *IEEE Communications Magazine*, May 1998.

KEEN99   Keener, R. "Voice, Data, Video Network Offered with One-Stop Shopping." *Health Management*, June 1999.

KHAR98   Khare, R. "The Spec's in the Mail." *IEEE Internet Computing*, September/October 1998.

KING99   King, R. "CLECs Get Moving in New York." *Inter@ctive Week*, January 25, 1999.

KIRB01   Kirby, R. "Telemedicine and the No-Brainer Bandwidth Bargain." *Network Magazine*, February 2001.

KRIS01   Krishnamurthy, B., and Rexford, J. *Web Protocols and Practice: HTTP/1.1, Networking Protocols, Caching, and Traffic Measurement.* Upper Saddle River, NJ: Prentice Hall, 2001.

LARO02   LaRocca, J., and LaRocca, R. *802.11 Demystified.* New York: McGraw-Hill, 2002.

LEUT94   Leutwyler, K. "Superhack." *Scientific American*, July 1994.

LIEB95   Liebmann, L. "Keeping Inn Control." *LAN Magazine*, June 1995.

LIEB98   Liebmann, L. "CLEC Provides Alternative Medicine." *Network Magazine*, March 1998.

LIEB99   Liebmann, L. "Bandwidth Fuels E-conomy." *Information Week*, May 10, 1999.

MADA98   Madaus, J., and Webster, L. "Opening the Door to Distance Learning." *Computers in Libraries*, May 1998.

MART88   Martin, J., and Leban, J. *Principles of Data Communication.* Englewood Cliffs, NJ: Prentice Hall, 1988.

MCDY99   McDysan, D., and Spohn, D. *ATM: Theory and Application.* New York: McGraw-Hill, 1999.

MILL01   Miller, B., and Bisdikian, C. *Bluetooth Revealed.* Upper Saddle River, NJ: Prentice Hall, 2001.

MILO00   Milonas, A. "Enterprise Networking for the New Millennium." *Bell Labs Technical Journal*, January–March 2002.

MUSI02   Musich, P. "Project Gets Helping Hand." *eWeek*, November 25, 2002. www.eweek.com.

NORR03   Norris, M. *Gigabit Ethernet Technology and Applications.* Norwood, MA: Artech House, 2003.

OHAR99   Ohara, B., and Petrick, A. *IEEE 802.11 Handbook: A Designer's Companion.* New York: IEEE Press, 1999.

OZSU99   Ozsu, M., and Valduriez, P. *Principles of Distributed Database Systems.* Upper Saddle River, NJ: Prentice Hall, 1999.

PAHL95   Pahlavan, K., Probert, T. and Chase, M. "Trends in Local Wireless Networks." *IEEE Communications Magazine,* March 1995.

PERL00   Perlman, R. *Interconnections: Bridges, Routers, Switches, and Internetworking Protocols.* Reading, MA: Addison-Wesley, 2000.

PFAF98   Pfaffenberger, B. *Building a Strategic Extranet.* Foster City, CA: IDG Books, 1998.

RAO02   Rao, K.; Bojkovic, Z.; and Milovanovic, D. *Multimedia Communication Systems: Techniques, Standards, and Networks.* Upper Saddle River, NJ: Prentice Hall.

RAPP02   Rappaport, T., *Wireless Communications: Principles and Practice.* Upper Saddle River, NJ: Prentice Hall, 2002.

REAG00a   Reagan, P. *Client/Server Computing.* Upper Saddle River, NJ: Prentice Hall, 2000.

REAG00b   Reagan, P. *Client/Server Network: Design, Operation, and Management.* Upper Saddle River, NJ: Prentice Hall, 2000.

REGA04   Regan, P. *Local Area Networks.* Upper Saddle River, NJ: Prentice Hall, 2004.

REGE96   Rege, J. "A New Face For Florida." *Oracle Magazine*, July/August 1996.

RENA96   Renaud, P. *An Introduction to Client/Server Systems.* New York: Wiley, 1996.

RIVE78   Rivest, R.; Shamir, A.; and Adleman, L. "A Method for Obtaining Digital Signatures and Public Key Cryptosystems." *Communications of the ACM*, February 1978.

RODB00   Rodbell, M. "Bluetooth: Wireless Local Access, Baseband and RF Interfaces, and Link Management." *Communications System Design*, March, April, May 2000. (www.csdmag.com)

RODR02   Rodriguez, A., et al. *TCP/IP Tutorial and Technical Overview.* Upper Saddle River: NJ: Prentice Hall, 2002.

ROSE98   Rose, M., and Strom, D. *Internet Messaging: From the Desktop to the Enterprise.* Upper Saddle River, NJ: Prentice Hall, 1998.

ROTH93   Rothschild, M. "Coming Soon: Internal Markets." *Forbes ASAP*, June 7, 1993.

SACH96   Sachs, M., and Varma, A. "Fibre Channel and Related Standards." *IEEE Communications Magazine*, August 1996.

SCHN96   Schneier, B. *Applied Cryptography.* New York: Wiley, 1996.

SCHU98   Schulzrinne, H., and Rosenberg, J. "The Session Initiation Protocol: Providing Advanced Telephony Access Across the Internet." *Bell Labs Technical Journal*, October–December 1998.

SCHU99   Schulzrinne, H., and Rosenberg, J. "The IETF Internet Telephony Architecture and Protocols." *IEEE Network*, May/June 1999.

SEIF98   Seifert, R. *Gigabit Ethernet.* Reading, MA: Addison-Wesley, 1998.

SEVC96   Sevcik, P. "Designing a High-Performance Web Site." *Business Communications Review*, March 1996.

SEVC03   Sevcik, P. "How Fast Is Fast Enough?" *Business Communications Review*, March 2003.

SHEN95   Shenker, S. "Fundamental Design Issues for the Future Internet." *IEEE Journal on Selected Areas in Communications*, September 1995.

SHNE84   Shneiderman, B. "Response Time and Display Rate in Human Performance with Computers." *ACM Computing Surveys*, September 1984.

SHOE02   Shoemake, M. "IEEE 802.11g Jells as Applications Mount." *Communications System Design*, April 2002. (www.commsdesign.com)

SIMO95   Simon, A., and Wheeler, T. *Open Client/Server Computing and Middleware.* Chestnut Hill, MA: AP Professional Books, 1995.

SING99   Singh, S. *The Code Book: The Science of Secrecy from Ancient Egypt to Quantum Cryptography.* New York: Anchor Books, 1999.

SMIT88   Smith, M. "A Model of Human Communication." *IEEE Communications Magazine*, February 1988.

SPIR88   Spiram, K., and Whitt, W. "Characterizing Superposition Arrival Processes in Packet Multiplexers for Voice and Data." *IEEE Journal on Selected Areas in Communications*, September 1988.

SPOH02   Spohn, D. *Data Network Design.* New York: McGraw-Hill, 2002.

SPOR03   Sportack, M. *IP Addressing Fundamentals.* Indianapolis, IN: Cisco Press, 2003.

SPUR00   Spurgeon, C. *Ethernet: The Definitive Guide.* Cambridge, MA: O'Reilly and Associates, 2000.

STAL99a   Stallings, W. *ISDN and Broadband ISDN, with Frame Relay and ATM.* Upper Saddle River, NJ: Prentice Hall, 1999.

STAL99b   Stallings, W. *SNMP, SNMPv2, SNMPv3, and RMON 1 and 2.* Reading, MA: Addison-Wesley, 1999.

STAL00   Stallings, W. *Local and Metropolitan Area Networks,* 6th edition. Upper Saddle River, NJ: Prentice Hall, 2000.

STAL02a   Stallings, W. *Wireless Communications and Networks.* Upper Saddle River, NJ: Prentice Hall, 2002.

STAL02b   Stallings, W. *High-Speed Networks and Internets.* Upper Saddle River, NJ: Prentice Hall, 2002.

STAL03   Stallings, W. *Cryptography and Network Security: Principles and Practice,* 3rd edition. Upper Saddle River, NJ: Prentice Hall, 2003.

STAL04   Stallings, W. *Data and Computer Communications,* 7th edition. Upper Saddle River, NJ: Prentice Hall, 2004.

STEI02a   Steinmetz, R., and Nahrstedt, K. *Multimedia Fundamentals, Volume 1: Media Coding and Content Processing.* Upper Saddle River, NJ: Prentice Hall,

STEI02b   Steinert-Threlkeld, T. "MasterCard Tools Up Data Handling." *Baseline Magazine,* June 17, 2002.

SUBR00   Subranamian, M. *Network Management: Principles and Practice.* Reading, MA: Addison-Wesley, 2000.

SULL99   Sullivan, K. "Interim Help Yields Long-Term Lucre." *PC Week,* April 19, 1999.

TEGE95   Teger, S. "Multimedia: From Vision to Reality." *AT&T Technical Journal,* September/October 1995.

THAD81   Thadhani, A. "Interactive User Productivity." *IBM Systems Journal,* No. 1, 1981.

TSUD92   Tsudik, G. "Message Authentication with One-Way Hash Functions." *Proceedings, INFOCOM '92,* May 1992.

UHLA00   Uhland, V. "The Turbo-Charged Enterprise." *Satellite Broadband,* November 2001.

WEXL03   Wexler, J. "Irrepressible Frame Relay." *Business Communications Review,* July 2003.

WHET96   Whetzel, J. "Integrating the World Wide Web and Database Technology." *AT&T Technical Journal,* March/April 1996.

WILS00   Wilson, J., and Kronz, J. "Inside Bluetooth: Part I and Part II." *Dr. Dobb's Journal,* March, April 2000.

XIAO99   Xiao, X., and Ni, L. "Internet QoS: A Big Picture." *IEEE Network,* March/April 1999.

INDEX